Culver's Exemplar
The Remarkable Life of Leigh R. Gignilliat

By Kelly C. Jordan

This volume is dedicated to **Paul Charles Gignilliat.**

A true son of Culver – in mind, body, and spirit – he is every bit
the honorable gentleman I found his remarkable grandfather to be.
I have equal measure of admiration for both grandfather and grandson.

As the scion of the subject and patron of the project, this book could not
have been completed without his interest, advice, and support.

My hope is that this work is in some ways an embodiment of The Spirit of
Culver.

The Spirit of Culver
The home to win, the zeal to dare,
Contempt for what is base and mean;
Pride in achievement that is fair,
And high regard for what is clean;
The Strength that is in brotherhood,
The courage that proclaims success;
The will to strive for what is good,
And first and always, manliness.
Samuel Ellsworth "S. E." Kiser

Author's Preface

After being inspired by Ron Chernow's magnificent biography of Alexander Hamilton to create his blockbuster Broadway show *Hamilton* using the medium of rap music, Lin Manuel Miranda remarked that he felt he had been chosen by Hamilton to tell his story in a most unusual way. In much the same manner, I believe that Gignilliat in some respects "chose" me to tell his story.

The writing of this book has been a labor of love that began with a "cold call" I received on July 1, 2008 from then-Head of Schools at the Culver Academies, John N. Buxton, asking me if I would be interested in becoming the Commandant of Cadets at Culver Military Academy, one three schools comprising the Culver Academies. After agreeing to serve in this position, Buxton gave me a copy of a book entitled *Arms and the Boy*, written by a former superintendent of Culver, Leigh R. Gignilliat. In the book, Gignilliat made the case for the value of military training in schools by describing the unique system he helped to create and the remarkably innovative approach CMA used that resonated with me as profoundly in 2008 as it had when the book was published almost a century prior. Gignilliat was a graduate of Virginia Military Institute who was captivated by military schools and had served as the Commandant of Cadets at Culver Military Academy prior to becoming its Superintendent, and I, as a fellow VMI graduate captivated by military schools and former CMA Commandant of Cadets, became enchanted by him. The more I learned about him, the more fascinated I became.

As my own interest in Gignilliat grew, I began using my skills as a professional historian to learn more about him. A stroke of good fortune in July 2016 led me to find a trove of documents related to Gignilliat that had only recently become accessible and also a curator who was an expert with the collection. My research expanded to include nine separate archives, locating many more documents to which previous Culver historians had not had access. These discoveries convinced me that writing a biography was the best way to bring together all of this information in a way that could be shared with others. This is how this book came into being.

I read hundreds of letters and documents that few if any others had seen since they were first written, and it was exhilarating. At times I felt a bit like I was eavesdropping on a century-old dialogue, as the letters in particular contained information and insights that were meant for only the author and the intended recipient. I developed a vision of Gignilliat sitting at his desk poring over documents and thinking deeply about ways he could enhance the practices and reputation of the school he loved so passionately. The photograph on the back cover of Gignilliat working at his desk evokes the sentiment and also conveys this image so well. It served as a kind of touchstone and talisman for me in my own efforts.

Reading his own letters, along with consulting the works of previous historians, enabled me to reconstruct the events of his remarkable life and allowed me to gain a level of insight into the identity and character of Gignilliat that I could have scarcely imagined. I became privy to his most unguarded thoughts and greatest areas of insecurity, and what I found confirmed that he was truly a gentleman of dignity, respect, and goodness who was honorable and worthy of respect. As a result of experiencing this level of unanticipated intimacy, I came to admire Gignilliat even more.

The many instances of good fortune I experienced during the research and writing of this manuscript mirrored those experienced by Gignilliat in many respects, and the feeling of simpatico and of being kindred spirits continued to mount throughout the entire period of writing. Each of these instances reinforced the notion that Gignilliat had chosen me to write this work. I became convinced that I was being called to do the work necessary to tell an important story that I was perhaps uniquely suited to relate and which needed to be shared with others.

When it came time to shift from writing the narrative to casting a critical eye on the man and his life, I discovered that my new-found relationship with Gignilliat emboldened me and inspired me to write what needed to be written, even if it was somewhat critical in places, because I was certain that it was what Gignilliat would have wanted me to do. Just as there was a symbiotic relationship between Gignilliat and Culver, so too was there a similar relationship between me as an author and Gignilliat as my subject, and both of these relationships were positive, constructive, supportive, ennobling, and uplifting. I know that I have benefited from the experience of researching and writing this book, and I hope that I have produced something that would have made Gignilliat proud.

As Miranda felt privileged to be chosen by Hamilton to tell his story, so too do I feel privileged to be chosen by Gignilliat to tell his story. I am deeply grateful to have had the opportunity to experience this relationship with someone now long gone from this earth, and I hope that readers will sense this connection and appreciate its impact on the resulting book.

Kelly C. Jordan
February, 2025

Acknowledgements

Writing a book like this one is a labor of love, and I could not have completed this multiyear project without the steadfast support of many people. While I am indebted to all of them for their help, assistance, and support, I am solely responsible for any errors that may reside in these pages.

The idea for this book began in summer 2017, and it became animated by the generous support of Paul C. Gignilliat. He and his extraordinary wife Ellen have been the most steadfast of supporters, sharing my milestones and providing constant encouragement along the way.

Mary Margaret Gignilliat, the keeper of the Gignilliat family archives, allowed me access to family photos unavailable anywhere else and which helped me illustrate aspects of General Gignilliat's life that would have otherwise been lost.

Culver Archivist Jeff Kenney rivals Paul Gignilliat in terms of his ceaseless support for this project, agreeing to serve as my expert peer reviewer and going even further by volunteering to format the manuscript for publication. His knowledge of CMA history rivals mine in some areas, and his expertise in the history of the city of Culver and the area far exceeds my own. He also did much to improve my prose, divide up many of my far-too-long sentences, and help me identify and incorporate the best possible photographs for the book, ensuring that we used the highest quality images. This book may not have taken form without his assistance.

Carol Saft, of the Culver archives, provided me with several important photos, and she also read the entire manuscript, correcting my prose and letting me know where I needed to make revisions.

As Sir Issac Newton conveyed so aptly, all works of discovery are indebted to the work of those who went before us, and this book is no different. I am particularly indebted to the works of longtime Culver educator Charles Mather – who wrote the first history of Culver based upon much firsthand knowledge and also documented some aspects for which we no longer have tangible evidence, along with the many and varied works of former Culver Historian Bob Hartman – whose work in capturing the anecdotes that animate the history of an institution – and the doctoral dissertation of longtime Culver teacher Richard Davies – whose work provides the first elements of critical analysis of much of the period covered in this biography. I benefited greatly from the work of each of these gentlemen, all of whom deserve recognition as Culver's "giant historians."

My interest in Culver's history began on July 1, 2008 -- the day I received a call from then-Head of Schools John N. Buxton – and John nurtured it consistently during the five years I worked for him as Culver Military Academy's Commandant of Cadets. His font of knowledge was deep, and he never tired of sharing it with me or engaging in my many endeavors to learn more about the people and events that have made Culver what it is today.

Whether she knows it or not, head librarian at the time Susan Freymiller – who began working at Culver on the same day as I did – planted the initial seed of this book by providing me with the first document that piqued my interest and got me started researching the life of Leigh Gignilliat.

I consulted with at least nine different archives while conducting my research, and I found someone at each who provided support far beyond what I could have expected. These individuals include:

Sarah McElroy Mitchell at Indiana University's Lilly Library, who provided me with the first trove of letters related to Gignilliat that made this project possible;

Allison Dillard, Reference and Cataloging Librarian at the Georgia Historical Society, who provided me with much of the foundation for the Gignilliat family history;

Monique Bolan, historian and historical researcher of Emerson Preparatory Institute, who granted me access to Gignilliat's secondary educational records;

Mary Laura Kludy, Archives and Records Management Specialist of the Virginia Military Institute archives, who provided me with Gignilliat's academic records and also combed the VMI archives for any scrap of paper mentioning him as a cadet;

Anne Foster, Archivist of the Yellowstone National Park Archives, whose assistance was essential to helping me discover the powerful impact of this relatively short period of time on Gignilliat's development as an educator and leader;

Jean Tabbert of the Glacier National Park museum and archives, whose resources allowed me to tell the story of the quixotic and perplexing Skyland Camps endeavor more thoroughly that ever before;

Members of the Cass County Historical Society, for providing me with information regarding the 1913 Logansport flood that had never been incorporated to Culver's treatment of this seminal event, and

Elenor Brinsko, a historical researcher I hired, who diligently searched through the holdings at the Wisconsin Historical Society to identify any material related to Gignilliat.

The material provided by these people enabled me to corroborate many of stories told about Gignilliat using multiple sources, producing a work that is methodologically rigorous and which can both serve as the basis and also stand the test of scrutiny by future historians.

Publication of *Culver's Exemplar* culminates a seven-year effort during which I spent much of my precious free time paying attention to some-one I never knew at the expense of those who I do know and love. I owe my wife, Roberta, an enormous debt for her unflagging love and support. While she had every right to demand more of my time and attention, she chose instead to be an unselfish ally who listened to my endless stories, lifted me up, and helped me continue to move forward to complete the project. I remain grateful to her and as fortunate to have her as my life's partner as Gignilliat was to have his beloved Minnie.

Table of Contents

Part II – The Lengthening Shadow

Part III – Reconciling Brightness and Shadow

Part IV –Documenting the Journey

Culver's Exemplar:
The Remarkable Life of Innovator, Leader, & Educator Leigh R. Gignilliat

No boy who wants to do the right thing will go very far wrong at Culver.
--Leigh R. Gignilliat

The presence and spirit of Admiral Horatio Nelson pervaded the British Navy and provided it with a collective understanding of what was expected of a naval officer for well over 100 years. After proving himself to be perhaps the very best naval commander in British history, Nelson's saying that, "No captain can do very wrong by placing his ship alongside that of the enemy," became both dogma and dictum for the British Royal Navy. It also provided the British Navy with an unparalleled and enduring competitive advantage.

In much the same manner, the presence and spirit of Leigh R. Gignilliat at Culver provided the institution, faculty, staff, and graduates with a common understanding of what was expected of a Culver man/graduate for over 100 years. In a somewhat analogous manner, and after becoming one of the most influential persons during Culver's first century of existence, Gignilliat's oft-repeated saying that, "No boy who wants to do the right thing will go very far wrong at Culver," encapsulated both the educational philosophy and practice for Culver, forming the canon and doctrine of the institution.

Ralph Waldo Emerson wrote that, "an institution is the lengthened shadow of one man," and it is my contention that Leigh Robinson Gignilliat was that man for Culver. He therefore deserves a full-length biography based upon his own tremendous accomplishments and because of its value to contemporary readers – educators, leaders, and innovators – who have much to learn from his approach and example.

As an innovator, Gignilliat was perceptive, bold, prescient, and ahead of his time. He successfully created a "learning organization" 70 years before Peter Senge coined the term. A self-trained educator, Gignilliat developed an approach that emphasized character formation and "preparation for life" as the primary goals of secondary education, reflecting the pragmatism of the period's most influential educator, John Dewey. He adopted the highly unusual (for the time) belief in the inherent goodness of adolescent boys and created a method based upon the premise that they responded best to guidance that was positive, constructive, and respectful to become their best selves. This was diametrically opposed to the prevailing approach of the time, which characterized boys as being little more than savage "brutes" who needed to be "civilized" via strict control and rigid discipline.

A progressive, experimental, blended, and pragmatic educator, Gignilliat demonstrated the Five "E"s of Educational Effectiveness – Engagement, Enhancement, Extension, Enrichment, and Excellence. He was among the first to adopt a "holistic" approach, characterizing the learning that occurred in the barracks and outside the classroom as having immense value and a positive impact on the development of boys. He used the Tactical Officers or "Tacs" (later counselors) to fulfill this function and take advantage of this opportunity. Gignilliat's unique blend of didactic, experiential, and Socratic approaches combined to create a distinctive and effective educational method that brought out the best in his cadets. He embraced the then-unusual technique of using curricular differentiation, to allow students to learn in ways best suited to their abilities and needs.

As a leader, Gignilliat was courageous, authentic, and effective, function-ing successfully in a variety of leadership roles in many types of organiza-tions to help promote Culver and as a way of serving. He was an exemplar of the ideal leader as described by contemporary leadership scholars Jim Kouzes and Barry Posner – authors of *The Leadership Challenge* – who was others-oriented, imbued with character, innovative, and able to achieve, providing both a model of and framework for what a Culver grad-uate could be and should become.

Gignilliat was a self-made man of character in Henry Clay's very best sense of the term, which made him a genuine and idealistic romantic (i.e., hearkening back to an earlier period) for his time and all the more fascinating for it. As a middle child of a Southern family who grew up essentially parentless, he made the most of his talents and opportunities to become something far greater than he could have ever imagined for himself.

True to his nature, Gignilliat was more of a beloved father-figure who used discipline and love to gain the willing obedience of his charges than a demanding taskmaster who coerced compliance at any cost. In doing so, Gignilliat provided a personal example of the Culture of Character pro-moted by Culver, showing that a person of civility, gentility, and sincerity could not only thrive but also flourish in the America of his time.

Trained as a civil engineer and something of an introvert, Gignilliat was nevertheless an intuitive, committed, generous, and masterful marketer and promoter. He consciously and deliberately helped build the Culver brand, and by personifying it he promoted awareness of Culver's distinctive and successful method of educating boys. He freely and eagerly shared the techniques, approaches, and successes experienced at and by Culver with the broader educational community in many novel forums. Gignilliat enhanced Culver as an institution by his willingness to make and re-make himself into the model of what he wanted to be, what he needed to be, and what the school and the nation expected him to be.

These characteristics combined to allow Gignilliat to become extraordinarily successful, amassing an exceptionally impressive string of individual accomplishments that brought national renown to his institution. His achievements also helped to solidify Culver's reputation as one of the very best educational institutions in the country, placing him in the first rank of American 20th century secondary educators.

My decade-long study of Gignilliat shows him to be exceptional in his own time, and I have found that he holds up remarkably well from a modern perspective, making him all the more impressive. Douglas Southall Freeman found, after reading, by his own estimate, 1,200 unpublished letters and reports, that Robert E. Lee's private correspondence did not contain even "the echo of a liaison, the shadow of an oath, or the stain of a single obscene suggestion." The same can be said of Gignilliat's private correspondence, which I have examined extensively, that it contains nary a hint of vulgarity, impropriety, or prejudice.

No written account can sufficiently convey the complexity and nuance of an individual's thoughts, motivations, fears, and concerns in their entirety – which is rather like trying to render a three-dimensional object in only two dimensions – but there have been some commendable attempts to do so that provide a solid foundation from which to proceed.

The unpublished works of Charles C. Mather and Richard Davies provide an excellent introduction to such an endeavor, but Mather concentrated on Culver as an organization and Davies focused on a particular portion of Gignilliat's adult life as an educator.[1] A traditional biographical approach is better suited to provide a more thorough portrayal of him, addressing his entire life and scope of activities.

The immense value of the work of former Culver historian Robert B. D. "Bob" Hartman to preserve stories about Gignilliat cannot be overstated. However, the somewhat anecdotal nature of Hartman's work leaves room for a more rigourous scholarly approach that will be more comprehensive almost certainly provide the treatment that the remarkable life of Gignilliat deserves.[2]

So capable, accomplished, and admirable a man warrants an extensive scholarly treatment to explore how he became such a person and what others can learn from his example. A biography that is both a chronicle of his life and a narrative of the influence of this remarkable innovator, leader, educator, self-made man of character, marketer, promoter, and man of Culver is therefore quite warranted.

It is said that the lifespan of our effective memory of others is about two generations, or roughly 70 years. After that span of time, a person's presence and influence begin to wane substantially. Those for whom recognition endures beyond this period of "collective amnesia" tend to experience a renewal of attention on the century commemoration of their passing that perpetuates their memory further and long into the future.

The task of the biographer, according to renowned biography expert Paul Murray Kendall is "to perpetuate a man as he was in the days he lived," referring to it as "a spring task" of bringing the essence of someone from the past "to life again." These have been the thoughts that have animated my efforts on this biography project: to ensure that Leigh Robinson Gignilliat is not only **not forgotten**, but **remembered**.

Chapter 1 – Historical Background of Gignilliat Family & Early Life of Leigh R. Gignilliat

As was true of most military schools during the late-19th and early 20th centuries, there was usually one man who defined an institution and set the course of its trajectory through long service and innovative approaches. This individual came to embody the ideals of the school, ensuring that his influence would be both pervasive and enduring. For Culver Military Academy, this person was Leigh R. Gignilliat.

Gignilliat's Heritage

Born Leigh Robinson Gignilliat in Savannah, Georgia on July 4, 1875, he was the sixth of seven children (six sons and one daughter) of William R. Gignilliat and Harriet Walker "Hattie" Gignilliat (*née* Heyward). The Gignilliat family was of French Huguenot descent, and marriage brought in both English and Scotch heritage. Seeking to avoid religious persecution, the Gignilliat family fled France to Switzerland and then came to America in the 1680s, settling on a large tract of land in South Carolina. Shortly after the end of the American Revolutionary War, the family moved to Georgia and settled near Savannah on a bluff overlooking the port city of Darien among Scotch immigrants in the area.

Gignilliat's grandfather, William Robert Gignilliat, was a college-educated graduate of the University of Georgia. He became a leading citizen of Darien, serving as the Senior Warden of St. Andrew's Episcopal church. He had three sons, all of whom served in the Confederate army during the Civil War, including Gignilliat's father, William Robert Gignilliat Jr. William Robert Sr. was present when the town was burned by Union troops on June 11, 1863 (as depicted in the movie, *Glory*).

Gignilliat's Father – William Robert Gignilliat

Gignilliat's father, William Robert Junior, was born in Darien on June 21, 1839. He was raised to be something of a "dandy," but he had a good mind. He graduated from his father's *alma mater* and also from the University of Virginia Law School, and his mother was quite learned as well, drawn especially to the sciences.

William Robert Junior married Harriet Walker "Hattie" Heyward around 1860 and began a family. They had seven children: (William L. (1861), Thomas H (1863), Helen Mary (1865), Arthur M. (1868), Robert D. (1873), Leigh R. (1875), and Ravenel (1879)). Harriet died as a result of complications from childbirth in 1879. William Robert Jr. also died young on November 25, 1885.

William R. Gignilliat Jr.[1]

Shortly after they married, the Civil War broke out. As a good and loyal son of Georgia, William Robert Jr. immediately considered volunteering for military service. Based upon his rather "soft" upbringing, a physician recommended that William Robert Jr. "turn his back" on the entirety of the Civil War for health reasons and sit out the war taking in the "restorative influences" in the south of France. As a proud southern gentleman who was anxious to prove himself and also to do his duty, William Robert Jr. disregarded this advice out of hand on the principle that "such advice was unworthy the consideration of a man in the hour of his country's need," and he promptly enlisted as a private in the Confederate army.[2]

Already in uniform and being "strikingly handsome" and also quite charming, a lifelong friendship with the organizer of an artillery battery, Captain John M. Guerard, brought William Robert Jr. the fortuitous opportunity to become an officer quickly. Based upon his friendship with the unit's commander and also on his educational background – which was far beyond that of a private solider – he was offered a commission and became the first lieutenant of Guerard's Battery.

A typical Confederate artillery battery consisted of four guns, frequently of mixed caliber weapons. Each gun had a crew of nine men and was

A typical Civil War artillery battery similar to Gerard's battery.[3]

transported using six horses, making the size of a battery approximately 40 men and 30 horses. It was the first lieutenant's job to provide for the logistical requirements of the battery, ensuring that the men had sufficient food and equipment, that the guns had sufficient amounts of ammunition, and that the horses had enough fodder and water to subsist. The first lieutenant also saw to the welfare of the men and the horses, and to the serviceability of the weapons and equipment.

The loading, aiming, and firing of Civil War artillery pieces was both a highly technical task and also a quite physical one. Understanding the fundamentals of ballistics, the impact of different gunpowder charges, and the characteristics of the types of projectiles used – which included solid round shot, shell (an exploding round shot), cannister rounds comprised of smaller solid round shot (referred to as "grapeshot"), and shrapnel – and being able to compute the different coefficients rapidly and make the necessary adjustments, all while being under fire by opposing artillery and also musket fire, put a premium on both mental acuity and the ability to remain calm under fire.

Training crews to service the guns rapidly and efficiently required an intimate understanding of human nature and also an ability to rely on the force of personality more so than coercive force to get soldiers to perform at their best under the most trying of circumstances.

When the war began, Confederate batteries were generally attached to infantry brigades, placing them in the thick of the action. Later in the war, four Confederate artillery batteries were grouped into an artillery battalion, and they were assigned to provide direct artillery support to infantry divisions. Regardless of how it was assigned, William Robert Jr. spent much of the war in very close contact with the enemy.

Due to Guerard's frequent absences serving on high-level staffs, William Robert Jr. often commanded the artillery battery in Guerard's absence, doing so with distinction at the battles of Ocean Pond, Florida (also known as Olustee), and Honey Hill, South Carolina. He served under then-Major J. Lamb Buist at the battle of Ocean Pond, and he was promoted to the rank of captain just before the war ended. The newly promoted Captain William Robert Gignilliat Jr. closed out the war serving on the staff of Buist, who himself had been promoted to the rank of General. William Robert Jr. compiled an admirable war record and served with distinction by all accounts.

After the war, Leigh Gignilliat's father intended to return to Savannah or move to Atlanta and establish a law practice, but he soon determined that he could best serve his community by returning to Darien and helping to work through the challenges of reconstruction. He became a pillar of the community, as his father before him had been, and also an acknowledged leader, serving as Senior Warden at St. Andrew's Episcopal Church (like his father), a master Mason, and chairman of the Democratic Executive Committee of McIntosh County, Georgia, which encompassed Darien. He became heavily involved in the contentious reconstruction that occurred in Georgia after the war.

According to this contemporaries, William Robert Jr. lived a life of "devoted unselfishness around the sacred hearth of home as well as in the wider arena of public life." As a result, he was well respected by his peers and held in high esteem by many, serving in a variety of important elected positions. He was renowned for his "high sense of duty and absolute loyalty to country and friends," and he left to his surviving heirs a legacy of "high character, patriotism and zeal." It was reported that his was the largest funeral that ever took place in McIntosh County.[4]

Leigh Robinson Gignilliat[5]

Leigh Robinson.[9]

While studying law at the University of Virginia, William Robert Jr. met fellow law student Leigh Robinson. Robinson was a native of Richmond, Virginia, and he enlisted in the 1st Virginia's Richmond Howitzers Light Artillery Battery as a private on February 15, 1862. Gignilliat's unit and Robinson's battery served in the Virginia campaign that occurred later in the war, and the two almost certainly became reacquainted during this period. The friendship remained intact after the war and deepened such that Gignilliat named his sixth child after him, christening him Leigh Robinson Gignilliat upon his birth in Savannah on July 4, 1875.

This choice of name was a particular honor, as young Leigh, of all the Gignilliat children, most closely resembled his father in appearance. It was also quite fortuitous, as William Robert Jr.'s untimely demise at the young age of 45 led to the newly married Robinson and his wife – he married Alice Morson in 1882 – becoming young Leigh's adoptive parents, and he lived with them for a time in Washington, DC.

Little is known of young Leigh's first decade while living in Darien with his father, mother, and five siblings (William L "Willie," Thomas H, Helen M. H., Arthur M, and Robert Deas). His mother died on February 5, 1879, one month after giving birth to Leigh's youngest brother, Ravenel, on January 9, 1879. Thus, Leigh grew up in a motherless house beginning at the age of four, without even the influence of his sister Helen, who, as her mother's dying wish, was sent to live with family friends to become a proper Southern woman. The rest of the family remained together in Darien afterwards until the untimely death of Leigh's father on November 25, 1885.

Leigh's older brothers and sister were no longer living at home and had begun their adult lives. Willie was apprenticing as an attorney in Savannah, and Thomas, a graduate of the US Naval Academy who had resigned his commission, was putting his remarkable mathematical talents to use designing and building airplanes in Hartford, Connecticut. Helen was married to a prominent attorney in Darien. Thus, the Savannah area remained the Gignilliat family homestead.

The more pressing question was where the younger children – Arthur, Robert, Leigh, and Ravenel – would live now that their parents were deceased. The answers were as varied as the individuals.

Having just reached his majority, 18-year old Arthur embraced the opportunity for adventure, struck out on his own, went to Texas, and became involved in building railroads and bridges. He returned to Georgia after several years, became a civil engineer, and was involved in the construction of the bridge across the Savannah River when he died on December 11, 1890 from a shotgun blast to the face he received during a quarrel that turned violent.[6]

Both Robert and Ravenel remained in Georgia, perhaps living with relatives or family friends. It is not known where Robert resided, but being in adolescence it would have relatively easy to find either a relative (older brother, uncle, etc.) or friend of the family with whom he could live until he reached his majority. The task of placing seven-year old Ravenel, however, was more delicate. Once married, it is likely that Ravenel moved in with his sister Helen and was essentially raised by her, allowing him to remain in Darien and avoid further upheaval in his young life. Both Robert and Ravenel remained in Georgia and became successful civil engineers.

Living in Washington, DC and Attending Emerson Institute

Being older than Ravenel but too young to be on his own, Leigh was sent by his father at the age of nine to attend the well-regarded and all-male Emerson Institute in Washington, DC, living in a boarding house nearby. The move to Washington, DC took young Gignilliat away from the rough sort of reconstruction occurring in Georgia and in which his father was involved. Rather, he grew up in the more genteel environs of the nation's capital, which had become far more refined and developed during the first nine years of his life.

Although Gignilliat remained proud of his southern heritage and conducted himself as a southern gentleman, this move might have stunted any tendency for him to become virulently anti-union during his youth and promoted instead an embrace of a broader conception of citizenship that focused on shared beliefs instead of ideological differences. Having spent five of his formative years in close proximity to the White House and other DC landmarks, it would also engender a lifelong attachment to and comfort within our nation's capital that would be important later in Gignilliat's life.

In an unpublished chapter of his memoirs, Leigh tells a story from this period, providing some of the only insight available during these years of his life. Gignilliat related events from 1884 or 1885 when he was nine years old and had just begun attending Emerson Prep school in Washington, DC. As part of the school uniform, all the boys had to wear long stockings. While the more well-off boys wore black stocking that did not fade, Gignilliat's gray stockings faded to a dreadfully ugly hue, making his already thin legs look even skinnier. Besides making him extremely self-conscious of his appearance, this unfortunate combination also resulted in him being teased by the other boys at the school.[7]

Demonstrating a trait that would characterize him throughout his entire lifetime, Gignilliat wanted to be noticed more for what he did than for what he wore. He determined that he needed to do something to shift the attention from his appearance to his deeds. In perhaps an unusual choice for a shy boy living away from home, he began declaiming, which involved memorizing notable works of prose and presenting dramatic performances of them in public. Gignilliat reflected on this choice while writing this chapter, relating that he had some inexplicable yearning from an early age to speak in public as a young boy, which was unusual, since such a desire did not remain with him as an adult.

Becoming a Declaimer and Learning How to Speak in Public Effectively

He traced the impetus for declaiming to a girl he met at the boarding house. Gignilliat became captivated by watching and listening to her practice her orations, and he learned to recite dramatically a poem called "The Drum." What he most enjoyed about reciting the poem was that each verse ended by repeating the word "drum" three times, which, when performed, involved pronouncing each one with an increasing roll of the "r" as follows: "*The drum, the drrum, the drrrrrrrum.*" According to Gignilliat, the girl at the boarding house rolled the r's on her tongue "as a snare drummer rolls his sticks on the drumhead."

Reciting such a poem dramatically and in public was precisely the type of action Gignilliat believed would shift the focus from his appearance to what he could do. He worked hard to memorize the poem and learned to perform it as the girl did, waiting for the opportunity to make use of his new abilities. The chance for him to do so came in the form of the Friday afternoon declamation contest at Emerson Prep.

When the time came for him to recite the poem, he did so with enthusiasm and found that many of the other boys were as captivated by the rolling "r" in the word drum at the end of each verse as he was. In fact, more and more of his classmates joined in repeating the final words of each verse with gusto. When he finished, there was a great round of applause, replacing the incessant teasing that he usually received.

Gignilliat performed the work exceptionally well and won the top prize of a delicious chocolate cake. According to Gignilliat, he was elated not because he loved cake but because he wanted to prove his worth to his peers at Emerson Prep by winning something and shifting focus from his dingy stockings and skinny legs to his abilities. This same desire would become expressly manifest in his approach to running Culver and the system of rewards and recognition he set up for both the winter and summer schools.

His initial success encouraged him to continue declaiming at Emerson, which he did. He reported that he developed quite a repertoire and participated in the declaiming contest sponsored by the school at the end of each academic year, earning a silver medal for his performance in his final year.[8]

Living with His Namesake – Leigh Robinson – A New Home

Gignilliat's namesake – Leigh Robinson – was a prominent attorney living in Washington, DC. He lived in a handsome house at 1831 G Street in the Northwest quadrant of Washington, DC, where he had established a household with his wife Alice Morson since their marriage in 1882. Upon hearing of William Robert Jr.'s untimely death in late-1885, Leigh Robinson invited young Leigh to live with him and his wife while he continued to attend the nearby Emerson Institute. The childless couple welcomed him into his home, accepting custody for the boy, and raised Leigh as their own son in Washington, DC.

Meeting President Grover Cleveland

Gignilliat tells of meeting the newly elected President Grover Cleveland with Leigh Robinson, when he was nine years old. The meeting took place in Washington, DC at a reception for the Bar Association, of which his father had been a member as was Robinson.

Gignilliat reported that he was "greatly thrilled by the experience of shaking hands with the President of the United States," especially since Gignilliat remembered "the great rejoicing and bonfires" that occurred in his home town of Darien, Georgia celebrating the first Democrat since the Civil War to be elected president of the nation. The nine-year old Master Gignilliat, when shaking Cleveland's hand, told the Democratic President of the United States proudly that he, too, was a Democrat! Robinson was "greatly amused" by the episode, and it provides a hint of the ease in which Gignilliat would interact with dignitaries as an adult.[10]

This is a delightful story, but there are several inconsistencies with it in terms of timeline that make it somewhat problematic. Gignilliat's father didn't die until he was 11 years old, so it seems strange that he refers to Mr. Robinson as his "guardian" when he was only nine years old. In addition, Cleveland was elected president on November 4, 1884 and took office on March 4, 1885, and Gignilliat was nine years during the period July 4, 1884 to July 3, 1885 and still living in Georgia, leaving him a small window of eight months during which he could have traveled to Washington, DC and met Cleveland while he was nine years old. Perhaps Gignilliat was mistaken about his age at the time of the meeting and/or the year of the meeting (as he does elsewhere in his reminiscences and which is the more likely explanation), or perhaps he met Cleveland before he was actually elected president (which would have mattered little to the starry eyed nine-year-old boy).

Nevertheless, the story, which he uses to begin a chapter in his reminiscences about important people he had the opportunity to meet throughout the course of his life, does well illustrating the point of the story from Gignilliat's perspective: he was more interested in getting to know people beyond the superficiality of merely meeting them and instead getting to know them and being able to "gain even some small insight into their philosophy of life." For Gignilliat, it was not celebrity but relationships – substance – that mattered.

Meeting the Garnett Girls

Leigh Robinson's wife, Alice, was a Virginian who had a sister named Marion married to a prominent Virginian named Henry Wise Garnett. Gignilliat got to know the Robinson's nieces, known as the "Garnett girls." Leigh considered that he had "practically grown up" with them in Washington, D.C.[11] Getting to know the Garnett girls would prove to be quite fortuitous when Leigh arrived at Culver in early 1897.

Attending Emerson Institute

As Gignilliat's de facto guardian, Leigh Robinson agreed to allow his young ward to continue attending the Emerson Institute for his secondary education. Located in downtown Washington, DC at 914 14th Street, NW (near Franklin Square between K and I Streets; about six blocks from Robinson's home), this small, nonsectarian school had been in existence since established in 1852 by noted educator Charles Bedford Young, Ph.D. With a faculty of five, a student population of a little over 50, and a modest library, Emerson's academic reputation was nevertheless excellent. It excelled at delivering both scientific and classical education courses designed to prepare boys for college. Ulysses S. Grant had two of his own sons educated at Emerson during his time as president.[12]

This academic excellence came at a price, and fortunately for Gignilliat, Robinson could afford to pay his tuition. Taking an active role in guiding his education while young Leigh lived with him, Robinson insisted on an emphasis on studying Latin and higher-order math, and Gignilliat became adept at both. While at Emerson, Gignilliat read both Virgil and Cicero in Latin, and he became proficient in logarithmic algebra. The former would be of particular use when he began working at Culver with a noted classicist, and the latter prepared him well for the demands of a collegiate engineering curriculum.

Unfortunately, the records of Leigh's time at Emerson were not stored properly, and they now consist of a sheaf of worthless blank pages, the ink having long ago disintegrated leaving no discernible trace of him on any of the pages. According to contemporary newspaper accounts, published periodically, Gignilliat was an excellent student, earning the top award for recognition of his "scholarship and punctuality" at least twice (1889, 1891).[13] Gignilliat did, however, remark in his reminiscences that he "spent his boyhood in Washington, DC," indicating that he considered it somewhat of a home and also that he enjoyed his time there.[14] He graduated with distinction as one of 11 boys from this excellent college preparatory school on June 16, 1891, demonstrating promise as a student and a desire to further his own education.[15]

The Decision to Attend VMI

When it came time to select a college, it was quite natural for Gignilliat to express an interest in studying engineering, given that all of his brothers except Willie (a lawyer) had done so. It was, however, Leigh Robinson who urged him to consider attending the Virginia Military Institute. As a fellow Virginian who studied law, Robinson knew VMI's superintendent, Scott Shipp (a fellow member of the Virginia Bar), and he thought highly of the school. Shipp had an excellent reputation in Virginia, having replaced Thomas J. "Stonewall" Jackson as VMI's Commandant, led the VMI Corps of Cadets in the fighting at the 1864 Battle of New Market, and served as a respected faculty member before becoming

VMI Superintendent General Scott Shipp, 1890-1907.[16]

Superintendent in 1890. Beloved by alumni and revered on post, Shipp was just the kind of man to whom Robinson would have entrusted his ward during the most important formative years of his adolescence.

Having spent almost 30 years serving as VMI's Commandant of Cadets, Shipp tended to be thought of as more of a disciplinarian than an educator, interested in using the school's military structure and the faculty and staff's close monitoring of cadets in and out of the classroom to mold their character and shape their intellect. It is true that Shipp, who had a serious demeanor and had been an "old soul" since he graduated from VMI fourth in the class of 1859, was keen on ensuring that tradition remained a powerful force at the school, especially the custom of allowing the cadets a high level of autonomy to determine what occurred inside the barracks.[17] Shipp believed strongly that obedience was essential to effective military development and achieving academic distinction.

Being a somber disciplinarian was not, however, mutually exclusive with being an educator. Shipp was also a learned man, earning a Juris doctorate from next door Washington College, and a talented educator, chairing VMI's Latin department and also teaching Math while serving as the Commandant of Cadets. A capable administrator, Shipp did much to improve the course of instruction during his time as Superintendent.[18] According to several authoritative histories of VMI, the engineering curriculum during the period of Gignilliat's attendance was academically excellent and quite well regarded, and the faculty was comprised of many fine educators who both guided their students while also challenging them consistently.[19]

As it had been recognized for several decades before he became Superintendent in 1890, VMI was thus a respected institution of higher education that was also a vestige of the Confederacy in the late-19th century, functioning as somewhat of a "disciplinary finishing school" under his direction that provided young Southern gentlemen a last bit of "polishing" before they took their place in society.[20] These two essential components – military discipline in the organization and way of living, and higher education through rigorous classroom learning – combined to produce an environment that was highly structured, conducive to learning, effective, and well regarded by learned men of the period like Leigh Robinson.

Confident in the institution, Robinson wrote to Shipp on June 5, 1891, inquiring about the prospect of sending Gignilliat to VMI. Considering Leigh suitably prepared academically, Robinson queried Shipp about sending a 16-year old to VMI immediately or waiting a year for him to become a bit more mature.[21]

Shipp's response was apparently positive in terms of Gignilliat's academic preparation from Emerson, and it also seemed to encourage Robinson to send him to VMI in September of 1891 at the age of 16. Accepting an applicant of this age was not unusual at the time, as VMI had only recently (1890) raised the minimum age requirement from 14 to 15 years of age, and the average age of the class entering VMI in 1891 was 17 years of age (16.94, as it would remain until around 1920).[22] Also working to

Gignilliat's advantage was VMI's recent decision to accept more cadets from outside the state of Virginia.

Since his brother Thomas had graduated from the US Naval Academy, the prospect of attending a military school was neither foreign nor objectionable to Leigh Gignilliat. VMI also provided the opportunity for the young Gignilliat to become a proper Southern gentleman, which was important to Robinson. Based upon these many considerations, Gignilliat and Robinson reached an accord regarding the choice of college: Leigh Gignilliat would attend VMI.

As with Emerson, VMI's excellence came at a price. Fortunately, Robinson was again willing and able to pay Gignilliat's tuition, which equated to roughly $8,000 each year in today's terms. For Robinson, the cost of educating his young charge and also providing him with the opportunity to become a proper Southern gentleman by attending a renowned military school was well worth the price of admission. Robinson agreed to pay Leigh's tuition, and he also provided Gignilliat with pocket money in the amount of $2.50 each month (which equates to a little over $80.00 in 2024 dollars).

Gignilliat at VMI

With fewer than one-third of American adolescents completing high school in the final decade of the 19th century, less than ten percent graduated from college.[23] Despite being out of the norm, pursuing a college degree was largely a foregone conclusion for Gignilliat. He

matriculated into the Virginia Military Institute in fall 1891 at the age of 16 to study civil engineering.

When he matriculated in September of 1891, there were 104/204 cadets from the state of Virginia, and only 11 cadets from his

VMI Cadets preparing for a parade, circa 1893.[24]

home state of Georgia. It is worth noting that far more Georgians attended The Citadel, another prominent Southern military school located closer to home in Charleston, South Carolina.

Despite being highly focused on discipline, the program of academics and military training at VMI was also quite challenging, as it was meant to be, and it was particularly challenging for first-year cadets, known as "Rats." Gignilliat was one of 78 cadets to enter as freshmen that year. Though young, Gignilliat possessed both the temperament and determination to be an excellent cadet. His challenge would be to not allow his lack of maturity to work to his detriment.

VMI's General Order of Merit – The GOM

To assess cadet academic performance and allow cadets to determine how they were performing relative to their peers, VMI rank-ordered its cadets at the end of each academic year using a unique General Order of Merit (GOM) system. This system averaged academic performance in the classroom and served as an antecedent of our modern cumulative grade point average.

VMI also used a system of assigning demerits to cadets for infractions of the school regulations. These demerits could be assigned for offenses as trivial as "lint on blouse" during an inspection, missing class, or more flagrant violations of the school rules. For serious acts of indiscipline that could result in suspension or expulsion, VMI convened military style hearings to determine a cadet's culpability and assign the appropriate penalty. While demerits and disciplinary hearings did not factor in to the GOM ranking, they did provide an indicator of general military conduct and discipline.[25]

Gignilliat's "Rat" Year at VMI

When he arrived at VMI, Gignilliat was paired with Miles Standish Deming, another non-Virginian, from St. Paul, Minnesota, as his roommate and partner to navigate the demanding first year. As with any system that is challenging and somewhat adversarial, one develops a bond that is deep and enduring with those with whom they share such an experience. Surviving the rigors of VMI's first year together, Gignilliat became especially close to Deming.

During his first year, Gignilliat did quite well in the classroom. He finished third in his class out of the 68 cadets who managed to complete VMI's demanding first year and earned recognition as being "distinguished in general merit." Demonstrating an aptitude for both Latin (2/68) and Drawing (4/68) that he would maintain throughout his entire four years, Gignilliat also ranked in the top ten percent of his class in Mathematics (6/68) and English (7/68), and he showed himself to be quite capable in the classroom.[26] Affable and bright, he acquired the nickname of "Jimmy," likely a play on his unusual last name. By the end of his first year, it was obvious that the preparation he received at the Emerson Institute and as a result of Robinson's insistence and generosity were paying off for him in college.

From a maturity perspective, however, being away from home and parental influence began to present some challenges for Gignilliat by the end of 1891. Gignilliat's tendency to become ill became something of a trend during his time at VMI, as did his decision-making due to lack of maturity.

A sickness broke out among the members of the Corps in December 1891, and Robinson wrote to Shipp expressing his concern and letting Shipp know that if the Corps was furloughed because of the sickness he desired Gignilliat to come to Washington, DC. Gignilliat became ill and was furloughed to Robinson, returning to VMI in early January 1892.[27] Perhaps he had not completely recovered, and Robinson wrote to Shipp again letting him know that he wanted Gignilliat to be furloughed to him again if the physician and Shipp determined that Leigh's condition warranted another absence from VMI. Gignilliat ended up remaining at VMI, but perhaps from a maturity perspective it would have been better had he gone home to Robinson instead of remaining on post.

Having remained at VMI and apparently recovered from his illness, Gignilliat was feeling better and began exploring his boundaries and "feeling his oats." He ended up straying a bit too far and faced a serious discipline issue in February 1892 that could have resulted in his expulsion. On February 22, 1892, Gignilliat was caught drinking with two third-class cadets. All three cadets admitted to the charge and offered to make a pledge of "total abstinence" from all "intoxicants" for the remainder of their time at VMI to be allowed to remain. As an indication of the popularity of all three cadets, all members of both the third and fourth classes agreed to make the same pledge of abstaining from all "intoxicants" for the remainder of the academic year as a show of support for the accused cadets and in hopes of influencing the superintendent to allow all three cadets to remain at the Institute.[28] This was common practice at military schools, especially at West Point and VMI.[29]

Based upon the three accused cadets' willingness to swear off of all intoxicants and the remarkable willingness of two entire classes of cadets to agree to abstain from all intoxicants for the remainder of the school year as a show of support for them, Shipp felt "at liberty in his discretion to withhold the extreme penalty" of expulsion and instead released Gignilliat and his two compatriots from close arrest and allowed them to remain at VMI under confinement "to the limits of the Institute or Camp" for the remainder of the year.[30]

In a letter to Shipp on March 7, 1892, Robinson acknowledged the "leniency" of Shipp and the "generosity" of Gignilliat's classmates that allowed him to "avoid incurring "the shame and lasting injury of expulsion," writing that "I trust [Gignilliat] has received a lesson which will make a lasting impression on him." Determined to make good on this surprising and welcomed second chance, Robinson insisted that Gignilliat "redeem himself in the estimations and good reports of his professors" substantively and rapidly.[31]

Declaiming at VMI

One way for young Leigh to do so was to find ways to contribute positively to cadet life on post. Doing so would also provide him with more constructive ways to occupy his time.

Having experienced success declaiming at Emerson, Gignilliat had developed quite a repertoire by the time he entered VMI. As it turned out, and since declamation was a popular activity for students at the time, VMI's Dialectic Society sponsored a declamation contest during his first year, which he entered and performed one of the selections he had learned at Emerson.

Exhibiting his penchant for perfectionism and the high standards to which he held himself for any public appearance (and later for the Culver corps of cadets), Gignilliat practiced incessantly in front of a mirror, perfecting his enunciation, voice modulation, and facial expressions. Presaging his gift for showmanship, he also arranged for a subtle violin accompaniment from a fellow VMI cadet during his recitation to set the appropriate mood and provide atmosphere music for the performance.

His performance won him the contest's top prize of a gold medal, satisfying Robinson's demand for Gignilliat to "redeem himself in the estimations and good reports of his professors." However, the impact of his performance has a slightly different impact on his cadet peers, earning him the enduring nickname of "jessamine flower," based upon one of the more memorable phrases of the poem he recited.[32]

Insights on the Faculty-Cadet Relations at VMI

In an unpublished chapter from his memoirs, titled "The Old Rat," Gignilliat related a series of stories from his first year at VMI in 1891. The stories center around the first professor at the Institute who was neither a graduate nor a veteran, and was thus considered to be a kind of "old rat" by the cadets at the time.

The stories provide a flavor of VMI during Gignilliat's time as a cadet, conveying a somewhat good-natured relationship between cadets and faculty.[33] This is noteworthy, as this type of relationship was quite different from the cadet-faculty relationships at many other military schools at the time, which tended to be more formal and infused with much more of the military hierarchy characteristic of the US Army.

His recounting makes it clear that Gignilliat thoroughly enjoyed this aspect of VMI. This relationship both impressed Gignilliat and stayed with him, almost surely establishing the notion of "playing the game" and the friendly, respectful, and cordial relations between cadets and faculty at CMA that Gignilliat insisted on establishing and maintaining.

Evaluating Gignilliat's First Year at VMI

Militarily, Gignilliat earned a total of 43 demerits during his fourth-class year, which was well below the class average of 75 demerits for that year.[34] As would be the case throughout his four years at VMI, while Gignilliat never accrued an excessive number of demerits, he acquired more than others rated as highly as he was on the GOM, indicating that he tended to take his academics a bit more seriously than the VMI disciplinary regulations, perhaps owing to his relative youth.

Gignilliat departed VMI in June 1892 after graduation and spent the summer in Washington, DC with the Robinsons.

Summer Furlough and an Amusing Experience with His Brother Robbie

During the summer after his first year at VMI, Gignilliat had a memorable adventure with his brother Robert "Robbie" Deas Gignilliat, who was two years older than him and with whom he was close. This episode is interesting on its own, and it also provides some portends of Gignilliat's actions and behavior at Culver.

According to Gignilliat, Robbie concocted a money-making scheme that involved purchasing a stereopticon machine that showed slides in a projector-like manner, allowing the owner to charge admission for providing presentations. The stereopticon machine was as expensive as it was technologically advanced. The projector was quite advanced for the age, with light to illuminate the slides coming from an arc light of jets of ignited oxygen and hydrogen gas, combined in a small cylinder of calcium just behind the lenses that produced a very intense light used to illuminate slides and provide an audience with an unusual and exhilarating viewing experience.

Robbie had worked out a way of paying for a stereopticon machine that required Leigh's assistance. To accompany such a spectacular visual image, it was standard practice to provide music and/or narrative to enhance the experience. Robbie wanted young Leigh to put his declamation abilities to good use as a public lecturer by providing the narration for his visual presentations. Having just completed the demanding first year at VMI, Leigh was only too happy to oblige the request of his older brother. The endeavor also promised adventure and fun.

Robbie christened their partnership by forming the Boston Stereopticon Company. Showing his gift for marketing at an early age, Gignilliat recalled that they included "Boston" in the name to reflect the city's reputation as a center of learning and education and for the prestige associated with it, which sounded more impressive to them than either the Savannah Stereopticon Company or the Georgia Stereopticon Company. Believing they could make a fortune, the two set out like enterprising salesmen on what became an epic adventure for both.

To attend to his part of the venture, Gignilliat memorized two canned lectures to recite as accompaniment to the slides Robbie would project. Robbie had secured two groups of slides, showing pictures of either the cathedrals of England or images from "moonlight in Venice." The brothers added two mechanical slides to the presentations—a kicking donkey and a snoring man -- to provide comic relief.

To sustain the illusion that he was a lecturer from Boston, Gignilliat wore a brown suit that belonged to one of his older brothers as his costume. However, the young Gignilliat forgot to bring a good pair of pants with him, so he had to wear a pair of Robbie's old corduroy trousers that looked presentable in the dark. Such were the expedients required at the time of shoestring operations of the nascent Boston Stereopticon Company!

Robert "Robbie" Deas Gignilliat, circa 1900.[35]

Literally taking their show on the road, the boys traveled to neighboring towns to share their presentation, renting suitable venues and charging admission for viewings. Business started slow for the young entrepreneurs, but they managed to make just enough money to cover their expenses. Nevertheless, word of their powerful viewing experience began to spread around the area (buoyed perhaps by the misconception that it might have actually been a burlesque show from Boston, according to Gignilliat), and by the time they reached Waycross (about 60 miles Southwest from Darien), they played to a full house.

In Waycross, the lighting fixture malfunctioned when a sandbag broke loose and smashed all of the slides of the cathedrals of England with enough force to shatter an empty chair and break through the floor before coming to rest. Mortified by the accident and a bit shook up by the close call, young Leigh was unable to face the stunned onlookers, and it fell to Robbie to inform the audience about the accident and refund their money. Nevertheless, they made a small profit from the show. More broadly, Gignilliat learned from Robbie's example the necessity of retaining the presence of mind to speak up and do the right thing in a time of hardship. It was a lesson he would put into practice well and often at Culver.

Next, the pair headed next to the coastal town of Brunswick, which was near their hometown of Darien, hoping that the residents would be intrigued by their remaining slides of "moonlight in Venice." However, a competing venue caused the audience to be quite small (six, as Gignilliat recalled), including one Italian gentleman who winced at Gignilliat's mispronunciations of the Italian cities during his lecture. They failed to make enough money to pay for all their expenses, and the sheriff arrived to arrest them. However, one or several of the uncles who resided in the area arranged to pay their debts, and the two were released from jail.

Gignilliat ended the tale marvelously, relating that his oldest brother Willie, who was a lawyer in Savannah, asked Leigh to take a client of his out to lunch several years later. It turned out that this person was supposed to be seated in the chair that was crushed by the falling sandbag in Waycross. Gignilliat admitted that it was the same show put on by him and his brother, but the man refused to believe him, likely due to Gignilliat's still youthful appearance, and also since he was convinced that the presentation had come all the way from Boston![36]

The story provides a wonderful glimpse into Gignilliat as a youth and his relationship with his brother Robbie. It also shows that Gignilliat could tell a good story, accounting for his skill in smaller social setting and with finding ways to establish and sustain rapport with others.

Tragic News – The Death of His Rat Roommate

Upon his return to Darien after the adventure with Robbie, Gignilliat received tragic news. His Rat roommate from VMI, Miles Deming, had contracted Typhoid Fever earlier that summer and died from it. Having survived the rigors of VMI's first year together, Deming's death must have been devastating for the 17-year -old Gignilliat.

Gignilliat's Sophomore Year at VMI – No Longer a Rat

Gignilliat returned to VMI in September, 1892. With the death of his Rat roommate, he needed to find someone else with whom he could live. While classmates generally roomed together, Gignilliat ended up rooming with a Second classman (junior) from Ohio named Charles "Charlie" Kilbourne, a fellow civil engineer who was also an excellent student. Kilbourne had a stellar career at VMI, winning one of the Institute's highest award for scholastic achievement – the Jackson-Hope medal – presented annually to the two most distinguished graduates of the Institute. Kilbourne served in the Army after graduation and fought with distinction in both the Spanish-American War and in WWI, and he later became VMI's sixth superintendent.[37] This was a fortunate pairing for both cadets, and although they roomed together for only one year, they formed a lasting bond and remained lifelong friends, corresponding regularly and especially when both were running two of the nation's top military schools.

Although he did not finish in the top five percent of his class, as he had during his freshman year, Gignilliat continued to perform quite well academically at VMI. He finished his sophomore year ranked a respectable sixth out of 46 classmates on the GOM, placing him in the top 13 percent of his class and earning him recognition for a second consecutive year as "distinguished in general merit," although just barely.[38] As during his fourth-class (freshman) year, Gignilliat continued to excel in both drawing (2/46) and Latin (3/46), also performing quite well in Astronomy (4/46) and Descriptive Geometry (4/46). Physics (15/46) and English (16/46) were his relatively lowest-ranked subjects.[39]

In terms of military performance, Gignilliat was promoted to the rank of corporal, which was and still is the highest rank available to sophomore

Members of VMI faculty, 1892-1893.[40]

cadets at VMI. While serving as a cadet corporal, he accrued 61 demerits during his third-class year, which would be his highest total while at VMI and reflected the relative increase for all of his other classmates, as the class average for demerits was 88 despite having fewer cadets in the class. To counter the inevitable relaxation of discipline that follows the completion of its demanding first year, VMI has a tradition of holding its sophomores particularly accountable for adhering to its regulations. This practice results in its third-classmen almost always accumulating the greatest number of demerits over the course of a given year, as it did in 1892-1893 for Gignilliat and his Brother Rats.[41]

Robinson was sufficiently pleased with Gignilliat's performance that he included some additional "pocket money" for Leigh in fall 1892. This must have made life a bit better for Gignilliat, allowing him to avail himself of some of the area's finer pleasures, such as they were available to him.

During the course of his time at VMI, Gignilliat was interested in sports but unsuccessful in his attempts to earn a spot on and compete with the school's varsity teams. VMI fielded varsity teams in football, baseball, gymnastics, as well as a tennis club.[42] While baseball had been a staple of the Institute's athletic program since 1866, football had only begun being played on post in 1891.[43]

Gignilliat played football for a time, which, given his slim build, was quite courageous, as college football during this period was exceedingly dangerous. Learning that Gignilliat had suffered a broken jaw and lost a tooth as a result of his involvement in a football game on Thanksgiving Day of 1892, Robinson wrote Gignilliat soon afterwards and forbade him from any further participation in this dangerous sport while at VMI. Robinson informed Shipp of his decree as well.[44]

With football now out of the question, gymnastics, baseball, and tennis were Gignilliat's only viable athletic options. While his interest in any and/or all of these sports is unknown, Gignilliat admits that he was not successful in making any of the teams in which he may have been interested.

Gignilliat reported that the "varsity teams were the only outlet for a modestly aspiring athlete" during his time of attendance. VMI's gymnasium was quite

Early VMI football players, circa 1893. [45]

meager during Gignilliat's time, housed in "a small frame building with a tan bark floor, a set of parallel bars, a pair of flying rings, and a trapeze" with little else. Besides "rough-housing and raising hell (since youthful animal spirits can't be entirely bottled up)," there was no intramural program to speak of at VMI, leaving young Gignilliat with no outlet for his athletic ambitions, modest though they were.[46] As a true Southern gentleman, however, he did become quite proficient on horseback, and riding horses well would be a source of pride and exercise for him throughout his entire life.

Lacking an athletic outlet for his ambitions, Gignilliat turned instead to more cerebral pursuits during his college days. This approach became especially prominent after his sophomore year.

Summer Furlough After His Sophomore Year – A Return in Doubt?

After departing VMI in June 1893, Gignilliat spent much of the summer of 1893 in Georgia with his family. While traveling to Georgia, Gignilliat had his travel money stolen and was stranded without means. Robinson wrote to Shipp on July 1, 1893, asking for his assistance to help Gignilliat get access to money and also a ticket to Georgia.[47] With Shipp's gracious assistance, Gignilliat was able to travel to Georgia and spend time with his family members.

While in Georgia, something happened that caused Gignilliat's return to VMI for his junior year to come into question. Gignilliat wrote to one of his professors from Savannah, Georgia on August 11, 1893, asking that his drawings be packaged up and sent to him in Savannah, since it was "doubtful," in his own words, that he would return to the Institute.[48] Gignilliat provided no explanation for his request, but the most likely reason was financial. Perhaps the 18-year-old Gignilliat experienced a bout of youthful rebellion with his guardian that elicited a threat to discontinue paying for his tuition, causing Gignilliat to question his ability to continue attending VMI. The problem – whatever it was – was apparently resolved, and Gignilliat returned to VMI for his junior year as his company's First Sergeant, the highest rank available to junior cadets.

Gignilliat's Junior Year at VMI

Returning to VMI for his junior year, Gignilliat roomed with his solid if unremarkable classmate and Virginian Ashby Brooke "Book" Taylor. Taylor was an athlete, playing football, baseball, and tennis for VMI. His nickname may have been somewhat facetious, indicating that he preferred the athletic field to the classroom. Taylor graduated from VMI and had a successful career in real estate.[49] Branching out a bit, Taylor and Gignilliat began exploring extracurricular activities at VMI, joining the German Club together.[50]

During his second-class and most academically demanding year, devoted almost exclusively for engineering students to highly challenging courses in science, engineering, and math, VMI did not rank-order cadets using the GOM, opting instead to recognize them for superior academic performance in each of their courses separately. Gignilliat continued to perform quite well in the classroom, earning recognition as being "distinguished" in both Engineering (in which only four cadets were so recognized) and Physics (in which only five cadets were so recognized). He was also ranked fourth out of 32 in both General Chemistry (in which only three cadets were recognized as "distinguished") and Mechanics (in which only one cadet was recognized as "distinguished"), and fifth out of 32 in Mathematics.

Gignilliat had a better year militarily, accruing only 47 demerits, which was 19 fewer than the class average of 66.[51] Overall, Robinson was pleased with his ward's performance and progress. [52]

In mid-January 1894, Gignilliat again spent time in the VMI hospital. Although he had a high level of energy, Gignilliat also had a tendency – like many other high-achieving young men – to work himself too hard and

become vulnerable to illness. The cold of the Virginia winters also likely contributed – he tended to get sick during the winter – and Robinson shared with Shipp that Gignilliat complained about the cold.[54]

Despite the increased academic challenges he faced in the classroom and serving as his company's First Sergeant, Gignilliat

VMI professor Robert A. Marr (standing), Gignilliat's drawing instructor.[53]

expanded his intellectual horizons significantly during his second-class year. He joined the somewhat haughtily named Virginia Dialectic Society at VMI, which was a debating club that provided oratorical training and leader development. Gignilliat resumed his role as a "Declaimer" for the organization, delivering the speeches of famous historical figures in dramatic fashion and as a performance.[56] The ideal disclaimer elevated mind over temperament, and demonstrated application, industry, mental and moral improvement, perseverance, judgment, and reason, all of which are the components of mental prowess, referred to by educator Thomas Williams as "intellectual manhood."

By reading works on rhetoric and eloquence, and by declaiming exemplary historical orations, students received not only an education in speech but also an education in ambition and self-fashioning."[57] Gignilliat again excelled in this role, earning official recognition for his oratorical prowess during his junior year.[58]

VMI hospital (left) and mess hall (right), circa 1890.[55]

It took hard work, discipline, and perseverance to become an effective declaimer. It also required the speaker to expose one's self to the criticisms of one's peers, which takes a special kind of courage in adolescence, and to create and maintain an atmosphere of trust and respect to ensure that peer feedback remained constructive and supportive. This type of interaction produced a remarkable characteristic of 19th century literary societies: "students took the reins of oratorical training."[59]

It was in this way that members of this club became peer educators, and it is likely that Gignilliat formed his earliest ideas of the power of peers to train, educate, and elevate one another based upon his involvement with the VMI Dialectic Society. As a younger member of the corps and of the society, this experience showed him how peer educators could be effective, especially high school juniors and seniors who were about the same age as Gignilliat when he became involved in the society.

Toward the very end of his junior year, Gignilliat became convinced for some reason that he would not be able to return for his final year. Generously and in a flourish of adolescent overreaction, Gignilliat gave away all of his VMI uniforms and equipment at the end of the school year, "thinking he would not return" to VMI for his final year.[60] Word of Gignilliat's actions reached Robinson, who telegrammed Shipp with the following very direct message: "Is Leigh in trouble? Wire at once."[61] There is no record of any disciplinary or academic troubles for Gignilliat at the Institute during this period, leaving one to wonder what precipitated Gignilliat's actions. Robinson appears to have been legitimately concerned, and based upon his response to this incident, it is clear that Robinson remained somewhat connected with and concerned about Gignilliat through the end of his junior year at VMI.

Summer Furlough After His Junior Year – A Return in Doubt (Yet Again!)

Perhaps Gignilliat had done something that disturbed Robinson, or perhaps the youthful rebellion from the previous summer ignited into a full-blown fissure, but for whatever reason, Gignilliat's return to VMI remained in doubt during the summer between his junior and senior year. The first inkling of this came in a letter Gignilliat wrote to Shipp on July 2, 1892, while in Georgia and not in Washington, DC (and therefore not residing with Leigh Robinson), informing Shipp that he had decided to return to VMI for his fourth and final year "if possible," but that he was having difficulty acquiring the necessary funds to pay his fall tuition. This is the first such letter of which there is record, as Robinson had dutifully paid Gignilliat's tuition for each prior semester, indicating that Gignilliat was no longer willing to accept the financial support from Robinson.[62]

Gignilliat followed up with another letter to VMI on July 6, 1894, asking for the addresses of his professors so he could write to them about getting copies of his textbooks for the lowest possible cost.[63] This entreaty appears to be more serious than Gignilliat's request of the previous summer for his professor to send him his drawings, indicating that Gignilliat was more concerned about this financial status in summer 1894.

Gignilliat's Senior Year at VMI – A Falling Out with Leigh Robinson and Willie Steps Up

By September 1894, Gignilliat had not found a way to resolve his financial crisis, and he wrote to Shipp requesting an extension to his leave until Robinson returned from Europe on October 1, 1894. The implication is that Gignilliat had decided to ask Robinson for tuition so he could return to VMI for his senior year, despite their apparent falling-out that appeared to have occurred sometime during the spring of his junior year or perhaps in the summer afterwards (mentioned above). Gignilliat moved down to Lexington, Virginia sometime during the next two weeks and was living in town while waiting for Robinson's return.[64] In September 1894, Gignilliat was elected by his classmates to serve as the Chief Marshall of the Final Ball, indicating that he had found a way to re-join the Corps officially, resume his studies, and serve as the captain of D Company.

Gignilliat's oldest brother, Willie, assumed guardianship duties for Gignilliat for the 1894-1895 academic year, indicating that Gignilliat's relationship with Robinson was damaged beyond repair. By mid-October 1895, Willie had managed to reach an agreement with Robinson for Robinson to pay the $150.00 for Gignilliat's fall tuition.[65] Upon receipt of the check from Robinson, VMI informed Willie that Gignilliat owned an additional $290.00 to replace the "effects" he had dispensed with at the end of the previous school year when he was convinced he would not be returning to VMI. This meant that even though Robinson had belatedly paid the $150.00 for fall tuition, Gignilliat still owed VMI an additional $290.00.[66] This outstanding balance was somehow paid.

While Gignilliat's relationship with Robinson had apparently deteriorated, the resulting financial troubles brought about a closer relationship with Willie. Gignilliat likely welcomed this development, since Willie was 14 years older and he almost certainly never really got to know Willie while growing up in Darien. As the family's first-born son who was also a lawyer,

Willie very likely also reminded Gignilliat of his deceased father. Willie paid for Gignilliat's spring 1895 tuition without Robinson's assistance, and he began taking a more active role as Gignilliat's guardian.[67]

Rejoining the Corps a bit late in September, owing to his financial difficulties, Gignilliat roomed with Virginia classmate Goldsborough "Keith" Serpel, perhaps more by convenience than by choice. He spent the year living with the sturdy Serpel, who played right tackle on the VMI football team and was also in the German Club. Serpel had a distinguished career in banking in Norfolk, Virginia, after VMI, and he shared Gignilliat's love for VMI, graduating with a degree in engineering and serving on the VMI Board of Visitors.[68]

All of Gignilliat's hard work over the previous three years paid dividends during his final year. In the classroom, Gignilliat excelled in Descriptive Geometry (1/25), Latin, Drawing, Astronomy, Surveying (2/25), along with General Chemistry, Ordnance and Gunnery, and the purportedly philosophical Art of War (3/25). He struggled somewhat in Minerology (19/25) and Geology (15/25).[69] Although he acquired just 23 demerits during his first-class year, his total of 174 demerits over the course of his four years at VMI was more than the 124 average number of demerits for the members of his class. This number of demerits placed him in the bottom 30 percent of his class in terms of military deportment, but

Gignilliat (circled) and the first-classmen of the VMI Class of 1895.[70]

his relatively few number demerits assigned during his first-class year contributed to an overall performance that was exemplary, earning him the honor of holding the highest possible rank of cadet captain for his final year.

Gignilliat also hit his stride as a leader with the VMI corps of cadets during his senior year, during which he served as a cadet captain (the highest rank a cadet could earn), president of the Dialectic Society, editor-in- chief of the yearbook (*The Bomb*), president of the newly founded Dramatic Club – earning him the new nickname of "Tragedian" – and was the elected Chief Marshall of the Final Ball, which was a particularly important commencement event (as it would be also at Culver under Gignilliat's direction). Gignilliat was also a member of the VMI Glee and Minstrel Club, serving as its interlocutor, who is the person in the middle of the line in a minstrel show who questions the end men and acts as the leader. He was a member of the German club and served on its floor committee, responsible for planning and conducting club events.[71] Besides athletics, it is hard to imagine how Gignilliat could have been more involved.

In reviewing his academic performance, Gignilliat excelled consistently in Drawing, Latin, Astronomy, Descriptive Geometry, and General Chemistry. He appears to have done best in subjects that were dynamic, somewhat hands-on, and which could be mastered through hard work and dedication. He proved himself to be very capable in the curriculum's military subjects as well, likely because they were similar to the academic subjects that engaged his interest. The more inanimate subjects like Geology and Mineralogy seemed not to capture his interest.

In terms of his military performance as a cadet officer, while Gignilliat managed to accrue a relatively modest number of demerits each year, he was clearly recognized as a leader among his peers. He also faced at least one significant challenge in this role. While serving as the senior ranking cadet responsible for monitoring the discipline in barracks on the night of January 2, 1895, a cadet "riot" of sorts erupted. This event – which may or may not have been planned in advance – precipitated an almost complete breakdown in discipline, and it caused much unrest in barracks and consternation among the school's leadership.

Deemed to be an incident that was "prejudicial to good order and discipline," Gignilliat was suspected of condoning the event tacitly by pretending to be unaware of it when it occurred, and he was formally charged with dereliction of duty. At the ensuing disciplinary hearing, Gignilliat was found "not guilty" of the charge and exonerated of all wrongdoing, thereby retaining the trust of the school's leaders in his ability to function effectively in his role and enabling him to retain his rank as a cadet captain.[72]

Perhaps feeling that he had earned the right to relax the standards of his personal conduct in his final semester at VMI, the disciplinary challenges for Gignilliat at VMI continued in January 1895, although these were not related to the performance of his duty as an officer. He was charged with two serious violations in early January 1895.

The first charge was making a "false official statement" to the Officer in Charge regarding whether Gignilliat had permission to enter a certain room for "visitation" with another cadet. Gignilliat asked the cadet Officer of the Day for permission to visit the room of his company First Sergeant, and there was a disagreement about whether the cadet Officer of the Day granted the requested permission. The presiding officer, after hearing testimony from both Gignilliat and the cadet Officer of the Day, acquitted Gignilliat of the charge of making a false official statement.[73]

Gignilliat was also charged with "abuse of the Sick list" on January 12, 1895. Gignilliat had been sick again in early January, and his brother Willie had written to Shipp on January 11, 1895 concerned about his younger brother's condition. Willie shared that Gignilliat had a tendency to catch bronchitis and that his condition would get serious if not treated quickly.[74]

According to the report of the incident, Gignilliat had been excused from all academic duty on January 12, 1895, due to his illness, and he was supposed to remain in his room for the remainder of the day. However, Gignilliat left his room and visited "other places around barracks" instead of remaining in his room as required by being on the Sick list and excused from academic duty. Gignilliat was found guilty of being absent from his room when he should not have been, constituting "abuse of the Sick list," which was a very serious violation of VMI regulations, especially by a cadet captain. As a result, Gignilliat was reduced to ranks and lost his captaincy.[75]

This came as a crushing blow to Gignilliat, who informed his brother Willie of the outcome. In his custodial capacity, Willie wrote to Shipp on January 29, 1895 asking for an explanation about the incident. Willie also expressed his support for the decision, sharing with Shipp that he had counseled his younger brother that "adversity, if rightly taken, develops finer traits of character than are called into play by success," and that he had urged Gignilliat to keep doing what he needed to do and "not to indulge in any bitter feelings or vain regrets" in the wake of the decision. Acknowledging that the ordeal had taken a toll on the young man, Willie confided to Shipp that he had "every confidence" that Gignilliat's "true manhood and better nature" would assert themselves and, as befitting a conscientious guardian, asked Shipp to provide all possible support to help him get through the challenge. Shipp provided Willie with the information he requested on February 1, 1895, and Willie was sufficiently placated to let the matter drop.[76]

Gignilliat, however, refused to accept the outcome despite Willie's acceptance of it, feeling that he had been unjustly convicted and wrongly reduced in rank. After receiving a petition of support for his reinstatement signed by every member of his company that surely fueled a sense of righteous indignation, Gignilliat began engaging with Shipp about the possibility of regaining his rank. Shipp responded by referring Gignilliat to the Board of Visitors, and Gignilliat crafted and submitted an impassioned appeal for the Board's consideration on February 6, 1895, based upon his belief that the hearing officer was not presented with all of the facts of his case, that the outcome was inappropriate, and that the rank that he felt he had rightly earned should be restored.[77]

There is no record of the Board considering Gignilliat's appeal, and it is likely that he graduated VMI as a cadet private and with a bit of a chip on his shoulder about the incident that robbed him of his coveted rank. Gignilliat does not appear to have had any ill-will towards Willie for his acceptance of the outcome, as the two remained close and Gignilliat asked Willie to stand with him as his best man at his wedding three years later.

These episodes, along with his immaturity that manifested itself periodically in acts of indiscipline that resulted in the acquisition of a few demerits each year even while performing well in the classroom and holding high cadet rank, might explain his willingness in later years to view cadet performance more holistically. While at Culver he insisted on maintaining the high level of military discipline expected of the period, but Gignilliat also allowed Culver cadets to have fun, and he was inclined to excuse acts of indiscipline he considered to be trivial in nature and/or effect and also to work with cadets who committed more serious violations of regulations from which he believed they could recover.

In terms of his extracurricular performance, it appears that Gignilliat left VMI more confident in his speaking abilities than in his writing abilities, owing to his involvement with the Dialectic Society and perhaps also the Glee and Minstrel Club. Perhaps most remarkably, Gignilliat helped to establish the VMI Dramatic Club in winter 1894/95, putting on a performance of the prophetically named farce comedy, "A Sea of Troubles," on February 23, 1895.[78]

Compiling an admirable record of academic, military, and extracurricular achievements, along with an uneven disciplinary record, Gignilliat graduated in June 1895 with a BS in civil engineering ranked fourth in his class of 25 on the GOM, thereby earning recognition for academic distinction again during his fourth and final year.[79] He would treasure his *alma mater* for the rest of his life, remaining in contact with the institution, basing much of the Culver system off the VMI approach, and returning to Lexington, Virginia for a visit whenever he had the opportunity.

As the editor-in-chief of the VMI yearbook, Gignilliat provided the following preface on behalf of himself and his other three editors, which he likely had a major hand in writing and serves as an appropriate epitaph for his time at VMI:

> *Before submitting to you the modest result of our labors, THE BOMB of '95, we the editors, beg leave to claim your attention for a moment, while we enumerate the difficulties that have beset us in its preparation. Out object has been to revive the old BOMB, the pioneer of Southern Annuals which in '85 assailed the public for the first and last time. During the intervening ten years the Institute has been without an Annual, and we undertake this second edition with no experience and many misgivings as to its ultimate success. The first difficulty encountered was the securing of adequate funds for the enterprise, the second, the selecting from a body of men pursuing an almost exclusively technical course, a staff of literati to whom might be entrusted the preparation of a book worthy of the Institute. The first, despite an unsuccessful appeal to the Board of Visitors for aid, and the difficulty of reaching our Alumni, we have in some measure surmounted; the second, we know only too well we have not. We are conscious, however, of having made an honest effort of having done our best. To the Faculty we are indebted for the several contributions which lend our book the only literary merit to which we can lay claim. To succeeding classes we hope our efforts may prove an incentive, and that profiting by our errors and shortcomings, they may in future be more successful.[80]*

While perhaps not written entirely by Gignilliat, the hallmarks of his early writing style are clearly present. The first is his almost complete discounting of his own ability to produce anything of literary value, including many self-deprecating references throughout all of his writings. In this case, there are several present. The second is his constant use of the plural pronoun "we," seeking to share credit and ensure that credit for the product was shared with others widely and generously. There is also a hint of his perseverance, alluding to the difficulty of obtaining funding for the project and the persistence in locating a source of funding for it.

After VMI

The 19-year-old Gignilliat graduated from VMI in May 1895, bringing to a close the many challenges he faced at the Institute for much of the year. The relief must have been tremendous, and he likely returned to Georgia to celebrate with his family and contemplate the next phase of his life.

Given the financial challenges he had experienced over the previous year, it was likely not long before he began looking for work in Georgia and perhaps also in Washington, DC before deciding to take the recently instituted Civil Service exam in Washington, DC, hoping for a position in the US Patent Office.[81] The Patent Office seems like a good fit for Gignilliat, as a patent clerk needed to have a scientific or engineering background to evaluate patent applications, and the US Patent Office was in DC, which was a city he both knew and liked. Working in such a capacity would have also allowed for a career of service, which many in his family had pursued and likely appealed to him. He almost certainly hoped to land a job as quickly as possible to start earning his own way in the world and also to begin his professional career.

Gignilliat probably took the civil service exam in Washington, DC in early 1896. It was an exam that was well-suited to his talents and intellect, as it was practical and not theoretical, designed to test aptitude for the specific job and not for overall general knowledge.[82]

The Powerful Yellowstone Experience

While waiting for the results, and as a way to earn some money, Gignilliat made use of his education and took what was likely a seasonal job as an Assistant Engineer at Yellowstone. Given the rather adventurous nature of some of his brothers – Thomas involved in the very early stages of powered man flight and Ravenel heading to the untamed west in Texas for a time – it is not surprising that Leigh jumped at the opportunity to become a surveyor in the wilds surrounding Yellowstone National Park.

Working at Yellowstone also gave him something meaningful to do. Yellowstone National Park was established on March 1, 1872 in the far northwest corner of what was then the Wyoming Territory, before the determination of official boundaries for future states in the area. The admission into the Union of the state of Montana on November 8, 1889 as the country's 41st state and the following year of Wyoming on July 10, 1890 as the country's 44st state made it important to establish precisely the northwest boundary of the park with respect to the newly established state boundaries of Montanan and Wyoming.

Yellowstone Park Superintendent Horace M. Albright in his "office." [84]

Gignilliat likely embarked on his Yellowstone adventure sometime in spring 1896, just after serving as Best Man at his brother Robbie's wedding in Georgia, and when weather became suitable for surveying. [83] He began working in the rugged country, posing a challenge to his health that had proven to be somewhat precarious during his time at VMI. In addition, he was also putting his engineering expertise to work and leading a small survey team, which gave him his first professional leadership experience.

Gignilliat's "office" must have looked something like the set-up Park Superintendent Horace M. Albright used above. The three "tame" black bears surrounding him illustrate the abundance of wildlife in the area and also the dangers faced by those working in the park during its early period. [85]

Working and living in the area required Gignilliat and his team to be away from the area's town, Fort Yellowstone, for extended periods of time while they did the work necessary to locate the park's northwestern boundary. The park's undeveloped infrastructure and poor roads meant that they were traveling on horseback and camping at night. The leadership aspects of this included selecting suitable campsites, pitching their tents, cooking their food, locating potable water sources, responding to the weather, keeping watch for the many dangerous predators living in the area, maintaining morale, and settling the inevitable disputes that arose

among the team members working under such conditions. This placed Gignilliat in a position of being immediately responsible for a small team of men who were likely older and more experienced than he was, and in a situation in which he had to confront every challenge facing the team directly and effectively or risk losing the confidence of his men.

Detailed pictorial map of Yellowstone, 1904. [86]

Yellowstone was established soon after the completion of the first transcontinental railroad in 1869. Its remote location made it quite difficult to visit, and the park only hosted 300 visitors during its first year of operation. In the early 1880s, and as tracks were being laid off the main line to extend its reach, the Northern Pacific Railroad built a rail line that connected the park's northern entrance with a train station in Livingston, Montana. From Livingston, visitors would travel by stagecoach to cover the final 60 miles south to the part's northern entrance. Livingston became a major source of visitors for the park, helping to increase the number of visits to 5,000 by 1883. By 1908 visitation increased enough to attract a Union Pacific Railroad connection to West Yellowstone.[87]

The natural beauty of the park was breathtaking, moving the naturalist John Muir to describe the park in 1898 as follows:

> *However orderly your excursions or aimless, again and again amid the calmest, stillest scenery you will be brought to a standstill hushed and awe-stricken before phenomena wholly new to you. Boiling springs and huge deep pools of purest green and azure water, thousands of them, are splashing and heaving in these high, cool mountains as if a fierce furnace fire were burning beneath each one of them; and a hundred geysers, white torrents of boiling water and steam, like inverted waterfalls, are ever and anon rushing up out of the hot, black underworld.*[88]

For young Gignilliat, it must have been a nirvana-like experience to live and work surrounded by such awesome natural splendor.

After being in the wilderness for a period of time – likely several weeks – the team returned to the Army's newly established Fort Yellowstone at Mammoth Hot Springs within the boundaries of Yellowstone National Park to report their progress, replenish their provisions, and enjoy the comforts of civilization briefly, such as they were at the time. Established in 1891, Fort Yellowstone was a permanent post that grew from the temporary cavalry post of Camp Sheridan the Army established when the War Department took over administrative responsibility for the area from the Interior Department in 1886. The Army's main purpose was to establish control over the rampant poaching and destruction of natural resources that the Department of Interior was unable and ill-equipped to address.

A private environmental group, the Boone and Crockett Club, became involved in the conservation efforts as well. Led by Theodore Roosevelt and noted American anthropologist, historian, naturalist, and writer George Bird Grinnell (for whom Glacier National Park's Mount Grinnell is named), the group sponsored legislation to preserve that nation's national parks. On May 7, 1894, the Park Protection Act was signed into law largely through the active support from the Boone and Crockett Club, which, combined with the Army's efforts on the ground, provided the necessary means to preserve Yellowstone's grandeur and beauty.[89]

Given the Army's mission at Yellowstone, the recently passed Park Protection Act, and Gignilliat's training at VMI, he was likely involved in these efforts as well. With perhaps several soldiers as part of his team, all of this added even more complexity to his surveying duties and increased his leadership responsibilities substantially.[90]

During one of his extended forays into the wilderness, the results of Gignilliat's Civil Service exam reached Fort Yellowstone, likely sometime around mid-July 1896. The duration of his wait was not completely unprecedented, as it took approximately four months to grade the exams because of lack of sufficient numbers of qualified graders and an increase of almost 20,000 (19,392) people taking the test.[91] While Gignilliat did have to wait for a long period of time to receive the results, it was not as long as the six months it took in 1893 to grade the exams and notify individuals of the results.[92] However, when the results arrived, Gignilliat was out of contact and remained unaware of their arrival until his return to Fort Yellowstone in late-August 1896.

Gignilliat returned to civilization during the third week of August 1896 to find a telegram, dated mid-July 1896, offering him the Civil Service position he desired. This outcome indicates that Gignilliat did very well on the exam, as the overall pass rate for exam for that year was only 58.3 percent and patent clerk jobs were highly sought after, meaning the competition for them was even keener.[93]

The telegram also requested immediate acknowledgment from him. Fueled by his excitement over the results and desire to accept the offer, Gignilliat almost certainly wired acknowledgment of acceptance to Washington DC immediately. However, given the length of time that had passed since being notified, combined with the already lengthy period of time the position had been vacant during the grading of the exams, he was likely informed that he was too late and that the position offered to him was no longer available.

During this period, it was common practice for vacant Civil Service jobs to be filled by "reinstatement or assignment of personas already employed," if a suitable candidate could not be identified and hired within a reasonable amount of time.[94] If he had done particularly well on the exam, he may well have been told to try again the following year, which would explain his decision to seek a short-term position before returning to DC to apply again for a job in the US Patent Office in summer 1897.

Gignilliat must have been quite disappointed by this outcome, and he used his time away from the wilderness in Mammoth Hot Springs to reflect on his situation and consider his options. Looking to one of his mentors for advice, Gignilliat wrote VMI Superintendent Shipp on August 22, 1896 to ask for his help in finding a job as a teacher or commandant in a military school. According to his letter to Shipp, Gignilliat wanted to work in such a capacity "...until the resumption of the work in The Park on which I am now employed as Assistant Engineer."[95]

Reacting in the moment, it appears that Gignilliat intended at that point to remain at Yellowstone as an Assistant Engineer. It also appears that he remained committed to engineering. Perhaps, however, the taste of leadership he had leading his survey team appealed to him, suggesting that he might have an aptitude for leading others, and inspired him to seek out a position "as a teacher or commandant in a military school."

Gignilliat's work at Yellowstone ended for the season sometime in late fall 1896, likely when the winter weather set in and made it impossible to continue surveying. Perhaps he had signed on for only one season of work in this capacity, but by the time of his departure it appears that Gignilliat no longer intended to remain/return to his position as an Assistant Engineer at Yellowstone National Park. The reasons for this decision are myriad, including perhaps his dislike of the cold weather (which was well-known prior to and afterwards), a disdain for the mundane and meticulous work of surveying, the unpredictability of the work and the pay, and/or a burgeoning desire to work at a military school in some type of leadership capacity.

What is clear is that Gignilliat also remained committed to working at a military school as either a teacher or commandant, as he had indicated in his August 1896 letter to Shipp. He was drawn to such work at this point in his life perhaps because he felt that he was well-trained to do it, he enjoyed serving in a leadership role, and also because it was more stable and predictable in terms of pay. Departing Yellowstone in late 1896, he was still thinking that working in a military school would be a temporary pursuit and that he would get back to some type of engineering, perhaps intending to re-apply to the US Patent Office in 1897.

Culver historian Robert Hartman believed that even though he spent several months on a surveying team in Montana, Gignilliat found the practice of engineering not to his liking and that "he was searching out a position that would better suit his interests and military training."[96] However, it is just as likely that Gignilliat didn't yet know he did not like engineering, and that once he had tried it, he thought that maybe doing the other thing he felt qualified to do – work at a military school – would be more to his liking. What we do know is that it took until June 1897 for Gignilliat to give up on the idea of applying for a job with the US Patent Office, and much of the reason for him doing so had to do with his situation at Culver and meeting his future wife.

This suggests that Gignilliat's actions during this period were less about a dislike for engineering and more about a young man being engaged in the process of finding himself after college (he was only 21 years old!) and figuring out what he really wanted to do with his life.

Gignilliat left Yellowstone without a job, and he "returned to Georgia by way of Chicago where he registered with the Albert-Clark Teacher's Agency."[97] He still intended to look for work at a military school, and in "late fall of 1896, [Gignilliat] forwarded his credentials to a Chicago teachers' agency and initiated a job search" for suitable work at a military school.[98]

Upon his arrival in Savannah, Gignilliat took a harbor survey job. While working in this capacity, Gignilliat experienced yet another health crisis, becoming "violently ill as the result of a ruptured appendix." It took him some time to recover, and he acquired what he described as having a rather "persnickety appetite" as a permanent result of this serious health issue.[99]

Colonel Alexander F. "Fred" Fleet.[100]

Sometime after Gignilliat registered with the nationally renowned Albert-Clark Teacher's Agency in Chicago en route to Savannah, Culver's third superintendent, Colonel Alexander F. Fleet, had a short conversation with someone at the Albert-Clark Agency in late-fall/early winter 1896-1897 and encountered Gignilliat's application.

Fleet related in a subsequent letter to Shipp that he came across Gignilliat's application *"...purely by accident,"* but it is clear that this occurred as a result of quite deliberate action by Fleet. After several months at Culver, Fleet, according to Hartman, recognized his need for "an energetic and youthful graduate of a military college who could introduce and direct a 'system' of organization and leadership" to Culver and who was also capable of serving as Fleet's "second-in-command."[101] Based upon this recognition, Fleet engaged in the sensible professional practice of contacting search firms who could help him address and satisfy this need. Clearly, there was little serendipity in the manner in which Fleet came across Gignilliat's application other than timing.

Fleet found Gignilliat to be a perfect match for his search criteria and decided to offer him the job as Culver's Commandant of Cadets and Fleet's second-in-command. This is somewhat curious, since Fleet already had the very capable Bert Grenier and Hugh Glascock in his employ, and these were men with whom he had worked at Missouri Military Academy (MMA) and in whom he placed great trust.

Perhaps Fleet wanted to augment his existing staff with someone who had graduated from a military school, or perhaps CMA founder HH Culver urged him to look for such a person familiar with military schools. Regardless of his motivation, Fleet's search had to have been done with HH Culver's support and acquiescence, since he was paying all the bills.

According to Hartman, shortly after Gignilliat's vitae reached Colonel Fleet, he was offered the position as Commandant of Cadets.[102] It is not known what caused Fleet to have such a positive reaction/response to Gignilliat's application. This was during a period when in-person interviews were the exception, given the challenges of travel and distance, so all Fleet had to go on was what he could read on paper and perhaps a second-hand impression from someone from the agency who had met Gignilliat when he delivered his application.

Fleet, as a Virginian, likely had a very high opinion of VMI, which worked in Gignilliat's favor. Perhaps Gignilliat being a graduate of VMI and not West Point worked in his favor with HH Culver, given the recent unpleasant experience with West Point graduate Tebbetts. Perhaps the notion of bringing in someone new who was not associated with either Culver or MMA was attractive to both HH Culver and Fleet to help bring the two schools together, which would also explain why Fleet was looking for someone other than Grenier and Glascock (both of whom were quite capable), and also so quickly and in winter 1896/1897.

Gignilliat went from leaving Yellowstone in late-1896 with no job to receiving two job offers in January 1897. According to Mather, Gignilliat

> *received two offers from the Albert-Clark Agency. One was to teach mathematics at Michigan Military College at $150.00 a month; the other as commandant of Culver Military Academy at $80.00 a month. He chose the latter offer because it interested him more than the other, especially since it was his intention at that time to remain only for the school year and then to return to civil engineering.*[103]

The offer from Michigan Military Academy makes sense, given Gignilliat's academic performance, background, and status as a military school graduate. Both positions were in the north, where he would have to exist for at least part of the year in the cold that he did not prefer but was willing to endure, as he had at VMI and while working at Yellowstone.

Gignilliat considered both offers carefully. While the offer from Michigan Military Academy was far more lucrative, it does not appear that money played much of a factor in his decision-making. Gignilliat wrote that he accepted the Culver offer because it interested him more. This suggests that, even as a young man, Gignilliat was more interested in doing meaningful work than in salary, as the Culver job paid a little over half of what the Michigan Military Academy job paid. Perhaps because he had not yet decided to give up on engineering at this point, Gignilliat was more willing to accept the lower-paying position that seemed more interesting in anticipation of returning to an engineering position that paid more. Pragmatically, while less lucrative, he may have believed that he needed only to earn enough to subsist during the interlude before he returned to engineering work, perhaps as a patent clerk.

As it turns out, Gignilliat made a very good decision to decline the Michigan Military Academy offer. The school was founded in 1877 in Orchard Lake (30 miles west of Detroit) by Captain J. Sumner Rogers, who had been a Professor of Military Science and Tactics at Detroit High School, and it was modeled on West Point. Although better known than Culver and more successful at the time by virtue of winning national drill competitions and being involved in the 1893 World Columbian Exposition in Chicago, the school soon fell on hard times with the death of its founder in 1901 and closed due to bankruptcy in 1908.

Accepting the offer to become the Commandant of Cadets at Culver and work with Fleet had a transformative effect on Gignilliat, his professional career, and the institution making the offer of employment. His decision to accept the far more active commandant position also indicates that Gignilliat had recovered fully from the effects of his ruptured appendix in fall/winter 1896.

The die having been cast, Gignilliat embarked on the long trip from Savannah, Georgia to Culver, Indiana during the second week of January 1897. Robert Hartman describes Gignilliat's journey artfully, and his description is worth quoting at length:

> As his train slipped from the platform and headed northwest from the tidewater coastline, he watched the scenery change from January crispness to the deep winter harshness in the mountains around Chattanooga. He was not a stranger to cold weather having spent four years at VMI and his mental memory book contained recollections of the frigid winds that slashed across the expanse of the parade ground. Yet going to the hinterlands in the dead of winter – and Yankee country, too – was approaching cultural shock.
>
> The miles clicked by and Gignilliat's mind whirled with thoughts of what lay ahead. He had a degree in civil engineering, but was about to abandon his profession for a job that made no claims on transits, log books, chains, contours, and calculus.

The Depot, Culver, Indiana.

Vandalia train station, Culver, Indiana.[105]

    In Atlanta he changed trains, then again in Chattanooga, and three more times, Cincinnati, Indianapolis, and finally Logansport, Indiana. There, just as dusk had enveloped the rural landscape, he climbed aboard the Pennsylvania Railroad's Vandalia Line for the hour-long ride to Marmont, Indiana. It was January 13, 1897.

    As the train grew near the station, only a few lights identified a community that was to become part of Gignilliat's great adventure. He glanced out of the window to confirm that he had, indeed, arrived at the [train] depot [in Culver], gathered his hand luggage, and stepped from the warmth of the passenger car into the icy vestibule. The conductor opened the door, raised the cover over the steps, and lent a hand to Gignilliat as he climbed down to the platform. He glanced to his right and saw his trunk being unloaded from the baggage car.[104]

Arriving at Culver on the cold and snowy evening of January 13, 1897, as a 21-year-old young man, Gignilliat had little inkling that this was the beginning of what would become over four decades of devotion to an institution, a family, a way of life, a group of colleagues, and thousands of the nation's finest young men.

Chapter 2: The Situation at Culver at the Time of Gignilliat's Arrival

As much of a change as the situation represented for Gignilliat, Culver Military Academy had recently experienced both challenges and changes of equal or greater magnitude in the areas of personnel, organization, academics, and military training. It is important to address these aspects of Culver and to consider the school's new Superintendent, Alexander F. "Fred" Fleet, to better understand the situation into which Gignilliat arrived. It is also essential to consider the history of Culver Military Academy's first two years as a way of understanding the background and context of the situation.

A Brief History of Culver Military Academy, 1894-1896

The school that bears his name was founded by Henry Harrison "HH" Culver on the shores of Aubeenaubee Bay on 40 acres he owned on the northern bank of Lake Maxinkuckee. It had been his "castle in the sky" about which he had dreamed since 1888 (by his own account), and, after considering several different options (including a school for girls), he envisioned it as a military school for boys to prepare them for success in the world.[1] Although he does not address the reason for the school's military structure directly, it may have come from the first Superintendent (who came from Ohio Military Institute (OMI) in College Hill, OH) or from HH Culver's encounter with two boys at Lake Maxinkuckee who attended the same school and regaled the older man with captivating stories of their lives and adventures as cadets. Perhaps it was both.

Henry Harrison "HH" Culver – Known as "The Governor"

Henry Harrison Culver, named for the famous first governor of Indiana William Henry Harrison and thus called the "Governor" for all of his life by those who knew him, was a businessman and salesman who sold and then owned a company that made stoves (among other endeavors). Together with two of his brothers, they determined that cast iron was too brittle and wasn't durable enough, so they began the innovative practice of making ranges out of wrought iron, founding in 1881 the Wrought Iron Range Company in St Louis that produced and sold some of the most popular stoves in the country during the late-19th century.

To sell his stoves, the aggressive and energetic Culver organized his sales force in a hierarchical manner that bore some similarity to the military, and they spread out across the Midwest in wagons to peddle their wares and bring their products to the people. Unwilling to ask his sales staff to do something he was not willing to do himself, HH joined them on the

Henry Harrison "HH" Culver – known as the "Governor."[2]

road and worked his own sales territory. On one such trip, the sturdily build man of average height with sandy/reddish hair found himself in Wolf Creek, Indiana, which was about eight miles east of Lake Maxinkuckee in southern Marshall County, where he met a bright and vibrant school teacher named Emily Jane Hand. HH was smitten and the two soon married in September 1864, eventually having six children.

Emily Jane's father was remarkably intelligent, and she was known for her practicality and judgment. She owned property on the northeastern shore of Lake Maxinkuckee, to which HH added, and he loved to spend time there along the water fishing and enjoying the area. When his health failed in 1881 (perhaps due to heart problems and a slight stroke of paralysis), HH eventually moved to Emily Jane's property to recover in the wholesome environment of the lake.[3]

A summer of being in the outdoors restored his health. The independent-minded HH built a Chautauqua on the expanded property he and Emily Jane owned on the northern bank of Lake Maxinkuckee in 1889, intending to provide a gathering place for activities related to the Christian revival Chautauqua Movement of the time. This brought entertainment and culture in the form of prominent acts and speakers to local audiences for their own enjoyment and education. Culver's Chautauqua, located just east of what was then known as the town of Marmont (later renamed Culver in his honor), attracted some of the biggest names on the lecture circuit to perform and speak.

Emily Jane Culver.[4]

A man of forceful personality, HH Culver's dream was to establish a school where he could educate children, what he called his "castle in the sky." After declining a nomination to serve as his Missouri district's congressional representative and considering briefly founding a school

CULVER PARK ASSEMBLY

LAKE MAXINKUCKEE
(MARSHALL COUNTY, INDIANA.)

July 19 to August 1, 1889.

Advertisement for the Culver Park Assembly Chautauqua gathering in 1889.[5]

for girls, the very practical and astute businessman proceeded with his plan to create a school for boys and young men in which he could instill his own version of manliness to others on the banks of Lake Maxinkuckee. Indicative of his ever-present abundance of common sense, HH used the facilities of his former Chautauqua, comprised of a hotel, a smaller building (referred to as the tabernacle), and several cottages, to host all school-related activities.

The impetus for adopting a military system remains shrouded in mystery. It may have been the idea of the first Superintendent (who came from a military school) or a simple recommendation from the aforementioned interactions with boys from Ohio Military Institute, some combination of both, or it may have been more involved and complex. The "official" rationale has changed over the years, according to and reflecting current needs, but what is clear is that the inherent efficiency of such an organization appealed to the practically minded founder and was adopted.[6]

After a very small and unsuccessful summer program for 16 boys, none of whom enrolled in the winter program, Culver Military Academy opened on September 24, 1894 with an enrollment of 45 cadets. The cadets lived and studied in the Chautauqua hotel building under the direction of the experienced and proven educator Reverend John H. McKenzie. McKenzie had led the Ohio Military Institute prior to coming to Culver, and he had impressive credentials, including having earned a doctorate and been recently ordained as an Episcopal priest.

Unfortunately, the quick-tempered HH and the obstinate McKenzie had significant personality differences and fundamental disagreements about the direction of the school, with McKenzie wanting it to become more religious in nature and renamed as "Saint Paul's School," since, according to McKenzie, no one outside the area had ever heard of Culver or would send their sons to study at a place with such a name. HH wanted to incorporate some of the organizational aspects of his sales force into a military program for the school, believing that boys would enjoy and benefit from it. Given his background, McKenzie was supportive of such an approach and no doubt encouraged HH's notion to do so at Culver.

Reverend John H. McKenzie.[7]

The First Fire

As if personnel challenges were not enough – two contentious superintendents in as many years – the wood-framed Chautauqua that served as the school's main building and dormitory caught fire and burned to the ground on the afternoon of February 24, 1895.

Fortunately, no one lost their life, and most escaped with minor injuries. Rushing from St Louis to the school, HH made arrangements to house the students in various locations around the community (including his own local home on the northeast shore of the lake) while continuing their education at his school.

To rebuild the structure, HH brought with him from St. Louis a Swiss architect, Albert Knell. After agreeing on the design of the three-story building, HH set Knell loose to construct

The Culver Chautauqua hotel building.[8]

a building with "accommodations for [around] ninety cadets, a dining room, classrooms, offices, infirmary, library – and a power plant, called the 'Engine Annex,' which contained heating boilers and generators to produce the Academy's electric power" and power the entire campus.[9]

To properly anchor this new and heavier structure on the shifting sands and underground springs that existed near the lake, Knell had to shore up the foundation on the building's northwest corner where the Engine Annex would sit using an entire trainload of crushed stone to provide a proper foundation that could also distribute the weight of the equipment (e.g., boilers and generators) evenly.[10]

HH also vowed to restore his school in a building made of brick, steel, stone, iron, concrete, and other non-flammable materials throughout that would be "fireproof." All girders, studding, and lath were made of steel, and while he could do little about the wooden window frames and doors in the building, the aesthetic wooden floors were set on expensive nine-inch-thick concrete foundations. A fire in such a structure could burn only the floor and casings of the room in which it ignited.[11]

According to architect Knell regarding the construction method:

> "All exterior walls are of stone and brick laid in cement and resting upon heavy concrete foundations; stairways are spacious and built of iron; the interior supports for the floors and roof throughout being heavy steel I-beams, filled between with arches of concrete. The partitions are composed entirely of steel lathing fastened to concrete and steel studding, and covered with two coats of Agatite cement plaster and one coast of plaster of Paris, the whole forming a thorough and complete system of fire-proofing, which guarantees against fire, regardless of its origin, and insures (sic) perfect safety to the occupants of the building."[12]

It is hard to imagine a more "fireproof" method of construction, indicating HH's resolve to prevent any such future occurrence of fire at Culver.

This approach to construction, along with the practice of using crushed stone to establish a stable foundation in less-than-stable areas and of using an iron frame and concrete to "fireproof" the building, were in line with the most modern construction techniques being developed in Chicago's skyscrapers and around the world. Culver benefited from the impact of a of second fire – the great Chicago fire of 1871 – in terms of the new fireproofing techniques that became incorporated into the designs of buildings as a result.

In fact, the building was considered to be so impervious to fire that it was (somewhat surprisingly!) not even insured. This being a period during which the threat of fire was especially acute, CMA's early promotional material took special care to highlight this aspect as one of its most attractive selling points.

Culver's distinctive looking "fireproof" main building was constructed in an astonishing four months, the challenges of the foundation notwithstanding. The cornerstone was laid on May 16, 1895, and it was ready and capable of housing as many as 100 cadets by the time the new school year began on September 24, 1895. These measures represented the efforts of HH to protect his school and all involved with Culver Military Academy from ever having to face the scourge of fire on campus.[13]

Given rather free reign regarding the outward look of the structure, Knell began the process of creating Culver's unique architectural style. To convey the school's military character and Indiana location, Knell finished the building using a red brick façade trimmed with Indiana limestone, a crenelated roofline, faux towers, and a welcoming front porch made of brick and stone that led to "an entry constructed of limestone and crowned with a large keystone" for Main Barrack that would be become the signature look of Culver's buildings. It would be HH's third son, Edwin Raymond "ER" Culver, who would take an abiding interest in the outward appearance of the school and work with Knell to create and perpetuate the distinctive Tudor-Gothic architectural style of many of the institution's buildings.[14]

Engineers were able to solve the foundational problems with the building, but the foundation of the relationship between HH and McKenzie continued to erode and reached a point that was beyond repair by the end of the year. Despite their apparent shared purpose, the two men agreed on little else and never really got along. After his unsuccessful attempt to rename the school, McKenzie recommended that it be affiliated with the Episcopal church. HH staunchly opposed this idea, preferring it to remain a non-sectarian institution.

In addition, it became clear that McKenzie may not have had the same understanding of the purpose of the school's military program as HH Culver had. While McKenzie ended up working at three different military schools throughout his career, helping to start and/or incorporate a military program at each, it appears that he did not know very much about the particulars of how best to do so. For example, at Culver, he hired a law student from the University of Michigan who was an exceptionally athlete but who had no military experience to serve as his

Commandant of Cadets. While he was a good man, he focused most of his efforts on the school's athletic program (even going so far as playing on the football team, which was not unusual for the period), and the school's military program floundered.

The disagreements between the two strong-willed and determined men continued to mount in other areas as well, and it became increasingly apparent that the pairing was less than ideal. Each recognized the situation for what it was, and by mutual (if also self-interested) decision McKenzie left to run Howe Military School after one year.

Clinton H. Tebbetts -- A Second Superintendent

While capacity on campus increased, enrollment was dwindling. HH was spending far too much money on his "castle in the sky," especially after putting up the new building. He could ill-afford another year of losses, and he needed to increase enrollment to keep the school in operation. The situation for HH was growing desperate, and he hired Clinton H. Tebbetts as superintendent, hoping that a West Point graduate would better support his military program and run his school more effectively.

Major Clinton H. Tebbetts, Culver's Superintendent & Commandant, 1895-1896.[15]

As a seasoned Army officer, Tebbetts decided to function as both Superintendent and Commandant. He embraced HH's military ideal a bit too eagerly, and his view of discipline was that of the Army and not of an educator. As a result, he treated the cadets as mature soldiers instead of the devolving adolescents they were. This approach rubbed HH the wrong way, and he developed a powerful dislike for Tebbetts' way of handling "his boys."

Tebbetts' approach had a detrimental effect beyond retention, and enrollment dwindled during his first year in charge. By the beginning of his second year, Culver Military Academy's enrollment was down from 37 to 29 cadets, and the school was facing the real prospect of having to close its doors unless its enrollment could be increased quickly and substantially.

In addition, Tebbetts' health was not good, calling to question his ability to shoulder the dual responsibilities of superintendent and commandant. He further frustrated HH Culver with his lack of aggressive recruiting and unwillingness or inability to learn from the founder's impressive sales experience how to better market and promote the school. According to Hartman, Tebbetts' failure to learn from a master grated on every fiber of Mr. Culver's body, and by the beginning of Culver's third year of operation the tension between the two had reached a boiling point.

Unfortunately, Tebbetts' methods were not as expeditious as the construction of the main building, and when the school began using the new structure, the lowered enrollment of 29 boys left rooms for around 70 cadets vacant and unused.

The fire of February 1895 provided Culver with a brand new "fireproof" building. This building would serve as the foundation of its survival, but it took a second fire to build up Culver to a level that ensured its survival.

1896 – A Year of Change

Just as the new school year began at Culver in September 1896, and knowing that her husband was displeased with Tebbetts and disappointed with the state of CMA, Emily Jane brought to his attention a newspaper article reporting that a terrible fire on the evening of September 24, 1896 had destroyed Missouri Military Academy (MMA).

While it was a miracle that no one had died in the fire and few had been injured seriously, due in part to the heroism of cadets and faculty members alike, the MMA community was nonetheless left destitute and without a school at which to study after having been in session for only two weeks.

News of the destruction of MMA went coast to coast, which was unusual for a school in a very rural area and with an enrollment of around 80 cadets. The school was located in the town of Mexico, MO, which was about 90 miles west of St Louis. The reason the tragedy received such

Missouri Military Academy destroyed by fire on September 24, 1896.[16]

attention was because the school was led by a well-known and exceptional superintendent, Alexander Frederick "Fred" Fleet, and Emily Jane encouraged her husband to contact him.

Fleet's Dilemma

Fleet had served in the Confederate army during the Civil War, ending up on the staff of General Henry A. Wise, and he was present at Robert E. Lee's surrender at Appomattox. A scholar of the Classics who was also a devout Baptist, Fleet's academic publications were widely respected in learned circles, and his popular Sunday school lessons were used by many in churches across the country.

As both owner and founder of MMA, Fleet lost everything in the fire. He reported his total loss at around $90,000 (equivalent to roughly $1.5 million in today's value), which wiped out his entire investment in the school and life's savings. In addition, his extensive personal library was destroyed, which, as a scholar, troubled him most deeply. Fleet had prudently insured as much of the property as possible from at least 15 different entities, but it covered only about 40 percent of his total loss. In terms of the contents of the building, insurance would cover just under $3,000 of the much greater losses, including almost all of the government-issued military equipment. Fleet would be involved in processing and litigation for the next three years before finally settling all of his claims and being relieved of personal liability for the fire-related losses.

Faced with such a catastrophic loss, Fleet determined that there was no prospect of rebuilding in Mexico, despite the willingness to support such a project by some of the locals. In the immediate aftermath of the tragedy, Fleet believed that he had already "taxed the good will of the people of Mexico as far as [he] should," and determined that "it would be asking too much of them to contribute again towards building a new school." Having ruled out the option to rebuild from the ashes, Fleet began looking elsewhere for a suitable place to relocate and provide his charges with the semester's worth of education for which most had already paid.

Reflecting the high esteem he had earned, Fleet received numerous offers of assistance from patrons willing to host his school at their locations, including two from within the state of Missouri and others from three different states. He had to accept one of the offers quickly or face the prospect of losing students to other schools, refunding tuition and boarding fees, and becoming unable to keep his school in operation.

The In-State Offers

Fleet received two generous offers to relocate his school within the state of Missouri. One was from the Meremac Highlands Inn, near Kirkwood, Missouri, and the other from the Hotel Estes at Pertle Springs, Missouri. The Meremac offer had much intrinsic appeal for him, but Fleet was careful to give each equal consideration.

After visiting the most promising location near Kirkwood, Missouri the day after the fire, Fleet rejected the offer from the Meremac Highlands Inn because its buildings did not have brick or stone exteriors and were even less fireproof than his structure at MMA had been. (Meremac was destroyed by fire in 1926.) Fleet was unwilling to subject his students and faculty to the threat of fire again, and he was determined to find a location that provided safe "fireproof" buildings for his school's new home.

The other location in Missouri, the Hotel Este, met this condition, but it was not acceptable because it also served as the location of the spring encampment for Wentworth Military Academy, one of his most successful competitor schools in the state. Fleet could ill-afford to relocate somewhere that would likely expose his institution to yet another risk to its survival. Thus, Fleet determined that there would be no "Missouri Compromise" regarding his decision to relocate MMA anywhere in the state of Missouri.

The Out-of-State Offers

The out-of-state offers came from Illinois, Kansas, and Indiana. While it is not known if Fleet even considered the offers from Illinois and Kansas, the offer from Indiana caught his attention. It was from HH Culver, who came from a prominent St. Louis family, and St. Louis provided the majority of MMA students. While the Missouri connection was convenient, the fact that Culver's recently constructed main building was a true "fireproof" structure likely had much greater appeal to Fleet. Emily Jane urged HH to contact Fleet, and the telegraphed message from HH struck just the right chord with Fleet, saying, "*You have the boys and I have the buildings. Let's get together.*"

HH had summed up both of their situations splendidly, and despite the tragic circumstances of the situation, it is hard to imagine a better opportunity for him or Fleet receiving a more appealing offer. After corresponding with HH via telegraph, and within four days of the destruction at MMA, Fleet determined that Culver was the best location to move his school, at least in the short-term. By accepting HH's offer so quickly, the MMA cadets had little time to consider enrolling elsewhere. The cadets were able to reassemble, remain together as a corps, and complete at least the first semester of their school year under Fleet's expert tutelage.

Agreeing to Merge MMA and CMA

Fleet took a tremendous leap of faith to accept an offer that was almost too good to be true, from a man he had never met, to run a school he'd never seen, in a state he had never lived. Fleet and HH had a "gentleman's agreement" for how they would integrate their resources, and in those days that was enough for men of honorable character and intentions to enter into such a significant arrangement. Thus, on the strength of what was little more than a virtual handshake at the time and the promise of potential benefit borne out of mutual desperation did the merging of the two schools commence.

Remarkably, Fleet was able to convince his entire faculty and staff of five individuals to agree to uproot their families on scarcely more than a moment's notice and accompany him to Indiana. Fleet also convinced the parents of 72 of the 78 cadets enrolled at MMA at the time of the fire to allow their sons to relocate almost 400 miles to the northeast to continue their education. Of the six who did not make the move, we know that three had already enrolled elsewhere (as Fleet had feared) and that two were recovering from their injuries from the fire and not yet able to join their peers. The status of the single other cadet is not known. This equated to a remarkable retention rate of over 90 percent.

HH Culver's response via telegram to Fleet's acceptance conveys an enthusiasm that almost certainly appealed to the Classics scholar in Fleet. He wrote, "*Veni, vidi, vici. The academy is at your disposal. When will your party start? Answer quick.* HH Culver." The first three words are Latin for "I came, I saw, I conquered," a famous saying attributed to Julius Caesar and intended to indicate a quick and decisive victory, which this most assuredly was for both parties. It is an erudite and entirely appropriate response from HH Culver to Fleet that must have helped reassure Fleet that he had made the right decision.

Extinguishing Other Embers at CMA

On the very same day as the fire that destroyed MMA, and after returning from a long, expensive, and largely unproductive recruiting trip, Tebbetts wrote HH a letter expressing his despair with various aspects of the situation at the Academy and his own unhappiness with the current state of affairs. This was the last straw for HH, who was fed up with employing a superintendent who he felt did not treat his beloved boys well and also could not sustain, let alone increase, enrollment at his school. Their relationship was strained beyond repair, and HH finally surrendered to his mounting frustration and took decisive action.

Based upon archival sources, it is clear that HH was also unsatisfied with Tebbetts as a financial manager for the school. Sometime in early September 1896, HH detailed his highly capable business manager, F. T. "Sam" Neal, from the Wrought Iron Range Company to take over these responsibilities and bring some semblance of order to the financial chaos that reigned at CMA in fall 1896. Upon receipt of Tebbetts' letter, HH (who was in St. Louis) directed Neal (who was on campus at Culver) to fire Tebbetts immediately.

Neal met with Tebbetts on September 28, 1896 and fired him as directed. However, and as was to be expected, Tebbetts was not happy about being let go and argued with Neal for three hours before accepting his dismissal. While Neal held firm in terms of the decision, Tebbetts was able to wrangle agreements for HH to pay out the remainder of his contract – totaling $800.00 (equating to approximately $30,000 in 2023 dollars) – and for Neal to allow him to remain in his house on campus until October 7, 1896 (due to his wife's illness).[17]

The decision by HH to fire Tebbetts was almost certainly influenced by Fleet's acceptance of his offer to superintend Culver Military Academy. Despite the acrimonious manner of Tebbetts' separation as Culver's superintendent, it nevertheless cleared the way for Fleet to assume the superintendency of Culver upon his arrival.

Wishing to move on from the Tebbetts' administration, HH was able to get Fleet's agreement to arrive at Culver on October 5, 1896. To ensure the campus was prepared for his arrival and that of the MMA Corps, Fleet sent his own wife, along with several other faculty wives, to Culver a few days ahead of main body. HH appreciated all of this, but he did not have a place for the Fleet family to live upon their arrival, since Neal had agreed to allow Tebbetts to remain in the superintendent's quarters until October 7, 1896. HH wrote to Neal to ask if Tebbetts could be out of the house any sooner, perhaps in time for Fleet's wife to be able to move in immediately upon her arrival in the first days of October, and by October 5, 1896 at the very latest, when Fleet was scheduled to arrive. Neal did not think Tebbetts would be out by October 5, 1896, and the truculent Tebbetts appears to have stayed in the house until the agreed-upon date of October 7, 1896.

Contemporary records also indicate that Neal was concerned that Tebbetts might take some type of adverse action against Culver after reading about Fleet and MMA coming to Culver. Neal also reported hearing rumors that Tebbetts had connected with McKenzie and that the two were trying to lure CMA cadets away to Howe via parents.[18] Lacking corroborating evidence to support Neal's concerns, we are forced to rely on his man-on-the-ground-at-the-time perspective and make our own determination accordingly. Given the level of acrimony his separation produced, it seems nevertheless likely that Neal's concerns regarding Tebbetts' possible actions/reactions were worth taking seriously, regardless of their legitimacy.

The MMA Group's Arrival

After collecting MMA cadets spread from Denver to Pittsburgh, Fleet, his staff of five, and 61 of his cadets arrived in Culver on a train provided gratis by the Vandalia Rail Line around 5:00 pm on Monday, October 5, 1896. They were met by a small party of Academy officials, cadets, the Culver band, and community members, who cheered their arrival. Two lake steamboats were moored at the pier to ferry the newcomers across the lake to their new home at the Academy, where the wives of some of the MMA faculty had arrived a few days prior to ensure all was ready for their arrival.

When the ships completed their short journey across Aubeenaubee Bay and the MMA group stepped off the boats, Culver Military Academy's enrollment increased immediately from 29 to 90 cadets. Culver's faculty

The view the MMA group had when they arrived at CMA.[19]

and staff were also strengthened significantly by the arrival of MMA's academic staff of capable instructors, and HH Culver had one of the very best and most respected superintendents in all the land to run his distressed school.

Over the course of the remainder of October, 11 additional MMA cadets arrived. In addition, with the departure of Tebbetts, the parents of several other CMA cadets allowed their sons to return to the school. With their arrival, total enrollment reached around 100 cadets sometime in late-October. As a result, Culver's main barracks became overcrowded, requiring cadets to reside in another frame building on campus. Apprised of the situation, HH decided to build another building with room for 40 cadets and two staff members that would become West Barrack. Construction began in late-October 1896, but HH's desire to have it completed by January 1, 1897 proved to be too ambitious.

Contemporary accounts report that the cadets from MMA and CMA "merged with very little friction or jealously," but rumors surfaced that "the Missouri boys, being more than twice the strength of the Culver Corps, took control on the first night and ducked all of the CMA cadets in the lagoon." Given what we know about the officers who accompanied Fleet, it seems highly unlikely that the MMA cadets had any opportunity to depart the barracks in the evening and take all of the CMA cadets to the lake to dunk them. Rather, one suspects that the barrack was a flurry of activity that first evening and that all collapsed in exhaustion at the conclusion of a very long and stressful day for the MMA group. What is certain is that the senior cadet captain from MMA, Donald Smith, assumed the role of senior captain of the combined MMA-CMA corps.

Within one week's time, the *Culver City Herald* reported, based on first-hand observation, that, "Under the new order of things everything is running as smooth and regular as clock work (sic) at the Culver Military Academy." The reporter went on to write that, "The boys from the 'sunny south' are delighted with the academy and its surroundings, and are especially pleased with beautiful Lake Maxinkuckee." Remarking on the conditions he observed, the reporter wrote that he "found every department as clean and tidy as a band-box," but was a bit disappointed to find Colonel Fleet present but too busy for an interview.

Later in October, MMA contributed several cannons that had survived the fire and new government-issued rifles to replace those destroyed in the fire, augmenting Culver's existing military equipment. Within one month of the second fire, and largely as a result of its own fire of 19 months prior, Culver Military Academy had astonishingly been built up and "saved" by a second terrible fire, like a Phoenix rising from the ashes.

Dousing the Financial Fire

Despite the infusion of cadets, faculty, and equipment, Culver also faced a tremendous increase in its expenses.

Unsatisfied with Tebbetts as a financial manager for the school, HH detailed his highly capable business manager, F. T. "Sam" Neal, from the Wrought Iron Range Company to take over these responsibilities and bring some semblance of order to the financial chaos that reigned at CMA in fall 1896. While his love for his school was unbounded, HH could ill-afford a third year of financial losses from his "castle in the sky" and remained hopeful that it could remain in operation.

Neal discovered that CMA was critically short of cash to pay its own expenses and those it assumed from MMA. Neal worked very hard with HH and HH Jr. to make good on all its debts. While Fleet and others focused on integrating MMA into CMA, Neal and HH Jr focused on keeping CMA afloat financially.

Many of the expenses came as a surprise to those at Culver, but HH was adamant that Neal make payment for all bills during this very challenging period. HH also began construction on a second barrack during this period, making things even more challenging for Neal.

As an expedient, Neal asked all Culver parents to pay their son's tuition immediately instead of waiting until later in the semester as was the usual practice. MMA did not have as structured a process for paying tuition, and Neal found that Fleet had made many different arrangements with individual parents for the amount of their son's tuition and when it needed to be paid.

HH Jr. monitored the transactions closely from the Wrought Iron Range Company in St. Louis, making the most efficient use of the funds Neal forwarded to him and supplying the remainder from the Wrought Iron Range Company assets with the approval of his father.

Neal worked tirelessly to address these issues, and along with assistance from HH Jr., managed to acquire enough cash to meet all of Culver's tremendous financial obligations in the final three months of 1896.

Fleet Takes Charge

One of the first things Fleet addressed was the school's motto.

The School Motto: A 19th-Century Mission Statement

Soon after his arrival, Fleet changed Culver's motto from its original "If God is with us, who can be against us" (*Si Deus nobiscum, quis contra nos*; from Romans). This motto was very likely adopted by McKenzie and reflected his religious perspective. It is unknown if Tebbetts shared McKenzie's religious focus, but Tebbetts did follow McKenzie to Howe after Culver, so he was at the very least not opposed to it.

Fleet changed the school's official motto almost immediately to the more earthly "Not many [things], but much," (*Non Multa sed Multum*) which can be stated more colloquially as "quality over quantity." The more academically inclined and Classics scholar Fleet retained the Latin vernacular of Culver's motto, keeping with the prevailing practice within academe, but altered the focus of the motto significantly, making it both more secular and pragmatic.

The idea it was meant to convey was that it is *the quality with which a task is done* – the "muchness" of it – *that is more important than number of things* – the "many" – *one does*. It was an elegant expression of Fleet's shrewd recognition that Culver, at the time of his arrival, was a school of limited resources that needed to differentiate itself by becoming distinguished in a few important areas rather than striving to match the broader offerings of institutions that possessed more resources.

Fleet's Vision for Culver

In Fleet's emerging whole-boy educational approach, his motto meant identifying important aspects in the areas of mind, body, and spirit upon which the institution could focus effectively, and then enhancing existing programs or implementing new ones to help boys become distinguished in these areas. As long as the school identified the correct aspects in each area and the administrators remained focused on achieving distinction within the identified aspects, the school would be successful in producing graduates who were highly competent in a certain few but essential areas, preparing them to excel in society. In comparison to the righteous tone of McKenzie's dictum, Fleet's motto for Culver was more in line with a mission statement of today, indicating that the institution's focus would be on preparing boys for success on earth by enabling them to do a few important things exceptionally well.

For Fleet, this effort began with facilities. The Culver catalog devoted much attention to the calamity of the fire that destroyed Missouri Military Academy and its buildings in the catalog, with over five pages containing a listing of fires that had occurred at other schools and the cost of the damage they caused. Setting Culver apart from the many examples provided, the catalog makes special and repeated mention of Culver's "fireproof" buildings.

HH Culver Passes Away and Three of His Sons Step Up to Support CMA

HH Culver died at his home in St. Louis on September 26, 1897 after a six-month illness. Coming one year after the fire that destroyed MMA and which resulted in the salvation of CMA with the arrival of Fleet and his MMA cadets, Culver was far more stable and financially secure at the time of his death. The Culver community mourned his loss and took solace in the rejuvenation of CMA that HH had managed to achieve.

Determined to perpetuate Culver Military Academy as a living memorial to their father, three of the Culver sons – Henry Harrison "HH" Jr. (b. 1870), Edwin Raymond "ER" (b. 1872), and Bertram Beach "BB" (b. 1875) – committed to ensuring that CMA remained in operation. HH Jr. assumed responsibility from providing primary oversight of the Wrought Iron Range Company in his father's stead, while ER and BB took over the role of HH Jr. by providing direct oversight of CMA: BB Culver from the time of his father's death in 1897 through 1899, and ER Culver from 1900-1902. This arrangement allowed HH Jr. to focus his attention on keeping the Wrought Iron Rang Company functioning, profitable, and capable of providing continued support for CMA.

The Personnel Situation at Culver at the Time of Gignilliat's Arrival

The personnel situation at Culver was perhaps of greatest import to the institution at the time of Gignilliat's arrival. Glascock, with Fleet's direct involvement, was charged with arranging the school's academic program to achieve Fleet's vision. This required Glascock to attract and retain first-rate scholars who were also able to be successful teachers of young boys. The school's curriculum, pedagogy, and facilities had to be as impressive as its faculty, and the students had to be both committed to and capable of responding successfully to the rigor required of them by their instructors in the classroom, whether preparing for college or to enter society or the business world upon graduation.

Fleet required a similar level of expertise to bring the school's military and student life programs up to the desired standard. There had been little deliberate effort made in this area in Culver's early years. McKenzie hired Culver's first commandant in fall 1894, Warren W. Holliday. Holliday was a young, highly educated graduate of the University of Michigan's law school and a superb athlete, but he had far more expertise playing football and boxing than he did in developing boys outside the classroom. While popular during his stay, Holliday had no military experience and departed after one year at Culver.

Warren W. Holliday, Culver's first Commandant of Cadets, 1894-1895.[20]

Since Mackenzie's successor, the West Point-trained Tebbetts, had served as his own commandant of cadets during his time as Culver's second superintendent in 1895 to September 1896, the position of commandant was vacant when Fleet arrived in October 1896.

To achieve the desired level of performance in the military and bring student life programs up to the desired standard, Fleet determined within his first 90 days at Culver that he needed to hire a very capable full-time Commandant of Cadets to oversee these crucial areas.

One reason that this position was so important was that Fleet had been quite fortunate to rely on a very talented individual to handle all things military at MMA. Kenneth G. Matheson served as Fleet's Commandant of Cadets from the time the school opened in 1890 until the end of the school year in summer 1896 just before it burned down.

An 1885 graduate of The Citadel, Matheson was an experienced commandant, having served in this capacity for three years at Georgia Military College and directing the military training at the University of Tennessee for two years before joining Fleet at MMA. In addition to being responsible for matters traditionally addressed by commandants – including housing, barracks order, and cadet discipline – Matheson was also responsible for providing and directing military training at MMA, since the school did not have an Army officer detailed for such a purpose during the period of his tenure as commandant.

Fleet described Matheson as being "very excellent" at serving as a commandant, and he came to rely upon him quite heavily.[21] In doing so, Fleet did not develop his own expertise in any of the areas overseen by a commandant or in providing military training to young cadets, relying on Matheson's expertise in these important areas.

George W. Goode as a US Army Captain in 1906.[25]

After MMA's commencement exercises concluded in June 1896, Matheson resigned to enroll at Stanford University and earn an MA in English. Matheson earned his degree and returned to the South to marry Fleet's younger daughter, Arabella or "Belle," and took a teaching position at Georgia Tech in Atlanta, Georgia, later becoming president there and also of Drexel University.

Fleet succeeded in convincing the Army to assign a serving officer as a replacement for Matheson (which was somewhat unusual). The Army assigned First Lieutenant George W. Goode, a West Point graduate (1880) and serving cavalry officer, as MMA's Professor of Military Science and Training on June 11, 1896.[22]

Goode demonstrated his bravery and coolness under pressure during the MMA fire when he carried an unconscious faculty colleague (Captain Rolla McIntyre) to the third floor and leapt out of a window with McIntyre in his arms, both amazingly surviving the fall uninjured.[23] A cadet reported that the 1896 school year got off to an excellent start under Goode's direction, indicating that he was a quality individual who could pick up right where Matheson left off.[24] Cadets were drawn to him, as was quite "manly," along with being both affable and approachable.

When MMA burned down, Goode traveled to Culver with Fleet and others on October 5, 1896. Uncertain if the Army had the same arrangement with Culver to provide a Professor of Military Science and Training, Goode requested and was granted a one-month's leave of absence to sort out the situation of MMA, Culver, and his own beginning on October 10, 1896.[26]

While on leave, the remarkably dedicated Goode served as the CMA commandant and "succeeded in bringing the Military Department to a very high state of efficiency" and also "wining the esteem and respect of the cadet officers to an unusual degree." During this period, MMA made the decision to close, and since Culver did not yet have authorization for a PMS&T, Goode needed a new assignment. The Army, therefore, reassigned Goode back to his active-duty cavalry regiment stationed at Fort Riley, KS, with a report date of November 18, requiring him to depart Culver on November 7, 1896.[27]

According to the cadets, "Major Goode was a man of superior ability in every way, and has left his impression upon the corps, which we hope will be an inspiration to them throughout the coming year."[28] Along with the MMA cadets, Fleet must have accepted the loss of Major Goode quite reluctantly because he did not feel that any of the other members of the faculty and staff who came with him to Culver or those who were already at Culver were qualified to serve in this important position. In the near-term, he needed an immediate replacement, and in the longer-term, he needed to determine how he would acquire a capable commandant of cadets and cope without an Army officer at Culver.

As potential commandants, Fleet had high hopes for two of his own staff who came with him from Missouri. Captain Hugh Glascock was a talented teacher and administrator. While possessing no lack of personal courage, as demonstrated during the fire when he, "though himself badly injured, ran from room to room and literally dragged out the terrified boys" who might have otherwise not made it out of the building alive, he was better suited to run the faculty.[29] Based upon his overall soundness of character and demonstrated commitment to the school and cadets, Fleet appointed Glascock as the Acting Commandant upon Major Goode's departure; however, Fleet both wanted and needed him to direct the academic component of the academy (which he did spectacularly well for many years).

Fleet's other hope was for Captain Bert Greiner. Greiner was quite comfortable in the classroom, and he had been injured helping to evacuate boys from the burning barracks at MMA. As a result, he was well-thought of by both the cadets and Fleet. However, Greiner was not yet a capable trainer or suitably experienced to assume the important responsibilities of the commandant, especially as envisioned by Fleet. Nevertheless, it appears that Fleet was not convinced that Greiner had the ability to do for the military what he was asking of Glascock in the academic realm and implement a system of military discipline and training that would produce highly capable graduates of military distinction. Greiner's subsequent distinguished service in the Spanish-American War and close working relationship with Gignilliat upon his return helped him to earn Gignilliat's trust, and Gignilliat groomed Greiner to serve with great success as his successor as commandant beginning in 1910.

As far as the other two MMA staff members, the haughty Englishman and Royal Military College Sandhurst graduate J. R. Lewin, and Rolla M. McIntyre (about whom little else is known), neither returned to Culver for the 1897-1898 academic year.

Fleet also used his first 90 days to assess the other members of the Culver faculty and staff to determine their capabilities as educators and potential commandants. Dr. William Jaeger was a talented German scholar and educator who taught languages and sciences, and also served as the school's Athletic Director, but was not suitable to serve as the commandant. The Scotsman Robert Eaton taught Latin, Greek, and English, and like Lewin and Jaeger, his foreign status exempted him from consideration as commandant. The final member of the Culver faculty was a young Amherst graduate named Arthur Stuart, who taught physics, chemistry, and math but was too inexperienced to assume the commandant's role, in Fleet's assessment.

It is also important to realize that Fleet had spent much of his professional career working with college-aged students. As a result, while he had some experience with adolescents, he had not developed the type of expertise that he had with older students. After observing Matheson and Goode in action, Fleet realized that he needed someone who could address the areas of responsibility traditionally associated with the commandant's purview and also someone who could relate well with adolescent boys. Since Culver did not have an Army officer assigned to provide military training for the cadets, this commandant might also, like Matheson and Goode, have to be able to provide military training to the cadets as well.

Accordingly, Fleet made hiring a commandant of cadets a top priority upon Goode's unavoidable departure. This action of seeking to hire a permanent commandant is also significant for another reason: it indicates that Fleet was already thinking of remaining at Culver beyond the period of his initial agreement and that he needed a qualified permanent commandant to help him do so.

Culver's faculty and staff, early 1897.[30]

Since he did not find a suitable person to serve as his commandant from among the available candidates, and since he was becoming increasingly aware of how important the position was, Fleet took the natural next step to begin searching outside the organization for a suitable candidate: He sought the assistance of a talent agency. Given his location, it made sense for Fleet to use an agency in Chicago, and he contacted the renowned Albert-Clark Teacher's Agency. In one of the more fortuitous twists of fate for Culver, this was the very same agency with which Gignilliat had registered on his way home from Yellowstone, and Fleet reached out to them at around the same time that Gignilliat had engaged with them. After laying out his parameters, he was presented with Gignilliat's credentials, along with perhaps others as well.

After receiving the response from the Albert-Clark Teacher's Agency, Fleet must have believed that he had found a suitable candidate to help him achieve his vision in the school's military and student life programs in the person of Gignilliat. Although he was quite young, Gignilliat's southern background likely appealed to Fleet as a Virginian, and Gignilliat's relative youth may have been attractive on the promise of allowing a younger man to establish a more collegial bond with the cadets. Fleet wasted little time in extending Gignilliat an offer of employment as Culver's Commandant of Cadets, which Gignilliat accepted in January 1897.

As Culver's first truly full-time commandant, Hartman tells us that Gignilliat was hired specifically to develop and implement a system of military discipline and training that would produce highly capable graduates of military distinction and in line with Fleet's vision for Culver. Given the success of MMA, this program was almost surely based off the work of Matheson and Goode. Fresh off the clarifying experience of Yellowstone, Fleet's vision likely had an appeal to Gignilliat that was as powerful as it was visceral. Gignilliat spent the first 13 years at Culver pursuing this ideal and creating the military system that could bring Fleet's vision into being, and it helps explain Gignilliat's relentless pursuit of the coveted "honor school" status in the eyes of the US Army and his passionate drive to retain this distinction for the institution.

Shortly after Gignilliat's arrival, Fleet succeeded in obtaining from the US Army an officer assigned to teach purely military subjects. This was no mean feat, as the Army had agreed to provide such officers to only 100 schools in the entire nation, and the school to which such officers were assigned also received a standard issue of equipment from the government to allow the instructors to have access to the items they would need

John Q. Adams, US Army, Retired.[32]

for their training. Securing an officer and equipment with which to train thus became a hallmark of the best military schools in the country.

As he had done at MMA, Fleet succeeded in having Culver added to this auspicious group of institutions to receive both military equipment from the US government and an Army officer assigned to the school as the Professor of Military Science and Training (PMS&T).[31] Captain John Q. Adams reported for duty as the PMS&T at Culver on March 25, 1897, and with him came the government-issued military equipment he would need to instruct the cadets properly.

The Organizational Situation at Culver at the Time of Gignilliat's Arrival

Another insightful perspective on the organizational status of the institution Gignilliat joined in 1897 comes from the 1897 and 1898 school catalogs, both of which were very likely written largely (or at the very least influenced heavily) by Fleet.

The original 1894 catalog was a quite serviceable document written by HH Culver himself, and it reflected a businessman's attention to efficiency and succinctness. However, the catalog changed significantly with Fleet's arrival. Reflecting Fleet's academic background and experience, Culver's catalogs beginning in 1897 provided a far more comprehensive presentation of the school's many offerings, academic and otherwise. Fleet also understood the entrepreneurial nature of the business of running a school, and the catalogs had a much more promotional flavor during this period as well. This may have been as result of the influence of the public relations expert Fleet hired in early 1897, H. E. Cook, a real estate man from Cleveland, Ohio who possessed a vivid imagination and had the vision and ability to see how to make things grow.

Fleet's influence is manifest in the 1897 and 1898 catalogs, and the portions related to the school and its philosophy of operation are almost exactly the same. A pair of indications that Fleet was heavily involved in the writing of the CMA catalogs (if not the primary author) are apparent in the content of two particular areas. The catalog devotes six entire pages to the relationship with Missouri Military Academy (MMA) and the fires that plagued American boarding schools at the end of the 19ᵗʰ century. The page devoted to MMA is quite complementary, beginning its account in 1890 (which was prior to Culver's opening) and has the tone of someone who not only knew the school well but was also quite proud of it.[33]

The next four pages are devoted exclusively to the danger fire presented to American schools. In making the case for the safety of Culver's brick, "fire-proof" structures, this section lists 71 schools (32 in 1896 and 39 in 1897) that had been "partially or wholly destroyed by fire during the period August 25, 1896 to April 22, 1897, involving, in some instances, the loss of life and serious bodily injuries; entailing upon students great damage to personal effects, necessitating a repayment of tuition in other schools, the expense incident to such changes, and the destruction of nearly two million dollars' worth of property," which, in contemporary value, equated to around $61 million dollars.[34]

The other section that strongly suggests Fleet's influence on the cata-log relates to the colleges and universities to which graduates had been accepted and/or were attending. This section conveys that graduates had gained admission to at least 11 institutions of higher education, includ-ing: The United States Military Academy at West Point, the United States Naval Academy at Annapolis, Yale, Princeton, Stanford, Clark, DePauw, Washington and Lee, the University of Michigan, the University of Virgin-ia, and the University of Missouri.[35] While impressive, this listing had to include MMA graduates in its accounting, as Culver had graduated a total of six cadets by 1897, making it impossible to have placed graduates in the 11 schools identified in this section. The inclusion of presumably MMA graduates in this list only makes sense if it was prepared or at least influ-enced by Fleet.

Moving to the substance of the catalog's text regarding the school's edu-cational philosophy and its philosophy of operations, one is again struck by the sophisticated and nuanced character of both the content and prose of these sections that could only have been written by someone with an extensive background in education and school administration. In addi-tion, nothing like these sections appeared in the 1894 catalog written by HH Culver, meaning that it could only have been produced by McKenzie, Tebbetts, or Fleet, with Fleet being the most likely author.

Asserting that "the critical years of every boy's life are those between twelve and twenty," since "home influence begins to lose its hold, and the restlessness and lawlessness of young manhood [begins] asserting itself even in the noblest and most generous natures," the aim and scope of Cul-ver, in part, was to shield boys from the perils of society in every possible manner during "this period of greatest danger," referred to memorably by the pioneer of the study of adolescence G. Stanley Hall in 1904 as "storm and stress" (*sturm und drang*).[36] Subtlety embracing the military program as a metaphor through the use of the notion of "shielding" boys was either the deft touch of an exceptionally skilled author or an exceptionally fortunate word choice. Given the deliberate nature of almost every activity at Culver that began with Fleet's arrival, one suspects that it is more a case of the former than the latter.

Pre-dating the school's turn towards becoming a college-prep institution but conveying a noble aspiration, the catalog asserts that the "boys who usually succeed best at college" were those "to whom poverty teaches the stern lessons of self-denial and self-control" to develop within them "a discipline which will take the place in part of the severe discipline of life."[37] Embracing the notion of want as a motivation, the Culver catalog champions the twin virtues of "self-denial and self-control" promoted by the school's military discipline as the best means to prepare boys for the rigors of life. Drawing on experience with preparing boys for college and also on life experience, Fleet's background seems to be almost perfectly suited to provide an author with the context necessary to craft such an explanation.

In conjunction with "mental training" and athletics, the catalog touts Culver's ability "to keep the Cadets fully occupied" and "to stimulate mental activity and promote intellectual growth by all means in the power of the best teachers," and "to preserve a careful oversight of the physical health" highlighting the "military feature" as "the wisest solution of the even more important question of the development of a character based upon right principles, without which all else is vain."[38]

Based upon a belief that every boy had a natural fascination with the military, the idea was to use this affinity to exercise over him a restraint under which he would surely chafe if it came from any outside source. The military system, therefore, played upon the boy's "every noble impulse and by every incentive of honor and ambition to learn first the self-control and implicit obedience to orders, by which alone he can prepare himself in turn to command and control others."[39] This explanation makes the point that Culver's military system, at this point, was much more of a means to the end of preparing boys for manhood than it was an end unto itself to train boys to serve in the military.

Culver was a decidedly nonsectarian institution in 1897. Indeed, one of the disagreements between McKenzie and HH Culver had been McKenzie's desire to make Culver into an Episcopalian institution, which HH

Culver opposed strongly. While Tebbetts likely supported McKenzie in terms of a proper religious foundation for the school, there is no evidence that he tried to challenge HH Culver on this front, preferring instead to focus his efforts on the military aspects of the school. By 1897, the catalog stated, under the heading of "Moral and Religious Instruction," that, "The Academy is not conducted in the interest of any religious denomination, and yet its officers will do all in their power to make it a decidedly Christian school." While espousing a Christian foundation, it is clear that Culver was also largely Protestant, reflecting the beliefs of both HH Culver and Fleet.

Expanding on the school's moral and religious instruction, the catalog stated that, "The faculty are all active Christian men, representing several churches, and they will spare no effort to give a high moral and religious tone to the school." One of the ways in which this would be accomplished was through daily chapel services and by requiring all cadets to attend Sunday religious services in the Academy chapel.[40]

While forming the foundation of the school's moral and religious instruction, chapel services in 1897 were more akin to the present-day all-school meeting, during which "eminent ministers and laymen" would visit the school and deliver addresses to the cadets, while at other times the superintendent read them sermons "appropriate to young men" supported at times by readings and music provided by the cadets themselves. It is clear that the school embraced a Christian tradition and that it adopted a fairly conventional approach to providing cadets with their moral and religious instruction that would have been both familiar to and comfortable for a man like Fleet.

Not being overly religious himself but identifying as an Episcopalian, Gignilliat would have almost certainly have been comfortable with this aspect of Culver. This approach also largely reflected his own VMI experience and religious preferences.

Culver's Academic Program

The catalogues from this period began addressing the school's academic program with a short section on admissions. Eschewing a special admissions examination, Culver determined the placement of those accepted after considering the course for which he was best suited based upon an assessment of what his previous studies had best prepared him. Mirroring the section concepts used at West Point and elsewhere during the period, each course had multiple sections in which an increasing level of rigor was used. A cadet was placed initially into a section based upon his perceived ability to perform, and if it proved to be too difficult or easy for him, he was moved until he found the section best suited for him to learn the material and succeed.

Of note, the catalogs also mentioned in the initial treatment of the school's academic program that Culver placed a high priority on teaching boys not only how to study, but also "the reason for rules and principles, as well as the rules themselves." Conveying this message in this manner indicated the integral nature of the school's military discipline to its pedagogy and educational philosophy.[41]

At a time when children were expected to do as they were told and when there was little impetus for adults to provide any rationale beyond "because I said so" to adolescents, this focus on emphasizing "the reason for rules and principles, as well as the rules themselves" represents an enlightened approach to both pedagogy and education.

It implies that teenaged boys were capable of higher-order thinking and understanding at a time when this level of cognitive ability was little associated with young males. It also establishes at Culver a tradition of viewing boys as being highly capable and of proceeding from a premise that they were able to understand and reason at a high level, presenting a marked difference from the more common approach of the period of viewing their abilities in more base terms and believing that they had little interest in or ability to grasp the higher purposes of a school's approach and intentions for them. While it is clear that HH Culver delighted in the company of boys, Fleet appears to have respected them.

Culver held students accountable for their learning and performance using monthly reports that summarized the class standing and deportment of each cadet based upon the results of daily recitations in class and inspections in the barracks. To pass to a higher class or complete a course of study, cadets were required to attain a final grade of at least 60 percent, based upon the results of daily recitations, monthly exams, and final examinations.

Culver followed a fairly standard practice of the day by granting three different types of diplomas – A, B, and C – in accordance with excellence in scholarship. Earning an "A" diploma required a cadet to earn an academic average of at least 85 percent as juniors and 90 percent as seniors, while those qualifying for the "B" diplomas earned academic averages between 82-84 percent during their senior years. Both the "A" and "B" diplomas indicated that a graduate was prepared for college-level work. Cadets earned a "C" diploma by earning academic averages of at least 75 percent during their senior years, but these graduates were not considered to be ready for college-level work without additional remediation.[42]

Culver aligned its curriculum with the influential "Report of the Committee of Ten," appointed by the National Teachers' Association in 1894 (on which Fleet served as an advisor regarding the place of Greek in secondary schooling), and focused on ensuring that its college-bound students received adequate preparation in their elementary and secondary schooling to ensure their readiness and ability to complete college-level work upon matriculation.[43] Owing to special agreements, the catalog noted that "Graduates of this Academy are admitted without examination to Wabash College, and the Universities of Chicago, Missouri, Stanford, Purdue, Indiana, [and] Virginia," presumably for those who earned "A" or "B" diplomas.[44]

Culver's "Classical" academic program in 1897 prepared cadets for success during their first two years of college, and its "business" curriculum prepared cadets for success in a "business or commercial" line of work, depending upon the cadet's goals and abilities. Remediation was available for freshmen, and advanced courses were also available for cadets pursuing the Classical academic program.[45] For example, Fleet taught a section of Advanced Greek for interested and capable cadets.

The Culver of 1897 did not privilege the college preparation course over the more vocationally oriented business track, giving unbiased and equal weight to both tracks.[46] Approaching both tracks in the same manner, Culver used small class sizes that allowed for much personal contact and mentoring to focus on teaching the proper process for study and reflection. Believing that it was during adolescence that the foundation for real learning was established, this approach allowed boys to acquire a deeper knowledge that went far beyond the acquisition of the superficial knowledge available to many and those without the benefit of a more rigorous education.[47]

The Academy's Classical course was referred to as a special feature of the school, based upon Fleet's tremendous qualifications as a Greek scholar and teacher. Fleet was so confident in the program that he was comfortable in stating that "no school in the country can give better classical preparation for college or university."[48] Coming from a former president of a college with such a distinguished academic background, this was a powerful statement that surely persuaded some parents that Culver was the right place for their sons to be educated.

It is clear that Culver's academic expectations of its students were high from almost its very beginning, regardless of whether they pursued a college preparatory or vocational type of education.

Culver 's Military System

The military system at Culver had equal value in preparing students for college or to enter society or the business world after graduation. The description of the Military Department began with the subheading of "Great Lack in American Character." This section began by stating, "A lack of system or order is perhaps the most serious defect in the American character," and went on to state that, "Hence the necessity in our schools for a discipline which will develop and train to its fullest perfection this trait in the youth of the country."[49]

The 1897 catalog extols the ability of the military system to fix the defect of the great lack of character in America and that military drill was very effective way of doing so for boys aged 14-20. This was the same age-range highlighted as the most important time for boys' the development.

The section regarding the school's military program also emphasized the value of having a US Army officer assigned to the school to train the boys and the equipment provided by the government to support the training.[51] This type of official recognition from the Army allowed a school to identify its top three graduates each year for specific mention in the *US Army Register* and consideration for admission to West Point and/or a commission.[52]

This information provided evidence to show that Culver was one of only 100 or fewer schools in the country that enjoyed such benefits, distinguishing it from its many competitors.

The CMA corps of cadets on parade, 1897.[50]

Fleet's Vision of the Type and Role of Discipline

Channeling West Point, the military section quoted General Schofield's famous "fixed opinion" definition of discipline from West Point on the value of military training: *"I give it as my fixed opinion that but for our graduated cadets, the war between the United States and Mexico would have lasted some four or five years, within its first half more defeats than victories falling to our share; whereas, in less than two campaigns, we conquered a great country, and a peace without the loss of a single battle or skirmish."*[53]

At the time it was published, discipline was best defined as "a habit of obedience," with the rationale that learning the habit of obeying in a school environment would habituate one to following orders and doing what was required in more trying times and in the hierarchy of industry. There was little dispute about its meaning; however, the larger disagreement regarded how best to instill discipline. The two notions involved either an intelligent appeal to reason (i.e., persuasion) or the use of force to coerce compliance. While some viewed it as the rigid enforcement of rules and a demand for compliance, more enlightened views conceived of it as a form of mutual respect and based on the eliciting of an intelligent response to the requirements of a position and the demands of a situation rather than the more brutish recourse to coercion.

The University of Virginia developed a notion of how a student-run school would operate during its first 20 years (1825-1845) that had matured and was in place by the time Fleet attended 15 years later. The system included the use of an innovative "honor" system to restrain and curb behavior.[54] The idea was to make it part of the school's culture of honor that obeying the rules and refraining from egregious moral offenses such as lying, cheating, and stealing would not be condoned among the group of gentlemen at an institution, and that it was not only allowable but expected for students to inform on other students who had violated an important school rule and/or committed a serious breach of honor.[55]

This approach was much more successful at getting student buy-in and support, allowing the school to shift its focus elsewhere and beyond simply obtaining student compliance.[56] Perhaps the most important aspect of this approach was that it helped to avoid a punitive rule-based approach that engendered an "us-vs-them" relationship between students and faculty, allowing the school to appeal to the higher nature of students and engage in a more developmentally based approach that promoted a greater sense of unity between students and faculty.[57]

Beyond his formative experience at the University of Virginia, as a classical scholar, Fleet would have known that the word discipline came from the Greek word *paideia*, meaning to instruct (esp. children) via educative discipline, and from the Latin word *discipulus*, which is the Latin word for pupil and also of disciple, or follower, and also from the Latin word *disciplina*, which means teaching. It generally deals with governing one's behavior, study, and instruction, and is based more upon persuasion than on coercion, which was most likely the manner in which he used the word and meant for it to be understood in this context.

The quotations below from a somewhat contemporary military manual offer further evidence in this regard.

> *"Discipline has been described as 'the habit of obedience.' It implies a control of the inner man. A disciplined man is self-controlled, especially during emergencies, when the undisciplined man goes to pieces."*

> *"Discipline cannot be acquired in a day or a month; it is a growth. The main object of drills is to teach the habit of obedience. As soon as you obey properly, promptly, and at times subconsciously the instructions of your officers; as soon as you can cheerfully give up pleasure and personal privileges that conflict with your duty, you will then have become a disciplined citizen."* [58]

It is highly likely that HH Culver's ideas regarding discipline were much more in line with Fleet's (i.e., persuasion), and that Tebbetts' notion of discipline was more focused on using it to enforce compliance (i.e., coercion), which was not what Culver wanted or had in mind for his boys.

Ending 1896 on a High Note

Despite the real challenges faced in the final months of 1896, the match between CMA and MMA suggested by Emily Jane turned out to be providentially good fortune for HH Culver, Fleet, and the communities of both MMA and CMA. Upon hammering out the details of his contract five days after his arrival, Fleet commenced a 90-day assessment of Culver to determine if it was indeed a viable and suitable long-term solution for him, his faculty, and his students. The financial challenges that Neal and HH Jr. were addressing notwithstanding, Fleet found an institution with tremendous potential, and HH found in Fleet a man he could respect and feel comfortable having in charge of his beloved school.

By the time of the Christmas break in December 1896, Fleet had determined that Culver was both viable and suitable for him, his faculty, and his students, and HH had determined, after two disappointing attempts, that he had finally found the right person to run his school. Almost every member of the MMA group that arrived at Culver in October 1896 returned in January 1897, and by the time of graduation enrollment had increased further to 122 cadets, elevating it into the ranks of the largest prep boarding schools in the nation at the time.

The Foundations of Greatness

Having established the foundation for realizing his desired vision for Culver, what was needed was a synergizing agent to bring it all together into a complete, coherent, and functioning whole. In Fleet's mind, this was the role of the Commandant of Cadets, who also served as his second-in-command. This was the role for which Fleet had recruited Gignilliat and in which he expected him to function. It was expansive, challenging, and just the sort of opportunity that might appeal to an ambitious young college graduate fresh off the exhilaration of an adventure akin to Gignilliat's own Yellowstone experience.

However, the dynamics would have to play out for themselves, and both Fleet and Gignilliat would have to come to their own determinations as to whether it was either desirable and/or practicable. In addition, HH Culver would have a significant say in the arrangement as well. Thus was the situation on campus as of January 13, 1897.

Chapter 3: Gignilliat Takes Charge as Commandant, 1897-1900

Gignilliat's Arrival at Culver – An Eventful First 48 Hours

In the final decade of his life, Gignilliat recorded many of his memories from Culver. We are in deceased Culver historian Robert Hartman's debt for retaining such a detailed record of Gignilliat's first hours on campus at Culver.

Based upon Gignilliat's own recollections, Hartman wrote,

> *As the train grew near the station, only a few lights identified a community that was to become part of Gignilliat's great adventure. He glanced out of the window to confirm that he had, indeed, arrived at the [train] depot [in Culver], gathered his hand luggage, and stepped from the warmth of the passenger car into the icy vestibule. The conductor opened the door, raised the cover over the steps, and lent a hand to Gignilliat as he climbed down to the platform. He glanced to his right and saw his trunk being unloaded from the baggage car. Facing him were Donald Smith and Gordon Cox, cadet captains, shivering with nervous anticipation as they waited to meet their new commandant.*[1]

Lake Maxinkuckee was frozen over, and the snow drifts from a recent storm had closed the main roads in Culver, which was something Gignilliat had not experienced since his time at Yellowstone. As there was no transportation available, cadets Smith and Cox carried Gignilliat's personal baggage (leaving this trunk to be delivered the next day) as they escorted the southerner Gignilliat, arriving from the warmer climes of Georgia wearing only a light overcoat, to campus by following the railroad until it crossed Academy Road (known then as Indiana Avenue) at what was called Bogardus Crossing. The intrepid little group walked east along Academy Road until they reached campus in the vicinity of what is now Logansport Gate. Hartman tells us that "Gignilliat observed two shaved cedar posts and in the near-darkness" supporting a hand-painted wooden sign emblazoned with the name "Culver Military Academy."[2] Gignilliat had arrived at what would become his home for the next 42 years.

Campus showed little signs of life when he arrived, and "only a few lights were visible since the electric power was turned off at 9:30 pm" to coincide with the conclusion of the cadets' scheduled day. The only light came from kerosene lamps that shone through the frost-covered windows

The path Gignilliat and his cadet escorts walked as it looked in 1897.[3]

of the rather large and imposing edifice known as Main Barrack. To the right of this building, Gignilliat viewed "a vast expanse of white against the black sky" littered with shapeless snow-covered piles of building materials – mostly stone, brick, and timber – for the construction of Culver's second building, West Barrack. By fall of 1897, this building would be complete, and its first floor would provide science classrooms while cadets resided on the second and third floors.[5]

Hartman continues to narrate the arrival of Gignilliat as follows:

Gignilliat as he looked upon his arrival at Culver, January 1897.[4]

> *"[Gignilliat] and his cadet escorts entered Main Barrack and stood in the central foyer. Ahead was the stairway that led to the upper two floors and to their right a darkened hall led to classrooms and a room used on Sunday as the chapel. Glancing to his left, a closed door was identified by Smith as the entry to the Mess Hall. Quietly, they climbed the stairs. Facing them at the second floor was a large lounge which would soon be altered to contain*

CMA in 1896.[6]

Steps on first floor of Main Barracks circa 1897. [8]

the Academy's first library. Along each hall, cadets were probably listening intently to learn from a word or sound something about their new commandant. They would begin to find out the next day how their lives would change. A door from the lounge was Room 213 and it was identified as the office of Colonel Fleet. Smith and Cox excused themselves and hurried to their rooms, relieved that their assignment was over. Gignilliat tapped on the open door and saw the Superintendent for the first time." [7]

In his collection of recollections, *Unfurling the Colors*, Gignilliat relates the story of his first meeting with Fleet. Gignilliat recalled that Fleet "was a somewhat portly man of fifty or thereabouts, wearing a green eyeshade and was reading at a roll-top desk. He had a close-cropped gray beard, thinning gray hair, and was wearing a double-breasted navy blue coat. There was a lump in his right cheek which I learned later was a piece of horehound candy," a bag of which was ever-present on his desk..

Colonel Alexander F. Fleet during his days at Culver. [9]

Gignilliat continues relating the event as follows:

As I approached him, feeling very much chilled in body and spirit, he rose and greeted me with a smile like a benediction. Somehow I forgot that I was cold, and felt glad to be there shaking his hand.... He was Colonel A.F. Fleet, Culver's Superintendent. Curiously enough, I remember the look of the man's eyes as he spoke to me. Whether they were grey or blue, I do not recall, but they were keen and sparkling, and there was something in their depths that registered with me subconsciously even in the absorption of the moment."[10]

Taking his initial measure of the man with whom he was destined to work for and with for the next dozen years, Gignilliat concluded that, "somehow I knew my line had fallen in good water."[11]

The well-manner Fleet chatted cordially with Gignilliat until his two most important subordinates arrived at Fleet's office. Hugh Glascock and Bert Greiner had accompanied Fleet to Culver from MMA, and the three of them, known collectively as the "three G's," would have a profound impact in setting Culver's academic and operational principles for the next three decades.

Marmont, Ind., January 14, 1897.

Gen. Orders.

I. Capt. H. G. Glascock is hereby relieved from duty as Act. Com'd't of this Academy.

II. Major L. R. Gignilliat is appointed Commandant of the Culver Military Academy, and from this date he will be obeyed and respected accordingly.

By order of
Col. A. F. FLEET,
Supt.

General Order appointing Gignilliat as Culver's Commandant of Cadets, Jan 14, 1897. [14]

After exchanging a few pleasantries, all four men agreed to meet for breakfast at Colonel Fleet's table the following morning.

Gignilliat was shown to his quarters, located in Room 212, which consisted of a single room with bath. Containing a folding bed and a table with "a cracker box on it subdivided into pigeon holes, Room 212 would serve as both his office during the day and as his bedroom at night.[12] The simplicity of his quarters delighted Gignilliat, and he remarked that "I simply needed to fold up my bed, sit down at my table, and carry on as Commandant of Cadets..."[13]

Arising the next day, Gignilliat began his official tenure as Culver's Commandant

CMA Dining Hall as it looked in 1897. [15]

of Cadets, based upon his authority granted by the General Order that appointed him to that position.

Gignilliat's appointment as Commandant of Cadets must have come as a great relief for three men: HH Culver; Fleet, and Glascock, who had been serving double duty as both Headmaster and Acting Commandant since the departure of the previous commandant in early November, 1896.

Breakfast the next morning with Colonel Fleet turned out to be a momentous occasion for Gignilliat.

It was then that he met the Colonel's two daughters, his eldest child Mary, "known to her family as Minnie," and his second daughter Belle. Born on January 27, 1875, Minnie was just six months older than Gignilliat, while Belle was several years younger. Gignilliat recalled that both young women were "lovely and intelligent," but that when he first met them, he "regarded them as two very pretty and attractive young girls, but nothing more."[16]

Miss Mary S. "Minnie" Fleet, as she looked when Gignilliat met her. [17]

Reflecting on his first meeting with Minnie, Gignilliat recalled that:

"That part of my spirits which had not been thawed out by Colonel Fleet's warm and friendly reception was completely thawed out by Miss Minnie. Both girls, but Miss Minnie in particular, I thought, resembled the Garnett girls with whom I had practically grown up in Washington, D.C., and who were nieces of my adopted parents, Mr. and Mrs. Leigh Robinson. When I commented to Miss Minnie on her fancied resemblance to the Garnett girls, she smiled and said, "They are my cousins.".... What interested me more was that she had once visited in the home of the Robinsons, in Washington. Alas, I was in Georgia, and I had just missed meeting her. Still more interesting was the fact that she had attended the Commencement activities and final ball at VMI in 1895, the year of my graduation."[18]

It was indeed a pleasant surprise to learn of this unexpected connection with Fleet's attractive daughters.

An Initial Inspection of Campus

In what became a familiar grouping in subsequent years, Gignilliat, Glascock, and Greiner departed from breakfast to inspect the campus.

They began in the Main Barrack Annex, meeting the chef and his assistants, checked the kitchen and food storage areas for cleanliness, and exited into the adjacent Engine Annex. The Engine Annex contained large coal-powered steam boilers,

Culver's faculty and staff upon Gignilliat's arrival in 1897. Glascock and Greiner are seated to Fleet's left. [19]

alight and hissing, that provided heat for Main Barrack and powered two large steam-driven generators that produced electricity for the entire campus. A rail spur off the main line of the Vandalia Railroad allowed coal to be delivered directly to the annex to keep the boilers fueled, which was convenient, but the vibrations disrupted the kitchen operations, and the dust and ash from the boilers seeped under the doors and windows, making it difficult for the kitchen staff to maintain an appropriate level

of cleanliness. The trio returned to the east wing of the barrack to check the first-floor classrooms and observe the behavior of the cadets in an academic setting.

Climbing the central stairway to the second floor, Gignilliat was introduced to the Academy physician, Dr. Oliver Rea, and his

Cadet room circa 1897. [20]

nurse, Matron Elizabeth Howard. Rea was a handsome and engaging man who had attended medical school and established a practice in what became known as the city of Culver after serving as an enlisted soldier in the Union Army during the Civil War. During their initial meeting, Dr. Rea informed Gignilliat that it was his practice to confine cadets to their own rooms when recovering from minor ailments and to move cadets requiring more substantial care to the home of a faculty member where they could be attended to by an Academy wife. The medical staff was not able to provide dental care at the time of Gignilliat's arrival.

Moving to examine the cadet living quarters, Gignilliat found much that he disliked. His VMI experience had habituated him to expect simple furnishings and a high level of orderliness. Gignilliat observed that "the cadets had too much latitude in selecting furnishings, particularly wall hangings."
Gignilliat was even more disturbed in the second and third floor latrines, where he found several toilet stalls without doors, floors of rough-finished concrete, ceramic basins for washing and shaving, and three bathtubs separated by slight partitions. Gignilliat determined that these facilities were inadequate to support and encourage the level of personal hygiene he planned to demand from the cadets, and he made the first of many mental notes to address the conditions of the cadet rooms and bathrooms in the barracks immediately.

Continuing his inspection of the barrack's facilities, Gignilliat exited the third floor through a trap door into a powerful gust of cold wind from the lake that almost knocked him over, to gain purchase to a view of the entire campus from the roof of Main Barrack From this vantage point, Gignilliat saw "a large wooden water tower near the northeast corner of the roof [and] took in his first bird's eye view of the lake, allowing him to gain a better understanding of the Academy's water system.[21] During this part of his inspection, Gignilliat "learned that other than wells for drinking water, the principal source of water was Lake Maxinkuckee." His training as a civil engineer allowed Gignilliat to recognize and appreciate that the Academy's physical plant was impressive.

After lunch with Colonel Fleet and his daughters, Gignilliat and his companions continued on to complete their tour of the campus. At the end of his first full day as commandant, Gignilliat had acquired a good appreciation of the institution's physical plant and facilities, and he had also made his first measure of Glascock and Greiner, both of whom had impressed him greatly.

Gignilliat's First Disciplinary Challenge

After an initial night in the barracks that was uneventful and a day of touring facilities largely as a spectator, Gignilliat's second night in the barracks would provide him with the opportunity to assume his official role as the Commandant of Cadets and begin instilling the level of discipline he believed to be appropriate for the corps.

Perhaps because of his youthful appearance, or simply because they were typical adolescent boys, many of the former MMA cadets hatched a plot to test the mettle of their new commandant and allow them to both size him up for themselves and also compare him to the highly respected former MMA commandants Matheson and Goode. In preparation, the cadets had smuggled into the barrack one of the large, white-painted rocks about the size of a man's head that lined Culver's walkways. Around an hour after taps on January 14, 1897, "a rumble began at the far end of the second floor hall...[that] grew closer to Gignilliat's room, passed by, then banged along the sidewall before coming to a stop."[22]

As one who had likely partaken in such shenanigans as a cadet at VMI, Gignilliat knew instantly that he was being tested and that his response to the situation would largely set the tone for his ability to maintain good order and discipline among the cadets and within the barrack. Donning his robe, Gignilliat stood by the door of his room and listened for a few minutes. Again, he heard the rumbling of a large rock rolling down the hall and right past his room. Several of the culprits also ignited a smudge fire in the lavatory, filling the corridor with smoke in an effort to add to the disturbance and enhance the impact of the ensuing confusion.

Opening his own door to take measure of what was happening, Gignilliat saw the head of an innocent and unknowing first-year cadet sticking out of his room. Gignilliat recounted that, "I grabbed him fiercely," and demanded, "What is this all about?" The stunned cadet stammered in response, "I d-don't know," perhaps unsure of whom he was addressing. Gignilliat believed him and forgave the lapse in military protocol in the young cadet's response.

Finding all of the cadets on the floor in bed and feigning slumber, Gignilliat recognized the futility of determining who was responsible for these actions. Knowing the cost of inaction in such a situation, and surrendering to his growing ire at such a thoughtless action of setting a fire deliberately in a building after the experiences of both Culver and MMA related to fires, Gignilliat was determined to address the situation forcefully to establish his own authority in the barracks and also to ensure that the prank would not be repeated.

After extinguishing the smoldering substance, Gignilliat roused all of the cadets and ordered them into formation in the halls. In what became his standard practice when addressing new situations at Culver, he relied on his VMI experience for guidance and implemented the approach used at VMI that he believed to be appropriate for the situation. Since conducting guard duty was an essential aspect of the VMI cadet experience, Gignilliat decided to implement the practice at Culver. He proceeded to select "three reliefs of sentries, three corporals of the guard, and an officer of the day." Gignilliat immediately posted sentries on each end of the two hallways with orders to preserve order in the barrack, and he appointed an Officer of the Day to supervise the guard team.

The cadets placed on guard duty were instructed to maintain the peace for the remainder of the night, and Gignilliat threatened each with dismissal if there were further disturbances. This was the very first instance of placing cadets on guard at Culver, and it must have surprised them greatly. Having addressed the situation sufficiently, and likely gaining the shocked attention of the entire corps, Gignilliat returned to his room and went to sleep. That night the first of Gignilliat's "traditions" – guard duty –was initiated.[23]

When he arose the next morning, Gignilliat set to work processing what he had learned and observed during his first days at Culver. He knew that he needed to develop a plan to transform the institution into a "proper" military school along the lines of his own *alma mater*, and he was determined to make use of a chain of command – which is the backbone of any military organization – to do so. According to Hartman, Gignilliat made use of the chain of command for the first time at the day's lunch formation (called Dinner Roll Call, or DRC, at both VMI and Culver) by having the Regimental Adjutant announce that the corps was to assemble in the gymnasium that afternoon after classes in lieu of military drill.[24]

At 3:30 pm, the cadets assembled as instructed, along with several members of the faculty, and Gignilliat explained to them the purpose of military discipline. In what became two of the common themes of his time at Culver, Gignilliat told the cadets that military training, properly delivered, brought "poise and bearing [and] things that would be lasting assets to them throughout life," and he asked them, "Do you want to play at this business of being soldiers? Or do you want the real thing?," suggesting that the real benefit came from engaging in military training seriously and with purpose.

Expressing his willingness to work with them, Gignilliat surprised the cadets again by not telling them what he wanted them to do, but rather vowing to work with the cadets to determine how to achieve the types of results they all evidently desired. Reinforcing the chain of command, Gignilliat committed to working with the officers and noncommissioned officers in one group to help them improve the military performance of the corps by providing them instruction on the proper ways to give commands that helps improve the performance of those receiving the orders.

As a second group, the remainder of the cadets would be given intensive drill sessions designed to improve their performance in the areas of marching and the manual of arms. Gignilliat concluded by assuring the cadets that with proper training, they could make Culver into an excellent military school of which they could be quite proud. Decades after this episode, Gignilliat said that he could "still remember with deep gratitude the response of those boys to that talk," and that "their spirit of cooperation from then on could not have been finer."[25]

Unbeknownst to Gignilliat, H. H. Culver was in attendance, and he was quite impressed with both the content and delivery of Gignilliat's remarks to the cadets. This reaction suggests, by treating them with respect and engaging with them, that Gignilliat's approach was quite different from his predecessor's (Tebbetts) and much more in line with how H. H. Culver wanted his cadets to be treated.

The cadets at Culver appear to have been impressed by their new young commandant as well, and they let him know by welcoming him to the institution in a very cordial mention in their monthly campus publication, known then as *The Culver Vedette*.

In behalf of the Corps we wish to extend our hearty welcome to our new Commandant, Major L. R. Gignilliat, and express our hope; which we are sure will be realized, that the battalion will make an enviable reputation for itself during the coming five months.

The cadets as a body, should take more pride in the Military department and organization, and should do all in their power to raise the standard, so that this school may be inferior to no Military school in this country.

Vedette article welcoming Gignilliat. [26]

Fleet Begins Building His Military Team at Culver

As a seasoned administrator, Fleet had experience in hiring and surely knew how to build effective teams comprised of individuals who complemented one another. Recognizing the value of Gignilliat's youth in allowing him to be very approachable to the cadets, he could also see that there were viable ways of countering Gignilliat's inexperience by bringing on a more seasoned person to help with the military training. The process of acquiring an experienced Army officer to serve as the Professor of Military Science and Training (PMS&T) was either ongoing (having been initiated by Fleet's predecessor) or was initiated by Fleet himself (which is more likely), and this was a clever way of countering Gignilliat's youth and lack of experience in terms of military training.

Captain Philip Pendleton Powell, US Army.[29]

The Army assigned Captain John Quincy Adams to serve as Culver's first PMS&T. Adams was "a cavalryman who had fought in the Civil War as a lieutenant in Sherman's Signal Corps," and thus had all of the long experience for which Fleet had been searching.

Adams' brush with fame was that it was he who had "dispatched the famous message which was the inspiration for the song 'Hold the Fort for I am Coming.'"[27] When Adams arrived on campus on April 5, 1897, Fleet thought he acquired a combination that provided Culver with a perfect blend of youth and experience.

Adams turned out to be somewhat of a disappointment for Culver. While the cadets accepted him as a lovable old man who told interesting stories and did not ask much of them, Gignilliat viewed him in more professional terms and was not impressed by what he observed. According to a somewhat disapproving Gignilliat, Adams "never actually took up residence at Culver," living instead in the northern Ohio town of Norwalk that was equidistant from Toledo and Cleveland and almost 300 miles away, where he had settled after his retirement from the Army to farm.

In compliance with the minimum requirements of the War Department at that time, Adams came to campus once a month "to deliver his minimum one lecture a month to the cadets." Gignilliat was not impressed by Adams' performance when presenting these lectures, which Gignilliat characterized as being, for the most part "yarns about his Indian fighting and frontier days."

While the cadets enjoyed Adams' lectures greatly, especially the more sensational episodes he related, he was not functioning as the experienced military trainer to partner with Gignilliat that Fleet desired.

The two men did not get along personally either. In an episode certain to attract Gignilliat's ire, Gignilliat related that, "On one of his monthly visits to Culver [Adams] brought my wife a quart Mason glass jar full of radishes, which he knew she liked. Although she thanked him graciously for his gift [as one would expect from the refined Minnie], he did not think that she was appreciative enough. 'Madame,' he told her, 'I raised those radishes myself, and I figure that in time and energy expended they cost me a dollar apiece,'" in effect demanding payment for what was obviously considered to be a gift by its recipient.[28]

Having crossed his beloved spouse in such a discursive manner, and given the paucity of time he actually spent on campus or value he providing to enhancing the military capabilities of the cadets, it is unlikely that the cordial Gignilliat spent much time cultivating any type of meaningful relationship with Adams. Adams stayed at Culver until 1901, when he departed for another assignment.

Adams' replacement was US Army Captain Philip Pendleton Powell, an aged Confederate veteran from Virginia who accepted a commission in the US Army Cavalry and served with distinction in the Cuba campaign in the Spanish-American War. Fleet must have had higher hopes for Powell (a fellow Virginian), who served at Culver for three years (1901-1903).

Powell, however, apparently made little impression or improvement during his time at Culver. Mention of him is notably sparse in Culver documents from the period, including Gignilliat's annual military report.[30] He resigned his position in 1903, dying in early May 1905.[31]

Only with the arrival of the redoubtable, youthful, and energetic Captain George L. Byroade in fall 1904 did Culver finally acquire the PMS&T it needed (more about him later). Functioning as the ideal pairing Fleet had been seeking for seven years, the team of Gignilliat and Byroade cracked the Army's code for its annual inspection. They co-taught lessons on the theory of Military Science to the first classmen during the winter drill period, which provided the impetus for Culver's military system to be nationally recognized by the Army as one of the six best schools in the nation, referred to on campus as joining the "Big Six."

Gignilliat's Initial Thoughts on Discipline

It was in the 1898 CMA Catalog that we get our first insight into Gignilliat's own thinking about the purpose and value of a military system.[32]

In his "Report of the Commandant" section, Gignilliat provided a thorough description of the military program he had designed and implemented for Culver to accomplish Fleet's objectives.

This description showed that Gignilliat's understanding of the meaning of discipline when he arrived was very basic, more akin to that of Tebbetts, and not nearly as sophisticated and/or nuanced as Fleet's. This may have been based upon his VMI experience, which involved the use of coercion almost exclusively to enforce discipline within the corps (as Gignilliat discovered on several occasions and much to his own dismay!).

However, Gignilliat began to see the value of persuasion while working at Yellowstone with Captain Bromwell, which opened his mind to the possibility of the value of discipline if used appropriately and for a good purpose. Fleet became an outstanding teacher of this method for the next 13 years upon Gignilliat's arrival to Culver.

An Effective Military System Needs a Regimented Schedule

The schedule for the cadets was highly regimented, intended to provide them with the structure and routine Gignilliat believed to be essential to maintaining good order and discipline within the corps.

Beginning with Reveille at 6:10 am and ending with Taps at 10:00 pm, the cadets were kept occupied and gainfully employed during the majority of their days on campus.

During the course of the day, half of the time (eight hours) was devoted to classes and study, and almost three hours were dedicated to drill and ceremonies of some sort (e.g., formations, inspections, drill, and parades). Taken together, this accounted for almost 70 percent or 11 of the almost 16 hours of structured time during the week Tuesday-Saturday (Culver's weekends were Sunday and Monday during this period).

This rigid structure compared favorably with the standard US Army schedule for the same period and was even more regimented than the schedule adhered to by soldiers serving on active duty at the time. The table below provides a side-by-side comparison of the two schedules.

EVENT	US Army	Culver Military Academy
Reveille	5:00 a.m.	6:10 a.m.
Breakfast	5:30 a.m.	7:00 a.m.
Sick Call	6:30 a.m.	6:40 a.m.
Work/Class Call	7:00 a.m.	8:15 a.m.-12:00 p.m.
Guard Mount	7:50 a.m.	12:00 pm (replaced Drill in 1904)
Drill	10:00 a.m.	12:00 pm (1897-1903)
Lunch	12:00 p.m.	12:30 p.m.
Work/Class Call	1:00 p.m.	1:30-3:00 p.m.
Drill	2:00 p.m.	3:00 p.m.
Evening Parade	20 mins before sun-set	4:00 p.m.
Dinner	6:00 p.m.	6:00 p.m.
Free Time/Study	Free time: 7:00 – 9:00 pm	Study: 7:00 – 9:30 pm
Tattoo	9:00 p.m.	9:30 p.m.
Taps	9:30 p.m.	10:00 p.m.
Length of Day	**16.5 hours**	**~16 hours**

Daily schedule comparison, Army (1874)[33] and Culver (1898). [34]

Gignilliat and Culver Begin Creating Culver's Unique Military System and Training Program – The Black Horse Troop

With the arrival of a qualified Commandant of Cadets and PMS&T, Colonel Fleet began turning his attention to the pressing matter of enrollment.

Touting the advantages of a small school as enthusiastically as possible was not having the desired effect, and, "hoping desperately" to grow the school's enrollment to a level that the Culver family would not have to "dip so deeply" into their own pockets to support the school, Fleet made the bold and innovative decision to hire a public relations expert in early 1897. Fleet hired H. E. Cook, a real estate man from Cleveland, Ohio who possessed a vivid imagination and had the vision and ability to see how to make things grow.

According to Gignilliat, the establishment of Culver's famed Black Horse Troop occurred as follows:

> *"On March 4th, 1897, when William McKinley was inaugurated as President, [the 80-horse] Troop A of the Cleveland National Guard, which possessed title to the name the Black Horse Troop, escorted the newly-inaugurated (sic) President down Pennsylvania Avenue and to the White House. Every horse of the troop had been purchased in the bluegrass region of Kentucky, and each was coal black. After the inauguration, [the experienced horseman] Mr. Cook suggested to Mr. Culver, and Colonel Fleet, that the Culver Military Academy buy the mounts of the Black Horse Troop that had escorted President McKinley in Washington" with such aplomb and success. "Mr. Culver shook his head. 'We can't buy eighty horses,' he said. 'We can't spare the money right now.' 'You don't have to,' replied Cook. 'Leave it to me.' Instead of purchasing the full eighty horses of the troop that had escorted McKinley, he purchased only sixteen of them, but he saw to it that he got generous space in the press for his purchase," which both Fleet and Gignilliat appreciated. "The press notices said that the famous horseman, H. E. Cook, having critically inspected all of the mounts of Cleveland's Troop A, and having rejected those that were deemed unsafe for youth to ride, had purchased the troop for the Culver Military Academy. No reference was made to the exact number acquired, but the purchase included title to the name 'Black Horse Troop,'"* which Culver would make great use of to bring attention to the school and increase its enrollment.[35]

Far from resenting Culver's actions, the commander of Cleveland's Troop A and his senior horse advisor wrote to Fleet on March 19, 1897, expressing their "most earnest appreciation of your patriotic and enterprising venture in buying the troop of black horses for your Cadet Cavalry."[36]

The letter went on to state that, "Your idea of securing these horses and holding them together where they will not only have the best of care, but will furnish a daily incentive to patriotism for the boys of the cavalry squads of your excellent school, met with cordial sympathy on the part of every member of our troop, and we accordingly resolved to accept your offer on the horses."

Expressing their delight in Culver's decision to create a Cavalry Department, and acknowledging their support for the idea of integrating horsemanship into the curriculum and the tacit support of the Culver family financially the authors wrote, somewhat patronizingly, that, "You are to be congratulated on having a school so high in its educational feature and general equipment as to require such unusual excellence in its Cavalry Department in order to place that department on par with our other fine facilities," and also for having such an enlightened board able to appreciate the greater physical benefits that the training in horsemanship and the conduct of cavalry exercises can have on boys.[37]

Having purchased the 16 horses, Gignilliat recalled that, "The arrival of the black horses was a great occasion. [Culver] declared a half-holiday" so the boys could see the horses unload at the rail spur north of campus.[38] Gignilliat was impressed with the look of the animals, and he was especially taken by one particular horse.[39] When Gignilliat inquired about the animal, the English hostler informed him that the "spirited and mettlesome" horse was called "Airy," which was the way the Cockney-speaking man pronounced the horse's actual name of "Harry." Regardless of this communication discrepancy, Gignilliat and the horse connected instantly, and Airy would become his preferred mount for many years.[40]

As an experienced horseman, Gignilliat was convinced that the addition of a Cavalry Department would bring "great advantages" to Culver in a number of areas, including as "an additional means in the complete development of its Cadets," along with promotional, marketing, and recruiting benefits. He also had an instinctive understanding that the horses would have great appeal to boys and could help entice many to enroll at Culver. Beyond the allure of horseback riding that is powerful for boys, the military tradition and role of horses provided an immediate injection of energy and excitement into the school's military activities.

Since he was a cavalryman, Gignilliat recalled that even the nominally engaged Adams was also "greatly pleased" with the arrival of the horses and the creation of the Black Horse Troop (BHT) at Culver.[41]

The color and quality of the horses were striking, but their size – at least 15 hands high – was also quite remarkable. Challenging for an adult rider to handle, these steeds would be even more difficult for teenaged boys to control, especially if they were not experienced riders. To be effective, Culver needed a training program for its cadets that was of the highest quality to succeed in melding the boys and the horses into effective pairings that could perform at a very high level. This was no easy task.

Wanting to take immediate advantage of its new organization, Culver accepted an invitation for the BHT to make its first public appearance during the Civil War veterans' organization, known as the Grand Army of the Republic (GAR), annual encampment May 12-14, 1897, serving as the escort for the governor of Indiana and leading the GAR parade in eastern Indiana town of Richmond. Since it was about 200 miles southeast from Culver, both the cadets and the horses would have to depart on May 11, 1897, and travel by train, which added to both the excitement and complexity of the event, to arrive in time to escort the governor to from the train station to his hotel that evening,

Having little other choice, Cook took charge of training the 16 new troopers for the event. Relying on his own training and sense of showmanship, Cook "trained the cadet troopers in some fancy maneuvers for the parade that were not to be found at all in the U.S. Cavalry drill regulations," which included "spirals and cross-crosses and other more or less intricate evolutions."[42]

However, the army-trained cavalryman Adams disapproved of Cook's methods of instruction, "which emphasized more the technique of park and cross-country riding, in which Mr. Cook excelled, than the army technique."[43] Since VMI had not yet established its own cavalry department, Gignilliat could contribute little to the effort at this point.

The persnickety Adams made one of his required monthly visits to campus a few days prior to the BHT's departure for Richmond, and he let it be known that he was "thoroughly disgusted" by what he termed as "Cook's horse cotillion." As Gignilliat related the incident, with "his white goatee bristling with indignation, [Adams] declined positively to appear on the streets of Richmond with a 'damned circus act.'"[44]

Without Adams, command of the BHT for its first public appearance at the parade on May 12, 1897, fell to Gignilliat, who was fortunately an able horseman. Seeking to enhance the appeal of the troop even more,

Cook received approval to acquire a snow-white pony on which to mount a cadet bugler, which was a nice touch that provided a stark contrast to the 16 magnificent black horse of the BHT. With a cadet named Maxwell (hailing from the Culvers' hometown of St. Louis) providing the commands for the troop via bugle call, Gignilliat had only to ride at the head of the column wearing his impressive Governor's uniform and present the command to the reviewing officer, Civil War General Lew Wallace (who was also the author of *Ben Hur*). [45]

A mounted Gignilliat resplendent in his impressive Governor's uniform. [46]

Ever the opportunist, Cook captured a photograph of the BHT in formation and included it in Culver publicity material.[47]

The BHT's appearance provided Culver with some excellent publicity in Indiana's newspapers, including twice on page two in the May 12, 1897 edition of the *Indianapolis News* (the most widely read newspaper in the state). According to an unattributed newspaper account appearing in the 1898 CMA catalog, "One of the most striking features of the parade was that of the Black Horse Troop of the Culver Military Academy." While spectator expectations were high, given how well the unit had performed at McKinley's inauguration as part of the Ohio National Guard, the author offered that "we doubt if any one (sic) expected to see such a display of riding and maneuvering as was given by the Cadets of Culver, who handled the fiery blacks with such ease and dignity and soldierly bearing." The author observed that "the Cadets handled their beautiful steeds with the ease and grace of Arabs, and through the entire encampment their conduct was most becoming, gentlemanly, and courteous…,"undoubtedly pleasing all at Culver and perhaps especially Gignilliat.

The author concluded by writing that "It is doubtful if any troop of horses in the world is so well and favorably known as these matchless blacks, and it speaks well for the appointments of the Culver Military Academy to require the purchase of such a troop of horses for its Cavalry Department," justifying Cook's idea and the Culvers' investment.[49]

Gignilliat and the original Black Horse Troop at the GAR parade in Richmond, Indiana on May 12, 1897. [48]

Perhaps just as importantly, the performance of the BHT impressed Indian's governor, James A. Mount, quite favorably. In a letter to Fleet dated June 14, 1897, Mount wrote the following: "I was much impressed when I met the Black Horse Troop at Richmond. They won universal favor, and from me the highest admiration. The boys were soldierly in their bearing, their drill was executed in the best possible manner, and they truly deserve the many encomiums they received." After inviting the BHT to be with him at the upcoming July dedication of the Logan monument in Chicago, Mount closed with the following statement that could have hardly brought more joy to Fleet, Cook, and Gignilliat: "I assure you I shall ever feel a deep interest in the Cadets and in the Academy, and shall gladly do what I can for its promotion."[50]

Given the response to this initial performance of the BHT, it is hardly conceivable that anyone at Culver could have dared hope for a more positive response or better return on their investment.

The Army was also favorably impressed by the performance of the BHT. After being in existence for a little over one year, Culver received full equipment for cavalry drill from War Department at the beginning of the 1898-1899 school year.[51] This, along with the completion of the new riding hall in 1898, providing the Cavalry Department at Culver with the very best equipment and facilities available in the nation. This support allowed the BHT to realize Fleet's dream of "quality over quantity" rapidly, while also helping to advance the renown and interests of the school.

Writing to the VMI superintendent in 1902, Gignilliat shared that while the BHT did not make any money for Culver, it was nevertheless "a splendid advertising medium," allowing the BHT and Culver to be featured in appealing photographs in magazines as a result of much work done by Cook and Gignilliat.

Photographs of mounted cadets were far more appealing to magazines, and they were also more effective in getting Culver noticed than pictures of cadets simply marching and drilling with rifles, which did not convey the same sense of adventure and excitement. In addition, Gignilliat found that work with the horses was quite beneficial for the cadets physically, echoing the sentiments of many horsemen for as long as people had been riding horses.[52]

Culver and Gignilliat could have used Adams' expertise to prepare the BHT for this important event, but, as Gignilliat pointed out, Adams lived almost 300 hundred miles away and appeared on campus only for his once-monthly required visits, making him unavailable to contribute meaningfully. This must have surely chafed at Gignilliat's sense of duty and responsibility to the institution, further reducing any respect he may have had for Adams.

Gignilliat's Decision to Remain at Culver

From the moment of Gignilliat's arrival at Culver on the cold and snowy evening of January 13, 1897, his plan had been to remain at Culver for a brief period of about six months and then return to the east with the hope of landing the position in the US Patent Office he had been offered in 1896. However, several circumstances conspired to cause him to question this course of action and ultimately change his plans to instead remain at Culver.

Courting Minnie

The first and most powerful influence was Colonel Fleet's eldest daughter, Mary. Known as "Minnie" to her birth family, it was a nickname given to her by her brothers that she disliked but tolerated from her most intimate associates.[53] Gignilliat learned to call her Minnie because that was how she was introduced to him and was also what her family called her when he first met her. Gignilliat lovingly called her "Myn" or "Minnie" for the rest of her life, but she preferred to be called Mamie, and that is what she had most at Culver and the cadets call her for her adult life.

Minnie and her younger sister Belle attracted much attention at Culver upon their arrival. Gignilliat first met Minnie at breakfast on January 14, 1897, and he recalls thinking of her as an attractive woman and nothing more."[54]

However, Gignilliat became more interested in her during the winter months for several reasons. Dining regularly at Colonel Fleet's table in the dining hall, Gignilliat fell into the routine of sitting beside Minnie at virtually every meal, providing him with the opportunity to carry on a sustained discourse with her on a very regular basis. During their conversations over meals, they discovered that they shared some "kindred tastes."

Since his time at Emerson Prep, Gignilliat had been interested in declaiming, which was the practice of delivering dramatic presentations of works of literature one had memorized, and he coached some Culver cadets for several declamation contests in 1897. Having grown up accustomed to such events in the house of her highly educated father, Minnie joined him in this endeavor because she enjoyed such presentations and knew how they should be delivered correctly. In addition, Gignilliat and Minnie collaborated to help the cadets stage a short play during Commencement festivities, identifying another shared interest.[55] Both of these activities allowed them the opportunity to spend more time together and, perhaps more importantly, away from the watchful eye of Colonel Fleet.

The burgeoning relationship began to take form, and Gignilliat started trying to impress Minnie. As an experienced "declaimer," Gignilliat had mastered the ability to deliver dramatic recitations of different works of literature, and he decided to try to use this to his advantage in his efforts to impress Minnie. According to Gignilliat, his efforts did not go as planned. Writing after WWII, Gignilliat related the episode as follows:

> I remember on one occasion reciting for Minnie and Belle in Colonel Fleet's parlour (sic) a piece entitled 'Lasca.' In the poem there was one line in which Lasca 'drew from her garter a dear little dagger.' References to garters in those days were supposed to be indelicate, so I decided to substitute the word 'girdle,' which today has itself taken on a more indelicate meaning. As I recited the poem in their presence I was evidently thinking of 'garter' when I came to the line in question. Instead of saying, 'She drew from her girdle a dear little dagger,' I declaimed it, 'She drew from her girdle a dear little garter.' This was too much from the girls, who could not restrain their laughter. In fact, Minnie told me afterwards that they both laughed themselves to sleep at my painful embarrassment."[56]

This anecdote helps give an idea of the innocence of their relationship and the charming nature of their courtship.

Instances like this led Gignilliat to begin courting Minnie sometime between January and June 1897, which certainly influenced him to remain at Culver.

Learning from and Being Mentored by Fleet

Besides spending time with Minnie, Gignilliat also spent many hours of each day with Colonel Fleet. His relationship with Fleet was another influence on Gignilliat's decision to remain at Culver.

Knowing nothing about his new boss prior to arriving at Culver, Gignilliat was gratified to discover Fleet's "nativity" as a Virginian and fellow southerner. Gignilliat was also quite pleased to learn that Fleet's wife was related to the wife of his guardian, Leigh Robinson. As a result, Gignilliat felt that he had unexpectedly landed not in some "distant Siberian land," as he had first feared, but instead "among friends and almost relatives" at Culver.[57]

Working so closely with Fleet provided further impetus for Gignilliat to remain at Culver. As an experienced educator, Fleet had become an able mentor who taught Gignilliat the business of education. Kindly and professorial, Fleet's southern and gentlemanly mannerisms almost certainly appealed to Gignilliat. Fleet's age, being close to that of the father he never got to know, also allowed Fleet to become a sort of father-figure to the young and impressionable Gignilliat, who, isolated from all family contact, was sure to crave some type of paternal counsel and support.

The Satisfaction of Working as Commandant

As further incentive to change his plan of returning East, Gignilliat found that he truly enjoyed the work of being a commandant, much more than he had ever enjoyed the work of engineering. Perhaps even more unexpectedly, given the somewhat tenuous relationship he developed with military discipline at VMI, Gignilliat discovered that he was very good at being a commandant. Gignilliat's ability to establish and implement the highly effective military structure and system of discipline that Culver needed amazed Fleet and brought him success at Culver almost immediately.

Gignilliat attributed part of his rapid success to the fact that he possessed a "more than usual aptitude for dealing with the difficult problems of military discipline as applied to boys and young men."[58] In the short span of two months, Gignilliat had impressed Fleet so greatly that Fleet reported to the superintendent of VMI that Gignilliat was "unquestionably the best Commandant I have ever seen" and better even than his "very excellent" MMA Commandant, Major K. G. Matheson.[59] This was high praise from a well-respected educator, and it had to have brought Gignilliat great joy, along with equal measures of comfort and pride.

This high level of confidence emboldened Fleet to give Gignilliat broad authority and much autonomy, creating an exceptionally appealing professional environment within which he functioned. Gignilliat was also "pleasantly surprised by the [physical] surroundings" in which he found himself.[60] These unexpected motives further influenced his decision to remain at Culver.

The Decision to Stay at Culver Is Made

It may well have appeared that the universe was conspiring to have him remain at Culver. He was among friends, enjoying the work, and courting Minnie, and all of these influential factors combined to bring about a change of heart. As a result, Gignilliat changed his mind about his desire to pursue the plan he had when he arrived at Culver in January 1897, and he reported that by June 1897, "all thoughts of applying for a job at the U.S. Patent Office had vanished."[61]

In fact, Gignilliat had been looking forward to taking a long vacation back east since he stepped off the train at Culver, and he planned to spend two months away from Culver at the conclusion of the school year in June 1897. However, after being away from Culver – and Minnie – for two weeks, Gignilliat returned to Culver six weeks early and asked her to marry him. Minnie accepted his proposal of marriage, much to Gignilliat's delight. However, in keeping with the custom of the time, Gignilliat still had to work up the nerve to ask the formidable Colonel Fleet for his permission to marry his eldest daughter.

One immediate impact of Gignilliat's betrothal was a rather significant improvement in his appearance. He began his time at Culver looking much like he did as a rather unkempt VMI cadet who had grown a mustache. However, when he began courting Minnie, he cleaned up his appearance and began looking more professional and presentable.

A young Gignilliat looking serious and more professional. [62]

Gignilliat's early return must have puzzled Fleet somewhat and perhaps tipped his hand. After procrastinating for several weeks, Gignilliat scheduled a meeting with Fleet at which he was determined to ask for the hand of his boss' daughter in marriage. According to Gignilliat, who could not have been more nervous, they talked of "cabbages and kings and many things that had no relations to matrimony" until he could no longer avoid the topic of his meeting. With his anxiety causing him to squirm in his chair in a most unmilitary fashion, he "blurted out the object" of his mission and asked Fleet for Minnie's hand in marriage.

Regardless of how obvious it should have been to him, given the increasing amount of time Gignilliat had been spending with Minnie, this unexpected request caused Fleet to regard Gignilliat in an entirely new manner. He paused for a moment to consider the situation, shifting his habitual mint-flavored "candy drop from one check to the other" as he took Gignilliat's measure as a potential spouse for his beloved oldest child. After having given Gignilliat's request due consideration, Fleet replied by telling Gignilliat that he had always told his girls that he "would not stand in the way of their marriage to anyone either was in love with," but that if the object of their affection was a "knothead" to not even bother to ask for his blessing.

Gignilliat concluded rather drolly, since he was not asked to tender his resignation as a result of the meeting, that Fleet did not consider him to be a"knothead" and was content to keep him around as both commandant and as a son-in-law. As a result, Fleet, who had already become a father-figure to Gignilliat, was now also his future father-in-law.[63]

Gignilliat Commits to Culver

Military training was most certainly on Gignilliat's mind after his first semester at Culver and upon his return. After the mid-year break, and while betrothed to Minnie, Gignilliat wrote to VMI Superintendent Scott Shipp to inquire about the possibility of becoming the Commandant of Cadets at VMI.[64] While there is no record of Shipp's response, the somber and serious Shipp, who had also served as VMI's Commandant, likely recalled the bright but somewhat immature cadet Gignilliat had been while at VMI. It is doubtful that such an individual would have appealed to Shipp as a legitimate candidate for the position of Commandant of Cadets. Rebuffing Gignilliat's somewhat impulsive inquiry, Shipp possibly counseled Gignilliat to focus on gaining more experience at Culver to become sufficiently prepared to take on the responsibilities of being VMI's Commandant, which would also allow him time to age and mature to separate the youthful Gignilliat a bit further from the cadets he would lead at the Institute.

After the excitement of the 1897-1898 school year, Gignilliat married Mamie on August 2, 1898. The following account appeared on the front page of *The Culver Herald* on August 5, 1898, under the heading, "Wedding at the Academy: Miss Fleet Becomes the Wife of Major L. R. Gignilliat," and it is worth quoting at length:

> *It was a quiet home wedding, but a more appropriate and tasteful ceremony, which at high noon on Tuesday, the 2nd instant, united in wedlock Miss Mary Seddon Fleet, and Major Leigh Robinson Gignilliat.*
>
> *The bride, a daughter of Col. A. F. Fleet, superintendent of Culver Military Academy, and a descendant on her mother's side of the Seddons of Virginia, is a young lady as sweet in disposition and bright in mind as she is charming in person, and the groom, a young Georgian of Huguenot ancestry, is the commandant of the academy and an aid on the staff of the governor of Indiana, in both of which positions he has made many friends by his soldierly accomplishments and genial disposition.*
>
> *The home of Colonel and Mrs. A. F. Fleet was beautifully decorated for the occasion with flowers, potted plants and evergreens, festoons of smilax and a profusion of water lilies, rendering the room in which the ceremony was performed particularly attractive.*
>
> *In this room and back of the raised dais the colors of the academy were draped in easy folds, while to the front and just over the position to be occupied by the bride and groom hung a wedding bell of gracefully entwined evergreens and water lilies. At the first strains of the wedding march, which was rendered with much expression by Miss Ayres, of Chicago, the Rev. Wm. W. Raymond, of the Plymouth Episcopal church, entered the room closely followed by the groom and his best man, William L. Gignilliat, of Savannah, Georgia.*
>
> *Then from the opposite entrance came the two little pages, Charles P. Fleet and Wm. R. Gignilliat [eldest son of Best Man William L. Gignilliat], and the attendants (all brothers of the bride), J. Seddon Fleet, Henry W. Fleet and Wm. A Fleet, and immediately following them the lovely maid of honor, Miss Belle Seddon Fleet, accompanied by Major Kenneth G. Matheson.*

The happy couple on their wedding day, August 2, 1898.[67]

As the attendants separated and formed on either side, the bride, a vision of grace and beauty, entered leaning on the arm of her father, and advanced to the dais, where the groom stood awaiting her.

And now followed the solemn and beautiful service of the Episcopal church, rendered more impressive by the subdued strains of music from the organ and the low, but firm, responses of those who pledged themselves to take life's long journey together.

The bride's gown was of white tulle, trimmed with lace – a costume which set off to the best advantage her petite figure and classic features.

The maid of honor was attired in tulle, trimmed with pink ribbons – a costume equally becoming to her winsome grace.

The groom, in full-dress uniform of his rank, was strikingly handsome – while the three young attendants, in full dress cadet uniforms, erect and soldierly to their bearing, and the flag draped in the back ground (sic), lent to the occasion a semi-military aspect peculiarly appropriate and altogether pleasing. The whole constituting a picture which will ever linger in the memory of all who witnessed it.

Many handsome pieces of silver and cut glass and other beautiful presents evinced the interest taken in this event, both here and in the old family homes in Virginia and Georgia.[65]

Recalling the event decades later, Gignilliat offered a humorous anecdote about the day of his wedding. According to Gignilliat, "My oldest brother, Willie, came up from Savannah to represent the family and to act as my best man. As he was approaching Colonel Fleet's cottage shortly before the wedding, he saw two of Minnie's brothers carrying a five-gallon water bottle and heard one say, 'Minnie, these are smelling salts. You'd better keep them handy.'" Gignilliat also recalled that it was Minnie's brothers and Matheson who gathered the water lilies for the decorations in Fleet's house.[66]

Immediately after the wedding, Gignilliat and his new bride left for their honeymoon in Washington, DC. Gignilliat felt very much at home in Washington, DC, having spent a good part of his youth there while attending Emerson Prep and living with Leigh Robinson. It was also an affordable option, since he could stay with this bother Thomas (who he referred to by his middle name of "Heyward") for free.

Traveling by train, Gignilliat recalled that he and Minnie were joined in their double seat by J. M. Studebaker, the founder of the Studebaker Company, during the journey from Culver to South Bend. Studebaker later related to Fleet that he found Minnie to be "a delightful conversationalist," but that Gignilliat himself was rather "uncommunicative." Gignilliat confirmed that this was most absolutely the case, as he considered Studebaker's presence to be an intrusion and referring to it as "one occasion when three was certainly a crowd."[68]

Another amusing episode from their time on the train occurred at breakfast the following morning. Gignilliat told the story in the following manner:

> *I asked my bride if she had ever heard that if you grasped an egg end to end in your hands that no matter how hard you squeezed, the egg would not break. She admitted that she had never heard of that interesting experiment in dynamics. I undertook to demonstrate. The theory evidently didn't hold for soft-boiled eggs. The egg explored like a bomb, squirted into my hair and my ears, and pretty much bespattered my new pearl-gray suit which I had strained my budget to purchase for my wedding trip. I should like to be able to say that she was properly sympathetic, but she giggled even more than she had over the "dear little garter' episode."[69]*

Even at the very beginning of their life together, Gignilliat and Minnie didn't take one another too seriously and found ways to enjoy each other's company regardless of the circumstances.

The weather in Washington, DC was as uncomfortably hot and humid as one would expect it to be at the beginning of August, but the newlyweds made the best of it. Gignilliat served as the tour guide, showing Minnie "all of the points of interest," and he also recorded their adventures by taking photographs of her in various settings.[70]

Intriguingly, Gignilliat made no mention of visiting or spending time with his guardian while in Washington, DC, and it does not appear that Robinson attended the wedding. While there may have been some reconciliation since their falling out in 1894, it does not appear that their relationship was fully mended by the summer of 1898.

Gignilliat Begins Hitting His Stride at Culver

Upon his return to campus from his honeymoon in 1898, and following up on the success of the BHT's performance at the GAR encampment in May 1897, Gignilliat arranged for the entire CMA corps of cadets – numbering 158 cadets – and the Black Horse Troop to march in the Chicago Peace Jubilee on October 19, 1898 as the escort for Indiana Governor James A. Mount. Commemorating the conclusion of the Spanish-American War, President McKinley and other heroes of the war would be on hand to witness the culminating public event of the week-long celebration.

The Culver group traveled on a chartered Nickel Plate train, arriving at the Dearborn Street Station in time to take their place within the line of march for the grand parade that began at 11:00 am.[71]

Culver Cadet Corps and Black Horse Troop at Chicago Peace Jubilee, October 19, 1898. [73]

Marching at the rear of the Second Division in a cold and driving rain, the battalion followed the route north on Michigan Avenue to Van Buren Street, turning west to State Street, north to Randolph Street, west to Dearborn Street, south to Adams Street, west to La Salle Street, north to Washington Street, west to Franklin Street, south

Culver cadets marching at the St. Louis Dewey Day parade, May 5, 1900 Gignilliat is mounted on the lead horse turned to the left.[75]

Culver cadets escorting Admiral Dewey at the St. Louis Dewey Day parade, May 5, 1900. Gignilliat in mounted in the center just left of the Colors.[76]

Culver cadets escorting Governor Mount at the GAR Encampment Parade in Indianapolis, May 17, 1900. Gignilliat is mounted in the center just behind the Cadet Band.[77]

to Jackson Boulevard, and east past the President's reviewing stand at the Union League Club to Michigan Avenue, where the parade ended and the units were released.

According to Culver's own account of the event, "the soldierly bearing of the Corps of Cadets elicited high commendation from distinguished observers," including Governor Mount and the Commanding General of the US Army, Nelson A. Miles, despite the terrible weather. Mount specifically mentioned Gignilliat in his letter of commendation, and the letters all made clear that Culver had made a positive impression.[72]

Around this time, Gignilliat and Minnie learned that she was pregnant and that they could expect the arrival of their first child in mid-May 1899. After an anxious winter and early spring, Leigh Robinson Gignilliat Jr was born on May 13, 1899. This opened another chapter in Gignilliat's life: that of a father.

Within 10 days of the birth of his first child, Gignilliat took the entire corps on another trip. Traveling even farther, Gignilliat chaperoned 160 cadets and the BHT to the GAR encampment in Terre Haute, Indiana, during the period of 23-26 May, 1899.[74]

Gignilliat's military system began to take hold and produce results during the following school year, 1899-1900.

Culver was invited back for another opportunity for the cadets to demonstrate their increased proficiency on May 5, 1900, when a troop of cavalry, the cadet band, and a battalion of infantry served as the official escort for US Navy Spanish-American War hero Admiral Dewey at the St. Louis Dewey Day parade. Their performance was impressive, and both Admiral Dewey and the grand marshal of the parade wrote laudatory letters of commendation to Culver's leadership praising the cadets for their outstanding performance in the parade.[78]

Less than two weeks later on May 17, 1900, the cadets served as the official escort for Indiana Governor James A. Mount at the annual GAR encampment in Indianapolis. [79] The following day, the cadets gave an exhibition of drill that impressed the governor and the many spectators greatly.[80]

At the close of the 1899-1900 school year, Gignilliat had much to be proud of in terms of the results of his efforts. The military program he had designed and implemented was beginning to take hold, and it was succeeding in bringing positive recognition to Culver and helping to increase enrollment. From the time of his arrival, enrollment at Culver had increased by over 120 cadets, going from 122 in 1897 to 242 by the end of the 1899-1900 school year.

In addition, cadets were succeeding despite the increased rigor of the military program, with the number of graduates doubling from 7 in 1897 to 15 in 1900.[81] While he was challenging them outside the classroom, the cadets were accepting the program and excelling militarily as a result of it.

Gignilliat's First Real Test – The "Big Fire"

With almost four years of experience as commandant and a slew of successful public appearances to his credit, Gignilliat's leadership ability had yet to be tested in a crisis situation. His ability to handle the boys appeared to have no limits, and all were amazed by the effortlessness with which he appeared to command their respect and loyalty. The vicissitudes of adolescences, however, are quite fickle, and in fall 1900 Gignilliat faced his first true test as a schoolman.

On the evening of Tuesday, October 30, 1900, two cadets left their rooms without permission and went into the town of Culver. For this offense, they were expelled. In defiance of Culver's rules, over 100 cadets formed up and marched themselves to the train station to bid them farewell the next day, Wednesday, October 31, 1900 (Halloween), absenting themselves from campus without proper authorization.

When Major Gignilliat learned of the cadets' actions, he rode his favorite horse "Airy" to the train station and confronted the cadets. One somewhat sensationalized account alleged that the very proper Gignilliat acted quite unprofessionally by calling the cadets "brutes" and "ruffians," and by referring to the entire group as "a mob."

However, Gignilliat says that his remarks were actually directed towards a group of local town boys who were "jeering at me and urging the cadets to disregard my orders." Acknowledging that we was, however, somewhat agitated by the episode, Gignilliat recollects that "only once was I moved to violence of language, and threatening horsemanship, and that was toward a group of depot loafers," when he spurred his horse at them and "turned a somewhat unrestrained vocabulary in their direction," "whereupon they scattered."[82]

Having gained control of the situation, Gignilliat order the cadets into formation and marched them back to campus. Upon their return, all were were placed on room restriction, and Gignilliat told them that he was going to recommend that they all be dismissed for their egregious breach of discipline.

When Gignilliat reported the incident to Fleet, it became apparent immediately that he and Fleet were not aligned with how to respond to the situation appropriately.

- Since his days at the University of Virginia, Fleet's view of dismissal as a punishment applied mostly to egregious offenses and honor violations. Indeed, in Fleet's own experience, students at the university had rioted and not been dismissed. As a result, he likely did not see it as good business sense for a school to consider dismissing one-half of its student body for a relatively minor offense like this.[83]

- By contrast, Gignilliat's experience at VMI had taught him that the only possible response to episodes of mass disobedience was to dismiss all who were involved in the incident.[84]

These drastically differing perspectives put Gignilliat at odds with Fleet.

Gignilliat discussed the situation with Fleet "until a very late hour," noting that there were "several angles to the situation," and discovering that he and Fleet viewed the situation quite differently. This may have been the first significant difference of opinion the two had experienced, creating a situation between the wound-up young Gignilliat and the courtly and seasoned Fleet that was as awkward as it was unaccustomed. After getting nowhere in their own deliberations, Gignilliat reported that Fleet concluded their discussion by saying, "Major, we will do what is right to be done, but first we must consult the Culvers. After all, it is their school, not yours, not mine." This indicates that Fleet did not agree with Gignilliat's recommendation and that the two could not come to a consensus, requiring Fleet to request guidance from the Culver family.[85]

The following day, Thursday, November 1, 1900, both ER Culver and BB Culver (and perhaps other brothers) arrived in the evening and met with the members of the administration to consider the situation. During the first eight years of its existence, 1894-1902, the Culver family owned the

Copy of a telegram sent to the parents of one of the dismissed cadets on November 2, 1900. The text reads: "Your son leaves for home today. Expect him next train. Letter follows later with full explanation. A.F. Fleet." [90]

school and used an "Association" model for governance. Three different men had official overall responsibility for the Association: HH Culver from 1894 until his death in September 1897 ; BB Culver from the time of his father's death in 1897 through 1899; and ER Culver from 1900-1902.[86] Thus it was ER Culver who was nominally in charge of the Association at the time of the "Big Fire, but BB, who had recently relinquished control of the Association to his younger brother, remained quite engaged with the school.

```
                        Headquarters
                 Culver Military Academy
                    Culver, Indana.
                 (Lake Maxinkuckee.)


                                              November 3,1900.

My Dear Sir:
      On Tuesday night,October 30,two cadets absented themselves from
their quarters in the Barracks without permision,and were absent from
the Academy grounds for two hours or more.The paragraph in the Academy
Regulations covering this point reads as follows:

           "225. Any cadet who shall absent himself from the
                 Academy at after call to quarters,without permiss-
                 ion,and go beyond the limits,shall be dismissed."

      The two cadets had hearing on Wednesday,and were dismissed and
instructed to leave on the Vandalia train going south at7:50 p.m.
      One of the dismissed cadets was very popular,and his friends were
naturally distressed at his leaving.It was determined among them,
doubtless under the guidance of some of the older boys,to give him a
demonstration as he went away.
      After supper,therefore,over a hundred of the cadets moved quietly
away from the grounds,and went down to the railroad station,ostensibly
to see the two dismissed cadets off on the train,but in direct violat-
ion of the very regulatoin under which the two cadets had been dismiss-
ed.
      In a few minutes the absents was discovered and the Commandant
mounted his horse and rode rapidly to the station and ordered the
cadets to fall in and march back to the Academy.After some hesitation
and with murmurs of dissatisaction they fell ir and returned under
orders.On Thursday they were all kept under close arrest and were ex-
amined by the Commandant to see if there were any extenuating circum-
stances.The whole matter was carefully investigated from every possible
side and the decision reached that the only course to adopted in order
to preserve the integrity and the discipline of the Academy was to
dismiss all the cadets involved in the disorder and send them at once
to their homes.
      The matter was one of such grave moment that the Board of Trustees
were summoned from St.Louis and arrived Thursday night.The whole trans-
action was laid before them,and their unqualified decision was to sus-
tain the Academy authorities,and that the cadets implicated should be
dismissed.This was done,and the cadets sent to their homes by the noon
trains Friday.
      No words can express the grief felt by myself and the Commandnat
and the other officers of the Academy at the occurence.Because of the
previous excellent conduct of the greater number of the cadets this
action was entirely unexpected and could not have been anticipated.
      On account of the unusual pressure upon us this matter could not
e previously reported in detail.
      Hoping to hear from you at the earliest possible moment,and with
indebt,regards,I am,

           Very truly yours,
                 A.F.Fleet,Supt.
```

Letter Fleet sent to the parents of a dismissed cadets on November 3, 1900. [91]

The Culver brothers discussed the situation with Fleet and Gignilliat (and perhaps others) at great length, spending much of the night in deliberation. They determined, at Gignilliat's recommendation and with the support of ER Culver, to dismiss all 105 of the offending cadets for willful disobedience of the Academy's rules and authority.[87] This was one half of the 210 cadets enrolled at Culver, placing the school (and Fleet) in great peril.

On Friday, November 2, 1900, the cadets were dismissed. Addressing the cadets being dismissed after chapel on that morning to show his support for the decision, the head of the CMA Association ER Culver remarked that:

> *"My father [HH Culver], when he started this school, expected the faculty and not the boys to run it. Rather than have it otherwise we would prefer to convert these buildings into barns and fill them with hay."* According to Gignilliat, ER Culver went on to say that *"in matters of discipline there could be no safety in numbers, that a hundred boys could not violate a regulation and, since they were a hundred, escape the penalty exacted of an individual."* ER Culver concluded by saying, *"The cadets involved in this episode are dismissed from the school. The Quartermaster will furnish each with transportation to his home."*

Gignilliat recalls that a palpable silence followed ER Culver's remarks.[88]

Hartman tells us that Fleet followed up on ER Culver's sobering remarks by sending telegrams to parents (collect!) telling them to expect their son on the next train and that a full explanation would follow shortly.[89]

The actions of Fleet and Gignilliat attracted national attention for Culver because it was a remarkable act of fearless discipline and commitment to character development. The institution's "stand for respect for authority" and determination to show that there was "no safety in numbers when it comes to disregarding the authority of the school" held fast to ensure that all current and future cadets were convinced beyond any doubt that the school's rules must be obeyed individually and *en masse*.

The letter Fleet sent on November 3, 1900 with the full explanation is worth considering carefully.

Whether Fleet personally agreed with the decision or not, the content of the letter he sent to the parents of the dismissed cadets communicates very clearly the school's position on the affair. Fleet adopted unusually direct wording in the first six paragraphs to provide a very matter-of-fact account of the main aspects of the incident, which Gignilliat may have helped him draft. The more muted tone of the letter's final three paragraphs, especially the concluding sentence that began, "Hoping to hear from you at the earliest possible moment...", seems more likely to have come directly from Fleet's own pen.

Expressing the irrevocability of the decision in a manner that cadets could more readily understand, Gignilliat published orders on November 2, 1900 to reestablish the CMA chain of command. In this order, Gignilliat replaced the dismissed cadet leaders with those who remained enrolled at Culver. The finality of this order communicated very effectively that there was no going back on this decision. [92]

Eventually, around 80 of these cadets who requested readmission were allowed to return in December, 1900 under certain carefully crafted conditions. To be considered for readmission, a cadet had to have amassed a good record at Culver prior to the incident, and they could not have been either expelled or dishonorably discharged from the Academy as a result of the episode. The latter-two characterizations applied to the 15 or 16 ringleaders of the incident and indicated that the cadet had played a significant role in the event that prevented them from being reinstated. [93]

The conditions of their readmission were fairly specific. First, those who were dismissed from the Academy were allowed to return, all of whom would be on some type of restriction and some on probation as well, depending upon their previous record and actions during the episode that led to their dismissal. The restrictions included the denial of privileges until after the Christmas holiday and being ineligible to hold cadet rank until the second semester. As an incentive to reenroll, all reinstated cadets were allowed to return without prejudice, meaning that they did not have to serve punishments imposed prior to their departure and any actions of indiscipline that had not been adjudicated prior to their departure would be forgiven, allowing cadets who returned the opportunity to start fresh, overcome the episode, and succeed at Culver based on their subsequent performance. [94]

The episode and outcome were, as one might expect, the talk of the campus for many weeks afterwards. *The Vedette* reported one particular impact that the "Big Fire" had on the CMA Corps of Cadets.

Culver played a football game against the powerful Lake Forest Academy team on Saturday, November 3, 1900. Many of the cadets who had just been dismissed were members of the crack football squad that had an undefeated record up to this point in the season. Without most of their starters and even enough players to field a complete team for the game, Culver played against the very accomplished Lake Forest team using second- and third-stringers, and even some boys who had never before played football. The patched together squad lost to Lake Forest 10-0, but they demonstrated a remarkable spirit and put up a tremendous fight that impressed their opponents and spectators. The outcome was couched in terms of how well the less-experienced players competed against the perennially good Lake Forest Academy team, and it helped to buoy the morale of the dispirited cadets in the wake of the "Big Fire." Both The *Vedette* and *The Chicago Tribune* characterized the loss as a victory for the plucky Culver team. [95]

Parents of the dismissed cadets in both Indianapolis and Chicago – Culver's two largest sources of cadets – were very upset with Gignilliat, Fleet, and Culver. They were not as able to move forward as quickly as the cadets had. Several penned unflattering articles about Culver that appeared in larger newspapers, and others, according to Gignilliat, threatened the school with lawsuits. The Culver family, however, remained steadfast in their support for the administration and the school through it all. This was a remarkable statement of leadership for Culver, both in terms of what was decided and said, and also in how it was communicated.

In many respects, the "Big Fire" was not one of Gignilliat's best moments. This was a somewhat – in Gignilliat's own words – "impetuous" series of actions and decisions that showed Gignilliat to be the 26-year-old rather inexperienced man that he was. Gignilliat learned much from the experience, and we do not see another such remarkable lapse in judgment from him for another 13 years (during the Logansport episode).[96] Accordingly, it is worth investigating why he responded to it the way he did.

Gignilliat had learned how to address episodes of mass disobedience during his time at VMI. Cadet uprisings – called "mutinies" at VMI – occurred with some frequency in the post-Civil War period, including episodes in 1873, 1880, and 1899.[97] The lesson he learned was one of uncompromising accountability and focus on the institution's long-term principles over the more immediate short-term concerns of enrollment and finances.

Regarding the 1880 mutiny at VMI, the result of which ended with VMI dismissing 27/~130 cadets (all but four of the entire Third class; nine were later reinstated) that put the school in "dire financial straits," one historian wrote, "This illustrates a continuing policy of the Institute – to hold the prescribed line, regardless of the immediate effect upon attendance and finances." [98] About another episode, occurring ten months prior to the "Big Fire" incident at Culver, the same historian wrote the following:

> *"On January 3, 1899, the class scheduled to graduate the following June was dismissed en masse for mutiny and insubordination... This 1899 rebellion was the first since 1880, and General Shipp was true to the principle laid down in an order published when he was commandant in the 1860s. It said: 'Absolute, unqualified obedience is an essential principle in military administration. However hard, or severe or unjust an order may be, a good solider will obey it, and afterwards seek redress.'"* [99]

It is also worth noting that all 35 of the dismissed cadets were later reinstated by VMI but with strict penalties. [100]

Based on these episodes, one can conclude that Gignilliat was simply responding to the October 31, 1900 incident of mass willful disobedience at Culver as he had been trained to do and had seen VMI do. While ER Culver supported Gignilliat's recommendation to dismiss the offending cadets, it is likely that Fleet, whose experience at the University of Virginia suggested a quite different approach and who had lost everything just four years earlier at MMA, was less enthusiastic about Gignilliat's recommendation for how to respond. This was even more likely the case with the ensuing negative press Culver's response to the episode generated and the threats of lawsuits from parents that followed. Personally, Gignilliat's immaturity was also exposed by his response to this incident. By applying the VMI approach – which was based on a 40-year-old policy designed for college-aged young men – blindly and rather indiscriminately to the situation, Gignilliat was acting more by rote than reason. It was an unusual gaffe that upset many parents in Indianapolis and Chicago because it seemed to them to be so out of character for an institution that prided itself on making sensible and reasoned decisions in all areas.

The outcome could have been disastrous, and it put the school at great risk by dismissing 105/210 cadets for such an offense. That it turned out well with 80 of the 105 returning to the school by December 1900 was

Gignilliat's good fortune. That the episode worked to the institution's favor in showing it to be uncompromisingly committed to its values was of even greater fortune to Gignilliat, for had it not turned out that way, he would have been a young married man with one child and another on the way out of work, and the outcome would have been truly disastrous for Fleet (and Minnie, as his daughter).

One has to believe that as a result of this episode, and the close call to the Academy's survival and even though he had the support of ER Culver, Fleet began mentoring Gignilliat even more diligently, having witnessed the level of his maturity and having been shocked out of being lulled into believing that Gignilliat could handle much more than he was perhaps ready for based upon his ability to do good things with the corps when they were largely compliant to his wishes. It is also apparent that Gignilliat realized the folly of his actions (as he indicated in his memoirs) and took the appropriate measures to learn for himself to control his impetuousness. Whatever the reason, as a result of this crisis, the professional relationships between Gignilliat and Fleet, and between Gignilliat and ER Culver, had to have changed somewhat.

A significant institutional consequence of the "Big Fire" was that Culver did not march in President McKinley's inauguration parade on March 4, 1901. Culver had fully expected to appear at the event and had begun planning for it. The cadets were excited about going and looked forward to the event. [101]

Gignilliat inspecting a cadet room circa 1899. [105]

In Gignilliat's account, the parent of one of the dismissed cadets who was not readmitted was a prominent Indianapolis attorney who was friends with the Senate Sargent of Arms, responsible for planning the inauguration. Upset with Culver's decision and the outcome for his son, the attorney apparently told the Senate Sargent of Arms not to invite Culver, and Culver did not receive an invitation to this important occasion. [102]

According to the cadets, however, the reason they did not attend the event was due to "the unwillingness of a number of the cadets to take the trip," causing it to be "practically abandoned." [103] This may have been a somewhat true and more convenient story to tell the cadets in lieu of sharing with them the actual reason they were not going to the inaugural.

Regardless of the cause, and given the effort Culver had put into getting the corps invited to important events like this to gain attention for the school, was a great disappointment for all at Culver to not participate.

Gignilliat's Military System Begins to Take Form and Hold

At the beginning of the 1898-1899 school year, Culver received full equipment for cavalry drill from War Department. [104] Following up on the success of the BHT's performance at the GAR encampment in May 1897, Gignilliat put this new equipment to good use when he arranged for all 151 Culver cadets (the entire CMA corps) to march in the Chicago Peace Jubilee on October 19, 1898.

His system began to take form and hold and produce results during the following school year, 1899-1900.

At the beginning of 1899, ER Culver took over directing the Culver Board of Directors, beginning the development of a tremendously strong and powerful relationship between Gignilliat and the younger Culver brother.

By fall of 1900, Gignilliat had directed Adams to inspect the cadets during each of his monthly visits. While the BHT performed well during the 1900 Thanksgiving Exhibition at Culver, the cadets themselves recognized that they needed to improve their performance in their infantry drill. They were not happy with the results of Captain Adams' battalion inspection on December 8, 1900, reporting that, "We are sorry to say that the battalion review and inspection was decidedly poor and the corps did not do itself justice." The lack of "snap and precision" is what concerned the cadets most.

Reflecting the positive impact the many trips that Gignilliat took them on was having on their desire to excel militarily, the cadets also noted that, "We all want to go on some trip this year – but how can we show off away from school if we are not good enough to show off at school."[106] It is clear that the use of trips had elicited the desire to perform well militarily among the cadets. Having created the necessary pre-conditions, it was now up to Gignilliat and his military staff to find effective methods of translating this desire into action that would improve the battalion's military performance.

Gignilliat also figured out how to get the tents he needed to support field training. Working on the staff of the Indiana Adjutant General, he met officers who controlled the state's military resources, and he obtained permission for Culver to use enough tents to allow entire corps to establish a military camp -- referred to as "castrametation" -- and train on this skill. As a result, the military training program implemented and administered by Gignilliat and Adams as PMS&T improved, as did the cadets' proficiency.

On the personal side of his life, sometime during the summer of 1900, a little over a year after the birth of Leigh Jr., Minnie discovered that she was expecting the Gignilliats' second child. Frederick Fleet Gignilliat was born on March 4, 1901.

Reason For Optimism At the Turn of the 20th Century

The challenge of the "Big Fire" notwithstanding, Gignilliat began the new century in a very positive status in terms of his professional and personal situations. He and his family had every reason to look toward the future with great excitement, anticipation, and enthusiasm.

Chapter 4: Creating Culver's Unique Military System and Achieving "Distinguished Institution" Status, 1900-1906

Foundation of Success Established in 1898-1899

Gignilliat's sustained focus on improving the corps' ability to parade and raising the level of proficiency to a very high level produced results that were quite evident and impressive for its military program, leading to even greater benefits for the school at the dawn of the new century.

Beginning in 1900, Culver began using the "Great Lack in American Character" argument as justification for the military system and military drill in its catalog.[1] This theme linked the military system and program directly to the school's mission at a fundamental level, further increasing its influence, importance, and appeal.

Using events from the previous several years to validate the capability of the military program he established, Gignilliat felt justified in turning his attention to the bigger dreams he had for Culver's military program. He did all he could to begin realizing those dreams during the period 1898-1899, but his efforts were hampered because the corps was simply too small.

To be able to march and train as a regiment – comprised of at least two battalions – required the corps to have at least 250 cadets. With fewer than 250 cadets, the cadets could not drill effectively at the regimental level. They could only march in a single rank instead of the traditional double-rank formation, and the corps was not large enough to form a regiment, requiring more than a single battalion.

Beyond the limitations the corps' small size imposed on drill, equipment limitations prevented Gignilliat from conducting effective field training with the cadets. More specifically, Culver did not have any tentage to allow the cadets to train on establishing a military camp, which was an important component of military training at the time.

Gignilliat's Military System Begins to Take Form

Under Fleet's mentorship and influence, Gignilliat's military system for Culver began to reflect Fleet's "whole-person" approach to education. For Gignilliat's military system, this was manifested in a military program that focused on the Body, Mind, and Spirit of the boy.

Military System and Training Program Improvements

By the beginning of the 1900-1901 school year, Culver's enrollment had increased to 260 cadets. This was the highest number of cadets yet enrolled, and it was also the first time it had ever been above 250.[2]

The CMA Corps of Cadets on parade, 1900. Gignilliat mounted third from the left.[3]

This number of cadets provided Gignilliat with the opportunity to begin the next phase of transforming Culver's military program along the lines of Fleet's desire for "quality over quantity."

For the military program, the focus was on improving in those areas included in the Army's annual inspection. While the Army was inspecting all schools at which it assigned an Army officer and provided equipment, it had not yet begun its practice of identifying distinguished institutions, providing them with special recognition, or designating any number as "distinguished" units.

1900 – 1902 – Focusing on the "Body"

Gignilliat's efforts to transform Culver's military program into one of the nation's premier programs began by focusing on drill and the "body" aspect of the "body-mind-spirit" construct.

Building upon the success of the Black Horse troop (mentioned previously), the CMA Corps of Cadets grew to a total enrollment of over 250 cadets, allowing for the creation of seven cadet companies of sufficient size (~ 35 cadets marching in each). This size was sufficient to allow for the conduct of company drill in double ranks and also to form two single-rank battalions. These developments were significant because they allowed the corps to engage in regimental drill, using its two battalions. For military schools at the time, the ability to conduct regimental drill represented the acme of both efficiency and effectiveness.

Drill was the main focus of Gignilliat's military system in the fall, teaching the new cadets the rudiments of military drill and also working with the entire corps to improve its proficiency. As part of his military training program, Gignilliat began staging an annual Thanksgiving Exposition at Culver to provide the cadets with a focus for their training efforts and to demonstrate their proficiency to the Culver community.

1902 – Changes in Personnel, Governance, and Approach

As the military program began to take hold, Captain Adams departed Culver at the beginning of the 1901 school year. He was replaced by Captain Philip P. Powell as Culver's PMS&T. Powell was not a particularly effective military trainer and did not understand much about the best ways to excel on the Army's annual inspection.

Also, at the beginning of 1902, the Culver brothers incorporated Culver Military Academy. This new administrative structure was more orientated towards the business aspects of the running of a school. While ER Culver remained deeply involved in the administration of the school, the more experienced businessman BB Culver took over as president. It was thus BB Culver and Fleet who focused on transforming Culver into a thriving and sustainable educational institution for the next decade.

By 1902, Gignilliat had learned much about how to train cadets effectively, and he understood that much of the Army's annual inspection standards were based on how cadets were trained at West Point. So, while much of the daily activities at Culver remained based upon VMI practices, Gignilliat began basing Culver's military training program on the practices of West Point. This added vibrancy to the program and brought its approach much more in line with the best practices of the day.

To support this training for the 250 cadets Culver was able to enroll during the 1900-1902 period, Culver petitioned the War Department and received 50 additional cadet rifles and accoutrements, 20 NCO swords, and 20 more cavalry sabers and 30 cavalry carbines.[4]

Using West Point as a model required a staff capable of presenting training well and functioning at a very high level, higher than had been the case at Culver thus far. Accordingly, Gignilliat secured Fleet's support to assemble the most effective military staff possible from among the members of Culver's staff and faculty. Being restricted by the available choices, the first group he selected was not as effective as it needed to be, but it was a first step in the right direction. It also began the practice of having staff and faculty members from across the entire institution serve as members of the military staff, further connecting the military program to the rest of the school and establishing Gignilliat as a very important leader at the institution.

Demonstrating his innate ability as a trainer and his deft touch in finding ways to create community, Gignilliat focused on improving the performance of the worst-performing cadets instead of enhancing the performance of the best-performing cadets, with the belief that, "the general efficiency of the Battalion is determined not by its best, but by its weakest members."[5] This approach almost certainly appealed to his newly formed staff, as it served a shared purpose of devoting their energies to helping those who most needed their assistance while also contributing to the overall improvement of the corps' military proficiency.

Furthering the focus on improving the "body," Gignilliat also added ten minutes of "setting up" exercises to reveille formation to help improve the posture and appearance of the cadets. In a period overly concerned about the "softness" of its contemporary times, this was another brilliant addition of Gignilliat's. The setting-up exercises had the additional intent of helping to improve the overall health of corps, addressing another concern prevalent among parents of the time. While outwardly beneficial and a savvy marketing move, Culver's medical officer, Dr. O. A. Rea, determined that this addition was also having a positive impact on the cadets' health.[6]

1902 Army Annual Inspection – An Auspicious Beginning with Room for Improvement

After almost two years of making changes to the military program intended to improve the corps' military performance and appearance, Culver has its first significant, acknowledged, and official annual inspection by an Army officer on May 16, 1902. According to Gignilliat, "The Cadets acquitted themselves admirably. The efficiency of the Corps and the excellent condition of the arms received the highest commendation from the Inspector." The inspector's report also highlighted the battalion parades, the regular in-ranks and barracks inspections, the weekly marching reviews, and the corps' public appearances as evidence of military prowess and excellence.[7] While very positive, the report had little impact outside of Culver, as the Army was not yet identifying the top performers as "distinguished institutions."

While the results had to be gratifying, there was still much that needed to be done to bring Culver's military training program up to elite status. Gignilliat had succeeded in securing the number of tents necessary to support the end-of-year field encampment, but the training during this event only included instruction on establishing a camp, practice marches, and guard duty. The inspector's report made no mention at all of any type of field training, as Culver focused more on promoting the health benefits of living outdoors for a few days instead of conducting effective military training.[8] While the drill and inspection aspects had become quite good, the field training needed significant improvement.

Culver's Summer Naval School

Enrollment remained one of the highest priorities for Fleet since his arrival. When the school completed its session each June, Colonel Fleet and Mr. Cook would travel around the region to meet personally with parents to recruit their sons for Culver.[9]

According to Gignilliat, Culver started its Summer Naval School in 1902 as a program in its own right and also "in the hope that eventually the summer school boys would fill the barracks left vacant by the cadets of the winter school." Fleet hired one of Gignilliat's older brothers– Thomas Heyward – to run the Summer Naval School.[10] Twelve years older than Leigh, "Heyward" (as Leigh called him) was a graduate of the US Naval Academy who served as a Lieutenant on active duty in the US Navy and fought in the Spanish-American War. He was also a competent engineer, active in both civil and aeronautical projects, and an educator, serving as principal of a public school in Savannah, Georgia. Since he was no longer a US Navy officer at the time he was hired, the state of Indiana appointed Heyward as a Commander in its Naval Reserve force.

The first year of the program was not a rousing success from almost every perspective. Enrolling only 25 boys, the revenue it generated was not sufficient even to cover the operating costs for the program. From

Gignilliat and Minnie at the Summer Naval School, 1904.[13]

a recruiting standpoint, only three of these boys enrolled in the winter school. As a result, Colonel Fleet wanted to abandon the venture at the end of the first summer, feeling that his summers could be much better spent by focusing on developing the winter school than in devoting himself to administering a dubious summer program of questionable value to the school.[11]

However, the ever-enthusiastic Gignilliat – operating, in his own words "more from optimism than foresight" – asked the Culver brothers and Fleet for permission to try and make the summer program successful, and they granted his request. Sensing an opportunity, Gignilliat set to work "with the enthusiasm of a young man given the opportunity to win his spurs on his own."

While capable in terms of the subject matter, Heyward had little of Leigh's flair for marketing and promotion. Showing many of the hallmarks that would distinguish him as a marketer and promoter at Culver, Gignilliat applied all he had learned about marketing from H. E. Cook and added his own ideas to the summer program.[12] He created an "alluring" catalog for the program and appealing magazine advertisements with photographs, which was quite innovative (and perhaps even a bit edgy) for the time. Playing off the then-novel ideas of an organized vacation for boys at a naval program in the middle of land-locked Indiana, combined with the illustrations, made the advertisements a smashing success, eliciting a "record-breaking flood of requests for the summer catalog."

In his marketing material, Gignilliat characterized Culver's Summer Naval School as something that takes a boy away from the unhealthy city and "places him amid beautiful and healthful surroundings" for what would be "an ideal substitute for the aimless summer" under the "tactful supervision of men whose life work is the development of the personal honor and manliness of boys." Overall, Culver's Summer Naval School promised to give boys "a summer of maximum enjoyment and the maximum good."[14]

Gignilliat focused on emphasizing the purpose of the Summer Naval School, which was, "To solve for parents the problem of what to do with their boys in summer in a manner acceptable to both the parent and the boy"; "to make the summer vacation a season of healthful and profitable activity"; "to afford the discipline needful during this period of relaxation for the growing, active boy of modern times"; and at the same time "to give him all the enjoyment and recreation that should be a part of his vacation."[15]

Culver's Summer Naval School accomplished these objectives by providing boys with plenty of "wholesome open-air exercise" in a picturesque environment with a "touch of romance" that had a strong appeal to boy's imagination and interests and which "affords him the change of thought and action that he requires when his regular school work is over." This approach was touted as being quite restful because it gave boys the "right amount of play" while avoiding the injurious "loafing" of summer by helping them learn things they want to learn, which never felt like work.

Gignilliat taking the Summer Naval School review, 1905.[16]

Spending time outdoors would make boys straight, strong, tanned, and healthy, while also giving them the opportunity to make up work from school and also learn new things.

After spending the summer in an environment that "offers the advantages of proper associates, a healthy moral atmosphere, personal supervision of experienced teachers, a special system of tutoring, and a beautiful and healthy location, free from the temptation and bad influences of the city, town, or large watering place" that offered "wholesome pleasures" in abundance," parents could expect their boys to return with a "coat of tan and hardened muscles that every boy considers a necessary part of a successful vacation."[17]

Gignilliat's appeal resonated with parents, and enrollment in 1903 tripled to 78 cadets. Perhaps even more importantly, 21 of those cadets enrolled in Culver's winter school, contributing significantly to the institutional purpose of the program and also to Culver financial viability.

The program also provided opportunities for Culver to host visiting dignitaries in the summer, furthering the network of influential people who knew about Culver and its programs.

With Gignilliat's involvement, Culver's Summer Naval School not only generated revenue that was more than sufficient to cover the operating costs of the program but also contributed significantly

Gignilliat participating in the "Culver Anchor" figure at the Summer School ball.[18]

Gignilliat with Vice President Charles W. Fairbanks, July 1905. Fairbanks was also an Indiana Senator 1897-1905; VP for TR, 1905-1909.[19]

Cadets of the Summer Naval School, 1906 from 28 states, China. Mexico, and Ecuador.[20]

(i.e., ~8 percent) to the enrollment of the winter school. These results achieved the two most significant goals for the summer program.

With the US Navy agreeing to establish a Naval Reserve unit at Culver in 1909 and to provide Culver with state-of-the-art equipment, the program's survival was assured.[21]

This episode provided powerful evidence of Gignilliat's innate ability to identify what appealed to boys and to create innovative ways to market and promote the institution.

It also provided a glimpse of the Midas touch he exhibited when placed in charge of an organization.

Perhaps based upon his early success with it, the summer program held a special place in Gignilliat's heart for the remainder of his time at Culver. In fact, he often delayed his summer vacation to remain at Culver until the end of the summer program, preferring to be away from campus for the beginning of winter school instead.

Translating Experience into Prose – The Start of Gignilliat's Career as an Author

Gignilliat's first published articles were as a result of his summer camp efforts, one of which appeared in *Scientific American* in 1903. Despite a rather scathing assessment of Culver's summer naval program appearing in one of the three Logansport newspapers at the time,[23] enrollment continued to rise significantly.

Enrollment in Culver's Summer Naval School increased to 120 in 1904 and to 188 in 1905. By 1906, Culver's summer Naval program was enrolling over 200 boys, surpassing the first five years of the winter school enrollment.

Culver Summer Naval cadets being mustered into the US Naval Reserve, summer 1909.[22]

The Summer Naval School also contributed approximately 10 percent to the winter school enrollment each of these years, further amplifying its value and helping to ensure its success.

The Winter School Military Program in 1902-1904 – Engaging the "Mind"

At the beginning of the 1902-1903 school year, the military program focused on drill at the individual, company, and battalion levels, and with the increased enrollment was able to practice some of the regimental exercises by forming the entire corps of cadets into a single rank. While perhaps not as effective as desired, it nevertheless allowed Culver to practice drill at every required level.

However, Gignilliat had learned from the inspection in May that the training had to be enhanced and made more effective to impress the inspector and bring it more in line with Fleet's "quality over quantity" ideal. He could also make use of the two artillery pieces larger than those ordinarily issued to military schools -- 3.6-inch breech-loading rifled steel cannons with carriages -- to support artillery training.[24]

Seeking to find ways to improve the military training program he was implementing, Gignilliat either determined on his own or was advised by the inspectors that the cadets needed some form of theoretical instruction added to Culver's military program to improve their performance on the Army's annual inspection.

In a bold move, since he had received little theoretical instruction in Military Science himself, Gignilliat began teaching Military Science theory to 1st classmen during the 1902-1903 winter drill period, adding a "mind" component to the "body" aspect of drill.

Gignilliat used two of the leading theoretical texts of the time – Wagner's *Elements of Military Science* and *Theoretical Principles of Small Arms Firing* – and covered most of both with the First class officers.[25]

This was innovative because Gignilliat took the military program's training beyond the focus on marching, drill, and appearance to include a mental component that exposed the cadets to the intellectual aspects of military training. By engaging the mind, Gignilliat began distinguishing Culver's military program from most of the other military schools in the country while also broadening its appeal to older cadets bored with the monotony of marching and drill. The founder of the US Naval War College, Stephen B. Luce, had done something similar at the nascent institution in the mid-1880s, and it had revolutionized the training of naval officers in America, so Gignilliat was in very good company with his radical approach.

To enhance the end-of-year field training, Gignilliat added instruction on outpost duty and patrols, and he had the companies begin training "in the formation and duties of an advance guard as described in Wagner's 'Security and Information,'" to the existing instruction on establishing a camp, practice marches, and guard duty.[26] Besides enhancing the training, adding field work to the military training program allowed the cadets to apply the theoretical concepts they had learned during the winter drill period to actual situations, especially the first classmen. It is here that we begin to see Gignilliat's effectiveness as a trainer and ability to grasp the higher-level aspects of the intent of the Army's inspection program.

After the departure of Captain Powell at the end of the 1902-1903 school year (who was little missed) and not receiving a replacement from the Army for the 1903-1904 school year, Gignilliat also made some changes to the military staff to improve its effectiveness, drafting two of the more capable young members of the faculty to join him in his efforts. H. F. Noble, a veteran of the Spanish-American War and expert marksman, and John S. Fleet, a Culver graduate and son of Colonel Fleet, joined the tactical staff and began helping with rifle marksmanship training. Culver's rifle range was functional, but it was deemed inadequate by Noble to support achieving excellence in rifle marksmanship.[27]

In addition, H. J. Noble, who had served with the 4th US Cavalry Regiment, arrived to command the BHT, bringing a wealth of military experience with him to share with the cadets. Culver graduate Captain J. A. Given helped Gignilliat provide theoretical instruction by teaching the NCOs.[28] While not a member of the tactical staff, Captain C. A. Thomas joined Culver as the Director of Gymnasium. Thomas began working with

Gignilliat to improve fitness and strength of cadets, which would pay off handsomely in the years to come.[29]

The program began gaining momentum by the end of the 1903 school year, and Gignilliat added a bit of a beard to go with his mustache in an effort to present an even more military mien.

By the time of the first Army annual inspection that identified the top six units as "distinguished institutions" in spring 1904, Culver did well but did not earn "Big Six" recognition. The results had

Gignilliat circa 1903.[30]

to be gratifying, but Gignilliat was not interested in delivering a "good" performance when the prospect of earning "Big Six" recognition loomed just beyond his reach. He needed some assistance to take the program to the next level, and the help he needed came in fall 1904 with the arrival of Captain George L. Byroade.

The 1904 Louisiana Purchase Exposition and World's Fair – Proof of Concept

Culver experienced a special treat at the end of the 1903-1904 school by attending the Louisiana Purchase Exposition and World's Fair in St. Louis, Missouri during the period May 23-June 3, 1904. The ten-day trip to and from St. Louis was made in a special 12-car train composed of seven Pullman sleepers, three horse-cars, and two baggage coaches. The trip took about 25 hours each way. On the evening of their arrival, May 24, the cadet battalion was reviewed and addressed by the president of the Exposition, former Mayor of St. Louis and Governor of Missouri David R. Francis.

While in St. Louis, the cadets were quartered in comfortable barracks provided by the Exposition authorities.

CMA parading at the St. Louis Plaza at the Louisiana Purchase Exposition, 1904.[31]

Rather than eating in the military mess hall provided for troops, the cadets instead took their meals at one of the best restaurants on the grounds by special arrangement.

The greater part of each day was devoted to seeing the exhibits, systematically supervised at first and then on their own after proving their ability to conduct themselves as gentlemen on the grounds.

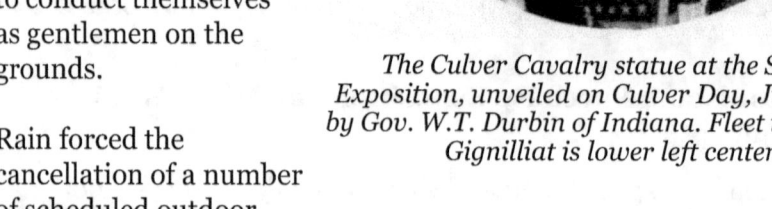

The Culver Cavalry statue at the St. Louis Exposition, unveiled on Culver Day, June 2, 1904, by Gov. W.T. Durbin of Indiana. Fleet is on the left; Gignilliat is lower left center.[32]

Rain forced the cancellation of a number of scheduled outdoor drill performances, but on several evenings, the battalion provided a dress parade on the magnificent Plaza of St. Louis appreciated by thousands of spectators at each performance.

CMA was especially honored during the visit with the distinction of having June 2nd designated as "Culver Day," which had to be especially meaningful to the Culver family living in St. Louis as well. The focus of attention at the Exposition was on Culver on that particular day, and Gignilliat was determined to take full advantage of this important opportunity to show as many people as possible how proficient a properly trained unit of prep school cadets could execute a multitude of military skills and tasks.

The weather, however, had different plans, and the morning began with a downpour that soaked the cadets in their gray blouses and white duck trousers. Since the rain prevented the cadets from performing outdoors that morning, Gignilliat secured a large fire hall and transitioned to presenting a modified indoor program of activities. There, in the presence of the Governor of Indiana and over two thousand spectators, and despite a last-minute change in venue, the cadets provided impressive exhibitions in drills of the cavalry, artillery, Gatling gun, and infantry maneuvers.

The cadets also demonstrated their skills in rough-riding, bridge-building, and wall-scaling, all of which amazed the observers with their precision and daring.

In the afternoon, a magnificent statue called the "Culver Bronze Equestrian Group," created by the renowned sculptor George Julian Zolnay, was unveiled in a public ceremony in the Palace of Education. The statue shows a fearless cadet rider standing Graeco-Roman style on three magnificent horses in the act of racing over a low hurdle.

Zolnay considered the creation to be his masterpiece, which was high praise for such a prolific artist. The unveiling elicited applause from the crowd and school cheers from the cadets. The 1906 CMA Catalog offered that the statue "in a way typifies the comprehensive education imparted at Culver education that endows the body with health and strength, and trains nerves, muscles, and judgment at the same time that it trains the mind."

The unveiling ceremony included addresses by President Francis, Indiana Governor Winfield T. Durbin, Colonel Fleet, and the Honorable John L. Griffiths of Indianapolis, who served as Consul General of the United States to Britain. Gignilliat was present but did not speak. Immediately after the ceremony, Governor Durbin and his staff, accompanied by Union Civil War officer Major-General Peter J. Osterhaus, reviewed the Culver battalion on the Plaza of St. Louis. Somewhat unusually, Governor Durbin assembled the cadets before him after the review to deliver remarks conveying his admiration for their performance and skill.

The day concluded with a grand military ball in the Hall of Congresses at which the cadets opened by constructing 27-foot spar-and-rope bridge in four minutes and 27 seconds for the battalion to cross over in a very precise set of military maneuvers to the delight of the crowd.[33] With Emily Jane Culver and Colonel and Mrs. Fleet in the receiving line with Governor Durbin and other dignitaries, Gignilliat and Minnie performed the essential duty of presenting the guests to those in the receiving line. As expected, they performed their duties with dignity and aplomb.[34]

After participating in the dedication of the Indiana building at the Exposition on the following day, June 3, the corps boarded the train for the 25-hour return to Culver, arriving home on the evening of June 4 just in time to occupy the field camp and prepare for commencement exercises on June 9, 1904.

It is clear that Culver made a profound and positive impression on Indiana's governor at the Exposition. During his remarks at the military ball on June 2, Durbin "expressed the favor with which the people of Indiana regarded the Culver Military Academy, stating that it was "a matter of pride that the generosity of a citizen of St. Louis should have enabled the State [of Indiana] to possess a school which stood in the front rank of institutions of its kind," and lauded Culver as "a place where good citizenship was taught."[35]

In a letter from Governor Durbin to Fleet dated June 13, 1904, Durbin wrote that, "It was the general comment of those competent to judge that no cadet corps at the Exposition, barring West Point Academy, approached [Culver] in equipment, bearing, discipline, or precision and thoroughness in drills." Expressing his support for Culver's methods, Durbin offered "that there is no better method of training youth than is afforded in such institutions" as Culver, and that "among such institutions, barring only the National Military Academy (sic), Culver Academy has no equal in the United States" Durbin closed by writing that, "As Governor of the State within which Culver Academy is located, the impression manifestly made by [the Culver] cadets at the Exposition was a source of gratification and pride to me."[36]

In a newspaper article appearing several days earlier, Durbin was even more forceful in his praise, remarking that the Culver cadets "clearly outclassed all other cadets, save those from West Point, and in many respects, they compared favorably with the West Pointers. A number of regular army officers spoke in the highest terms of the Culver Cadets, their discipline, soldierly bearing, and proficiency in drills and exhibitions."[37] Having taken West Point as the model for its military training program, Gignilliat could have scarcely dreamt of any higher forms of praise for his unit.

Culver received a slew of similarly congratulatory messages from other individuals of note who had taken favorable notice of its presence at the Exposition. These messages and laudatory comments affirmed that Culver had made its mark at the Exposition and confirmed that its military training program was having the desired impact on improving the corps' military proficiency and enhancing the gentlemanly qualities of its cadets.

According to the 1906 CMA Catalog, the educational value of the trip was readily apparent, but it was also valuable for other, less obvious reasons beyond simply the pleasure of the experience or "because of the most pleasing words that were showered on the cadets for their efficiency in their military maneuvers."

From Culver's perspective, the value of the experience was also because it was "at once a test of the discipline of the Academy, and at the same time a most gratifying proof of the soundness of the principles under which this discipline is administered."[38] The powerful words of Indiana's governor confirmed this assessment, while also being been much appreciated.

According to Hartman, the Culver family was so pleased with the experience for the winter school that they sponsored a trip to the Exposition for the cadets of the Naval School during the second week of August 1904. This provided Gignilliat with a similar opportunity to show off his 78 summer sailors of the two-year-old summer Naval School, and he responded with a flourish.

The summer naval participants departed on a Vandalia "Culver Special" along with four of their 28-foot cutters. At the Exposition Park, the boys toured the exhibits and entertained visitors with a series of parades and naval exhibitions on the man-made lagoons. Response was similar to the June reception, bringing more notice and renown to Culver's military training programs.[39]

Gignilliat learned much from these trips about the logistics but also the promotional and marketing potential of such events. Playing to his natural strengths, they prepared him well to lead similar high-profile trips in 1907 and 1908.

These trips also provided powerful affirmation of his efforts and confirmation of his military training program for both the summer and winter school. Application in public further honed proficiency.

Upon his return to campus for the 1904-1905 school year, Gignilliat was ready to make the final push necessary to attain national recognition for his military system, military training program, and for Culver.

Culver Summer Naval Cadet boat drills at the 1904 Louisiana Purchase Exposition.[40]

The CMA Military Program in 1904-1906 – Engaging the "Spirit"

The 1904-1905 school year brought with it a substantial improvement and enhancement in Culver's military program. One of the most significant improvements was the arrival of a tremendously qualified and talented PMS&T, Captain George L. Byroade.

US Army Captain George L Byroade.[41]

Born in 1871 in Pennsylvania, Byroade graduated from the University of Pennsylvania before joining the Army. He saw active service in Cuba and the Philippines before being taken ill and sent home to convalesce. While receiving treatment, the Army determined that he was no longer fit for active duty, and he was retired from active service as a captain. However, he remained on the Army's list of officers and continued serving by teaching tactics and functioning as a PMS&T, so he should have been eligible for advancement. Sadly, and despite his eventual recovery and tremendous physical prowess, a clerical error wrongly characterized him as an invalid and a cripple, and he was passed over time and again when considered for promotion.

While in the Philippines, Byroade was commended for his gallantry in action, and his superiors were quite impressed with his performance. Undoubtedly, his intellect honed with an Ivy League education helped him master the intricacies of Army operations and apply them effectively in conflict. While at Culver, Byroade took some classes at the University of Chicago Law School, further attesting to this intellectual merit. His cognitive prowess would serve him well later in his career when he completed the US Army's challenging School of the Line as an honor graduate, was invited to remain for a second year of study, and was offered a highly coveted instructor position at the US Army Command and General Staff College, in which he excelled. While all of this was in the future, it is nevertheless indicative of his ability as both a solider and his intellect.

Immediately prior to his assignment to Culver, Byroade serve as the PMS&T at the University of Kentucky from 1902 to 1904, where he started a very successful military band that became an important part of the school's culture and still exists as the renowned Wildcat Marching Band. He was a professional infantry officer who knew Army drill exceptionally well, and his age and military experience may have evoked in Gignilliat memories of Captain Bromwell, the Army officer who had impressed him so greatly during his time at Yellowstone. This combination would have elicited great confidence from Gignilliat and set Byroade up for success immediately.

When he arrived at Culver in fall 1904, Byroade was an intelligent, vibrant, fit, and experienced Army officer who had been successful at teaching. His time at the University of Kentucky had allowed him to become well versed in the Army's doctrine, theoretical material, and training methods for cadets. Byroade had also been inspected annually by the Army at least twice while at the University of Kentucky, so he was quite familiar with the standards and knew what the inspectors expected. Having just turned 33 years of age on September 11, he was full of energy and ideas for the burgeoning military school. He was also perhaps the ideal colleague for Gignilliat, and, given all the work that had been done over the previous four years, his arrival at Culver could not have been timed any better.

Gignilliat and Byroade made some important changes to Culver's military training program. The biggest change occurred during the winter drill period, where they refocused their training efforts. First and most importantly, Gignilliat and Byroade placed significantly more effort on improving the capabilities of the cadet leaders, especially the commissioned officers.

Byroade was a gifted trainer and a compelling lecturer, and he took responsibility for training the cadet officers. Perhaps at Byroade's urging, Culver also adopted an excellent text to support the leader training that was more suitable for high school students and which used a question-and-answer format that was very effective at engaging the cadets and keeping their interest.

Gignilliat remained involved in the training, Together he and Byroade provided effective education in the theory of military science that both enabled and empowered the first classmen to begin making sound tactical decisions during field training.

Gignilliat and Byroade also increased their efforts with the rest of the cadets, endeavoring to improve the performance of the individual cadets and of the smaller units, especially the squads. Using the other members of the tactical staff and cadet drill masters, Culver instituted an intense squad drill program to increase the proficiency of the individual cadets and the smallest collective unit, reasoning that the better each cadet and each squad could perform, the better the entire corps could perform.

Both Gignilliat and Byroade understood that competition appealed to boys, and they instituted a series of competitions at the individual cadet and squad levels to enhance the level of engagement among the cadets. They also provided the winners with awards and special recognition as incentives to further increase the appeal of the competitions. This approach transformed something that was once viewed as "drudgery" into something that the cadets looked forward to and to which they gave their best efforts to excel, in hopes of winning awards and earning perhaps the most valuable reward among male adolescents: peer recognition.

Taken together, these two changes tapped into some of the very foundations of boys, created ways for every cadet to participate and contribute to the corps' success meaningfully, and provided ways to channel their enthusiasm for competition and their desire to belong to a distinguished organization effectively. This provided a jolt of energy and excitement within the school that translated into even better performance on the drill field, parade ground, and field exercises.

To support their enhanced training program, Gignilliat persuaded Fleet to allow more time to be devoted to military training. Taking advantage of this opportunity, Gignilliat found ways to devote as much as 1.5 hours each day to military training in some form, taxing the cadets even further in their already crowded schedules but making excellent use of this most precious resource.

It is worth noting that during this period, Culver's "weekend," such as it was, occurred during Sunday and Monday, as Saturday was considered to be a normal duty day like Tuesday through Friday. While Sunday included mandatory chapel, the afternoons of both Sunday and Monday were largely unstructured, and it is likely that Gignilliat made use of some of the free time on Monday afternoons to provide additional time for drill and other military activities.

1905 Army Annual Inspection – Tantalizingly Close to "Big Six" Recognition

By the time of the 1905 Army annual inspection, Culver did even better than it had done on the 1904 inspection, but it was not yet at the level it needed to be to earn "Big Six" recognition. Performance in most areas improved, but not enough to place Culver in the "first rank" of military schools. Given all the effort put into its military training program, the results must have been somewhat disappointing for Gignilliat, but they also may have motivated him to strive even harder for this recognition.

The 1905 inspector surprised the cadets by asking first classmen who were not commissioned officers or high-ranking noncommissioned officers to

Cadets executing strength drills during winter drill.[43]

drill the battalion. While somewhat out of the norm and perhaps beyond reasonable expectations for high school cadets, he noted in his inspection report that the commissioned officers were quite proficient in this area but that not all of Culver's first class noncommissioned officers could drill the battalion properly.

This indicated that Gignilliat and Byroade needed to ensure that all officers – commissioned and noncommissioned – could drill the battalion with the same level of proficiency. It also provided additional incentive for every cadet leader to aspire to excellence when directing drill exercises.

Adding the Final Pieces – The 1905-1906 Military Training Program

Having created an extensive military training program for the school, Gignilliat added an additional member to his tactical staff to help direct and supervise the many activities occurring daily. He also ensured that the program was fully resourced in terms of funding, equipment, personnel, time, and priority, reasoning that only by devoting the full resources of the institution could Culver achieve the objective of earning "Big Six" distinction.

Having a much better idea of what was required to achieve this objective, and with the advice and counsel of Byroade, Gignilliat reorganized the members of his tactical staff to make the best use of their talents and abilities, and to give the cadets the best chance of excelling on the 1906 annual inspection. His most impactful move was to place the recently hired Captain Robert Rossow in charge of the cavalry training, creating one of the most effective fusions of purpose and practice at Culver during its first 50 years.

Robert Rossow was a legendary figure at Culver for almost 40 years, from 1906-1945. A Regular Army officer in the Cavalry, he served in the Philippines just after the Spanish-American War and also in WWI. At Culver, he led the Black Horse Troop and exemplified the spirit of the cavalryman, inculcating its distinctive swagger and spirit into its members. Rossow also served as the CMA Commandant of Cadets for a decade (1926-1935) and as Director of the Woodcraft Camp (1935-1945). He led Culver cadets in the 1913 Logansport flood rescue effort and was one of the most memorable figures during CMA's first 50 years (more about him later).

Using these changes to improve, Culver did again all that it had done during the 1904-1905 school year that had brought it tantalizingly close to earning "Big Six" designation, only better. The cumulative impact of its efforts began producing even greater dividends in the area of cadet leadership, which was perhaps the main intent of the Army's annual inspection of cadet leader development programs.

This improvement in cadet leadership occurred because the class of 1906 first classmen had been exposed to portions of the enhanced training program since they were third classmen, and they had seen for themselves the impact since the spring 1904 annual inspection. Watching the first classmen function each spring under the conditions of the annual inspection and functioning under their command, the class of 1906 witnessed firsthand what worked well and what was not as effective. Combined with the excellent training provided by Byroade and the additional time devoted to military training, they learned how to be even better leaders than the first classmen of 1904 and 1905

One particular area that challenged the younger Culver cadets was the strength required to perform the wall-scaling exercises and to dig their own field entrenchments to standard. While the older cadets had little difficulty hoisting themselves over the wall and digging their own trenches, many of the younger cadets had not yet developed the musculature necessary to be able to do the same on their own. The result was that the older cadets had to help the younger cadets get over the wall and dig their field entrenchments, slowing the units down when performing each of these activities.

Accordingly, the 1905-1906 winter drill period focused on improving the strength and fitness of the younger cadets to address these areas. Under the direction of Captain Thomas, the cadets completed a rigorous strength and fitness regime using dumbbells and working on gymnastic apparatuses. These efforts resulted in improvements in their posture and appearance, which enhanced their soldierly bearing and increased in their strength, improving significantly with their ability to scale walls quickly and also dig their own field trenches to standard. As a way of incentivizing performance in this area, Gignilliat began the practice of issuing special pins – known as "Culvers" – to recognize and reward those who were especially proficient in setting-up exercises and drill as an incentive to strive for excellence.[42] These pins, became (and remain) highly coveted by cadets.

The resulting program created the conditions for success by ensuring that Culver acquired and devoted the resources necessary to achieving "Big Six" recognition. This included increasing the number of tactical staff member from eight to nine, devoting as much as 1.5 hours each day to military training, acquiring the best equipment from the Army for training, including rifles and artillery pieces, making the best use of their existing facilities, especially the parade field and riding hall, and capturing and retaining cadet interest and inducing their buy-in by presenting compelling training, using competition, and providing awards and recognition for excellence.

While somewhat all-encompassing, Gignilliat believed that the longer cadets were under military discipline (both daily and cumulatively), the better cadets they became, and the military program provided him with the opportunity to increase the amount of time cadets were under formal discipline each day. The results of the enhanced training program provided further support for this belief.[44] Being able to create, resource, and implement such an impressive and comprehensive military program also demonstrates Gignilliat's ingenuity and executive abilities, showcasing his ability as an educator in Body, Mind, and Spirit.

Gignilliat, with Byroade's help, had hit upon the very method of training used with such success by the British navy at the zenith of its effectiveness and especially during the time of Nelson.

Just as the Royal Navy owed its ability to fire its guns faster and better than any other navy afloat – which was its most valuable advantage – to its commitment to intensive training and belief that the best way to train sailors effectively was to keep them at sea and constantly under ship's discipline, Gignilliat believed the same for cadets: the longer they were kept under military discipline – both daily and cumulatively – the better cadets they would become. This approach allowed for a far more intensive level of training that provided immediate feedback, the opportunity to correct mistakes, and the chance to enhance performance at the most opportune times. Just as British naval crews were pitted against one another in competition, cadets were placed in constant competition individually and collectively, bringing out the very best in them.

The long periods of drill turned out to be the best possible training for cadets, working them into a high state of efficiency and effectiveness. With constant repetition and practice, every maneuver became second nature, and the cadets learned to work together, to anticipate one another, and to carry out flawlessly the countless finely timed and intricate procedures required by the Army's annual inspection.

Whether deliberate or not, the system Gignilliat developed and implemented during this period had precedence for producing success that translated from the decks of 19th century British warships to 20th century cadet military units at Culver. It was based upon time-honored practices that would have been quite familiar to military organizations of the past who had embraced them and enjoyed similar levels of success.

Just as British naval captains discovered when using the same methods and rewarding the winners with awards and recognition, the ensuing level of performance and pride that resulted from this approach transcended previous levels of achievement, and the ensuing outcome and team spirit transformed both the British gun crews and the cadet units into remarkably high-performing and finely tuned military organizations that could outperform almost any other similar groups against which they were pitted.

Coincidentally, Gignilliat also had much in common with Nelson, being taller but also similarly slim, and being quite cordial in social situations but rather rigid and imposing when exercising command. Each had an insatiable desire to win and an incomparable duty ethic and sense of responsibility. Nelson's dying words – *Thank God I have done my duty* – could have served as an equally suitable epitaph for Gignilliat.

Visitors to Culver could scarcely believe the precision achieved by the young men as a result of this system of training, and they were mightily impressed by what they saw. The contrast with other military organizations, even those comprised of college-aged cadets, was powerful and stark. Culver cadets and units performed with far greater precision, were more highly disciplined, and consistently functioned at higher levels than any others they had observed.

Cadets executing Artillery drill around the time of the 1906 Army Annual Inspection.[46]

1906- Achieving "Big Six" Recognition

The long-prepared for inspection occurred at Culver during the period of May 13-14, 1906. Major John S. Mallory, of the US Army General Staff, served as the inspecting officer. The report of his inspection was sent to the War Department on June 6, 1906, and it was exceptionally flattering. When compared to the results of the other approximately 100 annual inspections conducted in spring 1906, it was evident that Culver had made tremendous progress since the 1905 annual inspection and was clearly among the very best military schools in the nation. As a result, the War Department acknowledged that Culver was one of the six best military institutions in the entire country and recognized officially by the War Department as a "distinguished institution" in the Army General Order Number 125, dated July 9, 1906.[45] Culver had done it!

The cumulative impact of the sustained efforts of over five years came to fruition for the spring 1906 Army annual inspection, and it showed in both the inspection report and the results. The inspection report is worth addressing in greater detail to get a more accurate sense of just how well the institution performed during this inspection.

According to the inspection report, Byroade oversaw battalion drill, and it was executed superbly. Rossow obtained the same results with the cavalry drill, as did Noble and Thomas with the engineering drill. The inspector made special mention of the speed with which the cadets were able to complete both the engineering tasks and the wall scaling. Thomas' work with improving the strength of the younger cadets was evident in both the excellence and speed with which the cadet teams – comprised of cadets of all ages – were able to scale the walls.

Cavalry drill at Culver around the time of the 1906 Army Annual Inspection.[47]

Cadet Engineering drill around the time of the 1906 Army Annual Inspection.[48]

Cadets Wall-scaling drills around the time of the 1906 Army Annual Inspection.[49]

The increased strength of the younger cadets was also helpful in the field exercises, which were overseen by both Gignilliat and Byroade, and characterized by the inspector as being "excellent." The work of the military staff paid off as well, earning the inspector's highest accolades in the areas of guard duty, discipline, and barracks appearance.

Culver Military Academy Battalion of Cadets passing in review around the time of the 1906 Army Annual Inspection.[50]

In perhaps the highest compliment of all, the inspector rated the cadets' appearance as "very favorable" and being "strongly suggestive of West Point," which served as Gignilliat's model for the military program.

Attuned to the impact of the training on the cadets in terms of attitude, the inspector was quite favorably impressed with both the bearing and demeanor of the Culver corps. He remarked that the school did a wonderful job of developing and nurturing the cadets' military spirit "to a very great extent," and that they performed their military duties with a "great deal of zeal."

The inspector commended the cadets for their exceptional precision in drill and manual of arms," for being "highly disciplined," "enthusiastic," and for manifesting an admirable "soldierly spirit" for being so relatively young. Combined with their high levels of proficiency and discipline, the inspector's overall impression of the cadets was exceptionally favorable.

Cadets executing a "charge" during open-order field drill around the time of the 1906 Army Annual Inspection.[51]

The inspector characterized the cadets as being uniformly "neat, well mannered, unusually intelligent" and quite "fond of military life." Clearly the cadets had embraced the training sincerely and engaged with the inspection process fully.

Commenting more directly on the program designed and implemented by Gignilliat and Byroade, the inspector remarked the Culver's military instruction was "provided along broad practical lines," indicating that it was not simply limited to drill. Combined with the extensive amount of time devoted to military training that "largely exceeded War Department requirements," the program delivered an exceptionally high quality of military training that was "sufficient to qualify cadets as lieutenants and also in higher grades" of commissioned officers. Nothing could have pleased Gignilliat and Byroade more than such an assessment.

In only two areas did the inspector give Culver less than superior marks, both of which were related to the youth of the cadets: their relatively "boyish" appearance in uniform, and the rather "elementary" nature of the military curriculum. Gignilliat did all he could to address the former by hiring tailors to fit the uniforms as well as possible, and he could do little to address the latter and also keep the instruction at an appropriate cognitive level for the cadets enrolled at Culver.

At the completion of the two-day assessment, the inspector offered his overall impression of school that is worth quoting at length:

Culver Military Academy is a "splendidly equipped and abundantly resourced up-to-date military school and also a prep school of a high order patterned after West point. It has most of the diversified features of West Point in its practical course.

Its daily routine is similar to West Point and Army posts, and it has all necessary buildings and accessories to support its outstanding military training program that was evident in the performance of the cadets and the dedication of the military staff."[52]

Gignilliat leading Culver Cadets on a practice march around Lake Maxinkuckee.[54]

After coming so close to earning Big Six recognition in 1904 and 1905, Gignilliat could not have been more pleased with the inspector's report and the outcome of the 1906 inspection. Validating his own beliefs, the 1906 inspection report ranked Culver as one of the six best military schools in the entire country.

By earning this recognition, Culver joined VMI, Norwich, Pennsylvania Military College, St. John's School (Manlius), and Shattuck, in the top rank of American military schools, becoming just the third prep school to achieve such a distinction (St. John's School (Manlius) and Shattuck were the first two in 1904).[53]

The outcome was the result of an institution-wide effort to achieve excellence led by Gignilliat. With Byroade's help, Gignilliat developed the program, identified the right men and placed them in the right positions (sometimes requiring change), and educated himself to be able to teach military science theory to the first classmen. He developed his own military capabilities without the benefit of Army schooling or serving in an Army unit to become a capable military officer, and he was recognized as such by the 1906 inspector.

Gignilliat and the Institutional Impact of Achieving "Big Six" Recognition

In this expansive endeavor that required the combined efforts of staff, cadets, and trustees to achieve success, Gignilliat showed his effectiveness at an institutional scale by quarterbacking this venture, paying attention to details as diverse as finding tailors to fit the cadets' uniforms, ensuring that the cadet store had adequate stocks of polish and other essentials, working with the buildings and grounds staff on the upkeep of the parade ground and the members of the horsemanship staff to take care of horses, with the farriers to make shoes for the horses, with the parents to provide money for the cadets to purchase needed items, and with the business office to purchase needed items and let the necessary contracts. In aggregate, this required an explicit, extended, and dedicated focus on Body, Mind, and Spirit to achieve excellence.

Striving for "Big Six" recognition gave the military program purpose, and it helped to give form to what had been somewhat inchoate prior by providing a tangible goal as an objective. This effort benefited the entire school, and it served as an example of the power of Culver's efforts to educate the whole boy and Fleet's focus on quality over quantity.

Chapter 5: Institutionalizing Success and Serving as Acting Superintendent, 1907-1910

1907-1910 Retaining the "Big Six" Distinction

Perhaps as a show of support for his great achievement, Gignilliat's oldest brother Willie came for a visit on January 10, 1907. This allowed Gignilliat to bask a bit in the adulation of the relative who meant the most to him, along with his sister Helen. However, the strain of the effort caught up to him, and Gignilliat became severely ill with a cold in the last week of February 1907, laying him low during the vitally important winter drill period.

Gignilliat recovered and resumed his tremendous efforts to prepare the corps for the upcoming 1907 Army annual inspection and a bid to replicate its stellar 1906 showing. In an equally impressive feat, and with the same team largely intact, Culver earned Big Six recognition again in 1907.

Never satisfied with the status quo, Gignilliat brought Captain Ralph H. Mowbray and Captain H. Lawrence Durborow (CMA 1902) into the effort to begin working with infantry in field exercises.[1] Going beyond the requirements of the annual inspection, Gignilliat convinced the Culver family to build a new fully equipped gymnasium (to replace the original one built in 1903-1904 that had been destroyed by fire on June 1, 1906) and an indoor rifle range, both of which were better suited to the school's needs and enabled even more effective training during the winter drill period. He also brought Captain William R. "Duke" Kennedy – a veteran of the Spanish American War and US Army infantryman who served at Culver 1905-1944 and is recognized as one of Culver's "giants" – on to the military staff to work with the cadets to improve their rifle marksmanship.

The acquisition of two new state-of-the-art artillery pieces – 3.2 in breech-loading rifled guns with limbers and harnesses – piqued cadet interest in the artillery.

Cadets firing on the new rifle range around the time of the Army Annual Inspection 1906.[2]

In response, Gignilliat engaged the popular Captain Harold C. Bays – who served at Culver 1904-1932 and is also recognized as one of Culver's foundational 18 "giants " – to work with the guns and gunners. The combination of the new instructor and new equipment

Cadets firing on the new rifle range around the time of the Army Annual Inspection 1906.[3]

increased the number and level of cadet engagement in this arm.

The irrepressible Captain Robert Rossow, another Culver "giant" who served from 1906 to 1945, began making his mark on the program's cavalry training, bringing it to national prominence. The capable Captain H. F. Noble took over responsibility for the program's engineering training.

The most influential change, however, came from the 1907 first classmen. Having been part of the process of earning Culver initial "Big Six" designation, they were personally committed to retaining it during their final year.

Even with all of these changes to the military training staff and program, all at Culver were quite anxious during the two-day period of inspection on May 9-10, 1907 by US Army Captain Julius A. Penn.

1907 CMA Battalion Inspection by US Army Captain P. D. Lochridge. [6]

According to an account in *The Vedette*, "Everybody connected with the Academy...awaited with eager interest in the official orders from the war department (sic) containing the results of the spring inspections."[4] In the Army General Order Number 156, dated July 25, 1907, Culver was again named as one of the nation's six distinguished military institutions.[5] Culver had done it again!

Sharing this honor with Culver was the perennially named VMI, along with Norwich and Pennsylvania Military College, St. John's School of Manlius, NY, and Shattuck School of Faribault, MN, all of which were superb institutions making repeat appearances in this august company.[7]

Summer Cavalry School

Having been a popular and distinctive part of the winter school for ten years, and seeking to find a way to make use of the mounts of the BHT in the summer months, Culver came up with the idea of offering a summer cavalry school beginning in July 1907 to appeal to the "many youngsters throughout the country who would welcome the opportunity to spend a summer in the saddle" and perhaps enroll in the winter school as a result.

According to Gignilliat, the actual basis of the decision was economic, based largely on the success the Culver Summer Naval School had in fulfilling its immediate purpose so successfully during its five summers of existence, increasing its enrollment from 25 to 207 cadets. In terms of the larger purpose of increasing enrollment in the winter school, there were at least 126 cadets who had attended both programs during this same five-year period, helping to increase winter school enrollment from 257 to 349 cadets. The decision was also impacted by a "more immediate desire to make an elaborate showing at [the upcoming] Jamestown [exposition]."[8]

The cavalry program had been one of the most popular features of the regular session at Culver, prompting many requests to have it included in Culver's summer offerings. Based upon a belief expressed by a somewhat altered version of the Scottish poet James Thomson's verse – Give a boy a horse to ride and a boat to sail, and on land nor sea his health shall fail – Culver thus extended its thinking regarding its summer programs to appeal to the boy who loves horses, believing that the Culver Summer Cavalry School would "prove as attractive and as beneficial as has the Culver Summer Naval School to the boy who loves boats."[9]

Applying his promotional skills to this program as he had to the Summer Naval program in 1902, Gignilliat wrote the catalog for the Summer Cavalry program. According to that source, "The purpose of the Culver

Summer Cavalry School is to provide boys an organized vacation of the most beneficial and enjoyable type, and to give them a substitute that does away with the retrogression and injurious effects of the aimless summer."

Organized and conducted along the same principles as the naval school, the program would simply substitute "the drills and organization of a troop of cavalry for the boat drill and organization of the naval battalion," while providing boys with the same healthful and wholesome experience of the Summer Naval School cadets.[10]

Armed with such foundations, the first session of the Summer Cavalry School ran from July 2 – August 31, 1907, with an enrollment of 46 cadets. Combined with the 336 cadets enrolled in the Summer Naval School, Culver had a total of 382 cadets enrolled in its 1907 summer programs, eclipsing its winter school enrollment of 349 cadets for the 1906-07 session by 33 cadets.[11]

Jamestown Exposition – A Chance to Show the Nation What a "Big Six" School Could Do

As the "crowning feature" of the 1907 session of the Culver Summer schools, 374 cadets from both the Summer Naval and Cavalry schools embarked on a two-week trip to the East in conjunction with the Jamestown Expedition, commemorating the 300th anniversary of the establishment of the settlement at Jamestown, Virginia. The official party included ER Culver and his wife, Gignilliat and Minnie, Gignilliat's brother Thomas (who he called by his middle name of Heyward and who also brought his two children), Major Adams, Captains Bays, Glascock, Greiner, F. L. Hunt, Noble, Rossow, Kennedy, and the school surgeon (Dr. Parker) and nurse (Miss Stewart).[12] H. H. Culver's widow, Emily Jane, did not travel with the group, but she did join the excursion for one special day.

Because of the number of cadets and the number of stops and events included, many of the members of the faculty and staff were needed on the trip (some of whom were also accompanied by their wives). The manifest included Dr. Parker, bandsmen Harry Menser and Arthur Swigart, Quartermaster Hand and his assistant Arley Cromley. To care for the horses, horsemanship workers Ollie Baker, Frank Seltzer, and Ed McFeely of the barn force, and farrier Fred Cook came along. In addition, about 30 relatives of cadets who wanted to participate were welcomed as well at a cost of $20.45 for each (which they paid themselves).

To ensure all was coordinated properly, Gignilliat and the very recently returned Adams departed a week ahead of the trip on August 12, 1907, to see to all of the necessary arrangements at the main stops on the trip (Washington, DC, Jamestown, and Annapolis). Gignilliat would have almost certainly preferred to have taken Byroade with him, and he likely spent time setting Adams straight on his expectations upon his return as PMS&T.

The cadets departed on August 19, 1907 on two trains, and the logistical sophistication of the planning was evident from the start. One train led by Rossow and Kennedy departed early around 7:30 am and contained "the baggage cars, horse cars, and a pullman" for the approximately 30 relatives of cadets who decided to come along, arriving at each destination several hours ahead of the other train carrying the cadets. The other train consisted of ten cars, with the first nine containing the cadets and the rear car being reserved for the executive staff and their wives (of which there were only two: Minnie Gignilliat and Mrs. F. L. Hunt). The train carrying the cadets departed a bit later at 11:30 am, after allowing time for the cadets to eat an early lunch.[13]

Traveling along the Pennsylvania railroad, the first stop was in Cincinnati for dinner. From Cincinnati, the train next traveled through the picturesque mountains of Virginia and West Virginia on the Chesapeake & Ohio railroad, stopping for breakfast at the famous Greenbriar Hotel in White Sulphur Springs, WV. The next leg of the trip took the cadets up the Shenandoah Valley and across the Blue Ridge Mountains right past

The Jamestown Exposition, 1907. [16]

Charlottesville, VA en route to Richmond, VA for dinner and a bit of sightseeing on the evening of August 20. During their three hours in Richmond, from about 6:00 – 9:00 pm, which included dinner in shifts at the famous Jefferson Hotel and a parade through the streets of Richmond by six cadet companies, the cadet band, and the Black Horse Troop, the cadets were met with an enthusiastic reception and were dubbed "the

Culver cadets at the Government Pier, manning boats and making sail, Jamestown Expedition, August 1907. [17]

toast of the town" by a reporter.[14] After posing for a photo in the ornate lobby of the Jefferson Hotel, giving a series of rousing cheers, and marching back to the train, the party was once again under way, bound for their final destination of Newport News.

Reaching Newport News on the morning of August 21st, the entire party took ferryboats to Jamestown Island, where Rossow and Kennedy had an entire camp set up for them as a headquarters and base of operations throughout the duration of their stay.[15]

The cadets spent the next four days – 21-24 August – involved in the festivities related to the Jamestown commemoration.

The exposition was a grand affair, perhaps even more grand than the 1904 Louisiana Purchase Exposition, and there was much for the cadets to see and do. As with the 1904 excursion, the Culver chaperones were determined to balance the educational opportunities, ceremonial and performance responsibilities, and opportunities for individual and group discovery in ways that would make the event as beneficial as it was fun and exciting for the young men. Having demonstrated in 1904 that they could be counted on to behave themselves and trusted to make good decisions on their own, this played out as a schedule of events that allowed the cadets to demonstrate their military proficiency to others in attendance while also having time to take in the sights and wonders surrounding them on their own and with groups of friends.

The outcome of this approach allowed Culver to become even more well-known while allowing the cadets to enjoy themselves.

During this period, the cadets gave many demonstrations of naval skills, including manning the boats and making sail in their cutters..

Friday, August 23 was designated as "Culver Day," and the events of this day were particularly memorable. Joined by Emily Jane Culver, the CMA contingent played host to the Honorable George E. Foss, the US Representative from Illinois' 10th Congressional District (covering the northern suburbs of Chicago) and Chairman of the House of Representatives' Naval Affairs Committee, along with other members of his committee for the day.

The Honorable George E. Foss reviewing the Culver cadets with Gignilliat at the Jamestown Expedition on "Culver Day," August 23, 1907. [18]

After the Culver battalion paraded and passed in review for its visitors, which also included the Lieutenant Governor of Virginia, James T. Ellyson, and veterans of the Mexican War, and the playing of a stirring patriotic song, both Gignilliat and his brother offered "happy speeches." Thomas Gignilliat introduced Foss, who offered the following praise for Culver:

Summer Naval School Cadets aboard the USS Minnesota anchored at Hampton Roads, August 1907. [20]

I want to congratulate you upon your splendid appearance at the Exposition. I have heard your praises on every hand, from men of civilian and military life. An army officer said to me, 'The best equipped and best disciplined military school next to West Point and Annapolis.'"

"I wish to pay a tribute of praise to the philanthropy of the founder, Mr. Henry H. Culver, and to his no less patriotic widow who is here today."

"You are doing a splendid duty to the country, for you are preparing yourselves as reserves which the navy so much needs as well as the army."[19]

These remarks must have had Gignilliat beaming, especially the favorable comparisons to West Point and Annapolis, and they likely served to reinforce all the work he and others had done to raise the school's military training program to such a high level of effectiveness.

Most of the rest of Foss's remarks related to US naval preparedness. A luncheon attended by many dignitaries at the Exposition followed the remarks. The long days and multiple activities began taking their toll on the cadets, and the tired boys had little energy left to dance and enjoy themselves at the ball that evening, especially since the lateness of the event resulted in there being very few girls available as dance partners. The cadets, however, gave it their all, dancing hard until midnight before returning to their tents for some much-needed rest.

During this period, they were enthralled by the sight of 15 of the Navy's most impressive battleships at anchor at Hampton Roads. They visited the USS Minnesota and the USS Missouri on the morning after the ball, "inspecting the big guns, the galleys, the ward rooms, the compass and engines," enjoying the rare privilege of seeing the "flower of the American navy" in such intimate fashion.

The Summer Naval Cadets competed against a U.S. Navy crew from one of the ships in a cutter race and won a "stirring victory" for Culver. According to Gignilliat, Emily Jane Culver was so pleased with the victory that she later presented each member of the winning crew with "a handsome gold ring that she had specially designed by a leading jeweler."[21]

Culver Summer Naval and Cavalry School cadets on the steps of the US Capitol during the 1907 Summer Jamestown Exposition Trip, August 27, 1907. Gignilliat is first on the left of the front row.[22]

At the conclusion of their participation, the cadets boarded a steamboat – the good ship Newport News -- early on the morning of August 25 bound for Washington, DC by way of Chesapeake Bay and the Potomac River. The Culver Glee Club gave a repeat performance of the songs they had sung at the Exposition to a large and appreciative crowd on the vessel during the journey. The afternoon provided the opportunity for much-needed naps, and the band serenaded Mount Vernon as the ship passed by Washington's revered home in the evening twilight. The trip ended with the entire Culver party checking into the Ebbits House hotel, and the cadets were in bed by 11:00 pm for taps.

The next day – August 26 – the cadets spent in "systematic sight-seeing" of the nation's capital, beginning with three hours at the Smithsonian Institution and the National Museum. A specially arranged guided tour of the US Treasury building was next on the agenda, where the cadets witnessed the stamping of US currency and the gold and silver vaults during their hour-long visit. The afternoon included visits to the Washington Monument and the US Capitol building, along with treats of ice cream and other delicious snacks available on the mall. At 5:00 pm, the cadets paraded in the area between the White House and the Washington Monument, reviewed by the Assistant Secretary of the Navy Truman H. Newberry.

On Tuesday, August 27, the cadets again visited the capitol, the Library of Congress, Statuary Hall, the chambers of both the House of Representative and the Senate, and the Supreme Court, followed by an automobile tour of the city, returning to their hotel in time for lunch. The afternoon consisted of a voluntary trip to Mount Vernon under the supervision of Captain Mowbray or free time for the Summer Naval School cadets while the Summer Cavalry School Troopers traveled to Fort Meyer to be reunited with their horses. While at Fort Meyers on August 28, the Summer Cavalry troopers provided a demonstration of cavalry drill in the open field and a rough-riding exhibition in the riding hall for the soldiers at Fort Myers..

The cadets of Culver's Naval school, including the band, traveled by train to Annapolis on the evening of August 27 for an overnight visit to the US Naval Academy. On August 28, they toured the school and paraded for the Naval Academy community (which included the approximately 300 USNA midshipmen) on the Naval Academy's impressive parade ground. The reviewing officer was the Naval Academy's Superintendent, Captain Charles J. Badger, who complimented the cadets on their "splendid military appearance." According to the *Annapolis Capital*, this was the first time in the history of the Naval Academy that a private military school was reviewed on the parade ground. The article went on to describe the Culver cadets as "probably the crack military body of the kind in the country," noting also that "there was nothing but words of commendation from Superintendent Badger and others attached to the [Naval] Academy for [Culver's] splendid military accuracy and the discipline of the visiting battalion."[23]

Later, the Culver cadets selected two 10-man cutter crews to compete against two similar crews comprised of the youngest USNA midshipmen in a rowing race of one mile in length. USNA graduate Thomas Gignilliat served as the official starter for the race between the fairly evenly matched crews. While the race was close, the two Culver boats eked out a narrow but hard-fought victory of about a single boat length over the older and larger Annapolis students.

After the race, the cadets marched to the Maryland State House in downtown Annapolis, where they were received by Governor Edwin Warfield, who addressed the group briefly and also complimented them on their military bearing. The Culver cadets responded with three rousing cheers for the governor, and the band serenaded him with the entirely appropriate song, "Maryland, My Maryland." The cadets departed Annapolis by special train just after noon for their return trip to Washington, DC. The cadets affixed a broom to the final car of its train upon departing Annapolis, indicating that they had completed a "clean sweep" of the USNA middies. Acknowledging the glory Culver gained, Emily Jane Culver also presented each member of the victorious crews with the same special gold rings she had given to the members of the cutter crew that defeated the U.S. Navy crew in Hampton Roads several days previously.

The Summer Black Horse Troop at Jamestown

With only a few weeks to train before the big event, many – including Gignilliat – were concerned that the summer troopers would not be able to achieve the level of proficiency expected of the more well-known BHT of the winter school. In typical Culver fashion, the summer troopers were informed of the concerns and "told that it could not be very well explained to the public that they were just a summer organization" and not

Summer Cavalry School cadets on the USS Minnesota at the Jamestown Exposition, August 1907. [25]

the actual BHT of such renown. Made aware that they were expected to maintain the BHT's reputation for expert horsemanship and high levels of precision in their drills, and also that many did not believe that they

were up to the task, the boys dug in, committed to doing what it took, and got to work learning about their mounts and mastering the intricacies of cavalry drill.[24]

Summer Cavalry School cadets in Washington, DC, August 1907. [27]

According to Gignilliat, "They were told that it was up to them to do the impossible, and to sustain the Black Horse Troop's reputation for horsemanship," and the boys did just that at Jamestown, showing themselves to be true men of Culver. Gignilliat was amazed by the ability of the summer troopers and he remarked that, "At Jamestown they gave a splendid account of themselves, not only in parades and reviews and in troop evolutions, but even in rough riding and jumping."

In talking with a US Army Cavalry officer at the Exposition about how little training the boys had, the officer characterized their performance, in view of their short period of training, as a "military miracle." While perhaps a bit of an overstatement, as a result of the summer troopers' performance at Jamestown, all doubts about continuing the Summer Cavalry School were completely dispelled.[26]

The group began its trip home on August 29, 1907. After stopping for dinner and a brief tour of the University of Virginia in Charlottesville, VA, the trains returned to Culver via Cincinnati on August 31, completing the 1,000-mile journey.

Comments regarding the impression of the cadets during the trip included (from the *Annapolis Capital*):

- Major Sylvester, Chief of Police, Washington, DC: *"Culver cadets were the best behaved military organization that has ever visited Washington."*

- Mr. Foss: *"The Culver cadets were the whole show during their visit."*

- The *Baltimore American* newspaper: *"Culver school is probably the crack organization of the kind in the country."*

- Unnamed Jamestown Exposition officials: *"No organization, not even West Point or Annapolis, has attracted more attention at the Exposition;"* and, *"It was heard at the Exposition that [Culver's] band played the best military music on the grounds this season."*

- Assistant Paymaster McMillen of the US Navy: remarked that he was *"sorry that he had been appointed to the navy at a time to cut him off from a share in the glory of Culver's achievements at Jamestown."*

- US Army officer Major Mallory: *"Culver academy, in its military work, compares favorably with the battalion at West Point."*

- US Naval Academy Superintendent Captain Badger: *"I must acknowledge that I am surprised at the showing made by the Culver cadets."*

- The Culver battalion was also honored by an in-person visit by US Navy Admiral Harrington to bid the battalion farewell and was accompanied by US Federal judge Christian C Kohlsaat from the pier to Old Point, both of which are gestures considered to be compliments of the highest order.[28]

The total cost of the trip was approximately $25,000, which was about one-third of the entire summer revenue (and equates to a little over $830,000.00 in 2023 dollars). Each cadet paid $40, amounting to almost $15,000, and Culver provided the remaining $10,000 (which is over $331,000.00 in 2023 dollars). However, as Culver publicist H. E. Cook would have undoubtedly observed, the benefit of getting Culver better known in the East was incalculable, and the publicity gained from the trip for Culver was priceless.[29]

It is noteworthy that Fleet did not accompany the cadets on this trip, trusting Gignilliat to oversee the entire affair and indicating his high level of confidence in his Commandant. It was also somewhat unusual that Minnie did not accompany Gignilliat on the trip and instead remained in Virginia, where Gignilliat joined her upon the conclusion of the summer session.[30]

Major Adams (center left) and Gignilliat (center right) inspecting a pontoon bridge. [31]

1908 – A Year of Change and Portent

Earning recognition as one of the best military schools in the country yet again in 1908 – which now included eight schools owing to the increasing number of military schools in the country -- without the assistance of Byroade (who departed in fall 1907) institutionalized success for a third year in a row.

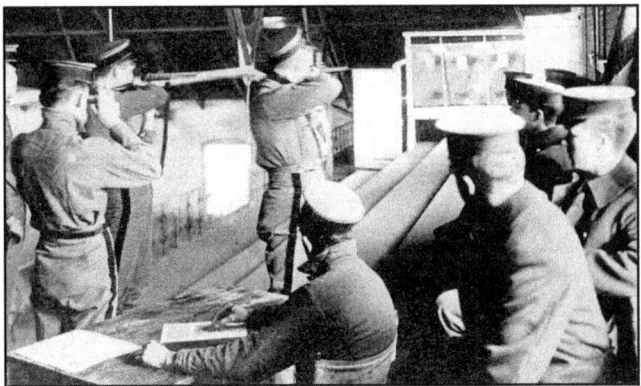

New CMA indoor rifle range. [32]

The tremendously popular (with the cadets) Captain J. Q. Adams returned to replace Byroade, and he learned what it took to perform at the level demanded of maintaining national recognition. Adams fully supported the program and the efforts required to do so.

CMA Corps of Cadets, fall 1909. [33]

Fully resourced to sustain excellence, it became the expectation within the corps that Culver would earn "Big Six/Eight" recognition each and every year without fail.

Culver also began expanding its facilities and size as word of its successful programs spread. One of the most important enhancements to the military program was the completion of a brand new, state-of-the-art indoor rifle range, allowing cadets to practice marksmanship year-round and compete among themselves during the winter months. According to Gignilliat, this range, and the excellent marksmanship instruction provided by Captain Kennedy, aroused the highest degree of interest among the cadets he had ever seen, furthering the cadets' zeal for excellence.

The enrollment in the winter school also grew, cresting 350 for the first time in the school's history. A corps of cadets of approximately 370 cadets made Culver one of, if not the, largest schools of its kind in the country at any level of education, furthering its claim to be one of the nation's very best military schools..

One of the unexpected outcomes of the effort was that the practice of hazing largely fell out of favor among the corps, since everyone had to cooperate to earn and retain Big Six recognition, and hazing detracted from these efforts. Just prior to the Army Annual inspection in May 1906, Culver dismissed 13 upper-class cadets and suspended several others for hazing incidents that had occurred in April 1906 and was motivated by practices at West Point and Annapolis. Byroade served as the presiding officer for the inquiry, providing explicit support for Gignilliat's determined efforts to abolish the practice of hazing at Culver once and for all.[34] Indeed, Gignilliat believed that by the beginning of the 1907-1908 school year he had succeeded and that "hazing as a practice" no longer existed in the Corps.[35]

Another important outcome of the Big Six effort was its impact on the Culver family. The success of the school in this endeavor and the national

Cadets providing a drill exhibition in Cleveland for approximately 10,000 spectators in Wade Park, Cleveland, OH, August 1908. [37]

recognition it brought to the school they viewed as a living monument to their deceased father and was a contributing factor to the board's development of its "Greater Culver" plan announced in March 1909. Under this plan, the Culver family committed to providing between

Cadets parading through the streets of Cleveland, OH, August 1908. [38]

$300,000 - $400,000 to the school over a five-year period to sustain its new-found level of excellence by providing the funding for additional building and more and better equipment for the academic, military, and athletic programs. Akin to a modern strategic plan, the Greater Culver program was a visible show of support for all the institution had achieved and a promise to provide the necessary resources to sustain that level of achievement.

The Great Cruise of 1908

During the final week of August 1908, Gignilliat took 250 Summer school cadets on another epic trip, dubbed the "Great Cruise" of 1908. The official party included the following individuals: ER Culver and his wife, Gignilliat and his wife, Gignilliat's brother Thomas "Heyward " Gignilliat, Culver Summer School Commander Admiral Albert Ross, USN, and Culver Captains Bays, Crandall, Durborow, Glascock, Greiner, Hunt, Kennedy, H F Noble, Mowbray and Rossow.

Departing Culver on August 21, the trip began with a parade in Grant Park in Chicago before boarding the good ship Northland for a one-week

excursion during the period August 22-29, 1908.

Heading north on Lake Michigan, the first port call was at Mackinac

SS Northland, ship for the 1908 Great Cruise. [36]

Island, where the cadets drilled and paraded for an appreciative audience before having some free time to explore the fort. Entering Lake Huron, the ship headed south, and the party made its way to the city of Cleveland, where the cadets again drilled and paraded. In addition, the troopers put on a cavalry drill land rough-riding demonstration but were disappointed to not be able to engage in a riding coemption with their spiritual unit of origin – Troop A of the Cleveland Army National Guard.

Continuing to Lake Erie, the group reached the farthest eastern point of their trip at Niagara Falls, NY, where they drilled and paraded one day and spent another day of leisure, riding the Maid of the Mist to the base of the falls and enjoying many other of the area's enticing opportunities. The return trip included a single stop in Little Traverse Bay to drill and parade at the charming city of Wequetonsing, MI (near Harbor Springs), where the only foul weather of the trip soaked the cadets in formation but did little to impact their remarkable discipline.

While under way, the cadets learned about naval operations, relaxed, ate, and napped, having a thoroughly enjoyable time. According to one report, the prevailing sentiment among the cadets was best expressed by the saying, "And should I live a thousand years, I should never forget it."[39]

After sailing 1,500 miles across three of the Great Lakes (Michigan, Huron, and Erie) and making port in four locations, (including Mackinac Island, Cleveland Niagara Falls, and Wequetonsing, MI), and with an additional 500 miles of travel across the ground, the group ended is 2,000 mile odyssey where it began in Chicago on August 29, 1908 before returning to Culver that evening.[40]

It is notable that the official party for this trip again did not include Fleet, indicating that at this point in 1908 he may not have been up to the rigor of a one-week cruise covering approximately 2,000 miles. It is also important to note that seven of the captains included in the official party – including Glascock, Greiner, Hunt, Bays, H F Noble, and Mowbray and Rossow – were fast becoming the operational leaders of Culver under the guidance of Gignilliat.

Upon his return to campus at the conclusion of the Great Cruise of 1908, what a tremendous sense of accomplishment and validation Gignilliat must have felt upon achieving this recognition for a second consecutive year. The effort to do so helped to both develop and show the effectiveness of Culver's whole-person approach – Body, Mind, and Spirit – applied to the military system. It also supported Fleet's "Quality over Quantity" approach for the military system. This successful and prolonged effort also helped to crystallize two of Gignilliat's cardinal educational tenets

Gignilliat in 1909. [41]

that he would later articulate in his 1916 book, *Arms and the Boy*: Training must be given properly to be effective; and training must be made real for the cadets so that it is meaningful.

Taken together, the effort to attain and retain Big Six recognition taught Gignilliat how to be an effective trainer, and he also began learning how to become an effective administrator. Gignilliat grew a full van dyke beard during this period, enhancing his military countenance and showing his new-found confidence.

Serving as Acting Superintendent

Throughout the process of earning Big Six recognition, Gignilliat's reach across the institution expanded, bringing him into contact with varied aspects of the school that also enhanced his base of knowledge and increased his level of experience as an education administrator. Working with the service areas of the school, including horsemanship, buildings and grounds, the tailor shop, and the business office, was very beneficial, as it showed him how each of these elements functioned and brought him into closer contact with the people performing these duties. He got to know them, and they were able to take their own measure of him as well. Combined with Fleet's mentoring, there could scarcely have been a better program to begin preparing the approximately 30-year-old Gignilliat to learn how to run an academic institution.

More specifically, Gignilliat benefited professionally from the experience in the following ways: He had to coordinate for each annual inspection and also arrange for the resources required to support them, causing him to become more adept at coordination and logistics.

Being responsible for bringing national recognition for military excellence to Culver, he learned much about marketing and generating publicity for the school by publicizing the results of the inspections and writing articles about them for national publications. Gignilliat's article appearing in the February 1907 edition of *The Times Magazine* was essentially a recap of the inspection results that brought Big Six recognition to Culver in spring 1906, along with a description of the process Culver used to earn it. Gignilliat also had to become a more public figure, and he promoted the military aspects of the program on his own via exposure, performance, and publication.

Having learned that a larger corps was beneficial for the inspection, Gignilliat had to work with admissions to recruit and grow the corps, and he had to work with the members of his own staff to improve the retention rate for those cadets already enrolled. A major component of the recruiting effort was to provide a desirable military system that was appealing to parents and cadets, and which admissions and others could use to promote the school.

Organizationally, he learned how to get internal resources (time and personnel) and the buy-in from his colleagues for the common benefit of the institution. Perhaps just as importantly, Gignilliat learned how to get external resources (e.g., tents and military equipment) to support the school's drive for excellence. Each of these endeavors helped develop him into a more capable administrator, and his overall success in accomplishing these varied tasks showed that he was and had become a good manager of resources and people, along with sharpening his ability as a shrewd judge of capability in others. More broadly, his performance provided tangible evidence of his growing effectiveness as a capable educator who could apply a whole-person education approach – Body, Mind, Spirit – to the military program to achieve superior results.

These efforts also contributed significantly to Fleet's focus on "Quality over Quantity" by developing a way of earning "Big Six" recognition for Culver, furthering one of his superior's most important objectives and further endearing himself to Fleet as an exceptionally capable colleague. Indeed, it was during this period that Fleet provided his extraordinarily positive assessment of Gignilliat to the VMI superintendent, showing that Gignilliat's efforts were both noticed and appreciated by Fleet.

All of this served as the context within which Gignilliat began taking on additional administrative duties beginning in winter 1908. Fleet became ill in December 1908 and departed campus to convalesce in the warmer climate of the south. Gignilliat was named Acting Superintendent in Fleet's absence, compelling him to begin putting into practice much of what he had learned during the drive to earn Big Six recognition.

He also began developing his executive ability, as he continued to serve as Commandant while also functioning as the Acting Superintendent. This was a significant increase in his level of responsibility that exceeded his individual capacity, and it required Gignilliat – who preferred up to this point to do most things himself – to become more diplomatic, more focused, and to learn how to delegate effectively.

As the Acting Superintendent, Gignilliat was acting in Fleet's stead and had to run the school as Fleet would have. This meant that it was imperative that he maintained relations with Fleet and the Culvers (especially ER Culver) that were positive and productive.

Given that Fleet was 66 years old by the time of his illness (born June 6, 1843), it was unlikely that he had many productive years remaining (he had already served about as long as he had predicted when he accepted the job in 1896). Realizing this, Gignilliat also had to keep the progress initiated by Fleet going to show that he was an effective administrator who should at least be considered as a candidate to replace Fleet if and when the time came to do so. This thought was almost surely weighing on the minds of both Gignilliat and the Board (especially Board President BB Culver) at the time of this episode.

Not knowing how long he would serve in this dual capacity, Gignilliat decided to get some help addressing his enhanced role. Given the success he had experienced working together, Byroade would have almost certainly been his first choice to fill this role had he not departed in fall 1907. He had an excellent alternate in the person of Bert Greiner, however, and Gignilliat brought Greiner to his side to serve as his aid almost immediately. Besides the assistance he received from doing so, this allowed Gignilliat to begin grooming Greiner to replace him as commandant, should Gignilliat become the actual superintendent.

The trust that Gignilliat had developed in Greiner gave him great comfort that, should Greiner replace him as commandant, he could be certain that Greiner would maintain the military training system Gignilliat had spent the previous eight years so painstakingly developing and implementing. This move was a sign of both his growth and increasing maturity, and it allowed Gignilliat to focus more of his attention on the relatively unfamiliar requirements of the superintendent's

Artist's rendering of the new Dining Hall, a centerpiece of the Greater Culver Plan. [43]

job confident that his cherished military system would be left intact and stewarded carefully.

Gignilliat served in this capacity almost continuously from December 1908 until he was appointed as Fleet's replacement in September 1910. During this 19-month period, which served as an extended job interview, Gignilliat performed well. The school continued to thrive, enrollment increased, and it maintained its string of earning recognition as a "distinguished military institution" throughout, providing the Culver community and the board with discernible evidence of Gignilliat's executive abilities and ability to function effectively in the role of superintendent.

The "Greater Culver" Plan

Partly due to the school's success in gaining Big Six recognition, and also in an effort to not only sustain but enhance its overall excellence, the Culver Board of Trustees announced its plan for a "Greater Culver" in a letter dated 12 March 1909 to Fleet, who was convalescing in Florida. At the time of its release, it is likely that the board expected Fleet to recover and begin the process of implementing their vision for the school. However, this was not to be the case, and the responsibility for implementing the plan and realizing its inspiring vision fell to Gignilliat, which turned out to be a fortuitous turn of events for both Culver and its new superintendent.

The "Greater Culver" plan was essentially a commitment by the Culver family to provide Culver with best facilities in country during the period 1909-1914 by pledging $300,000 to $400,000 to support new construction and the purchase of additional equipment. The first priority was to build a dining hall worthy of the school, which was completed in 1911.[42]

This plan served as the Culver family's "marching orders" for the institution that were operative when Gignilliat was functioning as the acting superintendent and when he took over as the actual superintendent in September 1910. It was Culver's first strategic plan, and Gignilliat's role was to implement it, much like school heads of today. As we will see, Gignilliat embraced this program wholeheartedly, took personal responsibility for seeing that it was implemented effectively and as planned, and combined it with Culver's endeavors related to the coming Preparedness Movement and the military camps sponsored at Culver to create an even "Greater Culver."

Fleet returned to campus from Florida where he had been recovering from illness on April 1, 1909, but he had not fully recovered and soon fell ill again. In June 1909, Gignilliat became Acting Superintendent again, as Fleet spent much of the summer recovering away from campus near the University of Chicago.

After closing out the summer programming, Gignilliat departed on August 23, 1909 for what had become by now his customary vacation at the end of August and for part of the month of September. Rather than spending time in Virginia, he took his beloved Minnie and the boys to England for a month-long vacation, leaving Glascock and Greiner in charge.

This overseas trip indicates that he likely expected Fleet to resume his duties and be functioning as superintendent for the coming school year. However, by the time winter school began on September 16, Fleet had still not returned to campus.

Gignilliat returned on September 30, 1909, and Fleet returned to campus soon thereafter on October 7, 1909, after an absence of almost four continuous months. By May of the following year, Fleet's health had failed again and he was not on campus.

Gignilliat functioned as both Commandant and Acting Superintendent for the important annual inspection by the Army on May 7-8, 1910 and for the remainder of the school year including for the commencement exercises that occurred on June 16, 1910. Missing these two important events was indicative of the severity of Fleet's infirmity.

Being gathered on campus for the end-of-year festivities, the board had to be concerned and surely discussed the situation among themselves that summer. It appears as though the board expected Fleet's condition to improve sufficiently to allow him to resume his duties as superintendent at the beginning of the 1910-1911 school year, and he was listed in the catalog published in July-August 1910 as the school's superintendent. However, his health must have taken a turn for the worse later in the summer of 1910, and Fleet informed the Culvers that he would be unable to resume his duties and had decided to retire and remain in the warmer climes of Atlanta with his daughter Belle and son-in-law Kevin Matheson, who was an English professor at Georgia Tech.

When Fleet's condition failed to improve sufficiently to allow him to resume his role as superintendent over the summer of 1910, the board had little choice but to begin searching for a suitable replacement. After observing how well Gignilliat had functioned as Acting Superintendent for the previous 18 months, and certain of his commitment to the school to avoid a repeat of the short-term disasters of MacKenzie and Tebbetts, it must have been a relatively easy decision to name Gignilliat as the school's fourth superintendent on September 18, 1910, which was just prior to the beginning of the 1901-1911 school year that began on September 21, 1910.

Gignilliat also expected Fleet to recover, and he saw no reason to alter his custom of joining his wife in Virginia for some relaxation after the conclusion of Culver's summer camp. As a result, Gignilliat was away from campus when the announcement of his appointment as superintendent was made. He had departed campus on September 1, 1910, having concluded yet another successful summer session. He was looking forward to enjoying a well-deserved respite from his significant responsibilities and was confident in the abilities of his able lieutenants – the redoubtable Glascock and Greiner – to manage the affairs of the school until Fleet's return.

Gignilliat was informed of his new appointment while away from campus in Virginia. While perhaps apprised of Fleet's worsening condition, the appointment as superintendent must have come as somewhat of a surprise, producing equal amounts of pride, concern, and anxiety in him. After informing Minnie of this development, which did not bode well for her own father, Gignilliat likely made plans to return to Culver quickly and begin functioning as superintendent in his own right while Minnie considered traveling to Atlanta to be with her infirmed father.

Gignilliat was still quite attached to his role as commandant and the military training program he had created when he returned to campus to assume his new position, and his initial inclination was to not fill the commandant's position and continue serving as both superintendent and commandant with the help of his staff. This arrangement had not worked well for Tebbetts, and BB Culver, as board president (and perhaps ER Culver as well), must have shared with Gignilliat his/their concerns about the dim prospects for success of repeating such an approach. After assessing the situation for himself and taking the counsel of the Culver brother into consideration, Gignilliat relented and named Bert Greiner Acting Commandant on September 28, 1910, relinquishing his treasured role somewhat reluctantly with the expectation that Greiner would function in his own stead much as he had done for Fleet for the preceding year and a half. Greiner would serve in such a capacity for an entire year, being named Commandant in his own right almost exactly one year later on September 27, 1911, and shortly after Fleet's death on September 3, 1911.

Thus began a new chapter in Gignilliat's service to Culver.

Chapter 6 - Assuming the Mantle of Leadership and Adjusting to a New Role, September 1910 – December 1912

Gignilliat's Living Situation in Fall 1910

Gignilliat's life had certainly changed by fall 1910. According to the US Census data from 1900, Gignilliat and Minnie were living Culver in the same household as his in-laws, Colonel and Mrs. Fleet. In terms of family, Gignilliat and Minnie had a one-year-old son, Leigh Robinson Gignilliat Jr.[1]

However, by 1910, Gignilliat and Minnie were living in a cottage next door to his in-laws with his two sons, Leigh Jr and Frederick "Freddy" Fleet Gignilliat, born March 4, 1901. To help run the household, the family also employed a two-member staff. The 25-year-old Bertha Byrd was the housekeeper, and her 26-year-old sister, Anna, was the cook.[2]

Moving into their own house and employing a small household staff allowed Gignilliat to support Minnie in the manner to which she was accustomed and also focus more of his attention on Culver and what was becoming his burgeoning writing career. It is worth reviewing his published written works briefly during the period 1903-1911 to get a sense of his thinking and state of mind before turning to his involvement with Culver as its new superintendent.

Gignilliat's Early Published Works, Outlining the Culver Way

For one who did not consider himself to possess any talent for writing, Gignilliat had been remarkably active in education circles since as early as 1903, publishing at least six articles by the time he became Culver's superintendent in 1910.[3]

His first published article was a very thoughtful one-page piece titled "What We Leave Behind," and it appeared in January 1903 in CMA's own student publication, *The Vedette* (which was more of a digest that contained a mix of news articles and opinion pieces until 1913, when it became a conventional student newspaper), addressing the graduating cadets and providing them with some context within which to consider the influence they leave behind at CMA.[4] His next article appeared in the popular *Munsey's Magazine* in June of 1903, containing equal measures of text and photographs (five photos in all).[5] Titled, "An Inland Naval School," the three-page article was very practical in championing the value of using naval training as a positive way to develop young men.

This is a theme to which Gignilliat returns often over the course of the next two decades.

His next two articles appeared in the highly respected and widely read *Scientific American* in March and May of 1905. They were mostly descriptive accounts of the use of military training in educating boys.[6] In fact, both articles essentially described Culver's approach in its winter and summer programs, respectively, serving as excellent marketing material to reach a very different audience of readers. Each article was well illustrated, with the March article presenting nine photographs of military training at CMA and the May article using five different photographs from the Summer Naval School to illustrate its content. In addition, two photographs of Culver Summer Naval School cadets appeared on the cover of the May 6, 1905 *Scientific American*, no doubt to the great delight of Gignilliat and the Culver family.

These two articles are significant because they present the core of Gignilliat's thinking regarding the value of military training in an educational institution at the time he became Culver's superintendent. They also show how far his thinking had progressed from his belief as a VMI cadet that the military had little contribution to his education and was largely a game he enjoyed playing, with both great success and equally devastating setbacks.

A decade removed from his own cadet experience, the 1903 and 1905 articles indicate that Gignilliat's thinking regarding the value of military training in education had changed substantially, reflecting the positive contributions the military system could make. Perhaps the example of Captain Bromwell in Yellowstone coupled with the mentoring from Fleet and his experience as commandment combined to alter his beliefs, but it is clear that the ten years that had passed since his graduation from VMI had been quite impactful.

Cover of Scientific American, *May 1905.*

By 1905, as his published works show, Gignilliat had become both a supporter of and articulate proponent for the value of military training in schools.

Lest one question the genuineness of his first three articles in support of military training as an effective educational approach for young men, Gignilliat's next two works belay any doubts about his sincerity on the topic. His article, which appeared in February 1907 edition of *The Times Magazine*, was likely written in 1906 soon after Culver first achieved "distinguished institution" recognition from the US Army.[7] Although titled "Military Schools in America," this article focuses exclusively on Culver. It is essentially an eight-page description of Culver's approach that succeeded in earning it "distinguished institution" status during the 1906 Army Annual Inspection. The content addresses both the winter and summer school activities at Culver, and it is illustrated with seven photographs, five of which relate to CMA and the other two depicting activities of the summer naval program.

The substance of this article contains the strongest argument Gignilliat had put forth in support of Culver's unique approach to military training up to then, using the Army's recognition as validation of its effectiveness. As such, it is essentially a synthesis of his 1905 separate articles and serves to provide a comprehensive description of Culver's entire military program involving both military and naval training, explaining how and why it earned its place in the first rank of what were referred to as "essentially military schools" in the nation.

Gignilliat's final article of this period was written in 1910, and it was his best work to date. Titled "The Purpose of the Boys' School," it published in 1911 in the book, *A Handbook of Schools*.[8]

The 1910/1911 article demonstrates a more literary approach and with far more eloquence that hints at the writing style Gignilliat would come to adopt in his later publications when he had the proper amount of support and time. For example, Gignilliat made excellent use of a metaphor for the forming of character as being akin to the "setting of bolts in concrete." Arguing that the proper focus for educating high school boys was developing business efficiency, character, and good citizenship through the proper use of discipline, by which he meant discipline that was meaningful and to which the boy submitted voluntarily and willingly, Gignilliat addressed some of the main elements he would continue to emphasize throughout his entire career.

Building on his earlier works, these two articles embrace military training of all types and present a more full-throated argument for the value of military training in schools. Along with the practical advantages he highlighted previously, Gignilliat also made a case for ways that military discipline was an effective – and even preferred – way to develop young men, characterizing it as being the "crying need" of teenaged boys.

Gignilliat also presented his early thoughts on how to address hazing, citing both constructive ways (build a spirit against it within the corps) and more direct ways (dismissing perpetrators immediately) of controlling it. Finally, Gignilliat began to rely on his own well-earned expertise, citing the basis for many of his ideas as being grounded in 15 years of experience with over 4,000 boys. Perhaps he felt himself finally ready to lead the school in his own right, as he had been doing on an interim basis since late-1908 when Fleet's health began to fail.

It is in these two articles that Gignilliat begins to acknowledge his belief in the power of the immersive experience of the boarding school to mold a boy's character and of the benefits of a "whole-boy" educational approach like the one used at Culver. By the time he became superintendent, as shown in his professional writings, Gignilliat had developed his own ideas about how a military system could and should be used in schools, he had formed his ideas sufficiently to convey them to others, and he was ready to begin sharing his ideas more broadly and also trust his own judgment to implement them effectively at Culver.

This brief review provides a good indication of Gignilliat's thinking as an educator when he assumed the superintendence of the institution. His published works show the development he experienced as a writer during the first decade of the 20th century that parallel his development in other aspects of his professional life and which he would continue to refine and enhance in his new role as Culver's chief executive administrator. As with his talents as an administrator and educator, the number and length of his published works would continue to grow, and their quality would become increasingly more sophisticated throughout his long tenure as Culver's superintendent.

The Open-air Barrack – Gignilliat's First Demonstration of Institutional Innovation

Gignilliat was determined to take advantage of the unexpected opportunity of becoming Culver's superintendent, He decided that innovating in the cadet living quarters, which he had come to know so well during his time as commandant, was a good place to begin. This also made sense for a boarding school, where living arrangements mattered.

Open Air Barrack at Culver, 1910.[10]

In 1910, convinced that an abundance of fresh air was beneficial physically and intellectually, Gignilliat persuaded the Culver family to fund construction of a temporary "Open Air Barrack."[9]

This structure was intended to be an experiment to determine if allowing for increased exposure to additional oxygen would sharpen their minds and academic performance, if it was beneficial for cadet health, and if it would fortify their physiques.

The wooden construction of the barrack attests to its temporary and experimental nature, as the Culver family and the administration would never have agreed to the construction of a permanent structure that was not fireproof. If it turned out to be demonstrably beneficial, the plan was to erect a larger and more permanent structure (presumably of fireproof material) that would be the best of its kind.

The two-story Open-air barrack contained 12 rooms with space for 24 cadets who volunteered to reside there (cadets did not begin living by unit until 1913). The larger, steam-heated rooms had running water and contained individual wash basins, large windows to allow in ample light, separate study desks of special design, and spacious closets with laundry compartments. The doors also had large glass panels (which became standard in all cadet rooms in 1912), making it easier to inspect the rooms and also to check on cadets without disturbing them.

The custom desks in the Open-Air Barrack.[11]

The awnings over the sleeping alcove in the Open-Air Barrack.[13]

The concept was to provide cadets with an exceptionally healthful living environment by having "all beds enclosed in an alcove which was separated from the inner room by a window and, likewise, from the outside by a second window," allowing the cadet to essentially sleep in the outdoors. The bed in the alcove was protected from inclement weather by large awnings over each window.[12]

In practice, the beds were placed along the outside wall in two adjoining open-air sleeping porches enclosed entirely in glass and accessible from the room by means of a dormer window, the sill of which was level with the floor. Raising the inner window automatically lowered the outside window, which smacks of the application of Gignilliat's training as an engineer to the innovative design of this feature. The idea was to open the outer window while sleeping to expose the cadets to the healthful benefits of fresh air while keeping the inside window closed to keep the living room comfortable.

It was an innovative design unique to Culver and almost surely developed in part or perhaps entirely by Gignilliat.

A cadet living in the Open-air Barrack followed a set procedure at Taps.

To go to bed, he raised the inside window, got in bed, and closed the window behind him.

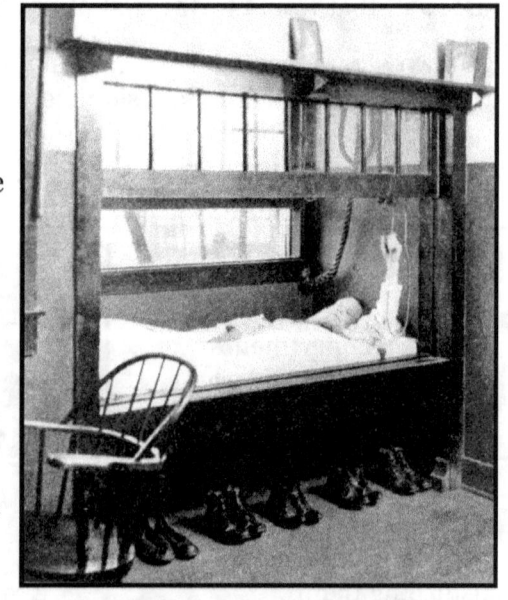

The sleeping alcove in the Open-air Barrack.[14]

Closing the inside window raised the outside window, allowing the cadet to receive the benefits of fresh air. The Taps inspector could check the cadet's status without having to open the door by peering through the large window in the room's door.

During the day, the outer window was closed and the inner window was opened so that the bed and porch were included as part of the room.

Pleased with the inventive design of the sleeping alcove windows, the Culver family secured a patent for the design and offered it at no cost to any interested worthy

The innovative window system in the Open-air Barrack sleeping alcove.[15]

organization. Several sanitariums expressed interest, but there were no takers.

By the early 1920s the novelty of the Open-air Barrack had worn off for both the cadets and Gignilliat, and, despite needing rooms desperately for the tremendously expanded corps, the experiment was deemed as being unsuccessful. Instead, Culver built the two more traditional barrack buildings of Argonne and Chateau Thierry.

During the construction of the Recreation Building in 1923, the Open-air Barrack building was moved and began serving other functions. Most notably, it was home to the Culver Band for around five years (~1925-1931) before being torn down to make way for other facilities, its construction providing an unwarranted fire hazard to the Culver campus.[16]

Gignilliat's Health Plan for Cadets

The slogan, "You send us a boy, and we'll return him as a man" was an important theme in the early 1900s at Culver. Taking advantage of the school's military program, Culver focused on improving the posture of boys using the idea of military posture.

"Military posture" included the requirement to stand up straight with "shoulders back, chest out, chin in." Gignilliat took the lead in this endeavor, and by 1910 he had put in place a program designed to correct any "deficiencies" related to posture.

As a way of measuring the impact of this program, Gignilliat had each boy photographed from the side at the beginning of each school year. He also had the cadet's height, weight, and chest measurements, inhaled and exhaled, recorded.

Based upon the assessment of his posture, the staff developed a program for each cadet to correct any deficiencies and improve his overall bearing in a manner that supported the military ideals of the school and program. Gignilliat repeated the process at the end of the year and sent copies of the before-and-after photos and measurements to the parents, along with grade reports, to show the progress cadets were making inside and outside the classroom. This practice was quite welcomed by parents and continued after Gignilliat's departure and well into the 1950s.[19]

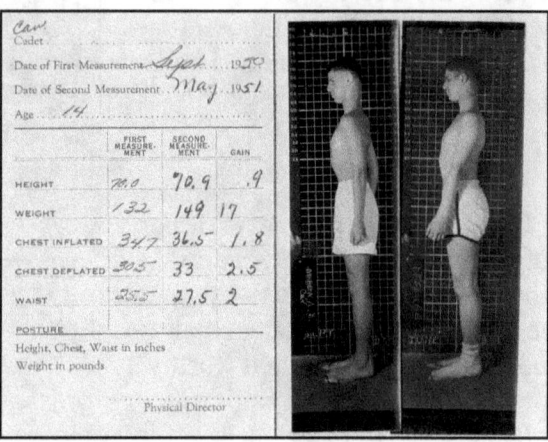

Example of Posture Report sent to parents.[18]

These efforts were continuing in the same vein Gignilliat had started in 1907 when he developed and implemented a novel shower system for cadets as another way to focus on their physical health and development. Showering daily was a fairly new practice in American society at the turn of the century, as some believed that it was actually detrimental to one's health based upon outdated ideas about the body's "humors" and specious beliefs regarding the nature of germs. Gignilliat, however, was convinced that it not only contributed positively to a cadet's health but also, and in keeping with the ideas of Progressivism that he embraced and which were popular at the time, that there was an efficient way to do so.

According to the 1907 CMA catalog, the shower system was "designed, or might be said invented, especially for the gymnasium" so that after exercising, "an entire battalion could be given a shower in a very few minutes." The cadets "marched through a U-shaped gallery of parallel rows of pipes," and "on completion of the circuit, had received a scientifically regulated shower bath, warm on entrance and gradually, by an ingenious arrangement, decreasing in temperature so that the water at the end is an invigorating coolness."[20] This approach was not popular with the cadets (not surprisingly), and the experiment ended in 1909 or 1910.[21]

Gignilliat's "Scientifically Regulated Shower Bath" system, circa 1907.[22]

1911 – A Year of Loss for Gignilliat and Minnie

As one of his first acts of the 1911 winter school year, Gignilliat hired a new surgeon. After the school's first surgeon, Dr. Oliver Rea (hired 1897), retired in 1905, the Academy relied on local physicians to cover the health concerns on campus. This trial practice confirmed that having a dedicated Academy physician on campus was both a much better and much preferred approach. As a result, Dr. E. E. Parker was appointed school surgeon in 1907, serving until 1911. Gignilliat appointed Dr. C. E. Reed, a former missionary doctor in China, as the school surgeon just prior to the beginning of the 1911 winter school session. Reed served in this role until 1928, working closely with Gignilliat to attend to the health of the cadets and see to their wellbeing.[23]

Rea had practiced in a room on the first floor in Main Barrack until 1898, when the infirmary was moved into a four-room suite on the second floor in the new East Barrack. When Culver built its new medical facility in 1907, Rea moved the entire medical enterprise (including the dentist) into the new facility.[24]

The new hospital showed how Culver's influence was growing, as competitors attempted to use it to portray Culver in a negative light. As a luxury that few similar institutions could afford, other schools suggested that Culver needed such a facility because it did not take good care of its students. The very capable Rea responded to this challenge by offering evidence of Culver's substantial health and medical programs. This approach quickly silenced the critics and served to help bring even more and better publicity to the decision to construct a first-rate health center based on the desire to provide the best possible care for the hundreds of cadets attending the Academy for its renowned winter and summer programs.[25]

The Loss of a Brother – Thomas "Heyward" Gignilliat

Gignilliat's brother, Thomas, called by his middle name of "Heyward" by Gignilliat, completed his final year as the Director of Seamanship and Navigation at the Summer Naval School in 1910. By the end of the summer of 1910, and although of robust moral character, Heyward's physical health was failing, preventing him from continuing in this role. Heyward died the following year in Asheville, North Carolina on July 5, 1911 at the age of 48.

Thomas "Heyward" Gignilliat.[26]

Compared to his very grounded brother, Heyward was more of a dreamer. Gignilliat's brother lived a life of respectable accomplishment that also fell tantalizingly short of greatness. Being 12 years older, Gignilliat really only got to know Heyward well during the period of their mutual association with Culver's Summer Naval School, 1902-1910.

Heyward graduated from the U.S. Naval Academy and served as a Lieutenant in the U.S. Navy in the Spanish-American War. He left active service as a result of an illness contracted in the Philippines, and he had performed solidly and honorably in the Navy.

Joining the US Corps of Engineers as a civilian, Heyward put his engineering degree to work on coastal fortifications. He became interested in the idea of mechanical flight, and his observations of seagulls in flight and mathematical investigations led him to the idea of developing a flying machine. In the fall of 1890, he began experiments in Hartford, Connecticut to develop such a machine. This was one year before Professor Samuel P. Langley's "Experiments in Aerodynamics" (*Smithsonian Contributions to Knowledge*, XXVII, 1891) was published, which is the basis for the claim that Heyward Gignilliat was the first to announce the correct mathematical principles governing aerial navigation.

Heyward returned to Savannah and established the American Aeronautic Machine Company in 1892, which was the first company ever chartered for the commercial manufacture and sale of airplanes. Unfortunately, his experiments from 1890 until 1893 – a decade prior to the Wright brothers' success at Kittyhawk, North Carolina – never produced a machine that would fly.

In 1895, Heyward proposed an agreement with the Venezuelan government for it to finance his experiments to develop a successful flying machine for military use, citing Great Britain's' recent encroachment on Venezuelan territory as one justification for the request investment of funds. Receiving no responses from Venezuela, Heyward taught in Savannah public schools, becoming a long-serving and beloved principal of the Barnard Street School.

Gignilliat brothers Thomas (center) and Leigh with Navy Secretary Truman H. Newberry.[29]

Beginning in 1902, Heyward spent his summers working for his younger brother serving as the Director of Seamanship and Navigation at Culver's Summer Naval School. He was also a commander of the 3rd Division Naval Battalion of the Georgia State Troops.[27]

Less an example of transparent nepotism, Gignilliat wrote of his own brother that he had "a knack for handling boys" and for making seamanship "attractive and interesting to them." Gignilliat also credited his brother with introducing the popular rowing and sailing races that have become staples of the summer naval experience at Culver, and with inaugurating safety provisions that "appealed to parents without restricting too much the freedom of the boys in the water."[28] These observations from the exacting commander of the summer experiences indicate that Heyward deserved his position in Culver's Summer Naval School based upon his qualifications and retained it as result of his abilities as a capable educator and effective trainer of young men who functioned within the expected manner of Culver faculty.

The following description comes from Heyward's obituary:

> *"...it may be said that from earliest boyhood he was noted for
> a disposition singularly sweet but coupled with unflinching
> resolution. Not aggressive, but of unfailing physical and moral
> courage, he sought in a quiet way to impart to all with whom
> he came in contact his own love for all that was noble, true and
> beautiful in life, and his aversion to everything that tended to
> lower and degrade. Thus lived and thus has passed away, too
> soon, a son of the south, true to its best traditions – un chevalier
> sans peur et sans reproache."* [a fearless gentleman who was
> above reproach]"

With the passing of his brother, Gignilliat lost a family member, capable educator of boys, and good friend. Unfortunately, this would not be the only loss he would suffer in the next six months.

The Loss of a Mentor and Father-figure

Just as the 1911 summer session ended and the 1911-1912 school year was about to begin, word came that Culver's Superintendent Emeritus, Colonel Alexander Fleet, died at his daughter Belle's house in Atlanta on September 3, 1911. While perhaps not a surprise, as Fleet had been ill since December 1908, his passing was still received by the Culver community with great sadness.

Glascock, who had been with Fleet since 1894 at the Missouri Military Academy, recalled that the success of Culver during Fleet's tenure had been a labor of love but that that labor had been of the "hard and unceasing" variety. According to Glascock, "Colonel Fleet...had an almost oppressive sense of the great responsibility of his task," yet he applied his abiding faith in his own abilities to serve the school exceptionally well.[30] Glascock spoke for many who rightly credit Fleet with not only saving CMA but also developing it and allowing it to prosper and grow under his stewardship. Indeed, HH Culver's wife Emily Jane, along with sons BB and ER, could scarcely have been more pleased with Fleet's success in enhancing the living memorial to HH Culver.

Gignilliat led a formal delegation from Culver to attend the funeral in Atlanta in his official capacity as superintendent. The loss must have impacted him greatly, as he not only lost a mentor but one who was somewhat of a father-figure to him. It might have been even more impactful than the loss of his own father when he was 11 years old.

Minnie lost her beloved father. Although six months pregnant at the time, Minnie traveled with the official party to Atlanta. Her younger sister

Belle had married the former Missouri Military Academy Commandant Kenneth Matheson, who Fleet respected highly. Matheson was serving as an English professor at Georgia Tech, and the loss must have impacted him deeply as well. Given the pain of the loss to her mother, sister Belle, and Matheson (who Minnie knew well), Minnie stayed in Atlanta a bit longer to comfort her family and help with the postmortem requirements.

Upon his return to campus, and as evidence of the impact Fleet's passing had on him, Gignilliat published a special order at the opening of the winter school session on September 26, 1911. The order directed that the Culver colors be draped in black mourning cloth for a period of 30 days and that the officers of the military staff and cadet officers wear a knot of black crepe on the hilt of their sabers. These actions were traditional signs of respect for a fallen comrade in the military, and Gignilliat did well implementing them to honor one who had meant so much to the Academy and him.[31]

Greiner Named Permanent Commandant

Culver's first Mess Hall on the first floor of Main Barrack, 1895-1902.[33]

Gignilliat also made another significant decision at the beginning of the 1911 winter school session. Having watched Bert Greiner closely while functioning as temporary commandant in his own stead over the preceding 12 months, Gignilliat was evidently pleased with what he had observed and impressed with Greiner's performance. Gignilliat also likely realized that his initial plan of serving as both superintendent and commandant simultaneously was as impractical as it was unrealistic.

As a result, Gignilliat published a special order on the second day of the new term – September 27, 1911 – appointing Greiner as CMA's permanent Commandant of Cadets and promoting him to the rank of major.[32] While his two principle deputies – Glascock and Greiner – had been Fleet's men, each now owed their positions to Gignilliat and had earned his full confidence. They were and would remain among his staunchest supporters as Culver's leader.

The New Mess Hall – The Culver's "Greater Culver" Plan Put in Action

As the cornerstone of the "Greater Culver" plan, the Culvers initiated their work by beginning construction on a new mess hall for the campus in 1910. This was important for two reasons:

Culver's old Tabernacle building and second Mess Hall, 1902-1911.[34]

- It was a much-needed improvement for the campus, with its expanding corps; and

- It provided a visible demonstration of the Culver family's commitment to its "Greater Culver" plan announced in spring 1909.

The new Mess Hall represented a giant leap forward for the Academy in terms of facilities. After the Chautauqua burned down, the earliest dining hall was on the first floor of the rebuilt Main Barrack. The kitchen adjoined it but was located in the annex, along with the power plant. As Gignilliat mentioned in his memoirs, the superintendent and his staff took all their meals there with the cadets.

Exterior of Culver's new Mess Hall in 1911 (looking west).[35]

Following the construction of the first gymnasium in 1902, the Mess Hall was moved from Main Barrack and relocated in the Academy's old gymnasium, formerly the Chautauqua tabernacle.

The Tabernacle building served as the Academy's Mess Hall until mid-April 1911, when the new Mess Hall opened.

Planned and constructed during the period 1909-1911, the new Mess Hall brought major construction to the grounds and altered the layout of the campus. Its size wholly dominated the west side of the campus, but gaining consensus on its design was somewhat challenging.

According to Hartman, "Construction of the Mess Hall in 1911 had its genesis in 1909, when James I. Barnes, a contractor from Logansport, Ind., submitted the winning bid. Correspondence between the Culver family and architect Albert Knell indicates an on-going argument over several aspects of the design, including the tile floor and certain decorative aspects of the interior." Architect Knell supported contractor Barnes, and the Culver family reluctantly agreed in August 1909 to accept Barnes' bid of $86,600 to construct the building (equating to almost $3 million in 2023 dollars).

Outfitting the structure with furniture, kitchen equipment (including ranges from the Wrought Iron Range Company), and a state-of-the-art refrigeration system brought the total cost of the new Mess Hall to an astonishing $150,000 (which equates to just a little over $5 million in 2023 dollars). The Culvers thus made an extraordinary statement of commitment to the school by funding its construction, along with a tremendous show of support for the first phase of their 1909 "Greater Culver" plan.

As Acting Superintendent for much of this period, Gignilliat was involved significantly in the discussions regarding the planning for the new Mess Hall. As a trained engineer, he was almost certainly on site most days reviewing the progress, overseeing costs, supervising the construction of this massive project, and managing its impact on campus.

The new Mess Hall was a remarkably well-designed structure. The east tower was later modified to support the clock donated by the Class of 1927, and the south entrances were remodeled to provide easier access to the ground floor. Despite these minor changes, this exceptionally well planned and constructed building remains much as it was when opened in spring 1911.

As it turns out, it was also a wise investment by the Culver family that provided incalculable returns for CMA for many reasons. The new structure displaced the rail spur leading to the annex of Main Barrack and the coal dumping location for campus further north to a new power plant facility, which was a welcome aesthetic and functional change.

It also allowed for the creation of a useful quadrangle in the newly open ed area vacated by the rail spur and coal dumping location. Cadets held formations on the newly created quad just east of it until the Administration building was built in 1913 (see photo).

With an interior area measuring 90 x 130 feet, the expansive hall, much larger than the whole Tabernacle building, was able to seat the entire corps of cadets at once and capable of providing seating for around 1,000 people. State-of-the-art food preparation facilities, including a spacious and very modern kitchen equipped with Wrought Iron ranges, a bakery annex on the third floor where the kitchen staff produced all of the Academy's bread and baked goods, and a refrigeration system that kept vegetables fresh, milk (piped in from the dairy room to the dining hall) cool, and ice cream (also made by the kitchen staff) cold, allowed the cadets to eat family-style. Meals were served by an impressive staff of waiters held to strict standards of appearance and conduct on par with those of the cadets. The ever-pragmatic ER Culver personally designed a metal frame for the back of the chairs to hold the folded overcoat and hat of the occupant.

Opened in 1911, and as impressive as its exterior was, its interior grandeur was even more remarkable and immediately evident to visitors. Entering through large double-doors into a functional vestibule serving as a barrier to the outside conditions, the most striking feature was the broad expanse of floor without supporting pillars – a revolutionary (for its time) free-standing ceiling, allowing for an exceptionally large undisturbed area for

seating. The ceiling itself was supported by 100-foot steel trusses and divided by three 25-foot skylights, thus providing ample natural lighting, reducing its weight, and supplementing the light provided by electric sconces.

The sidewalls, wainscoted in white marble broken at intervals by green marble pilasters, were beautiful,

Interior of Culver's new Mess Hall, opened in April 1911, looking west.[37]

and the addition in 1934 of four murals depicting scenes from Indiana history contributed by the graduating class of 1928 further enhanced the attractiveness of the interior and have become important parts of the building's heritage.

The main floor of the Mess Hall was constructed of small green, wine, and white tiles made in Georgia. They were laid in 1911 by a family from Elkhart and became a focal point of the expansive floor. In 1986, structural flaws in the sub-floor required its virtual demolition, but it was replicated exactly in color and design by the same company that had installed it originally.[36]

A mezzanine at the east end of the new Mess Hall contained comfortable wicker furnishings and provided a more intimate area for guests to dine while also allowing visitors to gaze over the entire structure with a view much like that in the accompanying photograph. Ever pragmatic, this feature was and is also used frequently for more routine meetings over a meal.

The magnificent new Mess Hall was dedicated on April 17, 1911 with an equally impressive ceremony. Indiana Governor Thomas Marshall (later to serve as Woodrow Wilson's Vice President, 1913-21) was the honored guest. Along with Marshall, Gignilliat also in invited the President of Purdue University, Dr. Winthrop E. Stone, and noted Indiana author Meredith Nicholson Stone, along with the former President of DePauw University, Dr. Hillary A. Gobin, to ensure they were aware of the Culver facilities and assist in Culver's marketing and college placement efforts.

An ulterior motive may also have been to show his invited guests that Culver's physical plant was impressive and on par with the two other Indiana educational institutions represented.[38]

After reviewing the corps, Gignilliat hosted a sumptuous banquet to christen the new facility. Ever the gracious host, Gignilliat invited every local dignitary

Gignilliat escorting Indiana Governor Thomas Marshall and others in an inspection of the Corps of Cadets as part of the dedication ceremony for the new Mess Hall, April 17, 1911.[39]

Banquet for the formal dedication of the New Mess Hall, April 17, 1911.[41]

to the banquet, filling it to capacity and demonstrating its remarkable ability to feed such a large number of people so quickly and efficiently.

Governor Marshall was the primary speaker, and at the time he was beginning to be mentioned as a possible candidate to become the next President of the United States. When Gignilliat introduced Marshall, he said the following:

"We have long wanted Governor Marshall to visit Culver. We have especially coveted the honor of having him address the young men of this corps. We took a great deal of pleasure showing him around today, in letting him see our new Mess Hall, but we especially wanted him to see the Black Horse Troop and its possibilities as a presidential escort. ("Great applause," the official record here remarks.) Governor Marshall, the organization is a direct descendant of a famous inaugural escort. It is subject to your orders, sir, either for the Mexican border or Pennsylvania Avenue."

According to Gignilliat, Marshall responded somewhat laconically by saying, "If I go, you go."[40]

Throughout the day, Gignilliat and Marshall got along exceptionally well. Their meeting on this day and continued association afterwards, along with Gignilliat's periodic urgings in 1912 and 1913, set in motion a chain of events that resulted in the entire Culver Corps of Cadets marching down Pennsylvania Avenue in March, 1913 as Marshall's official escort in the presidential inaugural parade.

Military Equipment in 1911

At the beginning of the 1911 school year, Gignilliat's untiring efforts promoting the quality of Culver's military system again bore fruit. The War Department recognized the excellence of Culver's military training system by providing the school with a new supply of excellent equipment to support the training of its winter school military battalion. This included 320 of the Army's .30 caliber 1898 magazine-fed rifles, field equipment including web belts and suspenders, haversacks, canteens, and other items; four 3-inch breech-loading field artillery pieces equipped with harness for mounted drill; 60 pistols, 60 sabers, and 60 magazine-fed carbines for cavalry drill. To support training, the government also furnished an abundant supply of blank ammunition for field exercises and live ammunition for marksmanship practice.

The Navy also recognized Culver's value, issuing new equipment to support the training in its Summer Naval School that supported the summer naval battalion organized as Indiana's official Naval Reserve force as of 1909. This equipment included a sub-target gun designed to teach cadets how to fire a rifle that could be used indoors and without ammunition; the latest model of its 4-inch naval gun with telescopic sites and an electrical priming device; state-of-the-art Morris tube equipment for target practice; and four 1-pounder rapid-fire Hotchkiss guns.

Demonstrating its own commitment to maintaining its military training programs at the highest levels, Culver spent much to supplement the government-issued equipment. This included providing complete sets of tack and other required horse equipment for the Cavalry department, and field telephones, telegraphs, and other portable wireless equipment for signal training. In conjunction with the state of Indiana, Culver also managed to provide sufficient tentage, cots, and field kitchen equipment to support the cadets field training.[42] In aggregate, Culver's military programs were as well equipped and supplied as any in the nation, allowing it to deliver exceptional training and make it "real" in accordance with Gignilliat's convictions.

The Iron Gate Ceremony – Gignilliat Establishes a Hallowed Academy Tradition

The story of how the tradition of the Iron Gate ceremony came into being is fascinating, and it provides another illustration of the innate natural partnering between ER Culver and Gignilliat, along with Gignilliat's own uncanny appreciation of the power of ceremony and sense of what appealed to boys.

ER and his wife found the gate while traveling in Europe sometime during the first decade of the 20th century. Given the family business, ER was particularly struck by the handsome wrought iron gate, so he purchased it and brought it back to Culver without any specific purpose but certain it would be used in one of Culver's new buildings. This was entirely fitting, since it was made out of the very substance upon which the Culver family's livelihood had depended for so long. However, the gate did not fit in any of the existing structures at Culver, and it was placed in storage for some later, unspecified use, and largely forgotten.[43]

As Culver's new Superintendent, Gignilliat was searching for a way to incorporate some meaning into the June Week festivities overall and especially in the commencement ceremony itself. Hartman wrote that Gignilliat was "determined to structure the closing of a Culver experience and the state of a new life as a very special event, " which, along

Photo of an early Final Formation in front of Main Barrack.[45]

with all of the other June Week events and the final ball, would ensure that it would be indelibly etched into the memories of all who witnessed it, especially the graduating cadets.[44]

Sometime during his first year as superintendent, Gignilliat discovered the Iron Gate in storage (without the eagle, which was not added until the 1960s) and recognized it as the symbol for which he had been searching. The idea was simple: graduating cadets would depart from the final formation, march to Gignilliat, receive their diploma from him, and then proceed through the Iron Gate and into their new lives.[46]

Possessing a keen eye for meaning and symbolism, Gignilliat believed that there could be no better way for a graduate to "pass through the outer gate of secondary education and to the broader paths of university life" metaphorically than by physically passing through a symbolic gate at Culver as the cadet's final act during June Week and after leaving the corps assembled for the emotional Final Formation. To make it useful for his purpose, he took this rather simple gate and had a stand built for it, instantly creating an icon of the Culver experience.

Ever the showman, Gignilliat did not bring out the Iron Gate until the day of graduation, June 8, 1911. As part of the solemn ceremony, Glascock was to come forward and unlock the gate to allow access to the cadets who had earned the privilege of passing through it during their special

The Iron Gate circa 1915 and much as it looked when Gignilliat "discovered" it.[47]

day. Alas, Colonel F. L. Hunt recalled that the event almost did not go as planned, as Glascock broke the key off in the gate's large padlock during a practice held immediately prior to the actual ceremony. Knowing how important the symbolism of this event was to Gignilliat, the excitable Glascock hurriedly summoned John McCormick, the Academy's longtime carpenter, to break one of the links on the chain using a file to allow the gate to be opened. Thus, from the very first was the unlocking of the Iron Gate ceremonial, but many remembered the high level of anxiety regarding the event decades later.[48]

During the actual commencement ceremony, Henry Clay "Easy" Anderson, by virtue of his last name and the alphabet, was the first Culver graduate to pass through the Iron Gate. Anderson led the other 47 members of his class on this historic symbolic passage during which they passed through the Iron Gate from the life of a cadet into a world filled with new experiences.[49]

Ever mindful of the importance of the moment, Gignilliat took advantage of the opportunity available during his final moments as their "commander" to make the occasion even more meaningful. As he handed him his diploma, Gignilliat charged each cadet to remain cognizant of what it meant to be a Culver graduate – a "Culver man" in the parlance of the period – out in the world and able to look him in the eye and state with utter certainty that, "I have been dependable" to what it means to be a Culver Man (which would shortly be identified as the Spirit of Culver) to be allowed access to the campus as an

Culver's First Iron Gate Ceremony, June 8, 1911. [51] Gignilliat is in the center to the left of the Iron Gate.

alumnus of the institution. Cadets never forgot these parting words, which served to remind them of their greater responsibilities to society and the institution as they completed their time at Culver.

This symbolic passage immediately became a hallowed Culver tradition at the winter school commencement exercises. Gignilliat rightly gauged the visual impact it would have on the spectators, but he was perhaps not as prepared for the emotional impact this relatively simple act had on the graduating cadets, becoming, as Hartman told it, "an image burned into the brain of every cadet," along with "the most prized of all his marches," and perhaps "the most treasured of all cadet memories."[50]

Culver's First Alumni Association

During his first year as superintendent, Gignilliat also determined that the school's alumni needed an organization to allow them to remain connected to the institution and keep abreast of its affairs. He decided to form the Culver Alumni Association for the more than 400 graduates

Gignilliat with his two sons, Leigh Jr. (left) and Fred, which Henry Joined in December 1911.[55]

of the school as a way of enacting his policy for maintaining close contact with alumni and to leverage the great strength of his close personal relationships with many of them. This relationship had been fostered and enhanced by the hospitable and kindly personality of Minnie, who endeavored to have every cadet in her home at least once a year during their time at Culver.[52]

Gignilliat invited about 100 alumni to return to campus for June Week 1911. They observed the performance of the corps, participated in the festivities, witnessed the first Iron Gate ceremony, and became reconnected with the Academy just at Gignilliat had hoped.[53]

During the 1911 June Week, Gignilliat formally initiated the Culver Alumni Association as a permanent entity at a business meeting in the new Mess Hall by establishing a constitution and by-laws, and electing officers. Dues were set at $2 a year. With that, the organization was up and running. Growing rapidly, there were more than one hundred active members by 1914. This organization would become the Culver Legion in 1916.[54]

Birth of Gignilliat's Third Child – Henry Culver Gignilliat

1911 came to close on a joyous occasion for the Gignilliat family. Just after the winter recess began, Minnie gave birth to the Gignilliat's third child on December 23 in Culver, a healthy baby boy named, fittingly, Henry Culver Gignilliat, and called "Hank" by the family. Although there was quite a large age gap between Henry and his two brothers, Leigh Jr. and Fred, the Gignilliat family was now complete and quite happy in their Indiana home.

Bertram Beach "BB" Culver.[56]

The Gignilliat family was living happily in their cottage next to Fleet's previous home, their household was served faithfully by their housekeeper and cook, Anna and Bertha Byrd, and after the sadness of loss of Gignilliat's brother and Minnie's father earlier in the year, the joy of Henry's birth helped them to end 1911 happily and look forward eagerly to the promise of 1912.

1912 – The Partnership with ER Culver Begins, and the Founding of Woodcraft Camp

Despite his hopes for a brighter year, 1912 began with yet another death. HH Culver Jr died unexpectedly on January 22, 1912, at the young age of 41 years old. Gignilliat, accompanied by Greiner, led a detachment of cadets that included all of the company commanders and the color guard to attend the funeral services in St. Louis and represent the school. This death, while tragic on its own, was to have tremendous impact on Culver as an institution and on Gignilliat himself.

Since HH Sr's death on September 26, 1897, and because his eldest son, Walter Llewellyn, was not involved in the family business, HH Jr. had been running the Wrought Iron Range Company in St. Louis. With the death of HH Jr, the very business-minded Bertram Beach "BB" Culver was the family's best choice to assume responsibility for running the Wrought Iron Range Company. A little organizational history is in order to help understand the formal relationship between the Wrought Iron Range Company and CMA, and the impact of HH Jr's death.

For its first eight years from its founding in 1894, CMA had been organized and run by the Culver family somewhat informally as an association. During the period of its status as an association, HH Culver Sr. served as the head until his death in 1897, followed by BB Culver from October 1897 to December 1899. Edwin Raymond "ER" Culver took over as its head in January 1900. This arrangement explains why it was ER Culver who made the final decision supporting Gignilliat's "Big Fire" recommendation to dismiss the 100-plus perpetrators in November 1900.

Five years after the death of HH Sr., the family decided to formalize the association by incorporating the school in 1902. Upon incorporation, BB Culver became president, putting his business expertise at the disposal of the Culver family's second most significant business interest. To provide assistance, ER Culver became the corporation's secretary. Since it was a family-owned entity, the corporation's stock was divided equally among the six children of HH Culver Sr.: Walter Llewellyn, Henry Harrison Jr, Edwin Raymond (ER), Bertram Beach (BB), Ida Culver Wintermute, and Knight K. Culver.

While the Culver siblings remained stockholders, it was only BB and ER who were involved with CMA (Walter sold his stock to ER and BB in 1909, and Knight made occasional appearances at Culver events on behalf of the family). In 1928, ER and BB bought out all of their siblings' shares to create the non-profit Culver Education Foundation and make a gift of the school to it as an enduring monument to HH Culver Sr. This was intended to occur in 1930, but ER's untimely death delayed the process until June 1932, and the CEF assumed sole ownership of CMA by summer 1933.[57] More will be said about this process in a later chapter.

Edwin Raymond "ER" Culver.[59]

While ER was involved somewhat in decisions regarding the Academy for the first ten years of the corporation, from 1902 until his permanent departure in 1910 it was BB Culver and Superintendent Fleet who made all substantive decisions about CMA. As a result, BB Culver and Fleet developed a close professional and personal relationship. However, during this period Gignilliat traveled on corps' trips with ER (e.g., 1907 Jamestown, and 1908 Great Lakes cruise), and the two established a firm foundation of collegiality and mutual respect.

With the untimely death of HH Jr., BB vacated his position as President of the CMA corporation to assume responsibility for running the Culver family's principal business, the family-owned Wrought Iron Range Company. This moved ER up from his position as Secretary of the CMA corporation to become its president in early 1912.[58]

This change in governance was significant and benefited Gignilliat by allowing him to work closely with the more creatively oriented ER, a man with whom he shared much in common in terms of vision, character, and temperament. While Gignilliat had a good relationship with BB, the kinship that had developed between him and ER was more substantive and intimate, and it provided a basis for Gignilliat to establish the kind of relationship with ER as President of the CMA corporation that Fleet had been able to do with BB during Fleet's tenure as superintendent.

Of the same mind and of unerringly similar thinking, the pairing of ER and Gignilliat in their respective roles proved to be both effective and fortuitous for the school over the ensuing 18 years of their association. The quiet and reserved ER was content to support Gignilliat's ideas and remain inconspicuously in the background, allowing the more flamboyant and energetic Gignilliat to implement his ideas and bask in the attention he attracted as the face of Culver and its frontman. This relationship certainly contributed significantly to Gignilliat's own successes and that of CMA by securing the backing of a corporate president who readily eschewed the limelight and shared his imagination, supported his endeavors, and trusted his judgment.

Founding of Woodcraft Camp

Hartman tells us that, "In his monograph saluting the Woodcraft Camp's 75th anniversary, Major Dick Zimmerman noted that the success of the Naval and Cavalry schools was so impressive that parents asked the trustees if they would not bend on the age requirements and let younger boys attend. Gignilliat and Rossow heard their requests but determined that handling 28-foot cutters and managing cavalry training would be too strenuous for boys under 14. However, the die was cast. Gignilliat saw a 'beautiful lake, unlimited opportunities for the study of trees, flowers, birds, fish, and all outdoor things,'" and on this basis the idea for the Woodcraft Camp began to take form.

What happened next, as Gignilliat remembered it, was that he became quite impressed by a group of "smart, trim-looking youngsters in khaki shorts, and with neckerchiefs knotted about their shoulders" he noticed while on holiday in London with his wife in fall 1911. After asking a great many questions and talking to some of the boys, he learned that they were members of the World Scout Movement, founded by the dynamic Sir Robert S. S. Baden Powell in England. Gignilliat purchased a Scout manual and other pamphlets about scouting activities, along with an entire Scout uniform in London. He credits this encounter with the inspiration for establishing the Woodcraft Camp at Culver along the lines of Baden-Powell's group of Boy Scouts.[60]

The 1912 Woodcraft Camp catalog provides the following justification for the founding of the Woodcraft Camp, influenced heavily by Gignilliat if not written completely by him:

> *"Each summer between three and four hundred boys, coming from almost every state, many of them even from the Pacific coast, gather at Culver for the eight weeks' session of the naval and cavalry schools. Each summer also many applications have been received from boys under the required age and size. Some of these applicants have been accepted as an experiment, but it was found that they could not enter satisfactorily into the full activities planned for the older cadets; such things as the handling of fourteen foot (sic) oars in the navy cutters and the mounted exercises of the cavalry school are rather heavy work for boys under fourteen. Yet there are many things in the summer at Culver that these younger boys would enjoy and from which they would gain much in muscle and all round training and development. For this reason the officers of the school have spent much time in planning a course that would be as interesting and ideally suited to boys between twelve and fourteen as the naval and cavalry schools have proven for boys between fourteen and twenty. The woodcraft school is the result. It is to be entirely distinct from the other schools. It gives just the things that will be of natural interest to red blooded (sic), wide wake (sic) boys in their early teens and it is to be under the personal direction of a man who of all outdoor men in America is perhaps best fitted to make the course a splendid success."[61]*

Upon his return to Culver in fall 1911, Gignilliat discussed his idea for the Woodcraft Camp with members of the Culver family. Overcoming concerns that such a venture might be too "juvenile" for the Culver system, Gignilliat secured approval and funding for his idea "with the understanding that the Camp should be entirely separate from that of the older boys of the Naval School and should have its own separate staff of instructors."[62]

The change in governance in early 1912 did little to impede progress of establishing the new summer program, as ER Culver proved to be quite supportive of it. Named the Culver Woodcraft Camp, it opened in the summer of 1912, and according to Gignilliat, "flourished from the first." In fact, Gignilliat observed that, "many of the finest boys who have graduated from the winter school got their first introduction to Culver at the Woodcraft Camp."[63]

The connection with the Boy Scouts was explicit, deliberate, and significant from the start. According to Gignilliat, "When the first Woodcraft Camp at Culver was started, we enlisted the services of Dan Beard as its head," and it was Beard to which the 1912 Woodcraft Camp catalog referred as "a man who of all outdoor men in America is perhaps best fitted to make the course a splendid success."[64] Serving as the director of the Boy Scouts of America after having co-founded the organization in 1910, Beard became the "officer in immediate charge" of the Culver Woodcraft Camp. The influence of Beard planted the seeds of a burgeoning scouting movement at Culver that remains strong to this day.

"Uncle Dan" was a man after Gignilliat's own heart, as he was a great showman who wore a beaded buckskin shirt while presiding over the Woodcraft School's council fires, a touch that the showman in Gignilliat appreciated. Beard also subscribed to Gignilliat's firm believe that boys wanted things to be "real" in order for them to have meaning. According to Gignilliat, "Under [Beard's] spell there was not make-believe in anything the Woodcrafters did. For the moment at least, they became real Indians, real Daniel Boones and Davey Crocketts."[65]

Culver took advantage of Beard's name recognition, titling the first Woodcraft catalog as Culver's "Summer of Woodcraft under Dan Beard." Culver also took advantage of its own brand recognition, highlighting on the second page of the catalog that the Woodcraft Camp was "under [the] same management as the well known (sic) Culver Military Academy, Culver Summer Naval School, and Culver Summer Cavalry School," and noting that "the Culver Summer Schools (Naval and Cavalry) have acquired a world-wide reputation for their success in providing a really well-organized, profitable and

"Uncle Dan" Beard in his beaded buckskin shirt.[66]

CULVER,
Summer School of Woodcraft

Under Direction of Dan Beard
Culver (On Lake Maxinkuckee) Indiana
NINETEEN HUNDRED AND TWELVE

Culver Military Academy   Culver Summer Naval School
Culver Summer Cavalry School

Inside cover of 1912 Woodcraft Camp catalog.[68]

interesting summer for boys."[67] Finally, the catalog reflected the influence of Scouting, featuring a boy dressed in a scout-like uniform enjoying himself in nature. It was a powerful and effective image created by Beard that also smacks of the influence of Gignilliat.

Writing specifically to parents, the 1912 Woodcraft Camp catalog quoted from Beard as follows: "A boy like a tree grows best with his toes in the ground," making the point that the environment of nature will be more beneficial than the urban areas in which many of the boys lived. The catalog also identified the ages of 12-14 as a period in the development of every boy in which he is "peculiarly susceptible to the influences of the open," creating the opportunity for attendance at the Woodcraft Camps to make use of "Nature herself [to] become his teacher, imparting to him lessons of resourcefulness, courage, and patience, and planting in him a love for the open such that he may return to it in after years for refreshment and inspiration."

The message closed by suggesting to parents that they "will find [that] the course here offers something better organized and far more purposeful and effective than the ordinary type of summer camp," and that they will be both "gratified and surprised by the remarkable results obtained in the eight weeks at Culver." This final element of the message reflected the purposes of Culver's other summer programs quite closely, along with Gignilliat's own views. Given Gignilliat's involvement from the initial conception,

Ernest Thompson Seton enthralling boys with stories.[72]

it also indicates that if he did not draft it himself, he was closely involved with the writing of it.[69]

Not satisfied with bringing only one of the country's most prominent scouting advocates on board, Gignilliat also hired the renowned Ernest Thompson Seton to work at Culver's Woodcraft Camp. It was Seton's influence that was responsible for the Woodcraft focus on Indian lore, which paired nicely with the Woodcraft council ring that inspired many a boy and set their hearts afire in such an enchanted environment. Seton was also responsible for the totem poles brought in from Alaska that marked the Woodcraft streets, and he sketched the designs of Indian symbols that adorned the Woodcraft tents.

Gignilliat appreciated Seton's uncanny ability to "make things along the trail [come] gloriously alive" by making a story out of every tree, flower, rabbit track, and nest of turtle eggs baking in the sand. Dick Zimmerman, who wrote a monograph saluting Woodcraft's 75th anniversary, highlighted Seton's remarkable ability to "teach the secrets of the wild, impart the wisdom of the Indians, preside at the Council Ring, and inspire campers to see the wonders and beauties of the forest and field" that appealed to them and made their Woodcraft experience so memorable.[70] This approach not only succeeded in capturing the boys' interest, but they remembered the stories and learned from them, promoting a lasting interest in nature that transcended their Woodcraft experience.[71]

These abilities of Seton appealed to Gignilliat's desire to hire staff who could make every aspect of the Culver experience contribute positively to the development of the boy in ways that were lasting and meaningful.

The first Woodcraft Camp was located just east of the current Riding Hall. The proximity of this site to the stables and riding hall made this site ideal for the Summer Cavalry School since 1907. However, out of desire to keep the younger campers as close to the main campus as possible, this location, defined by a nearby quarter-mile running track and known as the Oval, became the site of the Woodcraft Camp. The Summer Cavalry School was moved across the road (old US 10) and north of the new infirmary.

Woodcraft Camp tents.[74]

The eight-week Woodcraft Camp ran from June 27 to August 22, 1912 for boys between the ages of 12 and 14. The first 36 boys were called "Woodcrafters," and they lived in pairs in weatherproof tents with flies extended over the front and sides, raised floors, and mosquito netting. Reflecting the shared belief of both Gignilliat and Beard regarding the positive contribution of fresh air to the health of boys, the catalog noted that while occupying these relatively permanent structures, "the boy sleeps as it were in the open air, flaps being opened around the entire upper part of the tent so that there is perfect circulation of air without draft." Two adult instructors lived on-site with the boys to provide guidance, oversight, and care.[73]

"Uncle Dan" Beard at Woodcraft Camp.[75]

The boys learned about a variety of subjects, including camping, birds, fish, and forestry. Instruction in camping addressed the selection of a proper camp site; how to purify, drain, and store water in the wilderness; proper waste disposal in nature; building temporary tents, shelters, and camp beds in the wilderness; the proper use of camp utensils; first aid; taking care of health in camp; suitable camp clothing and outfits; and even the building of a canoe. Woodcrafters were also taught how to recognize various species of birds, fish, trees, and shrubs, along with how to take and preserve specimens of each and record their observations efficiently. The boys were taught how to swim and fish in Lake Maxinkuckee, which they surely enjoyed. Woodcrafters participated in their own versions of Culver's athletic and non-sectarian religious services, rounding out their program of instruction. This was a tremendously practical curriculum that allowed for much activity and placed emphasis on having fun and learning by doing.

The Scouting-based Woodcraft approach of earning badges by learning about and demonstrating abilities related to outdoor activities was similar to the TUXIS system of development and advancement already in place in the Summer Naval and Cavalry schools since 1908. However, the TUXIS system was specifically designed for older boys (aged 14 and up), whereas the Woodcraft approach was designed to be more appropriate for the younger boys aged 12-14. The similarities helped to make the more developmentally appropriate Woodcraft approach a seamless addition to Culver's summer programs.

By all accounts, the first session was quite successful along the lines of the Summer Cavalry School in 1907 and not like the disappointing first session of the Summer Naval School in 1902. It is worth noting that Gignilliat had been intimately involved in the first sessions of the two successful camps and not with the first session of the less successful Summer Naval School, although it, too, flourished once Gignilliat became involved with it after its first iteration.

Gignilliat had succeeded in not only finding ways to make summer programs related to Culver's existing programs successful, but with the establishment of the Woodcraft Camp, he had gone beyond the particular niche of effectively developing boys aged 14-20 that Culver had established, adapting and expanding it to work well with boys aged 12-14. This helped to enhance the Culver brand, increase its stature and financial sustainability, and extend its reach to an entirely new population of boys and their patrons. This was quite a remarkable feat to accomplish within the first two years of his superintendency, and it must have confirmed the Culver's family's confidence in turning the school over to him.[76]

Gignilliat's Involvement with Scouting and Baden-Powell's 1912 Visit to Culver

In conjunction with establishing the Woodcraft Camp at Culver, Gignilliat became involved with the burgeoning Scouting movement in America. The background of Scouting helps shed light on Gignilliat's interest in and attraction to the Scouting movement.

The international Scouting movement was established by Baden-Powell as an outgrowth of his experiences in the Boer War when he organized a group of boys to serve as messengers and scouts. Like Gignilliat, Baden-Powell believed in the capabilities of boys, and he saw the important contributions they could make in times of crisis and when the conditions were real.

Scouting was designed to appeal to restless, impulsive, and unpredictable boys approaching their teens, using the outdoors as a way to channel their energy, give them purpose, provide them direction, and develop their character. In America, Dan Beard, with his "Sons of Daniel Boone," and Ernest Thompson Seton, with his "Seton's Woodcraft Indians," among others, were doing similar things with boys. While these programs and others like them were quite popular in America, it was Baden-Powell who, while acknowledging that he acquired many of his ideas from the programs of Beard and Seton, succeeded in putting the whole concept into the usable form of the Boy Scouts that transcended national interests and garnered international appeal.

James E. West was perhaps the person most responsible for the success of Scouting in America, and, at Gignilliat's invitation, he made use of Culver's Woodcraft Camp "as an early laboratory for Scouting and as a locale for one of the first, if not the first, schools for the training of Scoutmasters and Scout executives" in the country.[77] It was this association that led to Gignilliat being asked to lead the American delegation of Scouts and Counselors to the first International Boy Scout Jamboree in London in 1920.

Reviewing the first Boy Scouts of America Handbook, one is struck by the congruence between Scouting's principles and Gignilliat's system at Culver. On the first page of the original 1911 edition, scouting executive John L. Alexander succinctly expresses the purpose of Scouting as follows:

> *"The aim of the Boy Scouts is to supplement the various existing educational agencies, and to promote the ability in boys to do things for themselves and others...The method...is a combination of observation, deduction, and handiness, or the ability to do things...This is accomplished in games and team play, and is pleasure, not work, for the boy."[78]*

The "games and team play" were intended to prepare boys for the competition and combat they would likely face in life as adults.

It is important to note that this program depended upon competent adult leaders to be successful. Scouting was also something that boys could do with their fathers, adding a further positive appeal and attraction to it.

For the boy, "to be a scout means to be prepared to do the right thing at the right moment," along with being chivalrous, manly, and gentlemanly.[79] Gignilliat could have written these requirements himself, as they reflected some of the core tenets of the program he had designed and implemented at Culver.

Scouts needed to be physically fit, patriotic, good citizens, friendly and accepting, and imbued with an unshakable sense of honor. Honor was of particular importance in Scouting, considered to be a sacred thing that served as the basis for all of Scouting's values. A Scout's honor was his promise to do his best in all situations and to demonstrate manliness at all times.[80] This accomplished the other main purpose of Scouting – to help mold the character of the boy – along with preparing him for the competition and combat of life as an adult. These aspects of Scouting also resonated with Gignilliat deeply, and he could not fail to realize the complementary nature of Scouting and Culver.

It was not enough to know how to be good; a Scout had to demonstrate his commitment to Scouting by doing "a good turn daily," quietly, with the proper motive, and without boasting, to develop the habit of helping others, to honor God, and to demonstrate to others his commitment to following the Scouting way. This was in direct response to the prevalent belief that society overall – and most especially its boys – was in a general state of moral decline as a result of (among other influences), urbanization and industrialization.[81]

To counter these sinister influences on America's youth, Boy Scouts emerged with the audacious and lofty goals of creating an idealistic movement that would restore the moral fiber of the country's boys and help them become honorable, capable, and effective citizens and men.

To help Scouts do so, its guidelines they had to memorize and recite on command were phrased positively and in terms of what a Scout should do, not what he should avoid doing (as was much more common during this period).[82] Scouting promoted the triple tenets of brotherhood, good citizenship, and friendliness as returns for adhering to its guidelines.[83] In these ways did Scouting develop the entire capacity of the boy, very much akin to Culver's whole-boy educational approach, and help Scouts to become well-formed, well-informed, and well transformed.[84]

British Sir LTG Robert S. S. Baden-Powell.[86]

Following the Scouting path gave boys much-needed direction, allowing them to begin their preparation to become substantial men and achieve meaningful accomplishments. According to Scouting's approach, "the way for achievement in big things is the preparing of one's self for doing the big things – by going into training and doing the little things well."[85] These are sentiments echoed by Gignilliat during his time at Culver, making his strong attraction to Scouting quite understandable.

Scouting used an effective organizational method of small patrols (~ 8-10 boys) within a larger troop structure (~ 30-40 boys in several patrols) as a way of allowing boys to lead other boys within the troops and also provide a small group (i.e., the patrol) for each to belong while having fun, learning teamwork, acting with discipline, and developing leadership. According to the 1911 Boy Scout Handbook, "The patrol is the character school for the individual" – echoing Gignilliat's notion of CMA's units being "schools within a school" for many of the same reasons behind the Boy Scouts troop and patrol method of organization.

The Scouting approach was also inherently respectful of boys, allowing them to lead themselves, and it gave them permission to be boys, have fun, and be a little loud and rowdy (within limits). The mixture of discipline, fun, teamwork, and leadership may have differed in degree, but the intentions of Scouting and Culver shared many common elements and were far more similar than different from one another.

Scouting's organization and ranks appealed to boys' intrinsic attraction to both. The troop gave him something to belong to that was larger than himself, and reciting the Scout Oath in public allowed him to demonstrate his commitment to the organization and enjoy the feeling of belonging. The ranks provided him with the ability to know his place in the hierarchy and to improve his status through his own merits and advance forward in the Patrol file and troop without being in direct competition with his peers. Scouting's competition came in the form of teamwork and group projects, making them constructive bonding experiences instead of destructive ways of identifying winners and losers (the latter of which terrified young boys above all else). Scouting also came at just the right time when boys were beginning to ask life's big questions. To the question of "Who am I?," Scouting provided the answer of "A Scout." To the question of "What do I believe?", the answer was the Scout Law.

The Culver system offered similar appeals. Culver's organization and ranks appealed to boys' intrinsic attraction to both. The unit gave him something to belong to that was larger than himself, and wearing the Culver uniform and performing military drills in public allowed him to demonstrate his commitment to the institution and enjoy the feeling of belonging. The ranks provided him with the ability

PROGRAMME

Of Exercises on the Occasion of the Visit of

Lieutenant General

Sir Robert S. S. Baden-Powell, K.C.B., K.C.V.O.

to the

Culver Military Academy

CULVER, INDIANA

February 7, 1912

Program cover for Baden-Powell's visit.[87]

to know his place in the hierarchy and to improve his status through his own merits and advance in Culver's military system without being in direct competition with his peers. Culver's competition focused on the unit and came in the form of military teamwork and athletics, making them constructive bonding experiences. Culver also came at just the right time when boys were beginning to ask life's big questions. To the question of "Who am I?," CMA provided the answer of "A Culver cadet." To the question of "What do I want to become?", the answer was a Culver man.

Taken together, it is little wonder that Gignilliat became enamored with Scouting and cultivated a relationship with its leaders. Gignilliat hired the Chief Scout in America, Dan Beard, to establish the Woodcraft Camp in 1912. Securing perhaps an even greater coup, and demonstrating again his prowess at marketing, Gignilliat succeeded in having the well-known founder of the Scouting movement, British Lieutenant General Sir Robert S. S. Baden-Powell come to Culver in early 1912. Given the importance of this visit and his desire to make a positive impression on Baden-Powell, Gignilliat did all he could to showcase Culver to its distinguished visitor in the best possible light.

Upon his arrival at noon on February 7, 1912, Gignilliat, Glascock, and Greiner welcomed Baden-Powell to campus with the corps formed up in double ranks on either side of the walkway leading to the impressive new Mess Hall. As Baden-Powell passed by, the cadets executed a smart rifle salute, coming to "Present Arms" with remarkable precision while the artillery sounded a 15-gun salute in Baden-Powell's honor.

After lunch with the entire Culver community, the honored guest was escorted to the riding hall at 2:00 pm for an impressive program of military exercises that included a review of the corps, a demonstration of the manual of arms, a performance of the silent manual of arms set to music, a demonstration of cavalry exercises set to music, a rough riding exhibition, belt calisthenics, flag drill, roping, wall scaling, construction of a spar bridge, and Graeco-Roman races, concluding with a pyramid of riders on horseback to close out the performances.

The cadets were well aware of the significance of the occasion, and they took pride in the precision of the staging and execution of their performances. According to *The Vedette's* review of the military exercises, "The boys never showed to better advantage than in the various drills and exercises which followed one another without a moment's delay and which were performed with the snap and ginger only looked for in the spring after the drills in the field have begun to tell."[88]

The signaling drill, which involved around 200 cadets conducting semaphore messaging with flags, was new, thrilling the crowd with its precision. During the demonstration, the cadets wigwagged the Scout Motto, "Be Prepared" (a brilliant touch arranged by Gignilliat), which elicited both a smile and enthusiastic applause from Baden-Powell, proving to be "one of the most effective" demonstrations of the entire program in the assessment of the cadets.

At 3:45 pm Gignilliat introduced Baden-Powell, a hero of the Boer War, to present his address, "Scouting in War and Peace" by "very happily" (according to *The Vedette*) describing him as one who was "as distinguished in the pursuit of peace, viz.: the making of men, as he has been in war, and who by his effort in this direction has placed the world in his debt." Baden-Powell spoke mostly about his experiences in the Boer War, incorporating elements of Scouting into his accounts of his own experiences in war and peace.

According to *The Vedette*, the main idea that Baden-Powell wanted to convey was that "War between civilized people is a crime, and the scout qualities are to be cultivated for their value in making peaceful and valuable citizens," which was as interesting coming from a man with his background as a solider as it was for being delivered in the venue in which it was presented. Baden-Powell was apparently a captivating speaker, peppering his talk with memorable sayings such as, "You should carry, as well as paddle, your own canoe," "You gain character by doing things, or, in other words, by playing the game," and "A smile and a stick will carry you through almost any difficulty in life," which sounds a bit like Theodore Roosevelt's famous quote, "Walk softly and carry a big stick."

It is clear from *The Vedette's* account that the cadets enjoyed Baden-Powell's presentation. At the end of his presentation, the cadets delighted Baden-Powell by singing the Culver hymn and cheering him with nine boisterous "rahs," which was as unexpected as it was appreciated by their guest.

Baden-Powell ended his visit by paying Culver perhaps the ultimate compliment, stating, "I have seen the cadets of all nationalities at their work, and I must say that you beat the lot."[89] This was precisely the type of impact Gignilliat had hoped to make on such an influential dignitary, and he likely beamed with pride when Baden-Powell spoke these words.

During the visit, Gignilliat discussed his idea to establish a Woodcraft Camp at Culver, and Baden-Powell not only supported the idea enthusiastically but also suggested that certain elements of the scouting movement be incorporated into Culver's newest camp to curb any perceived military bent to the program. This overt association with Scouting was exactly what Gignilliat had hoped to establish, and having the name of Baden-Powell associated with the Woodcraft Camp brought instant recognition and creditability to the new program.

Gignilliat's Long Hunting Trip at the End of 1912

The remainder of 1911-1912 winter school session concluded without episode and with the second Iron Gate ceremony, now a Culver tradition. Then with little respite Gignilliat was heavily involved in the first Woodcraft Camp for 36 boys, which ran from June 27 to August 22, 1912. Gignilliat enjoyed this work and delighted in spending time with the boys outdoors, but the complexity of Culver's summer session – now comprised of three separate camps and two distinct age groups of boys – meant that the demands of direction and coordination increased significantly.

While he could certainly find time to go on a hike with the troopers, spend time on the water with the naval cadets, and attend campfire sessions with the Woodcrafters, the requirements to provide for, schedule, support, provision, and deconflict the activities of three separate camps presented greater challenges for Gignilliat during the 1912 summer session. However, he made good use of his enhanced skills as an administrator to make the opening of Woodcraft Camp and the 1912 summer session Culver's most successful to date.

Gignilliat's custom had become one in which he would work the week following the closing of the summer session before taking a vacation of three to six weeks with Minnie and his children, leaving the opening of the winter school session to the other two "Gs" on campus – the very capable Hugh Glascock and Bert Greiner. However, he did not follow this pattern in 1912 for any number of reasons. Perhaps he wanted to spend some time with his son Hank, who would turn nine months on September 23, 1912.

It may have also been a result of Culver welcoming its largest winter class ever of 385 cadets – comprised of 219 new cadets and 90 percent of the old cadets eligible to return – when the winter session began on September 18, 1912. This required the administration to find creative ways to house so many students, and the military department determined that it needed to increase the number of inspections significantly to ensure proper discipline and decorum was maintained within the corps.

At the start of the 1912-1913 winter school session, Gignilliat also rolled out what was called a new "polydeinic" system of rewards that he viewed to be very important. Based upon the TUXIS system used in the summer programs, the new winter school system supported all cadets to become better all-around students, soldiers, citizens, and athletes by rewarding merit for all who qualified and replacing the more competitive and less popular system that recognized few winners at the expense of many other losers. Implementing a system that "shares the honor with all who are willing to work hard without in the least decreasing its value" was very much in keeping with Gignilliat's own educational philosophy and likely took much effort and attention to make it effective. Given its importance to him and to the school, Gignilliat met with cadet representatives on October 4, 1912 "to discuss and settle the rules" for the new system before departing the next day for his trip.[90]

Most likely, however, was that Gignilliat remained to accompany the corps on its trip to Plymouth, Indiana on October 4, 1912 to hear an address by the New Jersey Governor and Democratic candidate for president of the United States Woodrow Wilson. The battalion traveled to the event by special train, but the BHT, with a record 100-plus troopers enrolled, 60 of whom were new, rode overland on horseback, perhaps accompanied by Gignilliat. Once in Plymouth, the BHT escorted Wilson from the courthouse to his private automobile, where gave a short address. The avowed advocate of peace Wilson said, "I am always glad to see the uniform worn in connection with education. To me it has a deeper meaning than as an attribute to war. It means discipline, of course, but in addition it signifies that a man is not living for himself, but for the social life at large," emphasizing that serving others is the greatest good a citizen can perform in a democracy.[91] Gignilliat would later quote from Wilson's address in *Arms and the Boy*, indicating that had a profound and lasting impact on him.

Whatever the reason for the delay, Gignilliat departed campus on October 5, 1912 for almost seven weeks to hunt moose, deer, and birds in Maine without Minnie, who remained a Culver with baby Hank. After stopping by the USS Arkansas anchored at New York City for a tour by a former Summer Naval School instructor (Ensign Ingram), Gignilliat arrived at a hunting camp in Glenwood, Maine, about 100 miles northeast of Bangor close to the border with New Brunswick.

The group stayed in cabins but spent as long as a week at a time in the woods on the hunt, where they slept "on fir branches and huddled together like pigs for warmth" while trying to stay dry and out of the snow. Freed from pressures of the unrelenting responsibility he faced at Culver, Gignilliat reported that he spent much of the time "laughing and joking and having a perfectly beautiful time out of hardships that would kill us anywhere else except outside in the Almighty's temple of health and good spirits – the great silent pine woods."[92]

Still, he sent back periodic dispatches to Culver that were mentioned in *The Vedette*, and he sent a very long account of his adventures that he wrote on November 17, 1912 to Culver, which appeared

A happy and rested Gignilliat (at left) with his hunting party and game in Maine, 1912.[94]

in *The Vedette* in its entirety on the same day of his return to campus, November 23, 1912.[93] The description of his physical exertions during that final week provide evidence that he was in very good shape at 37 years old.

Having worked virtually nonstop for the year since he returned from his vacation in London with his family in October 1911, the time away seemed to be very beneficial for him. He returned after seven weeks away "in the best of health," rested, and ready to re-engage with the demands of Culver. According to *The Vedette*, "Officers and cadets rejoice[d] over his home-coming," just in time for him to settle in for a month prior to the winter recess and enjoy the holidays with his family and the Culver community.[95] This restful reprieve would prove to be fortuitous, as he would have one of his busiest and most eventful years at Culver in 1913.

Looking Towards 1913

During his first two years as Culver's chief executive administrator, Gignilliat had developed as an administrator, refined his philosophy of education, and enhanced his capabilities as an educator by experimenting with new approaches and implementing innovative programs. With ER Culver as Culver's president, he gained a like-minded partner on whom he could rely upon for unconditional support in these endeavors. By the end of 1912 and after over two years of very hard work, Gignilliat was comfortable in his new role as Superintendent and in his relationship with ER Culver, and he was poised to begin putting his own stamp on Culver in ways that neither he nor any of his predecessors could have foreseen or imagined.

Chapter 7 – 1913 – The Year of Destiny: Moving Culver Beyond the Reign of Fleet and Finding the Spirit of Culver

After focusing intensely on the internal workings of Culver during his first years as Superintendent, Gignilliat began shifting his gaze beyond campus to some of the larger happenings around the country in 1913. These events included the presidential inaugural celebration, the devastating Midwest flood in early spring, and the country's burgeoning military preparedness movement. He also began to get a sense of the international situation during his Mediterranean cruise with the US Navy at the end of the year.

The Invitation to Participate in the 1913 Presidential Inaugural Parade

Recall that the story of Culver's involvement in the 1913 Presidential Inaugural began at the banquet commemorating the formal opening of the new Mess Hall on April 17th, 1911, at which Thomas Marshall, then the governor of Indiana, was the guest of honor. Gignilliat concluded his introduction of Governor Marshall by stating that Culver's BHT was "a direct descendant of a famous inaugural escort" and that it was "subject to your orders, sir, either for the Mexican border or Pennsylvania Avenue," which elicited great applause from the audience at the time. Marshall's laconic response – "*If I go, you go*" – stuck with Gignilliat and remained in the forefront of his ceaseless promoter's mind.[1]

The two men next met in late August 1912, when Marshall was the principal speaker at the closing of Culver's enhanced summer session that marked the completion of the first iteration of the Woodcraft Camp, and Gignilliat again raised the issue with Marshall. While driving the future Vice President to the train depot in Culver, Gignilliat recalls saying, "Governor, I really meant what I said about that escort business." Marshall reaffirmed that if he was involved in the presidential inaugural parade in some fashion, he intended to have the BHT serve as his escort.[2]

Hartman tells us that, "The morning after Wilson's victory in November of 1912, Gignilliat wired the vice-president elect that Culver's offer still stood," to which "Marshall responded forthwith and confirmed the invitation."[3] Gignilliat had also made a formal application with the inaugural committee for the BHT to participate in the parade in this role on the assumption that it was somewhat *pro forma* and would certainly be approved.

General Leonard Wood.[4]

It seemed that all was set for the BHT to serve as Marshall's personal escort in the inaugural parade, and Gignilliat and his staff turned their attention to the planning and preparations for the event.

In early 1913, however, while in Washington making arrangements for Marshall's transition, Marshall's secretary was informed that Marshall was not authorized a personal escort and that Culver's request for the BHT to serve in that capacity had been denied.

Upon further investigation, Gignilliat learned that it had been General Leonard Wood, the US Army Chief of Staff serving as the Grand Marshal of the inaugural parade and responsible for its planning, who had denied Culver's request. Wood's decision was based upon precedent: the Vice President had never before had his own escort in the inaugural parade, and Wood saw no reason to buck tradition by approving Culver's request to do so on this occasion. Gignilliat was personally devastated by this outcome, and he recalled that, upon learning of this development, his hopes had been "shattered."

Unaccustomed to having his plans foiled and wanting sincerely to honor Marshall as a "dear friend" of Culver, Gignilliat quickly regained his composure. He contacted Marshall and asked, "Will it embarrass you… if we try to get that decision changed," to which Marshall replied, "Not in the slightest" and wished Gignilliat luck in doing so.[5]

Armed with Marshall's blessing, Gignilliat engaged in the effort to get the decision changed. Aware that General Wood had a reputation of being somewhat intractable at times, but ever respectful of the demands of military hierarchy and protocol, Gignilliat decided to send his aide to see General Wood in Washington, DC to get the denial reversed.

Gignilliat's aide at the time was Captain William A. "Will" Fleet, who was Colonel Fleet's son, Minnie's brother,

Captain William A. "Will" Fleet.[6]

and an all-around impressive young man. After graduating from Culver in 1900, Will Fleet, like his father, studied the Classics at the University of Virginia, where he became one of America's first Rhodes Scholars. Completing his studies at Oxford during the period 1903-1907, Fleet returned to America and joined the faculty at Princeton University for the 1907-1908 school year before coming to Culver to teach Latin and Greek. While at Princeton, Fleet was both a colleague of and became friends with Woodrow Wilson and his family, especially his daughters Margaret, Jessie, and Eleanor.

The meeting with the head of the inaugural parade was not successful, and Fleet was unable even to gain a personal audience with General Wood to make his case. A member of General Wood's staff informed Fleet that the General was far too busy to meet with a mere captain. Considering Fleet's request himself, the same staff officer replied that nothing could be done to reverse the decision backed by such strong precedent because such a thing was simply not done.

His hopes dashed yet again, Gignilliat was eager to find another way to overcome Wood's opposition. Deeming the chance of persuading Wood to reverse his decision with another direct approach to be slim at best and with a mounting sense of desperation, Gignilliat departed from the chain-of-command approach and sent Fleet to New Jersey to see Wilson in person and ask for his personal approval for the BHT to serve as Marshall's escort in the inaugural parade.

Showing resourcefulness in finding a way to gain access to the President-elect, Wilson received Fleet warmly at the capitol in Trenton, speaking fondly of mutual friends. As Gignilliat tells it, "When Will went to the State House in Trenton, Mr. [Joseph P.] Tumulty, Wilson's secretary, told him that the Governor was very busy and could not be interrupted, [and] that it would be impossible to arrange an interview" upon such short notice. Will asked if Tumulty would be willing to deliver a very brief note to the Governor that Fleet would type himself stating the nature of his visit. Tumulty agreed to do so and was astonished when Governor Wilson came out almost immediately to greet Will personally.

Woodrow Wilson while at Princeton.[7]

Getting straight to the heart of the matter, Fleet explained the reason for his unannounced visit. Responding to Will's dilemma, Wilson said that he would be delighted to dictate a note of support to General Wood for Will to hand-deliver.

While there are differing accounts of its exact substance, the mostly likely version of Wilson's concise note read something like the following:

> *"I am entirely ignorant about such matters, but if it can be done I would be pleased if the wishes of the friends of Mr. Marshall could be acceded to. WOODROW WILSON"*[8]

Regardless of the exact wording, it is clear that Wilson penned a note to General Wood conveying the President-elect's expressed wish that the request for Culver's BHT to serve as Marshall's official escort in the inaugural parade be granted as a way of honoring his running mate.

Buoyed by Wilson's support and with his note of support in hand, Will Fleet returned to Washington to discuss the matter with General Wood personally. Determined for a face-to-face encounter this time, the young captain remained steadfast in his efforts even though he was kept waiting for over an hour after he arrived. According to Gignilliat, "Will was one of the most polite and considerate young men that I ever knew, but he had a quiet determination in his makeup, and when he had a mission to perform he was not easily deterred."[9]

The usually placid Will retained his composure while cooling his heels, and when finally ushered into the General's office, "Will reached into his pocket for the letter and with almost the same cold incisiveness of the General himself said, 'Would you mind, sir, looking at this letter' from president-elect Wilson?" After reading it, and "without changing expression General Wood rang for his aide," who had become an expert on the practices and traditions of past inaugurals. Wood asked him if the Vice President had ever had an inaugural escort, to which the aide replied forcefully, "Never, sir!" General Wood took a moment to process the response and then replied, "Well, he will this time."[10]

Having agreed to support Culver's request, General Wood asked Will why he hadn't shown anyone Wilson's note on his first visit. Replying candidly, the young captain responded, "I didn't have it the first time, sir." The General reacted by giving Fleet "a grim, but nevertheless approving, smile."[11]

With that response, General Wood, who could be a bit of a maverick himself when determined to get his way, knew that Will had gone around him and over his head. Nevertheless, General Wood also couldn't help but admire the gumption required to acquire such authorization, perhaps seeing a bit of himself in the determined young man standing before him.

In Gignilliat's assessment of the episode, while General Wood typically frowned on such actions, "He, also, was evidently a believer in the 'stick-to-it-iveness' advocated by his great friend Theodore Roosevelt."[12] This explains how the disciplined general was able to put aside his pique at the manner in which Will had obtained Wilson's authorization to not only accept but also come to support the outcome of the engagement.

Armed with such support, and exploiting his momentary advantage, Gignilliat gained approval for the entire CMA corps of cadets to participate in the inaugural parade. While the BHT would have a special post of honor serving as Marshall's personal escort, the infantry battalion and band were placed in the main body of the parade to march with contingents from other military schools from across the nation.

1913 Inaugural Invitation Controversy

While audacious and effective, Gignilliat's efforts to secure an invitation for Culver to participate in the 1913 Presidential Inaugural parade were not universally admired or appreciated. A Washington newspaper correspondent for the *Chicago Evening Post*, Edward B. Clark, who was also a staff correspondent for the *Indianapolis Star*, somehow got wind of some version of the episode shortly after it occurred. He became righteously indignant about it and published an article scathingly critical of the Vice President-elect and of Culver under the provocative title, "Inaugural Will Set Precedent: Unique Features and Shattered Traditions Mark Incoming of New President."

Clark's article got all of the intentions and most of the facts about the episode wrong, and the article comes across as largely a hatchet-job on both Marshall and Culver. Incorrectly ascribing the efforts related to the use of an official escort to Marshall himself, and convinced that the decision to overturn precedent was both inappropriate and would damage the solemnity of the occasion, the article essentially accused Gignilliat of going around established channels to get what he wanted and bring publicity to Culver, implying that Gignilliat's actions were blatantly self-serving and appallingly inappropriate.

The article appeared in the *Washington Post* on February 4, 1913, in the *Chicago Evening Post* on or near the same date, and later in the *Indianapolis Star* on March 2, 1913. Gignilliat likely read the article when it appeared in the *Chicago Evening Post*, and perhaps someone in either Chicago and/or Washington brought the article to Gignilliat's attention when it first appeared in print. Regardless of how it came to his attention, Gignilliat was as incensed by its inaccuracy as he was mortified by its implications. He was determined to set the record straight and do whatever was necessary to defend the honor of Marshall and his beloved institution.

As soon as he became aware of the article, sometime between February 4-15 1913, Gignilliat wrote a letter to Clark expressing his concern for Marshall's reputation and his fear that some may conclude from Clark's article that it was Marshall who sought to have the BHT serve as his escort in the parade to inappropriately bring to himself "the same accompanying honors as those given to the President-elect."

To correct this misperception, Gignilliat went to great lengths to make clear that the arrangements for the BHT to serve as Marshall's escort in the presidential inaugural parade had been made "some time ago." This argument is quite reasonable, since the BHT had been providing official escorts for Indiana governors for over 15 years since its founding in 1897, which Gignilliat also pointed out.

Perhaps more importantly, Gignilliat stressed that Marshall was completely unaware that there was "any precedent to the contrary" when he accepted Culver's offer to provide him with an escort in the presidential inaugural parade. This, too, was an eminently rational argument, since very few citizens in the country had ever witnessed a presidential inaugural in person and were almost entirely ignorant of its conduct.

While it did not appear in print, Gignilliat's letter protesting the substance of his article apparently made quite an impression on Clark. Clark was a professional journalist and felt compelled to write a letter to the editor in response so that these issues would be addressed in print and in some of the same newspapers in which his original article appeared.

While moved somewhat by Gignilliat's response, Clark did not share Gignilliat's level of concern regarding the potential for readers to be misled by the content of his article. In his editorial response, Clark referenced Gignilliat's' two main concerns identified above but stated that he did not believe anyone could come to such conclusions in any way except by "indirection," thereby rejecting the fundamental premise of Gignilliat's concerns. Clark nevertheless wrote, "I feel that it is right to say that the suggestion of the escort came from [Marshall's] friends and that in adopting it [Marshall] was innocent of any breach of the rules established by precedent," thereby exonerating Marshall of any notion of wrongdoing and restoring his reputation. Preparing for the inaugural was important, but this exchange shows that matters of honor and reputation were paramount for Gignilliat.

Along with his actions during the Big Fire, a picture begins to emerge suggesting that Gignilliat embraced a fairly rigid duty-ethics approach when faced with a crisis. Characterized by doing the right thing above all (which sheds some light on his inability to accept criticism in some cases when he believed he was taking the right action), this situation must have mortified Gignilliat, as any suggestion, however slight, that he did something improper himself, or perhaps even worse, contributed in any way to harming the reputation of someone in authority, represented a deep blow to his character. It also helps explain the extraordinary lengths to which Gignilliat went to in order to right this perceived wrong on behalf of Marshall and for which Gignilliat felt himself to be somewhat responsible.

1913 Inaugural

The challenges related to Culver's participation in the event notwithstanding, Gignilliat and the corps got to work preparing to represent the school to the nation in the best possible light. In keeping with his meticulous attention to detail, the preparation was expansive and covered a broad range of areas.

Marching and horsemanship were, of course, prioritized, and the cadets put in a tremendous amount of practice for the event. Most of their preparations occurred outdoors to mirror the conditions the cadets would likely encounter, meaning that they occurred in rain or snow that comes with the weather in Indiana during this time of the year. According to Gignilliat, "

> *Ordinarily, outdoor drill was suspended in the winter months, Not so in the weeks preceding that Match 4th. Clad in overcoats, woolen gloves, and overshoes, the infantry marched and counter-marched over the frozen, snow-covered drill field. The band played until the instruments froze despite the alcohol in the valves, and the Troopers, with difficulty, controlled their*

nettlesome mounts who were prancing and blowing steam from their nostrils in the chilling winds of the Indiana winter."[13]

As it turns out, the training that occurred during such inclement weather proved to be invaluable preparation for the weather challenges the cadets faced during the actual inaugural parade.

To prepare the cadets for the experience of visiting the nation's capital, members of the Culver staff gave a series of lectures about Washington, DC to familiarize the cadets with its history and attractions. Given his intimate familiarity with the city, as a result of having lived there for seven years, Gignilliat gave his own presentation consisting of 34 pictures that showed his knowledge of city and was appreciated by the corps.

As with the Jamestown trip, several members of the board accompanied the corps, including the president, ER Culver, his wife, and Knight Culver, a younger brother of BB and ER Culver. As expected, the ever-present Minnie Gignilliat made the trip as well.

To plan for the inaugural, Gignilliat had the staff use the Jamestown trip as an example, mirroring its execution and incorporating all they had learned from the successful logistics of the event. This was especially helpful for determining how best to arrange the transportation for the corps and the BHT's horses.

Much of the month of February was consumed by the myriad preparations necessary for the upcoming inaugural, compounded by the participation controversy. According to Gignilliat, "Excitement ran high in the school. The trip to Washington was looked forward to as high adventure, more than a welcome break in the long stretch between the Christmas holidays and the close of school in June."[14] After relentless effort and ceaseless progress, the preparations were complete by the end of the month, and all was ready for Culver's next entre to the national stage.

The 1913 inaugural adventure began with the pre-dawn departure of the stable train with 64 horses on Friday, February 28, 1913. Led by Captain Rossow and accompanied by the horsemanship staff and hostlers, this train would precede the corps along the route and deliver the horses to their temporary home in the stables at Fort Meyer in Washington, DC.

Shortly afterwards, at around 7:00 am and after eating breakfast, the corps (minus a few stay-behinds) departed by special train. During this

12-hour leg of the trip, the band went through the train and played ragtime music in the cars throughout the afternoon.

The corps arrived that night in Pittsburgh, Pennsylvania around 7:00 pm. After assembling for formation at the train station, the corps marched in

Cadets departing Culver for the Presidential Inaugural.[15]

overcoats through downtown over fresh snowfall to the renowned Fort Pitt hotel, the flagship hotel of Culver graduate Eugene C. Eppley (CMA '01). The proud Culver grad Eppley graciously hosted the dinner provided for the cadets during their very short stay in the city. After consuming their meal, the cadets immediately marched back to the train and were under way within the hour by 8:00 pm. Their long day of excitement concluded with Taps on the train at 9:30 pm.

Culver cadets marching through Pittsburg to the Fort Pitt Hotel.[16]

Sleeping through the night, the cadets awoke early to be ready for their train's arrival in Washington, DC at daybreak (around 5:30 am) on Saturday. After assembling for formation at the train station, the corps marched through downtown Washington, DC to their home for the duration of their stay, the historic Ebbitt House Hotel. After quickly settling into their rooms and eating breakfast, the cadets wasted no time beginning their sightseeing adventures with a trip to Mount Vernon.

Cadets in formation in front of Mount Vernon.[17]

Cadets visiting George Washington's Tomb at Mount Vernon.[18]

The day ended by seeing a play that evening at the Chase opera house, where the cadet band performed a medley of popular tunes and Culver songs to the delight of the crowd.

The next day (Sunday) began with the group attending church services en masse at the Foundry church with Vice President-elect Marshall, followed by an invigorating tour around the city in touring automobiles, providing a very novel experience for many of the cadets who had never ridden in cars before this trip. The cadets also visited the Washington Monument, many climbing to the top to take in the splendid view of the city from this wonderful vantage point. Returning to the hotel, the cadets relaxed that evening before beginning a four-day nonstop period of activity.

Monday morning was devoted to preparations for the afternoon review on the White House lawn by US Army BG Albert L. Mills. Mills was a recipient of the Medal of Honor and a former West Point Superintendent who was serving as the Chief of the Army's Militia Affairs Division at the time of the review.

Given the background of the reviewing officer and the visibility of the event, Gignilliat was particularly eager to have the corps put on its very best performance.

US Army BG Albert L. Mills.[19]

Others observing the review included Vice President-elect Marshall, Indiana US Senator Benjamin Shively (who likely helped Culver gain approval to participate in the inaugural) and his wife Laura, along with ER Culver and his wife, Knight Culver, and Minnie Gignilliat.

General Mills reviewing the CMA corps of cadets on March 3, 1913.[20]

This review was excellent preparation for the next day's inaugural parade.

The CMA corps of cadets passing in review for General Mills on March 3, 1913.[21]

Tuesday was the day of the inaugural parade, and it was an early day consisting of long hours of waiting for the cadets. The line of march was led by the West Point band, followed by Grand Marshal Army General Leonard Wood and his staff, and the Essex Troop of horseback riders from New Jersey providing the mounted escort for President Wilson. Vice President Marshal was next, riding a carriage pulled by two black horses and flanked by BHT riders specially trained in mounted pistol marksmanship at each corner, with the entire BHT following immediately behind. The West Point corps of cadets and Naval Academy corps of midshipmen came next.

Being so close to the front, the Black Horse Troop's day started especially early. After preparing their mounts and joining the line of march, the cadets spent the next 12 hours in the saddle, most of which involved endless waiting.

BHT Riders escorting Vice President Marshall's carriage in the 1913 Presidential Inaugural Parade.[22]

Gignilliat recalled that it was sleeting on the morning of the parade, and the streets were "coated with ice" along the entire two-mile route of the parade. While marching on the parade route, the sleet and cold made the roads extremely slick, causing many of the horses to lose their footing and slip, with some ending up on their bellies.

Gignilliat related proudly that the troopers rode while "blinking a bit from

The Black Horse Troop escort on the way to report to Vice President Marshall.[23]

Gignilliat riding in the inaugural parade with Captain J. Q. Adams to his left.[24]

The BHT riding in the 1913 Presidential Inaugural Parade behind Marshall's carriage.[25]

the stinging sleet and controlling their mounts on the glassy pavement with expert horsemanship."

While some members of the Essex Troop fell off their mounts and their horses ran free on the parade route, Gignilliat reported that even though many horse slipped on ice-covered street-car tracks, going down on their bellies with legs sprawled, the Culver troopers "deftly brought their mounts to their feet," coming up erect in their saddles often to the applause of the spectators. As a result of their training and discipline, not one of Culver's riders were unhorsed, providing a memorable display of horsemanship that brought honor to the school. Captain Rossow reported that General Wood complimented the cadets' performance, saying that the BHT was "one of the smartest outfits in the entire parade." Nothing could have pleased Gignilliat or Rossow more.

Being farther back in the line of march and having fewer preparations to make, the infantry took their position and waited for three hours in the cold and sleet before beginning their own march along the two-mile route. The cadet account in *The Vedette* reported that the lines while marching were so straight that they would "put a carpenter's square to shame," indicating the level of pride they took in their own performance.

The cadets also commented on the power of the encouragement they received from the cheers of the estimated 500,000 spectators along the parade route and especially from the BHT troopers who, having completed their own arduous ride, returned to cheer on their fellow infantryman. Later in his life, Gignilliat recalled that, perhaps because of the "rigorous workouts in the Indiana winter... the cadets made a magnificent showing."[27]

The CMA cadet battalion marching in the 1913 Presidential Inaugural Parade.[26]

At Wilson's invitation, Gignilliat and his wife attended a White House luncheon sometime during the parade where Gignilliat had the opportunity to speak briefly with the new President. Gignilliat's pride in the school was no doubt bolstered by the superb conduct of the cadets during the entire trip. According to the cadets' own account, "So fine was the behavior and military carriage of the cadets" while at liberty on the streets of Washington that it did even more, perhaps, to establish a good name for the institution than did the unsurpassed lines which they presented in the inaugural parade itself. Receiving compliments on the comportment of the

The CMA Band marching in the Presidential Inaugural Parade.[28]

Gignilliat with Vice President Marshall and his wife on Inauguration Day, March 4, 1913.[29]

cadets before, during, and after the inaugural parade surely bolstered Gignilliat's confidence as he provided Marshall's escort and spoke with Wilson during the inaugural parade.

After completing their military duties, the cadets returned to their hotel to warm up, clean up, and prepare for the ball Marshall sponsored that evening at the famous Willard Hotel. A White House aide who also happened to be Gignilliat's VMI classmate, Captain Henry Coates, endeared himself to the cadets by arranging to have many of Washington, DC's most popular debutantes attend the ball. By Gignilliat's own account, this celebration was "the social event of the inaugural." Adding to the enjoyment of the cadets, many reported that they were able to stay up long after Taps that night telling stories, as the dreaded Taps inspector was noticeably absent that evening. One wonders if this unusual oversight was somehow intentional, meant to provide the cadets with some much-needed respite and as a well-deserved reward for their magnificent efforts during that day.

CMA cadets formed up while touring Washington, DC after the 1913 Presidential Inaugural Parade.[30]

By design, the corps remained in Washington, DC on the Wednesday following the inaugural to visit the Smithsonian National Museum, the White House, and other points of interest.

Having seen and done all they could during the allotted time, the cadets boarded their special train and departed at 9:30 pm. Their return trip was delayed somewhat when the locomotive had some mechanical difficulties, but the group arrived in Pittsburgh in time to parade through town to eat breakfast at the Fort Pitt Hotel, courtesy again of Eppley.

Arriving back at Culver late between 11:00 pm on Thursday (corps) and 1:00 am on Friday (horses), Gignilliat took several measures to recognize the cadets' performance. He had the dining hall prepare a steak dinner for the boys before allowing the entire corps to sleep until the (as yet) unheard of hour of 8:00 am on Friday, which was reported to be the latest reveille that had ever occurred on campus. This particular reward of extra sleep was so remarkable that it warranted mention in the school's yearbook the following year! In addition, the cadets had the following morning off from classes after they awoke late, using a half-day on Saturday morning to make them up. In addition, Gignilliat commutated or relaxed all of the existing Extra Duty penalties of the cadets. Gignilliat also produced a picture book as a souvenir for the cadets.

For one who placed such great value in keeping cadets under constant military discipline and was judicious with his compliments, these measures were quite remarkable and conveyed to the entire Culver community a level of pride, admiration, and appreciation for all that everyone had done to make the inaugural participation such a rousing . success. Adding words to bolster Gignilliat's actions, ER Culver, addressing the entire Culver community, remarked that, "You have written the greatest page in the history of 'Greater Culver' and have done more for its greatness than the future can possibly do."[31]

The Logansport Flood

Fresh off the success of the 1913 presidential inaugural, and during that same month of March, Culver experienced an event that influenced the school more than any other event during its first two decades: Assisting in the rescue efforts related to the devastating Logansport Flood of 1913.

Briefly, Gignilliat decided to send a rescue party of around 80 people – 60 or so were cadets – to man the naval cutters requested by the city of Logansport and assist in the rescue efforts of almost 1,500 citizens during the two-day period of March 26-27, 1913. This event, even more so than participating in the Presidential Inaugural, brought favorable national attention to Culver and Gignilliat. Given the significance of this event, it is treated in much greater detail in a separate chapter.

Other Significant 1913 Events at Culver

After the excitement of the Presidential inaugural and the Logansport Flood rescue operation, one might be tempted to think that the remainder of the 1912-1913 school year would be relatively mundane. However, this was not the case. The Military Preparedness Movement was emerging in America in 1913, and both the Culver family and Gignilliat became swept up in it.

Spring 1913 – Hosting, Travel, and Construction on Campus

Gignilliat hosted the Superintendent of VMI, General Edward W. Nichols, as the Sunday sermon speaker on April 13, 1913. Gignilliat and Nichols began working together closely during 1913 on matters related to military preparedness and the role of military schools and colleges in the country's military system, especially through the newly formed Association of Military Colleges and Schools of the United States (AMCSUS) organization. Both were members of the AMCSUS Executive Committee, by virtue of the size of the schools they led. Nichols returned to speak at the First- and Second-class banquet on the last Saturday of April 1913 (26

April 1913), and he spoke again at chapel regarding the value of military training.

Nichols' message was that military training's value was to train young men in "the prompt discharge of our daily duties," arguing that "the man who has that ingrained into his system has the 'stuff' that enables him to succeed in any line of human endeavor." He ended his address with the following charge: "Do your duty and be a man."[32] Contemporary accounts indicate that the cadets impressed Nichols with the speed and quality of a pontoon bridge they build for him on Monday morning as part of their training for the upcoming Army Annual inspection.

New Administration Building and Sally Port linking East and North Barracks.[35]

In April 1913, Gignilliat was on the road, traveling to Chicago, then to Greencastle, Indiana for the installation of the new president at DePauw, and then to St. Louis for a board meeting toward the end of the month. At the April 1913 board meeting, the trustees agreed to build a new barrack – North Barrack – on campus to provide additional rooms for the ever-expanding corps of cadets.

Returning to campus, Gignilliat announced the building of the new barrack on campus at the First- and Second -class banquet on the last Saturday of April 1913 (26 April 1913). The plan for the new barrack was to incorporate many of the best aspects of the Open-air Barrack – including its large windows on doors, larger rooms, lounges, drinking fountains in each hall, and modern furnishings – but not the open-air aspect of it, which was determined to be not as beneficial as anticipated and/or worth the cost associated with constructing the complicated sleeping alcoves.

In North Barrack, the first floor was to have offices for the headmaster and commandant, along with some additional classrooms. The upper floors contained additional cadet rooms, with one floor allocated for the Band quarters. This new building allowed for the expansion of the corps from four to five companies, adding E Company at the beginning of the 1913-14 school year, and for the corps to begin living by unit.[33]

Gignilliat's new office in the new Administration Building as it appeared in 1914.[37]

The new Visitors' Reception Room on the first floor of East Barrack.[38]

The meeting room in the new Administrative building allowed faculty to meet weekly.[39]

The construction effort also included the creation of a new Administration area as part of East Barrack, with an impressive Sally Port linking the two structures together. This feature, through which official visitors were to be welcomed, created the official "entrance" of the Academy and shifted the core of campus away from Main Barack.[34]

The Baker & Knell construction crew broke ground for the new buildings on May 12, 1913.[36] While construction progressed steadily over the course of the summer, neither building was ready by the beginning of the 1913-14 winter session. With 461 cadets enrolled – an increase of 29 from the previous winter session and Culver's largest enrollment to date – cadets were assigned rooms in the unfinished structure but lived in tents while waiting for it to be completed. Construction was completed in late-November 1913, and North Barrack was deemed ready for occupation on November 29, 1913.

The impact of the completed Administration building was also significant, since it allowed for the library to be moved from the first floor of East Barrack into the basement of the new Mess Hall. This move created space for Gignilliat's spacious new office. Gignilliat was dissatisfied with the office on the first floor of Main Barrack that he inherited from Fleet, which he felt was too cramped and not appropriate for the superintendent of a school of CMA's renown.

These moves also allowed for the establishment of a lovely visitor's reception room and several other offices and meeting rooms in the new Administration building.

The Administration Hall on the first floor of North Barrack.
(Culver Archives)

The new Message Center on the first floor in North Barrack was staffed 24 hours a day.
(Culver Archives)

Together, this established an impressive and functional headquarters for CMA apart from Main barrack and located directly across the new Sally Port from the offices of the headmaster and commandant, and the new main guard room.

Following the completion of the new Mess Hall in 1911 (Phase 1), the construction of North Barrack and the Administration building completed Phase 2 of the Culver family's "Greater Culver" construction plan for improvements on campus. They enhanced CMA's amenities and brought its administrative facilities more in line with the school's reputation for excellence. CMA finally had the type of administrative facilities it desired and deserved.

Culver stood for its annual Army inspection in early May 1913 (3-4 May), and it was conducted by West Point graduate and US Army Captain James P. Robinson. As expected, Robinson was well pleased with the level of preparation he encountered. He was also quite impressed with the "snap and pop" of the corps' manual of arms, which reminded him of his own West Point days. Reflecting on the overall performance, Robinson concluded that Culver had "maxed cold" the inspection, ensuring that it would retain its coveted "distinguished institution" recognition.[40]

Another occurrence during this period related to the athletic performance of Cadet Philip Stiles, who set the world interscholastic broad jump record at on 10 May 1913 at a track meet at Lake Forrest College. Stiles jumped 23 feet 7 1/5 inches, which exceeded the existing world record by 1 1/5 inches. Stiles then broke his own world record the following Saturday at a track meet hosted by Culver, jumping 23 feet, 7 3/4 inches. These feats brought significant attention to CMA in spring 1913, bolstering its reputation as a world-class educational institution.

Rounding out the eventful 1912-1913 winter session, Culver hosted the first meeting of the International Conference of the Boys' Secretaries of the YMCA during the period 17-30 May 1913. With 300 attendees from at least 15 different countries living in tents and eating with the cadets in the beautiful new Mess Hall, this two-week event brought significant exposure to Culver as well. Gignilliat hosted in his usual fashion, scheduling many performances, drills, and exhibitions for the visitors to observe, ending with a sumptuous farewell dinner and address by Gignilliat on May 29, 1913. This event was a success and indicates the growing influence of YMCA on Culver, which continued to flourish during Gignilliat's tenure.

Commencement 1913 and Kiser's "The Spirit of Culver"

Original hand-written copy of "The Spirit of Culver."[42]

Having come to the end of perhaps its most eventful year to date, Culver's always impressive commencement exercises had to take it to another level to appropriately mark the event. The resulting commencement address proved to be more than equal to the challenge.

Traditional Culver lore has it that "The Spirit of Culver" was hurriedly scribbled by Samuel Ellsworth, "S. E." Kiser right before he delivered it as part of his commencement address on June 5, 1913. It appears, however, that Kiser actually wrote the poem earlier in August or September 1912 after visiting campus to pick up his son, Palmer, who attended the 1912 Summer Naval School.

Kiser was a newspaper reporter in Cleveland who also wrote for the *Chicago Record-Herald* from 1900-1914. Much of his writing and poetry was either whimsical or inspirational in nature. His regular column, "Whimwhams and Sentiment" ("whimwhams" meaning "oddities") was syndicated widely, and his poems were quite popular. Some were along the lines of like Rudyard Kipling's "If," and William Ernest Henley's "Invictus," and they appeared in publications like *Harper's Magazine*. He was quite prolific, and his inspirational poem, "The Fighter," which channels much of the sentiment conveyed in "The Spirit of Culver" (first line : *I fight a battle every day*; last line: *And I am undefeated still!*) was included in at least one anthology of America's best-loved poems.[41]

Struck by the vibrant atmosphere he encountered at Culver in August 1912, Kiser was inspired to write the poem soon thereafter. In beautifully crafted verse, Kiser conveyed the ethereal yet essential meaning that the Spirit of Culver is to always do your best to succeed; to succeed by doing the right thing; to do the right thing to strengthen the brotherhood and honor Culver; and to honor Culver by being honorable, dependable, and respectable to perpetuate the Spirit of Culver, capturing the essence of what animates the very soul of Culver.

Kiser must have sent a copy of his poem to Gignilliat, who included it in a scrapbook he compiled for the Indiana Society in September 1912. Inadvertently but fortuitously, the poem also served to capture the essence of Gignilliat's Iron Gate charge to "be dependable" to the ideals of Culver. The poem stuck a chord in his soul, but it was the cadets who helped Gignilliat realize just how deeply Kiser's poem would resonate with the entire Culver community.

Culver cadets came across the poem somehow around the time Gignilliat departed for his hunting trip in Maine in early October 1912, and it evidently resounded with them powerfully as well. They had it published at the very top and in the center on the front page of the October 26, 1912 *Vedette* (which became a weekly campus newspaper beginning in fall 1912).

Introducing the poem on the second page, the cadets wrote:

> *"The poem which appears on the first page of this paper is reprinted from the Souvenir Scrap Book (sic) compiled by Colonel Gignilliat for the members of the Indiana Society. The poem was written and titled by Mr. S. E. Kiser of the* Chicago Record-Herald. *It represents the author in a spirit of frankness, sincerity and honest appeal, which is his most becoming form. It is at once a tribute and a standard – the first so far as it is deserved, the second so far as it shows something to be attained. The poem has a clear ring; it is as earnest as the advice Polonius gives his son, and more than that, is as worth living up to. Make your first step in this direction by committing to it."*[43]

It is clear that the poem resonated with the cadets immediately, and they recognized on their own its ability to capture the very essence of the Culver experience and also its inspirational power.

The cadets published a running commentary on the poem in November 1912 in *The Vedette*. Beginning on November 2, an article appeared on page two addressing the overall *"spirit of Culver,"* followed by another focusing on *"the strength that is in brotherhood"* on November 9, and concluding with a short piece dealing with "*the courage that proclaims success*" on November 23. In each short article, the author related the sunstance of the stanza from the poem to some relevant aspect of the cadet experience to illustrate its applicability.[44]

Upon his return from his hunting trip in Maine in late-November 1912, Gignilliat noticed the attention paid to the poem by the cadets and recognized the value they placed on the poem. Together with his prominence as an author and status as a parent of a Summer Naval School cadet, Kiser emerged in Gignilliat's mind as an excellent candidate as a speaker for the corps.

Turning his attention to the 1913 commencement activities, Gignilliat began searching for a suitable graduation speaker. With the rise of the Military Preparedness movement in America and the Culver family's support for it, US Army Chief of Staff and prominent preparedness proponent General Leonard Wood appeared to be the ideal speaker for Culver. Gignilliat forwarded an official request for Wood to speak at Culver's 1913 graduation exercises and remained hopeful that this would occur. However, a week before the event, Wood informed Gignilliat that he would not be able to make it to Culver for commencement, leaving Culver without a suitable speaker for its most cherished event.[45] It was within this context that Gignilliat must have turned to Kiser as a suitable replacement.

As it turned out, Kiser was the prefect selection to deliver the 1913 address. Kiser delivered "The Spirit of Culver" as a concise summation of the school's most cherished ideals at the conclusion of his remarks to the delight of the audience. This event fueled the popularity of the work among the alumni and parents in the audience.

As he had with the Iron Gate, Gignilliat recognized its value to the institution. With Kiser's gracious permission, Gignilliat began including the poem in official Culver material, starting with the 1914 *Roll Call* and *Message Center* (a reference booklet for cadets published by the Culver YMCA chapter). By 1917, it appeared on the first page of the CMA catalog and had become part of the Culver ethos, inextricably embedded in the very fabric of the institution it so aptly portrayed.

The 1913 Summer Session

The 1913 summer session unfolded as planned, with the operation of the Summer Naval School, Summer Cavalry School, and the Woodcraft Camp now constituting the main components of it. As he had experienced the previous summer, the responsibility of operating three seperate programs simultaneously placed increasingly complex demands on Gignilliat's administrative abilities. The smooth operation of each program and the overall enterprise provides compelling evidence of his ability to steward this multifaceted undertaking quite effectively.

Gignilliat continued to find innovative ways to market Culver's summer programs. The extended Summer Cavalry School's cavalry "hike," sending the troopers on horseback traversing about the region and camping along the way, helped to expose many to that program. Gignilliat also began sending Summer Naval School cutter crews to compete in national races. One of Culver's crews won the junior national championship in the Naval Militia cutter races held at Put-In-Bay, Ohio, on August 27, 1913.

1913 US Junior National Championship Crew.[46]

This impressive victory resulted in Culver receiving both the striking Perry Centennial Trophy Shield and the impressive Riggs Cup. Gignilliat wasted little time in making use of this accomplishment, featuring it in Culver's summer session advertisements in the widely read *Harper's Magazine* and elsewhere.

There was also talk of another summer cruise in 1913 for Summer Naval School cadets as a special detachment of the Indiana Naval Reserves. Planned in conjunction with a similar unit from North Carolina, the itinerary included sailing from Norfolk, Virginia to New York City, conducting some gunnery exercises in Gardiner's Bay on the eastern tip of Long Island, and returning to Norfolk, traveling to Philadelphia, and returning to Culver.[47] It is unclear whether the cruise occurred as planned at the end of the 1913 summer session, but it is apparent that Gignilliat continued to explore every possible opportunity to promote Culver's summer programs innovatively and to the best of his ability.

Fall of 1913 Brings More Innovation from Gignilliat – and More Activity!

Occupied with his summer duties, Gignilliat was not able to find time to get away for a vacation with his family. He had gone on the hunting trip to Maine in 1912 without Minnie, and it appears that he did not take much of a break between the summer and winter sessions in fall 1913.

During this period, Gignilliat was coping with the transition from summer to winter school, welcoming a record-high number of 461 boys into the winter school, including his eldest son, Leigh Jr, who matriculated into Culver as a new cadet in fall 1913. As if this weren't enough, Gignilliat was also trying to complete a 15,000-word manuscript regarding the value of military training in schools on which he had been working for some time.[48] He succeeded in the first two endeavors, but the manuscript was far from complete by the middle of October 1913.

His editor appreciated the demands under which Gignilliat was operating and extended the deadline for the manuscript's submission to April 1, 1914, indicating that Gignilliat could have until June 1914 to compete the project if necessary.[49]

Despite the tremendous press of duty he experienced at the beginning of the 1913-1914 winter session, Gignilliat was excited to welcome the newly hired consulting psychologist – Dr. Truman H. Kelly from the University of Illinois – to begin his work at Culver in fall 1913. Highly credentialed with a doctorate from Columbia University, Dr. Kelly established a new department to "make a study of the natural aptitudes of the cadets." Reflecting the influence of the Progressive movement, the purpose of this pioneering department was to help "make each cadet in the battalion mentally more efficient," much as the military drills and athletics did for each of them physically.[50]

Responding to Gignilliat's desire to make parts of Culver's developmental programs as individualized as possible, the idea was to "try to work with the boy in finding out for what calling he is best fitted," and "to teach those who have not learned the art of study how to attack a lesson" while also improving the study skills of others who have already learned the basics. Kelly's department was therefore charged to provide advice and recommendations for the "course of study best suited to the individual" cadet after conducting a variety of psychological and intellectual assessments.[51] This endeavor represents the beginning of Gignilliat's efforts to expand Culver's programs to address academic issues and performance in the classroom.

While perhaps slow in coming, Gignilliat would continue introducing innovative approaches into Culver's academic programs, albeit sometimes more curious than effective, for the next 15 years. Exhibiting his belief in the ability of innovative approaches to develop boys positively and bring out the very best in them, Gignilliat's efforts occurred during a period when many schools adopted the opposite approach for educating boys based on a belief that they needed to be controlled and "tamed." While discipline was important at Culver, the manner in which it was imposed and respect for the boys were paramount.

For the military program, Culver received four new 3-inch artillery pieces in fall 1913. These allowed Culver to begin developing its effective four-gun artillery drill that would form the basis of the artillery's honor organization in later years. Gignilliat was also delighted to learn that the US Army agreed to upgrade the rifles for the infantry with the well-regarded M-1903 Springfield bolt-action rifle. Arriving in late 1913, these new rifles were issued to cadets upon their return to campus in January 1914. Together, these two equipment upgrades elevated the quality of Culver's military equipment substantially and in line with the "Greater Culver" improvement plan, allowing it to remain on par with the very best military programs in the country.

Culver and the Burgeoning Preparedness Movement

In the wake of the Spanish-American War of 1898 that heralded a new experience of so-called American imperialism, the beginning of the 20th century found America exploring many different ways to address the emerging national security challenges of the new century. One aspect of this issue involved the training and development of high school and college students as citizen-soldiers.

The nation's first Students' Military Instruction Camps, intended to provide training for students aspiring to become citizen-soldiers, occurred in summer 1913 at Gettysburg, Pennsylvania, and at the Presidio of Monterey in California. While they were not particularly well attended (~ 225 students in total at each; 160 at Gettysburg and 63 at the Presidio), lightly supported by the Army, and generated little public interest, the US Army Chief of Staff, General Leonard Wood, found in them something for which he had been searching for some time: The "machinery to reform the army and radically alter American defense policy."[52]

In Wood's mind, America needed to create and sustain a large standing army along the lines of the Prussian system, and he believed that camps like those that occurred in the summer of 1913 were an excellent way to train citizen-soldiers to be part of this force.[53] It was this idea that formed the core of the burgeoning Military Preparedness Movement in America, for which General Wood become one of the most visible and vocal proponents.

Determined to explore this idea further, Wood authorized four additional camps to occur with full Army support during the summer of 1914. These camps were planned to begin in the first week of July 1914 and last for five weeks to train around 200 boys at each location for a total of approximately 1,000 boys.

Wood did not, however, specify where these camps would occur. As a result, he received a "deluge of letters" from parties interested in hosting the camps, including the Culver family.[54]

The Culver family's interest in military preparedness became apparent during this earliest stage of the Preparedness Movement. Brothers ER and BB Culver began discussing the possibility of hosting a national summer camp for boys at CMA in early fall 1913. At their direction, Gignilliat had discussed with the War Department the possibility of having Culver host a military instructional camp for students in summer 1914.

In early November 1913, the Culver brothers officially offered the use of Culver's campus to the War Department to host one of the upcoming student military training camps.

With Gignilliat away from campus, Greiner took the lead in the initial stages of this endeavor. As the plan took shape, Greiner determined that CMA's own farmland was suitable to serve as the camping ground for 200 participants. However, Greiner also concluded that he would need to use some of the surrounding farmland to support the camp's field training. The solution was to ask Culver citizens to donate approximately two square miles of farmland for a suitable maneuver area for the field training.

The Secretary of War was intrigued by the Culver brothers' proposal and sent US Army Captain Robert O. Van Horn from his office to Culver on November 6, 1913 for a two-day visit to inspect the area and review the drill performance of the CMA cadets. Van Horn was quite impressed with the cadets' proficiency and with Culver's facilities.[55] During the period of Van Horn's visit, the charismatic Rossow succeeded in acquiring permission from all but one of the local farmers to use their land for the camp's field training.

Van Horn departed Culver with a very positive impressive of its cadets and facilities. Greiner forwarded Culver's final proposal to the War Department, hoping to obtain its favorable consideration.[56] While ultimately selecting the more spacious Lincoln Fields site at Ludington, Michigan for its 1914 student training camp within the region, the War Department was nonetheless "favorably impressed" with Culver's potential and began paying increased attention to the institution.[57]

1913 US Navy Fall Mediterranean Cruise

Perhaps as a result of the Logansport Flood rescue efforts or the success of Culver Summer Naval School, Gignilliat was selected in mid-October 1913 to serve as a member of an official government party for a Mediterranean cruise with the US Navy's North Atlantic Fleet scheduled for fall 1913. This prestigious honor took Gignilliat away from Culver during the period October 22-December 17, 1913, further delaying the completion of his manuscript but providing him with the opportunity to become more familiar with the Navy and spread the word about CMA among the delegates.[58]

The Mediterranean cruise included the involvement of fourteen US Navy Atlantic Fleet ships, described in that year's "Annual Report of the Secretary of the Navy" as being "arranged largely for the educational advantages to be derived by officers and enlisted men from an opportunity to visit foreign ports and to travel in foreign countries." The Navy believed such experiences provided a welcome diversion from normal sea duty, increased "contentment" of the crew, and generated more widespread interest in the Navy that it hoped would increase its popularity. In effect, it was a marketing endeavor, and Gignilliat was a perfect selection for this mission.[59]

While perhaps well-intentioned, the September 6 *Army-Navy Journal* reported that "officers of the vessels of the Atlantic Fleet that are to make the cruise to European waters this fall are almost unanimously opposed to the project, and little enthusiasm is manifest among the enlisted force, except in the case of the new men."[60] The main reason for the discontent involved the changes required to scheduled mandatory tactical training, which needed to be completed unnecessarily hurriedly and prior to the cruise.

The flotilla was comprised of nine battleships including *Wyoming*, Fleet commander Rear Admiral Charles J. Badger's flagship; *Arkansas*; *Utah*; *Florida*; *Delaware*; *Kansas*; *Vermont*; *Connecticut*; and *Ohio*. They were accompanied by the hospital ship *Solace*; storeship *Celtic* and three big colliers: *Cyclops*; *Jason*; and *Orion*. This flotilla operated essentially independent of shore support, conveying an element of strategic "reach" to what was otherwise a friendly sightseeing voyage.

US Navy Battleship Arkansas, *the "Ark," as she looked at the time of the 1913 cruise.*[61]

Gignilliat departed campus on October 22, 1913, bound for Newport News, Virginia. Upon arrival, Gignilliat headed to Hampton Roads, Virginia, where he learned that he had been assigned to sail on the battleship *Arkansas*, skippered by US Navy Captain Roy C. Smith. Gignilliat's seaborne home, universally referred to by the crew as the "Ark," was docked in Hampton Roads.

On board, Gignilliat settled into his own spacious stateroom, which included a Filipino servant to shine his shoes and run errands for him. He was delighted to learn that Lt (JG) Jonas H. Ingram, a former instructor in the Summer Naval School, was assigned as a gunnery officer on *Arkansas*. Gignilliat also obtained a copy of the ship's book that was chock full of information about the vessel, which he sent back to Culver before departing.

The fleet departed Hampton Roads on October 25, 1913. Cruising at around 12 knots, the Atlantic crossing was largely uneventful. After four days as sea, the flotilla passed the "grave" of the Titanic at midnight on 29 October 1913, sending chills through many of the crew as the disaster was still quite fresh in the minds of many.

Gignilliat documented this experience more thoroughly than almost any other episode in his life up to this point. Excerpts from the five letters he wrote to Minnie that were quoted

Ships in formation crossing the Atlantic on the way to the Mediterranean, as seen from the deck of the Arkansas, *October 1913.*[62]

in *The Vedette* during his absence from campus provide some details of his experiences and insights into his thoughts during the cruise.

From the contents of his letters, it appears that Gignilliat had a duty – assigned or assumed – to learn as much as possible about the duties and responsibilities of sailors, along with life aboard a ship at sea. He observed and participated in the training, stood watch, partook in drills, and even performed some shore duty during the cruise.

Gignilliat provided the following observations about observing and participating in training during the cruise in his letters to Minnie.

- *"Yesterday forenoon I spend an hour watching the calisthenics on deck. They are giving the sailors a new set of Swedish movements and then a run around the deck while the band plays"* (26 October 1913).

- *"Every afternoon the officers exercise on deck. Some of them manipulate the medicine ball very strenuously. The Admiral can outlast most of the officers"* (26 October 1913).

- *"Then I went into the after-turret with Ingram. He has a wonderfully trained crew, perfect co-ordination in loading the two big 13-inch guns. Ingram gives his commands in an electrical sort of way and pits one gun against the other, commending this man and checking up that one and making the whole bunch work like their lives depended on it"* (26 October 1913).

- *"A turret during a gun drill is a place of considerable action and some little clatter. The turret officer sings out 'Stand by, load.' The breech is thrown open and the great 13-inch shell comes up the ammunition hoist, heralding its approach with a tremendous clatter. It is yanked, shifted and shoved with lightning rapidity, a hydraulic rammer shoots forward, drives the shell into the breech and darts back with the swiftness of a lizard's tongue. Then three big bags of powder are passed in as quickly and adroitly as a juggler handles his balls, the breech block flashes into place and the big gun is ready to hurl its 870 pounds of steel through a target dancing on the waves 5 miles away, tickle a dreadnought in her steel ribs or do any other little playful stunt in its own particular line"* (13 November 1913).

- *"This morning I went down into the powder magazines and ammunition handling rooms below the turrets and saw them test the flood cocks for sprinkling and flooding the magazine in case of accident"* (26 October 1913).

- *"Then I went up and studied the range-finder and took readings on the hospital ship and the colliers, which are steaming in column about 8,000 yards off our port side. Then I went on the bridge and took an observation with the sextant. I had an invitation from the surgeon to see an operation in the sick bay, but I don't care much for operations"* (26 October 1913).

- *"I stood the morning watch with Ingram a couple of days ago (4 to 8 o'clock). It was cloudy and I didn't see the sun rise, but I saw something of the busy life of Uncle Sam's sailors beginning at 5:30. They were scrubbing decks and hammocks that morning. I was a little chilly on the bridge, but they were splashing around in bare feet on the deck and looking very fit physically and not at all uncomfortable. I had the best appetite for breakfast I have had yet"* (13 November 1913).

- *"On Saturday on the captain's invitation I accompanied him on his inspection of the ship. I used to think Sunday morning inspections of the barracks were pretty thorough, but they are not to be compared with an inspection of a dreadnought"* (3 November 1913).

The turret gun crew trained and commanded by Lt (J.G). Ingram (a future Medal of Honor winner) won the coveted gunnery "E" for excellence on the cruise and was presented with it on the return trip.

Life aboard ship was not all work, and Gignilliat had time to relax and enjoy himself at times. He provided the following observations about learning about life aboard a ship at sea.

- *"Monday night I went up with Ingram and the Admiral's aide to 'movies' on the deck. It was an interesting sight – the wash of the waves against the side, the lights and the blinking signals of the other ships astern, the men sitting on the deck, others standing and a number up on the after-turrets and guns, and the pictures running along steadily just like any nickelodeon show in Culver or Plymouth"* (26 October 1913).

- *"There have been some very pretty sparring matches during the cruise. Once a week they have had what is called a 'happy hour.' A ring is roped in on deck, or a reflector with lights in it is rigged above the ring, chairs are placed for the admiral, captain, and other officers, the men sit on the deck or mass themselves on the turrets. The bouts are usually three rounds, no decision – occasionally six or more rounds"* (13 November 1913).

Sketch by Reuterdahl of Gignilliat (right) and one of Arkansas' officers (Commander Riggs) drawn during the cruise.[64]

Henry Reuterdahl was an American painter known for nautical artwork who also had an extended relationship with the US Navy, and he was another guest on the cruise. Reuterdahl served as an officer in the US Naval Reserve, and he accompanied the voyage of the US Great White Fleet voyage in 1907. He wrote frequently on naval topics and was an editor of the authoritative *Jane's Fighting Ships*.

At the time of the cruise, Reuterdahl was an artist who drew for *Collier's* magazine. Gignilliat struck up a friendship with the artist, and he sponsored an exhibit of 40 of Reuterdahl's naval-oriented works and a talk by him during the 1914 summer session.[63]

After a 13-day crossing of the Atlantic on a more northerly tack, the ships made for the Mediterranean Sea. Gibraltar appeared to be of great interest to some members of the crew. Gignilliat wrote on November 3, 1913 that:

"We are considerably less than a thousand miles away from Gibraltar, or 'The Rock,' as they call it. Some of the younger and more gullible members aboard are hoping we will pass through in daylight so they will see the 'Prudential' sign. They have been told that it is quite a sight,

that Victoria opposed putting it there, but that Edward yielded for a consideration, etc." (3 November 1913) (Note: Prudential

Passing Gibraltar, November 1913.[65]

Insurance Company had adopted the Rock of Gibraltar as its iconic image in the 1890s, and it was well-known in America for it.).

They passed by Gibraltar and entered the Mediterranean Sea around November 6, 1913. Once in the Mediterranean, the fleet split up, with *Arkansas* and *Florida* going to Naples for three weeks, while the other ships visited Malta, Genoa, Villefranche and Marseilles.

On November 7, 1913, Gignilliat reported that, "We were detached from the fleet early yesterday morning and now with the *Florida* just astern we are rushing along toward Naples at considerably increased speed."

The calm weather experienced during the Atlantic crossing came to an end, and the conditions became a bit more challenging. Gignilliat reported that, upon entering the Mediterranean, they encountered some rough weather, characterized by him as the waters "kicking up her heels, scurrying foam and lashing waves on every side." On November 3, 1913, Gignilliat reported that the ship had "been rocked with a vengeance" for several days, remarking, "Talk about being rocked in the cradle of the deep!" Again on November 7, 1913, Gignilliat recorded that, "We came through a terrific gale last night."

The Ark arrived at Naples on November 8 for a three-week stay scheduled for the period November 8 through 30, 1913. According to Gignilliat, the ship docked around 9:00 am, arriving with what he called "the usual salutes, cannon popping away, national airs and all that sort of thing."

Arkansas in port at Naples, dressed out to honor the Italian King, November 13, 1913.[66]

Their arrival was not as impressive as it could have been, since the US government had apparently requested that the Italians downplay the event. As a result, the Italian ships had left the harbor, and Gignilliat commented, perhaps somewhat disappointedly, that, "the courtesies extended ashore have been of the most informal character."

Gignilliat was fairly busy during the initial days in port, with the first spent making official calls. He attended a formal dinner that evening, remarking that it was "a very fine and elaborate affair" that included the usual formalities of offering toasts to national leaders and the two navies. In an unusual coincidence, he sat across from the very famous VMI graduate and sculptor Sir Ezekiel Moses, a proud Southerner who lived and worked in Rome. Also in attendance were the Italian Minister of War, Paolo Spingardi, and several other high officials, all dressed in their most formal uniforms. Since this was supposed to be a lowkey affair, all of the Americans were dressed much simpler in plain black evening clothes.

The next several days were filled with other official duties, keeping Gignilliat in Naples during that period. One of the events that impressed him the most was the review of 10,000 Italian army troops he attended on November 11, 1913. According to Gignilliat,

Italian army parade at Naples, November 11, 1913.[67]

"I attended the review of about 10,000 troops day before yesterday, the king's birthday. It was a brilliant sight, much more impressive than the greater part of our recent inaugural parade. The officers are smart-looking fellows, dashingly uniformed and splendidly mounted."

Gignilliat was particularly impressed with one of the Italian units. He wrote that, "Especially inspiring were the *Bassiliere* with their patent leather hats, rakish-looking coque feather plumes, and their quick, swinging stride. All of their movements are executed at the double." He was likely referring to the well-known *Bersaglieri*, Italian light infantry troops famous for their distinctive hats and the jog they employ when passing in review instead of marching.

Bersagliere solider in uniform, circa 1900.[68]

Rounding out his official duties was a special audience with Italian Pope Pius V at the Vatican in Rome. Gignilliat recounts the event as follows:

St. Peter's Basilica in Rome in November 1913.[69]

> *"At 10:15 we presented ourselves at the bronze doors of the Vatican....A wait in one of the rooms was relieved by watching the functionaries and flunkies passing by – servants in crimson brocaded silk, a cardinal in his robes of state, a Syrian patriarch of the Greek church come to acknowledge the Pope, private secretaries, officers of the guard – all these were passing through from time to time. Finally we moved again, this time into the hall of tapestries where wonderful Gobelin masterpieces were hung on the four walls. From this we moved into the throne room. Very nearly two hours had elapsed since we entered the building... The Pope came in very silently, a striking looking figure, clad in white, a serious but pleasant face. Welcoming us the Pope spoke briefly in Latin. Monsignor Kennedy, who accompanied the Pope, translated."*

During his wait, Gignilliat became fascinated with another military group, the famous Papal Swiss Guard. He noted their "mediaeval parti-colored uniforms" and that they were carrying "ancient battle axes" known as halberds, even though a rack filled with modern rifles was close by. Gignilliat also observed that "two officers of the royal guard" wore uniforms "of a sort of Essex troop full dress effect," referring to the New Jersey unit that provided President Wilson's official escort in the 1913 presidential inaugural parade. From his vivid descriptions of their apparel, it is clear that Gignilliat took special notice of and was attracted by the many colorful military uniforms and other official trappings he saw in Italy.

The visit to the Vatican concluded with a call on the Papal Secretary of State, Spaniard Rafael Merry del Val. According to Gignilliat, del Val was a very cordial and "splendid-looking man" who spoke "English so beautifully as to make one feel rather ashamed of the way he speaks it himself." Gignilliat's impression of de Val is not surprising, as he was born at the Spanish embassy in London. He lived there for the first 13 years of his life and was educated by the Jesuits, which accounts for both his language proficiency and manners.

With fewer official duties and having secured the Ark, crewmen received leave for extensive sightseeing trips to Naples, Rome, Venice, Florence, and Pompeii. The ships in port were opened for visits by local residents, and officers and men were liberally entertained ashore. Gignilliat joined in many of these excursions.

Gignilliat continued performing the duties he had either been appointed or assumed during the period of shore leave. Serving as a shore patrol officer on several occasions, he reported that,

"Our blue jackets are having a good time and at the same time giving a fine exhibition of restraint and discipline. I have seen them in the museum and at Pompeii and on the streets at night enjoying the noise and color of the gay Neapolitan life, but orderly at all times."

During his frequent visits to local police stations while on shore patrol, Gignilliat recalled that he did not encounter a single member of the crew who got in trouble during any of the trips in Italy. This splendid performance must have harkened back to the admirable way that CMA cadets had behaved in Washington, DC during the presidential inaugural. Given his background as a commandant in concern for proper behavior, it is not at all surprising that this aspect of the crew's performance merited special mention by him.

The crew returned to *Arkansas* at the end of November 1913 to make preparations for the voyage home. The Ark and its sister ship *Florida* departed Naples and made a rendezvous with the rest of the fleet near Malta on December 1, 1913 for the return journey.

On 3 December 1913 the fleet passed Gibraltar, homeward bound, leaving behind a Europe that just nine months later would be convulsed by the first of the 20th century's pair of great world wars. At the time, however, the coming cataclysm was quite unanticipated. The Navy's larger concern was the Mexican Revolution, which, in the spring of 1914 generated a major U.S. naval combat operation at Vera Cruz, involving most of the ships that had enjoyed a peaceful trip to the "Old World" of Europe a short time before.

Having time to reflect during the trip to and from Italy, Gignilliat recorded the following observations in his letters to Minnie:

- *"The sea is wonderfully blue, the sky is filled with soft masses of clouds, and the gray ships with the bright spots of color on their signal halyards look like Reuterdahl's pictures."*

- *"This stupendous mass of guns and armor plate is so steady that you scarcely know you are in motion; there is none of the vibration of the liner."* [perhaps referring to their voyages across the Atlantic on ocean liners during their 1911 visit to England]

- *"These great dreadnoughts that could probably destroy anything on earth, look simply like specks amid the vastness of the sea and sky."*

With thoughts of Culver never far from his mind, Gignilliat recalled thinking of "Mr. Jensen's remark about the work of man in contrast with the work of God, when he saw the circular lagoon alongside the lake" as he gazed at the fleet at sea.

Norwegian Jens Jensen was a noted landscape architect brought to CMA by the Culver brothers to assess the status of the campus' grounds and landscaping. Surprising Gignilliat greatly, Jensen was not impressed by Culver's grounds during his first visit to campus in 1913.

A devoted naturalist, Jensen remarked that the geometry evident in CMA's lagoons was obviously the work of man, which could not compete with the work of God and detracted from it.[70] Jensen would later be hired by Culver in 1915 to fill in the lagoons and redesign much of CMA's landscaping as part of the "Greater Culver" strategic plan.

With an astute eye for the human dimension, Gignilliat observed the interactions of the crew and officers on Arkansas carefully, and he came away from the experience greatly impressed by what he saw. He offered the following assessments of the ship's personnel over the course of the cruise:

- *"I am impressed with the looks of the men. Put a lot of college and high school men in the same togs and you will have about the same looking crowd. They average a bit younger than I had anticipated. At first you notice the absence of the saluting and more formal intercourse between officers and men that one is accustomed to in a military post, but in the close quarters aboard ship too rigid adherence to that sort of thing would undoubtedly be inconvenient. Apparently nothing is sacrificed in efficiency."*

- *"If one of their number dies who has a dependent mother or other relative they make most astoundingly generous contributions from their small pay. There are many exceptionally good faces among the men."*

- *"One of Ingram's gunners, a chap named Reilly, who made with his gun the world's record of 6 shots in 57 seconds, is a fine type – clean-cut and alert, the sort of chap you like to think of as typically American, even if the name is Irish. I spent an interesting half hour in the turret with him at general quarters yesterday morning."*

- *"It is not a hard matter to tell a harmoniously and efficiently handled organization. You sort of feel it in the air. That is the case with the Arkansas. She has a splendid lot of officers. I do not know when I have been so uniformly impressed with a lot of men as I have with those officers I have been in close contact with in the wardroom of this ship."*

Gignilliat was so impressed by the crew of the Ark that he wrote an article upon his return titled "The Arkansas Spirit," lauding the attention to duty, efficiency, and teamwork of the crew. Consciously or not, this article channeled Kiser's "The Spirit of Culver," noting that "spirit is as valuable an asset in citizenship as it is in the naval service."[71]

On this voyage, Gignilliat acquired more support for the developmental approach he had instituted at Culver, finding that sailors under rigid discipline at sea were quite capable of conducting themselves respectably in port when freed from the strict discipline required on board. In fact, Gignilliat remarked on his impressions at the Logansport gate dedication ceremony on May 20, 1914, saying that he had encountered "a lot of the finest types of Indiana men" serving in the Navy while on the cruise, all of whom impressed him with their military bearing and proficiency.[72] This experience provided him with external validation of the value of the

The Brooklyn Bridge, photographed from the deck of Arkansas *on arrival in New York City, December 15, 1913.*[74]

discipline he sought to instill in Culver cadets.[73]

The 13-day return trip across the Atlantic was uneventful, ending with the fleet making port at the Navy yard in New York City late on December 15, 1913.

As he had the previous year, Gignilliat returned to campus just in time for the Christmas furlough. His homecoming was "hailed with delight by all cadets," and he was greeted on his first appearance in chapel in January 1914 with a "hearty yell which had nothing aqueous in its texture," quipped *The Vedette*.[75] His reunion with Minnie must have been especially welcomed, and he surely spent time talking with Leigh Jr. about his experiences as a new cadet at Culver. Fred and Hank must have also delighted in their father's return and reveled in his accounts of his many and varied experiences. The family was whole again and happy.

The Eventful Year of 1913 Comes to a Pleasant Close

During his absence, the cadets had begun exploring the establishment of a cadet-run Honor system, and the first classmen had been measured for their class rings that had been designed by Gignilliat before he departed for the cruise. Perhaps most exciting was the completion of North Barrack and the Administration building while he was away, allowing the cadets to move from their tents into the building and Gignilliat to move into his new office on the first floor of the new Administration building Readjusting to life on land, he resumed administering the Academy.

Chapter 8 –The "Schoolboy Epic Supreme" of the 1913 Logansport Flood Rescue Adventure

Fresh off the success of the 1913 presidential inaugural, and during that same month of March, Culver experienced an event that influenced the school more than any other event during its first two decades: assisting in the rescue efforts related to the devastating Logansport Flood of 1913. It is important to place this event in its proper context so that its true significance can be understood.

The 1913 Flood – Background and Context

According to author Trudy Bell, the Easter 1913 storm system and the ensuing flooding was "the most widespread natural disaster ever experienced by the United States (at least up to then), far wider in geographical extent than the Great Chicago Fire of 1871, the Johnstown flood in 1889, and the great earthquake and fire in San Francisco in 1906."[1] It was this level of devastation, brought on by a once-in-a-lifetime combination of floods and tornadoes, that impacted Logansport and caused Gignilliat to involve Culver in the episode.

The conditions that led to this flood developed over time and should have been more evident to those who study such things were it not for some particularly unusual circumstances. Bell offers that, "the winter of 1913 was unusually warm and wet," with widespread rains occurring throughout the month of January that produced flooding in Ohio by the end of month. Temperatures returned to more normal winter readings during the month of February, which also came with more precipitation in the form of snow.

However, in the beginning of March the temperatures were again unnaturally high (unlike the frigid weather the cadets endured during the same period at the presidential inaugural), topping a more June-like 70 degrees Fahrenheit during the week before Easter. These conditions resulted in the soil becoming saturated and "unable to absorb any more rainwater" by the week of Easter.[2]

All this changed dramatically and for the worse on the Thursday before Easter, when "an arctic high-pressure system swooped down from Canada across the Midwest," dropping the temperature nearly 40 degrees in just six hours. The system also brought with it "hurricane-force winds" that "topped 70 miles per hour around all of Ohio and Indiana," rolling carriages off roads and blowing down "signs, chimneys, and fences," along with "hundreds of telephone and telegraph poles around the Midwest."[3]

The U.S. Weather Bureau had been watching the system develop, and this change confirmed their worst fears about the potential danger of it. So certain had the government's meteorologists been about their predictions that they alerted the newly inaugurated President Woodrow Wilson on Wednesday of the likely catastrophic nature of its impact in the Midwest. This prompted the new president to dispatch immediate offers of assistance to the governors of the states that would bear the brunt of the storm – Ohio and Indiana.[4]

The heavy ice that settled on the wires further damaged the communications network in the area. By Saturday evening, which was calm, clear, and beheld a total eclipse of the moon, Bell estimates that around "8,000 [telegraph] poles and associated wires were on the ground," crippling communications across the entire Midwest.[5] This was particularly impactful in the era before commercial radio because it prevented the U.S. Weather Bureau from gathering the necessary information about the developing weather systems to create a coherent picture of the potential impact or issue timely weather warnings based upon such information.

Even if the communications network had been intact, the combination of weather influences in Logansport – especially the wind -- had destroyed the local weather instruments by Sunday evening, rendering them inoperable or no longer present. In addition, the damaged communications network prevented the governor of Indiana from receiving the offer of assistance proffered by President Woodrow Wilson on the morning of Wednesday, March 26, 1913.[6]

Record rainfall began moving across the Midwest on Easter Sunday, bringing an average of nine inches of rain to the area, which represented close to three months of normal rainfall for the region. Since the saturated and partially frozen soil could not absorb any of the moisture, it began flowing into the low areas and overfilling the rivers. Even if the people living near the rivers flowing through the affected areas had access to the information, the rainfall that occurred over the ensuing three to four days was unprecedented and would have overwhelmed any plans they may have had to react.

The conditions coalesced in a frightfully dangerous combination on Tuesday, March 25, 1913. On that fateful day, about half of the four-day rainfall total fell "with tropical intensity," amounting to around 4.5 inches of precipitation that caused some rivers in the area to rise as rapidly as a foot an hour. The frigid temperatures transformed much of it into ice. The water that wasn't frozen accumulated in terrific quantities in the rivers and streams that flowed toward Logansport, "putting the volume [of water] in the Miami Valley at something like a month's flow over Niagara Falls." The water came with such force on Tuesday that it "undermined building foundations," and it arrived so fast that "people did not have time to pack food or move precious possessions upstairs, or even to escape their office buildings or homes."[7] It seemed to many at the time that the Midwest was being torn apart by the sheer power of this unprecedented combination of natural forces.[8]

It was these conditions that bore down on Logansport with such force that it began lifting houses off their foundations and floating them down river in the rush of the exaggerated currents of the Wabash and Eel rivers, and trapping people in their office buildings and homes. Watching houses of his citizens floating away spurred the mayor of Logansport, David D. Fickle, into action, calling anyone and everyone for help. One of these calls was to Gignilliat at Culver on the dark and stormy evening of Tuesday, March 25, 1913.

The Schoolboy Epic Supreme – Culver's Role in the Logansport Flood of March 1913

The account of the actions of CMA with respect to the Logansport Flood are well known for the first day, but the actions of the second day are relatively unknown. Gignilliat provided a thorough account of the first day's events in fairly good detail, and it, augmented by other sources to provide context and greater breadth to the overall impact, forms the basis of the recounting of this part of the event.

Gignilliat titled his five-page account the event in his memoirs the "Schoolboy Epic Supreme."[9] It is worth quoting from in detail, as it illustrates Gignilliat's ability to write well, tell a good story, and his attention to detail in matters great and small related to this episode.

According to Gignilliat:

> *In March 1913, after a long and severe winter, there were thaws, and the vernal equinox brought much rain. On one occasion it rained steadily for several days and several nights. The lake, only recently ice-free [because of the unusually warm weather at the beginning of the month], was filled to*

the brim. The lawn and parade ground were veritable lakes in themselves, and innumerable tiny rivulets were slithering down the water-soaked trunks of the still leafless oaks and elms.

The storm broke in all its fury the night that [famous opera singer and mother of BHT cadet] Madame Ernestine Schumann Heink came to Culver to sing to the cadets [Tuesday, March 25, 1913, right after the Easter weekend on campus]. While outside the rain poured and there were flashes of lightning and great rolls of thunder, she sang to them, and in competition with the elements, enthralled them with her glorious voice and marvelous personality.[10]

Madame Schumann Heink poses with some CMA cadets during her visit.[11]

After the concert some of us went to the home of Mr. Edwin R. Culver, President of the Board of Trustees and host that evening to Madame Schumann Heink. Outside, the rain still came down in sheets; and there was wind and lightning. But inside by the big log fire in Mr. Culver's living room, it was very warm and cozy.[12]

Gignilliat continued, writing, "*Entertained by Schumann Heink's stories of her early life and struggles, and under the spell of her infectious laughter and richly accented conversation, we forgot the rain.*"

ER Culver's house on Culver's campus (which became the superintendent's home in 1919).[13]

*She was telling us, as I recall it, of how as a little girl when her
family was very poor she had sung in payment for a pail of milk
which she did not have the money to buy.[14]*

Shumann-Heink became very attached to Culver as a result of her
visit and experience. The cadets considered her their "patron saint,"
and she reciprocated, commenting that she loved it at Culver and that
she was a "full-hearted Culver girl." The cadets presented her with a
letter of appreciation for the Easter concert upon her departure from
campus on April 11, 1913.[15]

In fact, the storm had begun on the previous Friday (Good Friday) with
a powerful wind storm that had roared in from the west. The rain started
falling on Easter Sunday and continued for the next three days, raising the
spring-fed Lake Maxinkuckee's usually constant level by over two feet. By
Monday morning the water levels in rivers in the area had risen as much
as eight feet, with many being above flood stage of 12 feet. The result
caused the Wabash River to overflow its banks and begin flooding the
streets of Logansport in the lowest areas where the Wabash and Eel rivers
came together.

Over the next 36 hours, the water level in Logansport rose from an
already record-high 12 feet over the flood stage to as high as 22.5 feet in
some areas, washing away three or four bridges and numerous houses.
According to one account, "Practically one-third of the city was under
water, which forced 1 -200 families [~5,000 people] to leave their homes.
Twelve houses were entirely swept away and scores more moved from
their foundations."[16] Adding to the misery of the flood, six to eight inches
of snow fell on Logansport that evening.

Facing such daunting conditions over an area of 1.25 miles in his city,
Mayor David Fickle of Logansport sounded the alarm for any and all types
of assistance. CMA became involved in the rescue effort related to the
Logansport Flood as a result of a frantic telephone call, likely from one of
the mayor's representatives, James I. "Jim" Barnes.[17] Although attributing
the call to the mayor himself, Gignilliat recounts the rather dramatic
episode as follows, writing:

*As we were listening to [Madame Schumann Heink's] story,
Mr. Culver's house boy summoned me to the telephone to
receive a long-distance telephone call. It was from the Mayor of
Logansport, Indiana, the city whose newspaper had so ridiculed
our early efforts to start the Naval School.*

Logansport was in dire distress. It was situated some thirty miles to the south of us at the confluence of the Eel and Wabash Rivers, and a large portion of the city was under water, flooded. Those who were in the low-lying parts of the city near the angry, swirling, constantly rising waters were in very real danger. There were children and old people suffering from exposure and lack of food.

The Mayor wanted to borrow a trainload of our United States Navy cutters for his emergency.

"Have you anyone who can handle them?" I inquired.

" I don't know," he replied.

"Well," I said, "they are not row boats, you know. They are big and heavy and require a trained crew to manage them safely in swift currents. Maybe we can send you men as well as boats. I will call you back presently."[18]

It was probably Jim Barnes who orchestrated Culver's involvement in the rescue operation. There is something poetic about his involvement, as it had been Jim's father John who HH Culver had hired to build CMA's Main Barrack in 1895 to replace the Chautauqua that burned to the ground on February 24, 1895. Following his father into construction, Jim eventually took over the family business and built several buildings at the Academy in subsequent years. Barnes also served as mayor of Logansport from 1918 to 1921, and he owned a house on Lake Maxinkuckee later in life that he passed down to his descendants.[19]

Given his familiarity with Culver, it is therefore quite probable that the mayor tasked Barnes with reaching out to CMA for assistance. The *Logansport Journal-Tribune* offers corroborating evidence to support this notion, reporting in May of 1914 that "it was Barnes who started the whole thing when he shot a message to Culver on March 25, 1913, asking for the use of the Culver boats for flood relief work here."

The article goes on to state that it was Barnes who "took the Vandalia special train to Culver to get the boats" after securing Gignilliat's agreement to participate, and that Barnes was delighted to discover upon the train's arrival, that "Culver authorities were not only willing to send the boats but would send men to man them."[20]

Gignilliat himself acknowledged Barnes' significant involvement organizing the rescue effort during his welcoming remarks at the Logansport Gate dedication ceremony the following year.

Fickle's situation was certainly dire, and Logansport was not the only city in the area facing such peril. Something similar had happened in Peru, Indiana, which had a population of around 16,000 people (roughly equivalent to Logansport) and was 16 miles east – and upriver on the Wabash River – of Logansport. This is an area quite accustomed to seasonal flooding, so many Indiana residents were not terribly concerned about the rain or warnings about flooding because they had both seen and experienced it before, and they were oblivious to what was coming toward them. However, as Professor William R. Lazenby, the head of the department of forestry at Ohio State University at the time of the flood, offered, the intensity of a flood is directly related to its "rapidity," presenting its greatest danger and doing its greatest damage "when the surface water passes off quickly."[21]

This is precisely what was occurring on the evening of March 24, 1913 — the rapid passing of surface water – in the area around Logansport, Indiana. According to one account:

> "...on the evening of March 24 [1913], Peru residents had no idea what was coming. Nobody could turn to a 24-hour news network to learn that some random people had drowned in communities several hours away and start putting the dots together that this was not an average seasonal flood. There were no radio stations to listen to, although radio technology was making inroads into some levels of society, with the Titanic memorably using their radio room almost a year earlier. Information was dribbling into the local newspapers, which were preparing issues for the next morning. People could look out their window or get the occasional phone call or telegram to learn what was going on away from their home."[22]

With the damage to the telegraph poles in the area disrupting communication services, author Geoff Williams, who made an extensive study of the flood published in 2013, determined that the Wabash River "ambushed" Peru in a surprise attack, as the water "stormed the city all at once," instead of "gradually coming into the streets." The force of the "attack" devastated the town of Peru in much the same way that Logansport would be demolished.[23]

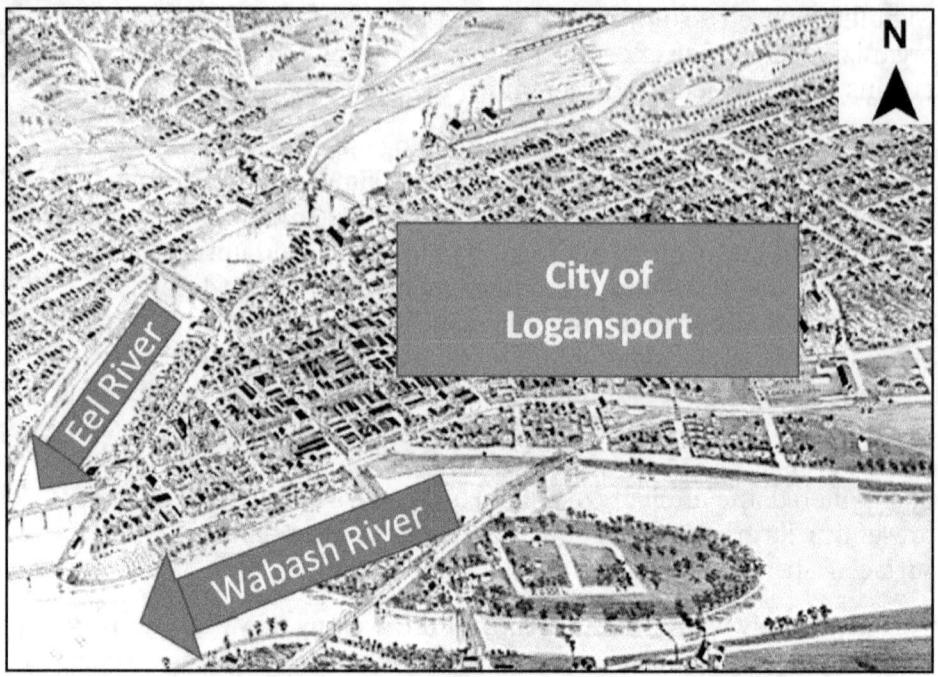

City of Logansport showing the confluence of the Eel and Wabash Rivers.[24]

It was this "attacking" wave of water that continued on toward Logansport, only it combined with the force of the smaller but still powerful Eel River at the very center of Logansport, where the two rivers join together.

As bad as the damage had been in Peru and even in the eastern portion of Logansport caused by the force of the Wabash River, the combined swell of the Wabash and Eel rivers was much more powerful, and it poured over the banks of the Eel River just as it bent to the south to join with the larger Wabash River. As a result, the water crested over the banks at levels of 12 feet and much higher, slamming into the flimsily built structures in the less desirable southwest portion of Logansport, submerging them instantly and tearing them from their foundations, setting them afloat. It was almost certainly these same houses that Mayor Fickle watched as they floated away downriver.

Faced with a dilemma of wanting to help the citizens of Logansport but determining how best to respond to the mayor's request for assistance while safeguarding his Culver equipment and cadets, Gignilliat turned to ER Culver for guidance and advice. As Gignilliat recalled, he "returned to the fireside, apologized to Schumann Heink, and asked E.R. Culver to come with me to his study. When I told him of Logansport's distress, he said to me, 'Do what you think best.'"[25]

Armed with ER Culver's discretion, Gignilliat decided to send four of Culver's cutters to Logansport and to supply the cadets to crew them. Unbeknownst to Gignilliat, President Wilson decided to engage the resources of the War Department in the recovery efforts early in the morning of Wednesday, March 26, 1913, directing the War Department to "extend the necessary aid to the suffers from the floods."[26] It is unlikely that Wilson could envision the role that cadets from Culver Military Academy would play in this effort or that boys far younger than the draft age of 21 at the time would become so involved in the effort.

Gignilliat informed his staff of his decision, and the campus began to spring into action almost immediately. As Gignilliat related,

> *It was after midnight [on Wednesday, March 26, 1913] when I turned out our campus crews to load the cutters on the flat cars which the Mayor of Logansport had sent up. I placed the supervision of this job in the capable hands of Captain Robert Rossow, Captain Howard Noble, and Captain Harold Bays. Then I went back to my office to pick, in collaboration with Major Greiner, the Commandant of Cadets, four crews to man the cutters in the flood. Since the boys who had been midshipmen in the summer schools were not quite sufficient in numbers to man the oars, I supplemented them with some brawn and muscle from the current football team.[27]*

Requiring a crew of ten oarsmen plus a coxswain for each cutter, Gignilliat and his staff selected 44 cadets to participate in the rescue efforts as crew for the four cutters. One smaller cadet who had not been selected, Elliot White Springs, refused to be excluded and found a way to become part of the first day's efforts by stowing away under one of the cutters on the train. Despite his well-earned reputation for enforcing strict discipline, Gignilliat reported that he "did not have the heart" to punish Springs, perhaps recognizing that he might have done the same thing in similar circumstances and respecting the young cadet's desire to be part of the adventure and willingness to face the danger it entailed. Gignilliat may have had an inkling that this rather slight teenager would distinguish himself in WWI as a pilot by shooting down a dozen German aircraft, becoming one of America's greatest aces.

Despite Springs' success in insinuating himself into the expedition, Gignilliat recalled that all of the other 44 cadets were "hand-picked" for their experience as oarsmen and/or brawn. He also found ways for cadets not selected to crew the cutters to contribute, using their tremendous "strength and will" aroused in the moment to help carry the heavy and unwieldy cutters from the boathouse to the rail spur on campus.

Amidst the confusion of excitement, Gignilliat placed the strong-voiced and charismatic Captain Rossow in charge of the loading detail. A veteran

Regular Army cavalryman who commanded the BHT with an inordinate level of pride and who had been instrumental in persuading Gignilliat to establish the Summer Cavalry School in 1907, Rossow was popular with the cadets and an extremely forceful and capable leader. The cadets reciprocated Rossow's deep love of Culver by dedicating the 1913 *Roll Call* to him.

The efficient Rossow organized the cadets into teams of 25 to carry the heavy and awkward cutters – which were 28 feet in length, eight feet wide and weighed 3,000 pounds – the half-mile

Captain Robert Rossow.[28] from the boat shed on the edge of the lake to the railroad spur on campus and load them on the railcars that had arrived around 1:00 am under the direction of Jim Barnes.[29] Working in the darkness of the night, and in a cold and steady rain, Rossow had several bonfires built to provide light and heat while they secured the boats to the railcars.

Once finished, the cadets who had helped carry the boats were quite disappointed to learn that they were not going to be part of the group to travel to Logansport. Adding to the confusion, another group of about 50 cadets arrived at the rail spur and tried to bluff their way on the train.

Knowing boys as he did, Gignilliat sympathized with the cadets, observing that,

You can't have a stir like that in a school without having boys wake up who are not being called or needed. Adventure was in the air that night, and danger. They both stir youth to action. There were many volunteers

Culver cutters secured to rail flatcars.[30]

clamoring to man the oars, all of them eager to serve. I was not abrupt with these surplus volunteers. I think that even in that absorbing moment I took time to tell them that discretion was the better part of valor.[31]

Despite his explanation and firm refusal, the cadets pleaded with good-cop Gignilliat to be allowed to participate. Bad-cop Rossow gathered the boys together and explained the selection criteria to them, emphasizing that all of the cadets who were going to Logansport had either experience in the Summer Naval School or were accomplished varsity athletes, and in some cases both. This mollified some and silenced further protests for the moment.[32]

Having placated the stay-behinds, Gignilliat, along with three adults and 44 cadets (and the stowaway Springs) boarded the train and departed for Logansport sometime around 3:00 am, leaving the very capable Majors Glascock and Greiner in charge at CMA.

Majors Glascock and Greiner around the time of the Logansport Flood.[33]

According to Gignilliat, the trip itself was somewhat precarious, since the conditions between Culver and Logansport were unknown and the rail men were unsure if the bridges along the route would sustain the weight of the fully loaded train. Accordingly, the train proceeded slowly and carefully along its southwesterly track.

> "Trestles, for those who don't have extensive bridge terminology, were bridges constructed for the railroad. They were sturdy to be sure, since trains passed over them, and usually constructed of timber and iron, but they were built hastily and never meant to be permanent thoroughfares. They were constructed cheaply and fast, as a stop-gap until the railroad could get around to spending money on stone or iron structures."[34]

All of this justified the caution demonstrated by the train engineer and crew.

Despite their slow progress, spirits were high among the train's passengers. From their position in the caboose, Gignilliat remembered that he and the group "talked in the high excitement of the adventure that had taken us out of our warm beds into the drenched blackness of a cold and windy March night."[35] It appears that Gignilliat was as caught up in the excitement of the moment as his cadets.

The normally one-hour trip might have taken twice as long, due to the caution of the rail men. Despite the high spirits of the group reported by Gignilliat during the trip, the adults also tended to business, talking with Barnes about the conditions they could expect to encounter when they arrived and dividing the cadets up into specific boat crews. Rossow reported that he made a special effort to ensure that his boat was crewed by "husky" cadets he knew and trusted.[36]

The train "crawled" into Logansport "just as dawn was breaking" on Wednesday, March 26, 1913. With the power knocked out, the city before them was dark, flooded, and covered with a fresh blanket of snow. According to the stowaway cadet Springs, the temperature was a bone-chilling 24 degrees, and it was snowing hard.[37] It was immediately apparent that the mayor had been right to ask for help.

According to Gignilliat, even though the train stopped far from the worst flooded areas,

> The flood waters were just about level with the floor of the flatcars, so that it was a much easier task to unload the heavy cutters than it had been to load them. They were readily skidded off into the water and held alongside the flatcars as at a dock, while the cadets, previously assigned to their boats and thwarts, clambered aboard with their oars.[38]

Having arrived at Logansport and disembarked from the train, Gignilliat and Barnes conferred with some of the local officials from a Citizens Committee that had been formed to coordinate the rescue effort while Rossow and the others formed the cadets into the agreed-upon boat crews. The committee had determined that each of Culver's boats needed to have an armed police officer on board to help control any unrest they might encounter. The somewhat irascible Rossow objected immediately, uncomfortable with allowing an armed, unknown person into his vessel. The ever-tactful Gignilliat recognized the wisdom of the decision, and, possibly encouraged by Barnes, agreed to it and welcomed the police officers to board the Culver boats.[39]

A good deal of the devastation Gignilliat observed was as much due to the actions of man as it was to nature. Arthur Morgan, an engineer who studied the flood area afterwards, determined that residents had been too "shovel-happy" in removing "innumerable little storage reservoirs" in the area and also of "improving the overgrown and obstructed paths of the water," allowing water to flow "much more rapidly into the main streams."

People had also chopped down too many trees in the area's forests and removed too much of the "surface layer of leaves and mold" that would have served to slow the flow of water had it been present. In their haste to improve the area, people had built "too much, too quickly" that brought with it the paving of streets and construction of sewage systems that "hastened the flow of storm water." Finally, the construction of dams had done more harm than good in times of anything other than usual water flow. Author Geoff Williams observed that the tremendous amount of garbage was a fifth factor not mentioned by Morgan but which contributed significantly to the conditions that allowed for the flood to become so destructive.[40]

However, the proximate causes of the flood were less related to the issues identified by Morgan. According to Williams,

> *"There was one last reason for the flood, and it does not allow for any real historical or scientific analysis: just plain bad timing. It was the end of winter. The ground wasn't frozen – which can be problematic when there's flooding – but it was still oversaturated with melted, and melting, snow. The rain that came with the tornadoes couldn't evaporate, or be absorbed, fast enough. Additionally, the melting snow already had rivers at a higher volume than was typical for this time of year."*[41]

A dashing Gignilliat temporarily commanding Cutter 12 during the rescue efforts.[44]

While the contributing causes to the devastation they encountered were relevant, the group from Culver focused on the task at hand and directed their efforts to the daunting rescue effort they were facing.

With their preparations complete, the adventure began. Gignilliat initially captained Cutter 6, Bays commanded Cutter 11, Noble took the helm of Cutter 12, and Rossow skippered Cutter 13.

As Gignilliat recalled,

At the tiller of each boat there was an officer of the school. I took command of the first boat and directed the others to shove off and follow me in column as we rowed toward that portion of the town close to the banks of the two rivers where citizens were in the greatest danger and need.

Captain Harold C. Bays, who commanded Cutter 11.[42]

At first we progressed nicely in a column of cutters, but as we came nearer to the river, the boat that I commanded was caught in a whirlpool at a street crossing and spun around like a top. Before I could give the orders to pull us out of the whirlpool, two of the heavy [14-foot] oars were snapped like toothpicks against a telegraph pole. Fortunately we had brought along spares.[43]

As soon as we gained the quieter waters in the middle of the next block, I had the other boats pull up within hearing distance. I explained that it was evidently no longer possible to maintain a group formation, that each boat should proceed on its own, taking off first the marooned citizens nearest the river, that refugees should be taken to a certain point on high ground where soup and coffee kitchens had been set up by a relief committee, and, finally, that we would all rendezvous at that point at noon for further instructions. Each officer was armed with a pistol, and the instructions were that if any boat got into trouble, three shots should be fired and the nearest boat would go to the rescue.[45]

Dispersing in different directions, each boat began conducting its own rescues of the imperiled citizens of Logansport.

Gignilliat recalled his first rescue as follows:

...we effected our first rescue of two men on the roof of a one-story cottage. The roof, which was steeply

Rossow's Cutter 13 in action after dropping off the flood victims to the right.[49]

pitched, was only about half out of water. The men had been clinging to the ridge pole all night in the cold and rain and wind. They were near collapse. One of them, overcome with fatigue and exposure, cried hysterically. They told me that there had been three of them, but that one had slipped off and been drowned.[46]

Later, Gignilliat and his crew found

...two women, one sixty years old, ...in the attic of a one-story house. They had been lying on the rafters for forty-eight hours without food, light, or heat. We could not see them, but could hear their calls for help. Because the water was over the doors and windows, the cadets tore a hole in the roof to remove the flood victims.[47]

Through experience, the Culver men found that they could accommodate approximately twenty adults and around 10 children (depending upon their age and size) before having to return to the drop-off point. They did their best to abide these guidelines, but it was not always possible to do so. On one such occasion, according to Gignilliat,

Rossow's Cutter 13 loaded with flood victims.[52]

...I was forced to load our boat a little more than I thought was prudent. At the last house we rowed up to there were five children, and their excited mother refused to leave any of them behind for the next trip. The current was swift in that particular section and as we tried to negotiate a street corner, our cutter was swept under a slanting guy wire of a telephone pole. The current jammed the side of the boat against the slanting wire and tipped the boat dangerously to one side. With disciplined cool-headedness in the face of the excited cries of the women and the children in the boat, the cadets in my crew kept their eyes on me, responding instantly to my shouted commands, not letting their attention be distracted by panic among the passengers or the predicament that threatened to capsize us. Nearly pulling their young arms out of their sockets, and with the help of the boy in the bow with the boat hook, who, without orders from me, did just the right thing on his own initiative, they extricated us from the guy wire.[48]

The prudence in selecting experienced oarsmen for this effort was paying great dividends as the rescue efforts progressed.

Gignilliat related other stories about a calm and cheerful woman rescued by his boat who had with her a baby born the previous day, and another woman who handed a cadet in his boat a bundle she reported as containing her baby but which was actually her beloved pet poodle. In yet another incident that must have resonated with Gignilliat, "One helpless old man in the arms of his cadet rescuer said, 'I am not afraid for you to carry me down the ladder, comrade. This is the third time that I have been carried by a soldier -- twice when wounded in the Civil War.'"

According to Gignilliat, "Each of the four boats had its own stirring adventures in the raging flood," and "[e]ach had more than one close call," but none of the boats experienced any situation that placed it or its crew in overly dangerous situation that would have required the assistance of others and/or placed the cadets in harm's way.[50] Rossow related a particularly harrowing encounter that had a good outcome but which was quite perilous at the time.[51] One suspects that each of the cutters had similar experiences while operating in such a precarious situation.

Regardless of how one characterized the experience, suffice to state that the day was certainly filled with many challenging and eventful encounters.

Gignilliat's Cutter 6 making rescues.[57]

In response to the Logansport Mayor's call for assistance, supplies also began arriving for the displaced residents. The city of Chicago sent 5,000 loaves of bread to the area, and the city of South Bend sent large quantities of bread and meat. Others provided wagons loaded with clothing and provisions.

The Citizens Committee took charge of organizing the supplies, using Logansport High School as a makeshift shelter, hospital, and distribution center.

In the same spirit of sharing credit, Gignilliat was careful to include the efforts of the Logansport citizens in his account of the episode, relating:

> *I don't mean to give the impression that the Culver cadets did all the rescuing in Logansport while the Mayor and the townspeople stood by in apathy and helplessness, because that was by no means the case. There were many willing workers among the citizens of the town, and there were a number of citizens of our own town of Culver who came down to help, and there were yard men from the Culver campus who rendered valuable assistance.*[53]

However, the decision to crew the cutters with cadets experienced in using them proved to be quite well-founded. According to Gignilliat,

> *Once, when our cadet crews were pretty well worn out, we tried an experiment by sending out a boat manned by some husky men from the city of Logansport who had volunteered for the job. They were willing enough but they did not have the knack of pulling together that our cadet crews had; nor were they accustomed to responding instantly to commands, and that was vital in the swift and treacherous currents.*[54]

As a result, the willing and husky men from Logansport proved to be ineffectual as cutter crews, which required a level of subordination and cooperation that came only as a result of discipline and training.

Besides their training and experience, Gignilliat explained that the Culver cadets "had something in their hearts that in emergencies gave them strength that they did not have in muscles alone." Even after three decades, Gignilliat wrote that he remembered "the look in their eyes, their coolness, their discipline, the heart in them that gave to their legs and arms strength they did not normally possess."[55] His comments regarding the cadets are filled with pride, respect, and admiration, providing much *a posteriori* justification for his decision to use the cadets to aid the citizens of Logansport.

Working steadily in the snow and cold, and with few breaks to eat the sandwiches provided by a local family and drink coffee from the jugs carried on each cutter, each boat made approximately 6-10 trips between the flooded downtown area and the drop-off point, and rescued around 200 people. By nightfall on Wednesday, March 26, 1913, Gignilliat determined, after consulting with his other boat commanders and officials in Logansport, that the Culver group had rescued more than 800 people.[56]

The first day of rescuing had been a remarkable success, both because of the contribution made by Culver and also because not a single cadet had been injured in the process. Returning to Culver by train that evening, Gignilliat and his officers must have discussed the situation thoroughly, sharing all they had learned. Upon arriving back at Culver, the exhausted cadets were released to eat, shower, and rest, likely having little time for any of these activities as they were hounded by their peers for descriptions of their adventures.

Captain William R. "Duke" Kennedy.[58]

Conferring with Captains Rossow, Noble, and Bays, along with Majors Glascock and Greiner, that evening, Gignilliat determined that it would be prudent to send two additional cutters to assist with the next day's rescue efforts (cutters 4 and 10). This would require an additional 22 cadets to crew the boats and two more adults to command them. Captain Kennedy and Lieutenant Rockwood were selected for these roles.

Keeping some experienced cadets in each boat, the Culver leaders also selected some cadets who had not participated in the first day's rescue efforts to replace some who had. Overall, a total of 90 cadets ended up participating in either one or both of the rescue efforts.[59] According to accounts from Logansport, Culver may have also brought some row boats with them on the second day to assist with the rescue efforts.

It was fortunate that the Vandalia Railroad was able to continue operating, as daily routines had ceased to exist in areas impacted by the flood. Along with the disruption of the communications network, there was also a "virtual shutdown of railroads throughout the Midwest."[60] However, the geography of the area worked to Culver's advantage, as the area north of Logansport from where the Culver group came was located on higher ground outside the flooded areas and thus largely free of impact from the damage. As a result, the Vandalia line was able to continue ferrying people and supplies into Logansport virtually unabated.

Returning on the morning of Thursday, March 27, 1913, the group from Culver resumed its rescue efforts with an augmented force of six cutters, 50 cadets, and perhaps some smaller row boats. No accounts exist that address the specific efforts on this second day, but it is safe to assume that they

Gignilliat in action on the second day of the Logansport rescue effort.[62]

proceeded much as the first day's efforts had but encompassed a larger area. Culver's rescue efforts concluded at around 4:30 pm on the second day, and the group had rescued almost 700 more people. By this time, the water has receded to such an extent that it was impossible to get the cutters back to the railroad, forcing them to be left behind and the cadets to "*march a long detour back to the depot.*"[61]

The endeavor was quite taxing on all involved. While possessing a high level of energy, the normally indefatigable Gignilliat recalled that he was "*unutterably tired and weary*" by the end of the second day of the rescue efforts. The youthful and energetic cadets were remarkably more resilient, giving fifteen rousing "rahs" for Logansport as the train departed after marching to the train station, and they "*were singing and joking*" throughout the entire return trip.

In recognition of their efforts, and despite their apparent zest, Gignilliat authorized the highly unusual reward of excusing the cadets who had worked so hard in the Logansport rescue efforts from the next morning's reveille formation.[63] This was such a remarkable occurrence that it warranted mention the following year in the 1914 *Roll Call.*

Upon his return to Culver, Gignilliat dutifully reported the episode to Office of the Naval Militia in Washington, D.C., noting that the cadets had helped to save over 1,400 people over the course of their two days of rescue efforts (1,492 by Rossow's account).[64] This contribution was part of the larger efforts orchestrated by the Wilson administration to make use of the government's resources to assist those impacted by the devastating floods, undoubtedly bringing more renown to Culver in the halls of Washington, DC.[65]

Perhaps reflective of this situation, Gignilliat was both surprised and gratified to receive subsequently several letters lauding the "magnificent work" of the cadets. Of note, Gignilliat received letters from the Vice President of the United States, Thomas Marshall, and from "the young and then relatively unknown Secretary of the Navy, Franklin D. Roosevelt."

Things went from bad to worse in Logansport, as thugs and sightseers alike descended upon the city. Martial law was declared on Friday as a result of rampant lawlessness and looting, along with threats of disease and typhoid. Police offers were authorized to "shoot on sight" anyone found looting. Gignilliat got the cadets out of the area in the nick of time.

Gignilliat sent the reliable Bays back to Logansport with a detail on Friday and Saturday to retrieve the cutters and other equipment left behind. Back on campus, Culver held a banquet on Saturday evening in honor of the cadets who participated in the rescue efforts. Gignilliat was still recovering and relinquished his toastmaster duties to Captain Noble. Cadets told stories and reveled in the memories. The banquet ended with the cadets giving the "leader and hero of the expedition," Gignilliat, their most heartfelt recognition – three rousing live "rahs" – as they had done so thoughtfully for Baden-Powell during his visit the previous year.[66]

Perhaps somewhat ironically, Gignilliat also received a note that was effusive in its praise of the cadets from the mayor of Logansport whose newspaper had ridiculed Culver's early attempts to start a summer Naval School. Gignilliat reported generously that, "the Editor of the paper made the *amende honorable* in a fine and most appreciative editorial in his paper."[67]

The Logansport Gate

Logansport went even further in showing its appreciation, presenting CMA on May 20, 1914 with a large and impressive red-brick and Indiana limestone gate a year later in appreciation of the assistance Culver had provided. Construction began in early October 1913, after Gignilliat and Fickle met to agree to the arrangement ,and cos around $500 (equating to around $16,000 in 2023 dollars). The construction of the gate itself, therefore, came as no surprise to the community, but it was somewhat surprising that the resulting structure so closely resembled the campus gate at Gignilliat's *alma mater*.

Anticipation for the formal dedication ceremony built steadily over the course of the 1913-1914 school year. Approximately 4,000 Logansport citizens, representing one-quarter of the town's total population, attended the dedication ceremony in Culver.

In what had become typical Gignilliat fashion, he marked the occasion by declaring it Logansport Day – "in recognition of services rendered by the corps of cadets during the floods of March 1913" – and he planned a full program of events for the event befitting the occasion.

The trains from Logansport arrived at 10:00 am, and the approximately 3,000 visitors were led to campus by a section of the CMA Band where they were greeted by a double line of mounted cadets posted as sentinels at the gate. Another 1,000 visitors arrived by automobile. The Logansport Citizens and Elks bands, and the CMA Band played while the audience assembled. Rossow's beloved Cutter 13 was installed in the gate for symbolic reasons and to serve as a speaker's platform.

The formal program was scheduled to begin at 10:30 am with a 17-gun salute for the Honorable Samuel G. Ralston, the new Governor of Indiana who had replaced Marshall. Since the Governor was unable to attend, Gignilliat began the ceremony by welcoming the crowd with the following words:

> *"You may think this a strange place to find a boat such as this, but I think that you must confess that it is no more strange than the main street of Logansport where it was forced to navigate in the day when your call for help came to Culver. At that time we heard Mayor Fickle and some others complaining because we had not given them a boat ride, and we have taken this opportunity to make good the deficiency,"* Gignilliat quipped.[69]

The Logansport Gate dedication ceremony, May 20, 1914.[68]

Restoring the solemnity of the moment, Gignilliat remarked that, "There is nothing better for a man or an institution to have than the esteem of his neighbors and to deserve well of them. It is because of this coming of yours today signifies such a regard on your part for the cadets of this academy that I am glad to welcome you to it."

Mixing humor with recognition, Gignilliat brought his introduction to an end, saying, "Logansport is, I believe, the only inland town that has sustained a naval invasion, but no other has had an admiral like Jim Barnes to call for the navy," his final statement providing well-deserved public recognition for Barnes' contributions to the episode.[70]

The Logansport Gate as it appeared at the time of its dedication in 1914.[74]

Continuing, Gignilliat commented briefly on the history and the use of cutters in the US Navy, and he mentioned an early attempt by the Academy to get the Navy interested in providing some for use on Lake Maxinkuckee, Gignilliat then remarked that it was the events related to the Logansport Flood that "finally gave to Culver its best opportunity to convince the department at Washington that the training received here might be of immense practical value." Gignilliat continued by saying that, "We people of the inland are likely to get out of touch with our navy and with the splendid work which it is doing. Yet when I made the Mediterranean cruise on board that magnificent battleship, the *Arkansas*, last fall with the North Atlantic fleet, I found on board that ship a lot of the finest types of Indiana men," of whom he mentioned two by name and lauded.[71]

Gignilliat concluded his remarks pensively and as follows,

> *"Citizens of Logansport, I must acknowledge that you have given us far more than the meager services which we were able to render you. By the light of torches on the dripping March night we loaded and sent down to you a trainload of boats and boys; you sent them back to us with a tradition that is imperishable in the school, a tradition of service to be handed down to all the coming generations of Culver cadets."[72]*

The dedication ceremony itself began at 10:45 am with an address by Mr. A. G. Jenkins, the chairman of the Logansport Relief Committee.

Jenkins said, in part, that

> *"Logansport in her simplicity and gratitude presents to this institution this gate as a memorial to perpetuate in the hearts and memory of the present and future generations the acts of heroism that brought rescue and life to thousands of her people; and imbued with the same purpose presents these medals to the individual cadets who played so important a part in this great work of rescue and humanity. To the cadets who took no part in this great work and to all the patrons of this institution present and past we extend our congratulations for their good fortune in being identified with an institution bearing the great love of humanity that is cherished by the officers and members of the Culver Military Academy, which as an institution is not only the pride of Indiana, but of the nation as well."[73]*

With the preliminaries completed, it was time for the main event. The gift was unveiled, revealing two red brick posts connected by a black chain.

The posts were adorned with large lantern lights atop them, and each had an inscribed bronze plaque affixed to it..

(Note: A simple chain suspended between the pillars
was used to control access until the Class of 2001
provided the actual gates currently in use.)

The bronze plaque on the post contains the following inscription:

"In recognition of the heroic and magnanimous service rendered our citizens by the Culver Cadets during the flood March 26, 27, 1913, this gateway is created by the City of Logansport. MCMXIV."

With a flourish that Gignilliat may have planned himself or inspired, but certainly appreciated, ex-Mayor Fickle's daughter, Helen Fickle, christened the gate by breaking a bottle filled with water from the Wabash and Eel rivers over one of the posts in much the same way that ships are traditionally launched. Helen recited the following words as she broke the bottle, "In commemoration of the heroic work of the Culver cadets and officers at our flood."

Miss Hellen Fickle christening the Logansport Gate, May 20, 1914.[75]

This action was a great show of respect, and it washed away any lingering resentment that may have existed related to the ridicule Logansport had directed at Culver for having an inland naval force.

In a show of unity, the combined bands of the city of Logansport and CMA accompanied these actions by playing Indiana's state song, "On the Banks of the Wabash." The gate was accepted formally on behalf of Culver by E. R Culver and the cadet Senior Captain, U. S. G. Cherry, Jr.

The gate instantly became an important symbol on campus, representing the valiant and courageous efforts of the cadets, and reflecting the symbolism of the Iron Gate.

For Gignilliat, the Logansport Gate served as a reminder to all who entered or left the Culver campus of "the value of discipline and efficiency and of the ideals of service to their fellow man."[76]

Immediately after the dedication ceremony, visitors were welcomed through the gate in three sections, each preceded by a portion of the CMA band, and were directed to various groves of trees on campus. In the comfort of the shade, they were provided with basket lunches, iced lemonade, and hot coffee to enjoy.

After lunch, Gignilliat opened the new Mess Hall, gymnasium, Riding Hall, Open-air Barrack, power plant, Administration building, and the new North Barrack to the visitors. The buildings were marked with signs so they were readily identifiable, and cadets were on hand to show the visitors through the buildings.

Next there was an impressive review of the corps of cadets at the Oval, where the cadets and officers who participated in the flood rescue were presented with special Logansport medals. They were distributed by Miss Helen Fickle, which surely enhanced their appeal.

The parade was followed by a series of impressive exhibition drills and exercises by various groups of cadets at the drill field. These included artillery drill, firing with blank rounds; Gatling gun drills, combined with field wireless and signaling; rifle calisthenics to music; troop drill and a cavalry charge; wall-scaling exhibitions; a music ride by the BHT; a rough riding exhibition by members of the BHT; and concluding with a sham battle. In addition, the Logansport Boy Scout troop performed their own drill exhibition.

Returning to the parade field, cadets impressed the visitors by building military bridges across the lagoons while they watched. Guests were also offered rides on the lake in the very same cutters used during the Logansport rescue efforts of 1913. The cutters were towed by launches past a representation of a partially submerged house similar to the hundreds impacted by the flood in which a figure appeared in an upper window screaming for help who was rescued by a nearby cutter to the cheers of the observers, who appreciated the reenactment. By 6:00 pm, trains began returning the visitors to Logansport with a renewed sense of connection and fellowship with their Culver compatriots.

Gignilliat was clearly moved by this event, and the program shows that he pulled out all the stops to put on the best show possible to mark the occasion. A reporter from the *Logansport Journal-Tribune* who attend the event provided the following dispatch:

"The delight over the complete success of Culver day is mutual between Logansport and Culver, although, in truth, it must be said that the Culver Academy authorities when a long route to make things nice for their visitors. Nothing was left undone: from the moment a Logansport person arrived the cadets took particular pains to make him welcome and make him comfortable. On no occasion have Logansport people making a holiday away from home been so well treated."[77]

Reflecting on the efforts of the cadets at Logansport later in life, Gignilliat conveyed his admiration as follows:

I shall never cease to marvel at the strength and endurance of these teenage boys, who labored at the oars for two days with scant time out for food or rest. Something else that I shall not forget about these boys was their tenderness with the old and the sick and the young. Maybe it was a woman with a baby, maybe a bed-ridden old woman with the stoicism of age, maybe a shivering and frightened child. All were helped into the boat with the solicitude that these boys might have shown their own mothers or grandmothers or little sisters in distress.

They took refugees from houses that the Department of Health had placarded with quarantine signs. They touched contagion and bore it in their arms willingly and unafraid. Yet no cadet became ill from the exposure to disease or cold or wet. All returned tired, but safe and well, to Culver.[78]

Several years later in a speech to the Wisconsin Teachers' Association, Gignilliat observed that the Culver cadets were able to sustain a "physical strain that most boys could not have stood, however willing," because the training they received at Culver had "hammered out of them the softness that is so insidiously creeping into our national life." As evidence to support his assessment, Gignilliat related the following story: "I heard a rather rough looking fellow whose family had been brought to dry land say: 'I though those cadets were a lot of candy legs, but they are rough necks just like we are.'" Far from promoting the dreaded "softness" that he saw creeping into American society, Gignilliat's cadets were proving that they were being trained in what Thucydides referred to as the "hard school."[79]

Indeed, Williams concludes that the great flood of 1913 seemed to have brought out the best in humanity, perhaps because it occurred in the Midwest and laid bare Midwestern sensibilities and decency in a time of unimaginable difficulty.[80] It served to remind residents of the power of nature and to caution them that one ignores such force at one's own peril.[81] The former was certainly true of Culver and its magnificent corps of cadets, and it reinforced Gignilliat's conviction that it was only through proper training and discipline that one could hope to withstand the latter. His time in the cutters watching his cadets do exactly that was therefore immensely gratifying and served to affirm, confirm, and bolster his unwavering belief in the effectiveness of the Culver system.

Insights into Gignilliat's Character – A Powerful Duty Ethic

Taken together, the controversy around Culver's invitation to participate in the 1913 Presidential inaugural parade and the decision to send cadets to help in the Logansport rescue efforts give us significant insight into the character of Gignilliat. We know that Gignilliat learned best by putting abstract theoretical concepts into concrete practical application, where he could observe them in action and appreciate their value. Furthermore, we know that he valued this type of learning experience and may have viewed the opportunity to participate in the presidential inaugural and assist the citizens of Logansport as just such opportunities for his cadets.

In action, Gignilliat demonstrated excellent leadership in both episodes and particularly at Logansport, where he went with the group, placed himself in the same amount of danger, and never asked of the group anything that he was not prepared to do himself. In this manner, he motivated and led more by action and example than by inspirational exhortation, which was in keeping with his personality and leadership approach.

Philosophically, we see from these and other events that Gignilliat had a very strong duty ethic that was triggered by the suggestion of impropriety from Clark that reflected poorly on the Vice President-elect and the request for assistance from the mayor of Logansport. Sometimes called "non-consequentialist" (being unable to justify an action by showing that it produced good consequences), duty ethics teach that some acts are right or wrong because of the sorts of things they are, and that people have a duty to act accordingly, regardless of the good or bad consequences that may be produced. Duty ethics are concerned with what people do, not with the consequences of their actions, and this surely provides an accurate description of Gignilliat's actions in these situations.

Duty-based ethics are usually what people are talking about when they refer to 'the principle of the thing,' and one suspects that Gignilliat justified his reaction to the inaugural controversy and his Logansport decision based upon "the principle of the thing" that compelled him to respond as he did. This approach also explains the extraordinary lengths he went to when addressing the inaugural controversy (e.g., contacting the author of the article and providing him with a lengthy written response) and largely negated any negative influence that the ridicule from Logansport regarding the Culver summer naval program may have had on Gignilliat's decision to help.

On a personal level, this was an acceptable and even admirable method for making individual decisions, but it may not have been as appropriate for an executive leadership decision involving an entire institution and other people, especially the Vice President of the United States and teenagers who might be exposed to danger unnecessarily.

Considering him from the perspectives of both action and philosophical beliefs, the decision to respond as he did to the inaugural controversy is understandable, but the decision to send cadets to assist the citizens of Logansport appears to have been somewhat unusual for Gignilliat.

In action, Gignilliat was concrete, realistic, practical, and unimpulsive, while also being honorable and principled. He prized security above all else, which was manifested in his demeanor and actions that were careful, cautious, orderly, practical, conservative, sensible, and stable. However, his duty-ethics approach meant that he also took a great personal interest in responsibility for his work, goals, and obligations, and such a request for assistance would have likely triggered this aspect of his personality.

This combination of traits led him to act in ways that consistently went above and beyond what was reasonably expected of him, doing everything in his power to exceed all expectations. However, his duty-ethics approach did little to help him reconcile conflicting duties, in this case the desire to assist the Logansport citizens vs. the duty to protect his cadets and school.

In such situations, Gignilliat came to rely on the advice, affirmation, and confirmation of trusted advisors like his older brother, Captain Bromwell, Fleet, and ER Culver. It was fortunate indeed that ER Culver happened to be present at the time he made his decision, and it was likely quite beneficial to have ER provide him with the latitude to *do what he thought best in the situation.*

As a practical matter, the Logansport incident was exactly the type of situation that Gignilliat believed Culver should be preparing its graduates to respond, making his decision to respond positively to a request for assistance natural and intelligible. Reflecting in his later years on his conversation with ER Culver regarding his decision to provide assistance to the citizens of Logansport, Gignilliat was struck by ER Culver's response to him to *"Do what you think best,"* and not *"Do what you think best for the school."* Such broad guidance was likely quite welcomed by Gignilliat at the moment, but it also required him to determine the correct prioritization of the conflicting duties he was facing.

Having served as superintendent for a relatively short period of time, this was perhaps the first significant decision Gignilliat had to make on his own in this role and without the ability to rely upon and/or consult with Fleet and his long experience. Given such discretion by ER Culver, and feeling the urgency of the situation, Gignilliat immediately felt the full weight of the responsibility for making the decision.

In terms of his relationship with ER Culver, this incident was also somewhat reminiscent of the 1900 "Big Fire" episode, during which Gignilliat adopted a duty-ethics position and ER Culver supported him. Gignilliat related that ER told him to "Do what you think is best," which is the very essence of a duty-ethic approach to a moral-ethical situation.[82] ER Culver adopted a similar stance during the "Big Fire" episode, telling the cadets that his father and family would rather have Culver's buildings used to store hay than to allow demonstrations of mass disobedience impact the running of the school.[83] ER Culver's responses in each of these episodes suggests that ER Culver also shared Gignilliat's support for duty-based ethics. Gignilliat's almost instantaneous response to the request suggests that the environment was supportive of such a decision, both from the Culver family and from the staff and faculty of CMA.

The initial decision to send equipment and cadets to Logansport was likely more of a spur-of-the-moment response based upon his immediate prioritization of the conflicting duties he was facing in the moment than a considered decision, reflecting what Daniel Kahneman refers to as "System 1" thinking. System 1 thinking is based more on instinct than reason, revealing much about one's foundational beliefs. It is quite susceptible to the influence of the environment at the time. Gignilliat's description of the situation in his memoirs supports this assessment well.

According to Gignilliat's recollection,

> *As Ed and I talked together, neither of us appreciated at the*
> *moment the hazards of the undertaking. Perhaps we were both*
> *still under the spell of Schumann Heink's voice and the recital of*
> *her brave life. I do not know.*[84]

Acknowledging that neither he nor ER Culver "*appreciated at the*
moment the hazards of the undertaking," and that they were both "*still*
under the spell of Schumann Heinks' voice and performance" are two
powerful indicators of System 1 thinking, meaning that the decision was
based largely on instinct. Gignilliat admitted as much in his memoirs,
reflecting on his uncharacteristically *impetuous* initial decision – meaning
"impulse-driven" and "without conscious thought" – indicating that this
was a System 1 response and thus largely instinctual. It was also along
the lines of his initial reaction to the situation he faced during the "Big
Fire" in October 1900.[85] This suggests that Gignilliat's instinct or "natural
reaction" was guided largely by his duty-ethics beliefs.

However, the decision at the end of the first day of rescue activities to
send the cadets back for a second day of action, and to send both more
equipment and cadets, was far more considered and indicative of System
2 thinking. System 2 thinking is based on reason and is largely divorced
from environmental influences, making it more logical and considered.
It also indicates a greater level of moral certainty, since Gignilliat was
making a far more informed decision regarding a dangerous situation
about which he was fully apprised and had a true appreciation of the
hazards that he did not possess when making his initial decision. It does
not appear that he had any second thoughts about his initial decision after
returning to Culver on the first day, as he determined that the group from
Culver had helped save around 800 people and that they could do more to
help the following day if/when they returned.

Turning to the question of whether he would have made the same decision
again, Gignilliat offers more interesting insights into his character.
Gignilliat muses in his memoirs,

> *I am considerably older today, and Ed is gone, and I wonder*
> *if now I would dare risk the lives of boys entrusted to my care*
> *without asking their parents' consent in advance. Probably*
> *today with our powerful motor-driven launches there would be*
> *no need for such risks.*[86]

It is intriguing that the normally straightforward and direct Gignilliat provides a somewhat evasive response in his memoirs that actually dodges the question of whether he would make the same decision again by saying that new technology would make it unnecessary for him to do so. He admits that he and ER did not properly "appreciate at the moment the hazards of the undertaking" when they considered Barnes' request for assistance and indicates that the environment had impacted the decision – Schumann Heink's voice and story of braveness when growing up – but he does not provide a definitive answer to this question.

In considering this same question eight decades later, Bob Hartman concluded that Gignilliat would not have sent the cadets, reasoning from a Consequentialist perspective. This is not in line with a duty-ethics approach to the situation.

In light of the influence of Gignilliat's duty-ethics approach to addressing moral-ethical issues, one can surmise that, while he might have been more cautious when making the decision, Gignilliat's reflective retelling of the story in his memoirs suggests that he still believed he made the right decision and personally would likely do the same thing again.

Perhaps he might have been influenced to act differently in his professional capacity as the school's chief executive, but from a philosophical perspective embracing the idea that some acts are right or wrong because of the sorts of things they are and that people have a duty to act accordingly, regardless of the good or bad consequences that may be produced, it is more likely that Gignilliat would have made the same decision again, even if it placed the institution in danger, as did his decision regarding the dismissal of one-half of the corps as a result of the "Big Fire" episode and for which he received the support of ER Culver.

One suspects that Gignilliat would stand by his prioritization of the conflicting duties he faced regarding the request for assistance from Logansport because they reflected his beliefs about "the principle of the thing" and that he was bound by duty to take the right action in the situation, regardless of the outcome.

This analysis suggests that by early 1913, Gignilliat's executive abilities might have been still developing and perhaps not fully developed but that his moral-ethical perspective was fully developed by March 1913 at the age of 38 and after being at Culver for 17 years. This moral-ethical perspective was based upon a belief that people have a duty to do the right thing, even if it has the potential to produce a bad result, and it became a bedrock principle that Gignilliat inculcated into the Culver cadets and institution.

Chapter 9 – 1914 - 1915 – Finding His Voice: Becoming an Evangelist of Military Preparedness

Getting Back into the Culver Groove

After readjusting to life on land, Gignilliat reengaged with life at Culver and on campus. As he had come to expect, there were myriad issues that required his attention and opportunities for his consideration upon his return.

Culver's First Honor Council Established – The Cadet Council

One of the more interesting developments that had occurred during his absence in the fall of 1913 was an effort by the cadets to develop their own cadet-run honor council. Current Culver lore holds that "the first mention of the Culver honor system appears in the 1921 Culver Instructor's Handbook, which describes a system established by the cadets themselves and administered by the Cadet Club" and that credit for the honor system that currently exists at Culver "belongs to [cadet] Bill Maxson," who helped develop it in the late-1930s.[1] It turns out that cadets had been working on this issue much earlier than previously acknowledged.

Mention of the honor system "established by the cadets themselves" sometime prior to the 1921 reference in the Culver Instructor's Handbook almost certainly refers to this system developed by the cadets during the 1913-1914 winter school session. The aim of the council hewed to the ideas expressed by Senior Cadet Captain Curt Anderson at an informal meeting in fall 1913 at which he presented the idea of taking ownership to ensure that the trust afforded cadets by the administration to behave honorably was upheld. Having established such a noble and appropriate purpose, the cadets worked on determining the appropriate scope, jurisdiction, and composition of the council to make it feasible into the spring of 1914.

Although Anderson had cited the renowned honor system at the University of Virginia as the basis of his own idea, according to the March 5, 1914 edition of *The Culver Citizen*, the cadets had shifted their attention in 1914 to consideration of the system used at the nearby University of Chicago. The student responsibilities of the University of Chicago Honor Council included investigating "all serious infringement of the regulations" and making recommendations to the faculty as to the character or severity of the punishment" to be imposed on the offender. This system made use of a council of ten students selected from each academic class: four seniors; three juniors; two sophomores; and one freshman.

Viewed as a way to improve the existing system of discipline at Culver, such an approach would allow Culver cadets to assume some of the responsibility for maintaining good order and discipline with respect to honor within the corps, adding value to the cadet experience. This was an approach that Gignilliat supported and nurtured. As a result, it began to form, with the first official meeting conducted by this nascent, self-appointed (at this point) organization on February 26, 1914. Support for such a body continued to grow among the cadets, and its development was followed closely by the entire community as it took form and matured throughout spring 1914.

Encouraged by the support from their peers and from Gignilliat, the cadets continued developing the cadet-run honor system they envisioned. According to an article in the March 7, 1914 edition of *The Vedette*, the organization, which had originally been named "The Student Council," had settled on the name for it: The "Cadet Council."

The Cadet Council aspired to "become the most influential group and the greatest power for good in the school" through its ability to "counteract any deteriorating influences which may arise" within the corps and to "elevate the standard of honor, fairness, and unselfishness in the cadet corps." Eight cadets, led by Senior Cadet Captain Anderson, worked closely with eight members of the administration and faculty (including Captains Hunt, Grant, Crandall, Mowbray, and Durborow) to design it.[2]

According to the Articles of Organization drafted by this group, the purpose of the Cadet Council was "to maintain within the corps a high regard for the principles of honor, truth, and fairness and to discourage any offenses or tendencies which in their nature reflect upon the moral tone of the institution or are derogatory to the best interests and the greatest efficiency of the corps."[3] A council format comprised of cadets provided inspiration to the cadets to make their honor system a "tangible and essentially successful" system and not "a mere shadow or sham" of a program. *The Culver Citizen* article noted that, "although the faculty may aid in establishing it, only through the efforts of the cadets themselves can the honor system become a reality and success."[4] Certainly this rationale struck a chord with Gignilliat, who believed that cadets would buy into things that were "real" and meaningful.

Taking the form of a "student court" functioning in an advisory capacity, the council was empowered "to consider and act upon matters arising in the Cadet Corps which may tend to detract from its prestige and standard of honor" in order to address influences that were "bad in the Corps" and which might "have the effect of injuring the Corps' influence or reflect unwarrantably on any number of the student body."

It is important to note that this body was not focused on addressing "minor breaches or discipline" or challenging the Academy's existing disciplinary process or outcomes; rather, it was "to be concerned particularly with offenses which are vicious in their nature and which tend to lower the standards of truth, fairness, and dependability in the school." By "vicious" in nature, the cadets meant of or pertaining to "vice," as opposed to virtue. The main way in which it achieved these objectives was through the authority it was granted via its charter "to investigate conduct and try cases in which there is involved a violation of honor or breach of trust."[5]

"The Articles of Organization of The Cadet Council" stated that it would be comprised of 13 cadets chosen through an innovative (at least for Culver) selection process. The cadets devised a process of election based upon years of attendance at the Academy to select eight of the members, with two members coming from cadets who had been at the Academy for at least three years, two members coming from cadets who had been at the Academy for at least two years, two members coming from cadets who had been at the Academy for at least one year, and two members coming from cadets new to the Academy.[6] The five cadet captains, "by virtue of their office," rounded out the council's membership.[7]

The cadets presented their proposal for official recognition to Gignilliat

CMA's first members of the Cadet Council.[8]

for his review and consent in early April 1914, which he approved. Elections were held on April 15, 1914, bringing The Cadet Council into existence.[9] In accordance with the Articles of Organization, Gignilliat appointed the president, vice president, and secretary of The Cadet Council from among the elected and appointed members.[10]

This organization instantly became a valued element of the Culver system. The Articles of Organization were reprinted in the 1914 *Roll Call*, and the founding of the Cadet Council was referred to in the class history as the "most important" accomplishment of the class of 1914 in their final year at the Academy.[11] The Cadet Council was also identified in the 1914 CMA catalog and incorporated into the standardized overview of the essential elements of the Culver program that Gignilliat had instituted in

1911, indicating the value he attached to it. According to the 1914 catalog, "this council was formed on the initiative of the cadets themselves," and it has been "most effective" in helping to eliminate "all vicious influences and to control those things which by their very nature might escape the knowledge" of the administration, however vigilant they may be.[12]

Both of these references pre-date the "first mention" of it in 1921 identified in the standard honor system text cited previously and provide compelling evidence for the establishment of Culver's honor council and system as dating to the 1913-1914 winter session and in conjunction with the creation of the Cadet Council.

While the form of this organization resembles the current Cadet Club, it appears that this was an initial step by the cadets to become involved formally in some aspects of the running of the school that presaged similar efforts that would occur in military schools across the country in the 1920s and 1930s, including at West Point.[13] It is clear that the issues that concerned them were centered around honor, truth, fairness, unselfishness, and honorable behavior, and that these concerns provided the impetus for the creation of the Cadet Council. One suspects that by Maxson's time as a Culver cadet in the late-1930s, the need for a separate cadet council to focus solely on honor-related issues had arrived (as it had at other military schools around the same time), prompting him to pursue the establishment of the Cadet Honor Council currently in existence.

Gignilliat's Work with the BSA Continues

Gignilliat also continued working closely with the burgeoning Boy Scout movement in America. Begun by Baden Powell in England in January 1908, the system caught on in America and the first troop was established on February 8, 1910. Since that time, and as mentioned earlier, Gignilliat and Culver had been quite involved with both the American founders of the Boy Scouts of America (BSA) and the movement itself. His first trip away from campus after returning from the naval cruise was to attend a national BSA conference in Washington, DC in late-February 1914.

Gignilliat's First Big Writing Project – Chapters for O'Shea's *Types of Schools for Boys*

Gignilliat was also working on a writing project with which he had become invovled several years previously by renowned Univeristy of Wisconsin education Professor Michael V. O'Shea. O'Shea had sent his sons to Culver's summer programs for several years and became acquainted with Gignilliat as a result. The two would become quite close, and O'Shea would eventually teach annually in the Culver summer program.

Impressed with his educational approach and in spite of his inexperience as a writer, O'Shea invited Gignilliat to become one of several authors in a book he was editing on different education systems for boys in America. Gignilliat's contribution described the value of using a military system in secondary education for boys in the 1917 book, *Types of Schools for Boys.*

During the first three months of 1914, Gignilliat completed the first draft of his manuscript, deliberately avoiding any specific reference to Culver, and sent it to O'Shea for review. Acknowledging his own inexperience and indicating his anxiety about writing for publication, Gignilliat asked O'Shea for his candid assessment of his work, writing "I do not pretend to be a writer and have none of the craftsman's sensitiveness about criticism of my work." He conceded that he had "very little facility" for writing and that he undertook the project "with considerable misgivings as to my ability to produce something that would be worthy of reproduction in permanent form." Gignilliat assured O'Shea that he very much looked forward to receiving his comments on the draft and hoped that they could collaborate to get the manuscript "licked into acceptable shape."[14]

O'Shea sent Gignilliat's draft to the publisher, Bobbs-Merrill out of Indianapolis, for review and comment in early April 1914. Robert Shafer, a senior editor at Bobbs-Merrill, read the manuscript. He was perhaps the ideal reviewer, having, by his own account, no idea about how a military schools went about its "mysterious work."[15]

Shafer was not impressed with the writing of Gignilliat's first draft, providing O'Shea with a stinging three-page critique of it. Shafer felt that the manuscript lacked structure and coherence, and that it was infused with a pervasive sense of self-consciousness on the part of the author. Gignilliat's own misgiving about his abilities as a writer were apparently quite evident, and his nonpartisan attempts to avoid any direct mention of Culver actually detracted from the readability of his manuscript.

In terms of content, Shafer believed that what Gignilliat had written was "not wholly bad," that it was "measurably successful" in terms of substance, and that "for all the amateurishness, school-boyishness even, the article sounds sincere and does carry real conviction with it." Shafer particularly liked the emphasis Gignilliat placed on character development in military schools and how he used concrete examples to illustrate the usefulness of the military school method of education. He was, however, disappointed with the rather scant attention Gignilliat had devoted to the academic curriculum of military schools (i.e., two short paragraphs).[16]

The gist of this assessment from an experienced professional editor indicates that what Gignilliat submitted for review at the end of March 1914 was truly a first draft of an inexperienced writer who clearly knew his subject well and had important information to share but who also lacked confidence in his abilities and needed direction. Given Gignilliat's background, experience, and training, this assessment appears to be right in line with what one would expect from him at this point in his career and development as an author.

O'Shea demonstrated tremendous tact by providing Gignilliat with his own three-page review of the draft in mid-April 1914 that highlighted the good aspects of it and also addressed the areas in which it needed to be improved. Providing a series of concrete suggestions along the lines of, "...show in the same concrete way that you have treated the rest of the article just how the training in the military school will connect up with the situations in real life," and "...give greater prominence to the intellectual life and training of the cadet," O'Shea showed himself to be adept at providing useful feedback in a manner that would be received positively by the author.[17]

O'Shea also provided Gignilliat with specific recommendations regarding organization and structure, and he provided Gignilliat with a copy of the completed draft of a chapter from an experienced writer to show him how a more polished work could look in its final form and to use as a framework for his own contribution. O'Shea suggested that Gignilliat work with one of Culver's English teachers to help him revise the manuscript and assured him of the value of his work. Overall, O'Shea provided Gignilliat with guidance that was both constructive and pertinent.[18]

Gignilliat expressed his appreciation for O'Shea's candor and agreed to make almost every change suggested. Gignilliat again mentioned his "lack of literary ability" and stated that he would not be upset if O'Shea decided to have someone else write the article, going so far as to recommend VMI's Superintendent General Edward W. Nichols "or the head of some other military school who has some literary talent" as possible replacements. Gignilliat was also expressed his concern about being able to meet the deadline for submitting his revised draft.[19]

The tone and tenor of Gignilliat's response to O'Shea's criticisms indicates that he was genuinely interested in producing a good article, that he was acutely aware of his own limitations as a writer, that he was undeterred by the challenge and game to revise the manuscript. This was an impressive demonstration of his own self-awareness, humility, and determination to succeed, especially in an area outside of his comfort zone.

O'Shea replied to Gignilliat at the end of the month with a strong statement of support, praising him for his response. O'Shea also told Gignilliat that he was free to work on the revisions at his own pace and to "do the work entirely at your own convenience." This guidance assured Gignilliat that there was "no hurry whatsoever" for him to complete the revisions, likely putting Gignilliat at ease and removing the time constraints as a source of stress for him.[20] Taking O'Shea at his word, Gignilliat focused on doing his best work on the article at his own pace, taking the remainder of 1914 to revise his manuscript.

Other Happenings on Campus

The annual Army inspection occurred during the period May 4-6, 1914, conducted by Captain Robinson for a second consecutive year. For this inspection, Culver presented 461 of its 463 enrolled cadets in another impressive showing that retained its status as one of the nation's "honor institutions."

Towards the end of May, Culver celebrated the dedication of the stately Logansport Gate (addressed previously), welcoming thousands on campus for the festivities.

Commencement occurred on June 11, 1914, with 66 graduates passing through the Iron Gate.

Leigh Jr. had a successful first year as a cadet, earning promotion to corporal for his efforts. Charting his own course, he also participated in the YMCA and won the new cadet doubles tennis tournament.

Summer Session 1914

Within two weeks after commencement, Culver's summer session began on June 30, 1914 with a total of 343 cadets in attendance. The Summer Naval School had 180 cadets enrolled, while the Summer Cavalry School was filled to capacity with 83 cadets, and Woodcraft hosting 80 young campers.[21]

Gignilliat made good on his promise to Henry Reuterdahl, hosting an exhibit of 40 of his works on campus and sponsoring a talk by him in August. The redoubtable Lieutenant Jonas Ingram, who had worked at the Summer Naval School and been with Gignilliat on the 1913 Mediterranean cruise, was married in Indianapolis, and both Gignilliat and Minnie attended the ceremony. Ingram coached one of Culver's summer crews to victory in the naval militia regatta hosted by Culver in late-August. O'Shea was also on campus teaching courses while his sons enjoyed their experiences as summer campers.

Winter Session 1914-1915

With little time for Gignilliat to catch his breath, the 1914-1915 winter school session began on September 21 with a record 463 cadets enrolled. Enjoying an impressive 85 percent retention rate of old cadets, Culver had to add another infantry company – F Company – to handle the increased number of cadets, expanding the battalion to an impressive six companies. This winter session also witnessed a new daily schedule for the fall consisting of six 45-minute recitation periods in the morning, with a 30-minute study hall towards the end, followed by chapel, a 15-minute spelling period (which was the only academic class occurring in the afternoon), and 30 minutes for cadets to meet with their instructors to received additional instruction, before reporting for drill and athletics.[22]

Having worked virtually non-stop since his return from the Mediterranean cruise in mid-December 1913, and not having had any opportunity to vacation with his wife and family since 1911, Gignilliat took the opportunity to take a well-earned and much needed vacation in fall 1914. Departing on October 8, Gignilliat took Minnie and young Hank (and perhaps also Freddy) on an extended five-week motor trip through South Carolina, likely visiting Minnie's family in Virginia and his own relatives in Georgia along the way. Although he visited two schools during this trip, he found plenty of time to rest, recharge, and spend time with a portion of his family. He returned to campus on November 19, ready to resume the demanding grind he had established for himself to lead his beloved institution.

Back to Work on the Manuscript

Gignilliat continued the work of revising his manuscript throughout the fall of 1914 and into the winter, but his concerns about Culver's enrollment became acute, and he was again forced to focus almost all of his attention on Culver during the 1914 holiday season. For a variety of reasons, many of which Gignilliat found unsatisfactory, Culver lost at least 20 cadets between the opening of winter school in September 1914 and the holiday furlough in late-December 1914.[23] Writing to ER Culver in early January 1915, Gignilliat reported that it was highly unlikely that he would be able to fill all of the vacancies that had appeared as a result of the loss of so many cadets.[24]

Entering the new year under-enrolled, Culver was in danger of lacking the revenue necessary to maintain its operations. This situation was somewhat grim when compared to its opening enrollment number, but Culver still began 1915 with more cadets enrolled than it had begun the 1913-1914 school year, indicating that this reduction in enrollment was more disappointing in terms of expectations than it was potentially financially catastrophic for the institution.

Despite having to address the ever-present challenges of enrollment that determined a portion of Culver's institutional survival, Gignilliat completed his revisions over the holiday break and submitted his revised manuscript to O'Shea for consideration on January 16, 1915, just prior to departing to attend the AMCSUS annual meeting in Washington, DC for the first time.[25] He assured O'Shea that he had worked very hard on this revision "for a number of months," giving it all the time he could afford and burning "a good deal of midnight oil" during the process of revision.[26] One suspects that Gignilliat adopted O'Shea's advice to obtain some assistance from a member of the English faculty, which may account for Gignilliat's perceptible satisfaction with the revised draft he submitted.

Captain Frederick L. Hunt.[27]

In all likelihood, then-Captain Frederick L. Hunt, the head of Culver's English Department who held a master's degree from the University of Chicago and had been at Culver since 1900, would have been an excellent source of support. Given the close relationship between Gignilliat and Hunt, he was the most likely candidate to have provided such assistance.

The Association of Military Colleges and Schools of the United States (AMCSUS)

Immediately after he submitted his revised manuscript to O'Shea, Gignilliat departed Culver to attend for the first time the annual meeting of the Association of Military Colleges and Schools of the United States (AMCSUS) in Washington, DC.

AMCSUS was the brainchild of Colonel John C. Woodward, then-president of the Georgia Military Academy, who, wondering why such an organization did not exist, wanted to form an association of the nation's military colleges, military junior colleges, and secondary military institutions having United States Army personnel detailed as instructors. Woodward believed that these schools were doing a "far greater service for education in general, and [in] the training of our citizen soldiery in particular" than was generally acknowledged and desired to create a forum for them to gather professionally and socially.

Considering his own quarter-century study of military schools, Woodward concluded that the schools needed such an organization to develop coordinated efforts to create and influence national policy, establish an effective relationship with the War Department to help them obtain more governmental support and assistance (among other things), and increase public awareness and interest in military schooling. These combined objectives fueled his drive to establish a "more definitely organized effort" to harness the influence of these valuable institutions, enhance their effectiveness, and increase awareness of their contributions and effectiveness.

Woodward believed that the "psychological moment" for such an organization had arrived in the second decade of the 20th century, perhaps as a result of the burgeoning "military preparedness" movement developing across the country, and he proceeded accordingly. He wrote to the presidents and superintendents of military colleges, military junior colleges, and military prep schools in America who had a US Army officer assigned to their schools on November 6, 1913, inviting them to a conference in Washington, DC on December 2, 1913 to discuss the prospect of forming an association of like-minded institutions.

The ornate "new" Ebbitt House hotel in Washington, DC (known informally as the "Army and Navy Headquarters" for visiting officers) served as the entirely fitting location for the conference. The meeting commenced with Colonel Woodward bowing cordially to the assembled members and posing the question, "Shall we gather around and talk about our common problems?"

The following year, and based upon the accord achieved at the December 1913 gathering, the Association of Military Colleges and Schools of the United States (AMCSUS) was established formally as the nation's first such organization.[28] So began the AMCSUS initial intent to engender "member school cooperation as the Association's chief function" by providing a forum in which to discuss common and enduring challenges faced by all.[29] This organization quickly established itself as exerting great influence on government military policy (especially regarding ROTC), and has served at the primary voice for the nation's essentially military schools and colleges since its founding.[30]

Being available for the AMCSUS annual meeting, scheduled for January 19-21, 1915, and somewhat intrigued by the organization's purpose and potential, Gignilliat wrote to ER Culver on January 11, 1915, asking permission to attend.[31] His initial assessment of AMCSUS, an organization that would become immensely important to both Gignilliat and Culver, was rather indifferent, writing,

"I do not know that we have a great deal to gain from this association, yet I believe that we should at least keep in touch with its movements. It is possible that just now when so much is being said about measures for national defense that the military schools through an organization of this kind can gain special recognition."

Gignilliat closed by writing, "I believe it would be well worth while (sic) to attend this meeting, and will do so if you approve." [32] ER Culver concurred and granted Gignilliat permission to attend the meeting.

Although initially skeptical, Gignilliat's assessment turned out to be quite prescient, and it was very fortunate for him and important for Culver that he attended this meeting and became so involved in the organization. It was at the January 1915 AMCSUS annual meeting where Gignilliat began forming the relationships that allowed him to become aware of the possibilities for Culver and for other military schools presented by the Preparedness Movement and to meet important individuals who would provide him with high-level access to the US military for years to come.

For example, the Secretary of War, Lindley M. Garrison, addressed the 1915 gathering. Garrison discussed the proposals being considered by the War Department addressing effective ways of creating a reliable reserve officer corps for the country. [33]   This was an issue of particular interest to military schools, whose graduates had begun serving in such capacities.

Members of AMCSUS had also offered their own plan, involving government-sponsored scholarships to attend military schools. While the members of AMCSUS were not united in their support of one approach over another, they provided the War Department with differing opinions and options to consider.

America's Historical Challenges in Obtaining Trained and Reliable Reserve Offices

Secretary of War Lindley M. Garrison.[34]

The Spanish-American War in 1898 reignited the simmering debate over US military mobilization stretching back to before the Revolutionary War. The War Department developed the idea of the "expansible army," comprised of a small professional standing army for its national defense with an excess of professional officers who had the necessary experience and leadership to command larger units when the army had to expand in response to emergencies, as its preferred method for wartime mobilization.

The searing experience of the American Civil War brought the weaknesses of a system that relied on such a system into sharp focus. The first year of fighting showed policy makers in graphic form (i.e., large numbers of needless casualties) the difficulty in obtaining adequate numbers of trained officers to lead Army units during times of emergency. The capabilities of volunteer officers were both suspect and found wanting, prompting action from Congress with the passage of the Morrill Land Grant Act on July 2, 1862.[35] Sponsored by Vermont Congressman Justin S. Morrill, this landmark piece of legislation gave each state 30,000 acres of land-script for each member of Congress that the states could sell under the condition that they used the proceeds to fund at least one educational institution devoted to the study of the agricultural and mechanical arts. To make the bill more palatable, the requirement to teach military tactics was added.[36]

In the Spanish-American War at the end of the 19th century, regular and National Guard troops performed adequately, and even volunteer units like the "Rough Riders" (led by the professional Leonard Wood and the volunteer Teddy Roosevelt) did well. However, the short duration of the conflict's major combat operations prevented many of the mobilized units from having a significant impact on the outcome.

In considering the performance of the US Army during the Spanish-American War, Army officers and the War Department worked to make corrections to the system of reserve officer procurement. By the first decade of the 20th century, the War Department succeeded in providing the foundation for a federally funded system capable of producing reserve officers with a modicum of training during times of crisis.

The Fight Over Reserve Officers: The Regular Army vs the National Guard

As the country began considering realistically how it would obtain the type of Army needed to fight modern industrialized wars, planners faced two significant human resource challenges related to quantity and quality. Conscription solved both problems in terms of enlisted personnel, but addressing these same challenges for officers proved to be far more challenging.

The dilemma regarding the source of soldiers had two options – the existing organized state militias known collectively as the National Guard and the newly proposed federal reserve known as the Continental Army.

There were also two options for obtaining the required number of officers – especially junior officers – for America's army. One option – encapsulated in the McKellar bill – proposed establishing a military school in each state capable of producing at least 100 officers each year and who would serve for ten years to create a national reserve of approximately 50,000 trained officers. Another another option – known as the "Ohio Plan" – proposed making use of the existing military training in land-grant colleges to supply reserve officers.

Left out were the country's private military schools and colleges, numbering over 170 at the time and with an admirable heritage of providing scores of trained officers who served effectively in virtually every American conflict since the Civil War. While some military schools initially supported the McKellar bill, the land-grant colleges strongly supported the Ohio Plan.

Gignilliat's Position and Involvement

As the defense establishment considered both plans, there were meetings in late 1915 and congressional hearings in early 1916 focused on considering each option. Gignilliat was quite vested in the outcome of these deliberations, and he showed a particular genius for ensuing that Culver was sure to benefit from the result, regardless of the decision.

Gignilliat liked the McKellar Bill's plan to create/support a military school in each state on the basis of the impact it could have on Culver for enhanced stature in the state, along with increased resources and the ability to commission Culver graduates as reserve officers.[37]

Gignilliat learned that the Army planners did not support the McKellar Bill and preferred the Ohio Plan. With a keen eye for detail, Gignilliat also recognized an opportunity for Culver and other military schools in the Ohio Plan. While somewhat dismayed with the assertion that only college-aged men were suitable candidates for reserve officers, the War College Division report stated: "In no other way than through our *military colleges* and land-grant institutions...can we so efficiently and economically obtain the large numbers of officers needed in times of great emergency."[38]

Continuing to view Culver as the equivalent of a military college, and able to persuade the War Department that this was a correct characterization of the school – despite Congress disagreeing explicitly with this characterization in early 1916 – Gignilliat seized upon these two words – *military colleges* – as the basis for making a stronger case on behalf of the nation's military schools. Referring to those institutions at the secondary and higher education levels whose students/cadets were under constant military discipline as "military schools," Gignilliat used the wording from the War College Division report to argue that the institutions he identified and defined as "military schools" were equivalent to the "military colleges" referred to in the War College Division report, meaning that they could and should serve as vital sources of supply for reliable contributions of trained reserve officers needed by the country "in times of great emergency."[39]

This approach supported the position that the discipline associated with military training was both desirable and effective -- enhancing civic virtue, patriotism, and above all, citizenship in young men -- because it impressed upon the mind of the student early "the first lessons of civil government and respect for law" without unduly promoting "militarism." This was an outcome that could be accepted by almost all and that would be quite difficult to counter and/or argue against.[40]

Gignilliat thus found a way to back the AMCSUS and the War College Division's recommendations while also positioning Culver to benefit from either the McKellar Bill or the Ohio Plan. Regardless of the outcome, Gignilliat had deftly navigated this challenging issue, finding a way to support both approaches with Culver's best interests in mind.

Gignilliat's Growing Involvement in Preparedness Movement

Armed with his zeal for advocating on behalf of Culver and other similar military schools as legitimate sources of reserve officers for the nation, energized by his involvement through AMCSUS, and with little ability to speed up the publication of *Types of Schools for Boys* and get the message contained in his contribution to the work released in print, Gignilliat turned his attention to other preparedness-related matters. Perhaps most remarkably and somewhat out of his comfort zone, Gignilliat continued helping to get the word out about preparedness by agreeing to appear at speaking engagements related to the issue.

This was unusual for him because, despite his long history of declaiming and his extensive involvement with the Dialectic Society at VMI, Gignilliat believed that he possessed only a limited ability for effective public speaking. He indicated this on several occasions, and he shared his concerns in this regard most directly in a letter to O'Shea in June 1915. Writing that his public speaking had been limited to speaking to the young cadets at Culver and simply introducing other speakers he brought to the institution, Gignilliat wrote, "I have had no experience whatever in general speaking to adult audiences," noting that this was the main reason he hesitated to accept offers to speak to adult groups in public.[41] Much like his lack of confidence in his writing ability, Gignilliat sought O'Shea's validation and conveyed to O'Shea his willingness to make an attempt at public speaking if O'Shea thought that Gignilliat could deliver a talk that would be of interest to others. Given the increased level of visibility he was experiencing, this lack of confidence in his speaking ability is somewhat surprising. Gignilliat's willingness to consider such opportunities and agree to accept some/many of them provides another example of his character and commitment to this important issue.

Beginning in late-February 1915, Gignilliat began having speaking opportunities offered to him regarding preparedness. Despite his reluctance, he accepted many, likely falling back on his experiences as a declaimer and interlocutor at VMI. The first such engagement occurred on February 23, 1915 at the University of Michigan at an event sponsored by the National Security League, one of the leading Preparedness organizations of the time. He was in fine company, as General Leonard Wood, Admiral Matthew C. Peary, Frederick R. Coudert of the New York City Board of Education, and former Secretary of War Henry L. Stimson also spoke at the event.[42] That he began receiving additional opportunities to speak about preparedness indicates that his message was of interest and that his presentation was effective.

By the middle of the next month, Gignilliat received another offer to speak publicly, but this time on his other great passion: education. O'Shea wrote to Gignilliat on March 15, 1915 and invited him to speak to approximately 6,000 educators at the upcoming Wisconsin State Teachers' Association meeting in November 1915.[43] Gignilliat also received an invitation to speak at the University of Wisconsin's Young Men's Christian Association (YMCA) in spring 1915.[44] For one who lacked confidence in his speaking abilities, Gignilliat recognized that these invitations provided him with the opportunity to reach a very broad audience. He was nonetheless quite intimidated by the prospect of addressing such large groups, and he questioned his own ability to present something of value to those in attendance.[45]

Gignilliat accepted O'Shea's invitation to speak in November on March 17, 1915, but he expressed great reservations in doing so. Concerned primarily with the anticipated size of the audience, Gignilliat shared with O'Shea that, to someone as inexperienced in public speaking as he was, "the thought of addressing six thousand people is a little staggering."[46] Searching for a way to make the experience more comfortable for himself and more interesting to the audience, Gignilliat asked O'Shea if it would be possible for him to arrange "to show some of the very excellent and interesting moving pictures that we have of the life of the cadets" at Culver so that Gignilliat "could present something that would appeal to them and at the same time tell them something of the value of military training from an educational standpoint."[47]

At the beginning of his public speaking career, incorporating movies into his presentations became a hallmark of Gignilliat's approach. While ostensibly for the audience's benefit, it is clear that presenting in this manner appealed to Gignilliat and helped him feel more comfortable speaking in public.

Agreeing to speak at the November 1915 Wisconsin State Teachers' Association meeting was a particularly astute decision by Gignilliat. With the sinking of the Lusitania on May 7, 1915, the influence of the Preparedness Movement began to increase significantly so that by November 1915 it was reaching its peak. This issue dominated the national press and permeated the country's on-going discussion regarding America's role in the World War being fought in Europe. This particular event and venue thus provided Gignilliat the opportunity to speak at a large forum and present his views on the value that military schools and military training in high schools could contribute to preparedness. Ever the shrewd appraiser of situations, Gignilliat took great advantage of this opportunity on behalf of both the Preparedness Movement and Culver.

Camp Woodrow Wilson

As one response to increasing the nation's level of military preparedness, Gignilliat noted that he had heard talk of introducing military drill into high schools across the country. Expressing the depth to which his philosophy had developed with respect to the capabilities of military schools and military drill in high schools, Gignilliat offered that he believed that merely providing drill to high school boys might have some modest value on its own but that doing so apart from other efforts to place the training in its proper context and allow for it to contribute to the development of useful discipline would result in little tangible or lasting value to either the boys or the country.[48] Reading Gignilliat's own words helps present the clarity of his thinking on this issue:

> *Of course there is something to be gained wherever boys or men are trained to move in mass in response to commands, but where boys are under discipline and in uniform only during the hours of the drill that come only several times a week and where more compelling interests largely counteract the influence of the drill in the meantime little is gained in real discipline.*[49]

It is clear that Gignilliat had begun to find his voice and feel more comfortable offering his own justifications for military training for high school boys that were cogent and persuasive. He used the reasoning referred to above as the basis to extend his argument to the value of military training in education and military schools as the influence of the Preparedness Movement continued to increase during the period 1915-1917.

Confident in the Culver family's interest in military preparedness as a result of the family's fall 1913 offer to host a student military training camp in summer 1914, and certain of their continued support for such efforts, Gignilliat began to demonstrate the clarity of his thinking and depth of his vision for the value of an educational environment infused with a military approach beginning in spring 1915.[50] Making an argument for the ability of a relatively constant military environment to transform military drill for high school boys into something of more lasting value, Gignilliat wrote, "I believe that where boys are continuously under discipline as they would be in a camp more can be accomplished in two weeks than in a whole year of intermittent drills."[51] Completing his argument along this line of reasoning, Gignilliat concluded by writing that he hoped to have the opportunity to demonstrate how such military training properly given could "be made of great value to the individual as well as to the country."[52]

Based on his knowledge of the American Civil War and his experience at Culver, Gignilliat was convinced that the teen-aged recruits would react more positively to military training and absorb it more readily than college students or men in their 20s and 30s. This opinion remains valid today, based upon all we have learned about cognitive development during adolescence.

In 1915, however, many in the country discounted the ability of high schoolers to make a significant contribution to the country's military preparedness. In Gignilliat's view, this was irresponsibly short-sighted because it resulted in preventing the country from taking advantage of one of its greatest sources of potential recruits to provide leaders for the exceptionally large armies required in modern warfare. A key component of Gignilliat's approach was thus to not only train teenagers but also to use Culver cadets who were of similar age to the boys being trained as drillmasters to provide the training and demonstrate their remarkable abilities.

Returning his attention to Culver, and demonstrating his remarkable ability to transform ideas into actions, Gignilliat informed O'Shea in

March 1915 that he had received approval from the Culver Board of Trustees "to conduct a free camp for two hundred high school boys of the state of Indiana at Culver between the dates of May 10th and 24th" in 1915.[53] Acknowledging Culver's excellent facilities and tremendous support from the Culver brothers, Gignilliat believed that Culver was in a unique position to demonstrate the feasibility of organizing short camps to provide high school boys with military training of value. Gignilliat was also quite confident that Culver's example could provide a plan for conducting such camps across the entire nation "with tremendous benefit to the boys and to the country itself."[54]

Undaunted by the War Department's selection snub of 1913, the Culver brothers sponsored their own student training camp on the Culver campus in 1915, paying personally the entire $3,742.06 sum to fund the operation of the camp (which equates to a little over $110,000.00 in 2024 dollars). While not officially part of the Army's efforts, the 1915 Culver training camp was quite successful and attracted attention across the nation and from the Army.

The 1915 camp was followed by other student training camps at Culver in 1916 and 1917, along with training camps for alumni in 1916 and 1917 to "brush up on their military knowledge" in case their country needed them on the Mexican border or in Europe.

These military training camps – five in all during a period of two years – made important contributions to military preparedness, galvanized the Culver community, elevated CMA's status even further with the Army, and brought much positive attention to Culver during this period. This was especially important, since the Midwest region of the country remained staunchly isolationist with respect to the war in Europe even as it also supported the notion of military preparedness.

Sustaining Its Designation as a Distinguished Military School

While simultaneously preparing for the Army's annual inspection in early May, Gignilliat worked tirelessly to prepare for the 1915 camp. Demonstrating his remarkable ability to multitask, the Army inspector, Captain Robinson, who was conducting his third consecutive inspection of CMA, offered the following assessment of Culver's military training program in his official report of his May 8-10 inspection:

"This institution gives more and better military instruction than any I inspect. It is about as near perfection as such an institution can be."[55]

The positive nature of this evaluation impressed even the cadets themselves, who were quite used to earning such accolades for their stellar performance. An account in the student newspaper offered that, "Of all the splendid things said by officers who have viewed the work of the academy, certainly no other has been more compressed in volume or more comprehensive in its tribute to the military department."

Acknowledging the team effort required to obtain such results, the cadets observed that this verdict was "all the greater testimony to the cadets of the last three Winter school battalions, to the military staff, to Major Greiner the commandant, and to Colonel Gignilliat the superintendent, who are responsible for the results secured."[56]

Immediately upon the conclusion of the Army's annual inspection, the "Camp Woodrow Wilson Schoolboy Military Camp" for 200 boys opened on May 10, 1915. Comprised of 100 boys from Marshall County

and another 100 boys from across the state of Indiana, the participants were hand-picked by their high schools on a competitive basis with emphasis on leadership qualities, resulting in a group of unusually able lads gathered together for this experiment.

High school cadet company in formation at Camp Woodrow Wilson.[69]

The high school cadets were issued khaki uniforms, lived in tent camps they established as part of their training, and ate meals prepared especially for them in a field kitchen. To function as drillmasters and inspectors, Gignilliat relied upon a cadre of hand-picked CMA cadets who had demonstrated exceptional

High school cadets washing dishes at Camp Woodrow Wilson.[70]

military bearing and special aptitudes for leadership. One of these cadets was his eldest son, Leigh Jr, who was a cadet corporal in his second year in CMA. These CMA cadets referred to the high school training event as the "Rookie Camp."

The training for the Rookie Camp was quite intense, lasting from reveille at 6:00 am to taps at around 10:00 pm on Monday-Friday, with a half-day of training on Saturday mornings and no training on Sundays. The emphasis of the camp was quite practical, reflecting Gignilliat's experience with the Boy Scouts. In addition to the military aspects of marching and rifle drill (i.e., close-order drill) and tactical field exercises (i.e., extended-order drill), it addressed such topics as first aid, signaling, camp site selection, shelter tent pitching, camp sanitation and personal hygiene, and general camp organization.

Despite the comprehensive schedule of instruction, the rookies had three to four hours of free time each day, during which they were allowed to attend special lectures, watch movies, and avail themselves to other entertainments available to CMA cadets.[57] This approach reflected Gignilliat's belief that "boys are not afraid of a few hardships if they are sure that they are getting the real thing" in terms of training.[58]

In all, the participants received approximately 172 hours of military training in the camp's two weeks of operations, and all were exhausted

General Leonard Wood and Gignilliat watching high school cadets drill, May 24, 1915.[73]

but satisfied upon its conclusion. ER and BB Culver provided the resources as promised and insisted that no expense be spared to make it successful. In addition, Gignilliat secured permission from the Culver brothers to offer a full scholarship to Culver's Summer Naval School to the participant who demonstrated exemplary performance at the high school boys' camp and interest in continuing the training.

General Leonard Wood and other notable educators visited the camp and were duly impressed with its operation, along with Culver's facilities and capabilities. After observing the rookies in action, General Wood commented that it was "tip top" and that what he saw was "bully." He offered that he hoped other schools would follow the "good example of Culver," providing a powerful statement of support for the school's contribution to the nation from one of the nation's strongest supporters of military preparedness.[61]

The camp concluded on May 24, 1915 and was tremendously successful by all accounts. Indeed, Gignilliat was so impressed with the top two cadets that he offered both full scholarships to Culver's Summer Naval School.

One contemporary description appearing in the *Salina Daily Union* out of Salina, Kansas, the day after the camp concluded made two important points about the experience:

- Gignilliat was quoted as saying that "in one summer he could train 1,000,000 men and boys by this method"; and

- General Leonard Wood stated that, "I have, and do now, most emphatically urge military training in our schools and provisions for this kind of a summer camp."[62]

Camp Wilson succeeded in many ways. It provided the Culver brothers with a way to show their support for national military preparedness, brought the attention desired by Gignilliat to Culver and its method of military training, and it made General Leonard Wood – one of the most influential supporters of the Preparedness Movement – into a believer in Gignilliat's approach to military training and in Culver's value as one of the nation's top military schools.[64]

A flattering review of the camp appeared in the September 1915 edition of the magazine of the Navy League of the United States, *Seven Seas*, which helped spread the word of the successful Culver camp. Gignilliat's genius for promotion was made evident in the text written by author William Mather Lewis (a politician and educator who was the mayor of Lake Forest, Illinois, at the time and who went on to become the president of two universities), which began with the following statement:

> *Among the numerous instances of patriotic effort which have recently been made throughout this country to advance our military preparedness and to demonstrate our capacity or incapacity to meet readily and efficiently any heroic situation which may suddenly be forced upon us, the one which has probably attracted greatest publicity is the Free Camp of Military Instruction for High School Boys, held at Culver Military Academy.*[65]

Describing the program of instruction, Lewis summarized it as follows:

> *Somewhat in line with Major General Leonard Wood's plan of holding summer camps of military instruction for college students, the Culver idea was to concentrate the efforts of a score of trained instructors on a large group of high school boys, endeavoring to whip them into military fitness within the shortest possible time.*[66]

After providing a more detailed explanation of how the camp was organized and run, Lewis commented on its remarkable effectiveness, attributing it to four primary causes:

1. The unnatural enthusiasm and genuine engagement of the boys attending the camp;

2. The excellence of the instruction provided by "wide-awake [and] intelligent" drillmasters, who were largely Culver cadets;

3. The inspiring example provided by the Culver cadets involved in the training; and perhaps most important of all,

4. The concentrated intensity of the experience that kept the boys engaged and allowed them to achieve a level of mastery and precision unattainable by the more prevalent approach of providing this type of training "scattered through a long series of infrequent drills."[67]

Lewis observed that, along with the proficiency of the Culver cadets providing the training, it was the concentrated intensity of the continuous two-week experience that truly set Culver's approach apart from other forms of training being offered around the country at the time. According to his assessment, the more prevalent custom of providing students with a series of infrequent drills over a longer period of time "often becomes a feature more demoralizing than beneficial in the training of young men."[68]

Justifying Gignilliat's confidence in the method he put into practice in May 1915, Lewis wrote that "[t]he successful operations of Camp Woodrow Wilson has suggested its extension throughout the country." Attributing the camp's success directly to the efforts of Gignilliat, Lewis supported Gignilliat's suggestion to organize "high school camps in the various States, utilizing fair grounds (*sic*) at county seats for the purpose" and using drillmasters from "Government training schools and military academies recognized by the War Department" as a way of realizing

Gignilliat's quite optimistic goal of providing training for up to 1,000,000 young men over the course of a single summer. [69]

After remarking on how impressed Major General Leonard Wood was with the Culver camp, Lewis concluded his article by providing the following testament to its significance:

> *If this nation is to depend upon "a citizenry trained and accustomed to arms," a scarcely more feasible plan could be evolved for acquainting our American youth with the first principles of military efficiency than through high school student camps."* [70]

Lewis' article helped to advance Gignilliat's argument that teen-aged recruits would react positively to military training and absorb it quite readily, especially if the training was provided properly by drillmasters of similar age to the recruits being trained. In analyzing the reasons for success he had observed, Lewis wrote that "[b]oys seem to respond to the leadership of boys more readily than to older men, and the psychology of [using] the boy drillmaster for young recruits is worthy of serious consideration." [71] Lewis concluded his assessment by offering that "boys of high school age react with more zeal to military instruction than those of collegiate years," which offered confirmation of one of Gignilliat's core beliefs regarding the ability of teenaged boys to play a significant role in enhancing the nation's military preparedness. [72]

While his analysis was likely influenced somewhat by Gignilliat's own fervent belief in his approach, Lewis nevertheless provided some much-desired validation of the essential underpinnings of Gignilliat's approach in a publication that reached a wide audience and which had significant influence at a critical time during the Preparedness Movement. Gignilliat and the Culver brothers could scarcely have conceived of a more effective method of drawing attention to their efforts, and they were undoubtedly thrilled with this type of publicity that their first military camp for high school boys at Culver received.

In light of the success Gignilliat had with Camp Wilson, the Army may have wanted to reconsider its decision to locate the Midwest student military training camp at Lincoln Fields in Ludington, Michigan. While the purpose of both camps was to promote patriotism – and explicitly not "militarism and/or aggression" – and provide participants with military training to help them become capable of serving as junior officers in times of national emergency, each experience was quite different. [73]

Military training camp at Lincoln Fields, Ludington, Michigan.[84]

In comparing the two camps, Culver's Camp Wilson had more students in attendance, was more rigorous, and cost the participating students less.

Expecting "a thousand or more young men" at Lincoln Fields, the Army actually trained 148 students during the period July 7 – August 6, 1915. The low attendance was ascribed to students making other summer plans due to a delay in securing the funding to ensure the camp would occur and to the cost of the training, which was $17.50 per student (equating a little over $400.00 in 2024 dollars).

Intended to "try to give the boys a chance for a real vacation" and allow them to enjoy the amenities of the area while participating in the camp, the training at Lincoln Fields was not designed to be overly taxing, lasting from reveille at 6:00 am to noon on Monday-Saturday, and no training on Sundays, allowing the participants to have each afternoon and the whole of Sunday to themselves. In all, the participants at the Lincoln Fields military training camp received approximately 162 hours of military training in the camp's five weeks of operations, which was 10 fewer hours than the participants' at Culver's two-week Camp Wilson received, and they paid more for the experience.[75]

Camp Wilson served as an important confirmation and influential validation of the Culver military system and Gignilliat's approach to the training of schoolboys. In terms of increasing preparedness, and using Lewis' review as a benchmark, it appears that the 200 students who trained at Culver's efficient Camp Wilson received much better training than did the 148 students who participated in the longer and more expensive military training camp at Lincoln Fields in Ludington, Michigan during the summer of 1915. This

Men training at Lincoln Fields, Ludington, Michigan.[86]

experience undoubtedly enhanced Gignilliat's enthusiasm for military preparedness and zeal to do all he could to make others aware of the Culver system. In particular, he was almost certainly more determined to have his contribution to O'Shea's *Types of Schools for Boys*, which provided an excellent description and explanation of this approach, appear in print at the earliest possible moment.

The Growing National Stature of Both Gignilliat and Culver Military Academy

Another event occurred during this period that was unrelated to preparedness but nonetheless indicative of the burgeoning national prominence of both Gignilliat and Culver Military Academy. Gignilliat was recognized, along with Orville Wright, with an honorary Master of Arts degree at the commencement exercises of Trinity College in Hartford, Connecticut on June 23, 1915.

No honor in the abstract, the president of Trinity College, Dr. Flavel S. Luther, was a frequent visitor to Culver and was thus able to see for himself the effectiveness of the Culver military system and the impact it was having on its cadets and graduates.[77] Luther persuaded Trinity's Board of Trustees to approve his recommendation to recognize Gignilliat for his accomplishments as one of the nation's most innovative and successful educators. This recognition further attested to his growing renown and influence in the world of education.[78]

Taken together, his involvement with AMCSUS in crafting portions of the legislation to create a reliable reserve officer corps for the country, the attention garnered by Camp Woodrow Wilson, the invitation to speak at the November 1915 Wisconsin State Teachers' Association meeting, and being awarded an honorary degree are all indicative of Gignilliat's growing national status, which also reflected well on Culver Military Academy. This enhanced attention added to the already considerable renown of the man and the institution, benefiting both substantially.

Continued Implementation of the "Greater Culver" Plan

Gignilliat also found time to work that spring with renowned Norwegian landscape architect Jens Jensen, brought in by ER Culver, to apply the "Greater Culver" plan to make the grounds of Culver more adequately reflect the quality of the institution. Hosting him during his initial survey of the Culver grounds, Gignilliat "had expected Mr. Jensen to expatiate on the beauty of the lakes" and was therefore quite surprised to learn that Jensen was wholly unimpressed by what he saw. Jensen criticized the appearance of the school's lagoon and the practice of storing the dismantled summer piers along the lakefront, marring its natural attraction.[79]

Exposed to an entirely different aesthetic, Gignilliat recalled that it was the first time he had ever considered the possibility that Culver's geometrically designed lagoon was "not a thing of beauty." Jensen championed the beauty of nature over the efforts of humans, remarking to Gignilliat that one should "never let the work of man run in opposition to the works of the Almighty."[81]

Culver's iconic lagoon and canal to which Jensen objected.[90]

Accordingly, Jensen recommended filling in Culver's somewhat iconic lagoon and canal, and replacing the foliage that was not indigenous to the area with the naturally occurring plants to further enhance the natural appeal of Culver's grounds. Doing so would allow for the creation of a "beautiful meadow sloping from [the] buildings to meet the lake," permitting the natural beauty and peace of Culver's landscape to emerge. ER Culver was both delighted with Jensen's vision for the grounds and persuaded by his recommendations, and he directed Gignilliat to implement them immediately. The process of transforming Culver's grounds into the more recognizable form familiar to contemporary observers took place over the next 18 months.[82]

The 1914-1915 Winter Session Comes to a Close

While busy working on the grounds' improvement project and after the success of Camp Wilson, Culver concluded its 1914-1915 winter session by graduating 86 cadets on June 10, 1915, eclipsing its previous highest output by 20 graduates. On hand to celebrate Culver's successes was Vice President Marshall, who delivered the commencement address.

Leigh Jr. had a very successful second year as a cadet, earning promotion to the prestigious rank of Color Sergeant for his efforts. He also furthered his high school athletic career, playing on both the Company C basketball and track teams. He continued to participate in the YMCA and also joined the Spanish club on campus.

1915 Summer Session

After a brief visit to VMI for his 20th reunion and receiving an honorary MA from Trinity College on June 23, 1915, Gignilliat returned to campus and transitioned to his summer work of directing Culver's summer school. Welcoming a record 535 summer campers to campus on June 30, 1915, Culver's summer session had 314 cadets enrolled in the Summer Naval School, 81 cadets in the Summer Cavalry School (including Leigh Jr.), and 140 Woodcrafters (including Freddy). In addition, Culver hosted a summer BSA scoutmasters' training course during the first two weeks of August and the naval militia regatta at the end of August, at which Culver crews won two major races.

The Charge of Enhanced Militarism as a Result of Military Training in Schools

Despite being so busy, Gignilliat remained acutely aware of the waxing interest in military preparedness around the country, and he recognized the tremendous opportunity this interest presented for Culver and for other military schools across the nation. There was little more he could do to influence the situation, but his interest in the value of military training for high school-aged boys and engagement in helping inform others about the contribution military schools could make to the country's military preparedness remained exceptionally high. Gignilliat therefore began considering alternative ways to get the message contained in his contribution to O'Shea's *Types of Schools for Boys* shared more rapidly with a larger audience.

Talk of increasing American militarism had been part of the anti-preparedness critique as far back as 1913, and it had been largely discounted as little more than inflammatory rhetoric. However, with the outbreak of war in Europe in summer 1914, these allegations continued to mount so that by summer 1915 they could not be so easily dismissed. Providing one of the most influential indictments regarding the militaristic impact on students fostered by military drill was an article published by University of Michigan student K. G. Karsten, president of the Collegiate Anti-Militarism League. Karsten's article was published in *The Cosmopolitan Student*, which was based in Ann Arbor, Michigan, and it was circulated widely in the region, demanding a response from Gignilliat and other preparedness supporters in the area.

The central proposition of Karsten's article was that "military drill fosters military spirit among students," which was both dangerous and intolerable because it prejudiced one against non-military solutions to international problems and promoted instead a narrow form of nationalism that was at best destabilizing and at worst destructive to international peace. Once radicalized in this manner, Karsten argued that it become the militarist's creed that wars were inevitable, which was "most repugnant to civilization," "most antagonistic to Christianity," and "most injurious to society."

The influence of Prussian militarism on the outbreak and conduct of WWI at the time undoubtedly contributed to both the idea and its influence. It was the avowed purpose of Karsten and the Collegiate Anti-Militarism League to cultivate a "positive attitude on the question of militarism" among the students of American universities, by which he meant an opposition to the supposed militarism he believed to be rampant and increasing on America's college campuses as a result of military drill.[83]

The portion of Karsten's argument that likely attracted Gignilliat's attention was his charge, largely unsubstantiated and supported with one-dimensional anecdotal evidence, that "the military training of students in America is one of the most significant menaces confronting the republic today." Based upon this belief, Karsten sought to "check the spread of this cancer in our educational system" and reduce it "to a nominal size such as does exist."

Rather than serving as a prudent and patriotic response to the war in Europe, Karsten argued that the military training of students was subversive of both "American policies and traditions," presenting the highest degree of significant "danger to American democracy." The danger was that, unchecked, the spread of militarism would become so rapid and pernicious that one could "expect to wake up some day and find America as militaristic as Germany" if it was allowed to continue to exist on its college campuses and spread across the country.[84]

In its totality, Karsten's argument took direct aim at many of Gignilliat's core beliefs about the value of military training in schools, targeting them as examples of undeniable, un-American, and dangerously subversive practices. For a patriot and true believer like Gignilliat, these charges were intolerable and could not go unanswered, especially appearing so close to home. As a result, he became both personally involved and invested in the efforts to counter such accusations that he believed to be wholly inaccurate.

Becoming an Evangelist of Military Preparedness

One of the methods for countering invalid charges of militarism was
to engage in speaking engagements with influential groups in hopes of
persuading those in the audience that this viewpoint was exaggerated.
Based upon the increasing attention being paid to preparedness topics,
along with the encouragement of O'Shea, Gignilliat began to receive and
accept invitations to speak to groups interested in learning more about
the contributions that military schools could make to preparedness.
Despite his relative inexperience and substantial personal discomfort,
his patrician manner and soothing voice may well have made the perfect
alternative to reach those not attracted to the "hard sell" of many other
preparedness advocates.

One such group was the Wisconsin State Teachers' Association, which
Gignilliat addressed in November 1915. O'Shea offered some guidance
to help Gignilliat craft his address to which Gignilliat responded
enthusiastically. Incorporating "moving pictures" with his own soft-
spoken manner of delivery allowed for an innovative mix of medium and
message that made his address to this important group a great success.

The 1915-1916 Winter Session -- Freddy Joins the CMA Corps

The winter session for the 1915-1916 began with a record-setting
enrollment of 465 cadets, of which 210 were new cadets. Assigned to the
newest of the six companies that were now standard at Culver with the
addition of Company F was a cadet of particular note: Frederick Fleet
"Freddy" Gignilliat, the second son of Culver's superintendent, who joined
Leigh Jr. as a member of the CMA corps of cadets.

The "Business and Professional Men's" Military Training Camp

After an eventful summer but just prior to the beginning of winter school,
Gignilliat embarked an unusual endeavor that was to have a substantial
impact on his thinking regarding military preparedness and a significant
impact on the locus of his actions for the next 18 months. Curious about
the ability of the Plattsburg-style camps to bring about substantive
changes in its participants, especially in comparison with the two-week
camp he ran at Culver for high school boys in May 1915, Gignilliat enlisted
in the Plattsburg-style military camp – the "Business and Professional
Men's Camp" – conducted at Fort Sheridan, Illinois in fall 1915 to study it
"from the inside."

Away from campus during the period September 20 – October 17, 1915,
the 41-year old Gignilliat, along with the much younger Captain Alexander

W. Fleet from Culver (Colonel Fleet's son and Gignilliat's brother-in-law), experienced the rigors of the month-long camp intended to provide "tired businessmen" with some fundamental military training to enable them to answer the nation's call to arms as officers should it come, for either service on the Mexican border, which seemed more likely in fall 1915, or in Europe in the World War.[85]

Clearly the training was not overly taxing, for Gignilliat found time to write an article for the *Chicago Daily Journal* describing his experiences and sharing his commentary about the training of officers and boys. Titled "Military Training for the Boy," Gignilliat's article was the ninth in the paper's university literary extension course on "The Making of a Soldier." The article appeared in print on October 6, 1915.

Gignilliat began the article by asserting that national leaders had failed to recognize the value of early training for boys. He presented a very Progressive-era argument that was right in line with G. Stanley Hall's idea of adolescence by arguing that youths show a particular zest in and for military training, and that people are most adaptable to change in their teenaged years, or what Hall referred to as "the bud of promise."

Channeling one of Hall's most famous sayings (and indicating that he was familiar with his work), Gignilliat observed that "the boy is the father of the man," when experiencing for himself how the "tired businessmen" with whom he was training at Fort Sheridan responded to the training as compared to the cadets with whom he had been working at Culver since 1897. Gignilliat offered that "[t]here is a difference between the zest and imagination of the fresh and enthusiastic youngster of 16 and that of the world-weary business man or sophisticated college senior," and that the imagination of boys under military instruction allows for "the thing [to be] real" and not make-believe.

Gignilliat attributed this difference to the enthusiasm for military training and a ready adaptability to it "that can never be equaled, perhaps not even approached, in the majority of cases in later life" that he had observed in boys. In his experience, "[the recognition of authority, the spirit of strict and immediate compliance with legitimate orders, the sense of responsibility, [and] the ideals of duty and loyalty" were all things much easier to inculcate in youths than in adults. Given that much of what Gignilliat identifies are aspects of one's identity – which we now know to be formed during the fertile developmental years for boys between the ages of 12-24 – his assessment was quite accurate and prescient when viewed from a century hence. Ever aware of the country's concern for the emergence of militarism in society, Gignilliat assured the readers that, "In making the boy a good solider, he is also made a better citizen."[86]

However powerful the boys' enthusiasm may be, Gignilliat was nonetheless doubtful that any type of training could produce an acceptable officer in a month or six weeks. Turning his argument in favor of military schools, Gignilliat noted that:

> *"[t]he semimilitary (sic) school that merely plays with military training and the land grant college that grudgingly gives a few hours per week to perfunctory drill merely because it is required by law to give military training, are apt from a military standpoint to do more harm than good. They pretend to do what they do not do and give the boy a slipshod and incorrect idea of a soldier's duties."*

By contrast, "[t]he really excellent military schools and colleges, however, are turning out a number of graduates each year who would make the most competent officers of volunteers available outside of the national academy at West Point." Attributing this difference to the practice of military boarding schools to have cadets under military discipline 24 hours a day for many weeks at a time, enabling them to achieve a form of learning we now term as "habituation," Gignilliat concluded that military schools were thus much better at producing graduates with the capabilities and aptitudes to become successful officers in times of crisis. He urged the government to both recognize and make use of this valuable source of supply of officers needed in times of emergencies.[87]

At this same camp, Culver cadets were brought in to serve as the "opposing force" to fight mock battles against those attending the camp, providing an opportunity to put their training into practice and see for themselves how well they could execute the drills they had been taught. While the camp "rookies" did manage to absorb a "rigorous body of fundamental and special instruction," they were given a dose of reality when they "fought" against the more thoroughly trained Culver cadets.[88] According to Gignilliat, "the superior training of the cadets enabled them to outplay the citizen battalion at every turn of the game," in part because, based on his experience, Gignilliat believed that "boys acquire this sort of thing much more readily than grown men."[89]

Perhaps reflecting some confirmation bias on his part, Gignilliat came away from the experience very unimpressed with the training and doubtful that effective officers could be made in one month's time. Gignilliat used the article to question whether it was possible that "an officer can be made in a month or six weeks, or even a thoroughly trained solider in that time, from adults already firmly set in their habits of thought and action."[90] Reinforcing this opinion the following month in a letter on November 24, 1915, Gignilliat reiterated that, "You cannot make a trained soldier – much less a trained officer – in the course of a month, or in several months for that matter. I am sure there are none who realized this more fully than the men who have been through these camps."[91]

An uncredited staff editorial appearing in *The Chicago Evening Post* on October 19, 1915 provided further support for Gignilliat's observations. Titled "Two Parables at Sheridan," the article presented the reader with two allegories to consider – one about Culver cadets and one about trained officers leading untrained men. In Parable 1, the unnamed author observed that two trained officers leading 125 trained Culver cadets easily defeated four times their number of the less well-trained officers and men attending the camp. In the second parable, the anonymous author offered that, "Trained officers with untrained men are not as effective as trained officers and trained men." Combining these two lessons, the author concluded that, "You cannot make a trained officer in four weeks' time; you cannot even made (sic) a trained private." Going a step further, the author closed as follows: "The Sheridan encampment, like the Plattsburg encampment, wants to supplant our national military cocksureness, our valor of ignorance, by the sterner and humbler consciousness of our national military helplessness."[92]

The gist of the article was that the real lessons the nation should take from the Plattsburg and Sheridan encampments were that the nation was not prepared for modern, industrialized warfare, and that the nation needed to look elsewhere for ways to train its soldiers and military leaders effectively. In the author's opinion, military schools like Culver may be the answer. These observations were right in line with Gignilliat's own beliefs, and he certainly supported them and was likely gratified that they appeared in print and under a by-line other than his own.

A Fire Devastates the BHT's Mounts and Stable

Just after his return from the Chicago military training camp, fire again ravaged Culver in late October 1915. The troop had returned late on the evening of Sunday, October 24, 1915 from a cross-country ride to Winamac. Wanting to get the cadets to their barracks so they could prepare for their Monday classes and get some sleep, the stable staff took care of the horses and settled them in for the night. The Academy's veterinarian, Dr. Gordon, was the last man out and had turned off the lights.[93]

According to an article in *The Vedette*, "Fire broke out in the long frame stable at the academy shortly after midnight of Sunday," October 24, 1915, sometime after the time the stable staff departed and prior to the arrival of the night watchman to make his checks of the facility. Captain Samuel T. Starbuck was the first to spot the fire from his quarters in the Open-air Barrack, but "before he could get out and give the alarm the wind had swept the flames through the 80 tons of dry hay" stored above the stalls, stoking a fiery furnace of such intensity that no one could get close enough to save any of the animals, despite "frantic efforts made by cadets, employees, and officers to do so."[94]

Although the rush of the flames was rapid, it is likely that most if not all of the horses had suffocated due to lack of oxygen before the fire reached them. Nevertheless, only five or six of the 65 beautiful black horses managed to break loose and survive the fire. The other horses were found lifeless in their stalls in regular rows with their halters still attached to their mangers, offering compelling evidence that they had not been burned alive when they perished.[95]

If a silver lining could be found to this tragic event, it was that it hastened further the implementation of the Greater Culver plan. The stable was one of the final frame buildings left on campus (along with the Open-air Barrack), and the trustees had already announced a plan to replace it with a fireproof structure in 1916 as part of the Greater Culver improvement plan. Both the horses and the structure were insured (since the building was not fireproof), and the Culver brothers acted promptly to begin replacing each (in conjunction with the work Jens Jensen was already doing on the campus' landscaping).[96]

Much as their father had done in the wake of the February 1895 fire that destroyed the original Chautauqua building, the Culver brothers immediately came to campus to begin addressing the situation. Leaving Gignilliat to arrange for the purchase of a new herd of black horses, ER and BB Culver met with architect Albert Knell on campus within 24 hours of the devastation on Monday evening. Shortly thereafter, Gignilliat and ER Culver announced plans to replace the deceased horses and begin construction on the new fireproof stables. While this news was welcomed by the community, all were overwhelmed by the loss of irreplaceable favorite mounts such as Abob, Agility, Ajax, and Apache. In fact, it would be months before the community could bring themselves to name the new horses.

According to Hartman, Gignilliat charged Captain Rossow and Dr. Gordon with the daunting task of locating and purchasing new mounts of "the same color, size, and spirit as had been lost" as quickly as possible to regenerate the herd. The energetic and resourceful Rossow proved to be more than up to the challenge, beginning his quest to do so immediately.

Early Tuesday morning, Captain Rossow and Dr. Gordon departed to begin their search for suitable replacement horses. Traveling across Indiana, Ohio, and Missouri in search of black steeds as suitable replacements, Rossow discovered that news of the tragedy had spread across the entire country, ensuring that he encountered many sympathetic suppliers.

Within the first week, replacement horses were arriving on campus. By late November and after inspecting more than 1,000 animals, Rossow and Gordon had accomplished their mission. They had selected, purchased, and sent to campus 64 black horses that were younger, better bred, more agile, and far superior to the previous herd, and cadets were beginning to train with them.[97] By Rossow's expert assessment, the horses he and Gordon had procured were "excellent animals" that were "sound and of good disposition."[98]

Meanwhile, Gignilliat made contact with colleagues at Fort Sheridan (from which he had just recently returned) to secure help from experienced Army cavalrymen with training the new horses.[99] In response, the commanding officer at Fort Sheridan sent four veteran cavalrymen to help train the new mounts.[100] Working together to obtain horses, trainers, and facilities, the Culver leadership successfully regenerated the Black Horse Troop in an astonishingly short period of time and set the conditions to perpetuate the highly popular Summer Calvary School.

In addition, Culver took the opportunity to implement its recently approved plan to move Route 10 north, eliminating its disruptive influence of running through campus and allowing for more coherent campus design and construction. The road relocation was a major endeavor that required the purchase of a steam shovel for the excavation required by the project.

In line with the Greater Culver plan, the Culver family took advantage of the opportunity to also begin construction of the new rifle range, riding hall and cavalry building, and the indoor swimming pool. In conjunction with the landscaping improvements being made by Jens Jensen at the same time, the Culvers also enacted the part of the Greater Culver plan of extending the drill and athletic fields.[101]

Out of the tragedy of the fire that destroyed the BHT mounts and the wood-framed stables, the Culver family found a way to turn it into an opportunity to make significant progress on campus improvements. All of these endeavors added immeasurably to Gignilliat's workload, but one suspects that he was very willing to accept the additional burdens in the service of both Culver and Greater Culver.

The Triumph of the Wisconsin Teachers' Association Presentation

While directing the numerous ongoing rebuilding efforts on campus, Gignilliat addressed the Wisconsin State Teachers' Association on November 5, 1915 using his method that combined didactic and experiential approaches. Beginning didactically, Gignilliat delivered his speech, "Building Character through Military Training," and provided the most complete explanation for his belief in the powerful ability of military training to bring out the very best in boys.[102] The speech was "a spirited defense of the military system as a basis for moral instruction and the development of character" in which he espoused that a daily set routine was "the best way to instill discipline in boys" using the learning method of habituation to make it effective.[103] It was this discipline, as long as it was done properly and in an appropriately respectful manner Gignilliat stressed, that served as both the basis of moral and ethical formation, along with the development of character.

Moving to the experiential, Gignilliat then shared with the audience the "moving pictures" of Culver cadets in action to provide evidence of the effectiveness of the system he had just described. Thus did Gignilliat succeed using a combination of didactic and experiential methods of "tell then show" to present the most complete description and effective explanation of the Culver military system. It is this argument, making use of the innovative method he used to train cadets so successfully at Culver, that served as the basis for much of his argument in *Arms and the Boy* and overall championing of the military system of education for boys in subsequent presentations and articles.

Commenting on his fellow participants at the Fort Sheridan military camp at which he had recently trained and with respect to military preparedness, Gignilliat observed that while the men "undoubtedly possessed initiative to a high degree," it was "the cadets, who had been under military instruction for a much longer period, [who] possessed something that made their initiative much more effective." That "something" was their "automatic responsiveness to authority under stress of excitement," which Gignilliat believed to be "a quality which cannot be imparted even to mature men in a month."

What's more, the Culver cadets, in Gignilliat's opinion, "possessed the ability to use their own heads when that was essential, and also the ability to let some one (*sic*) else superior to them use his head when that was more essential." Making the point that being "under military instruction" for a prolonged period imparted both judgment and discretion was the crux of Gignilliat's argument with respect to military preparedness, and he used this forum to present it effectively.[104]

This speech was truly remarkable, and it was the best prose Gignilliat had written or would write for some time. The reason for this was, going as far back as his time in the Dialectic Society at VMI, that Gignilliat has developed a better "ear" for the spoken word than he had for written prose. It appears that the process of writing and delivering a speech succeeded in bringing out Gignilliat's thoughts in a way that was more natural and conducive to him than occurred when he was writing an article. While his command of the English language was always excellent and his writing was more than adequate, it was during this speech that Gignilliat realized he was most persuasive when he was able to deliver prose he had written in an oral format. As a result, Gignilliat began searching out and accepting opportunities to speak where he could deliver his message about the value of military training in schools and its contribution to the nation's military preparedness.

The Continental Army and Distinguishing Between Military Colleges and Prep Schools

Two other contemporaneous episodes occurred related to military preparedness that warrant mention. In October 1915, Secretary of War Garrison presented his plan for a federal reserve, called the "Continental Army," to President Wilson. Proposing that this new entity would supplant the National Guard – comprised of long-standing state militias – this plan was bound to create unrest. Indeed, opposition to it was both immediate and intense, especially in the rural Midwest and south.[105]

However, and somewhat unexpectedly, Garrison's plan also obtained an unusually high level of initial support within Congress. On October 21, 1915, the Senate majority leader, John W. Kern of Indiana, expressed support for the Continental Army plan, followed by the chairman of the Senate Committee on Military Affairs, Oregon Senator George E. Chamberlain. On October 25, 1915, the chairman of the House Committee on Military Affairs, Virginia Congressman James Hay, expressed his own support for the plan.[106]

Thus by the end of October, 1915, it appeared that the country was moving towards a new model of military preparedness that did not include state militias and would be controlled largely by the federal government.

In November 1915, the Army War College released a study titled, "Educational Institutions Giving Military Training as a Source of Supply of Officers for a National Army." Included in this report was a conclusion from the authors that, "In no other way than through our military colleges and land-grant institutions, with military departments, can we so efficiently and economically obtain the large number of officers needed in times of great emergency." Reinforcing this conclusion, the report went on to state that, "Under our present-day conditions [our military colleges and land-grant institutions, with military departments] are thought to be unequaled as a dependable source for officers."[107]

Earlier in the report, and in a break with its past practice, the Army made a definite distinction between two general classes of educational institutions: "the university and college; and the preparatory type."[108] While valuing the contributions of military preparatory schools like Culver, which, along with St. John's, Manlius in New York, was mentioned by name in the report, the authors nonetheless determined that the "output" of such schools was, "as a rule...too young and immature to make the best officers."[109]

Reflecting a high level of respect for schools like Culver, the authors felt compelled to state that, "Exceptions to this rule will be found when the emergency exists," and they expressed their certainty that "there will be no trouble in deciding the different cases as they arise."[110] Given that the high school/preparatory school was a relatively recent phenomenon in American society – gaining prominence during the Reconstruction era and only fully coming into their own as viable institutions at the beginning of the 20th century – the introduction of this distinction is not surprising. However, one suspects that Gignilliat interpreted this particular passage somewhat differently from what the authors intended.

Even though it was clear that Gignilliat was quite aware of this distinction, he had been conditioned by the War Department to consider Culver as fully equivalent to a military college, since Culver had been designated, along with select other military colleges and schools, as a "Distinguished Institution" continuously since 1906. His awareness of this new distinction is evident in his contribution to *Types of Schools for Boys*, in which Gignilliat wrote in the year during which this distinction appeared (1914) that, "Prior to 1914 the selection was made from schools and colleges without discrimination and those selected were all designated as 'distinguished institutions.'"[111]

As a result of this new distinction, and despite being accustomed (perhaps rightly, given the effectiveness of Culver's military training) to being treated as an equal with the military colleges, Gignilliat was likely quite worried about the impact this change would have on Culver.

Accordingly, Gignilliat must have reacted to the first part of this report with great concern and to the second part of this report with some level of ambivalent hope. The hope arose because the second part of the report appeared to provide tremendous support for the valuable contributions to national security of military schools like Culver with respect to the training of reserve officers, along with a possible exception to allow Culver to be considered (perhaps rightly) as the equivalent of a military college in times of "emergency." Recognizing the opportunity presented by the report's determination that "there will be no trouble in deciding the different cases as they arise," Gignilliat's sense of urgency to share his message about military schools expressed in his contribution to *Types of Schools for Boys* had to have become all the more acute.

Thus, it appears not only possible but very likely that Gignilliat was aware of these two events and that they concerned him greatly. As a result, Gignilliat became convinced that both his ideas and Culver were in great danger of being left out of the most important argument regarding the role of military schools that had occurred during his professional life. As a determined man of action who cared passionately about Culver, educating boys, and military preparedness, along with having acquired a new-found confidence and ability in public speaking and writing, it was almost certain that Gignilliat renewed his determination to find a way to engage in this debate and make his voice heard on behalf of Culver, boy's education, and military preparedness. The manner in which he engaged, however, was quite unusual but turned out to be more effective than anyone – including Gignilliat – could have ever imagined.

The Impetus for *Arms and the Boy*

Recognizing Gignilliat as a determined man who was most comfortable at this point in this life of responding to challenges by doing something, along with his concern for Culver's enrollment and his awareness of the waxing of the military preparedness debate in fall 1915, it comes as no surprise that these influences triggered his inherent bias for action. Accordingly, he began searching for active ways to engage more effectively on behalf of his concerns and causes.

The result of his many and varied 1915 successes mentioned previously, combined with his impatience with the lagging publishing timeline for *Types of Schools for Boys* and the ever-increasing Preparedness Movement debates, coalesced in a realization that he needed to be more involved personally in getting the content of his work and his ideas about the value of military schools for adolescent boys out in a timely manner to contribute to the intensifying Preparedness debate and also to help Culver increase its enrollment.[112] Given Gignilliat's reluctance to draw attention to himself and/or be the center of attention in any capacity other than at Culver and on behalf of the Preparedness Movement, this explanation makes sense as to why he suggested publishing the substance of his contribution to *Types of Schools for Boys* separately at this time.

Finding His Voice: The Genesis of *Arms and the Boy*

As his first active measure in response to the combined influence of the tremendously impactful events in fall of 1915, Gignilliat wrote to the senior executive at Bobbs-Merrill overseeing the *Types of Schools for Boys* project, Hewitt Hanson Howland, on November 19, 1915, asking about the possibility of publishing his contribution to *Types of Schools for Boys* separately in order to get it disseminated more quickly. In justifying his unusual suggestion (which was likely quite difficult for Gignilliat to make personally), Gignilliat shared with Howland that, "There is at this time very great interest throughout the country in military schools" and that based upon the recommendations of the War Department report, the government would very likely in the coming year [1916] begin to utilize military schools "as a source of supply for an officers reserve corps."[113] As a result of these developments, and appealing to the publisher's business sense, Gignilliat wrote to Howland that, "I take the liberty of suggesting therefore that *if the contribution that I made over a year ago to the Childhood and Youth series could be published at this time and given some publicity, it would probably achieve a much wider circulation than if issued later on.*"[114]

It is important to note the Gignilliat suggested that Howland publish separately the contribution of 73 pages and approximately 15,000 words he submitted in January 1915 for O'Shea's *Types of Schools for Boys*. Gignilliat did not suggest that he expand or even alter his contribution, asking only that Howland consider publishing it separately on its own and as it had been submitted.

Sometime between November 20-23, 1915, Howland let Gignilliat know that Bobbs-Merrill would be interested in publishing Gignilliat's contribution to *Types of Schools for Boys* in a separate volume but that the contribution would have to be revised and enlarged to warrant a volume of its own.[115] The president of the company, William Conrad Bobbs, expressed his support for Howland's suggestion, writing that, "A good long (?) MSS on Military Training for Boys would be very timely if we could get it quickly."[116] Although they could not know it at the time, this decision reflected the thinking of the Army's Chief of Staff, Hugh L. Scott, who had written on February 8, 1915 (shortly after Gignilliat submitted his revised chapters for *Types of Schools for Boys*) that, "The subject of military instruction in high schools has hitherto not received the consideration it deserves...."[117]

In approving the publication of Gignilliat's existing work as part of a larger and expanded volume devoted to military training in high schools and colleges, the editors at Bobbs-Merrill affirmed the suspicions of both Gignilliat and the Army that there was a gap regarding the existing literature addressing military training in schools that needed to be addressed. This helped set the stage for the positive reception of Gignilliat's book.

This approach represented a departure from Gignilliat's suggestion to simply publish his contribution to *Types of Schools for Boys* on its own, and was instead an offer from Howland for Gignilliat to write his own book that was able to stand on its own. Without perhaps recognizing the full implications of Howland's offer, Gignilliat responded enthusiastically to Howland's suggestion. Writing on November 24, 1915, Gignilliat agreed to "revise and enlarge the manuscript in accordance with [Howland's] wishes." While his contribution to *Types of Schools for Boys* had focused largely on the educational value of military training in schools, a volume of sufficient length to stand on its own would also have to address the training aspect of military schools. In describing how he intended to incorporate the training aspect into the volume, Gignilliat shared with Howland that,

> *"Military training in the schools and colleges serves a two fold (sic) purpose: It has a distinctly educational value, which has already been sufficiently covered in the manuscript as submitted. It also has a military value to the Nation, which, in view of present developments, can be considerably amplified."*[118]

The "present developments" to which Gignilliat referred were clearly the Preparedness Movement and the associated debates regarding the source of supply for reserve officers.

Gignilliat's specific interest in the Preparedness Movement involved the source and training of officers for a reserve corps, which he believed should come from military schools, whereas the militia believed that reserve officers should be appointed from state militias (which was opposed vociferously by the Regular Army because of the unreliable and uneven quality of volunteer/militia officers who served in the Spanish-American War). Recognizing the opportunity it presented to Culver and for other military schools and colleges, Gignilliat informed Howland that, "The General Staff [of the US Army] is at present working on a plan whereby the graduates of the really excellent military schools and colleges might be utilized as a source of supply for an officers reserve corps," likely referring to the "Ohio Plan."

Gignilliat had been involved in many of these issues since he first attended the January 1915 annual AMCSUS meeting in Washington, DC, and he saw merits in both approaches for Culver and the nation. As a result, he came on the scene right around this time, and his work on his two most important published works – *Arms and the Boy,* and several chapters in *Types of Schools for Boys* – championed the educational and practical value of "essentially military schools" and thus supported either option. When it became clear that the government would make use of the existing military training in land-grant colleges and other private military schools across the country, along with obtaining some officers from the National Guard, Gignilliat's proposal to enhance the benefits of military schools already in existence in the states became more attractive to proponents on both sides of the issue and helped to find a middle ground for compromise that was acceptable to each side.

Illustrating his increased status within AMCSUS and the War Department, Gignilliat was invited to attend a special AMCSUS meeting, scheduled for December 2-4, 1915 in Washington, DC, to discuss the Ohio Plan with other AMCSUS delegates and members of the War Department. It is likely that Gignilliat also hoped/planned to discuss his plan for having reserve officers coming from military schools with officers of the General Staff and perhaps with Secretary of War Garrison. Garrison had been serving as Secretary of War since March 5, 1913, and although he knew President Woodrow Wilson well, the two had never meshed owing in part to the very different ideas they had regarding preparedness.

In making his case to Howland for the viability of having military schools and colleges serve as a source of supply for reserve officers, Gignilliat did not express much confidence in the citizen summer camps like the one's held at Plattsburg, New York and Fort Sheridan, Illinois, as good sources of supply for trained officers. Gignilliat believed that the public at large knew very little about the extent and scope of the training that was provided in military schools or of its value either from the standpoint of citizenship or national military preparedness.

Gignilliat believed that the public would undoubtedly accept military schools as not only viable but highly desirable sources of supply for trained reserve officers once they were suitably informed. Gignilliat offered that he knew Army leaders who realized that the graduates of the "better class of military schools and colleges" provided the best available material for reserve officers.[119] His confidence in the ability for military schools and colleges to provide trained reserve officers in sufficient numbers, however, was in stark contrast to that of Grenville Clark, a Wall Street lawyer who was among the most influential supporters of the Plattsburg Training Camp movement. Clark expressed his own reservations quite bluntly, writing that "Talk of officering 400,000 men by militia officers and men from military schools is *bunk*."[120]

Striking Out on His Own

Being the man of honor he was, Gignilliat also told Howland that he wanted to ensure that both he and Bobbs-Merrill let O'Shea know that Gignilliat was not "in any way trying to divert the manuscript from its original purpose."[121] In a separate letter to O'Shea on the same day that he wrote to Howland (November 24, 1915), Gignilliat informed O'Shea that he (Gignilliat) had felt compelled to contact Howland at Bobbs-Merrill and suggest that Bobbs-Merrill consider publishing Gignilliat's contribution to O'Shea's *Types of Schools for Boys* on its own.

In providing some justification for his action, Gignilliat shared with O'Shea that, "Some days ago I received a letter from the General Staff in Washington with reference to the utilization of graduates of military schools as a source of supply for an officer reserve corps." Knowing that O'Shea shared his own frustration with the publication delays for *Types of Schools for Boys*, Gignilliat offered that it was his own opinion that, "The interest that is at this time centered on military schools suggested my writing Mr. Howland in regard to the possibility of publishing my contribution on this subject some time (sic) in the near future." Ensuring that O'Shea' was fully informed, Gignilliat let O'Shea know that, "In [Howland's] reply he suggested the possibility of revising and enlarging the manuscript and publishing it as a separate volume." Being somewhat chagrined with having let himself be swept up in the moment, Gignilliat acknowledged that, "After receiving this letter I felt perhaps that I should have written through you instead of directly to Mr. Howland." Wanting to ensure that his action had not offended O'Shea, Gignilliat asked O'Shea to share his thoughts on the idea of publishing Gignilliat's contribution to *Types of Schools for Boys* on its own.[122]

Showing himself to be a man of magnanimity, O'Shea responded positively and enthusiastically to Gignilliat's news. Writing on November 29, 1915, O'Shea offered that "if you could enlarge your manuscript so as to make a separate volume I think it would be very timely and important and now is the psychological moment for a book of this type." Providing support for Gignilliat's belief, O'Shea wrote that "such a book at this time might play an important role in determining the direction which military training will take in this country," which was precisely what Gignilliat hoped would occur. Wanting to ensure that Gignilliat knew that he had O'Shea's full support, O'Shea wrote that, "I should think it would be advisable for you to proceed without delay to enlarge your manuscript into an independent volume," which was exactly what Gignilliat needed to hear from O'Shea. Showing himself to be a good colleague as well, O'Shea closed by letting Gignilliat know that he would ensure that Howland knew that O'Shea supported this decision.[123]

While O'Shea's influence waned from this point forward with respect to Gignilliat's work on *Arms and the Boy*, O'Shea nonetheless showed at this important juncture that he was a good colleague, mentor, and friend. In spite of witnessing how challenging it was for Gignilliat to complete his contribution for *Types of Schools for Boys* and his first-hand knowledge of the self-doubt regarding his own literary abilities Gignilliat had expressed repeatedly, O'Shea provided Gignilliat with the support and encouragement he needed to be confident enough to strike out on such a bold endeavor on his own.

On the same day he wrote to Gignilliat (November 29, 1915), O'Shea also let Howland know that Gignilliat had contacted him about publishing his contribution to *Types of Schools for Boys* on its own.[124] Howland responded to O'Shea on December 1, 1915, wanting O'Shea to know very clearly that "The suggestion that Colonel Gignilliat's contribution to *Types of Schools for Boys* be published as a separate volume came rather delicately from the Colonel himself." Providing an explanation on how the idea morphed into having Gignilliat expand his contribution to *Types of Schools for Boys* into its own volume, Howland acknowledged that he replied by expressing interest in Gignilliat's suggestion but that he would have to expand the manuscript considerably for this approach to be viable. Howland did not see any conflict with using Gignilliat's contribution to *Types of Schools for Boys* as the basis for the expanded and separate volume on the same subject, and, hoping to gain O'Shea's support, added that he believed that "a good big script on military training for boys would be very timely" if it was completed quickly, echoing Bobbs' own assessment of November 27, 1915.

It appears that O'Shea concurred with Howland in all aspects and supported the project. Perhaps O'Shea's support came in part from the fact that the contributions from two other authors for *Types of Schools for Boys* were still not complete, preventing Bobbs-Merrill from publishing his own work anytime soon. Since O'Shea had a history of supporting inexperienced writers, it is also likely that his support for Gignilliat's venture was genuine, as he remained a steadfast advocate of the project through its completion and beyond, and he remained a good friend of Gignilliat's for many years afterwards.

Gignilliat traveled to Washington DC for the AMCSUS meeting regarding the Ohio Plan that occurred December 2-4, 1915. During this visit,

Gignilliat took advantage of the opportunity to discuss his ideas for military training in schools with members of the US Army General Staff and General Leonard Wood, who, while no longer serving as the US Army's Chief of Staff, was nonetheless one of the two most well-known proponents of military preparedness (the other being Theodore Roosevelt).[125]

At the December 1915 meeting, AMCSUS found a way to incorporate its request for government-sponsored scholarships into the Ohio Plan. Since AMCSUS already preferred the Ohio Plan to the McKellar Bill, this development, along with the other revisions that were made to it, ensured AMCSUS support for the Ohio Plan in the Congressional testimony it would offer in early 1916.

Upon his return to Culver from this pivotal meeting, Gignilliat received an important letter from Howland on December 10, 1915 that provided him with the framework for expanding his work into a worthy book-length manuscript. Indicating that Gignilliat should use his contribution to O'Shea's *Types of Schools for Boys* as his base, Howland shared, on behalf of Bobbs-Merrill, that, "It is our feeling that a good book on military training for boys, covering not only military schools, but the introduction of military courses into non-military schools and the whole subject of the preparation of a citizen-soldiery through our education institutions would have a ready welcome."

This guidance must have been received by Gignilliat with great joy, since these were exactly the topics in which he was most interested and on which he had been speaking, writing, and advocating for most of the year. Howland went on to share that, "Aside from having a man prepared to fight, emphasis should be placed on the value that military training has in the boy's physique, to his sense of order and to his prompt and willing obedience to authority." Again, and whether by design or serendipity, Howland asked Gignilliat to emphasize those points about which Gignilliat was most passionate and knowledgeable. Howland closed by making the point that Bobbs-Merrill would like to publish the book as soon as possible and asking Gignilliat for an outline of the volume and the writing schedule he planned to follow. [126]

Given this propitious set of instructions, it is arguable that Gignilliat was perhaps the military educator best suited to complete such a manuscript. Whether someone other than Gignilliat was better suited to write this book at the time is beside the point; rather, the important point is that Howland had asked Gignilliat to write the book that he was most interested in writing. Thus, and despite his ambivalence regarding his own writing prowess, Gignilliat was able to draw on his impressive reservoir of passion and knowledge about the very subjects Howland had asked him to address, contributing, one must assume, to his willingness to engage in such a daunting literary task with such great enthusiasm. Howland's instructions also likely buoyed Gignilliat's confidence in his ability to deliver an acceptable product, while fueling his determination to complete the project as quickly as possible.

Gignilliat responded to Howland on December 13, 1915, requesting a complete copy of his manuscript for O'Shea's *Types of Schools for Boys* and promising to begin writing as soon as he received it. Gignilliat reported that he planned to work on expanding the manuscript as Howland suggested over the Christmas break. Demurring to provide Howland the outline and writing schedule he requested under the pretense of his preoccupation with Culver's end-of-year requirements, Gignilliat promised to speak with Howland by telephone about his outline once he had a better idea of how he planned to approach the writing of this work. Gignilliat did share that he believed that he would be able to address "both the military schools and the introduction of military courses in the non-military schools," as Howland suggested. Gignilliat also believed that he would be able to treat "the subject [of both military schools and the introduction of military courses in the non-military schools] from the standpoint of the preparation of a citizen soldiery through our educational institutions and from the standpoint of the moral and physical values of such training in the boy's general development."[127]

Despite not having a discernible plan for approaching the project, and reminding Howland that he wrote slowly, Gignilliat nonetheless offered that he would do his best to have the manuscript completed and in Howland's hands in early January 1916. Given the challenges he faced in completing the much-smaller manuscript for O'Shea's *Types of Schools for Boy* in 1913-1914, this promise to deliver the much-larger manuscript to Howland so quickly is both quite surprising and wildly unrealistic. Rather than being disingenuous or somehow misleading, this promise indicates Gignilliat's tremendous zeal for the project and his commitment to prioritize its completion.[128]

His letter to Howland of December 13, 1915 demonstrated that Gignilliat was clearly a strong believer in and evangelizer for the ability of military schools and military training for youths to transform young men into robust and capable citizens prepared to take their places in society and answer the call of duty if and when it was received. Gignilliat's reference to "the moral and physical values of such training in the boy's general development" also indicates the influence that O'Shea and the process of writing his contribution to *Types of Schools for Boys* had on him.

Indeed, it appears that Gignilliat had found his voice as a proselytizer in early November 1915 with his presentation to the Wisconsin State Teachers' Association and that he had become confident enough to agree to present his argument in a book-length volume that could be shared with the entire nation. This is certainly a dramatic and rapid transformation for one who less than a year prior had questioned his own ability to write even a portion of a book about the value of military training and balked at the prospect of addressing an audience of approximately 6,000 persons.

Howland sent Gignilliat a copy of his manuscript for O'Shea's *Types of Schools for Boys* on December 15, 1915. Howland also asked that the two of them arrange to meet in Indianapolis with owner William C. Bobbs to discuss the project when Gignilliat had developed an outline that he could share with them.[129] With Culver's holiday recess beginning on December 18th, Gignilliat was thus free to settle in for several weeks and begin work revising and expanding the manuscript he had written for O'Shea's *Types of Schools for Boys* into his own single-authored book that would become *Arms and the Boy.*

Chapter 10 –
Using His Voice: Publishing *Arms and the Boy* and Military Preparedness Involvement in 1916

Gignilliat spent the 1915 holiday season working on transforming his contribution to *Types of Schools for Boys* into a full-length manuscript of its own. As he discovered, the process of writing did not come naturally to Gignilliat, and he made headway slowly. Writing to Howland on January 15, 1916, Gignilliat provided an update on his progress that was not very promising.

Over the previous month, Gignilliat developed the idea to create a survey and send it out to every high school in the country's 48 states that was providing military training. This required taking the intermediate step of contacting the superintendents of education in each state and requesting a list of high schools with military training programs. In addition, Gignilliat also sent the survey to the heads of every military school in the country, which numbered around 170 at that time.[1] Despite his lack of training in such methodology, Gignilliat created a 24-item questionnaire to support his project.

The questionnaire included four questions addressing the value of military instruction in schools as instruction, six questions regarding the merit of military instruction in schools as a system of discipline, another six questions relating to the extent of military instruction in schools, and queried respondents via eight questions regarding their ideas related to the advantages and disadvantages of military instruction in schools.[2] This was a methodical and comprehensive approach that created the opportunity to transform his contribution to *Types of Schools for Boys* that was based almost exclusively on his own experience at Culver to something far more expansive and inclusive, and which could incorporate the ideas and experiences of many other educators across the country. While ambitious and academically admirable, this process was also quite time-consuming and delayed his work on the manuscript considerably.

In addition to the survey, Gignilliat was also scanning newspaper clippings from across the nation "to get an idea of the general sentiment" on the subject of military training in high schools. Gignilliat had requested and received information from the presidents of the University of Illinois and Massachusetts Agricultural College (now the University of Massachusetts Amherst), along with several other higher education institutions, regarding the role and functioning of the military officers on duty at these institutions. Completing his investigation, Gignilliat also queried General Wood and members of the US Army General Staff regarding the work of then-Lieutenant Edgar Z. Steever's "unique system of military instruction" in several Wyoming high schools, which was a structured program to allow public high schools to incorporate military training into their curricula relatively easily.[3]

Gignilliat received a request from William R. Austin, a trustee of Wabash College in Indiana, for information establishing a military department at his institution. According to Austin, at least a few and likely the majority of the trustees, including the Vice President of the United States, Thomas R. Marshall, desired to establish such a department at Wabash. Knowing the importance of gaining the support of Vice President Marshall, and wanting to do all he could to help other Hoosier educational institutions incorporate military training into their curricula, Gignilliat provided an exceptionally detailed response of five single-spaced pages to Austin. Realizing that this response contained information that would likely be of value to many other institutions across the country, Gignilliat determined that it should be included in his expanded manuscript as well.[4]

In terms of Culver's own program, Gignilliat continued an effort he had begun in late 1915 of adding additional theoretical instruction to the military science class for first classmen. He was able to augment this endeavor substantially in early 1916 when he secured the services of a serving US Army officer from the renowned School of Musketry, the very same Captain Robinson who had inspected Culver for the Army for the preceding three years, to provide additional theoretical instruction to the upper division cadets. Taking the entire program up a notch (and perhaps exceeding Gignilliat's own level of expertise), Captain Robinson introduced the cadets to more sophisticated aspects of marching and combat operations, along with providing them with advanced instruction in the areas of fire control and military history.[5]

As a result of his multifaceted approach and various activities over the holidays, Gignilliat informed the Bobbs-Merrill senior editor Howland that he would be unable to meet his ambitious (and perhaps unrealistic) goal of completing his transformed manuscript by early January 1916. After informing Howland of his decision to create and disseminate his survey (and including a copy of it in his letter), Gignilliat explained that while his progress had been slowed by the gathering of material, he expressed his belief that his approach was adding value to the project and would thus be worth the extra time it required. Being an experienced editor who was used to working with inexperienced authors, Gignilliat's letter likely came as no surprise to Howland.

While he was engaged in the activities he had identified and was in the process of collecting the material he listed, Gignilliat also suggested to

Howland that the promise of what he could acquire as a result of these endeavors was sufficient to warrant expanding the scope of the work so that it could "set forth suggestions and helpful information to these institutions that are seeking to organize military departments."[6]

By "these institutions that are seeking to organize military departments," Gignilliat meant both public and private high schools, along with colleges and universities across the nation. Compared to the scope of his initial contribution to *Types of Schools for Boys*, which focused largely on private secondary educational institutions, this represented a tremendous expansion of both the extent of its coverage and the intended audience for the manuscript Gignilliat proposed to deliver.

While ambitious, the approach suggested by Gignilliat in mid-January 1916 was likely more in line with what Howland had envisioned when he suggested that Gignilliat expand the scope of his contribution to *Types of Schools for Boys*. Determining that his plan would add value to the resulting work, even if it slowed down its completion somewhat, Howland approved Gignilliat's suggestion on January 19, 1916.[7]

Howland's decision cleared the way for the creation of an entirely new work that would become the most comprehensive assessment yet produced of secondary and higher education military training offered in schools. The cost of doing so, however, might end up coming at the expense of Gignilliat's own argument for the value of military training in schools (especially in secondary education institutions).

Gignilliat's Remarkable 90-Day Period of Productivity

In January 1916, Gignilliat began an almost unbelievable three-month period of intense activity that represents his zenith as an evangelist for Military Preparedness. His actions during this period laid the foundation for him to become the most respected spokesperson for military education in the country and for Culver to solidify its reputation as one of the premier military institutions in the nation. However, these actions also impacted his ability to complete the draft of *Arms and the Boy*, working against his desire to have the book published at the earliest possible time at the cost of increasing Gignilliat's exposure and national recognition.

Congressional Hearings Regarding Military Preparedness

One reason the writing for *Arms and the Boy* progressed more slowly than desired was Gignilliat's trip to Washington, DC for the AMCSUS annual meeting and his subsequent testimony to the US Congress on January 21, 1916.

In Washington, D.C., the House of Representatives Committee on Military Affairs began 1916 by hearing testimony related to endeavors to increase the efficiency of the country's military establishment. Secretary of War Garrison was the first to testify at 10:30 am on Thursday, January 6, 1916. Garrison began by presenting his assessment of the nation's current state of military preparedness, which he found to be quite lacking. He then presented his idea for establishing the Continental Army he had announced in November 1915.

In brief, this plan called for the establishment of a 400,000-man Federal Reserve force separate from the National Guard that could be kept trained and ready to respond to national emergencies in much the same way that state governors relied upon their own militias. There were a variety of problems with Garrison's Continental Army plan, many of which became apparent during the course of the two hours of his initial testimony. Of interest to AMCSUS and Gignilliat were the portions related to plans to acquire the approximately 70,000 additional commissioned officers needed to train and lead this new organization.

While Garrison mentioned in his opening statement that he envisioned using "graduates of military schools and colleges who qualify" as part of his strategy, he admitted under subsequent questioning that he did not have a detailed plan for this aspect of his proposal and preferred that Congress let the Executive Branch determine how best to accomplish this component.[8] However, when pressed by one member of the committee, Garrison offered that he would look to graduates of military schools and colleges who qualified as officers only after exhausting all other potential sources of supply, echoing Grenville Clark's rather dismal late 1915 view of military schools and colleges as viable sources of supply for reserve officers for the Continental Army plan.

The Secretary of War preferred to begin by relying upon the capabilities of existing educational institutions – civilian and military – to provide the requisite numbers of reserve officers. If, however, this approach proved inadequate, Garrison was willing to consider alternatives along the lines of McKellar's suggestions.[9]

Perhaps more promising, however, was the willingness of Hay, as the committee's chair, to consider the country's 173 military schools and colleges to be considered seriously as an excellent source of supply for reserve officers.[10]

The AMCSUS Congressional Testimony

Regardless of the plan adopted by Congress, the issue of how to provide trained officers for this federal military reserve force – whether in the form of the Continental Army or the National Guard – had yet to be determined. After gathering in Washington, DC for the annual AMCSUS meeting and electing Sebastian C. Jones, Superintendent of New York Military Academy, as its new president (replacing Colonel John. C. Woodward), the members of the AMCSUS Executive Committee remained in the nation's capital to testify before the House Committee on Military Affairs regarding the role of military schools in the nation's preparedness.

The AMCSUS Executive Committee was comprised of the heads of the five largest military schools, regardless of educational level, along with the AMCSUS officers (if not already a member). The members of the AMCSUS Executive Committee in early 1916 included Gignilliat as the head of Culver Military Academy, along with General Edward W. Nichols, Superintendent of the Virginia Military Institute; Dr. Thomas Fell, President of St. John's College, Annapolis, MD; past-president of AMCSUS Colonel J. C. Woodward, President of Georgia Military Academy; along with newly elected AMCSUS President Sebastian C. Jones, Superintendent of New York Military Academy, and Colonel O. C. Hulvey, President of Columbia Military Academy, TN and AMCUS Secretary.[11]

Establishing their purpose as presenting the committee with arguments for providing recognition and funding for the nation's military schools and colleges as viable and effective sources of supply for reserve officers, this group devised an approach that was both coordinated and nuanced. Beginning at 10:00 am, Jones, as the AMCSUS president, began by presenting the overall AMCSUS position that it and the institutions it represented felt that they were being overlooked in the preparedness discussion because of unfounded bias from the active military in favor of the federal service academies and were thus in danger of being forgotten entirely because of ignorance about their capabilities at the very time that they believed they could make their greatest contribution.[12]

Jones continued by making an effective financial argument, pointing out that cadets being trained at the military colleges and schools he represented were quite economical, costing the federal government "the great sum of $4 per year for each of the cadets now being given a (sic) military training in these institutions."[13] Since any approach would be costly, electing to provide a powerful argument showing the economic desirability of their position to the fiscally minded Congress was clever.

Getting to the crux of his presentation, Jones provided five requests that AMCSUS believed would not only conserve the great national asset represented by the nation's military schools and colleges but also make it possible to strengthen and improve the system and increase its output.

The five requests from AMCSUS were that the federal government:

1. Provide the AMCSUS schools with proper military equipment;

2. Recognize graduates of AMCSUS schools as valuable to any reserve army or reserve officer corps the government might create;

3. Designate the "essentially military" institutions represented by AMCSUS as "United States Reserve Army Training Schools" and the cadets attending these institutions as "United States Reserve Army Cadets," entitled to wear a standard military uniform recognized and adopted by the US Army;

4. Provide AMCSUS schools with "obsolete or historic ordnance" for display on their campuses to create a proper military atmosphere; and

5. Provide AMCSUS schools with federal scholarships to help attract cadets and increase output.[14]

These recommendations constituted an ambitious request for an organization that had been in existence for a little over two years, but the representatives appearing before Congress were able men used to aiming high and accomplishing great things.

Adopting a bold approach to their task, the members of the AMCSUS Executive Committee organized themselves so that each member addressed different aspects of the role of military schools in national preparedness that was particularly relevant to his institution and in ways that also complemented one another's testimony. In aggregate, the individual testimony presented by the members of the AMSCUS Executive Committee also served to reinforce the five main points outlined by Jones on behalf of AMCSUS.

The Superintendent of VMI, General Edward Nichols, provided compelling testimony regarding the value of the contributions to national defense made by schools like VMI throughout the nation's history by consistently producing excellent citizen-soldiers capable of serving the nation in times of war. Dr. Thomas Fell, President of St. John's College in Annapolis, Maryland, reiterated the point about providing scholarships for cadets at military schools and colleges to attract more students and increase their output. Colonel O. C. Hulvey, of the Columbia Military Academy in Tennessee and AMCSUS Secretary, provided the members of the committee with statistics from 1915 showing that 33,000 young men were in attendance in the nation's military schools and that there had been 5,200 graduates from military schools in 1915.

Colonel John C. Woodward, President of Georgia Military Academy and past-President of AMCSUS, offered that the work of educating cadets for citizenship and service done by the nation's military schools and colleges was perhaps the best way to spread the "gospel" of citizenship across the country. Woodward also expressed his agreement with one of the committee members that, based upon the heavy cost of casualties suffered by American forces in its previous wars, the nation dare not risk being unprepared for any future conflicts.[15]

On behalf of AMCUS, which had a membership comprised largely of secondary schools (over 80 percent), and Culver, Gignilliat made his contribution by endeavoring to make the case that military preparatory schools were also excellent sources of supply for reserve officers. Further, Gignilliat argued that preventing well-trained graduates of military preparatory schools from consideration as a potential source of reserve officers based merely on the fact that most graduated at age 18 or 19, when the age to become eligible to be commissioned was 21, was both short-sighted and ill-advised. The training they received would undoubtedly stay with them, but due to their relatively young age, these young men would of course have to prove themselves worthy of taking on such an important responsibility and leading soldiers effectively.[16]

The decision to discount the leadership abilities of young men who were under the age of 21 was largely arbitrary, stemming from the Progressive Era's subjective belief that higher education enabled one to manage others effectively. For its part, the Army extended this belief by equating management and "executive ability" with leadership, along with an erroneous belief that West Point taught leadership to its cadets (which it did not yet do in any formal sense), and concluded that those with college degrees or who had been accepted to college would therefore have better leadership abilities and were thus more desirable as officers.[17]

Based upon his knowledge of what was actually being taught at West Point, his faith in the training program he had installed at Culver, and his observations of what properly trained 18- and 19-year old Culver cadets were capable of accomplishing – especially relative to what he had witnessed at the Fort Sheridan and Plattsburg military training camps – Gignilliat was certain that the Army had drawn the wrong conclusion in the case of excluding military school graduates who were younger than 21 years of age from consideration as officers. He was determined to make this point, above all others, abundantly clear to the members of the Congressional committee during his testimony.

Based on the substance of his presentation, Gignilliat offered the very reasonable recommendation that graduates of military preparatory schools be granted probationary commissions and allowed to serve for six months to one year on probationary active duty with the Regular Army to determine if they had what it took to become successful commissioned officers and also to gauge the effectiveness of their training.

Those young men over the age of 21 and who had graduated from military preparatory schools should be considered as viable contributions to a supply of commissioned reserve officers for the country as well.[18] Believing that some of these graduates were the equal of West Point graduates (which may indicate as much about Gignilliat as a VMI graduate as it does about his confidence in the Culver system), Gignilliat was suggesting that military preparatory school graduates should be allowed to compete for commissions. The implication was that when given such an opportunity, Gignilliat's Culver graduates would prove themselves more than equal to the demands of active military service.

Writing to ER Culver two days after his testimony, Gignilliat was pleased with the outcomes and reported that he found the members of the committee "responsive and friendly to the interests of the military schools." Gignilliat acquired an acute awareness that "both the Army and the National Guard [were] somewhat unfriendly to the plan of utilizing military schools and colleges as a source of supply of volunteer officers."[19] He turned his attention to making the case that military schools and colleges were desirable sources of volunteer officers for a reserve army.

Demonstrating his relentlessness on behalf of Culver and AMCUS, Gignilliat followed up his testimony with individual meetings with several members of the Committee. During these meetings, Gignilliat made additional arguments on behalf of both military schools and Culver, bolstered by statistics he provided to make his points more compelling.

Still not satisfied, Gignilliat wrote that he wanted to meet with the Senate Committee on Military Affairs and that he planned to ask for Vice President Thomas Marshall's help to get him in contact with the Committee Chair, Senator George E. Chamberlain, a Democrat from Oregon.[20] It is unclear if Gignilliat managed to meet with Chamberlain or any other members of the Senate committee, but what is clear is that he was now in the thick of the preparedness discussion at the national level and that he was even more determined to do all he could to help Culver and other military schools have an appropriate stake in the most important national security issue of the day.

In the end, and based largely on the testimony offered during the January 1916 hearings, the McKellar Bill failed to gain the necessary support and was defeated in February of 1916. It was the recommendations of the War College Division, which integrated elements of the revised Ohio Plan that included the AMCSUS proposal and some influence from the McKellar Bill, that were incorporated into the Hay/Chamberlain bills and which eventually became part of the National Defense Act of 1916.[21]

Preparedness and Writing *Arms and the Boy* at Culver

Almost immediately upon his return to Culver, Gignilliat re-engaged with preparedness activities that characterized the three-month period of hyper-activity. By this time, preparedness had come to mean "the organization of the entire national strength so that it may be employed to the best advantage," in which military schools played an important part.[22]

Helping Start a National Preparedness Organization – the High School Volunteers of the United States (HSVUS)

Gignilliat was successful in making contact with the newly promoted Captain Edgar Z. Steever while he had been in Washington DC. This began a long and fruitful association between the two that resulted in making several significant contributions to the Preparedness Movement.

 The most important contribution was Steever's establishment, with Gignilliat's support and guidance, of the "High School Volunteers of the United States" (HSVUS). This was an organization devoted to promoting citizenship among high school students that preceded but which was very much akin to the Junior ROTC program. It offered a relatively simple way for public high schools to incorporate military training into their curricula meaningfully and effectively.

Edgar Z. Steever and the "Wyoming Plan" – Bringing Culver-like Military Training to Public High Schools

As a Regular Army officer assigned as an inspector-instructor of the organized militia of the Wyoming National Guard, Edgar Z. Steever took an interest in the burgeoning debate regarding Universal Military Training (UMT) that began in America early in the second decade of the 20th century. Similar to Gignilliat in many ways, Steever was convinced that high school students had much to offer and were quite capable of becoming proficient in basic military skills when properly presented to them.

Accordingly, Steever undertook, on his own initiative, to develop a system of training that could be incorporated into existing high school curricula that would also teach and promote good citizenship. His plan was founded on the premise that "good citizenship involves a willingness on the part of each able-bodied youth to make such effort and sacrifice" as was necessary to prepare for the obligations and duties of a citizen. Steever determined that this required students to be prepared in the areas of military, moral, civic, business, and education.

Democratic in form, meaning success through effort and advancement by merit, the approach also relied upon peer pressure to encourage boys to behave, since it would hurt their squad/team if they were unable to compete. Nor did the program appear to promote the militarism feared by some, as participation seemed to satisfy the curiosity about military service of many (echoing Gignilliat's own argument) and there was no appreciable increase in the percentage of enlistments between participants and non-participants. Adding further to its merits, General Leonard Wood, the Chief of Staff of the US Army at the time, gave the program high marks and supported it enthusiastically.

The military component of the resulting "Wyoming Plan" offered military training in the form of a series of games that included marching and infantry drills, wall-scaling competitions, rifle marksmanship matches, and competitive military problem-solving contests. The method of competition was the key to the program's success because it was all based on "games" between equally balanced teams so that every cadet who participated had the chance to win.

Steever also ingeniously allowed each squad to have a girl from the school serve as its official sponsor, adding an appealing chivalric element to the program that also allowed for sustained contact with members of the opposite sex. Steever's approach combined the teenaged boy's love of games with their competitive instinct, fascination with girls,

Edgar Z. Steever. (Public domain)

and their craving to belong in a group, making it almost irresistible to adolescent boys. Competitions could occur within the school and with other schools around the state, building pride in achievement, a shared sense of purpose, and a common experiential base, all of which combined to foster individual school spirit and a larger sense of camaraderie with fellow cadets from different schools.[24]

Steever also incorporated field aspects to the training, allowing the boys to spend a week or two outdoors living in military-style camps they constructed. He did not allow the one-dimensional task-oriented "drivership" of the "rock-crusher" style of drilling he had experienced in his own high school military program in Washington DC that tainted the experiences in such programs of so many boys (including himself), emphasizing instead that the purpose of leadership was acquiring "cheerful and willing obedience" of members. In addition, Steever wanted to elicit intelligent compliance instead of unthinking acquiescence. Accordingly, Steever ensured that the peer leadership employed by the boys was both respectful and democratic in nature, requiring the boys to "dope out" solutions together so that each understood the task and the reasons for it their actions.[25] In his program, the "how" of getting something done was at least as important as the "what" that was being accomplished.

Initially used at the high schools in Cheyenne in 1911, Steever's program met with opposition on a variety of fronts, including labor unions (who viewed it as nothing more than a military recruitment tool), parents and clergy members (worried that it would promote militarism in the children), and educators (concerned that it would stifle individual initiative in the students). To address the concerns of the labor unions, Steever made the program both entirely voluntary and separate from the state's militia. To the parents he touted the benefits of citizenship, and to the members of the clergy he argued that the training would actually prevent the students from becoming militaristic. As for the educators, Steever equated his program with athletics and challenged any of them to argue that athletics stifled initiative. This approach and these arguments won over his opposition, and the Cheyenne school board gave its consent to allow the program into its schools.[26]

Just as he was getting his program up and running in Cheyenne, Steever was ordered to the Mexican border for two years during 1913-1914. The organization remained active but made little progress during his absence. In response to requests to the government by parents and educators, Steever was allowed to return to Wyoming in 1915 and resume his work of establishing and enhancing his program throughout the entire state.

After gaining a foothold in Cheyenne, the Wyoming Plan spread across the state and enjoyed a high level of success in Wyoming – with 90 percent of the state's high school students participating in it voluntarily – by the beginning of 1916. Demonstrating the level of success he had in overcoming the initial opposition he faced, the high school principals of Wyoming offered their support in the form of the following statement:

> "Since the organization of the cadet corps, truancy is no
> longer a problem, nor do our boys quit school for a premature
> entrance into industry. School life has been made interesting,
> and we have no trouble keeping them for the complete course."[27]

Law enforcement officers and judges offered similar statements of support for his work, with one remarking that "if Lieutenant Steever gets them, I don't," meaning that the boys in Steever's program stayed out of trouble and jail.[28] It is hard to imagine a more powerful expression of support for Steever and his program.

Espousing many of Gignilliat's own and best ideas about developing young men and applying them to environments that were not "essential military schools," the Wyoming Plan made it possible to export a version of the Culver system and incorporate parts of it into public schools nationwide. The young and energetic Steever was also an outstanding trainer and a world-class marksman who knew how to connect with boys. All met with Gignilliat's approval, making Steever very appealing to him.

Created prior to the National Defense Act of 1916, the Wyoming Plan was remarkable for its unusual approach (teenaged boys in high school), innovative nature (games), and effectiveness (as Leonard Wood attested). An outgrowth of the pre-WWI Universal Military Training movement, the Wyoming Plan addressed "the growing feeling that America needed some new educational force, some organized effort which should produce in it a better sense of American citizenship, with all that that implies with loyalty to American ideals, unity of racial sympathies, better health, greater interest in our government, better business morality and sense of civic decency, etc."[29]

Steever's plan was particularly intriguing because it seemed to afford "a solution of that growing question in a peculiarly American way, a reconciliation of the ideals of America...with the necessities that seemed to be dictated by the peculiarities of her domestic problems, and by the emergence of America into the current of world affairs." It did so by ensuring that citizenship was addressed directly and explicitly in the schools, where it needed to be developed consistently and progressively for boys as they grew into manhood and prepared to assume the mantle of responsibly for citizenship.[30]

The Wyoming Plan – the Basis of the High School Volunteers of the United States (HSVUS)

After Steever's training program enjoyed five years of success, *Everybody's Magazine* published an article by George Creel in February 1916 extolling its virtues, titled "Wyoming's Answer to Militarism." Creel concluded that "no plan of an adequate national defense yet broached deserves larger consideration than the Wyoming idea" because it gained "every desired result with the slightest impingement upon American ideals" while also being both simple and economical.

Enthralled with the approach, Creel got behind the idea. After promoting it tirelessly for five months, the Wyoming Plan was crystallized by the pressure of the situation in 1916 into a national movement.[31] In recognition, and using the Wyoming Plan as its foundation, Creel proposed the establishment of the High School Volunteers of the United States (HSVUS) in July 1916, to be headquartered out of the iconic Butterick Building in New York City (which also served as home for *Everybody's Magazine*).[32]

According to its own literature, the HSVUS was "the first national organization of, by, and for high-school boys and girls, dedicated to the development of better citizenship through the uniform plan of training and system of district and national games, competitions, and reviews worked out by Capt. E. Z. Steever, in the schools of Wyoming, and now embracing the high schools of the country," which may discount the impact of the Boy Scouts of America and its own similar objective. In terms of duration, the Wyoming Program provided for three years of progressive training.[33]

The organization stated that "membership is open to all students of high schools which have adopted the High-School Volunteer, formerly called the Wyoming Plan of training as part of their curriculum." This indicates that both boys and girls could participate.[34]

In its initial stages, it is likely that the HVSUS included girls because it was the tradition in Wyoming to allow women to participate fully as citizens and in citizenship activities (voting and military training) due to a very small population and the need for all to be part of the body politic.

This was, however, not the norm elsewhere, and perhaps due to physical nature of training – as rifle drill and wall scaling require significant upper body strength – and in recognition of the cultural norms of the period that really did not welcome or encourage such activities for girls, the HSVUS became like the BSA and ROTC/SATC, a male-only organization (it remained open to girls only in Wyoming).

Thus, while ostensibly open to boys and girls when it was proposed and established, by the time the official handbook of the HSVUS was published in 1918 membership was limited to high school boys (although some thought was given to expanding the program to involve girls in 1918).[35]

Creel argued that this program was an important part of creating an effective national military reserve, urging it to be adopted by the War Department and established nationwide. In December 1916, the War Department "recognized the soundness of Steever's ideas and the practicability of applying in nationally."[36] Reflecting Creel's influence, the War Department rescinded Steever's new orders to report to the Philippines for duty on November 1, 1916, directing him instead to remain in the United States and focus on implementing his program domestically.[37]

Back to *Arms and the Boy*

At the beginning of 1916, Gignilliat had sent copies of the 24-question survey he created to every high school in the country and to the heads of all 173 military schools in the country, and the responses had been pouring in throughout the month. Supplied with "a raft of information from others states in which such training has been given," Gignilliat was busy with the time-consuming process of collating the information. However, after working diligently for two weeks, Gignilliat had made significant progress such that he informed Howland on February 16 that, "It will not take very long now to get the matter completed as I have all of the necessary material in hand."[38]

Gignilliat shared the general outline he had developed for the expanded manuscript. He also sent Howland a copy of the draft he had been able to complete and a copy of its working title – *Military Training in the Schools and Colleges* – and requested Howland's feedback to ensure he was on the right track. Gignilliat informed Howland that he planned to be in Indianapolis the following week upon return from a speaking engagement at Indiana University on the topic of military training in schools and indicated that he wanted to meet with Howland to discuss his progress.[39]

The year 1916 had thus far been a productive one for Gignilliat. He had developed a general outline for the book, gone to Washington, DC for the AMCSUS annual meeting, testified in front of Congress, spoken to many important people regarding preparedness, collated responses to his questionnaire in sufficient quantity to incorporate the results into his manuscript, and created a working outline and title for his new book.

Sometime during this period, Gignilliat found time to write a fairly long article about "Military Training on Our Colleges" for the *Fort Wayne Daily News*. Appearing in two parts on March 10 and March 11 of 1916, Gignilliat was able to expose other readers to his ideas about the best way to provide military training to students.[40]

Also in March 1916, Gignilliat was elected President of North Central Academic Association.

Taken together, these activities show Gignilliat's incredible capacity for work, and the accomplishments are indicative of his growing status as a respected educator.[41]

Bringing Preparedness to the Culver Campus

Gignilliat also began bringing his preparedness activities to Culver for the cadets. He shared his experiences in Washington, DC with the cadets in chapel on February 12, 1916.

On February 17, 1916, Culver cadets viewed the movie, "Battle Cry of Peace," which was a major statement on the Preparedness Movement in America.[42] The movie took place in a war-torn world, and it told the story of how enemies of the United States used pacifists as pawns to make sure that the United States did not spend too much on defense. Rendered vulnerable and unprepared, the enemies attacked America and took over the country. Presenting a partisan call for the US to join the Allies fighting World War I, the film was considered to be militaristic propaganda, and it was as controversial when released as D. W. Griffith's "Birth of a Nation," released that same year.

The film was based on the book *Defenseless America*, by Hudson Maxim, a U S inventor and chemist who invented smokeless gunpowder and the brother of the inventor of the Maxim gun, the world's first recoil-operated machine gun. It appears that both Theodore Roosevelt and General Leonard Wood, the two giants of the Preparedness Movement, were great supporters of the film.[43] By screening such a film on campus, it is clear that Gignilliat wanted to expose his cadets to its message, and his support for preparedness must have been known widely by all at Culver.

Completing *Arms and the Boy*

Returning from another preparedness-related speaking engagement at Indian University on February 23, 1916, Gignilliat settled in for an additional week of work on the manuscript. Unsatisfied with his ability to make suitable progress amidst the daily distractions of running Culver, and feeling acutely the pressure to complete his manuscript as soon as possible, Gignilliat wrote to ER Culver on March 4, 1916, telling him that he was going 100 miles west to the resort at Mudlavia, Indiana, for several days to complete the manuscript.

The amount of effort Gignilliat had been pouring into the manuscript becomes evident when he shared with ER Culver that he had been working "twelve to fourteen hours a day and often until considerably after midnight for the last few weeks" to complete the manuscript. Justifying the amount of time he was spending on the manuscript and his request for a brief leave of absence, Gignilliat shared with ER Culver that he felt that book will be "very advantageous to [Culver] if it can be promptly issued while the public interest is so intense on this subject."[44]

While close to completion, Gignilliat needed a few days to devote his entire attention to "go over the whole manuscript and get a bird's eye view of it," making sure it was accurate, complete, and of suitable quality for publication.[45] From the substance of this letter it becomes clear that Gignilliat had thrown himself completely into the task of finishing the manuscript, so much so that he was even willing to leave Culver in mid-session to complete the project. This is almost unheard-of behavior for Gignilliat, who prided himself on his devotion to the school and expected nothing less of his subordinates.

Gignilliat ended up having to postpone his trip to Mudlavia due to "matters that came up," and he instead traveled to Chicago on the evening of March 5, 1916. The "matters that came up" were likely the unexpected but very welcomed visit to Culver by Steever and a meeting of the North Central Academic Association in Chicago (which he had planned to skip).

Steever arrived at Culver on March 5, 1916 in preparation to meet with the Chicago School Board on March 6, 1916 regarding military training. Gignilliat had extended an invitation to Steever to visit Culver when they met in Washington, DC, in January 1916, and he must have been thrilled to learn of Steever's coming.

Gignilliat met Steever upon his arrival to Culver and prior to heading to Chicago on the evening of March 5, 1916 for the North Central Academic Association meeting occurring the following day. The two perhaps traveled to Chicago together that evening, since both needed to be in Chicago on March 6, 1916, and they would have had time to talk while on the train. Gignilliat's esteem for Steever remained quite substantial, and during their time together Gignilliat also hoped to go over some of the manuscript with Steever to get his feedback and reactions.[46] It turned out to be a good thing that Gignilliat postponed his trip to Mudlavia, as he was elected president of the North Central Academic Association meeting in Chicago on March 6, 1916 (adding yet more responsibilities to his already very full plate).

Taking time to send an update on his status to Bobbs-Merrill in light of these activities, Gignilliat wrote that he hoped to be able to send the completed manuscript to Howland "in a few days." Gignilliat also suggested a revised title – *Military Training for the American School Boy* – for the work, which he believed to be "less stiff" than his previous working title. Howland appreciated the update and was pleased with Gignilliat's progress. While he thought the new title was an improvement over the previous one, Howland urged Gignilliat to continue searching for an even better title for the book that would capture the reader's attention.[47]

Steever completed his business in Chicago and returned to Culver on March 9, 1916, where he met again with Gignilliat. That same day, Pancho Villa raided Columbus, New Mexico, and the neighboring Army camp in the early morning hours. It was almost certainly a hot topic of discussion at Fort Sheridan, IL (just north of Chicago), where Gignilliat spoke at the reunion of his fellow participants of the 1915 military training camp being held there on March 10, 1916, and it is likely that Gignilliat learned about the event that same day.[48] The excitement caused by this event, the largest foreign incursion on US soil since 1814, must have been quite palpable, generating even more enthusiasm for enhancing America's military preparedness.

The Pancho Villa Raid

Pancho Villa raided Columbus, New Mexico early on the morning of March 9. According to one account:

> "The raiders cut a swathe of destruction through the Columbus business district. Some of them ran into the Commercial Hotel, the only one in town, where they grabbed what loot they could and shot five guests. They set fire to the grocery store across the street, and the flames quickly engulfed the hotel as well. The Mexicans also fired into private homes, killing and wounding some residents of Columbus."[49]

The raiders also hit the nearby US Army Camp Furlong. In aggregate, Villa hit with a force of approximately 400 men in the two raids.

While there was little the stunned residents of Columbus could do other than protect themselves, at Camp Furlong one officer led a pursuit of the raiders approximately 15 miles into Mexico, killing 70-100 of them (by his own account) before having to return his exhausted horses and men to US territory. Despite Villa's audacity and having the element of surprise, his raid was a disaster. For what still remains a dubious purpose, he lost a total of 130 men, 100 of whom had been killed and the other 30 having been captured, which constituted just under a third of his entire force. On the American side, eight civilians and ten soldiers had died, and another seven soldiers and two civilians were wounded in the attack.[50]

The story flashed across the country almost instantly due the presence of an Associated Press correspondent who happened to be in town during the raid, with news reaching President Wilson late on the same morning.[51] Villa's raid and wanton acts of banditry violated America's territorial sovereignty in a manner not seen since the War of 1812. President Wilson decided quickly to authorize a Punitive Expedition to pursue the raiders, to be led by General John J. Pershing. Comprised of approximately 5,000 soldiers and charged with dispersing the band and capturing Villa if possible, Pershing's expedition (which would grow to over 10,000 soldiers) crossed the border into Mexico on March 15, 1916.

The Impact of Pancho Villa's Raid on Gignilliat and Culver – Proposals for Volunteer Units

Given the attention Gignilliat had devoted to enhancing the nation's military preparedness during the preceding several years, the Pancho Villa raid was undoubtedly upsetting for him. In the ensuing week during which President Wilson was determining how America would respond, Gignilliat apparently discussed the situation with many others, including the redoubtable and experienced cavalryman Rossow. Up to this point, American citizens were accustomed to flocking to the colors and forming volunteer military units in times of crisis. This type of response had occurred most recently during the Spanish-American War, which began with the sinking of US Navy ship and was spurred on by the rallying cry, "Remember the Maine."

Despite the excitement generated by Villa's raid, and determined to absent himself from the distractions, Gignilliat went to Mudlavia for a few days the following week to proofread his manuscript. Working at Mudlavia during the period March 12-15, 1916, Gignilliat was able to focus his attention and energy on completing the draft of his manuscript.

Proposing a Culver Volunteer Cavalry Regiment

It is evident, however, that Gignilliat and Rossow were appalled by Pancho Villa's incursion and felt that they had to act. The two determined that they should mobilize a volunteer cavalry regiment comprised of Culver BHT alumni.[52] A cavalry troop at the time consisted of 50 soldiers at full strength, and a cavalry regiment was comprised of 12 troops. This meant that Gignilliat and Rossow intended to raise a force of at least 500 men if the regiment was to be staffed at a level of at least 85 percent to be considered effective.

Cavalry units would become the "strike forces" of Pershing's 1916 Punitive Expedition, so they were not off-base from the perspective of force structure. Pershing's force had four US Cavalry units assigned to it – the 7th (of Custer's fame), 10th, 11th, and 13th – to conduct the pursuit of Villa and his band, along with two infantry regiments (the 6th and 16th) to protect its supply lines and additional firepower from artillery and machine gun units. The cavalry units used the traditional cavalry method of launching dispersed "flying columns" of troops that fanned out across a wide area to conduct reconnaissance and then converged upon enemy forces if/when contacted.

Upon his return to campus from Mudlavia, Gignilliat was compelled to send out a letter to BHT alumni on March 16, 1916 (the day after Pershing's Punitive Expedition crossed the border into Mexico), soliciting their participation and gauging their interest in such an endeavor. This action is somewhat surprising, as Gignilliat had learned that the US Army disliked the nation's practice of mobilizing volunteer military units in times of national crisis in favor of creating a formal and structured reserve force to serve just such a purpose. It was, however, very much in line with other preparedness advocates like former President Theodore Roosevelt, who also proposed raising a volunteer cavalry regiment much like the Rough Riders of the Spanish-American War fame.

In the letter, Gignilliat wrote that he and Captain Rossow were "seeking very quietly to see what can be done in the way of organizing a Culver regiment of cavalry" in the event of more serious trouble in Mexico. The nucleus of this organization was to be comprised of "old cadets 21 years of age or older who have received their training in the cavalry school at Culver," to whom Gignilliat reached out to determine "if they would be willing to identify themselves with such an organization."

Gignilliat also encouraged the recipients to feel free to "interest some of your friends who have some knowledge of horsemanship to join" as well, hoping to "fill up the ranks with the best type of men" available. Gignilliat offered that, "with the co-operation of the Culver men and the infusion of the good old Culver spirit," they could from "the best organization of this kind that was ever assembled."

According to the plan, Gignilliat would command the regiment and Rossow would serve as the second-in-command, with officers of the Regular Army commanding each of the regiment's three squadrons.

Rather than following the usual practice in volunteer units of electing their captains and lieutenants, Regular Army officers would command the 12 troops, and lieutenants would be "selected from the cadets of longest and most satisfactory service amongst those who joined." Rounding out the unit leadership, noncommissioned officers would come from "ex-Culver Troopers." For other BHT alumni for whom there were not leadership positions available, they would serve as regular troopers assigned to the units.

Once mobilized at Culver, the regiment would conduct its intensive preliminary training at Culver for some months as well. Based upon previous experience, this would mean that the troopers would live in tents and dine in their own field kitchen, while having access to the amenities available on campus as appropriate. The stabling of around 500 horses would present a challenge to the facilities, but they would likely join their riders in outdoor living arrangements.

The Redoubtable Captain Robert Rossow.[54]

One curious theme that runs throughout the two-page letter is the admonishment to keep the plan a secret. After beginning by stating that he and Rossow were "seeking very quietly" to ascertain the interest among BHT alumni in forming a volunteer cavalry regiment for service in Mexico, Gignilliat asked that the matter be treated "with entire confidence" and reiterated his caution to "keep the plan entirely out of the press" and to "not mention that the initiative has come from the Academy" when recruiting others for the regiment. Gignilliat closes the letter by reminding the recipient that the endeavor "must be treated with every confidence."

For someone who was so consistently straightforward in all of his dealings and had little tolerance for intrigue, these statements and this approach strike one as being both unusual and out of character for Gignilliat.

The rationale for such secrecy was based upon a concern that it might portray Culver in a negative light – *"We do not think it would be at all becoming of an institution of this class to make any rash statements or to make any announcements of any character until it was absolutely sure that they could be fulfilled in every particular"* – if word of this initiative got out and was either not successful or not accepted by the government. Wanting to avoid "making any premature announcement" and/or "any rash statements or to make any announcement of any character until it was absolutely sure that they would be fulfilled in every particular," he ended his letter by reminding the recipient again that "this organization is by no means an assured fact," depending "entirely on the response we get to this letter."[53]

This approach suggests two things: Gignilliat wanted to be certain that sufficient interest existed before proceeding any further, and that he was perhaps uncertain if this initiative would be well-received by the War Department. Both of these issues indicate a concern with maintaining Culver's sterling reputation with the public in general and more specifically with the War Department.

It may also indicate the romantic pull of volunteerism on Gignilliat, knowing with relative certainty that the chances of the War Department accepting the services of a volunteer Rough-Rider like unit for service on the Mexican border were very unlikely, even one coming from CMA.

We thus see evidence of Gignilliat's "guardian" nature, desiring to protect the institution from embarrassment or shame, along with the pull of romanticism (i.e., the appeal of the past and tradition) on the otherwise thoroughly modern gentleman.

Replying on March 22, 1916 to one BHT alumnus who appeared to be interested in joining the regiment, Gignilliat wrote that he very much appreciated the response and promised to keep him "advised of any developments" regarding this endeavor.

There is no more record of this initiative, and it appears that it never advanced beyond the conceptual stage. It and other efforts like it were almost certainly discouraged by the War Department, which was in the process of trying to get away from such practices and would instead mobilize National Guard units to augment the Punitive Expedition that summer.

The Punitive Expedition required many soldiers, and the initial response of the Army was to announce that the summer training camps it had planned for 1916 would have to be canceled. This caused much consternation, as many were looking forward to them.[55] While the Army ultimately found ways to staff its summer training camps, the impact for Culver was advantageous, as almost 100 additional boys signed up for its 1916 summer camp, pushing enrollment from the intended 500 to just under 600 cadets.[56]

Such developments as these -- both the potential cavalry regiment and the summer training camp for boos -- provide evidence of Gignilliat's tendency to think big and his penchant for action in times of crisis. In the Army of the time, a "penchant for action" was a highly desirable trait, indicating the internal workings of Gignilliat's mind and the organizational "fit" of his natural proclivities for military service and serving effectively as an officer. The subsequent 1917 proposal for a "Culver Division" led by Culver-trained officers and NCOs the following year around the time of America's entry into WWI suggests that this idea retained traction on campus and was almost certainly encouraged (and perhaps even originated) by the Culver brothers.

Despite such excitement, Gignilliat was able to finish his manuscript. While completing a massive amount of work on his own, Gignilliat could not write the entire book by himself. Having expanded to a somewhat unwieldy length that included 18 chapters and 22 appendices, Gignilliat, by his own admission, had allowed the scope of the book to expand beyond his ability to complete it on his own.

Despite his initial reluctance to O'Shea's suggestion that he consider involving other writers, the scope of the project, coupled with the extremely ambitious timeline Gignilliat had established, combined to outstrip even Gignilliat's own prodigious productivity. While Gignilliat focused on completing the book's 18 chapters -- all of which he wrote and were devoted to the "essentially military school" -- he enlisted help in completing the 22 appendices, devoted to other types of institutions providing military training.

Authors of appendices in *Arms and the Boy*

To complete the appendices, Gignilliat turned to three members of his staff for help, two of whom had been with him for more than a decade, and one eager young college graduate.

Captain Howard F. Noble wrote Appendix I, which contained suggestions for starting drill in the schools where the instruction had not been previously given."[57] Noble fought in the Spanish-American War and was a long-term Culver veteran, having been at the Academy for 14 years. In 1916, Noble served as the Senior Tactical Officer, and he also taught English and Mechanical Drawing as part of the faculty.[58]

Captain Howard F. Noble.[62]

Captain William R. "Duke" Kennedy wrote Appendix VII, "Suggestions for Rifle Practice in High Schools." Kennedy had been at Culver for 11 years, and he served as an instructor for both tactics and mathematics.[59]

Lieutenant Ralph G. Sickles authored Appendix XXI, "Military Instruction Camps for Students." [60] A recent graduate of Indiana Wesleyan University,

Sickles was fairly new to Culver, having arrived in late-April 1915 as a substitute for Captain A. R. Elliot, who taught English.[61]

The other 15 appendices were largely excerpts from previously published material, containing minimal introductions written by someone at Culver.

With the aid of these three men, along with the excerpted material from other institutions providing military training, Gignilliat was able to keep his own focus on the "essentially military schools" and complete the manuscript by the third week in March 1916.

Another one of the appendices -- Appendix II The Wyoming Plan – presented Steever's plan, based almost completely on a report written by Steever himself.[64]

By coordinating the writing efforts of the three members of his staff and taking a week to devote all of his attention to the project, Gignilliat considered the manuscript complete on March 22, 1916, and he mailed it to Howland on March 23, 1916. Gignilliat confided to Howland that, "The preparation of the manuscript has been a bigger task than I had anticipated and has consumed much more time than I at first estimated."

Gignilliat's own work completing *Arms and the Boy*

During his process of preparing the final draft of the manuscript, Gignilliat had reviewed what he had written often, re-writing portions of it several times. Consisting of 18 chapters and a remarkable 22 appendices, the manuscript had more than tripled in size from the contribution he submitted for O'Shea's *Types of Schools for Boys*, and its scope had also increased quite substantially. While satisfied with the draft he forwarded to Howland, Gignilliat shared that the final version probably had "too much appendix." He also thought that the order of the work's 18 chapters might need to be reorganized, reflecting the conflict he felt between making his own most effective argument versus optimizing the book's overall content.[65]

Most importantly during this final push, it appears that Gignilliat found his muse while at Mudlavia. Along with forwarding the completed manuscript, he proposed the much more lyrical *Arms and the Boy* as the work's main title, which added a more literary tenor, elevated the tone of the work, and relegated the descriptive but uninspired working titles of *Military Training in the Schools and Colleges* and *Military Training for the American School Boy* to subtitles at best.

Culver lore holds that the title came from the opening line of Virgil's epic poem, the *Aeneid*. Gignilliat was an excellent Latin student (as his academic transcripts from VMI demonstrate) who must have read the

Aeneid in school, providing some support for this legend. While no one can be sure, it is perhaps more likely that the title of the magazine that functioned as the National Rifle Association's contemporary weekly newsletter, *Arms and the Man* – that he read attentively because it often made mention of Culver – provided him with the contemporary inspiration for the title.[66]

To the main title, Gignilliat appended the more explanatory *A Study of Military Instruction in the Schools and Colleges.*[67] The editors at Bobbs-Merrill reacted quite favorably to Gignilliat's suggestion and accepted the pithy and elegant *Arms and the Boy* as the work's main title on March 25, 1916.[68] The editors were not as successful in selecting the work's subtitles. Trying too hard to convey its substance at the expense of brevity, the editors settled on the unimaginative and protracted *Military Training in Schools and Colleges; Its Value in Peace and its Importance in War With Many Practical Suggestions for the Course of Training and with Brief Descriptions of the Most Successful Systems Now in Operation* to augment the book's main title. It is, however, Gignilliat's title – *Arms and the Boy* – that has become the work's distinguishing identity. *

Revealing what would become one of his major concerns regarding the work's published form, Gignilliat included, along with the completed manuscript, many photographs for Bobbs-Merrill to consider using to illustrate the volume. While he felt that he may have sent Bobbs-Merrill too many pictures, he informed Howland that the collection of photographs included in the package represented a mere one-fifth of the number of pictures he had available to illustrate the volume.[69]

Continuing on the theme of illustrating the work, Gignilliat also got a bit ahead of himself and began making suggestions for the volume's cover before the editors had even had a chance to review his manuscript.[70] While perhaps somewhat premature, Gignilliat began to demonstrate his instinctive gift for recognizing the aspects of the military that appealed to the public and for incorporating his ideas into effective designs.

Among his first ideas for the book's cover, he identified photographs of either a Culver trumpeter, a formation of Culver cadets, the Culver color guard, or of the iconic Sally Port on the work's cover.[71] Each of these ideas was quite striking, and, as the editors at Bobbs-Merrill would discover, Gignilliat was not shy about providing them with his ideas and voicing his opinions regarding editorial decisions related to the book.

---

* When the Culver Education Foundation reprinted it in 2003, the work carried the much-improved complete title of *Arms and the Boy: Timeless Thoughts on Quality Education.*

Preparedness Concerns Take Center Stage

Around the time Gignilliat completed his manuscript, the country's preparedness concerns became focused on the impact of Pancho Villa's raid, shifting the nation's attention from the European war to matters closer to home. It turned out, however, that capturing the perpetrators and bringing them to justice sounded easier than it turned out to be, and the expedition lasted eleven frustrating months before ending disappointingly.

Following close on the heels of the Pancho Villa raid came the Sussex crisis. While ostensibly committed to protecting passenger ships, the German policy of unrestricted warfare and the sinking of the *Lusitania* in 1915 brought a heightened level of concern in America regarding this policy.

On March 24, 1916, the Germans torpedoed the French cross-channel ferry *Sussex*, damaging it severely and killing close to 50 people and wounding at least four Americans. This attack prompted President Wilson to threaten to break off diplomatic ties with Germany if these types of attacks continued.

The resulting Sussex Pledge of May 4, 1916, prolonged America's neutrality for another eleven months, but the combination of the Pancho Villa raid in New Mexico and the torpedoing of the Sussex reanimated the Preparedness advocates and brought greater attention to Preparedness issues in the first part of 1916.

The Telegram Campaign and Senator Reed Smoot

For Culver, getting the Hay Bill confirmed became of paramount importance in spring 1916 to ensure that military schools would receive appropriate recognition for the contributions they made to national preparedness and that their graduates would be allowed to be commissioned and put their training to good use serving the nation. Accordingly, one of the most unusual episodes in Culver history occurred that demonstrated the breadth of support and the depth of commitment the institution enjoyed.

In an effort to generate support for the Hay Bill, Gignilliat orchestrated a telegram campaign in April 1916 aimed at getting Culver supporters to contact their congressional representatives in support of the bill. To Gignilliat's way of thinking, the nation's "essentially military schools" deserved recognition for their efforts to keep alive military interest among the youth of the country "during a long period when military interest was at low ebb," and it made little sense for these institutions to be excluded from having the opportunity to continue doing so during a period of heightened military interest.[72] As the mainstay of the effort, Culver sent out "hundreds of telegrams to alumni and patrons throughout the country urging them to bring to the attention of their congressmen and senators the injustice about to be done the graduates of the high grade essentially military schools in denying them the opportunity for commissions."[73]

Senator Reed Smoot circa 1916. [75]

Gignilliat's efforts paid off more handsomely than even he could have imagined.[74] Senator Reed Smoot of Utah received a telegram from the parent of a Culver cadet urging him to support the Hay Bill, and he became intrigued. Smoot, who had been impressed with Culver cadets he had encountered previously, looked into the matter and was so moved by what he found that he decided to engage in the legislative process on Culver's behalf.

Smoot gained an audience with the Senate Military Affairs Committee, which was then debating the Hay Bill, and, on April 7, 1916, offered an amendment calling for the "creation of senior R.O.T.C. units in essentially military schools where the institution had been named as an 'Honor School' for the three preceding years and where there were more than 100 cadets over sixteen years of age."[76] In a performance that would have made Gignilliat proud, Smoot remarked that, "My amendment...is to provide for another class of civil education institutions," mentioning Culver by name in the very next sentence.[77]

Wanting to ensure that all good military preparatory schools, and especially Culver, received special acknowledgment of the value they added to national defense and recognition that their military training was as good as any in the country, Smoot offered that "there is no college in this country in which the military training equals that of Culver, either in scope or in thoroughness."[78]

The Hay Bill's sponsor in the Senate, Senator Chamberlain, responded that it was the committee's intention to include Culver in any such recognition, "because all of the members of the committee are familiar with the institution and know its worth as a military institution," and he agreed to amend the bill to ensure Culver was included.[79]

The Smoot amendment that was accepted called for graduates of "essentially military schools" like Culver who were under 21 years of age "to receive certificates exchangeable for commissions as Second

Lieutenants in the Reserve Corps upon reaching the age of twenty-one."[80]
While Gignilliat may not have been able to meet with members of the
Senate Military Affairs Committee in January 1916, his work on the
telegram campaign engaged the influential Senator Smoot in a manner
that may have been even more effective than his own personal appeal.

Preparedness Never Sleeps – And Neither Does Gignilliat!

Concurrently with the telegram campaign, Gignilliat gave an address at
the University of Michigan regarding preparedness and military training
on April 4, 1916. As important as the content of the address was that it
was sponsored by the National Security League, which was then one of
the most prominent Preparedness organizations in the country. As part
of a lecture series that included many national luminaries, it is clear that
Gignilliat had become recognized as one of the nation's authorities on the
military training of boys.[81]

While Gignilliat completed work on his manuscript, the Hay Bill
received House confirmation with relative ease on the same day as
Gignilliat sent his completed manuscript to Bobbs-Merrill. Moving to
the Senate, however, the bill languished for many reasons. Among the
more important reasons for the deadlock included disagreements over
the size of the regular army, the composition of the federal volunteer
reserve force, and a provision for the construction of nitrate plants.[82] After
several additional weeks of political wrangling that produced minor but
acceptable changes, the Senate voted to approve the Chamberlain Bill on
May 17, 1916, and the House voted to accept the Hay Bill on May 20, 1916.

President Wilson demonstrated his commitment to getting the bill passed
by "exerting vigorous leadership" using deft political maneuvering to
allow for the achievement of consensus through compromise regarding
the issues of the size of the regular army and the composition of the
federal volunteer reserve force, which would be the National Guard.
Wilson's efforts succeeded in breaking the deadlock on May 13, 1916,
and the Hay/Chamberlain Bill was signed into law by President Wilson
on June 3, 1916 as the National Defense Act of 1916.[83] The final result
was the product of much input from many people in meetings and
conferences, along with many refined ideas and significant compromises,
but the essence of Ohio Plan became the basis for the establishment of the
Reserve Officers Training Corps (ROTC) in America.

The remarkable success of his telegram campaign of April 1916
undoubtedly combined with his work on *Arms and the Boy* and
preparedness, especially in terms of identifying sources of supply for
reserve officers, to raise Gignilliat's profile across America, along with

that of Culver. In addition, the support he received from Smoot opened his eyes to the advantages of having high-level government patrons. It is likely that this episode inspired Gignilliat to seek the support of the newly appointed Secretary of War, Newton D. Baker, to provide the introduction to *Arms and the Boy*.

Editing and Revising *Arms and the Boy*

Returning to his work on the book, Gignilliat began referring to it as *Arms and the Boy* and devoting his efforts to promoting the completed manuscript and the issue of preparedness in America. Wanting to ensure that the resulting book was accurate and correct, Gignilliat reached out to two influential preparedness advocates to review the galleys. Because of his work with the Wyoming Plan and their work together training high school students, Steever was an obvious choice for one of the reviewers.

While demonstrably a training genius, Steever was neither a scholar nor an academic, so it was unclear if Steever would be an equally effective reviewer of a manuscript. Turning to someone who was both a scholar and an academic, Gignilliat asked the well-regarded president of The Ohio State University, Dr. William O. Thompson, to serve as another reviewer. Thompson was a great supporter of military training in schools, and he, along with his OSU colleague, Edward J. Orton, Jr., had been heavily involved in the Preparedness Movement since 1913. Both Thompson and Orton were also instrumental in creating the Ohio Plan and crafting the ROTC portion of the National Defense Act of 1916, so asking Thompson to serve as one of the reviewers for *Arms and the Boy* was equally prudent and shrewd. Both Steever and Thompson agreed to review the galleys for Gignilliat, with Steever focusing more on content and Thompson agreeing to pay attention to the work's larger argument.[84]

Revealing his inexperience with the publishing process, Gignilliat requested 12 copies of galleys to be sent out for review (which is quite a few!).[85] In addition, and with Steever was focusing on ensuring the accuracy of the content, Gignilliat requested that the galleys sent to Steever include the work's 22 appendices (which is also quite unusual), since so much important information appeared in them.[86] Gignilliat also provided additional material for the already extensive appendices, expecting this material to be incorporated in both the galleys and final printed copy of the book.[87] All three of these actions of an author unfamiliar with the publishing and printing process surely caused concern with the editors at Bobbs-Merrill.

Bobbs-Merrill sent Gignilliat his own set of galley proofs on April 7, 1916.[88] Seeing his creation in print must have been quite gratifying for Gignilliat, but it also brought more clarity to the ideas he hoped to convey in the manuscript. As a result, Gignilliat spent the next four days reviewing the galleys and making corrections. More importantly, he rearranged some of the chapters and moved the chapters dealing with military schools to the beginning of the work.[89]

It was during this four-day period, more than any other time over the preceding several years, that Gignilliat was able to arrange the material in a manner that made the most sense for the content, but these revisions came at the expense of crafting the argument he wanted desperately to present regarding the exceptional ability of the "essentially military school" in general and of Culver in particular to apply a military approach to education most effectively for both the student/cadet and the nation.

Once solidified in his own mind, Gignilliat edited and rearranged the galleys of *Arms and the Boy* accordingly to convey the material in the most logical arrangement for the overall content of the book and in the most persuasive manner of which he was capable. These efforts further diluted the persuasiveness of his own thoughts regarding the value of military training in schools.

The revised order of the chapters did, however, improve the manuscript's overall argument significantly, placing Gignilliat's best writing at the beginning of the book and providing a coherence to his argument that had been lacking in his original draft with respect to the overall content of the book. After acknowledging the major pros and cons of military training and making his own major point that military training, *properly given*, was of significant value, and acquainting the reader with the government's system of classification of military schools (which was likely more important to Gignilliat than to the reader), Gignilliat's reorganization resulted in having the work's next seven chapters address the "essentially military school."

Drawing examples from many "essentially military schools" across the country, this arrangement nevertheless provided a 70-page section that amounted to a powerful endorsement for Culver and its unique military system. After making the case for the superiority of the "essentially military school" in providing *proper* military training for young men, Gignilliat devoted the book's remaining nine chapters to making the case for the value of including military training in public high schools and land-grant colleges. Capping off his argument, Gignilliat devoted the work's final chapter to an assessment of the ability of land grant colleges and military schools' ability to produce effective reserve officers, concluding, somewhat predictably, that military schools were better suited to do so. The order of the book's following 22 appendices remained intact.

Returning the galleys to the editors at Bobbs-Merrill on April 12, 1916, Gignilliat offered that he was more satisfied with the revised arrangement of the work. Believing that it would "be more interesting to the average reader and will probably serve to carry him into the more general discussion that follows," Gignilliat closed by writing that he was quite sure "that the present arrangement will prove much more effective" in conveying the substance of his argument to the general public.[90]

Despite returning the galleys so quickly, Gignilliat continued providing additional corrections and suggestions to the editors. In addition, the editors at Bobbs-Merrill responded on April 15, 1916 that Gignilliat's request for 12 galley proofs was too great. Instead of producing such a large number of galley proofs, the editors at Boobs-Merrill offered to provide Gignilliat with 12 copies of advance sheets.[91] Advance sheets are rough copies of a new book that lack the formatting and binding of the finished product, and they typically contain all text included in the work, meaning that they would almost certainly have included the text of the manuscript's 22 appendices.

In addition, the text of advance sheets may also differ slightly from the published version of the book, as changes could be made rather easily to advance sheets as reviewers found errors and/or suggested revisions. Easier to produce than galley proofs, advance sheets were a much more economical method of providing Gignilliat with the number of copies he desired, and they also likely allowed for the review of the important contents contained in the almost two dozen appendices. Accordingly, Gignilliat accepted the offer of advance sheets for his reviewers.[92]

For the remainder of April, Gignilliat devoted tremendous attention to proofreading the galleys, approving photographs for the work, and providing the editors at Bobbs-Merrill with a steady stream of corrections, revisions, and suggestions.[93] Gignilliat was doing all of this while also continuing his preparedness activities – speaking at the University of Michigan on April 4, 1916 regarding the purpose of military training in schools as part of National Security League event and leading the delegation of the Navy League of the US at the National Defense Convention in Washington, DC during the period 10-13 April, 1916 – in impressive fashion. Both the National Security League and the Navy League of the US were important preparedness organizations, and the National Defense Convention was perhaps the premier preparedness activity that occurred in 1916. That Gignilliat was featured so prominently by these organizations and at their events indicates that he had achieved a national reputation as an important preparedness proponent.

On campus, Gignilliat hosted a larger group of high school principals from Chicago during the last week of April 1916 to discuss the conduct of Culver's high school military training camps and the value of military training in schools. He was also preparing for and undergoing the annual Army inspection during April-May 1916. While confident in Culver's ability to earn recognition as an "Honor School" for an unprecedented eleventh consecutive time, Gignilliat was nevertheless determined to do all that was necessary to achieve this distinction that was both an important point of pride for the administration and a valuable selling point for the school. As expected, Culver excelled yet again in the Army's Annual Inspection on May 1, 1916.

In the midst of all this, Gignilliat had completed the majority of his proofreading, approved the title page for the book, and signed a contract with Bobbs-Merrill to have it published by May 5, 1916. Recognizing that even he had limits to his own productive capacity, Gignilliat also accepted (somewhat reluctantly) an offer of assistance to index the volume.[94]

Secretary of War Baker Writes the Introduction

Wanting the book to be even more authoritative, Gignilliat hoped to persuade the newly appointed Secretary of War, Newton D. Baker, to write an introduction for the book.[95] As befitting Gignilliat's burgeoning audacity in matters related to *Arms and the Boy* and preparedness, he sent his aide, Captain William A. "Willie" Fleet, to Washington, DC (as he had done for the 1913 presidential inaugural) to obtain Baker's consent to provide a foreword for the book.

Secretary of War Newton D. Baker.[98]

Fleet was in Washington, DC during the week of May 7-13, 1916 attending to Culver business, and he brought a set of galleys with him to share with Baker. Acting on Gignilliat's specific instructions, Fleet hoped to get Baker to read chapters one and nine of the manuscript, dealing with "Some of the Pros and Cons of Military Training" and the "Ideals of the Military School." These are two of the best chapters in the book, addressing issues of significant importance to the preparedness debate as it related to the role of military schools. Baker, however, read *eight* chapters of his own choosing on the evening of May 9, 1916, including both chapters one and nine, and, after remarking to Fleet that it was "a mighty interesting book," agreed to write an introduction for the work.[96]

Baker appears to have been as enthralled with the book as Gignilliat had hoped he would be, and Baker asked to hold on to the galleys so he could finish reading the remainder of the work.[97] Baker's reaction might also have been the result of his relative unfamiliarity with the role of military schools with respect to preparedness. If so, his reaction also provided Gignilliat with a powerful affirmation of the value of his efforts and confirmation of the need for *Arms and the Boy* to be published as soon as possible, even if waiting for Baker delay the book's release.

Back to Preparedness and Camp Newton D. Baker

After devoting so much attention to the galleys, and likely buoyed by Baker's very positive reaction to *Arms and the Boy*, Gignilliat re-engaged with the preparedness activities that interested both him and the Culver brothers by conducting the second of Culver's military camps for high school students. Likely in recognition of agreeing to write the introduction for *Arms and the Boy*, Gignilliat named it the Camp Newton D. Baker Schoolboy Military Camp. The 1916 camp was twice as large as the 1915 camp, with 489 boys coming from nine states and 80 cities.

While the Culver brothers continued to provide substantial support for the camp, the larger size increased the cost of the endeavor significantly and beyond the Culver brothers' resources. Participants were required to pay $17.75 to help cover expenses (equating to a little over $400.00 in 2023 dollars), which was considered to be quite affordable and only $0.25 more than the boys who participated in the 1915 student military training camp at Lincoln Fields in Ludington, Michigan had to pay.[99]

The camp ran during the period May 15-29, using many of the techniques developed by Steever and supported by Gignilliat. Gignilliat incorporated many facets of the Wyoming Plan into the camp, especially the competitive aspects and the wall-scaling activities. This made the work more enjoyable for the boys and allowed Gignilliat to put some of Steever's ideas into practice. The results were excellent, and the increased size and scope of this camp brought positive attention to Culver.

The Hay Bill Becomes Law as the National Defense Act of 1916

The success of the 1916 camp coincided with the achievement of substantive comprise within Congress regarding the Hay Bill in May 1916. While the House compromised to accept a number of regiments for the Regular Army that was close to what was provided in the Senate's version of the bill was important, the compromises made in the Senate were both more substantial and effectual. In exchange for getting approval for a government-owned nitrate plant in place of the previously recommended privately owned plant, the members of the Senate Military Affairs

Committee agreed on May 13, 1916 to drop their support for Garrison's proposed Continental Army intended to function as the federal military reserve.[100]

By embracing the National Guard as the nation's primary ground military reserve force, the Senate gained the support of the powerful National Guard Association and the governors of the country's 48 states. Armed with such support, the passing of the Hay Bill into law as the National Defense Act of 1916 was all but assured.

The signing of the Hay Bill into law on June 3, 1916 as the National Defense Act of 1916 immediately evoked cries of outrage from the stronger preparedness advocates in the country. For example, Theodore Roosevelt termed the act "as foolish and unpatriotic a bit of flintlock legislation as was ever put on the statute books." Henry Cabot Lodge added his own commentary, offering that "Mr. Hay by his policy did more injury to this country at a great crisis than any one man I have ever known of in either branch of Congress."

Despite the objections from the country's staunchest preparedness advocates, the act did add considerable strength to the Regular Army, and it paved the way for a more rapid and efficient mobilization in 1917 and 1918 when the country marshaled for war. In addition, the provisions contained for the National Guard enabled this large body of soldiers to be incorporated as a federalized force into the nation's wartime plan and for the conduct of operations in Europe. Contrary to the dire predictions by many who opposed this approach, the National Guard soldiers and units fought well under the leadership of trained officers in WWI.[101]

This bill was not only advantageous to Culver but also quite desirable, as it assured that the graduates of Culver and the nation's other "essentially military schools" would receive special consideration for commissions as reserve officers. Gignilliat was undoubtedly pleased with this outcome, and he, along with the Culver brothers, viewed this portion of the bill as vindication for both the Culver military system of training young men and the results it was able to produce. Given that the bill was signed into law during Culver's first alumni military camp, one can only imagine the excitement and enthusiasm that surely permeated the campus.

Camp Leonard Wood for Culver Alumni

On the same day that Camp Baker ended (May 29, 1916), Gignilliat initiated a military camp for Culver alumni intended to help them "brush up" on any aspects of their military proficiency that may have waned since they had graduated from Culver. Named Camp Leonard Wood, this endeavor provided training for 75 men, May 29 – June 5, 1916.

Directed by Captain Howard F. Noble and Captain Charles A. Rockwood, the program of instruction covered the changes that had occurred in the drill regulations the cadets had mastered while at Culver, along with signaling, fire control, map drawing, and target designation. Delivered via periods of drill and lecture, along with demonstrations and some theoretical tactical problem-solving work, the

Culver alumni from the 1916 Camp Leonard Wood Alumni Training Camp.[102]

participants engaged with field work, tactical problems, an overnight hike, and target practice.

Augmenting the excellent training they had received as Culver cadets, and allowing for much social engagement that was both welcome and beneficial, the participants of this camp worked hard and enhanced their

Culver alumni enjoying some fellowship while off duty.[103]

military proficiency further through a program that was exacting but not exhausting.[104] As a result, they were particularly effective on the battlefields of Europe. In fact, 42 of the participants went on to serve in the Army, Navy, and Marines during World War I, with 29 serving as officers, 18 of whom served in Europe. Of particular note, two of these were decorated for gallantry in combat.[105]

Completing the Editing and Revisions

Howland confirmed his editorial desire to have the book released in summer 1916 but offered that he could not move forward until he received Baker's introduction. Howland also informed Gignilliat that his changes were further slowing the process down, causing Bobbs-Merrill to make corrections to the galleys and also create entirely new plates for the photographs to make the necessary corrections.[107] Apparently Gignilliat understood Howland's point, and he sent only one more set of corrections on May 25, 1916.[108] Howland sent the corrected galley proofs and completed index to Gignilliat on May 29, 1916.[109] Gignilliat was satisfied with the format and content of the pre-publication version of the book, and he accepted both the galley corrections and the volume's completed index the next day.[110]

Early Marketing Efforts for *Arms and the Boy*

Gignilliat wasted little time savoring the completion of the laborious and tedious pre-publication tasks, and he immediately engaged Howland on the topic of producing special leather-bound presentation copies of the published book.[111] Howland agreed to provide the requested volumes at no additional cost to Gignilliat and began working with the New York office of Bobbs-Merrill to have these volumes produced.[112]

Having witnessed glimpses of his genius for marketing, Bobbs-Merrill also asked Gignilliat to help publicize the book. They settled on the idea of producing a promotional circular for the book, creating proofs of it that they sent to Gignilliat, asking that he return them as soon as possible so they could be distributed prior to the end of the school year. Believing that Gignilliat's request would be reasonable, Bobbs-Merrill offered to provide Gignilliat with as many copies of the circular as he desired at no cost.[113] Even though he was consumed with the responsibilities associated with commencement, Gignilliat found time to review the proofs and approved the circular on June 5, 1916.[114]

The Close of the 1915-1916 Winter School Session

The closing of the 1915-1916 school year represented, in many respects, a high point for Culver and Gignilliat. The faculty, which numbered nine in 1896, had expanded to a remarkable 98 in the ensuring 20 years. With a beginning enrollment of 465 cadets organized into six companies, the 1915-1916 winter school commencement graduated 119 cadets on June 8, 1916. Graduation week witnessed both the adoption of the Culver Legion as the new name of the alumni association on June 5, 1916, and the cornerstone for the new riding hall (construction had begun in mid-March 1916) being laid by Colonel William J. Nicholson, US Army, in an impressive ceremony on June 7, 1916.

Laying the cornerstone of the new riding hall, June 7, 1916.[115]

Gignilliat, Minnie, and sons circa 1916.[119]

Gignilliat's sons also had successful years. Leigh Jr did very well as a second classman, assigned to Company D and serving as one of the corps' prestigious Color Sergeants for the year. He also participated in the artillery and served as a sergeant in the 1916 high school military training camp. Athletically, Leigh Jr. played on the 1915 championship Company D football squad and the Company D track squad in spring 1916. For the first time, he also played on the varsity basketball team, allowing him to put his height to good use for Culver. Leigh Jr. continued his involvement with YMCA and the Spanish club throughout the year as well.[116]

Freddy began his Culver career assigned to the relatively new Company F, and he also participated in Culver's newly created program for military engineering. Focusing his efforts on athletic endeavors during his plebe year, Freddy played on the company football, basketball, hockey, bowling, baseball, and tennis teams, and he won both the company individual and doubles tennis titles in spring 1916.[117] He would continue to excel as an athlete throughout his entire Culver career.

To Press, To Press! The Final Push to Get *Arms and the Boy* Printed and Released

As with the winter school, the summer session continued to grow at Culver. 1916 was particularly remarkable in this area, welcoming a record 910 cadets into the three programs. This was an astonishing increase from the 1902 humble beginning and almost doubling the number of boys enrolled in Culver's summer programs the previous year (1915).[118]

Neither Leigh Jr. nor Freddy attended Culver's Summer School in 1916 (as they had both done in 1915), indicating that perhaps the Gignilliat family made time for a family vacation in June 1916. It would make sense for Minnie to insist on a period of respite for Gignilliat after his whirlwind of activity during the first six months of 1916, both for his own wellbeing and to allow for the family to spend some time together.

While relaxing somewhat, Gignilliat also spent the month of June 1916 awaiting anxiously the release of *Arms and the Boy*.

By July 1916, however, Gignilliat's patience with the delays in publishing his own work was wearing thin, and he began pressing Bobbs-Merrill with additional requests. He asked for the advance sheets of the book to be sent out to the ten individuals he has identified as soon as possible, and he requested the production of a special leather-bound edition to be used as a gift for 20 selected individuals he had identified.[120] Offering further marketing advice, Gignilliat suggested that Bobbs-Merrill consider marketing *Arms and the Boy* as a text book for normal schools (schools created to train high school graduates to be teachers and known as teachers' colleges after World War II).[121]

All of these requests made sense to Gignilliat, as he was convinced that his book would sell very well if it was marketed properly. Based upon this series of interactions, one can surmise that Gignilliat had high confidence in the ability of his own marketing plan to generate sales that were more than sufficient to cover the large expenses required to fund his plan.

Up to this point, the editors at Bobbs-Merrill agreed to every one of Gignilliat's requests and suggestions. However, it becomes clear at this point that they did not share Gignilliat's optimism and that their own expectations for sales of *Arms and the Boy*, based upon their extensive experience as a bookseller, were far more modest. They had reached their limit of the support they were willing to provide to promote a book from a first-time author like Gignilliat until they had reliable sales figures on which to base further decisions.

By late July 1916, everyone was anxious for the book to be published. Howland explained to Gignilliat that printing the manuscript, with its many illustrations, was "quite a task" that would take some time to be completed properly.[122] A paper shortage in early August 1916 further slowed the book's production (and likely exasperated Gignilliat).[123] Expressing his impatience with the publication delays, Gignilliat asked the publisher if he might have at least a few copies of *Arms and the Boy* to offer for sale at Culver to the over 900 cadets and their parents before the summer session closed on August 24, 1916.[124]

In the meantime, Bobbs-Merrill completed the advance sheets and sent them on August 1, 1916 to the ten individuals identified by Gignilliat.[125] Later that same week, Gignilliat approved the final draft of the new version of the circular and let the publisher know that he had not yet received his own copies of the advance sheets.[126] All indications were that the book would be released shortly, and Gignilliat was quite anxious to see the fruits of his labor in its final form.

A Genius for Marketing: Gignilliat Promotes *Arms and the Boy*

At long last, on August 10, 1916, *Arms and the Boy* was released, and it was shipped to stores across the country on that same day. On the very next day, and likely in response to Gignilliat's impatience with the publication delays, Bobbs-Merrill sent copies of the special leather-bound presentation edition to the 20 influential people Gignilliat had identified in late-July 1916.[127] Bobbs-Merrill also sent 25 copies of the book to the Culver bookstore so that they could be offered for sale well prior to the conclusion of Culver's summer school.[128]

Gignilliat was in Chicago on Saturday, August 11, 1916, and he was delighted to find copies of the book for sale in stores there. Bound in a red buckram linen cover with gilded printing of the title and author's name on the front and spine and deckled pages, the published version of the book was attractive but a bit unorthodox in appearance for a military subject. Gignilliat was quite satisfied with all aspects of the volume's appearance.

The choice of deckled pages is surprising, as trimmed edges would have presented a more orderly and "military" look to the work. To the publisher, however, deckled edges are intended to mimic paper that is handmade and are usually reserved for their most premium releases that are considered to be something special. Given the cost of the 80 illustrations Gignilliat insisted on including, this may have also been a way for Bobbs-Merrill to reduce the overall cost of production.

The first printing had an attractive dust jacket designed by Gignilliat (that transposed his first and middle initials, identifying him as "R. L. Gignilliat"). The color photograph features a very military looking bugler standing erect in the distinctive cadet gray blouse and trousers, outlined in black, and wearing calf-high boots sounding a military call in the foreground, with two all-American cadets dressed similarly to the bugler and wearing white gloves, field belts and suspenders, and carrying rifles, looking relaxed and clearly enjoying themselves in the center. These two cadets are framed by Culver's iconic Sally Port abutted by crenelated turrets from which they are emerging (likely on their way to military drill), followed by several other similarly accoutered cadets in the background. All figures are bathed in bright sunlight and cast long shadows, indicating that the sun is low on the horizon and suggesting early morning activity. It is an image curated quite deliberately by Gignilliat himself to convey a very specific and explicit message to the reader of purpose and enjoyment within an environment of discipline and structure.

On the back of the dust jacket (which gets his initials correct), Gignilliat included an excerpt from the introduction provided by Secretary of War Baker. The passage states,

> *"Quite apart from any comment of my own upon this book, its merits will speak for themselves, and to those who want to know what the ideals are of a proper military training for boys, I am free to say that I know of no one to whom they could turn with greater confidence that the author of this book, no one who experience is larger, whose own ideals for peace are higher, or whose success in applying military education would entitle him to speak with more authority."*

Baker provides powerful affirmation of Gignilliat's ideas and confirmation of his expertise, characterizing him as valuing peace while touting the benefits of military training for boys.

Baker's quotation concludes as follows:

> *"This book is clear and frank and helpful. It is, moreover, especially timely just now when we are all measuring the possible content of the universal obligation of citizenship and considering what real preparedness may mean for America."*

Baker makes the point that the book is timely and that it relates to the obligations of citizenship and military preparedness in America. Taken in its entirety, it is little wonder that Gignilliat elected to have this excerpt showcased on the back of the dust jacket where it would be most accessible to the potential reader.

Encased in a plain, simple, red hardcover, which, combined with the striking photo on the dust jacket and the powerful endorsement from Baker, presented an aesthetic that was at once both appealing and elegant. Gignilliat reported that he was "very much pleased" with the "fine looking volume" that he believed to be both "attractive looking and elaborate." [131]

Gignilliat was overjoyed at seeing the published version of his work, and after waiting a bit longer (and somewhat impatiently!), he received his own copy by August 18, 1916. [132]

Having already sold all 25 copies sent to the Culver bookstore, Gignilliat ordered more to sell during the final week of Culver's summer school. [133] Howland responded by sending Gignilliat the first copy of the special leather-bound presentation edition of *Arms and the Boy*.[134] Gignilliat was quite pleased with the appearance of this more exclusive version as well, and with his acknowledgment of receipt of the volume he sent Howland a copy of a very favorable review of the book that appeared in the August 19, 1916 edition of the *Pittsburgh Press* newspaper.[135] From Gignilliat's perspective, these events provided him with indicators that the book was being received quite well and selling exactly as he had hoped it would.

Within one week of receiving his copy of the printed book, Gignilliat began making corrections. His corrections related to two very minor errors, but they indicate that Gignilliat continued to pay very close attention to the book and its content.[136] Gignilliat remained committed to getting copies of the book into the hands of the most prominent men in the land.[137] Gignilliat also encouraged Bobbs-Merrill to market *Arms and the Boy* more aggressively in New York, as the state had recently introduced military training into the public schools for the year.[138] Bobbs-Merrill responded on August 31, 1916 by sending copies of the *Arms and the Boy* circular to many high schools in New York.

Building Interest and Sales for *Arms and the Boy*

By early October 1916, and in response to a newspaper article stating that the University of Chicago "had just adopted military training," Gignilliat wrote to Bobbs-Merrill asking for a copy of the book to be sent to the school's president, Dr. Harry Pratt Judson, as a way of sharing with him "the only book in print dealing with the philosophy of military training in the schools and colleges."[139] A review of the contemporary literature by the author appears to validate this claim.[140]

Gignilliat was laid up for a week to ten days during the first half of October 1916 as a result of some surgery on his jaw that he had to endure. For a diligent worker like Gignilliat, being out of the office for such an extended period of time must have been difficult. By October 17, 1916, he was able to re-engage with his duties.

Gignilliat wrote to Bobbs-Merrill apologizing for being indisposed and then jumped right back into matters related to *Arms and the Boy*. Having been unavailable to review the proof of a poster Bobbs-Merrill created for the book, Gignilliat expressed remorse at not having pictures of larger universities, but he acknowledged that nothing could be done about it. He also noted that his first two initials had been reversed on the poster, as they had been on the book's dust jacket, and asked that this be corrected if more posters were printed.[141] Bobbs-Merrill acknowledged Gignilliat's request and promised to make the change if/when additional copies of the poster were printed.[142]

The *New York Times* Review of *Arms and the Boy*

During the latter portion of October 1916, Gignilliat became increasingly aware of the growing publicity related to *Arms and the Boy*, and he reported to an editor at Bobbs-Merrill that the publicity, especially the reviews in the eastern newspapers, had gotten a "novice" like him "a little puffed up" over all the attention.[143] In perhaps the most remarkable aspect of this publicity, *Arms and the Boy* was reviewed quite favorably in the *New York Times* on October 8, 1916 while Gignilliat was convalescing from his jaw surgery.

Titling the review, "Colonel Gignilliat discusses the value of military training in schools and colleges," the unnamed reviewer began by writing, "Military training in schools is a matter that may be better judged by effects that it has produced rather than by effects which it might produce." After noting that the Secretary of War Newton D. Baker was "fully alive to the many objections that are being urged against military training in schools" and yet still wrote favorably about the positive aspects of the obedience associated with military training in the book's introduction, the reviewer offered the following succinctly positive assessment of Gignilliat's work:

> *The precise value of Colonel Gignilliat's book is that he demolishes this objection to military training as a destroyer of initiative. He gathers facts and cases to show that, on the contrary, it is conducive of initiative and to the fullest development of individuality.*

According to this review, "Colonel Gignilliat devotes the greater part of his book to the personnel and working of the strictly military schools." While emphasizing the importance of having the instruction given properly by the highest quality of instructors, the reviewer offers that Gignilliat did not seek to compel "the so-called blind and unreasoning obedience" so often associated with the military, aiming instead to make use of thoughtful obedience to bring out the "initiative, individuality, and responsibility" which are indicative of "the true spirit of military training" and are therefore the desired outcome of the habit of learned obedience.

Regarding military training in high schools, the reviewer noted that Gignilliat believed it could be done with great effectiveness and that when done properly, it produced in young men the qualities of "truthfulness, purity, honesty, temperance, and a sense of the value of fair play – all qualities that go to make up a sturdy and righteous manhood." Calling attention to "what ha[d] hitherto been a matter of more or less academic interest with the romance of reality," the reviewer offered that *Arms and the Boy* "will be of value not only to teachers and instructors, but to parents and guardians" and others who were interested in citizenship and involved in developing the manhood of American male youths. Concluding that the volume was "copiously illustrated with excellent photographs," and that it was "an important addition to the literature of citizenship," Gignilliat could scarcely have written a more favorable review himself.[144]

It is no wonder that he felt "puffed up" after reading such an upbeat assessment of the work to which he had devoted so much energy and effort. This review seemed to affirm everything Gignilliat had hoped for when he began writing the text back in 1913, along with his decision to strike out on his own and have his work published as a separate volume apart from O'Shea's *Types of Schools for Boys*, which still had yet to be released. It was the policy of the *New York Times* at that time to treat books strictly as a form of news, meaning that the nation's most prominent newspaper reviewed Gignilliat's book because it deemed it to be newsworthy, providing a tremendous source of external validation for his work.[145] In fact, it would have been difficult for Gignilliat to anticipate any type of response from Bobbs-Merrill other than its unconditional support to market the book as aggressively as possible to take advantage of this unmatched source of publicity.

Balancing the Marketing Resources with Sales Revenue

The disagreement of marketing resources from the summer of 1916 continued to fester and became even more acute in the fall of 1916.

Gignilliat underwent jaw surgery in October 1916, which required "some rather sever treatment" and required almost an entire month of recovery before he was able to operate at peak efficiency.[146] Upon his surgical recovery, and buoyed by the very favorable *New York Times* review of *Arms and the Boy*, Gignilliat wrote to Chambers at Bobbs-Merrill providing copy for the revised circular he expected to be printed soon. He also urged Bobbs-Merrill to direct renewed marketing efforts for the book "with the school and college people" to take advantage of the fact that the War Department had "just issued its [own] circulars covering the courses for the Reserve Officers' Training Corps," which would almost certainly create an increased level of demand for the book if properly exploited.[147]

While Gignilliat continued to view all of his marketing ideas as not only sensible but desirable, the editors at Bobbs-Merrill, who were paying for these initiatives, did not share his optimism. When analyzing the sales performance of *Arms and the Boy*, the editors saw a book that was selling well but which did not yet warrant the additional marketing efforts desired by Gignilliat.[148]

The pushback began at the end of October 1916, when a staffer at Bobbs-Merrill wrote to Chambers to recommend against reprinting the corrected circulars and sending them out again so soon to the list of recipients Gignilliat suggested.[149] Acting on this recommendation, Chambers wrote to Gignilliat on November 9, 1916 informing him that Bobbs-Merrill was going to wait until January 1917 to send out the revised versions of the circular.

Chambers justified his decision by sharing with Gignilliat that the *"results obtained from the circulation already made have not been satisfactory"* (emphasis added) and that he could not justify sinking more resources into the marketing efforts for *Arms and the Boy* because he was afraid that "if we travel the same road again so soon, we shall not accomplish very much." In an attempt to soften the blow of this decision while also providing some context, Chambers informed Gignilliat that Bobbs-Merrill had already *"spent for promotion all that the sale of the book will warrant and then some* (emphasis added)." Based upon this assessment, Chambers offered that it would "seem wise to hold off until the sales catch up a little on the expense." [150]

In making this decision, Chambers, on behalf of Bobbs-Merrill, balked at providing any further marketing and publicizing resources for *Arms and the Boy* unless and until sales of the book caught up with the expense they have already incurred, which had already been greater than what they would normally provide for any of their other books. Given the level of support that Bobbs-Merrill had provided throughout the entire process up to this point, this appears to be a purely business decision based upon the actual sales performance of the book and had nothing at all to do with any real or imagined displeasure with Gignilliat as the author. This decision also provides the first indication that while *Arms and the Boy* may have been receiving much publicity around the country, this publicity did not translate into the type of sales it would seemed to have indicated. Combined, this information must have come as a terrible shock to Gignilliat, especially in the wake of the *New York Times* review.

Gignilliat was indeed shocked by this decision, and he wrote to Chambers the very next day on November 10, 1916 to let him know of his disappointment. From Gignilliat's perspective, the decision to wait until January 1917 to send out another version of the circular was ill-advised because Gignilliat believed that "the new circular [was] particularly timely just now [when] so many schools [were] undertaking the introduction of military training."

Given the opportune timing, Gignilliat was certain that the circular would be both helpful to and welcomed "by many school heads who are face to face [sic] with the new problem of introducing military training" into their schools. Pleading his case further, and seeking to take advantage of the positive publicity *Arms and the Boy* had received, Gignilliat argued that the revised version would "be more effective than the original circular since it contains extracts from the reviews of the book in addition to the statement of the publishers," all of which he believed would spur additional sales of the book.

Revealing that he was not only disappointed but also personally hurt by this decision, Gignilliat closed by writing to Chambers that he was "sorry that the sale to date has been disappointing to you." His tone and phrasing imply that he was also hurt that Bobbs-Merrill declined to provide the additional support he desired and thought necessary to improve the book's sales.[151]

Before sending this letter to Chambers, Gignilliat added a hand-written post script that is both illuminating and worth presenting in its entirety:

> *It is perhaps natural for me to feel confidence in my own book, but I firmly believe if you are willing to risk the outlay for a strong, vigorous attractive advertising campaign for this book that the sales will well repay you. The book <u>will not</u> sell however if dealers place it with technical war books. It must be popularized.*[152]

As this post script makes clear, Gignilliat was quite unhappy that Bobbs-Merrill refused to provide additional funding for marketing, and he also believed that the book dealers bore some of the responsibility for the book's disappointing sales by displaying the book improperly. Recalling the positive publicity the book had received, along with the positive feedback Gignilliat continued to receive from others regarding the work, one can understand his reaction and response.

Seeking to plead his case further, Gignilliat also wrote to Howland on November 10, 1916. In this letter, Gignilliat urged Howland to ensure that *Arms and the Boy* was marketed to the parents of boys, since restricting the market to "school men" would likely not produce very large sales.[153]

One can see by the post-script in his letter to Chambers and in the body of his letter to Howland, both written on November 10, 1916, that Gignilliat believed that the disappointing sales of *Arms and the Boy* were due largely to the mistakes made by Bobbs-Merrill in their marketing efforts and by the book sellers' placement of the book in their stores. Again, recalling the positive publicity and feedback he had received up to that point, one can understand how Gignilliat arrived at this conclusion. It is, however, somewhat telling that both of his explanations place the responsibility for the book's disappointing sales on external circumstances that were beyond his control and that he does not appear to have considered that the book's content and/or subject matter may have not had the broad appeal he believed it would.

Gignilliat was in Washington, DC working on ROTC issues during much of the next week from November 13-17, 1916, leaving the editors at Bobbs-Merrill free to determine how to respond to his letters criticizing their own marketing efforts and the actions of the book sellers.[154] Bobbs-Merrill determined that the cost of printing another 5,000 copies of the eight-page circular for *Arms and the Boy* would be $41.85 and $59.35 for an additional 10,000 copies.[155]

Armed with this information, Chambers wrote to Howland acknowledging that Gignilliat had "been after us to make another circular" and letting Howland know that Chambers had told Gignilliat that Bobbs-Merrill was going to "have to wait till the sales caught up before we could stand the expense." Chambers added that, "Maybe he'd like to pay for the promotion he desires," indicating that Chambers was comfortable with his own decision and suggesting that Chambers was of the opinion that Gignilliat's request was somewhat absurd.[156]

This exchange is telling, as it shows clearly that Bobbs-Merrill would no longer provide additional resources to promote *Arms and the Boy* unless and until it began to sell better. In addition, Chambers' final statement contains a bit of snark, showing that perhaps his (and maybe others') patience with Gignilliat as a collaborator was beginning to wear thin.

Since Gignilliat had written to both of them on November 10, 1916, Howland and Chambers each responded to Gignilliat the following week after discussing the matter and conferring with one another.

Writing on November 16, 1916, Howland provided support for Chambers' decision to delay production of the revised circular by sharing with Gignilliat that the amount of money Bobbs-Merrill had expended to promote *Arms and the Boy* to date had exceeded "the proper percentage" determined by the publisher. By doing so, Howland conveyed his support to delay production of the revised circular and also communicated to Gignilliat that Bobbs-Merrill was unwilling to provide the additional resources he requested unless and until sales of *Arms and the Boy* improved.

In addition, Howland offered that while he personally would have liked to have been able to produce an additional circular, he agreed with Chambers that Bobbs-Merrill would "have to wait a little bit until the sales catch up with the cost of advertising and promotion." Gignilliat was almost certainly disappointed with Howland's response when he read it upon his return from Washington, DC.

Chambers provided his own response to Gignilliat on November 17, 1916, showing that he was both a good editor and an astute judge of character. Sensing correctly that he needed some reassurance, Chambers assured Gignilliat that Bobbs-Merrill had not lost confidence in *Arms and the Boy*. Chambers reiterated that the decision to delay publication of the revised circular was simply in recognition that they had spent more than usual on the advertising and promotion of the book, and he offered that it would be irresponsible of them to spend more on the book unless and until its sales improved. Reflecting the information contained in Howland's letter sent the day before, Chambers shared with Gignilliat the remarkable fact that Bobbs-Merrill had *"spent more money in the promotion of your book than any other non-fiction title published this year* (emphasis added)," which was why Chambers could not "see how we can stand the expense of the new circular until the sales catch up with the promotion."[157]

In acknowledging that Bobbs-Merrill had spent more promoting *Arms and the Boy* than any other non-fiction work they published in 1916, Howland provided Gignilliat with information showing that Bobbs-Merrill had indeed done all they could be reasonably expected to do to promote the book. If the disappointing sales for the book could not be attributed to a lack of adequate resources devoted to promoting it, one must consider the possibility that *Arms and the Boy* may have lacked the appeal the Gignilliat anticipated and expected the work to have.

Having never received such a response to his requests for support from ER Culver, Gignilliat's response to being rebuffed would be hard to predict. However, the substance of the letters from Howland and Chambers appeared to have struck the right tone and persuaded Gignilliat that their decision to delay printing of the revised circular did not represent a lack of confidence in his book but rather the fact that Bobbs-Merrill had already spent all it could afford to promote his book.

This episode further revealed Gignilliat's lack of confidence in himself as a writer, and he must have recognized that this had occurred. Writing a somewhat conciliatory note to Chambers on November 18, 1916, Gignilliat thanked him for his support and expressed his happiness that Bobbs-Merrill had not lost confidence in *Arms and the Boy* as a salable work for the company.[158]

Chambers responded two days later by reassuring Gignilliat that Bobbs-Merrill had "not lost a particle of [its] enthusiasm" for *Arms and the Boy* and that the printing of the new circular simply had to "wait until the sales catch up before spending more money for promotion."[159] In providing Gignilliat with a second reassurance in such a short span of time, Chambers showed that he was quite adept at managing his authors. It also demonstrated that Chambers understood well the fragility of Gignilliat's self-confidence as a writer and the need to provide him with support that was positive, constructive, and supportive.

Ironically, this was exactly the type of support Gignilliat insisted the cadets at Culver received. Being on the receiving end of his own approach appears to have had the same desirable impact on him that he intended for his own charges, and Gignilliat turned his attention to other matters for the remainder of 1916.

Types of Schools for Boys Finally Released

After an usually long and tedious editorial process that had begun in summer 1913, Bobbs-Merrill was able to release O'Shea's *Types of Schools for Boys* in late-March or early April 1917. Gignilliat was somewhat responsible for some of the delays in publication. In contrast to the ambivalence he expressed regarding his own writing ability, he demonstrated a determination to provide content that was completely accurate and the confidence in his own ability to provide it. It also showed that he was at least as interested in ensuring that the information contained in his contribution was as accurate as possible as he was in helping the editors at Bobbs-Merrill move forward with the production of O'Shea's *Types of Schools for Boys*. While understandable, this episode suggests that Gignilliat was a bit short-sighted when considering the entire project, allowing himself to be distracted by the minute detail "trees" of the larger "forest" that comprised the substantial collaborative efforts necessary to get O'Shea's *Types of Schools for Boys* in print as soon as possible.

Coming out at least seven months earlier and having been circulated in galleys and advance sheets during the very height of the debate regarding the Hay Bill, Gignilliat's own *Arms and the Boy* attracted far more attention for the intended audience than one could have ever hoped for O'Shea's *Types of Schools for Boys*. Acquiring the influence he desired it to have as a result of the timing of its release, Gignilliat could be satisfied that his decision to strike out on his own and have his contribution published earlier and as part of a larger work of which he was the sole author was indeed both correct and fortuitous for him and for Culver.

Chapter 11 Gignilliat's Aeneid –

The Content and Argument of *Arms and the Boy*

Having devoted so much of his time and energy to the writing of *Arms and the Boy*, it is worth considering the book's content in detail to understand what Gignilliat was trying to convey, how he decided to present his message, and why he felt it was so important that he do so in this manner and at this point in time.

By doing so, one can gain invaluable insight into Gignilliat as an educator and into the heady issues related to preparedness with which he engaged. Many of these issues were quite critical and contained accusations of unpardonable distortions, inexcusable mental corruption, the intolerable promotion of militarism, and the unforgivable development of war mongers, intentional or otherwise, among the nation's impressionable youths, all of which demanded a forceful and persuasive response.

Front of Arms and the Boy *dust jacket with Gignilliat's initials reversed.*

Although intended to address all types of military schools equally and incorporate the views of many educators, the final version of the manuscript was decidedly focused on "essentially military" secondary schools and based largely on Gignilliat's own experience.[1] While his intention was to address the role of military training in schools comprehensively, and even though it included information from a variety of high schools and colleges, the actual content of the work belies Gignilliat's own preference for and experience with military high schools. As a result, the first 17 of *Arms and the Boy's* 18 chapters were devoted to military training in high schools and focused mostly, in accordance with his plan, on how this was done in "essentially military schools."

In addition, the reader will notice much overlap between the explanation of the Culver military system presented previously and the argument in favor of military schools and the value of military training in schools contained in *Arms and the Boy*. In many cases, the same quotations are used to support aspects of both systems. This was neither coincidental nor unintentional, and it allows one to recognize the areas in which Gignilliat drew from his Culver system and experiences and to highlight aspects contained in *Arms and the Boy* that are different from Gignilliat's system at Culver.

The Main Argument – The Value of Military Training in Schools

Gignilliat's overall intent for *Arms and the Boy* was for it to "make some small contribution toward the preparation of our young men for a more complete discharge of their duties of citizenship." This certainly included military service in times of peril, but it also involved the "effective and patriotic discharge of the normal civic duties of peace," such as leadership that contributes to the welfare and flourishing of the country.[2] Thus, it was citizenship more than either military training or leadership that formed the foundation of Gignilliat's efforts at Culver and as the basis of the system of military training he developed and promoted.

Gignilliat's stated purpose for *Arms and the Boy* was to bring together "some concrete information regarding the application of the military system to the various types of institutions," since there was such a "wide variation in the scope and character of such training" given across the country at the time he was writing.[3]

Gignilliat began by identifying and addressing some benefits and drawbacks of military training. This was a good rhetorical approach to highlight what is desirable at the very beginning and also address common criticisms up front to deprive them of their power. He used as his first sentence a citation from a presentation by respected Ohio State University Professor Edward J. Orton to assert that military training was "the most important tool in our whole educational kit." Gignilliat included statements of support from the Ohio State president, along with the presidents at the University of Illinois and Cornell University, as further evidence. After expressing his own level of support for military training in the preface, this was a deft rhetorical approach, as it uses the words of respected academics and university administrators, who the reader could assume to be professionally competent and relatively unbiased, to make the initial case for military training in the book.

Referring to the existing controversy about the wisdom and efficacy of military training in high schools, Gignilliat took special care to attend to the issue of drill in the high schools, endeavoring to do so objectively while also addressing "the objections that have been raised to such training." Responding to opinions that dissented from his own at the very beginning of the text, Gignilliat addressed the allegations that military training in high school had the dual deficiencies of destroying the initiative of boys while simultaneously developing within them an undesirable and unhealthy level of militarism, described as an inordinate fondness for war.

The former had little basis in fact, stemming mostly from the opinions of those opposed to military training in secondary education, and the latter arose from fears that such training might elicit the type of response that the Prussian system did for German youths fighting in Europe at the time.

For Gignilliat, neither of these negative outcomes were likely or possible if the training was given *properly*, which is perhaps the most important theme that runs throughout the work. Given properly, military training for high school boys induced the "higher ideals of citizenship for the student," which include "service, courage, discipline, and physical endurance," along with "more effective discipline and a better physical basis for educational training and life."[4] From the very beginning, Gignilliat argued that the benefits of military training in schools contribute positively to the development and perpetuation of the contemporary notion of "manliness," comprised of citizenship, character, and vigor.[5]

Citizenship over Leadership

Reflecting much of the rhetoric used throughout the debate regarding the National Defense Act of 1916, Gignilliat argued that the main value of military schools and military training was the ability of it to promote citizenship. Gignilliat wrote that "military training properly given means higher ideals of citizenship for the student."[6] In addition, the responses Gignilliat received to the 24-item survey he sent to virtually every military training program occurring with an educational context confirmed his belief that the main and best selling point for military systems in schools was citizenship.[7]

This focus of a military system on citizenship instead of leadership may seem somewhat strange a century removed from the situation unless and until one realizes several particular things about this period. Fifty years after the Civil War, and after the disastrous attempts to impose a Northern version of it on the South and West, America was just beginning to realize what a new national citizenship that was inclusive and constructive would mean for its citizens.

The "Pledge of Allegiance," developed by Francis Bellamy in 1892 for the 1893 Columbian Exposition world's fair in Chicago, was being recited in schools across the nation daily, and the study of civics was being introduced into the secondary curriculum to educate students about their rights and responsibilities as American citizens. A program that could contribute meaningfully to these efforts would therefore have substantial appeal during this period.

In addition, there was no formal leadership doctrine or recognized program of instruction that could be used as part of a school's curriculum. Using the data to guide him, Gignilliat also found in the responses to his survey that others were using the military program to promote citizenship in their institutions and not to teach or develop leadership among the students. It would be at least another generation before the explicit connection between the military system and leadership development began to develop at Culver, and several generations until this connection developed elsewhere in the country.

Origin and Classification of Military Schools

Gignilliat then addressed the origin and classification of the nation's "essentially military" schools, along with identifying the type of aid they received from the government. Tracing the growth and development of military schools in America from the founding of West Point in 1802 and showing how private military schools, land-grant colleges, and high schools contributed to national defense provided a succinct background and valuable context for the reader. Although certainly designed to provide cadets with military training, Gignilliat reiterated that in every school using a military system, the higher purpose was to help the cadet "acquire the disciplined will, the power of endurance, the sturdy physique, and the moral qualities of loyalty, devotion to duty, and self-sacrifice that become the citizen no less than the solider."[8]

Gignilliat identified the military personnel and equipment provided to military schools to support their training, and he concluded the chapter by explaining the Army's system of recognizing excellent military high schools as "Honor schools" and outstanding higher education institutions as "Distinguished Colleges," both of which afforded their graduates with preferential commissioning opportunities. The listing of schools receiving such recognition during the period 1904-1915 identified schools that performed exceptionally well in this regard, portraying Culver and several other schools in a quite positive light.

The Daily Life in the Essentially Military School

As O'Shea had suggested repeatedly during the writing of *Types of Schools for Boys*, Gignilliat next addressed the daily life in the essentially military school. It is in this chapter that Gignilliat begins making the case for the specific value of military training in schools by identifying particular aspects of it and their corresponding contributions. While existing under military discipline and living the life of a solider, the idea was to help the cadet understand how to apply the military training he was receiving to "the normal life of the citizen in times of peace."[9] Rather than aiming to make cadets better soldiers, military training in schools actually made them more capable citizens and better able to function in society.

Acknowledging that the average American boy was "impatient of restraint, undisciplined" and "notably lacking in respect for authority," Gignilliat was convinced that "continuous military training, with its exactness and precision, its rigid adherence to system and discipline, and its enforce (sic) exercise and regularity of life" would not only be effective in bringing "out the best that is in a boy," but would also develop "his sense of honor and of duty" by teaching him to obey, transforming the boy into the very ideal of manliness and citizenship desired by parents and the entire country.[10] Being soldierly in his barrack room, classroom, and drill field provided the boy with a sense of belonging and instilled within him the "military spirit of punctilious courtesy, of respect for authority, [and] of order and system" that made him habitually systematic and orderly.[11]

Cadets began by donning identical uniforms so they looked like soldiers and learning the rudiments of marching so they could march like soldiers. Almost any boy could dress himself and walk, but being required to do so in a military manner with precise standards was new to them and forced them to listen, learn, and concentrate to perform well. Starting with such simple tasks allowed for the cadets to experience success while also being transformed by the system. Once they had mastered these fundamentals, it was time to move to the next phase of training that involved learning to handle an instrument designed for war: the military rifle.

Beginning with the rifle, which Gignilliat believed had a natural attraction for all boys, the cadet was issued a piece of military equipment that could be lethal (many schools removed the firing pins from weapons used in drill to prevent accidental and/or negligent discharges) and for which he was held personally responsible. He could not lose it without facing serious consequences, and he had to keep it clean and serviceable at all times. In addition, he had to learn to execute the manual of arms well and precisely. This was particularly challenging for the younger boys, as the rifle they used was heavy and designed to be used by fully grown men. For many boys, the responsibilities of maintaining a rifle and drilling with it was "the first thing he has ever been made to do with precision and attention to detail," making it an effective tool upon which to base his military training.[12]

To counter the shared danger of fire, which was common to many schools of the period, cadets had to perform guard duty in the barracks to keep one another safe. While tedious and largely monotonous, Gignilliat advocated for using guard duty as a means of developing responsibility among the cadets. In his view, "it is a fine experience for a boy to be placed on post as a sentinel with definite orders to enforce and feel that he is occupying a position of trust and responsibility" within the organization that was unusual for boys their age.[13] Beyond standing a post, there was also value in supervising the conduct of guard duty. This was the purview of the older cadets, who obtained "a great deal of valuable executive experience" while doing so.[14]

According to Gignilliat, living an orderly life, taking care of his room, and learning to put things back where they belong had value beyond simply acquiring the habit of orderliness. Emphasizing the competitive advantage gained by boys trained in a military system, Gignilliat wrote that "a boy who has been taught to do things systematically will in his business life possess a decided advantage over boys who have not be so trained".[15] Whether addressing the aspects of individual drill, collective drill, or barracks living, the system of living under military discipline was "as complete and effective as that of any up-to-date business office," attesting to both its practical and development value.[16]

Educators and Academics

Turning to the educators, Gignilliat sketched out the roles and responsibilities of classroom teachers and the military staff at "essentially military schools." Gignilliat made clear that the academic staff and the military staff worked together in a system designed "not so much [to catch the boy] in breaches of regulations as in discouraging him from breaking them" in the first place, thereby reinforcing the habits of orderliness and honorable behavior that the military system was so well suited to promote.[17]

Using a military system required that the adult staff and faculty members demonstrate military courtesy when dealing with cadets. As one of the more distinctive aspects of a military system, Gignilliat argued that the value of "strict observance of military courtesy" was quite desirable because it helped in making transformative improvements in the average boy's "bearing and attitude" that was quite noticeable and beneficial.[18] In Gignilliat's view, this formality was not necessarily a barrier to establishing and sustaining authentic relationships with cadets as long as the adult possessed "the right qualities of tact, discrimination and good judgment." Used in this manner, a real level of respect and understanding could develop between adults and cadets, leading to a type of "friendliness" off duty without an undue level of intimacy that was detrimental to such relations and "so destructive of real influence."[19]

Gignilliat devoted the fifth chapter to a treatment of the studies and methods of instruction in the military school. Responding to criticisms that military drill wasted valuable school time that could be better used for academic studies, Gignilliat extolled the virtues of organization and offered that "the time given to actual drill is, in part, time that goes to waste in a less carefully organized schedule and in part it is time that the boy in the civilian school would have to himself," which may also be somewhat unproductive.[20]

In Gignilliat's view, boys needed "a normal wholesome atmosphere, regular hours, [a] simple diet and abundant exercise" to develop properly and flourish.[21] Indeed, one clear advantage of the military school was its ability to be very efficient, to make the best use of available time, and to provide students with predictability that many welcomed and found comforting.[22] The value of the uniform also became apparent, as it served as an effective way of putting all boys on an equal footing and used meritocratic performance as the basis for recognition and advancement.[23]

Recognizing the larger concern inherent in the criticism of having the features of a military system minimize and/or take precedence over academic activities, Gignilliat wrote that a shared commitment by all at the school to "place a high premium on scholarship and to guard against class-room (sic) duties becoming eclipsed by those military features which make a more ready appeal to the cadets' interest" was the best method to prevent such an occurrence.[24]

Addressing the modern notion of knowledge "transference," Gignilliat made the case that the benefits of military training extended to the classroom as well. He argued that the "high degree of accuracy and thoroughness" demanded of the cadet on the drill field must also be required in his classroom preparation and performance.[25] In the end, military training for high school boys, rather than dampening their initiative, crushing their spirit, and making them more militaristic, provided training for useful citizenship that was both constructive and desirable.[26]

Cadet Leaders and Discipline

Having addressed the role of adult educators and the methods of instruction in the military school, Gignilliat proceeded to explain the role of cadet leaders and the value of working with them cooperatively. The peer leadership responsibility inherent in the military system was of inestimable value to the formation of habits of honorable behavior and the development of character, and Gignilliat encouraged educators to take great care in selecting and training the cadet officers.[27]

Candidates for cadet officer positions had to be trustworthy so they could "resist the lure of popularity" and remain conscientious in the execution of their assigned duties. They also had to be "instinctively fair and honorable," reflecting an innate understanding of the destructive impact that unfair decisions and dishonorable behavior can have on groups of young men.[28] Given their importance to the overall running of a school's military system, Gignilliat was convinced that, "unless this phase of the cadet officer's duty is strongly emphasized, the system is of little value to either the school or to the boy."[29] While using cadet leaders contained some level of risk, Gignilliat argued that "service as a cadet officer furnishes a valuable opportunity for the rounding out of character and for the acquirement of executive experience," and was therefore worth the time, effort, and energy required to select, train, and supervise cadet leaders appropriately.[30]

Gignilliat next addressed the system of discipline in the essentially military school. For Gignilliat, the purpose of a military system in an educational institution was to instill two fundamental beliefs into cadets: support for a functional discipline, and a creed that embraced the value of character demonstrated by behavior that was honorable and gentlemanly. The practice of military drill under arms was an ideal vehicle for achieving these objectives while also holding the attention of the boy. It was ideal because boys were inherently attracted to military things and would be more inclined to accept the military system and its objectives.[31] A properly conducted military program could safely and effectively challenge a boy just enough while also appealing to his sense of honor without placing undue strain on his still-developing character.[32]

According to Gignilliat's educational philosophy, boys wanted and needed to be challenged if they were to become the men they were destined to be, noting that "boys are not afraid of a few hardships if they are sure that they are getting the real thing."[33] Conducted properly, discipline would inculcate a "real and permanent respect for authority" that would produce a man worthy of citizenship who would be well-equipped to assume his proper role in society and make contributions that were meaningful and worthwhile.[34]

Providing more specifics, Gignilliat identified and explained the rewards and penalties used in the military school's system of discipline. It is interesting to note that he used the term "penalties" instead of "punishments," indicating that boys were assigned penalties for violating the system under which they had agreed to exist, much like a player received when playing a game. Presenting the system of merits and demerits common to most military schools of the period, Gignilliat also explained how military schools addressed serious acts of indiscipline using a modified version of the military's courts martial system. This approach succeeded in gaining and holding the boy's attention, discouraging him from wanting to be subject to such a proceeding, and giving him a tangible reason for moderating his behavior accordingly.

Beginning with rewards, Gignilliat did well in emphasizing the positive aspects of the military system, noting that "foremost of incentives to boys in the military school are the opportunities for promotion," which he believed appealed to all boys equally. Other rewards included the awarding of uniform accoutrements in the form of badges and patches that were highly prized by most boys, along with merits as recognition for excellent performance and incentives to continue performing similarly. Clearly preferring to use methods of positive reinforcement, Gignilliat noted the effectiveness of these methods and how they helped make the system of discipline "work both ways" for the boys and the school, and in ways that were both effective and meaningful.[35]

Gignilliat acknowledged that rewards would not always be sufficient to maintain the level of good order and discipline desired in a military system comprised of teenaged boys. Accordingly, Gignilliat outlined the system of demerits and penalties used by many military schools. Calling attention to the value of demerits and penalties to keep cadets focused on the attention to detail required of them while under military discipline to ensure it remained "real," Gignilliat emphasized that the system of assigning punishment always included a hearing at which the cadet was provided the opportunity to respond to the charge(s) and relate the circumstances surrounding the alleged act of indiscipline.

If presented successfully, the charge(s) was/were dropped, and nothing more was said of the matter. If, however, the charge(s) were accurate, the cadet was assigned an appropriate penalty commensurate with the offense and circumstances, and he was punished accordingly. These penalties could take the form of demerits, loss of rank, confinement to quarters, the requirement to walk a specific number of "penalty tours" while under arms, suspension, and/or expulsion.

In every case from the most trivial to the most serious, due process was followed scrupulously and the results were made public for all to see.[36] The military system was perhaps most effective in developing citizenship among cadets in this particular aspect, holding them visibly and publicly accountable individually for the set of rules under which they had collectively agreed to exist and thus mirroring the American judicial system in many ways.

Addressing briefly the practice of hazing that appeared to be becoming more prevalent at the time, Gignilliat noted that "boys as s rule do not show much discretion in these things" and required clear and consistent guidance else "any latitude is apt to be abused" by them. Acknowledging its appeal to some and also believing that "real esprit de corps is not cultivated by hazing," Gignilliat observed that it must be the school, and not the student, that is in charge. To solve the challenge instead of simply driving its practice underground, Gignilliat was convinced that "hazing must be controlled largely by the sentiment of the cadets themselves."[37]

The Ideals of the Military School

In what is perhaps his most powerfully argued component, Gignilliat outlined in the book's ninth chapter the ideals of the military school from his perspective. Convinced that "the military instinct is natural to most boys," Gignilliat argued that military training was one of the best ways to produce capable citizens and to elicit good citizenship. Gignilliat believed that the "military training of boys, properly conducted, gives them the true fighting spirit," which was neither militaristic nor apt to increase one's desire for war.[38] In support of this assertion, Gignilliat wrote that a boy, having "gained some small conception of what the horrors of war may be" through military training "will be logically a greater lover of peace than the boy not so trained and a most stable citizen when the hysteria of war threatens the nation."[39]

Besides providing excellent training for citizenship, Gignilliat also argued that military training enhanced the "spirit of democracy" among boys by using a system that treated everyone as equals and which relied almost exclusively on merit for its recognition and rewards. Beginning on equal footing by wearing the same uniform and living in the same types of rooms, boys advanced in the military system on their strength of their own demonstrated level of proficiency, deeds, and performance. The military system also encouraged the ideal of service, requiring each person to "work for the general good of his squad, his company and his battalion," providing him with the incentive "to put forth more effort than he would be inclined to make for purely selfish reasons." As leaders in a military system, cadets needed to be willing to "make some personal sacrifices of time and pleasure" for the good of others to be successful.[40]

Countering explicitly the charge of exacerbating militarism, Gignilliat returned to his favorite theme, writing that properly conducted military training gave boys a "fighting spirit" that differed markedly from the detested militarism of the critics. Gignilliat felt that several years of military training would usually be quite sufficient to "gratify the boy's [innate] curiosity" regarding the military and also "satisfy his desire for [a] military life."[41] Testifying before Congress in January 1916 regarding the very same criticism, Mr. Sebastian C. Jones, Superintendent of New York Military Academy and President of AMCSUS, quipped that, "I think we may honestly claim to cure more military ambitions than we foster," indicating that military schooling probably did more to discourage military service than any other relevant institution.[42]

In a larger sense, Gignilliat related some comments that President Woodrow Wilson had shared with a group of Culver cadets in 1912, telling them that "using a sword or a rifle in battle" was inherently selfless service, and that military training helped cadets understand that they owed a duty to society which [was] above any interest you can have in [one's] self." In closing, Wilson shared that by service, he meant that each cadet would demonstrate a personal commitment to "do the greatest good to the world when you live in it to serve your fellowmen," which was quite evocative of Gignilliat's own notion of service and served as a fitting summary of the argument Gignilliat presented for the value of military training in schools.[43]

Expanding the focus of his argument, Gignilliat used the next chapter to address more broadly military training in high schools. Citing evidence gathered from his own questionnaire and other sources (primarily fellow high school educators), he argued that military training, properly conducted (always the caveat!), was of significant value to high schools and high school students.[44]

Gignilliat believed that educators of teenaged boys could and "should put emphasis on character building," which was most effective when the training provided was "made real and businesslike."[45] Expanding on his theme of the importance of providing proper military training, Gignilliat offered that, "the training must be real if it is to command the boy's respect and give him anything of real value, either as a citizen or as a citizen solider."[46]

Indeed, the problem Gignilliat observed with military training that was ineffective was that it was not given properly or made real. This was not only detrimental to the process, but it was also harmful to the boy and negated the value of the training, making it worse than providing no training at all. Gignilliat had made this point previously in his newspaper article of October 6, 1915 during his time at the Fort Sheridan Business and Professional Men's military training camp.

The Mental Value of Military Training – Transference

The mental value of military training was the focus of Gignilliat's next chapter. Citing input he had received from other like-minded educators, Gignilliat shared their views that "military training develops concentration," that military drill "awakens the stupid and puts snap into the whole student body," and that military training "quickens the mental processes and aids straight thinking," promoting quick responses to directions and creating a sense of order and accuracy within the classroom that was quite beneficial to both students and teachers.[47] Going further, Gignilliat believed that "the effects of military training carry over into the class room (sic) and result in a higher degree of attentiveness and more mental alertness," contributing constructively to cadets' learning rather than detracting from it.[48]

Regarding the mental value of military training, Gignilliat addressed what is known today as the process of transference when writing that, "our greatest task still lies in teaching the boy to apply the principles he has learned to new problems in whatever form he may meet them." Seeking to provide an effective link between the actions on the drill field and in the classroom, Gignilliat argued that, "military training may be so coordinated with academic work that it becomes, to a certain extent, a school of application," allowing the boy to learn how "to apply some of his formulas to practical things" and thus enhancing the learning significantly.[49]

The Physical Value of Military Training

Starting with Chapter 12, Gignilliat employed a didactic method of using a series of clarifying questions to provide clarity to his argument in the next four chapters.

This section addressed directly the guidance he received from Bobbs-Merrill in December 1915 to emphasize "the value that military training has in the boy's physique, to his sense of order and to his prompt and willing obedience to authority," along with the obvious benefits related to the acquisition of military skills provided by the training. [50]

The focus of Chapter 12 was to address the physical benefits of military training. This issue was of particular interest during the Progressive Era and in the wake of the nation's transition from a primarily agrarian society to an industrialized one and the resulting concerns about the detrimental impact of reduced physical activity on boys who now spent the majority of their days sitting in classrooms instead of working in the fields. Gignilliat did so by presenting the advantages of military training as a system of exercise and clarifying its relation to athletics.

Acknowledging that some questioned the value of military training as effective physical exercise, Gignilliat used the example of the "splendid physique" and "attractive carriage" of West Point cadets to counter this criticism. Drawing from his own experiences to provide further evidence, Gignilliat wrote that "the students of no civilian preparatory school in America can equal in set-up and superb physical condition the fourteen to eighteen-year-old cadets of our best military schools," using the contemporary term "set-up" to refer to posture and carriage.[51] During this period, poor posture was viewed as evidence of poor character, making this element of Gignilliat's argument particularly compelling.

After enumerating the positive benefits of strenuous military drill on the posture and carriage of young men, complemented by the appearance of the military uniform and the incentive to earn recognition for elevated levels of physical fitness inherent in all military systems, Gignilliat posed explicitly the questions: *What is the effect of military training on athletics? Is it a substitute for athletics?* Using examples of his own experiences at Culver regarding the impact of company athletic competitions and input from other educators provided in response to his questionnaire, Gignilliat offered that the most significant contribution that the military system could make to an athletic program was its ability to spur fierce levels of competition between and among military units. Since boys fought hardest to uphold the honor of their military units, athletic competitions that pitted military units against one another encouraged boys to give their all.

Accordingly, Gignilliat concluded that the military system complements an existing athletic program and should be used in conjunction with it and not as a substitute for it whenever possible.[52]

Military Training as a System of Discipline in Schools

Gignilliat made even greater use of his didactive methodology of using clarifying questions to highlight the merits of military training as a system of discipline in schools. Returning to the theme of transference, Gignilliat highlighted the positive impact military training had on developing a boy's initiative and willingness to think. In a properly conducted military system, when "a cadet is given an order, the emphasis is placed on what he is to do and not how he is to do it," and he is expected to "use his bean" to think through the problem to determine how best to solve it.[53]

Seeking to avoid an overemphasis on implicit obedience, Gignilliat believed that military training should also make use of reason to be truly effective. Besides countering the "dulling of initiative" that unthinking obedience could produce, such a system would also develop leadership that was of much greater value than mere "drivership" that regrettably ignored how results were achieved.[54]

Emphasizing process over content at a time when this was decidedly out of fashion for boys and in the classroom, Gignilliat argued that the properly conducted military program made allowance for mistakes based on inexperience. It also ensured that initiative was both encouraged and rewarded.

The Greatest Value of Military Training in Schools – Developing Citizenship

Making his most essential point, Gignilliat argued that military training was perhaps most effective in providing the basis for "more useful and effective citizenship" among adolescent boys. Learning respect for authority was highlighted as the first contribution military training made to enhancing citizenship, along with developing responsibility by being required to "do for the general good of his organization" things that he would not normally do so that he helped to further the general welfare of others by doing his duty "to something outside of and beyond himself."

Gignilliat argued that boys come to appreciate the value of doing things in a disciplined manner when they find that "things can be done where there is discipline that can not (*sic*) be done where there is not," and that "things run more smoothly with discipline" because it "saves time, saves lives, [and] gets team work (*sic*)." This process begins with boys realizing that "to control others, he must first control himself" by acquiring and appreciating discipline, which was one of the essential goals for boys during their adolescence.

Providing discipline of this type, Gignilliat made the point that military training also provided excellent training for business, as the discipline the boys acquired would go far towards distinguishing them from others who had not been so fortunate. Indeed, they could "take with them everything they got from the military training except the uniform" and put all of it to effective use in their professional lives. [55] In the end, military training for high school boys, rather than dampening their initiative, crushing their spirit, and making them more militaristic, provided training for useful citizenship that was both constructive and desirable.[56]

How To, How Much, and *How Often*

The next two chapters are largely unremarkable, engaging with the questions of assessing the military value of cadet training in the schools and the extent to which military training should be used in the high school. Regarding the military value of cadet training in the schools, Gignilliat makes an impassioned (and predictable) argument on behalf of the ability of teenaged boys to perform quite well in military environments based upon their interest, ability to learn quickly, "zest and imagination" for the training, and relatively higher levels of physical endurance.[57] He also observed that while large numbers of boys training in high school military program s were not currently joining state militias, this number could be increased by taking more deliberate measures to encourage such action.[58]

After rehashing information presented elsewhere regarding the impact of military training in high schools, Gignilliat tackled the issue of whether boys enjoyed the training in conjunction with addressing the extent to which military training should be used in the high school. Seizing on yet another opportunity to return to his favorite leitmotif, Gignilliat offered that when presented effectively, boys were more inclined to enjoy the training, as they had a sense of purpose when engaged in it and a sense of accomplishment after they completed a drill correctly.[59]

Chapter 16, regarding the process of securing competent instructors of military drill and the selection of duties of cadet officers, and Chapter

17, regarding uniforms, are largely procedural in nature and contain no insights regarding the value of military training in schools. Their placement is somewhat awkward, as they feel out of place and lack any appreciable connection to the preceding or succeeding chapters.

Land-Grant Colleges and Military Schools as Sources of Reserve Officers

The book's final chapter presents Gignilliat's assessment of the ability of the nation's land-grant colleges and military schools to serve as reliable and effective sources of reserve officers, along with the responses to the questionnaire Gignilliat sent out from a military officer involved in military training in California high schools, US Army infantry officer Captain W. B. Burtt. It is in this chapter that Gignilliat finally presents his argument for the inclusion of the nation's military schools and colleges as sources of supply for well-trained and effective reserve officers.

After discounting the contributions of an approach relying on using enlisted men and/or noncommissioned officers from the Regular Army and officers from the state militias as being unreliable and inadequate to provide the necessary quantity of officers in the case of a full-scale mobilization, Gignilliat didactically poses the question, *Can colleges train officers effectively?*

His treatment of this question is methodical if somewhat biased, determining, based upon his own experience, input from Ohio State's Professor Orton, and access he had to Army annual inspection reports, that land-grant colleges provide military training to their students grudgingly, since they are required by law to do so, and that their interest in doing so, even if it happens to be high at present, is subject to change and will likely wane when the current emergency passes. In addition, it was Gignilliat's assessment that the training provided by these institutions is, "for the most part carried out...so ineffectively...as to give rise to serious doubt as to the feasibility of training reserve officers in the colleges."[60]

Highlighting the advantages enjoyed by military schools for providing the necessary training, both by institutional temperament and resources, and using the examples of graduates from schools like Norwich and VMI, Gignilliat championed the McKellar bill's call for the establishment of a military school in each of the nation's 48 states as a preferred solution to the problem of providing a reliable and adequate source of reserve officers.

Touching all the bases, Gignilliat also lauded the current legislation in the form of the Hay and Chamberlain bills under consideration in Congress to create a Reserve Officers Training Corps based on college campuses that would be regulated such that it could provide adequately trained men to serve as reserve officers. Making the point that proved so crucial to getting the Hay/Chamberlain bills passed into law as the National Defense Act of 1916, Gignilliat closed by claiming that such a system, combined with the input of graduates from military schools and colleges, could produce a reliable and adequate source of supply for reserve officers on which the nation could depend.[61]

While the responses of Captain Burtt are thoughtful, they have little connection to the content of Chapter 18 and seem awkwardly placed. Since Gignilliat devoted an entire appendix to the condensed tabulation of answers to questionnaire sent to land grant colleges by the president of the Association of Land Grant Colleges (Appendix 14), it would have made more sense to include the questionnaire with Captain Burtt's responses in that section of the work.

The 22 Appendices – Mostly *How To*

Presented in 205 pages of text and 54 illustrations, the 18 chapters outlined above present the crux of the content of *Arms and the Boy*. The book's remaining 142 pages and 26 illustrations are divided among 22 appendices that are almost exclusively functional and procedural. While less philosophical and more practically oriented, the appendices reflected the guidance Gignilliat received from Bobbs-Merrill in December 1915 to address in the book "not only military schools, but the introduction of military courses into non-military schools and the whole subject of the preparation of a citizen-soldiery through our education institutions...."[62]

Gignilliat had little to do with the writing of any material appearing in the appendices, and his involvement was limited to the identification, collection, and selection of the material presented in them. While this information may have reflected some of his own thinking, one may conclude that Gignilliat's own thoughts regarding the value of military training in schools appear in the book's 18 chapters that he wrote, and that the material contained in the appendices, while valuable, is tangential to Gignilliat's argument and complementary at best.

Below is a listing of the book's 22 appendices, with the source of the material presented and/or author identified. Note that only three of the appendices are related to Culver.

> Appendix I. Suggestions for starting drill in schools where military instruction has not previously been given; prepared by Captain Howard F. Noble, Culver Military Academy.[63]

Appendix II. The Wyoming Plan; based almost completely on a report written by the plan's originator, Lieutenant Edgar Z. Steever, US Army.[64]

Appendix III. An ethical, physical, military system of training for boys; based almost completely on recommendations delivered in a presentation by Brigadier General Albert L. Mills, Chief of the Militia Division of the Army War College at a convention of the National Guard Association on November 11, 1915 from a written report.[65]

Appendix IV. Training and discipline of the Salt Lake City High-school cadets; based completely on a report written by Captain William C. Webb, US Army.[66]

Appendix V. Issue of rifles and ammunition to high schools and other institutions not having officers of the Army detailed as Professors of Military Science; based largely on extracts from a circular issued by the War Department, dated July 2, 1914.[67]

Appendix VI. California rules and regulations for the government of high-school cadets; based almost completely on extracts from a letter from the Adjutant General of the state of California, Edwin A. Forbes.[68]

Appendix VII. Suggestions for rifle practice in high schools; written by CPT William R. Kennedy, Culver Military Academy.[69]

Appendix VIII. Instruction of high-school boys in rifle shooting in the public schools of New York City; based almost completely on a report written by the Public Schools' Athletic League of New York City and provided by General George W. Wingate, the president and organizer of the league.[70]

Appendix IX. Rifle practice for high schools of California; based completely on the regulations for California high school cadets, published by Brigadier General C. W. Thomas, Jr., Adjutant General, State of California.[71]

Appendix X. Summer camps for high-school students; from Culver's own high school summer military camp in May 1915.[72]

Appendix XI. Certificate issued by the War Department to graduates of military schools and colleges to which officers of the Army are detailed as Professors of Military Science and Tactics, which is a reproduction of *War Department Bulletin No. 38*, dated December 6, 1915.[73]

Appendix XII. Securing military instructors, arms, and equipment from the government – purchasing uniforms economically; consolidated form various official sources.[74]

Appendix XIII. Table showing income of land grant colleges from the United States, time allocated to military instruction per year and money allocated to military departments; created from annual reports submitted to the War Department.[75]

Appendix XIV. Condensed tabulation of answers to questionnaire sent to land grant colleges; based upon extracts from "a condensed tabulation of the answers received to a questionnaire sent to all land grant institutions by the president of the Association of Land Grant Colleges."[76]

Appendix XV. Making a success of the military course in a university. Giving the organization and course of instruction of a successfully conducted military department at the University of Illinois; based almost completely on extracts from report written by Major F. D. Webster, US Army, Professor of Military Science and Tactics, and Commandant of Cadets at the University of Illinois.[77]

Appendix XVI. The Reserve officers' training corps in England; based on reports obtained from the US Army War College.[78]

Appendix XVII. A five-year combined military and classical or technical course for colleges suggested by President Edmund J. James of the University of Illinois; based on a letter written by Edmund J. James, President of the University of Illinois, dated January 11, 1916.[79]

Appendix XVIII. Suggestions for military courses in non-military educational institutions; based on a circular issued from the headquarters of the US Army's Eastern Department by direction of Major General Leonard Wood, Department Commander.[80]

Appendix XIX. Plan for military instruction at Harvard University; based almost completely on extracts from the *Harvard Alumni Bulletin*, dated December 10, 1915.[81]

Appendix XX. The organization of field artillery at Yale University; based almost completely on extracts from the *Yale Alumni Weekly*, dated March 10, 1916.[82]

Appendix XXI. Military instruction camps for students; written by Lieutenant Ralph G. Sickles, Culver Military Academy.

Appendix XXII. Compulsory military training for the boys
of New York; based on a report written by the New York
Legislature.

The Distinctiveness of the System Gignilliat Designed and Implemented at Culver – Formation Not Assimilation

As Gignilliat and most others recognized, Culver took on a significant
responsibility when it accepted teenaged boys. They arrive d on campus
talented, driven, ambitious, eager to be challenged, but still as adolescents
who were in the process of forming their own identities and character
upon which they relied in adulthood. The process on which it was based
was the most distinguishing feature of Gignilliat's system, embracing the
idea of formation that goes beyond assimilation.

The Developmental Challenges of Adolescence – A Modern View

Society at this time knew very little about the stage of life characterized
by *sturm und drang* (storm and stress) and recently identified by the
term popularized by G. Stanley Hall as "adolescence." Given the existing
level of ignorance about it, along with prevailing view that boys needed an
especially harsh level of discipline during their teen years to turn out well
as adults, it is all the more remarkable how and how much Gignilliat got
right in the system he developed and implemented at Culver.

According to renowned social psychologist Robert Kegan, one of the
greatest developmental challenges of this period is to complete the
formation of adolescents so they are able to meet the expectations
awaiting them in the adult world. This involves bringing about a
transformation from a very concrete view and literal interpretation of the
world around them to a more abstract and interpretive perspective, both
in terms of cognitive outlook and social maturity. Kegan determined that
this is best accomplished by providing an environment of high challenge
and high support, which is precisely the type of system Gignilliat
developed and implemented at Culver over a half-century before Kegan
arrived at this conclusion.

As becomes apparent, this process and the system he developed to
promote it was quite unusual for the time and also for military schools,
and it bears closer examination to appreciate its distinctiveness more
completely.

The term *formation* can be troubling for some, as it could suggest
a process of indoctrination and of imposing external values in a

standardized manner intended to produce students from an identical mold, failing to recognize and enhance their unique gifts and aspirations. Within the military context, however, the term formation relates to the periodic gathering of the members of a unit for any number of reasons (e.g., accountability, training, information, etc.). This perspective allows that it can also be a term that is both positive and constructive.[83] Referring to formation from this point of view characterizes it as being a process of individual inculcation of certain intellectual, social, moral, and behavioral values to cadets as worth acquiring and living by on their own terms, and which equips them with the knowledge and skills to understand and interpret critically the world in light of these values, while also respecting their freedom to discern how these ideals can be embodied in the decisions they make about their own lives.

Within the context of a military school, cadets acquire, through the process of formation, a greater sense of purpose, agency (i.e., the ability to act, fostered through ownership, commitment, and engagement), and the ability and desire to have an impact on others and society in ways that are positive, constructive, and values-driven. The goal of formation in a military school is to help bring about completeness – *wholeness* – through a continuous process of development that is positive, constructive, supportive, and intentional. While a tall order, this is the concept of formation adopted by Gignilliat and implemented at Culver.

Assimilation and Formation Compared

Assimilation and formation are two distinct types of development. The main difference is one of intention. Assimilation will likely happen regardless of intent and attention, whereas formation requires deliberate attention and intent.

Assimilation is generally defined as adopting the ways of another culture and fully becoming part of a different society. When one assimilates, s/he accepts the ways of the host and becomes, through education and experience, a full part of the community and can earn his/her way into the host culture and be seamlessly accepted as full members of their new community. Formation is a more deliberate and intentional type of assimilation that is more concerned with *how* the process of assimilation occurs. While assimilation cannot by itself bring about formation, because of the nuanced nature of formation, the process of formation is based in part on assimilation.

Assimilation requires some engagement, but it is less intentional and more akin to an inexorable process of acclimatization, as one is surrounded by the culture being assimilated and has little choice but to accept and embrace it or be cast out. It is something done to an individual, regardless of his/her desire for it, and it is accepted largely as being an inevitable outcome. The outcome is not as predictable in terms of the level of assimilation and acceptance by those being assimilated, with some embracing the outcome completely and others demonstrating a superficial level of assimilation in name only. Reflecting the rather passive nature of it, historian Lance Betros referred to this approach as development through "osmosis."[84]

Formation, by contrast, is more intentional and mutual, and it requires a higher level of engagement. It is something done with the individual, who chooses to be formed, is a willing participant who is part of the process, and who aspires to become transformed int o that which s/he is being formed. The outcome is more predictable in terms of the level of inculcation and acceptance by those being formed.

While the process of assimilation is relatively consistent with that which occurs with minimal participation and can be fairly one-dimensional, formation is more of an iterative process that requires sincere engagement, active participation, and continual reappraisal via information.

In addition, formation requires that one be re-formed or refashioned again and again in order to experience a series of transformations that bring one closer and closer to one's ideal self instead of the institution's desired version of one's self. Equally as all-encompassing as assimilation, it too requires and results in the conversion of one's habits, character, attitudes, desires, and unique purpose. As journalist Thomas Hritz put it, the transition from an assimilation model to a formation model reflects change from a "You will" doctrine to more of a "Will you?" attitude.[85]

Formation – An Intentional Process of Assimilation and the Distinctive Difference

In Kegan's view, "people grow best where they continuously experience an ingenious blend of support and challenge" because "the balance of support and challenge leads to vital engagement " that serves as an "evolutionary bridge" which "fosters developmental transformation," described as a "process by which the whole (*how am I*) becomes gradually a part (*how I was*) of a new whole (*how I am now*).[86]

The campus – its classrooms, administrative offices, barracks, dining hall, chapel, and athletic fields – become the principal settings for the critical years of formation and development as adults. While some development occurs on its own with the passage of time and in response to various

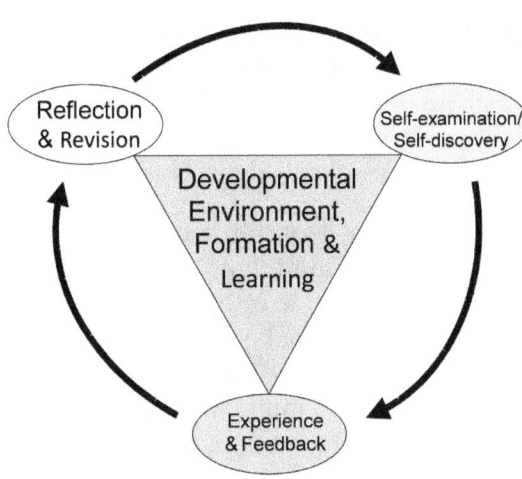

The iterative process of formation.

encounters, the process of formation – the intentional and deliberate shaping of a young person's being (identify and character) and worldview (including beliefs, virtues, values, and principles) – does not. Understanding what the institution needed to provide and how in needed to do so for this process to occur intentionally, effectively, predictably, and as intended, established the foundation for Gignilliat's system and his adoption (even if unknowingly) of formation as the process for implementing it at Culver.

Formation, therefore, has an intellectual, an individual, and a social component, requiring a whole-of-institution approach to its successful implementation. The intellectual aspect comes mainly through the learning processes that occur in classrooms. The individual aspect arises from the beliefs solidified and declarations made regarding a cadet's personal beliefs. The social aspect involves both the impact of living in community with shared values and the affirmation receive by the individual regarding internal conceptions that validate them and make them authentic.

Formation is best gauged by the quality of improvement, meaning that it is equifinal in that it can begin from many different starting points but that it has a finite number of acceptable outcomes (i.e., those that improve the quality of the whole within the parameters of the institution in which it occurs). When forming a tree, this means that it will not only grow but do so in a manner so that it is able to be healthy, bear fruit, and perpetuate its own existence.

The process of formation also emphasizes the essential roles of community and values in it, for which Culver was ideally suited and Gignilliat was quite fortunate. It also requires some level of willingness on the part of the cadet to embrace and support the process. Those few who made it through the close scrutiny of the admissions process and were unwilling and/or unable to do so found that there was no place for them at Culver and were quickly separated from the school.

The forward movement of the formational process is both iterative and cumulative, and the results become compounded as the three dimensions – intellectual, individual, and social -- coalesce into one and are manifested in the realization of more developed senses of identity, character, and beliefs.

As a process, formation occurs at different times for different individuals, at different rates for different individuals, and culminates at differing endpoints for each person. Because they are so disparate, dynamic, ever-changing, and unpredictable, the process must be flexible to allow for individual differences and outcomes, highlighting the challenges of incorporating such an approach into a structured military program. The diagram below illustrates the basic iteration of formation, of which there are many in this process that is both continual and continuous.

Formation, then, is primarily a dynamic process of willing integration that differs significantly from the more traditional method of forced and adversarial assimilation. It endeavors to engage cadets in a continuous developmental dialogue – occurring in the classrooms, drill field, athletic field, barracks, dining hall, and faculty offices, at social gatherings, scheduled meetings, presentations, and during athletics, informal exchanges, and casual encounters – in which they are both active and valued participants. It was used at and by Culver to give cadets "form" using discipline, education, example, and reinforcement to help them recognize and realize their own unique identity and purpose, while developing within them a more common notion of character and service.

It is important to note that many /most military schools of the era did not adopt developmental systems of formation, following instead West Point's lead and adopting/creating adversarial systems of assimilation based upon then-fashionable Darwinian notions of "survival of the fittest."[87] While such systems may have been appropriate for college-aged young men who willingly volunteered for them, they were wholly inappropriate for adolescent boys who may or may not have had a say in whether they attended such a school.

However, this distinction was lost on most individuals running secondary schools, captivated by the notion of creating their own smaller versions of West Point to turn high school cadets into polished graduates akin to the admirable gentlemen coming from the US Military Academy and for which parent were willing to pay.

Gignilliat's System and Culver's Progressive and Innovative Process of Military Formation

The process of formation used at Culver was designed and intended to help cadets progress toward the ideal of "completeness" in their own right and become well-formed persons of character who flourished and were able to go forth and help make the world a better place for all. Gignilliat's approach was far more appropriate for adolescent boys, allowing them to retain their dignity, enhance their own self-worth, and become the best versions of themselves at just the right time in their lives and in ways that adversarial programs did not or could not (and which caused lasting harm to many who went through them, even if/when successful).

The statement of purpose below sums up the main components of Gignilliat's approach concisely:

Forming, informing, and transforming the character, mind, and body of cadets in a caring community and disciplined environment of academic excellence and mutual respect that fosters moral citizenship, ethical leadership, and integrity for lives of purpose and service.

This approach fused the formation of intellect, identify, and character into a coherent and all-encompassing whole, and it used the educational setting and military system to inform all aspects of the process to lead to a transformation of cadets into graduates who will take seriously the challenge of living good and purposeful lives for the common/greater good.

In what later became Culver shorthand for it, this process may be summarized as follows: **Be, Show, Do**.

Be

- **Positive** – a belief in the fundamental goodness in human nature and the ability to remain upbeat

- **Constructive** – ability to be critical and caring, to focus on what matters and the bigger picture, to get the best out of one's self and others; not "*You're hopeless,*" but "*You can do better*"

- **Supportive** – manifest a sincere desire for success for self and others

Show

- **Dignity** – respect for self and others; not remaining distant, but keeping an appropriate distance from cadets, and always maintaining the self-respect of others

- **Differentiation** – awareness to select proper approach and adaptability to match behaviors to the situation, maturity level of those being formed, and to their individual differences; avoid temptation to homogenize and instead embrace diversity

- **Foresight** – ability to plan ahead, anticipate, and make the best and most ethical use of available means to achieve desired and moral ends with minimal risk

Do

- **Patience** – tolerance to allow others move at their own pace according to their ability while remaining supportive of their progress

- **Decisiveness** – acting with strong convictions, focused on definite purposes, and demonstrating command of one's responsibilities

- **Predictability** – ability to be consistent so others know what they can expect and produce anticipated result/outcomes; mood or feelings do not impact effectiveness and/or integrity.[88]

Under Gignilliat's leadership, the Culver community embraced the notion of formation explicitly in their approach, believing that virtuous people were formed (not made) through collaboration, example, and instruction over a long period of time and within a caring community. Under this system and Gignilliat's guidance, Culver engaged in the process of formation explicitly, viewing the process of cadet formation as intentional and deliberate, and requiring of a trusting relationship akin to that of a family to be effective and meaningful.

It was also guided by a shared vision of the qualities cadets *ought* to possess upon graduation. The work of implementing this system was noble and ennobling, and it allowed virtually all members of the community to be/become engaged in the efforts of helping cadets to thrive, flourish, and become the best version of themselves. This approach was as distinctive and innovative as it was effective and progressive, and it is a main reason for both Culver's and Gignilliat's renown.

An Influential Work That Did Not Achieve Commercial Success

Despite the value and effectiveness of the system it described, *Arms and the Boy* was not a bestseller by any measure, having one full printing of (presumably) 1,500 copies and selling a total of 1,297 copies. Nevertheless, the value of the book was less commercial (much to the chagrin of Bobbs-Merrill) than it was influential. In terms of longevity, the book remained in print for around 20 years and became *the* standard work in the field of military education during the first half of the 20ᵗʰ century. Its lasting durability and appeal allowed *Arms and the Boy* to continue drawing favorable attention to Culver throughout its long tenure in print.

While Gignilliat was successful in his aim to share his argument about the value of military training in schools with a wider audience as soon as possible in the pre-World War I period, the manner in which he did so was not as effective as it could have been. Containing much substance of considerable value, the style of presentation detracted from the message he worked so hard to convey. Gignilliat was a didactic educator who wrote a didactic book about a didactic system that he implemented using both didactic and experiential methods. Using this approach, Gignilliat wrote an unremarkable treatise in workman-like prose to convey an excellent philosophical argument regarding the value of military training in schools.

While this was perhaps appropriate for a how-to manual, Gignilliat's instructive approach detracted from his ultimate purpose by presenting the information descriptively and spreading it out across the entire work, which both diffused and reduced the power of his argument for the value of military training in schools.

It also shaped the structure and format of the book, making it less accessible, both to those interested in considering his more philosophical argument about the value of military training in schools and to those interested in learning about the more pragmatic aspects of implementing and/or conducting military training in schools according to Gignilliat's method. While the final form of the book may have felt right to Gignilliat, it was an unsuitable format to deliver the message effectively. The arrangement he used diluted his message, reduced the strength of his argument, and made it very hard for anyone to understand.

As had been the case since his days in at VMI in the Dialectic Society, while he was able to convey the substance of his argument effectively in person, the structure of *Arms and the Boy* skewed the substance in the written form and prevented readers from benefiting from the full power and persuasiveness of Gignilliat's ideas. This was particularly evident when addressing the mental value of military training and its ability to enhance both classroom learning and preparation for success in business. Presented together and as a collective whole, this argument is both potent and persuasive. However, presented as dispersed parts of a description of how to implement a military training program reduced its effectiveness, making it harder for the reader to grasp the crux of an argument spread across a number of chapters that is nowhere presented in consolidated form and as a coherent whole. If, as he had done with his speech to the Wisconsin Teachers' Association in November 1915, he had conceived of and written the book as an oral presentation he planned to deliver, it is likely that his book would have been both better received and more persuasive.

The Impact of the Truncated Pre-publication Editorial Process

One of the main reasons for the book's reduced effectiveness was that the process that helped him write his excellent contribution for *Types of Schools for Boys* was absent in the rush to complete the manuscript for *Arms and the Boy*. Gignilliat was a writer who benefited greatly from the input of others and the guidance of editors, and exchanges of this sort could have helped shape the manuscript in the positive, constructive, and supportive manner that had proved so beneficial to the *Types of Schools for Boys* project.

However, this process was conspicuously absent in the writing and publishing of *Arms and the Boy*, which impacted the resulting book negatively and detracted from its message. More specifically, Gignilliat's prose, the structure of the book, and the organization and presentation of the material were not nearly as effective as they could have been and should have been for a project of this scope and purpose. The haste to complete the manuscript and get it published as soon as possible overshadowed the substance of the work, and its effectiveness suffered accordingly.

In undertaking the writing of *Arms and the Boy*, Gignilliat expanded his contribution for O'Shea's *Types of Schools for Boys* from approximately 75 pages and 15,000 words divided among seven chapters to approximately 190 pages and almost 40,000 words divided among 18 similarly sized chapters, enlarging the manuscript by over 150 percent. Adding almost 25,000 words in the span of about three months while also running Culver and being heavily involved in preparedness activities equates to writing roughly an entire page of text each day (or at night, as Gignilliat attests) and is a truly astonishing achievement. In addition, Gignilliat collected an additional 30,000 words for the 142 pages included in the book's 22 appendices. Compared to his efforts for O'Shea's *Types of Schools for Boys*, Gignilliat in effect wrote more than three additional contributions of similar length, and that does not account for the effort expended to select and prepare the 80 illustrations included in *Arms and the Boy*.

Lacking the input and checks inherent in a disciplined editorial process, Gignilliat as an unconstrained writer allowed his "eyes to get bigger than his stomach" as he expanded the scope of the book beyond what was reasonable or advisable, the guidance he received from Bobbs-Merrill notwithstanding. As a result, during the halcyon first three months of 1916 when completing the manuscript, Gignilliat subsequently lost focus on the main purpose of the book, which was to present his argument on the value of military training in schools, and instead expanded its purpose, with Bobbs-Merrill's support and encouragement, to also provide information on how to start a military training program at a school. This development shifted his attention from presenting the most cogent argument possible and caused him to spend much of his already limited time in early 1916 unnecessarily collecting information for the book's appendices that was not essential to its central message and likely distracted from it.

It is likely that this occurred because of his involvement in the Preparedness Movement and the amount of time he spent responding to requests for information about how to start a military training program at various other schools. For example, his lengthy response to the Wabash College trustee regarding this very topic in mid-January 1916 both distracted him from completing the manuscript while simultaneously providing him with additional material for the book's appendices that was unnecessary and superfluous to his central argument.

This is not to say that the issue of helping other educators to bring military training to their schools was unimportant; rather, it was an essential part of Gignilliat's evangelization of this idea. However, this was a very different subject from addressing the existential value of military training in schools that appealed to a very different audience in a very utilitarian way. The functionality of the topic of how to bring military training to schools required an expository approach supported by myriad technical and specific details, much of which distracted the reader from Gignilliat's compelling argument for the value of military training in schools and detracted from its impact. Accordingly, Gignilliat did not need to and should not have elected to include it as part of his argument in *Arms and the Boy*.

The resulting book was "neither fish nor fowl," and while it contained much information of great value in both respects, the expository structure

Gignilliat adopted to present the material made *Arms and the Boy* more effective as a how-to manual than it was in accomplishing its intended purpose of presenting Gignilliat's argument for the value of military training in schools. This was unfortunate from a commercial sales standpoint, but Gignilliat's genius for marketing, willingness to promote the book's central argument, and active involvement in the Preparedness Movement ensured that the broader impact of *Arms and the Boy* was far greater than its modest commercial success.

Gignilliat used the argument regarding the value of military training in schools and the opportunity presented by the Preparedness Movement to spread his message and bring attention to Culver that was positive and beneficial. This argument was instrumental in helping to bring about the National Defense Act of 1916, which was the most substantial piece of militarily related legislation ever passed into law up to that point. As a result, Gignilliat quickly became one of the nation's leading figures in military education and education overall, helping to further bolster Culver's reputation as one of the nation's best military schools.

The Second Book Gignilliat *Should* Have Written: *Arming the Boy*

Instead of gratefully accepting the conditions under which Bobbs-Merrill agreed to publish his work as a separate book, Gignilliat should have insisted that Bobbs-Merrill publish his manuscript much as it was. The argument against expanding it as suggested was that it would detract from and dilute the value of the argument in the existing manuscript.

One suspects, had he been as involved in the production of *Arms and the Boy* as he was in Gignilliat's contribution to *Types of Schools for Boys*, that O'Shea would have advocated along these lines.

Had he had the continued guidance of O'Shea and availed himself to the editorial process of Bobbs-Merrill, one suspects, based on the process that occurred in the writing of Gignilliat's contribution to O'Shea's *Types of Schools for Boys*, that O'Shea and the editors would have had similar criticisms of *Arms and the Boy*. A reasonable suggestion would have been for Gignilliat to keep the focus of *Arms and the Boy* on presenting the argument regarding the value of military training in schools and to structure the work as a persuasive essay that would have been far more appropriate and effective in presenting the message, making it more accessible to and convincing for interested readers.

A work of approximately 200 pages would have permitted a much greater focus on Gignilliat's ideas regarding the value of military training in schools and allowed him to present his thoughts much more cogently.

Gignilliat would have certainly benefited from a more disciplined editorial process, and the resulting work would have surely been much improved.

To address the issue of how to bring military training to schools, Bobbs-Merrill should have allowed Gignilliat to write a second book. A volume of about 150 pages in length, supported by 25 illustrations, and divided into 22 short chapters (instead of appendices), would have been quite functional and procedural regarding how to start a military training program at a school.

This work could have been written in the more appropriate expository manner, used extensively in textbooks and how-to manuals and preferred by Gignilliat. Based upon Gignilliat's impressively rapid writing process in early 1916 to expand his manuscript, it appears that he needed less assistance when writing expositorily and could have proceeded largely on his own in this endeavor. To indicate its relation to the first book and suggest the continuity between the two volumes, the second work could have been cleverly titled *Arming the Boy*.

The advantages of such an approach would have been substantial. It would have allowed for the use of the appropriate writing style and structure to reach the intended audiences for each subject, making Gignilliat's ideas both more accessible and relevant. It also would have allowed Gignilliat to focus his efforts in early 1916 on crafting and presenting the most persuasive argument possible for his main purpose of supporting the value of military training in schools. Without having to devote precious time and energy to collecting the large and widely disparate amount of material for the unnecessarily large appendices for *Arms and the Boy* would have benefited Gignilliat greatly, giving him time to work with professional editors to improve his prose and arrange the book's material in a more effective manner.

While he may have still experienced the delay caused by having to wait until late-May 1916 for Newton D. Baker's foreword, it is possible that he could have completed the manuscript more quickly and thus negated this unfortunate lag altogether. This would have contributed positively and significantly to Gignilliat's desire to have *Arms and the Boy* published at the earliest possible moment, perhaps allowing it to be released as early as April or May of 1916, coinciding with the critical period of debate regarding the Hay/Chamberlain bill and exerting even greater influence.

Identifying the Specific Contributions of *Arms and the Boy*

These criticisms notwithstanding, *Arms and the Boy* was tremendously influential as a published work. One may characterize the more significant contributions of Gignilliat's *Arms and the Boy* as follows:

It provided a significant contribution to the debate surrounding the Preparedness Movement. Gignilliat used the manuscript as material from which he drew to support his many speeches and activities related to military preparedness. According to a review of the period's available literature, *Arms and the Boy* was the most referenced and likely the most substantial work produced regarding the value of military schools during the time of the Preparedness Movement and for the ensuing two decades.

It provided Gignilliat with the opportunity to testify before Congress on January 22, 1916 regarding the value of military schools. Gignilliat shared his efforts with other AMCSUS leaders and schools, often writing to request additional information for the manuscript and with offers to include aspects of their military training programs in *Arms and the Boy*. As a member of the AMCSUS Executive Committee, Gignilliat was on the team testifying before Congress on behalf of military schools. In addition, Gignilliat also used the manuscript as material to make the case for military schools to be considered as desirable sources of supply for officers for the burgeoning Organized Reserve Officer Corps.

It educated the new Secretary of War Newton D. Baker about Culver. Reading a draft of the book in May 1916 provided Baker with his first extended exposure to the Culver system, portraying it as one of the nation's premier military schools. Baker was so impressed with the institution that he agreed to write the introduction for the book. This positive engagement during the most critical period of debate in the Senate regarding the landmark National Defense Act of 1916 undoubtedly increased awareness of Culver within the War Department and also enhanced its reputation as a highly effective "essentially military school."

It helped to get the National Defense Act of 1916 passed into law by making the case for select military schools to be considered as desirable sources of supply for officers for the Organized Reserve Officer Corps and offering a way to compromise on the appointing of officers. Gignilliat made a forceful case that military schools designated by the War Department as "Distinguished Institutions" for three consecutive years and as a result of annual War Department inspections should be considered as legitimate sources of supply for reserve officers. The members of the Regular Army and the state militias/National Guard were at loggerheads regarding how best to appoint reserve officers. Gignilliat's solution was both elegant and practical, as it appealed to the members of the Regular Army, who could validate the qualifications of the cadets during their annual inspections, and to the states, since the designated "Distinguished Institutions" were all state-controlled and thus kept much of the appointing authority within the state. The debate regarding this particular aspect of the Hay Bill (which became the National Defense Act of 1916) coincided with Gignilliat's writing and publicizing of *Arms and the Boy*, making it almost certain to have had some level of influence among legislators considering the bill, given the high level of awareness Gignilliat was able to create for the book.

It helped to get Culver identified as one of the very first ROTC programs in the nation. The positive attention generated by *Arms and the Boy* with Secretary of War Baker and within the War Department for Culver as one of the nation's premier military schools resulted in Culver being designated as one of the first five institutions in the Midwest and one the first 20 institutions in the entire country authorized to host a unit in the newly created Reserve Officer Training Corps in November 1916.

It brought national attention to Culver by the very favorable reviews the book received across the nation in newspapers from Washington, DC; New York; Philadelphia; Atlanta; Springfield, MA; and Rochester, NY; along with Chicago, Indianapolis, and Cincinnati.

It enhanced significantly Culver's regional reputation. The numerous instances of Culver cadets providing excellent military training to other educational institutions in the Midwest during the spring and fall of 1917 served to solidify Culver' reputation as a premier military school and also to validate the effectiveness of the unique and ingenious Culver military system identified and explained in *Arms and the Boy.*

The increased attention and renown for Culver generated by Gignilliat and <u>Arms and the Boy</u> helped increase enrollment significantly so that by 1919, Culver had to build several new barracks to house its 728 enrolled cadets. Culver also experienced an increase of almost 50 percent in the number of cadets enrolled in Summer School for 1916, which equated to having well over 900 boys on campus for that period. This trend carried over to the winter school enrollment as well beginning in fall 1916, leading to a record enrollment of 744 cadets in fall 1920 that would not be surpassed until after World War II.

Characterizing *Arms and the Boy* as a Literary Work

Containing much information regarding both citizenship and leadership, it is a bit of a stretch to characterize *Arms and the Boy* as the country's first adolescent leadership manual. It certainly provided much in the way of instruction and advice in how to lead in a military environment, but this information was presented by treating leadership as more of an active and functional component of the larger ideal of citizenship upon which Culver and other military schools focused. It is, therefore, legitimate to conclude that *Arms and the Boy* provided readers with much in the way of "doing," which, in an Aristotelean sense, would lead to the development of habits of leadership that were both virtuous and excellent.

Considered in this manner, *Arms and the Boy* might best be characterized as a work promoting *applied citizenship*, incorporating the methods of a military system and peer leadership to achieve its objectives. Had it made no other contribution, this aspect alone made the work both innovative and unique. However, *Arms and the Boy* made many other contributions that allowed it to be of significant value when published and remain relevant for many years thereafter.

Chapter 12 – Preparing Culver and Himself to Answer the Nation's Call to Arms in 1916 and 1917

In conjunction with his work on the *Arms and the Boy* manuscript and publishing efforts, Gignilliat also became increasingly involved in military preparedness activities that would help get Culver, CMA cadets, and himself to answer the nation's call to arms that appeared to be coming increasingly imminent.

The 1916-1917 winter school session opened on September 20 with 522 cadets enrolled, an increase of 57 from the previous year. Over 80 percent of the old men returned, indicating a continued high level of retention. The increased enrollment also spurred the construction of two additional academic buildings (English and Math), along with what would become a state of the art 212 x 104-foot indoor swimming pool called the natatorium. With large Gothic windows and "resplendent with white and green tile," it was over four times larger than the average school swimming pool and perhaps the largest campus pool in the country at the time of its dedication during the 1917 Thanksgiving holiday.[1]

A Visit to the Plattsburg Military Camp and to Washington, DC for an AMCSUS Meeting

Gignilliat embarked on an adventure that took him on an automobile trip to the East for, among other things, a visit to the Plattsburg military training camp that was held in early September 1916. While there is no record of his impressions of the event, it is clear that Gignilliat made every attempt to involve himself in as many preparedness events as possible during this period.

The next month, Gignilliat left Culver to attend an AMCSUS meeting in Washington, DC scheduled to occur during the two-day period of October 20-21, 1916. The reason for convening this meeting was likely due to the government's impending announcement regarding the establishment of the Reserve Officers Training Corp (ROTC) across the nation, allowing for AMCSUS representatives to meet with members of the War and Navy departments to discuss the programs. It is also likely that Gignilliat discussed *Arms and the Boy* with fellow AMCSUS members meeting and visited with members of Congress during the trip.

Culver Becomes the Nation's First High School Army ROTC School

Despite not experiencing the commercial success for which he had hoped with the marketing and sales of *Arms and the Boy* in November of 1916, the influence of *Arms and the Boy* helped Gignilliat experience one of the greatest achievements on behalf of Culver while he was in Washington, DC that same month.

On November 15, 1916, Culver Military Academy, already acknowledged by the War Department as an "essentially military school," was designated as one of the nation's first five military schools in the central region of the country recognized as "Army training schools" under the new National Defense Act of 1916. This important designation established Culver as one of the first ROTC programs in the country.[2]

Culver shared this distinction with Purdue University, The Ohio State University, South Dakota State College of Agriculture and Mechanical Arts (now South Dakota State University), and St. Thomas College in Minneapolis, MN. In achieving this recognition, the War Department

Culver cadets training for trench warfare. [4]

acknowledged that Culver and the other designated institutions had "fulfilled the requirements necessary to come under the national defense act," and the schools possessed the equipment and ability to provide standardized instruction equivalent to the training provided by the United States Military Academy at West Point. It is significant to note that Culver was the only purely secondary institution to receive this distinction.[3]

Given the type and intensity of training conducted at Culver, the government's designation was understandable, made sense, and was widely supported. Going far beyond the typical drill-and-ceremonies approach of many military schools, designed to keep cadets busy and train them to parade well in public (if little else),

Culver cadets conducting open-warfare training. [5]

Culver's approach, based upon the program Gignilliat developed while serving as Commandant that had brought national recognition to Culver and which he continuously revised and refined, was far more extensive. It included both theoretical and practical subjects covering the full range of Military Art and Science as practiced at the time.

Based soundly on the best and most relevant literature, Culver cadets learned and practiced the very latest tactics and techniques developed in the active Army and elsewhere. Examples of training exercises regarding trench warfare and General Pershing's preferred "open-warfare" tactics appear below, attesting to the advanced nature of Culver's military training program and curriculum at the time of its designation as one of the first senior ROTC programs in the country.

The Army determined that it would divide its training schools into two divisions: a senior division for higher education institutions, and a junior division for secondary education institutions. The programs at Purdue, Ohio State, and South Dakota A&M included only infantry units designated as being included in the senior division, and the program at St. Thomas College had an infantry unit designated as being included in the junior division, as it was comprised of high school students.

In a remarkable decision made with the knowledge that it was a college preparatory school and also reflecting the proficiency and breadth of its military program, Culver was designated as having units devoted to the training of infantry, cavalry, and the field artillery in the senior division, and an additional unit devoted to the training of infantry in the junior division of the ROTC program. This noteworthy designation provided explicit recognition by the War Department that Culver was regarded by the Army as fully equal to the nation's military colleges (akin to schools like VMI), highlighting further the national esteem the school enjoyed. Reporting this achievement with justifiable pride to ER Culver, Gignilliat wrote that "our long fight to win for Culver equal recognition with the colleges in the matter of establishment of Senior Units of the Reserve Officers' Training Corps has finally been won."[6]

The orders also indicated that as many as 20 to 25 more schools would be designated by the War Department as "Army training schools" in the near future. Given this extraordinary designation, Gignilliat offered to ER Culver that, "It is now of course up to us to show that we deserve what we have fought for."[7] Accordingly, Gignilliat set about making additional changes to Culver's military training program to those he had already made in winter 1915-196 to ensure the school remained worthy of the special recognition it had just received, for which it had worked so hard to acquire, and that it was determined to maintain.

Coming out at least seven months earlier and having been circulated in galleys and advance sheets during the very height of the debate regarding the Hay Bill, Gignilliat's own *Arms and the Boy* attracted far more attention for the intended audience than one could have ever hoped for O'Shea's *Types of Schools for Boys*. Acquiring the influence he desired it to have as a result of the timing of its release, Gignilliat could be satisfied that his decision to strike out on his own and have his contribution published earlier and as part of a larger work of which he was the sole author was indeed both correct and fortuitous for him and for Culver.

Leigh Jr. – A Chip Off the Old Block

During the fall of 1916, Leigh Jr. was elected as editor-in-chief of the *Roll Call* (Culver's yearbook), following in his father's VMI footsteps. In another type of similarity, Leigh Jr. was also promoted to the rank of cadet captain and elevated from serving as an adjutant to command of Company B. However, unlike his father's demotion from cadet captain, his son retained his captaincy throughout the year.

1917 – A Pivotal Year for Gignilliat and Culver

A New Level of Influence: Gignilliat, Preparedness, and the Coming of the World War

Gignilliat re-engaged in his preparedness activities beginning in January 1917. On January 20, Captain Edgar Steever arrived at Culver to coordinate military training for all high schools in the Midwest that desired to incorporate it into their curriculums. While responsible for the military training in high schools across the entire Midwest region, Gignilliat arranged for Steever to base his operations out of Culver, an arrangement that was likely desirable and advantageous for both men.

Preparedness in High Schools, ROTC, AMCSUS, and HSVUS

In recognition of the War Department's December 1916 acknowledgment of "the soundness of Steever's ideas" and the practicability of applying them nationally, the Secretary of War assigned Steever to oversee the implementation of his program within high schools in the Midwest. Seizing on the opportunity this assignment presented for Culver, and based upon his own admiration for Steever, Gignilliat worked during the latter half of 1916 to persuade the Army's leadership to assign Steever to Culver to serve as his base of operations.[8]

Gignilliat's efforts were successful, and the Secretary of War ordered Steever to report to Culver on January 1, 1917 to take charge of the installation of military training in the public schools of the US Army's Central District, commanded by General Thomas Barry. Steever arrived at Culver on January 20, 1917 with a staff of 20 (four officers and 16 NCOs), where he was welcomed by Gignilliat and supported by the Culver family.

In terms of its contribution to national defense, the High School Volunteers of the United States (HSVUS) program provided the middle component of civic preparation and training for boys in high school that began in the Boy Scouts during primary schooling and continued in the ROTC/SATC in college. Gignilliat had been involved in the development of the Boy Scouts of America and also in the development of the ROTC, so basing the HSVUS out of Culver made immanent sense for many reasons. The HSVUS thus completed the civic training continuum for boys by linking the BSA of elementary schools with the ROTC/SATC of college.[9]

Upon his arrival at Culver, Steever wasted little time getting started. Steever's first action was to sponsor a conference at Culver on January 27, 1917 to introduce the HSVUS concept to representatives from high schools from Chicago, Kansas City, St Louis, and "such other centers as he could reach," which included South Bend, IN and a few other locations in northern Indiana. Representatives of high schools from seven different states attended the meeting, and Steever and his staff introduced the program as intended. [10]

As noted previously, the Wyoming Plan used competition as a way to make military training appealing to teenaged boys, with the wall-scaling competition serving as a centerpiece of this approach. Students formed teams and competed to see which team could get all of its members over the wall in the shortest amount of time. Emphasizing teamwork, planning, and tactical decision-making, the brilliance of this exercise was that it was a relatively low-cost way to provide training that was not overtly military in nature to high school boys in a way that it not only appealed to the boys but which was also transferable to both future military and non-military training. With his innate ability to recognize what appealed to teenaged boys, Gignilliat was captivated by Steever and the Wyoming Plan, and he had already incorporated its approach successfully into thew 1916 high school boys' military training camp.

A charismatic presenter imbued with the zeal of a true believer, Steever's initial presentation was very effective, generating both excitement of his idea and momentum for his efforts.[11] Very soon, the Wyoming Plan had gained purchase in Chicago, Kansas City, St Louis, as intended, along with Detroit, Cleveland, and Denver.[12]

In Cleveland, Ohio, for example, Steever and his assistant, Lieutenant James G. Ord, met with educators in the Cleveland school district on February 28, 1917 at the request of the school superintendent to present their military training program. Ord spent the ensuing week working with the district's high schools to explain the program and help them begin implementing it. Under his guidance, the school district hired a retired Army officer to put the program into action. The district conducted five weeks of very successful training beginning on May 1, 1917 using teachers with prior military service and/or who had attended military schools to provide the training.[13]

By June 1917, Steever had either established military training under the HSVUS program or transitioned existing organizations to provide HSVUS military training in at least 91 schools across 18 states and territories.[14] Gignilliat remained a staunch support of both Steever and his program, and Gignilliat was appointed as president of the HSVUS in May 1917. Sadly, he never had the opportunity to become truly active in it because he was called to active duty that same month. Due to his absence, he was replaced as the HSVUS president by someone not on active duty.

The day prior to the initial HSVUS conference, January 26, 1917, Reserve officer training began in the senior division at Culver. Focused on Culver's juniors and seniors, the training moved beyond the basic military training that all Culver cadets had mastered and began introducing concepts of military leadership and advanced military topics to the cadets.[15]

Intended for college-aged juniors and seniors, Gignilliat was determined to demonstrate that Culver juniors and seniors, although younger than their college-aged counterparts elsewhere, were more than capable of mastering the senior course of instruction with the same high level of proficiency that they had demonstrated with the junior course material.

On the day that Reserve officer training began in the senior division at Culver, Gignilliat was away from campus attending the AMCSUS annual meeting in Washington, DC. During this meeting, which occurred during the period January 25-27, 1917, Gignilliat presented an address to the members present titled, "Military Training in the Essentially Military Schools and Colleges." Likely drawing heavily from the content of *Arms and the Boy*, Gignilliat took advantage of this opportunity to share his ideas with his military school colleagues from across the country.

While some – and perhaps even many – present were familiar with the contents of *Arms and the Boy*, hearing the ideas expressed by Gignilliat in person must have been quite welcome and almost certainly generated a lively and engaging discussion among those present. Coming in the wake of the beginning of the nation's ROTC program and the AMCSUS special meeting in October 1916, AMCSUS members surely appreciated the opportunity to discuss Gignilliat's ideas, along with the larger issues related to military preparedness across the country.

Returning to Culver for a week, Gignilliat embarked on a trip with Steever around north central Indiana the next week to present and promote the Wyoming Plan of military training. They spent the period of February 5-10, 1917 visiting the towns of South Bend, Mishawaka, Goshen, Elkhart, Michigan City, and Valparaiso, meeting with high school administrators and teachers and bringing awareness of both military preparedness and Culver to each location.

This trip turned out to be particularly well timed, as the United States Army's Punitive Expedition in Mexico searching for Pancho Villa and followers came to end on February 7, 1917. While the expedition itself was not successful, it served to highlight the importance of military preparedness for the country regarding a threat not related to the war raging in Europe.

Having just returned from Washington, DC and conferring with military professionals who undoubtedly shared information about this expedition with him, Gignilliat likely had ample knowledge and opportunity to complement Steever's presentation with information that was both real-time and of immediate relevance to the audiences they addressed. Being informed in this manner made Gignilliat quite comfortable, and it is almost certain that he engaged with audiences more willingly during the course of this trip.

Captain H.L. "Lawrence" Durborow, Culver's director of academic coordination, had an article published in early March 1917 in the influential education journal, *The School Review*, published by the University of Chicago. Durborow's article, "Preparing While We Wait," addressed the value of military training in high schools. According to Durborow, the three most important advantages of doing so were the access to large numbers of young man provided by high schools (almost half a million men by his reckoning), the openness to instruction and appeal of challenges demonstrated by high school students, and the positive impacts that military training has on the physical development of teenaged boys.

Durborow also remarked on the positive influences military training has on the development of character and citizenship, and that it could be part of an effective developmental continuum for both beginning in the Boy Scouts, continuing into high school, and culminating in either post-high school military training or service or military training in college. All would serve to help America be and become better prepared for the challenges of modern, industrial warfare.[16]

Durborow's article was spectacularly well timed to provide support and reinforcement for all of Culver's preparedness activities. In addition, the substance of Durborow's article clearly reflects the thoughts and influence of Gignilliat. The final three pages of the article echo many of Gignilliat's main points, including a championing of Steever and his Wyoming program, the effectiveness of the country's honor military schools, the partnership between the Chicago public schools and Culver in the area of high school military training, and Culver's efforts to provide high school camps for military instruction, all predicated on Gignilliat's lodestar that military training can be and is effective for high school boys when delivered properly. In fact, for all its similarities in terms of content and tone, Gignilliat could have written the second half of Durborow's article himself.

In addition, Gignilliat kept up a constant stream of speakers on campus to address preparedness. Following investigative journalist S.S. McClure's absorbing talk on the situation in Europe on December 2, 1916, famed war correspondent Frederick Palmer spoke on February 7, 1917 regarding the Battle of Somme. Upon their return from the presidential inaugural, the Superintended of VMI, General Edward W. Nichols spoke on the general topic of preparedness on March 11, 1917. Thus did the drumbeat of preparedness continue sounding on campus.

The 1917 Presidential Inaugural

President Woodrow Wilson's second inauguration was a much more subdued affair for several reasons. The first was that it occurred during a period of tremendous international crisis for the US, as diplomatic relations with both Germany and Mexico were quite strained. Germany's decision to resume its practice of unrestricted submarine warfare in the Atlantic Ocean against all ships – merchant and passenger – sailing under the US flag on February 1, 1917, caused America to break off diplomatic relations with Germany two days later. The release of the Zimmerman Telegram to the American public on February 28, 1917, and its public confirmation by its author, senior German Foreign Service Officer Arthur Zimmerman, on March 3, 1917, exacerbated America's foreign relations with both Germany and Mexico.

This message was a coded telegram sent January 16, 1917, by German foreign secretary Arthur Zimmermann to the German minister in Mexico, announcing Germany's intention to resume unrestricted submarine warfare and proposing the formation of an alliance with among Germany, Mexico, and Japan if the United States declared war on Germany. Germany promised to return territory taken from Mexico by the US as a result of the Mexican American War of 1846-47 in return for joining the proposed alliance.

Intercepted by the British and passed on to the United States, both proposition s – the resumption of unrestricted submarine warfare and the return of territory to Mexico – outraged the American public when the terms of the proposed alliance were made public, and the American people demanded action.

American relations with Mexico had been strained since 1914, when the US attacked and occupied Vera Cruz in response to the Tampico Affair, which involved the unlawful arrest of nine US sailors. The Mexican government provided limited support for the US Punitive Expedition in response to Pancho Villa's March 9, 1916 raid into New Mexico, and US troops had only recently departed Mexican territory in late January 1916. At the time of the release of the Zimmerman Telegram, Mexico was involved in a civil war and its government was unstable, which were two of the main reasons it rejected the German offer.

Japan, already fighting on the side of Allies, also rejected the German overture, but the brazen nature of it caught America by surprise. The deliberate timing of the British release of the telegram exacerbated the tensions further.

Woodrow Wilson, along with his Vice President, Thomas R. Marshall, was sworn in for his second term of office as President of the United States in a private ceremony on March 4, 1917, and the public ceremony occurred on Monday, March 5, 1917 in Washington, DC. As they had done in 1913, the domestic women's suffrage movement staged a very peaceful and visible protest, taking up positions outside the White House holding signs demanding the right to vote. Conflict occurred between the women and the crowds in town for the inauguration, and press coverage of these clashes eclipsed coverage of the inauguration festivities themselves. It was with this period of crisis and heightened tensions that Wilson's second inaugural took place. It was, as one might expect, not a time that lent itself to celebration.

Based upon their wonderful experience in 1913, enthusiasm for the corps' trip to Washington, DC for the inaugural ran high on Culver's campus. Determined to prepare the cadets to get the greatest educational benefit from the event, and as he had done in 1913, Gignilliat initiated a series of lectures to orient the cadets, most of whom had not been on the 1913 trip, to the city and the sights they would see and the things they would experience. Compared to 1913, the plan for 1917 was for much more flexibility for cadets, who, having proved themselves worthy of such trust, would be allowed to venture out in squad-sized groups.[17]

Reviving the concept of 1913, Culver used two separate trains for the trip. Captain Rossow and 90 horses departed early on the morning of March 2, 1917 on the first train, and then 90 percent of the corps participating in the event departed a bit later that same morning after breakfast on the second train. While the first train with the horses continued on to Fort Meyer (near Washington, DC, where the horses would be stabled), the passenger train stopped for dinner in the midst of a snowstorm at the Penn Hotel in Pittsburg (as they had in 1913). The passenger train traveled through the night and arrived in Washington, DC on Saturday, March 3. The cadets spent the day getting settled in the Ebbits Hotel (where they had stayed in 1913), taking care of the horses, visiting with the many alumni staying at their hotel, doing some local sightseeing, and attending a theater performance that evening.[18]

Only two wives accompanied their husbands on this trip. Minnie came along to support her husband, as did the wife of another faculty member (Mrs. Hand). None of the trustees came with the cadets, but Knight K. Culver met the group in Washington, DC and hosted an alumni gathering.[19]

After attending religious services at the Church of the Covenant on Sunday morning, the cadets spent the rest of the day preparing for a parade and formal review by the Secretary of War, Newton D. Baker, and the US Army Chief of Staff, General Hugh L. Scott, at 3:30 that afternoon. The review went very well, but the storm and snow they had encountered in Pittsburg arrived in the form of a driving rainstorm, making the clean-up from it more demanding. The cadets spent the evening of March 4 ensuring that all was ready for the next day's inaugural parade.[20]

Most of the next day, Monday, March 5, was devoted to the inaugural parade itself. The cadets rose early, ate breakfast, and then attended to their uniforms and equipment, while the members of the BHT also prepared their mounts for the ride. Culver provided eight mounted riders as flank guards for Vice President Marshall's carriage, with the remainder of the BHT following immediately behind. Seated with Marshall was his wife, wearing the cavalry cape presented to her by the BHT in 1913.[21]

Close behind the BHT was the Culver battalion, marching with approximately 400 cadets divided into four company-mass formations. In a change from 1913, Gignilliat marched at the head of the Culver battalion instead of riding with the BHT.[22]

The parade itself was quite an ordeal, as the weather was particularly unpleasant. Strong winds and slashing rain pounded the cadets throughout the entire route of march, and it was a point of pride that the cadets' lines remained as straight and true as they were during garrison parades in better weather on campus.[23]

Given the somber period during which it occurred, Wilson decided not to host an inaugural ball. Vice President Marshall, however, had planned for some time to host a ball that evening in honor of Gignilliat, and his soiree became the most highly desired social event of the festivities.

The CMA battalion marching in the 1917 Presidential Inaugural, March 5, 1917. [24]

After recovering from the ordeal of the parade, seeing to their horses and equipment, and cleaning themselves up, the cadets arrived at the Willard Hotel for the Vice President's Ball. They were delighted to learn that they were outnumbered by the girls brought in for the event, and they sent word to the members of the BHT to join them as soon as possible to even the odds! The cadets danced until well after midnight, enjoying themselves immensely.[25]

The next day was filled with visits to the Smithsonian Institution, the Bureau of Engraving, and a very brief trip to Annapolis for those who were interested. Several social events occurred that evening, and the cadets had their choice of which and how many to attend. Knight Culver also hosted his alumni gathering that evening, and many cadets found their way to this event to visit with friends.[26]

The main event on their final day was a visit to Mount Vernon, after which they returned to their hotel to prepare for the trip home. Members of the BHT saw to their mounts, and the remainder of the cadets packed their gear and made their way to the train station, where they departed at about 8:00 pm. Minnie did not return with the Culver group, as she had planned to remain in the area for about a month to visit with relatives. She would return in time for the Easter carnival at the end of the first week of April (6-9) 1917.[27]

Arriving at Pittsburg for breakfast at the Penn Hotel, the entire group closed on Culver in time for dinner on Thursday, March 8, 1917. It was to be the last somewhat carefree episode for many of the participants, as America would enter WWI within one month of their return.

While somewhat somber, it appears that the cadets enjoyed the event and were proud of their performance. According to the review of the year's military activities in the 1917 *Roll Call*, "from a merely local standpoint the trip to Washington stands out prominently," noting that "Culver made a showing in the inauguration which will long be remembered by all those who witnessed the work of the Battalion and Troop."[28]

The Zimmerman Telegram, Unrestricted Submarine Warfare, and the Coming of War

The month of March 1917 was characterized by increasing tension between the United States and Germany, exacerbated by Britain's release of the Zimmerman Telegram in late-February 1917. In anticipation of Germany's plan to resume unrestricted submarine warfare beginning on February 1, 1917, the German Foreign Secretary, Arthur Zimmerman, sent a message to the German ambassador to Mexico, Heinrich von Eckhardt, to prepare him for the impact of this decision, which would almost certainly lead to war with the United States. Combined with the sinking of three other American ships in February 1917, calls for action in response to the German sinking of American ships become increasingly strident.

The impact of Germany's resumption of unrestricted submarine warfare on American shipping proved to be the final straw for both Wilson and the American public. After an extended period of discussion and debate, Wilson went to Congress on April 2, 1917 asking for a declaration of war against Germany. Congress responded, and on April 6, 1917, "after twenty-nine months of official neutrality, the United States declared war on Germany, formally entering World War I."[29] Suddenly, all of the attention regarding the country's military preparedness had an immediate level of relevance and urgency that was undeniable.

Gignilliat Renews His Efforts for More Marketing Effort from Bobbs-Merrill

As he had at the beginning of January 1917 (unsuccessfully), Gignilliat tried once more to entice Bobbs-Merrill to invest more resources in the marketing effort for *Arms and the Boy*. On March 23, 1917, he sent Bobbs-Merrill a design he had created for a window display cut-out for *Arms and the Boy*. Believing once again that "now is the vital time when we ought to be able to boom a tremendous circulation for this book," Gignilliat hoped that Bobbs-Merrill would produce the striking cut-out display that he felt certain was "unique enough to guarantee book sellers putting it in their windows, and that people will stop to look at it and study it," thus resulting in increased sales of the book.[30] Armed with the initial sales figures for the book, however, Bobbs-Merrill again demurred.

This episode makes clear that Gignilliat was determined to promote the book at almost any cost, and that he refused to accept the Bobbs-Merrill decision to limit promotional costs based upon sales revenue. This determination is likely indicative of Gignilliat's belief that promoting the book would bring about the increase sales desired by Bobbs-Merrill, and it exposes the belief by Bobbs-Merrill that they had promoted the book sufficiently and that the disappointing sales figures indicated that *Arms and the Boy* was simply not selling as well as Gignilliat and Bobbs-Merrill had hoped it would. This disagreement would continue and come to a head in April 1917.

Suitably rebuffed but far from defeated, Gignilliat embarked on his own marketing effort by reinvesting some of the royalties he received into purchasing copies of the book that he sent to those who he believed needed and would benefit from it. It is evident that Gignilliat was not intending to profit monetarily from this endeavor and that he cared little personally for the royalty payments he collected. Gignilliat sent a total of 43 copies of the book to individuals of his own choosing.[31] He had negotiated to receive ten copies of the book for free as part of the contract, meaning that he paid for the cost of at least 33 additional copies, along with the cost of shipping.[32]

In a copy of the statement making payment to Gignilliat for the first royalties generated by *Arms and the Boy*, Bobbs-Merrill subtracted a total of $21.64 for costs associated with "merchandise" that was presumably copies of the book, leaving $173.06 as the amount Gignilliat received from Bobbs-Merrill for his first royalty payment produced by sales of the book during the period August 10 – December 31, 1916.[33]

Both the subject matter of *Arms and the Boy* and the urgency with which Gignilliat sought to disseminate its message proved to be quite prescient in spring 1917. In the state of unpreparedness in which the country found itself as it began considering seriously the impact of going to fight in a total, modern war overseas, the War Department focused on the need to enlist, train, and lead at least two million young men who were to be called to arms.

Culver and Its Cadets Contribute Directly to Preparedness in Spring and Fall 1917

Despite the 1916 effort to recruit and mobilize a volunteer cavalry regiment in response to the Pancho Villa raid not coming to fruition, the effort associated with this venture must have generated a high level of response and been a positive experience for Gignilliat. According to Gignilliat, "Prior to the announcement of the Government's plan for the conduct of the war and before the plan had been made public for the creation of a national army [in which he was to serve for much of the war]...the Academy" gave "considerable thought to the means by which the services of men who had been trained at Culver might most effectively be made available to the Government (sic)."[34]

Gignilliat recalled that Steever and Howard Wheeler, the editor of *Everybody's Magazine*, suggested that forming an entire 25,000-man division "for which the company [grade] officers might be supplied by former Culver Men (sic) and field [grade] officers from Regular Army, and the men recruited through the efforts of Culver alumni, might be" a feasible and effective way to put the training of Culver men to its best use on behalf of the US government.[35] As with the plan for the raising of a Culver regiment in 1916, this endeavor also mirrored a similar but more ambitious effort by Theodore Roosevelt to raise a total of four volunteer divisions (one of which he would command), which was essentially an entire corps (to be commanded by Leonard Wood) and equating to around 100,000 volunteers.

Gignilliat contacted alumni throughout the country in early spring 1917 to gauge the level of interest in such an endeavor. Considering that this tentative call to arms occurred prior to America's entry into WWI (but during the tense period in early 1917 that preceded it), Gignilliat was quite gratified by the "immediate and enthusiastic response" he received in writing from almost 1,000 Culver men eager to participate.[36]

Armed with this level of support, Gignilliat presented his plan to form what would be an essentially Culver division to place at the government's disposal to the US Army's Assistant Chief of Staff, General Tasker H. Bliss, in the latter part of April 1917 after America had formally entered the war. By Gignilliat's recollection, "General Bliss explained the plans of the Government (sic), which very wisely eliminated all consideration of volunteer units and premised the organization of the vast army needs for America's participation in the war on the draft and a thoroughly coordinated and highly developed national scheme of defense" created by the National Defense Act of 1916.

As a result, the "plans for a Culver volunteer division were thereupon abandoned and alumni who had expressed interest in such an organization were urged to enroll in the first series of officers' training camps or to join one of the regular services or the National Guard," all of which were options pursued by many Culver men.[37] Gignilliat closed his recollection of this endeavor by offering that "such a division, if it had been created, and permeated with the spirit and tradition of the School (sic), might have written a glorious page in the history of the War (sic)."[38] As becomes evident, Gignilliat certainly had the organizational ability to pull off such endeavors, and testimony for those who accompanied him on the 1920 world Boy Scout jamboree attest to this.

Steever and (especially) Wheeler (who was an ardent preparedness supporter) were likely following the lead of Theodore Roosevelt, who had been advocating for and actively recruiting to create up to four volunteer divisions for the US war effort. Modeled on the "Rough Rider" volunteer regiment in which he served and ultimately commanded during the Spanish-American War, Roosevelt envisioned the creation of up to four 25,000-man divisions, with him in command of one and all ably staffed and led by experienced military men.

As one would expect, Roosevelt made his efforts known to the public, reporting that he was receiving word from around 2,000 men daily regarding their willingness to serve in such units. Wilson and the War Department opposed Roosevelt's efforts on personal (mostly for Wilson, who considered Roosevelt to be his archenemy) and mobilization (mostly the War Department) reasons, and they rejected Roosevelt's offer.

For the War Department, it was mostly based on its desire, after two decades of planning, to conduct a systematic mobilization that placed the right people in the positions in which they could do the most good for the country (and which was largely antithetical to the volunteer approach).[39] Thus, while the War Department had discounted the nation's tradition of raising volunteer units in times of crisis based upon its desire to conduct an orderly mobilization and in recognition of the complexity of the demands of leading men on the modern industrialized battlefield, it is evident that the spirit of volunteerism and belief in the American citizens' innate ability to fight was alive and well in the country in spring 1917.

Besides providing evidence of Gignilliat's tendency to think big and his penchant for action in times of crisis (as mentioned above,) both episodes are also indicative of the final vestiges of the pre-war struggle between the pull of the romantic past (i.e., support for volunteerism and the ability of the untrained American citizen to fight well in times of need) and his pragmatic realism evident in his constant theme of "proper military training" required to produce effective citizen-soldiers. The first indication of the pull of romanticism on Gignilliat appears in his knee-jerk reaction that led to the Big Fire, which was far more indicative of a romantic influence of his past (i.e., VMI) experience than a more pragmatic consideration of the existing situation (i.e., need to retain students to remain financially solvent). As became evident, when romanticism won out it was not for the best.

The next episode appeared in his decision to send Culver cadets to Logansport, which was a blend of the romantic and pragmatic that turns out better. This struggle was also evident in his personality as a desire to avoid calling attention to himself in the old tradition of a gentleman and embracing his introverted side and a need to be/become a public figure to support causes (preparedness) and bring positive attention to Culver by being/becoming more of an extrovert (but never a self-promoter). Again, the pragmatism of the latter won out after a prolonged struggle. This conflict was resolved in WWI in favor of a grim pragmatism with respect to military training, but its impact on him is undeniable during the period 1900-1917 (and it appears after the war regarding Culver, as will be address in subsequent chapters).

A Patriotic Offering of Culver to the US Government

During the week of April 23, 1917, when he went to Washington, DC to offer the Culver division to General Bliss, Gignilliat along with Culver Legion President Cal Chambers (representing the Culver alumni) called upon Secretary of War Baker (who both knew and was known by Gignilliat as a result of writing the Foreword for *Arms and the Boy* a year earlier) to present the Trustees' offer to place all of Culver's facilities "at the disposal of the Government."[40] The Army declined Culver's offer, believing that Culver could best serve the nation by continuing to provide military training to young men not yet of sufficient military age.[41]

The Navy, however, accepted Culver's offer and began making tentative plans for a training camp for 1,000 naval recruits from the Great Lakes Naval Training Center (north of Chicago) on the Culver campus. This camp was to be led by Read Admiral Albert Ross, who was ordered to report to Culver on April 30, 1917 to organize the camp. The plan envisioned using CMA first-class cadets and younger alumni to serve as drillmasters, which was right in line with Gignilliat's idea of effective military leadership. According to Gignilliat, "shortly before the camp was to open an epidemic of contagious diseases broke out at the Great Lakes Naval Training Station from whence the recruits were to be transferred and the Navy Department postponed the project" for what turned out to be an indefinite period of time. Admiral Ross remained at Culver over the summer before departing to serve as the "General Inspector of all naval training camps and stations in the United States"[42]

Closer to campus, Culver cadets provided remarkable evidence of their superb abilities as trainers during April and May of 1917, serving as military instructors at several locations. Cadets who volunteered for this duty "were placed on 'detached duty' for periods of two weeks to replace Regular Army military instructors who were being withdrawn from duty at the high schools."[43]

The specific results were quite impressive and included the following accomplishments:

Senior Captain James H. "John" Denny.[45]

- As a direct result of the process of writing *Arms and the Boy* (when replying to a request for assistance from a Board member of Wabash College), first class cadet and Senior Captain James H. "John" Denny provided military instruction for approximately 270 cadets at Wabash College during the three-week period April 28-May 18, 1917.[44]

- As a direct result of Gignilliat's efforts to publicize *Arms and the Boy* in Chicago, twelve Culver cadets provided military training for around 3,000 cadets in the Chicago public high schools for several weeks in May 1917.[46]

- As a direct result of the attention Gignilliat received regarding his efforts to bring attention to the Preparedness Movement and *Arms and the Boy* in Indiana, first class cadets Jack Schneider and Bob Anderson provided military instruction for approximately 400 cadets at DePauw University during the two-week period April 28-May 12 1917.[48]

- As a result of his success at Wabash College in spring 1917 and the renown gained for

CPT Steever with cadets selected to train high school students in Chicago.[47]

Culver by Gignilliat and *Arms and the Boy* in Chicago, Culver graduate James H. "John" Denny, with the help of 5 other Culver graduates, organized and supervised the training of about 3,000 cadets in the Chicago public high schools during fall 1917.[49]

The magnificent performance of these Culver cadets helped to both spread and solidify Culver's reputation within the Midwest as a premier military school and also to validate and confirm the effectiveness of Culver's military system.

Demonstrating the Value of the Culver Military System and the Impact of *Arms and the Boy*

The month of May 1917 saw both Gignilliat and Culver cadets putting their training into practice, but in roles that were somewhat reversed. The Culver cadets became the trainers, and Gignilliat assumed the role of a trainee as he began the process of qualifying for an active Army commission. In each instance, the value of Culver's military system was quite evident and the performance of those who had benefited from it was extraordinarily impressive.

By spring 1917, *Arms and the Boy* was also enjoying a substantial amount of influence. After being reviewed favorably in the *New York Times* in October 1916, the book attracted international attention. The idea of using methods to develop their youth that were positive, constructive, and supportive apparently terrified the German leaders, and they reacted accordingly. Presenting a developmental approach diametrically opposed to the Prussian method of unquestioning obedience embraced and used by the German army, *Arms and the Boy* was banned in Germany within eight months of its publication.[50] Coming around the time that American declared war on Germany, this development served to bring further renown to Gignilliat, Culver, and *Arms and the Boy*, especially as the author and his graduates prepared, along with the rest of the country, to go "over there" to Europe and fight in the World War.

Gignilliat Largely Completes the "Greater Culver" Construction Efforts by Spring 1917

As mentioned previously, the Culver family announced their strategic plan – the "Greater Culver" plan – in March 1909 as a way of ensuring that CMA remained in the front rank of all military schools in the country. The plan reflected the Culver family commitment to provide between $300,000 - $400,000 to the school over a five-year period to fund a series of strategic improvements to the Culver Military Academy facilities and campus, along with supporting high school training programs on campus,. In practical terms, this manifested in the form of additional building and more and better equipment for the academic, military, and athletic programs.

It was Superintendent Gignilliat's job to implement this audacious plan, monitor its progress, and ensure that it achieved its desired objectives, all of which fit perfectly with Gignilliat's temperament and training. The construction endeavors related to this plan were extensive and began on campus in 1910 with the new 90 x 130-foot state-of-the-art Mess Hall (with seating for over 1,000), and included the building of the new powerhouse, Admin Building (with the iconic Sally Port), and North Barrack in 1913; the major re-landscaping of the campus by Jens Jensen in 1915; the new Cavalry building and BHT herd (as a result of the late-October 1915 fire that destroyed the original herd and the existing stables), the new English and Math buildings and the new rifle range in 1916 ; the new Arsenal and 60 x 120-foot ultramodern Natatorium in 1917; and concluded with the completion of the new 104 x 212-foot best-in-the-nation Riding Hall in 1918 (construction on which began in March 1916 and cornerstone laid June 7, 1916).

Gignilliat's Call to Active Duty

Gignilliat received word from the War Department soon after America's declaration of war that he would soon be called to active duty to serve the nation. This call involved receiving the formal military training prescribed for all officers in the Organized Reserves Corps (ORC) established by the National Defense Act of 1916 before assuming his official duties. This training would be conducted at one of 16 regional camps established around the country. For Gignilliat and other ORC officers at Culver, this meant that his first duty station would be Fort Benjamin Harrison near Indianapolis.

The Army's plan was to train the officers for the newly created units first, in summer 1917, before having the drafted soldiers muster to receive their training. This meant that there would be two 90-day Officers Training Camps (OTCs) in summer 1917, with the most experienced of the ORC officers attending the first OTC scheduled for the period May-August 1917. Initially scheduled to begin on May 1, the start date was pushed back one week, and Gignilliat's orders had him reporting to Fort Harrison on May 8, 1917.

Given all that was going on at Culver and with his other preparedness activities, this gave Gignilliat little time to put his affairs in order before reporting for training. He was just able to complete the Alumni training camp for a little over 100 Culver graduates (now known as the Culver Legion) that occurred on campus during the period April 21 – May 5,

1917 and get the second alumni military refresher training camp started on April 30, and accompany the CMA corps to South Bend for a patriotic parade that had over 10,000 spectators cheering for them on April 21, 1917.

Gignilliat was also able to get the first week of training under way for the 600 high school boys from ten states (IA, IL, IN, KY, MI, MO, OH, PA, WI, WV) who were all part of the HSVUS and part of its first military training camp. Named Camp Thomas H. Barry (in honor of General Thomas H. Barry, who commanded the US Army's Central Department within which Culver was located), the two-week training camp began on April 30, 1917. Culver's own Major Harold C. Bays was in charge of the camp, and Captain Steever was the training officer. CMA cadets served as the officers for the camp, and NCOs came from the HS boys participating, all of which was very typical of organizational structures designed by Gignilliat.

The HSVUS Becomes a National Entity

Using the popular *Everybody's Magazine* (akin to today's *People* magazine) as a platform, Howard Wheeler, the editor of *Everybody's Magazine*, and influential journalist George Creel brought the message of the high school military preparedness to the people by their support and sponsorship of the HSVUS. Both Creel and Wheeler reflected Gignilliat's respect for boys and belief that they possessed a higher sense of responsibility regarding duty and patriotism than was normally acknowledged.

In the preface to *The Cadet Manual: Official Handbook for High School Volunteers of the United States*, Creel wrote that there was not a "hint of militarism" associated with the HSVUS, which provided a "safe foundation upon which national defense of democracy may be rested." Characterizing it as "working naturally as part of the educational plan" for young citizens as "merely a phase of the civic obligation," the system allowed boys to train as they grow into manhood to become trained defenders of the nation.

Assuaging concerns that such training would transform the male youth of America into Prussian militarists hungering to put their military training into practice by making war when and where possible, Creel observed that Steever's system presented the training that was a natural part of the normal education plan for boys in a manner that was both consistent with American values and which also avoids making it akin to Prussian military training for its youth that produced the "blood thirsty Huns" fighting against the Allied powers in Europe.[51]

Wheeler went even further, contending that Steever's approach represented "Wyoming's answer to militarism," arguing that "the final answer to militarism is Better Citizenship," which the Wyoming Plan promoted in the simplest and most direct manner in ways that were both appealing and effective to teenaged boys.[52] Steever adopted as the slogan for his program, "For Better Citizenship," in a move that was both astute and worthy of Gignilliat's own prowess in such matters. Besides being a deft move, the substance of the slogan surely appealed to Gignilliat for the very same reasons Steever adopted it.

Like Gignilliat, Steever was convinced that his system also developed leadership, writing in the HSVUS handbook that the training provided in military drill "improves good leadership and makes poor leadership good" if done properly.[53] Reflecting Gignilliat's own commitment to leading by example, Steever wrote that, rather than teaching others how to execute a drill properly using "long-winded orations, explanations, or recitations of the text of the drill book," the effective leader "jumps in and shows the man or men in error how to do it" properly, which is an active form of instruction that is far more effective with teenaged boys.

Recognizing as well that mastery takes time and that expertise is built up steadily over time, Steever also relates that, when teaching drill, "the natural leader is satisfied at first with the effort made, rather than perfection of the execution." Using a "show the way" methodology, Steever was confident that leaders could increase proficiency in their charges and improve performance steadily over time with direction that was positive, constructive, and respectful.[54]

Morning inspection during 1917 Army Annual Inspection. [55]

Given the many similarities between the Culver system and Steever's Wyoming plan, the respect for boys and attention to detail demonstrated by Steever, the spirit of competition ingrained into his approach, the positive, constructive, and example-based leadership approach he advocated, and his ability to connect positively with boys and train them effectively, it is little wonder that Gignilliat both respect ed and admired Steever as a peer and colleague.

The training camp at Camp Barry in spring 1917 was in many ways the culmination of work that began in February 1916, when *Everybody's* published an article extolling the virtues of Steever's training program, titled "Wyoming's Answer to Militarism." As mentioned previously, Gignilliat was appointed as president of this organization in May 1917, but his call to active duty prevented him from serving in this capacity.

The 1917 Army Annual Inspection

Gignilliat was also present for the 1917 Army annual inspection, conducted by Colonel Julius Penn during a cold and rainy two-day period of May 4-5, 1917. In fact, when Gignilliat paraded all of the cadets he was training on campus during the inspection – including 446 CMA cadets, 584 high school cadets, and 106 alumni – Colonel Penn had 1,136 cadets pass by him in review!

As had become the expectation, CMA again passed the inspection with flying colors and retained its designation as one of the Army's "honor institutions" and premier military schools in the nation. According to Colonel Penn's official report of the inspection, after witnessing the cadets' "excellent" conduct of guard mount, close-order drill at the battalion and company levels, extended-order drill at the company level, along with troop, riding, artillery, aiming and sighting, and wall-scaling drills, the inspector concluded that the cadets' marching and "set-up" (i.e., posture and bearing) "presented a credible appearance," and that the instruction the cadets both received and provided was both "splendid" and "commendable." In the reserved vernacular of the Army of that period, this evaluation conveyed the highest praise for the work of the cadets.

Regarding the staff, Colonel Penn singled out Captain Steever and his assistant (Lieutenant James G. Ord), and "the authorities of this institution" for special commendation for their excellent work and "enthusiastic, liberal financial, and patriotic efforts to encourage military instruction in High Schools (sic)." Colonel Penn noted that Culver was "splendidly equipped," especially in terms of facilities, and recommended that "every encouragement should be given to this School (sic) in the way of equipment." Highlighting the "systematic plan" being followed that will ensure that Culver remained "a splendid monument to its founder," Colonel Penn closed by noting that Culver was "helping in every way to further national preparedness." Such a determination certainly pleased both Gignilliat and the Culver family, as it affirmed the focus of their efforts over the previous decade to establish and maintain the school at the head of the high school military preparedness movement in the nation.[56]

This remarkable number of cadets and alumni receiving training at Culver in early May 1917 is a fitting testament to all of Gignilliat's tremendous efforts during the period leading up to America's entry into the Great War. Combined with being named as the president of the newly established High School Volunteers of the United States (HSVUS), it is difficult to imagine how anyone could have done more to promote an effective military training system for high school boys or on behalf of Culver and military preparedness during this period.

Gignilliat's Departure from Campus

Satisfied that he had done all he could to leave Culver in fine shape, he, along with at least 19 other members of the Culver faculty and staff, began turning over their campus responsibilities to those who would shepherd their beloved institution in their stead while they answered the call to the colors. Gignilliat himself was particularly gratified that the talented Hugh Glasscock would serve as Acting Superintendent in his absence, assisted by the dependable Bert Greiner as Commandant of Cadets.

Confident that his beloved institution was in capable hands, Gignilliat made his own final arrangements for his extended departure from campus. On May 7, 1917, Gignilliat was given a rousing send off by the entire community, He departed campus with four other officers also called to active duty for Fort Harrison, and headed toward a new adventure as a 41-year-old military officer trainee.[57]

1917 Commencement and Leigh Jr.'s Graduation from Culver

Gignilliat managed to return to Culver for one brief visit during the weekend of June 2-3, 1917. He had the opportunity to bid farewell to the corps, particularly the first classmen who would be graduating on June 7, 1917, but it must have been especially difficult for him to realize that he would miss Leigh Jr.'s graduation and passage through the Iron Gate.

Leigh Jr. graduated from Culver on June 7, 1917, as one of 96 graduates. The ceremony was notable because it was the first since 1897 for which Gignilliat was not present. Instead, it was Hugh Glasscock who gave the corps its final order for the 1916-1917 school year : "Dismissed!"

Leigh Jr. had amassed an enviable record at Culver, of which both he and his father were justifiably proud. It must have been difficult at times to be the superintendent's son and live up to the expectations many had for him. However, it appears that Leigh Jr. was more than up to the task, making a name for himself as a scholar, leader, and overall capable member of the corps. He was a very successful cadet, and he achieved many of the same distinctions as his father had at VMI during his final year, except that Leigh Jr. concluded his time at Culver on a much more positive note than had his father at VMI.

Leigh Robinson Gignilliat, Jr., circa 1917. [58]

In his entry in the 1917 *Roll Call*, one of his classmates wrote, "In Leigh Gignilliat we have the personification of energy as well as a whole string of other enviable virtues."[59] Leigh Jr's Culver career was characterized by steady progress in all areas, earning the highest possible rank in the military system, lettering in two varsity sports (football and basketball), and being elected as the editor-in-chief of the *Roll Call* and Secretary of the Hop Club (two notably important activities at Culver), all of which speak to his dedication and determination. He was recognized for his overall excellence at graduation with the alumni medal for excellence in scholarship and athletics as the athlete having the highest cumulative grade point average, and he was one of two cadets (along with 1917 Senior Captain James H. "John" Denney) recommended for commissions as second lieutenants in the US Army.

Leigh Jr. was quite well-rounded at Culver, earning two medals for wall-scaling and being active in the French and Mandolin clubs during his final year. Handsome and well-liked by his peers, he made his own way at Culver and was quite successful in all of his endeavors.

His 1917 *Roll Call* entry concluded as follows: "In every department Leigh has made good and leaves behind him a sterling record and a multitude of friends." He was indeed the personification of the ideal "Culver man,"

A Roll Call yearbook cartoon depicting the hard-working Cadet Leigh Gignilliat Jr.[60]

and the respect he had earned from both his peers and the members of the faculty and staff was evident during the 1917 commencement ceremonies.

Freddy was also thriving at Culver, completing his third-class year. He earned promotion to corporal in F Company as was elected as class treasurer. An accomplished athlete, Freddy played on the varsity basketball, tennis, and crew teams as a sophomore. He also played on the championship company football and baseball teams, along with the company hockey, track, bowling, and gym teams. As he had done the previous year, he won both singles and doubles company tennis championships. In addition to his athletic

Leigh Jr. in his final year at Culver. [61]

endeavors, Freddy was also active in the YMCA and participated in the wall-scaling competitions.[62]

There was much for the Gignilliat family to be proud of in the early summer of 1917, but their attention was almost surely directed toward Fort Harrison, where Colonel Gignilliat was being put through his paces as an officer candidate and aspiring active-duty Army officer. In the coming year – 1918 – his two older sons would join him in active military service, leaving Minnie and Hank free to rejoin Gignilliat as he continued preparing for the Great War.

Chapter 13 – Combining Voice and Action: Entering Active Duty, Training for War, & Fighting in the Great War, May 1917-July 1919

Part 1: Entering Active Duty and Training for War, May 1917-October 1918

Major Gignilliat (center) and his Culver staff on the eve of The Great War.[1]

After being so intensely involved in activities associated with the Preparedness Movement for several years, it came as no surprise when Gignilliat was notified in late-April 1917 that he was being called to active duty in the wake of America's decision to join the fighting in Europe.

Despite being a military school graduate, the officer's commissions Gignilliat held during the 19-year period 13 January 1897- 13 December 1916 were granted by the Governor of the state of Indian a and were not federally recognized. This meant that his authority as an officer extended to only those areas authorized by the governor of Indiana, which was limited largely to the Culver Military Academy corps of cadets and to the Indiana militia. On December 14, 1916, Gignilliat was commissioned as a Major in the newly created Officer Reserve Corps (ORC).[2]

This was the first federally recognized commission Gignilliat held, and it meant that his authority became much broader and extended from the limitations of his state-issued commission to the larger US Army. However, before the US Army would allow him to exercise this broader authority, Gignilliat would first have to prove himself both capable of doing so and worthy of such recognition by attending and successfully completing one of the recently instituted Reserve Officer Training Camps.

Despite having held some type of military officer's commission for almost two decades, Gignilliat had very little formal military training since he departed VMI over 20 years previously. Accordingly, the prospect of a

42-year-old man undergoing a demanding program of training with others who were almost half his age and making a good showing of himself must have produced equal measures of anxiety and excitement in Gignilliat.

Not only was Gignilliat unsure of what to expect when he reported to the First Officers Training Camp at Fort Benjamin Harrison (near Indianapolis) in early May 1917; the US Army was hurriedly implementing a brand-new method of training and assessing officers that it had never before used (or even attempted). As the Army implemented its mobilization plans, it would become readily apparent that despite the high levels of uncertainty among all involved in the process, both Gignilliat and Culver graduates were particularly well prepared for the demands of the officer training they completed.

Mobilization for the Great War and the New National Army

To mobilize a force large enough to meet America's objectives, Army planners determined that they would need to create a wholly new force for WWI. The Army used relevant provisions of the recently passed National Defense Act of 1916 to create the new National Army (NA) for WWI. This force worked off the same dynamic as the volunteer units, taking advantage of the enhanced zeal for military service that arose during times of crisis, but it focused instead on providing units for the massive number of conscripts called into service for this emergency and known as "citizen soldiers." Based upon its existing force structure and its projections for the size of the force it would need, the Army determined that it would need to create 16 National Army divisions.

To populate these new units, America turned to the draft. The WWI draft was designed to be very fair, and there was no opportunity to "buy out" of a draft notice like what had existed during the draft for the American Civil War. As a result, the attitude of the NA division soldiers was one that embraced the notion that every man had an equal chance for promotion to the ranks of the NCOs and officers charged with leading the organizations, producing a tremendously egalitarian spirit that viewed authority only in terms of necessity.

This rampant egalitarianism served as a leavening agent among the soldiers and created what some called "the real American melting pot." According to one author, "men from every class and social distinction... met as equals" in the NA units.[3] In many ways, this was a new model army born of the Progressive Era.[4] As a new model army, it would require a very different type of leadership to be effective.

Since the draft conscripted men from across the entire country, the Army established 16 cantonments – one per division – to serve as bases to mobilize, house, and train these new units. The regionally affiliated National Army divisions were based in newly established cantonments spread across the country and populated with men from the surrounding regions.

The Citizen-Soldiers of the National Army

The citizen-soldiers of this new model army prided themselves as being willing citizens of a democracy. They were all too happy to serve their country, and they expected to be recognized as citizens and led accordingly. For the officers of this new army, this meant that they would have to lead the citizen-soldiers of the National Army in a decidedly more "democratic" fashion.[5] One of the more significant manifestations of this approach was the expectation that leaders would share with their men the reasons for their orders along with the orders themselves.

Cognizant that they were leading fellow citizens and not professional soldiers, the leaders of National Army units could not and did not use the example of the Regular Army as a template for instilling discipline in their men. Believing that, "The citizen-solider of a democracy is entitled to understand the cause in which he fights, and the reasons and principles underlying the policy of the government, the very essence of the citizen-soldiers' relationship with Army leadership was fundamentally different."[6] Instead of relying solely on the formal authority granted them by the government, as their Regular Army counterparts were able to do, leaders of the National Army had to ground their authority in a carefully cultivated and somewhat fragile sense of trust sustained between leader and led.

In place of a rigid and unbending form of obedience, the citizen-soldiers of the National Army viewed discipline as something to be agreed upon rather than imposed, requiring techniques that were at once more persuasive and manipulative to gain compliance. Whereas the Regular Army could largely command obedience, National Army leaders had to negotiate it.[7] Faced with this situation, leaders searched for ways to persuade, rather than coerce, their citizen-soldiers to comply with their directives.[8] Realizing that "informed dedication to a cause was necessary for it to succeed," officers in the National Army relied more upon persuasion to gain the willing compliance of their military subordinates.[9]

Viewing this approach as little more than a social experiment, Regular Army veterans like General Pershing were quite skeptical that it would be effective on the battlefield. For those tasked with leading the men of the new National Army, however, there was no question that it was essential, and they had to find ways to make it equally effective.[10]

An organization considered by some to be a social experiment based upon a premise of leading citizen-soldiers democratically and also expertly must have appealed greatly to Gignilliat, as it was almost exactly the type of organization for which Gignilliat had designed Culver to produce leaders. Accordingly, it is little wonder that the Culver training he provided set Culver graduates up for success as young leaders in the National Army units.

Leading the Citizen-Soldiers of the National Army

To lead these National Army divisions, the Army needed to find a way to train and commission almost 100,000 officers for its expanded army.[11] The Army had never done anything like this, relying in the past on men commissioned in the militia and from the ranks of the Regular Army in the lower three ranks (Second Lieutenant, First Lieutenant, and Captain) and direct commissions of qualified specialists to provide junior officer leadership in times of crisis.

With mobilization of National Army units scheduled to begin in September 1917, the Army needed to create camps to train the large number of officers needed to organize, train, and lead these units in time for the new officers to be ready by the beginning of September 1917. Thus, the Army determined that it would sponsor a series of Officer Training Camps (OTCs) over the summer and fall of 1917. The first of these OTCs was scheduled to begin in early May 1917 at multiple locations across the country, with the goal of commissioning 25,000 trained officers in the grades of Second Lieutenant (O-1) to Major (O-4).

Referred to by at least one military officer as the "West Point" of the National Army, the Army's OTCs were crash courses designed to prepare civilians to become junior military officers in three-months' time.[12] Beginning with a physical assessment, these camps trained officers in the fundamentals of military operations in the basic arms – infantry, artillery, and cavalry – and assessed both their capability to perform and fitness for leadership.

Making Officers for the National Army

With the declaration of war on April 6, 1917, the nation began its process of force mobilization in earnest. The attention paid to acquiring officers to lead this large force over the previous decade was finally able to be put into practice. Within two weeks of the official declaration of war, the Adjutant General of the US Army, H. P. McCain, sent a telegram to

Army senior leaders informing them that the Army was establishing its First Series Officer Training Camps (OTC) in May 1917 and searching for "the 10,000 ablest leaders...from the whole country" to be mobilized and trained at these OTCs to prepare them to "officer the first half million troops."[13]

In a letter to Army senior leaders dated April 17, 1917, McCain provided specific guidance from the Secretary of War for the composition of the first OTC. According to McCain's letter, "Attendance at the proposed camps will be limited to the following citizens:

(a) Reserve officers.

(b) Members of the Reserve Officers Training Corps over 20 years and 9 months of age.

(c) Other students over 20 years and 9 months of age who are members of Cadet Corps.

(d) Graduates of military schools who are over 20 years and 9 months of age and under 44 years of age.

(e) Other citizens over 20 years and 9 months of age and under 44 years of age who are acceptable under paragraph 5 of the letter from The Adjutant General's Office...."

Paragraph 5 allowed applicants with little or no military training who "demonstrated in business, athletics, or other activity that he possesses, to an unusual degree, the ability to handle men" to be considered for a commission as a second lieutenant provided he was between the ages of 20 years and 9 months and 32 and was "a college graduate, or senior in college, or clearly a well-educated man." Regular Army officers were given wide latitude in selecting individuals they felt satisfied the Secretary of War's criteria and told to satisfy themselves "to the best of [their] ability" that the applicant was physically fit enough to serve as an officer, "procuring the aid of an Army medical officer or civilian physician if practicable" to assist them in their assessments.[14]

For its First Series OTC, however, the Army sought to find these leaders from an "experienced class of men" over the age of 31 who possessed exceptional mental and physical energy, along with an ability to instruct, manage, and lead the men assigned to the new units for which they were being developed.[15] The rationale for targeting more mature men was based upon the anticipated need for "officers who [could] be given higher grades when additional forces [were] organized."[16]

In addition, the Army encouraged "professors of military science and tactics to send their best men of suitable age," and urged college authorities to consider graduating immediately those seniors who had been selected as candidates for these camps.[17]

Once assembled, McCain's letter provided additional guidance for the conduct of the camps.

> *The first month in camp will be devoted to basic infantry instruction and instruction in those duties of officers that are common to all arms. At the end of the month those in attendance will be classified on the basis of past experience, aptitude, etc., and prorated among the arms (Infantry, Cavalry, Field Artillery, Coast Artillery, Engineers), and in each arm they will be divided into groups in such manner that there will be one group for each regiment, to be organized under the plan existing at the time of this division of the groups. The course for the last two months will be formulated accordingly.[18]*

The Army published a more detailed schedule for the First Series OTCs on May 5, 1917. Participants were expected to train for a minimum of 10 hours on each day of scheduled training, "usually 5 hours in the morning, 3 in the afternoon, and 2 for study in the evening." Training occurred Monday through Friday, with at least five hours on Saturday being used to bring "up to requirements work which has been interrupted by weather or other unforeseen conditions...and for additional instruction in such matters as the experience of the particular school renders advisable."[19] Sundays were left open as days of rest.

Looking to have the camps ready for the reception of selected reserve officers and candidates by May 1, 1917 to enable training to begin on May 8, 1917, and despite earnest efforts to meet these deadlines, the Army had to postpone these deadlines by one week. Accordingly, Gignilliat received his orders to report to the First Series Officers Training Camp on May 8, 1917, but the training did not begin until the following week on May 15, 1917.[20]

Gignilliat as an Officer Candidate

Reporting for duty at the age of 42 years old with a reputation for high levels of physical energy, mental acuity, and a gift for instructing and leading young men exceptionally well, Gignilliat fit almost perfectly the Army's desired profile for the initial officer candidates. More specifically, at 42 years of age when called to active duty, Gignilliat met at least two of the requirements specified for the First Series Officer Training Camp:

He was at the time commissioned as a major in the US Army Reserve over the age of 20 years and 9 months; and he was also a graduate of military school who was under 44 years of age.

Departing Culver on the morning of May 7, 1917, Gignilliat arrived at Fort Benjamin Harrison later that day with four other officers from Culver called to active duty, including Captains Rockwood, Miller and Elliot, and Lieutenant Watson. He was immediately put to work issuing uniforms, assisted by the others who had accompanied him. They worked 20 hours a day for two days issuing uniforms to others arriving at the camp. A muster formation of at least 5,000 men occurred on Wednesday morning, with most wearing the uniforms they had been issued by Gignilliat and his helpers.[21]

The more militarily experienced Rossow was amused by what he considered to be a rookie mistake of reporting in too early and paying the price for doing so by being put to work. Rossow waited at Culver and did not report until later in the week, avoiding much of the busy work that Gignilliat and others had to perform.[22] In all, at least 20 members of the Culver faculty and staff served on active duty during the war.[23]

A series of screenings recurred for the remainder of the week to ensure that those reporting for training met the criteria established by the Army. Having been judged physically capable during his first week on active duty, Gignilliat was accepted into the First Series OTC at Fort Benjamin Harrison. This meant that he began his period of active duty by undergoing the 90-day training program required for all Reserve officers – even those, like Gignilliat, who had attended a Plattsburg-style training camp previously – desiring active duty commissions in the grades of Second Lieutenant through Major at the First Series Officer Training Camp (OTC) conducted at Fort Benjamin Harrison in Indianapolis during the period May 15 – August 14 1917.

The training would challenge the officers "brains and courage" to determine if they had the physical and mental for the rigors of combat and the unprecedented challenges of modern industrialized warfare.[24]

Soldiers training at Fort Benjamin Harrison around the time of the First Series Officers Training Camp, 8 May – 15 August, 1917.[25]

Based upon a War Department directive of April 17, 1917, sixteen First Series OTCs were established at posts where new divisions would be formed to train approximately 25,000 officers in the grades of Second Lieutenant through Major. Beginning in mid-May, the idea was to complete the training and commission the new officers in mid-August 1917, just in time for them to meet the first groups of recruits reporting for training in late-August and early September.

The First Series OTC training was divided into two periods: a five-week first period; and an eight-week second period. The first period was devoted to drill, classroom instruction, practice marches, and evening study. It culminated with a small amount of field work devoted mostly to patrolling. Drill occupied most mornings and accounted for almost 30 percent (81.5/275 hours) of the training.

It consisted of calisthenics and instruction in basic soldiering, including the manual of arms, rifle marksmanship, bayonet and saber training, and semaphore signaling. Candidates were also instructed in the tactical employment of the squad, platoon, company, and battalion. Classroom instruction occurred mostly in the afternoons and accounted for about 23 percent (64/275 hours) of the training. Topics covered included reviews of the Army regulations, field service regulations, infantry drill regulations, guard duty, studies in minor tactics, and small unit tactical problem-solving. Early morning practice marches occupied 9 ½ hours, and evening study consumed another 46 hours of the candidates' time. In aggregate, this accounted for roughly three-quarters of the candidates' training time. The remaining 25 percent (66.5/275 hours) was devoted to administrative requirements (issuing equipment, physical exams, required paperwork, etc.), barracks maintenance, and additional training.[26]

Gignilliat managed to return to Culver for a brief visit during the first phase of training. Spending a very short time on campus during the weekend of June 2-3, 1917, he had just enough time to bid farewell to the corps, realizing that he would not be present for the following week's commencement festivities and would miss Leigh Jr.'s graduation and passage through the Iron Gate.

The second period of the OTC was devoted to more branch-specific training. Despite being a trained engineer and a superb horseman, Gignilliat remained with the infantry training program. For him and the other infantry officer candidates, this meant advanced training in marksmanship, tactics, and field work, along with classroom instruction regarding the roles and capabilities of cavalry and artillery. Weeks six through twelve followed much the same schedule as weeks one through five in terms of structure, culminating with a four-day field exercise.[27]

Candidates for commissions in the cavalry, artillery, and engineers followed separate programs of instruction during the second period, each of which also culminated with a four-day field maneuver exercise during week thirteen, presumably conducted in conjunction with all four programs operating together.[28]

The program of training, while of questionable effectiveness for the conditions they would face on the modern industrialized battlefields in Europe, was quite familiar to Gignilliat, as it consisted of much of what was taught at Culver. The training included "learning wig-wag and semaphore signaling and reenacting Civil War combat problems," all of which were emphasized in Culver's military training program.[29] Having incorporated such training into Culver's own military training program as the foundation of its decade-long "honor school" status, it is no surprise that Gignilliat demonstrated an easy mastery of most, if not all, of the required OTC tasks.

Despite the chain-smoking of his later years, Gignilliat was also apparently quite physically fit at this point in his life. Gignilliat commented that some of the older businessmen with whom he trained at Fort Sheridan and observed at Plattsburg were always "puffing and blowing" and "giving every unmistakable evidence of increased respiration as well as increased circulation" when engaged in mock battles and bayonet training.[30] Exhibiting almost inconceivably high levels of energy and stamina had been a hallmark of Gignilliat's deportment since he arrived at Culver in 1897, and the ensuing two decades had done little to reduce either quality or slow him down in the least, as his truly remarkable 90-day period of achievement during the first three months of 1916 had demonstrated compellingly.

In contrast to other men of his age, Gignilliat began most days with a vigorous session of horseback riding, which, along with the hiking and other physical activities that were part of his duties at Culver, combined to produce a level of fitness somewhat remarkable for a man of his age and during this period.

As a result of his familiarity with the subject matter, proficiency demonstrated during the training, high level of physical fitness, and experiences at Culver, Gignilliat excelled in the training. He impressed several of his West Point-trained instructors who were also professional officers. One of the instructors he impressed was the 27-year old Second Lieutenant Charles L Bolte (later a four-star general), who admitted that he was often little more than a half-day ahead of his charges in terms of the technical knowledge he was responsible for teaching them.[31] Gignilliat's base of knowledge in most areas was, by contrast, far greater, and as a result of his superb performance in the First Series OTC he was promoted to the rank of lieutenant colonel in the National Army infantry on August 15, 1917.[32] This is all the more impressive when one realizes that 17 of the 151 men assigned to his training company failed to complete the training, all of whom were far younger than Gignilliat.

The OTC was intended to commission officers in the ORC in the ranks of second lieutenant to major. Since he had shown himself to be worthy of a commission as a lieutenant colonel, Gignilliat was commissioned instead in the National Army.[33] This was the highest rank conferred upon any officer in the United States Army coming through the First Series OTC.[34]

Earning the only commission as a lieutenant colonel was remarkable. The Army received approximately 150,000 applications for the First Series OTC and selected approximately 43,000 for attendance, for an acceptance rate of around 29 percent.[35] Of those selected, 27,341 completed the training successfully, for a completion rate of approximately 64 percent.[36] This means that over two-thirds of the applicants were not selected, and over one-third of those accepted did not complete the training, making Gignilliat's success all the more impressive.

The First Series OTC at Fort Harrison not only allowed Gignilliat to demonstrate his own military prowess, it also served as a proving ground for the training program Gignilliat had designed and implemented at Culver. Training with him at Fort Harrison were 161 Culver men, many of whom made their mentor proud by excelling at the training as well.[37] In total, 511 Culver men attended the First Series OTC at one of the 16 locations at which it occurred.[38]

Newly promoted LTC Gignilliat, USA, congratulates Culver men who completed the Army's officer training and earned Army Reserve commissions, August 15, 1917.[39]

On the occasion of his graduation from the First Series Officer Training Camp and promotion to lieutenant colonel, Gignilliat had the pleasure of congratulating some of the Culver men who had also proved themselves to be very capable officers at the Fort Harrison OTC.[40] Many of these Culver men earned commissions as lieutenants and demonstrated the effectiveness of the Culver system that Gignilliat had designed and implemented.[41] Gignilliat looks sincerely happy in a contemporary photograph taken of this meeting, and having the opportunity to share this moment with some of his young graduates surely made the recognition he received for his own individual accomplishments more meaningful and satisfying.

In the months to follow, thousands of Culver graduates entered the ranks, with a vast majority serving in the US Army. However, Culver graduates also served in the US Navy and the notoriously selective US Marine Corps. Along with driving ambulances in the American Volunteer Services and enlisting in the state militias, Culver graduates also served in the armies of Canada, Great Britain, and France. Beginning with the young men at Fort Harrison, the Culver contribution to the Allied forces mobilized for the World War would be both substantial and significant.[42]

Gignilliat as an Officer Candidate Trainer

Most of the successful graduates of the Army's First Series OTC were given two-week leaves before reporting to their National Army cantonments on August 29, 1917.[43] A select few like Gignilliat, however, were pressed into service immediately as instructors for the Second Series OTC that began at the end of August 1917. One of his training officers had written on his evaluation that he was "highly efficient" and had shown "unusual ability for instructing and handling men."[44] Only one other officer candidate had received a similar assessment, making it clear why Gignilliat was selected to serve in this capacity.

With little time to savor his accomplishment, and as one of the Army's 27,341 newest officers, Gignilliat began fulfilling the purpose for which he had been commissioned in his new role as a Senior Instructor beginning on August 16, 1917. As an OTC Senior Instructor, Gignilliat was responsible for supervising the instruction provided to the officer candidates. The Army had determined that its new officers needed to become capable military managers, instructors, and leaders as rapidly as possible, and the OTC training program was designed to do so.

For Senior Instructors, making the candidates into effective military managers meant teaching them how to care for their men by having the officer candidates experience the same "mode of life" that their soldiers would endure as part of their units, supplemented with "instruction on the proper method of supplying, messing, administering, and disciplining organizations, and caring for the health, welfare, comfort, and sanitation" of their men.

The candidates were developed as instructors by experiencing "the same drills and individual training that they in turn must give to their future commands, with the same rigid discipline and attention to detail that they must exact when they become officers of an organization that is to be trained" so they could master the skills they would be responsible for teaching to their own soldiers. By leader, the Army meant a combat leader, and Senior Instructors would accomplish this aspect of their training mandate by "illustrating the tactical employment of troops and giving each [candidate] an opportunity for practice in tactical leadership" to develop within them a suitable level of tactical proficiency.[45]

In essence, the OTC approach for training officers was simply the Army's version of Culver's tried and true method of "know the way, show the way, go the way" that it had been using with such success for almost 20 years and which Gignilliat had implemented and supervised closely, especially during his 13 years as Commandant of Cadets. Gignilliat, therefore, knew the OTC approach intimately and supported it fully.

This broad and all-encompassing mandate for its leaders required the Army to select carefully the officers in whom it was willing to entrust this important mission. Ensuring that they remained engaged with the training and success of their charges, the Army made it clear that Senior Instructors were also responsible for achieving the desired results within the scope of their ability to do so.[46] Given his experience at Culver over the previous twenty years of doing almost exactly the same thing with boys aged 14-19, it is easy to understand why Gignilliat felt not only comfortable with the scope of his responsibilities but also confident in his ability to accomplish his objectives and succeed in this role.

The Army began its Second Series Officer Training Camps on August 27, 1917, scheduled to last 90 days and conclude on November 27, 1917. Acknowledging that it would need many younger officers to lead men into battle, and having achieved its objective of commissioning an appropriate number of older men who would be better suited to serve in higher grades during its First Series OTC, the Second Series OTC was populated with a much younger officer candidate.

The Army General Staff identified "men under 31 years of age" as particularly desirable candidates for its Second Series OTCs, meaning that almost all of the officer candidates would be men in their twenties. In place of the maturity sought in the officer candidates of the First Series OTCs, the Army looked instead for "brains, courage, and the physical ability to stand the test of war" as the desirable characteristics in its Second Series OTC candidates.[47]

Gignilliat served as a Senior Instructor in the Second Series OTC at Fort Harrison for 40 days until October 5, 1917. On October 6, 1917, Gignilliat was relieved of his duties training officer recruits, much to the chagrin of his superiors, both of whom were professional officers of long service and highly esteemed within the Army. Both the post commander at

Fort Harrison, Colonel E. A. Root, and the training camp commander, Lieutenant Colonel Alvan C. Read, contacted the War Department and protested Gignilliat's relief. Read argued that Gignilliat was "peculiarly fitted for the post of senior instructor, as he was for years commandant at Culver Military Academy and is an experienced teacher as well as an able military student."[48] The Army held firm to its decision to reassign Gignilliat, basing its decision on the need for field officers in the National Army.

For his part, Gignilliat commented that he disliked leaving any task "unfinished," be he added that he was "confident that [his successor] will be highly successful in its completion." Looking back on his time as an OTC Senior Instructor, Gignilliat offered, "I have been deeply gratified with the spirit of the camp on the part of students and instructor," and it was clear that he enjoyed his time training officer candidates and his role in the Fort Harrison OTC.[49]

It is worth noting that Gignilliat impressed a number of experienced professional officers during his time at Fort Harrison. Whether demonstrating his abilities as an officer candidate himself or functioning as a Senior Instructor and helping to develop other officer candidates, Gignilliat's acumen for military training was clearly evident and impressive. His performance during this five-month period served as a personal validation for his own abilities and as an external confirmation of the system he designed and implemented at Culver, and that he had described in *Arms and the Boy*.

Gignilliat Becomes an Intelligence Officer

On October 6, 1917, Gignilliat was assigned to the headquarters of the 84th National Army Division, as the purpose of the First Series OTC at Fort Harrison had been to produce officers for the 83rd and 84th divisions.[50] There he joined two of his former instructors from the Fort Harrison OTC who were senior officers in his new unit.[51] Assigned as the Assistant Chief of Staff, G-2, Gignilliat was responsible for the intelligence operations of a division of approximately 28,000 soldiers.[52]

The G-2 was responsible for developing and interpreting combat intelligence on the enemy front for a depth of two miles by collecting and processing relevant information.

84th Division Distinctive Unit Insignia.

Using a small section that included a deputy for combat intelligence, a commissioned interpreter, a topographic officer, and a number of enlisted men, the G-2 oversaw the division's interrogation of prisoners of war and collection of enemy documents. In addition, the intelligence staff supervised patrolling and other ground observations, controlled and distributed maps, and provided oversight for the intelligence officers of the regiments and battalions.[53]

Although he was not trained as an intelligence officer, this assignment indicates that Gignilliat's superiors must have had great confidence in his abilities. The Army was just developing its procedures for combat intelligence operations for division-sized units and above, and this position represented both a tremendous intellectual challenge and the opportunity to demonstrate his abilities as a solider and staff officer in an active division. This assignment also moved him farther away from Culver to Camp Taylor, Kentucky, which was just outside Louisville, Kentucky.

As a new National Army division, the 84th was starting from scratch organizationally as well as with respect to its soldiers. This meant that the division had to provide basic training to all of its new soldiers, train its officers, as well as train for proficiency at the seven collective levels of the echelons of the squad, platoon, company, battalion, regiment, brigade, and division.

Beginning with the end in mind, and acknowledging the intense pressure the Allied powers were applying for America to send its forces to the battlefield as quickly as possible, the Army realized that the larger goal was to achieve a level of training proficiency that would make it possible, "with a minimum of training in France for [divisions] to take their places on the line relatively quickly."[54]

The Army directed that it would be the division commander who would be held accountable for achieving the required training objectives. In addition to creating the necessary trench system for use in the training, the division commander was also responsible for creating a system of divisional schools to provide specialized training and supervising the "tactical instruction of brigade commanders, staff officers, and regimental field officers."[55]

Division commanders were directed to focus on instilling five basic principles in their soldiers to develop the required level of proficiency that would enable them to "render the most perfect service on the field of battle." These principles included:

- Patriotism

- Discipline

- Physical development

- Self-respect, self-reliance, and resourcefulness

- Professional knowledge.[56]

Similar to the OTC training programs, divisions were directed to devote four hours in the morning and four hours in the afternoon to military training. Afternoons on Wednesdays and Saturdays were designated as free time for the soldiers except for those requiring additional training, and no training at all was scheduled on Sundays.[57] This equated to approximately 640 hours during which a division commander was expected to accomplish the tremendous number of training objectives outlined by the War Department and train his soldiers to an acceptable level of proficiency.

Creating a leadership team capable of accomplishing the myriad tasks associated with these training requirements comprised largely of newly commissioned officers with little previous military experience and under the time constraints they were facing was as daunting a task as could be imagined. With the explicit statement that the " responsibility for the training of a division rests solely upon the division commander," it is therefore quite understandable that the Army would determine that an officer of Gignilliat's caliber and experience could best serve helping to bring one of its newest divisions to an acceptable level of proficiency as quickly as possible.[58]

In addition, the commander of the 84th Division needed the very best officers he could acquire to help him train his division to the level of proficiency established by the Army. Upon hearing of Gignilliat's background, experience, and performance as both an officer candidate and Senior Instructor at Fort Harrison from at least two of his more seasoned professional officers, the 84th Division commander likely made getting Gignilliat assigned as his G-2 as quickly as possible one of his highest priorities.

Gignilliat Begins a Gradual Movement Away from Culver

From the time he departed Culver on May 7, 1917, Gignilliat's time on active duty took him farther and farther away from Culver. Beginning at Fort Benjamin Harrison during the period May-October 1917, Gignilliat would spend time at Camp Taylor, Kentucky from October 1917 to August

1918, Camp Sherman, Ohio in August 1918, and Camp Mills, New York in September 1918 before departing the United States in September 1918.

Joining the 84th Division and Training for Combat

Gignilliat's American Travels on Active Duty, May 1917 – September 1918.

Formed on August 25, 1917, Gignilliat joined the 84th Division towards the beginning of its 16-week initial training cycle and began adjusting to his new duties. In October 1917, the division was in the early stages of progressing through the standardized training program required of all newly organized divisions. The training circular, *Infantry Training*, issued by the War Department on August 27, 1917, began as follows:

> In all the military training of a division, under existing conditions, <u>training for trench warfare is of paramount importance</u>. Without neglect of the fundamentals of individual recruit instruction, every effort should be devoted to making all units from the squad and platoon upwards proficient in this kind of training (emphasis added).[59]

To guide units in achieving this objective, the War Department created a 16-week program of intensive training it believed would be effective in bringing the squad, platoon, and company to "a reasonable degree of efficiency." This program consisted of many of the same elements included in the three-month OTC training program, including physical training, rifle marksmanship, bayonet and grenade training, and field living, along with training in trench warfare and open warfare for when the fighting move beyond the trenches. [60]

More specifically, the training plan directed that soldiers spend 57 hours in extended order and trench warfare drills, 56 hours in close order drill, 41 hours in bayonet training, 31 hours in hand grenade training, 27 hours in trench construction, 14 hours devoted to gas warfare, and six hours of familiarization training on machine guns and other weapons specific to trench warfare.

Coupled with up to 80 additional hours firing weapons on the range, almost half (~49 percent) of the available training time was devoted to developing proficiency in the basic tasks of soldiering.[61] Lectures that addressed army regulations, field service regulations, along with training on the Articles of War, machine guns, poisonous gas, and ways to sustain one's health and combat readiness in the field filled out much of the remaining hours during the first two months, along with physical training, barracks and equipment maintenance, and administrative requirements (physical exams and appointments, equipment issuing, personnel actions, administrative paperwork, etc.).[62]

Individual and collective training was intense during the first eight weeks, with proficiency evaluations occurring for the squads during the ninth week, for the platoons during the tenth week, and for the companies during the 15th week. Upon successful completion at the company level, training began immediately at the battalion level, with the 16th week containing at least three hours of night training.[63] The prescribed division training cycle was extended by two weeks in December 1917, with the direction that the additional time would be devoted to mastering the tactics and techniques of open warfare that many American officers believed would be decisive.[64]

Review of the 84th Division at Camp Zachary Taylor, November 10, 1917.[65]

Upon successful completion of the prescribed training program, divisions were free to develop their own training programs to develop proficiency at the battalion, regimental, brigade, and divisional levels with the time available prior to deploying overseas. While "the tactical training varied widely from unit to unit, all divisions tried to make their training as meaningful and realistic as possible for the soldiers."[66]

Adding to the challenge was the confusion created by the disagreement between General John J. Pershing, commanding the American Expeditionary Force (AEF) in Europe, and the War Department regarding the proper level of influence on trench warfare and open warfare. While Pershing was convinced that open warfare would prove to be decisive, the

War Department, based upon three years of evidence and the input from Allied countries, believed that trench warfare would "continue to typify combat in France for the foreseeable future."[67]

Lacking definitive guidance, it was left up to the inexperienced officers leading America's newly created divisions to determine the proper balance of training in trench warfare and open warfare operations, and to design the most realistic training they could imagine to prepare their soldiers for the rigors they would encounter while facing an experienced and deadly opponent in the modern, industrial warfare raging in Europe.

Gignilliat's Contributions to the 84th Division's Training

It is clear from his correspondence during this period that Gignilliat was enjoying himself, benefiting personally from his time on active duty, and quite proud of the work he was doing. In one letter, Gignilliat wrote that he was "in good physical shape" and that he was getting plenty of "outdoor exercise," which he believed was quite beneficial to him, writing "I really think it is doing me lots of good."[68]

He entreated ER Culver to visit him at Camp Taylor to see the new National Army that he was helping to form. Describing Camp Taylor as "a drab and somber place, grassless, treeless and on a windy day a rival to the desert of Sahara for dust and sand storms [sic]," Gignilliat believed that the National Army unit training there – his own 84th Division – would soon be able to overcome its initial mistakes and become a quite capable contributor to the National Army and the defense of the nation.

Keeping his focus on people, Gignilliat was proud of "the spirit of the men of our new National Army" and was confident that the men would "render a fine account of themselves" when called upon to serve.[69] In a later assessment, Gignilliat wrote that "everything is moving along finely and I think we shall undoubtedly have one of the finest divisions in the army."[70]

Gignilliat's new assignment placed him in positions of increased responsibility. In one letter he shared with ER Culver that he was simultaneously "commanding the second group of training battalions of the Depot Brigade, supervising instructor of the officer schools of the brigade and individually auditing the semi-annual returns of the supply officers of 53 Battalions," remarking that he had no reason to "complain of not having enough to do."[71]

Despite an increase in the level of responsibility, Gignilliat's new assignment was a bit less demanding in terms of the hours he was required to work and provided him with time to reconnect with Culver. Writing to ER Culver on October 9, 1917, Gignilliat shared that, while he had been tremendously busy since beginning his time on active duty, he nevertheless found himself "all the time unconsciously sorting out and putting away in my mind the new things I come into contact with that would be helpful back at Culver, both in administration and instruction. I hope some of these days I can get back on the job with all this new dope."[72]

Gignilliat was also still working on finding better ways to promote Culver, like having his Culver staff produce inspiring photos of Culver cadets working with artillery pieces as marketing items for the school. He also continued to advocate for raises for members of his Culver staff and was quite happy to be able to help them receive recognition for their good work.[73]

As a division staff officer directing his small section to assist in the training and development of a burgeoning National Army division, Gignilliat proved to be a dedicated and innovative trainer who treated his men with respect as he had done at both Culver and Fort Harrison. His didactic approach and patrician manner earned him the loyalty of his men and the appreciation of others.

One of the G-2 section's duties during training was to censor the news being reported to ensure that overzealous reporters did not share information with the public that could be detrimental to readiness. Gignilliat thought that there was much more to this responsibility and endeavored to engage with it more broadly, and, as he emphasized in *Arms and the Boy*, properly.

Instead of "confining the work of his department to censoring news" and ignoring or avoiding the reporters covering the 84th Division, as most of his counterparts in other National Army divisions did, Gignilliat "adopted a new policy of dealing with the little colony of newspaper correspondents [at Camp Taylor]" and working with them to help them get the actual stories "on the assumption that civilians [were] entitled to news of their friends in the army and that such publicity help[ed] the morale of troops and of the public."[74]

As with so many aspects related to the National Army divisions, Gignilliat's approach was quite appropriate, being quite egalitarian and democratic as expected in such an organization. As is clear from the article reporting this approach, correspondents and many others were grateful for Gignilliat's enlightened approach. They appreciated the equity with which he engaged, allowing for the release of additional information to their readers that was appropriate to be shared.

Another responsibility of the G-2 section was to help make training realistic by using the intelligence from Europe to portray enemy positions and actions authentically and prepare the soldiers for what they would likely encounter when they arrived overseas. Demonstrating another belief that he espoused in *Arms and the Boy* that training must be made as real as possible to have value, Gignilliat worked hard to add as much realism to the 84th Division's training as practicable.[75] He endeavored to acquire as much information as possible about what soldiers could expect to encounter in the trenches and to incorporate this information into the division's training exercises in ways that were appropriate and feasible.

One example of Gignilliat's efforts occurred during the division's time at Camp Sherman and received favorable publicity. Committed to maintaining the intensity of the training as their overseas deployment loomed in the near future, Gignilliat and his section created a firing exercise designed to expose the soldiers to what they would eventually see on the European battlefields. Endeavoring to create a realistic version of "no-man's land" – the extremely barren and dangerous area between the trenches of each opponent – Gignilliat had his section use a cable and pulley system stretched between two hilltops from which was suspended realistic airplane of the type being used in Europe to provide soldiers with lifelike targets to engage.

Containing a mannequin as the "pilot" and as the target for the division's sharpshooters, Gignilliat's section sent the plane from one hilltop to the other at terrific speed while soldiers fired at it trying to score hits on the dummy pilot. At least five bullets found their mark, providing the soldiers with an exceptionally effective training experience and tangible feedback on their proficiency. One correspondent reported that, "The night-firing was spectacular and accurate," offering that it was clearly evident that the 84th Division's intelligence section knew "a thing or two" about how to stage training events that were both realistic and effective.[76]

Seeking to provide the same level of realism for the division's training in night patrolling, Gignilliat had his section construct an accurate "enemy" trench in the middle of his "no-man's land" training

Machinegun training by the 84th Division.[77]

area and populated it with soldiers pretending to be Germans making improvements to their fighting positions. The object of the training exercise was for the 84th Division soldiers to get as close to the enemy position as possible to observe as much activity as they could while not being seen by the "Germans" and making it safely back to their own "lines," where they made their report to a member of the G-2 section.

Knowing what was actually occurring in the enemy position, Gignilliat's men could assess the accuracy of the patrol reports and provide the soldiers with feedback about the information they acquired and the stealth they demonstrated while collecting the intelligence. As with the firing exercise, the soldiers and leaders of the 84th Division appreciated the realism of the training event. Observers were impressed with the level of detail the G-2 section was able to achieve and the lengths to which Gignilliat and his section were going to prepare the soldiers for what they would face in combat.[78]

Building the 84th Division's trench system and No-man's Land training sites.[79]

Throughout this period, Gignilliat also kept up a steady stream of correspondence with ER Culver and members of his Culver staff. Adding to his description of Camp Taylor from October 9, Gignilliat wrote that, "It is more like Alaska here than the sunny south."[80]

He remained at Camp Taylor during the week and found ways to spend the weekends in an apartment in Louisville that he had rented for Mamie and Hank.

Although he was largely consumed with the challenge of preparing himself and his unit for war, Culver was ever-present in his mind. For example, and upon learning about a fire at Culver that destroyed the remaining original building on campus serving as a trunk room and which contained a substantial amount of cadets' unauthorized personal property, Gignilliat lamented that although the building was not particularly useful and that its loss will "probably improve the landscape," it was nevertheless "one of the landmarks of the old times" and to which many had a "sentimental attachment." This was especially true for Gignilliat, who shared with ER Culver that he had first met HH Culver in that building, first danced with his wife in that building, and also that he had "drilled his first detachment of cadets on its floor."[81]

It is noteworthy that thinking of Culver while preparing himself for war brought Gignilliat comfort. This is indicative of the deep and abiding connection he had developed with the school, and doing so provided him with some much-needed solace during this time of challenge and preparation.

Continuing to Promote *Arms and the Boy*

While engaged in the division's activities, Gignilliat also followed through on his intention to use his own funds to promote *Arms and the Boy*. He somehow found time to create and have printed a new circular for *Arms and the Boy*, titled "Aid from the National Government," that focused on how the book could be used to help schools and colleges implement military training and acquire both military personnel and equipment to support the training. Most of this work related to promoting *Arms and the Boy* occurred during the first three months of his time with 84th Division, when units were focused on establishing basic proficiency at the individual, squad, and platoon levels, giving Gignilliat time to focus on this project.

Gignilliat had someone from his staff at Culver send a copy of the circular to his editor at Bobbs-Merrill, HH Howland. Howland responded by complimenting the document, calling it "extremely attractive," and agreeing to distribute 1,000 copies of the circular that Gignilliat had printed using the resources of Bobbs-Merrill and "to bear whatever share of the cost of printing you may suggest."[82]

This was a magnanimous gesture by Howland, offering support to Gignilliat and his own promotional efforts for *Arms and the Boy* when he was serving on active duty and preparing to deploy overseas with his army division. This support from Howland also made good on Chambers' promise that Bobbs-Merrill would do all it could to help Gignilliat promote the book on his own. This episode shows both Howland and Chambers to be gentlemen of honor who were sincere in their efforts to help Gignilliat promote his book and willing to commit resources from Bobbs-Merrill to make good on their promises of support.

Gignilliat replied to Howland in a handwritten note from Camp Taylor on November 27, 1917, expressing his hope that the circular he had produced for *Arms and the Boy* would "help to stimulate interest in the book. As a sign of conciliation," he also conveyed that he would "be glad to accept [Howland's] offer to share expenses of printing."

Continuing his promotional efforts, Gignilliat asked Howland for four copies of *Arms and the Boy* to give to some officers of the 84th Division, showing that he was still thinking about ways to promote the book (and likely Culver as well) while serving on active duty and preparing for an overseas deployment.[83] This incident illustrates Gignilliat's sincere and very high level of commitment to the *Arms and the Boy* project and getting the book's message out to the widest possible audience, despite his own change in circumstance. With training and deployment preparations becoming increasingly pressing, Gignilliat had done all he could to promote *Arms and the Boy* from afar, and he had to cease further efforts to do so and focus his attention on helping to get his division ready for combat.

Completing the 84th Division's Training for Combat

The 84th Division, despite having worked through its required basic training and moving on to more advanced training on trench warfare and open warfare, was still not at full strength. In mid-April 1918, the division received its final quota of several thousand draftees from Kentucky and Illinois to bring it to full strength. To better integrate the soldiers into their units, the leadership decided to provide the new soldiers with some rudimentary training upon their arrival at the Camp Taylor recruit depot and prior to releasing them to their regiments for basic training. To ensure that the soldiers were trained properly at the recruit depot, the 84th Division established a series of schools to train the officers and non-commissioned officers who would receive the new soldiers in the best methods of instructing recruits.[84]

Having witnessed Gignilliat's prowess as a trainer, the 84th Division's leadership placed him in charge of this endeavor. Working under the command of the West Point-trained and experienced professional officer and depot commander, Colonel Sydney A. Cloman, Gignilliat's charge was to ensure that the new recruits received the best possible training upon their arrival to Camp Taylor, since Cloman was convinced that the initial reception and training were essential to creating good soldiers.[85] Taking what he had learned at Culver and described in *Arms and the Boy*, Gignilliat implemented the training approach that had served him so well up to this point and which would produce a similar level of success for the 84th Division.

Gignilliat's approach fit perfectly with this directive, focusing on imparting the "fundamentals of teaching" to his students to ensure that the new recruits were trained properly, as he had stressed throughout the Preparedness Movement and in the pages of *Arms and the Boy*.

Gignilliat began the training by addressing each class personally. During his initial presentation, he provided the students with a succinct summary of the approach they would be expected to master. Knowing the fundamentals of teaching was essential to getting the best results, but to be effective with the large number of draftees they would soon receive, the officers and non-commissioned officers also had to adopt an approach that was somewhat counterintuitive and which may have appeared to some as antithetical to the Army's normal way of doing things.

To be effective with America's newest soldiers, the instructors needed to be prepared to explain why they were being ordered to do what they were being told to do. The old Army adage holding that, "if the Army wanted you to have an opinion it would have issued it to you" would no longer suffice with the enthusiastic but questioning soldiers of the Progressive Era. Gignilliat had long experience with just these types of young men, and he had mastered the ability to inspire within them the "cheerful and willing obedience" that was the hallmark of the Culver military system and the benchmark he used to assess the quality of leadership.

According to Gignilliat, "The instructor must have patience, the ability to see mistakes and must be trained especially in making explanations. Recruits must not be 'bawled out' if they fail to understand the explanation the first time."[86] In other words, trainers had to engage constructively with the recruits and resist the temptation to use coercive methods to get their points across.

To accomplish these objectives, Gignilliat, with Cloman's support, implemented a didactically based "train-by-example" approach that would have been very familiar to any Culver cadet of the previous two decades. Based upon a belief that "a recruit learns much more rapidly through the eye than through the ear," instructors were urged to avoid talking about what was expected of the recruits and to show them instead. Using this approach, trainers introduced the skill to be learned, showed the recruits how to do it, and then let the recruits practice the skill.

Trainers would observe the recruits closely, making corrections professionally and without undue yelling or otherwise berating the recruits. To be an effective instructor using this approach, Gignilliat informed the trainers that they needed to study their men, learning their individual characteristics as much as possible, and ensure that the skills being learned were demonstrated properly and in ways that the recruits could readily understand.[87]

While somewhat unconventional, the 84th Division's investment in this method of training for its new recruits and decision to have Gignilliat train the trainers paid off. Using officers and non-commissioned officers trained by Gignilliat to implement the "train-by-example" method properly, one observer noted that the 84th Division had created a cadre of trainers who had become "experts and specialists" in the training of new recruits. As a result of this endeavor, Colonel Cloman was able to send good new soldiers to their regiments who were well trained and had "no inaccurate, slip-shod methods to unlearn" that would set the division's training schedule back unnecessarily.

In addition, unit commanders were pleased with the results of the new method because they received soldiers who had been taught how to do the right things in the proper manner.[88] This final result likely pleased Gignilliat the most, as it was quite evocative of the proper discipline he endeavored to instill within the cadets at Culver and which equated to doing the right thing in the proper manner at the correct time.

A Brief Visit to Culver

After being away from campus for over 11 months, and just after completing the "train-the-trainer" sessions for the 84th Division, Gignilliat finally found time for a visit to Culver with his wife, Minnie, during the period April 20-21, 1918. Arriving on a Saturday, Gignilliat attended the evening movie showing and consented to the requests of those present to giving a short speech between movie reels. On Sunday morning he inspected the barracks, and after church services, he addressed the corps. At 2:45 pm, Gignilliat attended a roughriding exhibition in riding hall, and at 4:00 pm he reviewed the garrison parade that was held in his honor despite the threat of rain. Needing to get back to Camp Taylor, he and his wife departed immediately following the parade for the trip down south.[89]

On to Camp Sherman with the 84th Division While Two Sons Join Up

The 84th Division completed its initial training at Camp Taylor at the end of May, 1918, and Gignilliat moved with the division to Camp Sherman, Ohio (which is near Chillicothe, Ohio) on June 9, 1918 to continue its training.[90] Taking him even farther from Culver, it is likely that the intensity of the unit's training and the press of his own responsibilities increased significantly and required his full attention during this demanding period.

In the midst of his training activities, both of his older sons had joined him on active service. Leigh Jr. entered West Point on June 14, 1918, as a member of the USMA class of 1920. Freddy elected to not return to Culver for his final year, deciding instead to qualify for a commission in the Infantry as a second lieutenant. Neither decision was surprising, but it must have made things even harder for Minnie as she and Hank tried to maintain contact with all members of the family.

A Final Visit to Culver

Despite the press of his duties with the 84th Division, Culver was never far from Gignilliat's mind. He found time to visit Culver with his wife a final time before going overseas during the period August 10-11, 1918. Arriving again on a Saturday, Gignilliat went to a Woodcraft council campfire. That evening, Gignilliat received a message from the 84th Division that he needed to return to Camp Sherman as soon as possible, as the unit had been alerted for overseas deployment and needed him back to help make the necessary arrangements.

Culver officials responded by arranging for a special 9:30 am parade on Sunday by the naval midshipmen and cavalry cadets that Gignilliat could review. Following the special parade, Gignilliat had time to conduct a general inspection of both groups in formation before he had to leave to return to Camp Sherman.

Since his unit was beginning the overseas deployment process, Gignilliat's wife and son remained at Culver and enjoyed the hospitality of ER Culver. Departing alone, Gignilliat returned to Camp Sherman and began the arduous process of deploying a division overseas.[91]

The Students Army Training Corps (SATC)

With America's entry into the war and in response to this demand, along with the acknowledgment that the newly created ROTC program was unable to provide sufficient numbers of trained officers for the coming combat operations, the War Department created the Students' Army Training Corps (SATC) as a temporary expediency and best way to respond to the situation. At the end of May 1918, the Army approved the SATC plan, and on June 29, 1918, the US Army Adjutant General released to all presidents of American colleges a circular detailing the organization of the SATC on the campuses.[92]

The SATC program called for students enrolled in the nation's universities and colleges to be organized into training units on campuses across the country, with the object of providing officers for the two million or more young men who were needed to meet the anticipated military requirements. To accomplish this objective, the SATC plan called for the establishment of a total of 763 SATC units in higher education and vocational institutions across the country in 48 states, two territories (Hawaii and Puerto Rico) and the District of Columbia.

These units included 527 collegiate Army units, 131 vocational army training units, 93 naval units, and 12 Marine units.[93] Training began at the designated units on October 1, 1918, but was suspended shortly after the armistice was signed on November 11, 1918.

While the nearby University of Notre Dame was selected to host both Army and Navy SATC units and enrolled approximately 700 students in these programs, Culver was noticeably absent from the list of participating institutions.[94] Given all the effort Gignilliat had devoted to getting Culver noticed around the country and ensuring that it received the recognition he believed it was due with respect to its magnificent military training program, it is interesting to speculate what might have been had Gignilliat still been at Culver when the SATC was organized and implemented. Based upon his past conduct, it is likely that Gignilliat would have lobbied successfully for the establishment of an SATC detachment at Culver, which would have made Culver one of a very few secondary schools in the country to receive such recognition.

Despite being away from Culver and engaged in preparing his division for war, Gignilliat found the time to remain appraised of the developments regarding the SATC.

Inspired by the activity regarding the SATC, Gignilliat wrote to ER Culver on June 29, 1918, to discuss the possibility of starting a post-graduate Military Science program at Culver that would lead to a commission. As he always had, Gignilliat believed that exposing men to Culver's mode of discipline would be most beneficial and would prepare them better than the officer training camps, in which he himself had both participated and excelled, were doing or could do.

Gignilliat also believed that post-graduate students at Culver could cover a great deal of material in a year's time that was more in line with what he believed aspiring officers should actually study. Gignilliat was so enthused that he wanted to present his idea to the Army in Washington, DC, but since he was unable to take leave of his current duties to do so, he wondered it ER Culver or someone else could do so.[95]

By the end of the summer, Gignilliat became even more concerned that Culver was being unwisely and unnecessarily bypassed in the discussions regarding the SATC. After having moved to the Port of Embarkation at Camp Mills, New York and prior to his departure overseas, Gignilliat wrote to letters to both ER Culver and to Captain Glascock on September 2, 1918, urging them to do all they could to get Culver involved officially in the SATC.

In his letter to ER Culver, Gignilliat wrote that, "I feel that any failure on Culver's part to participate to the fullest extent in this opportunity will be a serious blow to the prestige of the institution, and at the same time would deprive the Government of very valuable services that Culver is in a position to render." In his letter to Glascock, Gignilliat wrote that he "would not accept any compromise in this matter without putting up a very strenuous fight" and that he "would certainly go after this thing tooth and nail and see that Culver is given the full opportunity to serve the Government that it deserves."[96]

Gignilliat was so invested in getting Culver involved in the SATC that he considered "asking for a day's leave to go down to Washington to do what I could there personally." Gignilliat was convinced that "there was little question about our having the most highly efficient Senior Unit in the country," referencing the "tremendous fight" to get at Culver a Senior Unit of the Officers Training Corps," and citing the tremendously positive report from the Army's most recent inspection of Culver's military program as powerful evidence of his belief in the institution's value to the nation.

Convinced that Culver had the opportunity to give young men "the firm foundation of discipline, which approximates very closely that of the men trained at West Point and which cannot be acquired in several months in Training Camp," and believing that not enough people in Washington, DC knew about Culver or were aware of its value and capability, Gignilliat wanted to persuade the government to let Culver host an SATC unit.

Even though it was a secondary institution, Gignilliat's unwavering confidence in Culver's ability to train young men as capable military leaders, along with its "wonderful facilities" and all else that Culver had to offer, convinced him that he and everyone associated with Culver must fight to prevent the government from taking the easy route of simply lumping Culver in with all other secondary schools and treating them all the same.[97]

Deploying Overseas

Encampment of National Army soldiers at Camp Mills, New York awaiting transport overseas.[98]

Almost immediately upon his return to Camp Sherman, Gignilliat's division began the process of deploying overseas. The 84th Division moved to Camp Albert L. Mills, New York (on Long Island) on August 21, 1918, for overseas embarkation. His passion for the SATC issue notwithstanding, the demands of deploying his unit overseas and the rapidity of the decision-making required during this period prevented him from being able to address the situation as he wished or follow through on his desire to travel to Washington, DC to do so.

On September 8, 1918, Gignilliat and the 84th Division boarded the *SS Melita*, and at 8:40 am on September 9, 1918, the *Melita* set sail from New York bound for Liverpool, England.[99]

The SS Melita.[100]

After a two-week voyage, the 84th Division arrived in Liverpool on September 21, 1918.

Allowed a very brief respite in Romsey, England, Gignilliat boarded the SS Antrim at Southampton, England on September 24, 1918 bound for Le Harve, France in advance of the main body of 84th Division, which traveled on September 25, 1918.[102] Once in France, the 84th

Troops on deck of the SS Melita *during WWI.*[101]

Division consolidated at Siene-Infereure, France and was assigned to the American Expeditionary Forces (AEF) General Headquarter (GHQ). Three days later, the 84th Division moved closer to the front at Neuvic, France.[103]

Just as the unit was about to arrive within hearing distance of some of the fighting, the AEF GHQ made a decision on October 3, 1918 to "skeletonize" the 84th Division, breaking it up and using its soldiers as individual replacements for other units already in combat as part of the final Allied offensive to bring the war to an end.[104] Orders issued on October 4, 1918 reassigned the 84th Division from GHQ, to which the AEF's fighting division were assigned, to the AEF's Service of Supply

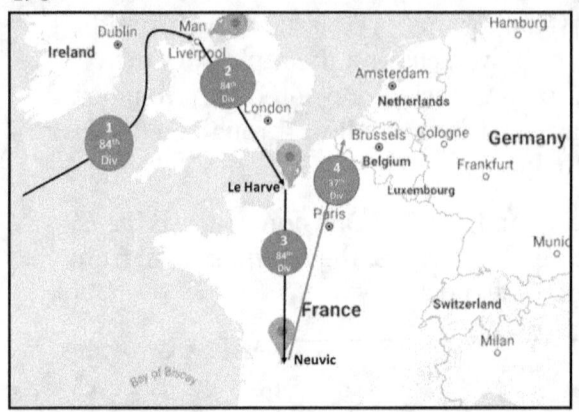

The 84th Division's route from Camp Mills, NY to Neuvic, France, Sep-Oct 1918.

(SOS), which provided supplies for the fighting units. This decision was quite different from the mobilization philosophy that led to the creation of the National Army divisions, and it surely came as a surprise to many.

This decision came largely as a result of the over 25,000 casualties American units had suffered in the first phase of the Meuse-Argonne offensive that occurred during the period September 26 - 3 October 1918 and as the 84th Division made its way into France and closer to the front. Since one division contained approximately 25,000 soldiers, the logic of the AEF's skeletonization decision, if not its significant impact on the units involved, was readily apparent.

Having been with the 84th Division for almost exactly one year, this decision must have been devastating for Gignilliat and for the soldiers of the organization. Reassigned from combat duty to the AEF Service of Supply as a source of personnel and equipment for other American units, the following month for the unit consisted of sending soldiers and equipment as replacements where they were most needed in theater.

After being almost completely depleted of soldiers and equipment, the remaining shell of the once proud 84th Division was moved to the major supply depot at Le Mans, France on November 6, 1918 to be further skeletonized.[105] Gignilliat must have despaired, after training so long and hard for combat operations, of sitting out the remainder of the war at a supply base sending others to do the fighting.

Part 2: Entering the Fighting and the Period of Armistice, Oct 1918-July 1919

Joining the 37th Division and Fighting on the Western Front

Despite his own personal disappointment at not being able to fight with his comrades of the 84th Division with whom he had shared so much over the course of the previous year, Gignilliat himself benefited professionally from this situation. Recognized as a valuable commodity, Gignilliat was relieved from his assignment to the 84th Division almost immediately, and he was assigned to the AEF GHQ on October 6, 1918, allowing him the

37th Division Distinctive Unit Insignia.

opportunity to participate in the fighting. After serving for one month on the GHQ staff, and based upon his work as the 84th Division's G-2, Gignilliat was selected to become the G-2 for the 37th National Guard Division on November 9, 1918.[106]

Fighting in the Flanders region of Belgium near Ghent, Gignilliat joined his new unit on the eve of an attack and what would become the final offensive action of the war.

Originally part of the First US Army's V Corps, the 37th Division was in the first wave of attacks during the initial phase of the Muse-Argonne Offensive and suffered tremendous losses in the fighting. Withdrawn from the fighting and placed into reserve on October 3, 1918, it became clear that the 37th Division and other units in the initial assaults needed extensive refitting before they would be ready to re-engage with the enemy. This situation led to the AEF's high-level reassessment that resulted in the decision to skeletonize the arriving 84th Division as the only practical method of reconstituting units like the 37th Division that had sustained such high levels of losses.

While the fighting continued during the second phase of the Meuse-Argonne offensive, the Allied high command was already looking ahead to what it hoped would become the war's final operation that would bring the four years of unimaginable violence to an end. Supreme Allied Commander French Field Marshall Ferdinand Foch's ability to issue orders to all Allied units helped encourage countries to consider helping one another to take advantage of this opportunity.[107]

In early October 1918 the French asked for an

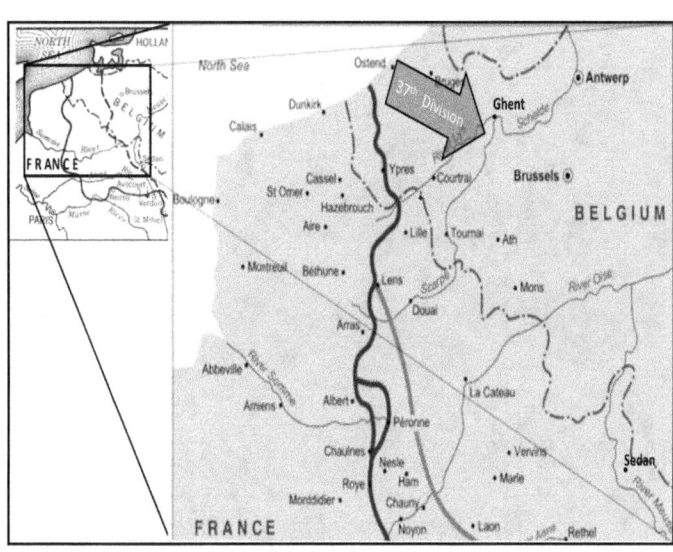

37th Division's area of employment, November 1918.

additional division to assist in its attack towards Brussels from Flanders, and the American's agreed to supply the requested division. The division selected for this assignment was the 37th National Guard Division that had just been withdrawn from the fighting and which was undergoing a fairly substantial refitting to replace the losses it had suffered and bring it back into fighting trim.

Accordingly, the 37th Division's reconstitution efforts were prioritized, making the assignment of a qualified G-2 of paramount importance. Fortunately, the AEF GHQ happened to have on hand a qualified G-2 officer available for immediate assignment. Just as the 37th Division was reassigned to the French Sixth Army's French XXXIV Corps to conduct an attack across the Escaut River as part of the on-going Ypres-Lys Offensive, Gignilliat was ordered to join the 37th Division immediately as its new G-2 on November 9, 1918.[108]

Joining a unit on the eve of an attack is perhaps the most challenging situation possible for a staff officer, and having to change plans almost immediately based upon the enemy's stubborn resistance made this situation even more difficult. Occurring at the very end of the war's active combat operations, it was vitally important to all of the Allied commanders that these final attacks succeeded in capturing and securing as much territory as possible. The impending armistice would almost certainly preclude further combat actions, and the Allies wanted to be in the strongest possible position with respect to the ground they occupied when the peace negations began.

Scheduled to attack in an area still heavily fortified by German forces, the 37th Division's initial attack encountered heavy resistance and was stopped almost immediately on the west side of the Escaut River. Slipping south, the division found and created bridges across the river, allowing its attacks on November 10-11, 1918 to succeed. The 37th Division advanced six miles east towards its objective of

Ypres-Lys Operation (Flanders) 37th Division
November 9-11, 1918.

Brussels before being halted by the armistice that commenced at 11:00 am on November 11, 1918. Suffering 1,648 total casualties during the operation, the 37th Division performed quite well as part of the French army and on behalf of the AEF.[109]

A review of the battle reports indicates that the G-2 section likely played an essential role in the success of this operation. When the lead brigade encountered an unexpectedly stiff level of resistance from the German forces defending on the east side of the Escaut River, it was almost certainly the actions of the G-2 section, working with the intelligence officers of the American and French units, scouting patrols, and information received from local inhabitants of the area, that helped the division commander conclude correctly that the planned attack would not be successful and also to determine how to revise the plan so that the attack could succeed without interfering with the attacks occurring on the left and right of the division.[110]

As a result of the revisions to the plan of attack, the 37th Division made greater progress towards Brussels than any other Allied unit involved in the attack. Given that Gignilliat was decorated for his service with America's second highest award, along with a highly respected award from the French, it stands to reason that his performance during this critical 36-hour period was quite remarkable.

The First Four Uneasy Months of the Armistice

With the cessation of hostilities, Europe settled into an uneasy period of armistice, during which it was not initially certain if the fighting would resume. Wary of the dangerous situation in Germany, and weary of the fighting, the armistice proceeded carefully and methodically.

During the period immediately after the armistice from November 11, 1918 – December 13, 1918, troops retained the positions they occupied when the armistice went into effect, remained in high states of tactical/ operational readiness, and occupied tactical defensive positions from which they could launch attacks immediately if necessary. Having survived an entire month without having the fighting re-erupt, both sides agreed to an extension to the armistice for another month covering the period December 13, 1918 – January 16, 1919.

Throughout this period, troops continued to train and remained in a high state of tactical/operational readiness. Another month-long extension of the armistice followed, lasting from January 16, 1919 – February 16, 1919. With the prospect of renewed fighting becoming more remote, troops retained their readiness and also began preparing to return home. A much longer extension was approved for the period beginning on February

16, 1919, and lasting until as late as January 10, 1920, as both sides negotiated a lasting peace treaty. During this period troops were moved into occupation zones and returned home.

All through the initial period of the armistice, the 37th Division remained in place in the area of the farthest extent of its final attack and assumed a defensive posture. If hostilities resumed, the 37th Division would attack to capture Brussels. During the period of the second extension, the 37th Division left the front and moved west into France (Hondschoote) to train and await further orders. When it became apparent in February 1919 that the fighting would likely not resume, the 37th Division was released from its tactical responsibilities and began redeployment operations during the period of the third armistice extension, departing France on March 12, 1919.[111]

During this early part of the armistice period, Gignilliat reported that he was "engaged in historical work for the Division which has involved considerable travel and personal expense." While perhaps challenging and expensive, Gignilliat nevertheless felt that, "[t]he opportunity was so valuable that I considered it well worth while (sic)," even though it caused him to deplete the personal line of credit he had established for his use in Europe.[112]

Also during this period, and perhaps somewhat unexpectedly, Gignilliat was promoted to the rank of colonel in the United States Army on of February 24, 1919.[113] Since his promotion to lieutenant colonel in the National Army on August 15, 1917, the Army had done away with the designations for differing types of commissions.

As of August 7, 1918, all new appointments and promotions were made in the United States Army, which helped to alleviate the confusion regarding the applicability of ranks held by officers commissioned into the ORC and National Army during the early stages of America's involvement in the war.[114] As a result, Gignilliat was promoted to the rank of colonel in the United States Army (and not in either the ORC, as he had been commissioned as a major, or the National Army, as had been commissioned as a lieutenant colonel) at 44 years of age, placing him on par with his regular Army peers and marking him, with so little time on active duty, as a very successful officer.[115]

While quite welcomed, this promotion elevated Gignilliat to a rank above what was required as the division G-2. The Army began looking for a new assignment for Gignilliat commensurate with his rank. The wheels of the Army's personnel bureaucracy, however, moved slowly, and Gignilliat was still assigned to the 37th Division – despite his position-rank mismatch – when it moved to port city of Brest, France on February 27, 1919 for embarkation and transit back to America and just as the Allied occupation of the German Rhineland got into full swing.

Allied Occupation of the German Rhineland During the Armistice

As soon as the armistice took effect in November 1918, French Marshal Ferdinand Foch, the Allied Supreme Commander, took the steps he determined were essential to prevent Germany from ever posing a threat to France again. Chief among his determinations was his conviction that denying Germany control over the Rhineland was essential to doing so. Given the resources available in the Rhineland, the Allies determined that German influence in this area had to be controlled tightly if the armistice was to have any possibility of success.

To put his plan into motion, Foch immediately ordered Allied and Associated Powers into the Rhineland to occupy it for several reasons:

- To deny the Germans access to it;

- To establish Allied control over it;

- To address the humanitarian crises related to lack of food and other issues;

- To prevent Bolshevik influence from taking control; and

- To explore notions of separatist movements (which he likely supported).[116]

Several Allied countries, including Belgium, Britain, the United States, and France were assigned specific areas to occupy within the Rhineland. These assignments would require some units from each of the occupying powers to remain in Europe as part of the occupation force while the rest returned home.

Shouldering such a tremendous amount of responsibility and with so many areas demanding his attention, Foch established a commission to monitor the armistice and administer the occupied areas, the Permanent Interallied Armistice Commission (PIAC). The PIAC was established to exercise general supervision of Armistice conditions and with maintaining formal communications with the German Government. The PIAC was also charged with the responsibility of supervising the occupation of the Rhineland to "ensure, by any means, the security and satisfaction of all

Allied Army Occupation Zones in the Rhineland.[117]

the needs of the Armies of occupation."[118]

To accomplish its objectives, the PIAC initially established a number of sub-commissions to monitor overall supervision of Armistice conditions, the most important of which, from Foch's perspective, was the Interallied Commission for the Rhineland (ICR). Charged with the general supervision of occupied territories, the ICR was authorized to appoint its own sub-commissions to deal with specific aspects of the occupation.[119] While operating as executive agents of the Supreme Allied Commander, the main interallied commissions reported directly to Foch and all decisions of the commissions had to be approved by Foch before they were put into execution.

French General Payot and the Interallied Commission for the Rhineland (ICR)

Given the importance of the ICR, Foch appointed one of his most trusted subordinates to lead it, General Charles Jean Marie Payot. Foch's confidence in Payot was based on their relationship during the war and also on Payot's performance. Payot controlled the French army rear area for three years, and his management of its supply and transportation was superb. Considered a born leader who possessed common sense, executive ability, great determination, and untiring energy, Payot was also intolerant of incompetency, grateful for honest effort, and an agreeable colleague.[120] His effectiveness was unquestioned, and it made sense for Foch to place Payot in this important supervisory role.

Payot's Management of the Occupied Areas of the German Rhineland

In his role as the head of the ICR, Payot exercised oversight of the affairs in all of the occupied territories, allowing Foch to have a single point of contact for all occupation-related activities.[122] Following the French custom, Payot established commissions to help him supervise the occupation.

For the starving inhabitants of the Rhineland, food-related issues quickly became paramount. With local production levels critically low, supplemental sources were imperative. The Interallied Food Council, an international humanitarian organization quite separate from any of Foch's commissions and led by the very capable Herbert Hoover, was one of the most important suppliers. Known as the "Hoover Commission," it was the only organization in the world capable of managing such an expansive project as the rationing of food within Western Europe. Hoover began bringing supplies to Europe through the ports of Rotterdam and Antwerp quickly, but until the security situation could be settled at sea and on land, these stocks were not available for distribution in the occupied zones.[123]

French General Charles Jean Marie Payot.[121]

The challenging issue of distributing the food in the occupied zones was beyond the Hoover Commission's capabilities. It became evident almost immediately that the Germans were not able to manage the distribution of the food either and that the Allies would have to provide access to the necessary transportation efforts to carry out the distribution plan in their respective areas of responsibility to ensure the delivery was fair and equitable. An inequality or partiality in the distribution of food in the areas occupied by any of the Allied or Associated Powers could lead to riots, corruption, and perhaps even create an opportunity for Bolshevik exploitation (all of which were already occurring within the unoccupied areas of Germany at the time), and it would also create a lasting prejudice in Germany against the nation responsible.[124]

The Interallied Military Food Commission

Armed with this knowledge, Allied leaders determined that a commission needed to focus solely on the effective distribution of food in the occupied areas. Accordingly, the Interallied Military Food Commission (IMFC) was established on February 24, 1919, to distribute rations within the occupied areas of the Rhineland. Given the dire situation regarding food in the occupied areas, the IMFC worked directly for the ICR, ensuring that General Payot would provide direct oversight for this tremendously important aspect of the Allied occupation of the Rhineland.

The initial intended duties of the IMFC included ascertaining the actual food situation in the occupied territories, calculating the amount of food needed to feed the population in each area, and providing supplements to the food available in each area to ensure the population was adequately supplied. This last duty required each occupation force to make arrangements for the importation, supply, and sale of the supplemental foodstuffs for their sector.[125]

An Unexpected Change of Plans for Gignilliat

In early 1919, as the prospect of renewed fighting reduced and just as Gignilliat began the process of returning to America, the Allied occupation plan got into full swing. The interallied commissions established by Foch generated requirements for experienced and capable officers who could be trusted to serve the allied cause and also represent the interests of their own country. Each of the occupying armies appointed representatives to the various commissions Foch established to serve as personal links between the Supreme Allied Commander and the territory being occupied by the various allied nations.[126] A newly promoted colonel like Gignilliat, possessing a wealth of administrative experience, an excellent service record in the war, and who had been overseas for around six months, would be especially attractive to serve in such a position for the United States.

On March 12, 1919, Gignilliat was in Brest, France on the pier preparing to board the USS Von Steuben with his 37th Division comrades and return to the United States via New York City, when a long-distance telephone call came from American Expeditionary Forces (AEF) Headquarters in Chaumont, France with orders to hold Gignilliat at the port "if he had not already sailed."[127] Gignilliat then received a telegram instructing him to remain at Brest and await further reassignment orders. Gignilliat was told that he was being considered with several other officers for a very important assignment of a diplomatic nature along the lines of a military attaché.

It is almost certain that Gignilliat's record had come to the attention of Army planners looking for qualified officers to serve as officials in the American occupation zone and that they were suitably impressed with his qualifications to serve in such a capacity.[128]

While he was somewhat disappointed to be denied the opportunity to return with his 37th Division comrades and eager to resume his duties at Culver "at the earliest opportunity," Gignilliat was nevertheless intrigued by the somewhat mysterious challenge he was unexpectedly facing.

Having performed exceptionally well while on active duty, and convinced that he may be provided with "the opportunity of rendering some worthwhile service" while he remained in Europe, Gignilliat wanted the opportunity to compete for the job or at least to show himself and others that he was capable of doing whatever might be asked of him "effectively" if selected for the position.[129]

After waiting in Brest for several days without any further contact, Gignilliat became convinced that he would not be selected for the position and believed that he would be heading back to the USA shortly. His waiting ended abruptly when he received a telegram instructing him to report to the Adjutant General of the AEF in Paris. The urgency conveyed by the communication was so insistent that Gignilliat dared not finish writing a letter he had begun until he arrived at his destination in Paris.[130]

While waiting in Paris, Gignilliat's thoughts again turned to Culver. Commenting to ER Culver on the impact of his service experience up to that point, Gignilliat shared that he would "return with a much broadened vision and with fresh and heightened inspiration from those with whom I have come into contact." Gignilliat also hoped that both his service and perhaps also his new assignment would afford him with opportunities "that may be worthwhile not only from the standpoint of personal satisfaction but from the standpoint of the Institution which his ever in my heart and thoughts."[131]

On March 15, 1919, Gignilliat's period of waiting ended when he learned that he had been selected to become the US representative on the newly created (as of February 24, 1919) Interallied Military Food Commission (IMFC) that was part of what would later become the Interallied Rhineland Military Commission.[132] When selected, Gignilliat did not think that his new assignment would cause him to remain in Europe for very long, but due to its importance, Gignilliat was committed to giving it his all and doing it as well as possible.[133]

During this period, pleas to lift the Allied blockade to ease the acute famine in Germany and Austria were rejected based upon a shared belief among many of the main delegates that they should first agree to the terms of peace being offered to Germany before lifting the blockade, since Germany had been both the principal aggressor and enemy in the war. The availability of food in the occupied sectors became steadily more limited as the negotiators wrangled with other issues, and by the end of February it had reached a crisis point.

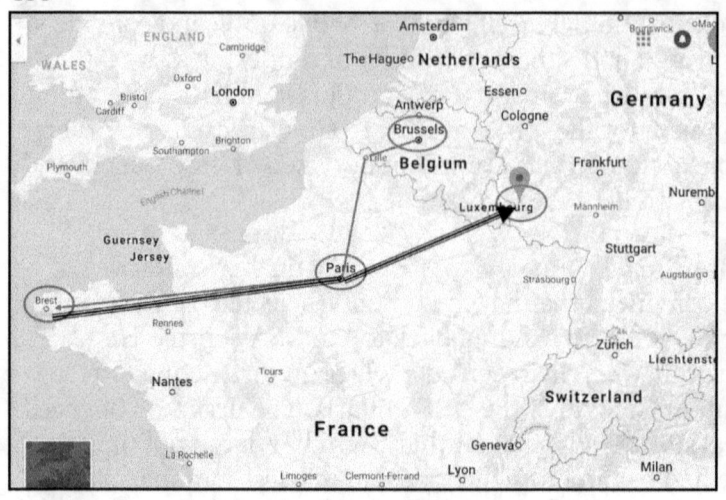

Reflecting this reality, in the first week of March 1919 the successful and highly respected British General Herbert Plumer, commanding the British occupation force in the Rhineland (initially the British Second Army and then the British Army of the Rhine (BOAR) beginning in March 1919) based out of Cologne and just north of the American occupation area based out of Coblenz, delivered a plea to the Armistice leaders urging the swift sending of food as his troops "cannot stand [the] spectacle of starving children."[134] The French faced a similar situation in their own sector, along with aggressive Bolshevik agitation around Mainz. This was the situation Gignilliat would encounter when he arrived in the American Occupation Zone in the Rhineland in March 1919.

Gignilliat's travels during the period February-March 1919.

The American Occupation Zone in the Rhineland

The American occupation zone in the Rhineland was between the British Occupation Zone to the north and the French Occupation Zone to the south. It covered 2,500 square miles, ranging from Luxembourg northeast along the Moselle (Mosel) River and extending across the Rhine to a bridgehead at Coblenz.[135] This area was more than twice as large as the state of Rhode Island, 20 percent larger than the state of Delaware, and roughly the size of the Netherlands in terms of land mass. The zone has a population of close to 1,000,000 people in 1919.[136]

Much of the American zone consisted of small agricultural villages, with a few industrial cities for production of steel and chemical. The two largest cities were Coblenz (sometimes spelled *Koblenz*) and Trèves (now known as Trier).

The largest city in the zone was the commercially robust city of Coblenz, with a population of just over 65,000. A city of varying sovereignty, it had been part of the German Empire since the end of the Napoleonic wars, allowing it to largely escape the WWI destruction that impacted so many other cities in the region. Located on the far northeastern side of the zone and with a pontoon bridge stretching 400 meters across the Rhine supporting large volumes of traffic in both directions, Coblenz served as the Rhineland's political center, the location of American Occupation Zone headquarters, and the focal point of the American occupation.[137]

The other important city in the American zone was Trier, located on the southwestern side of the American occupation zone. Trier became part of the German Empire during the Prussian-led unification of Germany in 1871, which, like Coblenz, allowed it to avoid much of the WWI destruction that impacted other urban centers in the region. This association with Germany supported a sustained level of growth in the area up to the beginning of WWII, with a population of just over 53,000 in 1919.[138] A vibrant and cosmopolitan city which, along with Coblenz, accounted for ten percent of the area's population, this was Gignilliat's base of operations and where he spent most of his time during this period.

Gignilliat's Actions with the IMFC

Gignilliat arrived in the American Occupation Zone on March 26, 1919.[139] The US Third Army had been created as the occupying force for the area, and its headquarters was in the large city of Coblenz. The American Occupation Zone was the most rural of the occupied areas, and owing to the transportation difficulties of moving within the sector, the Americans established an Advanced Headquarters (AHQ) roughly 200 kilometers to the southwest in the ancient city of Treves (Trier), which was in the very heart of the American occupation zone.

Separate from the US Third Army, the AHQ in Treves was responsible for maintaining liaison with the American members of the PIAC commissions and informing them of General Pershing's views on the various issues with which they dealt. Commissioners like Gignilliat were expected to represent America while carrying out their duties and to advocate for Pershing's views with their peers when possible.[140]

The situation he encountered upon arrival was both fragile and chaotic. Material shortages were perhaps the defining characteristic at this point, with foodstuffs being most acute. This was somewhat ironic for an area that was largely rural and comprised of small agricultural towns. Socialists and Bolsheviks took advantage of these shortages to foment unrest among the population, causing Pershing and his leadership to be gravely concerned about maintaining order in the American zone. Third

Army was aware of the challenges in the area but was not equipped to address them effectively.

Third Army's decision to decline requests to requisition foodstuffs for the German population was understandable but exacerbated the tension in the area. This was likely an important reason for the US Army's earnest search in early 1919 to find an experienced officer to address this concerning and potentially explosive situation and which led to Gignilliat being pulled off the ship in Brest and ordered to report to the American Occupation Zone instead of returning home with the 37th Division in March 1919.[141]

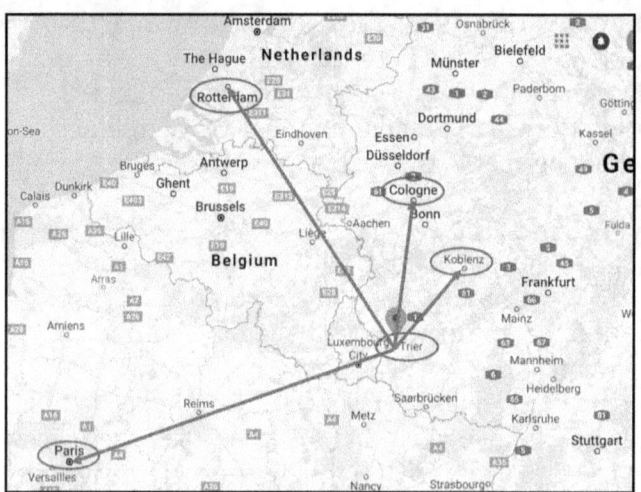

Gignilliat's range of travels with the IMFC, March–June 1919.

His new job was of a diplomatic nature that required the experience of a senior officer and also a great deal of tact. Gignilliat's specific role would be to address the issues related to the supply of and distribution of food to the approximately 1,000,000 German civilians living in the American occupation sector. With many Germans on the brink of starvation, food was a particularly important commodity, and addressing this situation effectively would be an important part of maintaining order and placating the inhabitants of the area.

Gignilliat's specific charge was to establish the policies and systems for food distribution to civilians within the American zone of occupation and also between the American zone and the other Allied zones of occupation to help bring desperately needed food to a population of almost 1,000,000 people. This required him to travel a great deal to places like Paris, Rotterdam, Coblenz, and Cologne (among others) to attend the bi-weekly IMFC meetings that rotated among the various Allied occupation sectors.[142] Attending these meetings brought Gignilliat into frequent contact with Payot and other members of the Allied and American occupation forces.

In his new role, Gignilliat functioned as part diplomat and part problem-solver, traveling extensively around Europe. While assigned officially to Coblenz, Gignilliat worked mostly out of Trier (Treve).[143] Gignilliat was the only non-general allied officer serving as a primary IMFC representative, and he worked closely with the other Allied general officers serving in these roles, especially those from Great Britain, based in Cologne and France, based in Paris.

Gignilliat initially thought that he would be able to get the various matters of policy determined within one or two meetings, but the challenges associated with the areas for which he was responsible were of such scope and complexity that it took him considerably longer to settle them than he initially expected.[144] He became intimately familiar with the trafficability of each sector during this period, and he acquired a special appreciation for the transportation difficulties within the American sector.[145]

By mid-April 1919, Gignilliat was fully engaged in the important and meaningful work of determining how best to feed the starving people of Germany. At one of the IMFC's meetings within the British occupied sector in Cologne on April 11, 1919, Gignilliat reported that he and his colleagues began addressing several of the most challenging issues for which they were responsible.[146]

The main issue involved a rather significant disagreement between the British and American leaders regarding the most appropriate level of restrictions for the trading of food between the American and British zones of occupation. The Americans preferred a more restricted level of trade involving food, based upon the transportation challenges of the more rural American sector, while the British preferred a less restricted level of trade involving food for the more industrial and more easily traversed area of the British sector.

In addition, the members of the IMFC had yet to agree upon standardized "methods of payment for supplies" or to many of the details related to the "utilization of the German machinery for distribution" of food and supplies within the occupied areas of the German Rhineland. Elaborating somewhat, Gignilliat shared that, "Food supplies come in part from the Hoover people at Rotterdam, also from local resources as well as from Army stocks, so there is much to be considered in securing the best results dialectically and economically and at the same time ensuring uniformity of treatment in the different allied zones."[147]

There could be no disparity regarding the availability of food within, among, and/or between the various Allied sectors. It was imperative that all aspects managed by the Allies were scrupulously equitable if they were to be effective and supportive of the peace negotiations.

While they apparently made some headway on these vexing issues at the next meeting on April 25, 1919, there remained two more months of substantial work for the IMFC until it had succeeded in resolving the many challenging issues it faced and established an effective policy and fair method for distributing food within the Allied zones of occupation. During this period, Gignilliat worked closely with Payot, and he developed great admiration for him. After the war, Gignilliat would show his respect by referring to Payot as "one of the Allies' masterminds." [148]

Gignilliat hoped that by late-April 1919 he would be able to "form some estimate of the time I will necessarily have to remain with the job" and that "after the work becomes a matter of routine" he could be released to return to Culver. Until such time, and despite his perpetual desire to return to Culver, he felt that the work he was doing as a member of the IMFC was of such importance that it would be "unwise" for him to depart while "in the midst of settling *mooted* points and determining a permanent policy" for the distribution of food in the occupied Allied areas.[149] Clearly the IMFC work was meaningful to him and gave him purpose.

Gignilliat's Main Contributions to the IMFC – Supplements, Ticketing, and Distribution

Gignilliat's three most important accomplishments during this period addressed the two main areas of his specific responsibility – to establish the policies and systems for food distribution within the American zone of occupation and also between the American zone and the other Allied zones of occupation – quite effectively, helping to feed the Germans and also curb unrest in the American occupation area. The shortages of even the most basic foodstuffs throughout Germany caused much social unrest, especially in areas where the occupation forces had plenty.

Food Supplements

Recognizing the potentially incendiary impact this could have in the American zone of occupation, Gignilliat successfully lobbied in April 1919 to make available for sale at cost price to the German population previously non-distributed stocks of flour controlled by the US Army. Gignilliat expanded this program to include other basic foodstuffs in great need, including milk, sugar, bacon, and lard, along with more limited supplies of canned beef and salmon, to augment the German per capita rations.[150] This program greatly reduced the scarcity of basic foodstuffs in the American occupation area and addressed one of the main sources of potential unrest in a positive, direct, and compassionate manner.

Ticketing

To control the purchase of American foodstuffs, Gignilliat's second major accomplishment was to spearhead the implementation of a ticket system to ensure fairness and equity. The system worked as follows:

> *Each person or head of family was issued the number of coupons to which he was entitled, each coupon authorizing [the bearer] to buy a certain quantity of a certain food within a certain period of time. There were also [more generic coupons for use in controlling more scarcely available types of food.] The coupons entitled the holder to register with some merchant of his own choice, who in turn registered his total requirements with the local Food Office. When the food arrived, each merchant was allotted the amount necessary to provide for the persons registered with him. Announcements of distribution were made in the daily papers. The merchant kept the coupons to indicate the amounts and regularity of his sales. Any allotment not entirely sold would be returned to the food authorities or debited against the next allotment.[151]*

The ticket system he introduced was fairly simple, and it did a reasonably good job of making the limited amount of food available as fairly as possible.[152] Using this system, people in the American occupied zone were usually able to get enough food to eat even though the variety may not have always been to their liking. It could also be made routine and administered easily.

Distribution

Gignilliat's third major accomplishment was to establish in early April 1919 a central purchasing agency – the Food Distribution Company (Limited) – formed and operated by civic-minded German citizens. The purpose of the company was "the purchase and distribution in the public interest of foodstuffs and other commodities of daily use" to improve the area's food situation.[153]

Practically speaking, the Food Distribution Company financed "the transfer of available foodstuffs from various sources to the civil population. It received requests from food officials, transferred these requests to the army or other source of supply sometimes making an advance payment, received the deliveries, and made payment for them."

The American foodstuffs included milk, flour, sugar, bacon, lard, canned beef, and salmon. It conducted all of these activities with transparency and in accordance with the directives of the IMFC.[154]

Serving the public interest, the company's employees were paid a fixed salary instead of working for a share of the profits, removing any incentive for corruption or personal gain. All profits were used to further the public interest as determined by a board of shareholders.[155]

While initially ineffective, Gignilliat applied his organizational expertise to its operations, transforming the Food Distribution Company quickly into an effective and efficient organization that contributed positively to the overall welfare of the citizens living in the American occupation zone.[156]

According to the US Army's official history, despite the rather cumbersome method of operation required by the situation that prevented the Food Distribution Company from being able to operate more like a similarly functioning American organization and some dissatisfaction with the types and amounts of available foodstuffs (causing irritation among both consumers and suppliers), "on the whole the system worked very well."[157] Another benefit was that this organization empowered the Germans and provided them with a way to contribute positively to their own recovery, giving them a stake in the FDC's success. Here was an area in which Gignilliat was particularly adept, and the successful results manifested his abilities well.

Gignilliat also helped to implement an intricate yet highly effective method of food distribution within the American occupation zone that used Army trucks to transport the food far more rapidly than was possible prior to his arrival. Before Gignilliat arrived, it could take as long as three weeks to get food distributed within the American occupied zone, aggravating the area's simmering unrest and leading to high levels of unnecessary spoilage and waste, along with negligent pilferage. Gignilliat was able to organize the available transportation assets so efficiently that food was usually delivered to its intended destinations within a few hours after its arrival to either Coblenz or Treves.[158]

The impact on the quality of life and morale for the Germans residing within the American occupied zone was enormously positive, and Gignilliat's method ensured the efficient circulation of food in the American occupation zone during the armistice.

By June 1919, Gignilliat's work had earned a very favorable reputation with the other members of the Allied occupation forces, especially with Payot. Payot expressed admiration for Gignilliat's abilities and accomplishments to both Foch and Pershing, setting the stage for future positive engagements with each important leader.

The End of the Period of Armistice

All of Gignilliat's work was essential to support the on-going negotiations occurring at Versailles during the spring and early summer of 1919. Maintaining control in the occupied territory in Germany was a crucial part of persuading the Germans to accept the harsh terms of the peace the Allies – especially France – were determined to impose. Effective administration of the occupation zones provided evidence that the Allies cared about the German people and could be trusted to adhere to the terms of any agreement Germany accepted.

While the occupation activities of the Allies had a direct impact on the peace negotiations, Foch was largely kept out of peace negotiations by politicians, especially the French Prime Minister Georges Clemenceau and the British Prime Minister Lloyd George, both of whom felt that "war was too important to be left to the generals" after the catastrophe of the previous four years of fighting. The resulting Allied peace terms were not at all to Foch's liking.

From his perspective, Foch was far more concerned about preventing the Germans from presenting a military threat to Europe and especially to France. He became increasingly frustrated with the attention focused on the peace negotiations that, from his point of view, were ignoring the very real issue of reducing the German's ability to pose any meaningful military threat to other European nations.

After six months of managing the armistice and having reached the limit of his patience, Foch insisted that the Allies issue Germany an ultimatum on June 22, 1919: sign the peace treaty or the Allies would renew the fighting. This was no idle threat, and the Allies meant it (especially Foch). Recognizing it as the best of the available options (all of which were bad), Germany's leaders determined that agreeing to the terms they had been offered was better than facing renewed fighting.

Despite Germany agreeing to the terms forced upon it by Foch and the Allies, Foch refused to attend the signing ceremony for the peace treaty on June 24, 1919. Foch remarked famously, "This is not a peace. It is an armistice for twenty years," which proved to be remarkably prescient.

On June 24, 1919, Germany and the Allied nations, including Britain, France, Italy and Russia, signed the Treaty of Versailles, formally ending the unstable period of the armistice and the war. The Great War was finally over.

Gignilliat's Contributions to the Peace Process

Since it was part of the Permanent Interallied Armistice Commission, the IMFC ceased to exist when the Peace Treaty was signed on June 24, 1919, which ended the armistice. As a result, Gignilliat was released from his assignment on June 23, 1919, the last day the Interallied Military Food Commission was in existence.[159]

In terms of IMFC operations, Gignilliat helped devise methods to overcome temporary difficulties caused by the hoarding of supplies by some and also by changes in either the supply of foodstuffs available and/or the availability of transportation assets to move the material efficiently and to where it was most needed.[160] By June 1919, the vexing problems he faced when he arrived in the American zone of occupation in late-March 1919 of providing food to almost 1,000,000 starving Germans had largely been addressed and resolved successfully. Fulfilling his duties, Gignilliat had devised and implemented systems that could be sustained with the available resources and managed easily and by routine.

Gignilliat's actions contributed significantly to America's ability to establish and maintain control of its zone of occupation during the uncertain period of the armistice and to prevent mass uprisings while the peace was being negotiated. His resourcefulness and deft negotiations to resolve the issues he faced were perhaps his most impressive accomplishments. The fact that he was decorated by four foreign countries who benefited from the work of the IMFC (Romania, Poland, Italy, and Tunis), provides further evidence that Gignilliat was exceptionally effective in this role.

Considering these significant contributions to the post-war period in Europe, along with Payot's personal advocacy on his behalf, it is little wonder that Foch and Pershing acquired a very high opinion of Gignilliat during his time as the American representative on the IMFC. As a result, Foch inducted Gignilliat into the highly selective French Legion of Honor and intended to send Payot to make the award during Foch's 1922 post-war American tour (though it was actually awarded by Payot in France on July 27, 1920, during visit in conjunction with BSA World Jamboree). In an equally impressive gesture of support, Pershing ensured that Gignilliat's name was added to the promotion roster for brigadier general in November 1921.

Pershing later agreed to come to Culver to decorate Gignilliat with the Distinguished Service Medal in December 1922, lending his considerable cache to Gignilliat and to Culver. Both Foch and Pershing were notoriously difficult to impress, making the actions each took on behalf of Gignilliat tremendously significant and indicative of Gignilliat's effectiveness while serving as the American representative on the IMFC.

Returning to Culver

By the end of June 1919 and with the period of the armistice ended, Gignilliat began the process of returning to the United States.[162] He certainly had much to be proud of in the service he had rendered. He demonstrated in several different roles and situations that he was an effective military officer, whether training officer recruits, working as an intelligence officer, or solving problems in an international forum working with

BG Gignilliat being decorated with the Distinguished Service Medal by General John J. Pershing at Culver, December 7, 1922.[161]

officers from foreign countries who outranked him. His wartime service had also provided him with the opportunity to personally validate the system of military training he outlined in *Arms and the Boy*, and he had to have been quite pleased with the results on both a professional and personal level.

Making his way from Coblenz, Germany to the northwestern coast of France, Gignilliat departed from Brest, France on the *USS Imperator* on July 7, 1919, bound for New York City.[163] Arriving in New York City on July 13, 1919, Gignilliat complied with his orders to travel to Washington, DC before arranging to return to Culver.[164] After spending several days in Washington, DC debriefing government officials on his own actions and the situation in the American occupation zone, Gignilliat arrived in Plymouth, Indiana on July 18, 1919.

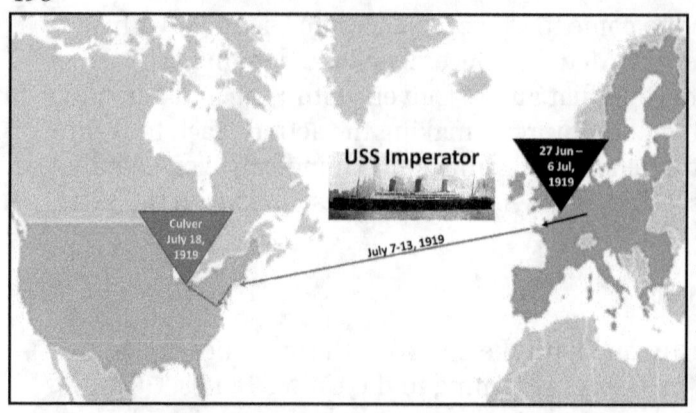

USS Imperator

27 Jun – 6 Jul, 1919

Culver July 18, 1919

July 7-13, 1919

Gignilliat's travel back to Culver, June-July 1919 from Coblenz, Germany, to Brest, France, to Camp Mills, NY, to Washington, DC, to Plymouth, IN, to Culver, IN.

Gignilliat was met at the Plymouth train station by Culver's Commissary Officer, E. V. Boblett, and transported to Culver. Upon his arrival in the evening, Gignilliat was met by a reception committee of faculty and staff members and their wives and escorted to the entrance near the infirmary by the magnificent Black Horse Troop.

On the parade field, the summer Naval and Woodcraft battalions awaited his arrival, and the entire assembled crowd cheered mightily and for an extended period of time upon his return. Once the cheers died down, his comrade-in-arms and decorated hero of the Spanish-American War Major Bert Greiner, who had selflessly (if also somewhat pragmatically, being too old for the draft and having suffered a disqualifying physical injury) agreed to remain at Culver to provide continuity and solace during Gignilliat's absence, marched the battalions into place, and members of the faculty welcomed Gignilliat home.[165]

After the battalions passed in review, Gignilliat greeted his family and was surprised by the new dwelling the Culver family had provided for him on campus after the cottage in which he and his family had previously resided had burned down in the winter of 1918 (March 25, 1918).[166] The sense of relief and accomplishment must have been palpable on campus, and Gignilliat had to have relished his return to Culver after a 27-month absence, nine months of which had been spent overseas and in extraordinarily challenging circumstances.

True to form, Gignilliat addressed the entire school population on the morning of July 22, 1919. He declared a holiday in honor of those killed in the World War and hosted a reception in his new quarters in the afternoon.[167] Gignilliat was officially discharged from active duty on July 31, 1919, and by mid-august, 1919, he was fully back in the swing of Culver, riding with the Cavalry during their ten-day summer hike. [168]

Reasons for Gignilliat's Success as an Army Officer on Active Duty

For someone who was on active duty for a total of 27 months, Gignilliat was a remarkably successful officer, earning two substantial promotions. As he learned at the OTC, the Army identified three roles in which it required officers to be proficient: *manager*; *trainer*; and *leader*.

Functioning as an effective military *manager* meant being able to care for one's men efficiently by becoming proficient in the proper methods of supplying, messing, administering, and disciplining organizations, and also learning how to care for the men's health, welfare, comfort, and sanitation. An effective *trainer* was an expert in instructing his men in the individual and collective drills while maintaining

Gignilliat back at Culver.[169]

an appropriate level of discipline to produce efficient soldiers, capable leaders, and effective units. By *leader*, the Army meant a combat leader, and officers demonstrated their ability in this aspect by becoming and remaining proficient in the tactical employment of troops and equipment on the battlefield, which could best be assessed during field exercises and also in actual combat situations.[170]

As a mature individual with over 20 years of executive experience and responsibility for training young men, Gignilliat had developed into an exceptionally competent manager and trainer while at Culver, and this expertise translated well when he functioned as an Army officer on active duty. The third element – leader – became apparent during the 84th Division's training period and also when he was in combat with the 37th Division. Gignilliat demonstrated that he was more than up to the challenge of combat, proving himself to be a capable and competent leader according to the existing standards of the US Army.

As a result, Gignilliat was able to demonstrate exceptional capability in all three of the Army's required areas for effective officers during his time on active duty. After exhibiting his proficiency as a major and officer candidate, Gignilliat was promoted to the rank of lieutenant colonel, and he continued to display his remarkable abilities of an Army officer.

After succeeding in the crucible of combat, the Army determined that Gignilliat possessed the abilities to be a successful colonel. His work as the American representative on the IMFC demonstrated his exceptional executive abilities, leading the Army to determine soon after the war that he possessed the necessary capabilities to be an effective general officer.

For a hierarchical organization like the US Army, promotion to general officer is the most visible and effective way it conveys to an individual and to others that the person possesses exceptional levels of patriotism, valor, and fidelity worthy of its highest level of recognition. This is precisely what Gignilliat was able to do during his 27 months on active duty, and the Army recognized that he had done so effectively and rewarded him accordingly with a highly coveted general officer's star for doing so.

The Culver Military System Proves Its Worth in the World War

Gignilliat's distinguished service while on active duty was indicative of the exemplary service provided by thousands of Culver graduates during the World War. Writing in 1930, Colonel C. C. Chambers, Secretary of the Culver alumni association, wrote that, "The Spirit of Culver was crystallized into a great surge of practical patriotism" and "found expression in the active service of a great company of Culver Men in training camps, on the high seas and on the battlefields of France, Belgium and Italy."[171] The challenge of a period of national emergency and the crucible of battle provided the opportunity to assess the value of Culver's military system and put it to the ultimate test.

After expending an enormous amount of effort, Gignilliat was able to determine by 1930 that of the 6,537 Culver graduates of either the winter school or summer programs who were of suitable age and eligible for military service, 3,500 served.[172]

Based upon these figures, Gignilliat concluded that an astonishing 54 percent of all living Culver graduates of military age were in active service during the World War.[173] The overwhelming number of those – 2,853 – served with Gignilliat in the US Army, which equates to approximately 44 percent of all living Culver graduates of military age.[174] What remains so impressive is that *over half of all of all living Culver graduates of military age served during the World War.*[175] Of those who served, 85 made the ultimate sacrifice and gave their lives while in the service of their country, becoming memorialized as Culver's first Gold Star men.[176]

As indicated, most Culver graduates served in the US Army, but Culver graduates also served in the US Navy and US Marine Corps, along with driving ambulances for the American Red Cross in the American Volunteer Services and in state militias. Adding a cosmopolitan aspect to

Culver's trench system created on campus to support training in trench warfare.[179]

these figures, almost two dozen chose to serve in the armies of Canada, Great Britain, and France.[177]

Of the 3,500 total, almost 1,400 (1,371, or almost 40 percent) became commissioned officers, serving in ranks of second lieutenant to colonel. Almost 700 (658) other Culver graduates were enrolled in officer training programs when the war ended. By the close of the war and following Gignilliat's lead, 53 percent of the Culver graduates serving in the war held commissions, 51 percent of them had served overseas, and 25 percent saw action on the field of battle.[178]

Culver Academies Historian Bob Hartman shares that 15 percent of Culver graduates were decorated for gallantry in action, which is a surprisingly high number. A remarkable 76 Culver graduates were decorated for conspicuous gallantry in action, receiving either the Distinguished Service Cross, the Navy Cross, or the Silver Star. Of these men, six were decorated twice for their conspicuous gallantry in action. Three other Culver graduates, along with Gignilliat, received the Distinguished Service Medal for exceptionally distinguished service during the war.[180]

By any measure, Culver's contribution to the World War was as remarkable as it was significant. It provided a visible and powerful demonstration of the tremendous effectiveness of its military system and method of forming, training, and developing young men who were capable citizens and able military leaders for the country in time of national emergency. Imagine what these young men could accomplish during periods of far less stress and with adequate resources and appropriate opportunity! Gignilliat and his colleagues at Culver were eager to explore this intriguing prospect during the period of peace and prosperity that followed the World War.

Chapter 14 – Resting His Voice: Basking in the Aftermath of His WWI Triumphs, August 1919 – December 1922

Changes at Culver During His Absence

When he returned to Culver in mid-July 1919, Gignilliat found that some things had changed during his absence. For one thing, construction on campus not started by him was occurring. The construction of two new, state-of-the-art barracks was underway, having begun as soon as practicable in early spring 1919. Replacing a smattering of self-standing cottages that had been pressed into service to house cadets, the new barracks were being built on the site out of necessity due to a significant increase in Culver's enrollment after WWI.

These two barracks would ultimately be named Argonne and Chateau Thierry, in honor of important WWI American battles in which Culver alumni had participated. In addition, the cornerstone of the Legion Memorial Building had been set on June 10, 1919 by his former division commander in the 84th Division, Major General Harry C. Hale. This structure would be built right next to the beautiful house ER Culver had gifted to the Academy as the new Superintendent's quarters that Gignilliat and his family would occupy (since his cottage had burned to the ground on March 25, 1918).

Just as significantly, the venerable Colonel J. Q. Adams retired as Culver's PMS&T, replaced at the beginning of March 1919 by US Army Infantry Captain Norman T. Findahl, who had been assigned to Culver since August 1918.[1] The Army also assigned US Army Artillery Captain John M. Fray to Culver. The assigning of two active-duty officers (which was somewhat unusual for an institution of Culver's size) indicates how valuable the US Army considered CMA's contributions to national defense.

The ever-popular Major Robert Rossow returned to Culver during the first week of May 1919. Rossow, who had trained at Fort Harrison with Gignilliat, also accompanied him to Camp Taylor with the 84th Division, commanding a machine-gun battalion. Once in Europe, Rossow assumed command of a different machine-gun battalion, and, like Gignilliat, remained in Germany after the war as part of the Allied Army of Occupation.[2] Based upon his service, Rossow was promoted to the rank of Lieutenant Colonel of Cavalry in the Officers Reserve Corps shortly after his return to Culver.

With the addition of Captains Findahl and Fray, and the return of Major Rossow, Culver had three very competent officers to instruct its major military branches – infantry, artillery, and cavalry – at expert levels by the time of Gignilliat's return.

Changes in His Own Family Upon His Return

Immediately prior to Gignilliat's return, Leigh Jr. made the difficult decision to depart West Point on July 11, 1919 after completing his first year in attendance. It had been an unusual year at West Point to be sure, with the early graduations of several classes as a result of the war, placing much greater levels of responsibility on the remaining underclassmen, and the compression of the education program for the remaining classes from the traditional four years to two years in anticipation of the war lasting into 1919 or perhaps even 1920 while attempting to retain a suitable level of academic focus and rigor. This situation altered the West Point experience significantly for all, creating a level of urgency and focus on warfare at the expense of a more traditional four-year experience that may have been unsettling for some.

The newly arriving USMA Superintendent, Douglas MacArthur, would make it a priority to establish a three-year curriculum and perhaps even reestablish the traditional four-year curriculum at West Point (which is what ultimately occurred), but there was no way for Leigh Jr. to know that any of this would occur or if it would apply to his class. While it is clear that Leigh Jr. had done well as a USMA cadet during his first year (it was rumored that he was slated to become the Regimental Adjutant for his second and final year, an important and quite visible position once held by George S. Patton), this charged, truncated, and uncertain wartime environment also helped to make it clear to him that the life of professional solider was not his calling.

Leigh Jr. made his decision prior to his father's return from overseas and perhaps while he was in transit across the Atlantic Ocean and largely unavailable for consultation, making it likely that he relied upon the counsel of his mother and received her support for leaving West Point. One can envision the redoubtable Minnie telling her first-born son to come home and that she would settle matters with his father when he returned.

Along with the generous gift from ER Culver of a new and impressive set of quarters, Gignilliat was perhaps even more surprised by Leigh Jr.'s presence upon his return to Culver, since he naturally expected his eldest son to be engaged with the training of new cadets at West Point. Minnie's considerable influence and his love for his son, coupled with his own euphoria at being back home after such an extended absence from his family (over eleven months) almost certainly combined to soften the blow, temper his disappointment, and help him accept the situation.

Making the situation more palatable, within a very brief period of time (and perhaps as a result of Gignilliat's own influence), Leigh Jr. was accepted at Princeton University and enrolled by September 1919. Owing to the education he received during his year at West Point and his own determination, he began as a legitimate sophomore and would graduate from Princeton in spring 1922, staying on track academically with the traditional four-year course of instruction for higher education.

Continuing His Preparedness Activities – Testifying Before Congress Again in August 1919

The day after the 1919 summer session concluded in late August at Culver, Gignilliat was back in Washington, DC, testifying before a subcommittee of the US Senate Committee on Military Affairs exploring options for reorganizing the US Army to sustain its readiness while also reducing its cost to the taxpayers (since it had become clear that popular opinion had turned decidedly against war).[3] During his testimony on the afternoon of August 28, 1919, Gignilliat made two important points based on what he had learned during the World War: One related to the effectiveness of military training provided at "essentially military schools;" and one about the length of time needed to train a young man in the basics of soldiering.

Regarding the effectiveness of military training at "essentially military schools" with respect to how well it prepared cadets to serve as officers in war, Gignilliat testified that, "those schools and colleges that have been giving military training in intensive form have been doing something very much worth while (*sic*) from the standpoint of the training of officers," and that "the output of those schools that have done the work thoroughly has demonstrated the tremendous value of the training they have received" when tested in the crucible of combat. The chairman of the committee, Senator James W. Wadsworth of New York, replied, based upon his own assessment of the value of the service provided by officers and soldiers who attended military schools and served in WWI, by stating, "There can be no question about that."[4]

When asked about the length of time it takes to make a good soldier, Gignilliat gave a nuanced response that demonstrated the depth of his understanding of the training process he had gained from his experiences at Culver and during World War 1. He believe that much could be done in three months, but it took six months to train a soldier properly.

Elaborating further, Gignilliat offered that he felt that "it would be desirable in a way to divide the six months into two periods of three months one year and three months the following year" to give the training time to sink in and also for the young man to have time to process the first three months effectively before undertaking the next three months. He closed by stating that young man would get more out of the training if it were broken up as he suggested and that "the sum total [of the training] would be better than if he had his six months all at one time."[5]*

By way of affirmation, the president and commandant of Bordentown Military Institute in New Jersey, T. D. Landon, who followed Gignilliat in that day's testimony, offered in response to a query by the chairman that he agreed completely with Gignilliat's assessment and recommendation.[6]

As was his practice, Gignilliat took the opportunity to emphasize that the military training had to be presented properly to be effective. Reinforcing one of his own long-held beliefs allowed him to make an implied case for the value of "essentially military schools," which would be better able to present the military training properly and therefore more effectively.

Recommissioned as a Colonel in the Organized Reserve Corps

Having been discharged from active duty on July 31, 1919, and based upon his exemplary wartime service and continuing stature as one of the country's premier military trainers, Gignilliat was re-commissioned as an infantry colonel in the US Army Reserves on December 19, 1919. It is unclear what his specific Army duties were for the next 18 months, but it is certain that he had impressed General Pershing during his time in Europe as the war ended and that he continued to serve with distinction in 1919 and 1920. Gignilliat was elected in June 1920 to serve as the Commander of Indiana American Legion for a period lasting until Oct 31, 1921.

Leading the American Delegation to Inaugural World Scout Jamboree in Summer 1920

In recognition of his stature and work with the Boy Scouts, Gignilliat was also personally selected by Boy Scout executives to lead the American delegation of 300 Boy Scouts to the first-ever World Scout Jamboree, occurring in London during the summer 1920. This assignment took

---

* It is interesting to note that in 1934 the USMC adopted two six-week periods of training over consecutive summers for its Platoon Leaders Course (PLC) program, developed as an alternative program for college students who wish to become commissioned officers in the United States Marine Corps, attesting to the enduring value of Gignilliat's 1919 observations.

Gignilliat and his two eldest sons Leigh Jr. (who had just completed his first year at Princeton) and Fred (who had just graduated from CMA in June 1920) for most of the 1920 summer, while Minnie and Hank summered at the Fleet family home in Virginia (which was how Minnie preferred to spend her summers when possible).

Gignilliat's two boys were doubtlessly excited by the prospect of their overseas adventure and getting to spend the better part of their summer with their father. Departing for New York City on the final day of June, Gignilliat arrived in New York City on July 1 with a cadre of assistants that included Major Charles Reed (Culver's surgeon) to see to the boys' health requirements and 11 CMA graduates (including Leigh Jr. and Freddy) to oversee the scouts.

Gignilliat met with Chief Scout Executive James West (who worked with Dan Beard and Ernest Seton, and accompanied the Culver party) before heading to Fort Hamilton, where the contingent of 300 Boy Scouts would be assembled and quartered prior to its departure. The scouts arrived the following day, and the Culver grads took charge, assigning them to one of eight troops of about 35 Scouts, each led by a CMA alum.

For the next three days while they lived in Army barracks and ate with Army soldiers, the CMA grads drilled the scouts in basic marching techniques, inspected their uniforms, and otherwise prepared them for their journey and the event. After supper, the CMA leaders took the excited scouts out for stimulating evening activities to places like Coney Island. As a culminating event for their preparations, Gignilliat held a final marching review of the scouts in Central Park on July 2 before loading them on the ship that same day for their ten-day voyage to England.

While at sea, the scouts were kept very busy by design to reduce their inevitable homesickness, cleaning compartments, scrubbing decks, and servings as KPs. Harking back to his own time on board a navy ship during his Mediterranean cruise in 1913, Gignilliat ensured that the scouts also drilled, stood guard, and did various other things that kept them busy from dawn to dusk. Recognizing that they were boys and not sailors, the scouts were allowed to have social engagements and attend dances in the evenings.

Sighting land on July 16, the party rested and was met at the Isle of Wright to be guided to the wharf by a steamer. Gignilliat was the first to disembark upon making landfall. Moving toward London, the scouts marched part of the way and then loaded into open-topped motor coaches for the remainder of the trip. The group arrived at their final destination late that evening to stay at the YMCA at Mildmay Park in North London, finally bedding down around 3:00 am on July 17th.

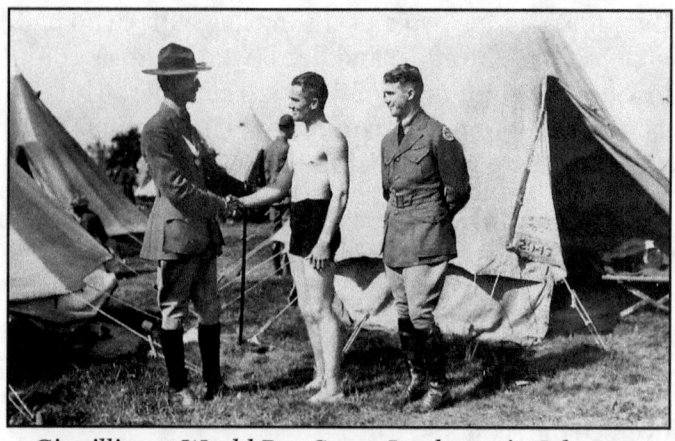

Gignilliat at World Boy Scout Jamboree in July 1920 shaking hands with Culver boxer Jimmy Hatfield (Fred Gignilliat is on the right).[7]

For the next ten days, the scouts rehearsed their scouting activities (Indian pageant, races, crafts, etc.) during the day and had a grand time visiting the sites of London at night. Their preparations complete and anxious to being their jamboree experience, the group departed London on July 27 for the site of the jamboree at an old British Army camp in Richmond (about 10 miles SW of the center of London on the outskirts) to join 5,000 scouts from 30 nations. Upon arrival, the boys pitched their tents and made camp, surrounded by fellow scouts from England, Scotland, and Ireland.

During the 10-day jamboree – occurring during the period 30 July – 8 August – the scouts performed their own scouting activities, observed the scouting activities of other scouts, participated and competed in the many individual events staged for their benefit, interacted with scouts from around the world, made friends, traded patches and neckerchiefs, and reveled in the camaraderie created by the largest group of scouts ever assembled to that point in history.

Making its own contribution, the Culver group also performed calisthenics in cadence and were recognized with a "world championship" for their efforts, as was the excellent Boy Scout band from Denver, Colorado. In terms of individual competitions, Culver cadet Jimmy Hatfield, who made the trip as a Scout so he could compete, also won his class in the boxing competition.

Indeed, according to an account offered by one of the CMA grads on the trip, the American contingent won just about every one of the jamboree's competitions. This individual also offered that the success of the American delegation was the "direct result of Colonel Gignilliat's work," and that

Major Reed (Culver's surgeon) ensured that the group remained in perfect health throughout the entire trip.[9]

Despite having experienced so much thus far, the adventure was far from over. After the jamboree, Gignilliat journeyed with the entire group to the European continent and took the opportunity to visit all the sites in Paris (as they had done in New York City) and also provide demonstrations of drills, parades, and other exhibitions (as was to be expected by a Gignilliat-led organization).

After three days in Paris, the group entrained for a visit to the important American battlefield at Chateau Thierry, where they were staggered by the amount of devastation still evident. The group visited the battlefield at Belleau Wood, the site of an important US engagement. Gignilliat led the group on a tour of some of the important WWI battlefields. Particularly memorable stops occurred at the Belleau Wood cemetery, where the group located the graves of Culver alumni and highly decorated Gold Star men Donald F. Duncan '07 and Charles H. Ulmer '16, and at the Verdun cemetery at the grave of the very popular John G. "Jack" Schneider '17, also a Gold Star man who was well known and liked by the members of the group.[10]

While the larger group remained in Antwerp, Belgium, and watched the Olympic events occurring there at the time, Gignilliat took the opportunity to take his two sons and several other CMA grads with him to revisit the areas where he had served during the war.

They visited both Coblenz and Trier, where his many friends showered him and his charges with every conceivable kindness. When his old comrade-in-arms French General Payot learned of his presence in the Allied Occupation Zone (which Payot oversaw), Payot surprised Gignilliat with a hastily arranged but nonetheless impressive ceremony at which he was awarded the French *Croix d'Officier de la Legion d'Honneur*. The ceremony was so spur-of-the-moment that Gignilliat had to borrow a uniform from an American captain, since he had not brought one with him for the trip.

The ceremony occurred in Wiesbaden, Germany

At the graves of Gold Star heroes, August 1920 (Gignilliat is third from the left).[11]

(which guarded the bridge into Germany at Mainz and was the headquarters of the French occupation zone) in front of an entire French regiment and huge crowd.

A sumptuous banquet followed the ceremony, during which Gignilliat was the guest of honor and feted by the many high-ranking dignitaries in attendance.[15] Although quite modest and humble by nature, Gignilliat must have nevertheless been quite proud to share this moment with two of his children.

After the ceremony in Wiesbaden, Gignilliat and his small band traveled to Metz in Payot's personal train car before rejoining West, Reed, and the remainder of the Scouts in Antwerp. The group traveled to several other places, including a final stop in Brussels, Belgium, where the Scouts put on a demonstration for over 20,000 people and the Culver men provided a roughriding demonstration. The Scouts embarked for the trip home on August 17 and arrived in New York City on September 4, 1920, having enjoyed the experience of a lifetime.

Once the scouts departed for their homes, Gignilliat returned to Culver to begin the 1920 winter school academic session, having missed virtually the entire 1920 summer session. Leigh Jr. made the short trip to Princeton to resume his studies.

Gignilliat in a borrowed uniform from a US Army captain being decorated with the French Croix d'Officier de la Legion d'Honneur, Wiesbaden, Germany, August 1920.[12]

According to one of the CMA grads on the trip, the majority of the credit for the success of the entire endeavor was due to Gignilliat's remarkable organizational abilities and attention to detail, both of which engendered a great amount of respect from all with whom he interacted. Another CMA grad on the trip went on to observe that Gignilliat was also successful in infusing the "Culver Spirit" into the group, which, in his opinion, also accounted for much of the group's success.[17]

French Croix d'Officier de la Legion d'Honneur with Rosette.[13]

Back in Stride – Returning to Culver for the 1920-1921 Winter Session

Returning to campus in time for the start of the winter session (which was somewhat unusual for him), Gignilliat

Gignilliat next to French General Payot at French Legion of Honor Ceremony in front of an entire French regiment and huge crowd in Wiesbaden, Germany, August 1920.[14]

assumed his old form and began the session with a flurry of activity. Two construction projects were already underway to build a new Commerce building and the Legion Memorial Library. However, construction was halted on both projects during 1920, and campus did not witness a resumption of further construction until 1923.

In terms of programs, however, 1920 saw tremendous changes. After laying the groundwork in 1919, Culver opened one of the nation's first secondary aviation schools, drawing much attention and high levels of enthusiasm across the country. Within the Corps of Cadets, both the BHT and the Culver Battery were admitted as permanent units to which cadets could be assigned, providing for choices among infantry, cavalry, and artillery units for the first time.

The admission of the battery and troop into the corps organization as permanent units was quite logical after having increased the corps from a one-battalion organization to a regiment composed of two cadet battalions in September 1919. The newly completed barracks were sufficient to allow for cadets to be housed by unit under this new organization, as they had been since the opening of North Barrack in 1913.

In addition, the cadets formally re-established Culver's Honor system that had been created before the war but allowed to lapse. It is likely that the dramatic increase in enrollment during the previous two years – growing from 548 in 1918 to 728 in 1919 to a record-setting 744 in fall 1920 (a number which would not be surpassed

Gignilliat on horseback in a borrowed uniform with Fred and Leigh Jr. on the day of the French Legion of Honor ceremony, August 1920.[16]

until after World War II) – was both the impetus and cause for these organizational and programmatic actions.

Achieving another important level of national recognition, Gignilliat was twice elected to serve as the vice president of AMCSUS during the period 1921 and 1922. AMCSUS continued to work closely with the Army to establish the ROTC programs mandated by the National Defense Act of 1916 but largely put on hold during WWI, and it remained quite influential. As a member of the Executive Committee by virtue of leading one of the nation's largest military schools and as an elected official of the organization, Gignilliat worked closely with AMCSUS president E W Nichols, Superintendent of VMI and close personal colleague, to reverse the declining membership of AMCSUS.

Using his genius for marketing, Gignilliat helped to increase membership from a low of 30 institutions when his tenure began in 1921 to approximately 45 member institutions during each of his years in office.[18] This remarkable level of improvement helped AMCSUS retain its level of influence as an important advocate on behalf of the nations' military schools and almost certainly attracted the Army's attention, which had come to rely on AMCSUS as a valued partner in its ROTC efforts.

His role as the commander of the Indiana American Legion, leading the American contingent to the World Scouting Jamboree, being awarded a prestigious French decoration, along with his successful efforts to increase membership in AMCSUS and the continued success of CMA as one of the nation's leading military schools were all important events that continued to bring honor to the Army and keep Gignilliat conspicuous to those in Washington, DC, especially Pershing. In May 1921 (almost certainly at Pershing's insistence), Gignilliat's name was placed on the eligibility list from promotion to brigadier general, and on June 29, Gignilliat's name was added to list of officers eligible to serve at the Army's General Headquarters (GHQ) by action of a board headed by Pershing. Shortly thereafter, Pershing became Chief of Staff of the US Army on July 1, 1921.

Pershing's support was essential for advancement to the general-officer ranks during his tenure, as the Army Chief of Staff had almost complete control of the general officer promotion list. Gignilliat continued to accomplish actions that sustained Pershing's existing support for him.

Upon his return from a reinvigorating vacation to Glacier National Park with son Fred in September 1921 (returning to his custom of vacationing after the completion of the summer session; more about the Skyland Camp endeavor later), Gignilliat completed a very successful tour as the Commander of the Indiana American Legion and hosted a visit by a delegation of the *Fédération Interalliée Des Anciens Combattants*, the Interallied Federation of World War I Veterans Organization known as FIDAC (more about FIDAC later), one member of which remarked that the discipline he observed at Culver was nothing less than "perfect."[19]

This was important, as Pershing was an ardent supporter of the American Legion, comprised largely of men who had served under him in Mexico during the Punitive Expedition and in Europe during WWI, and also of FIDAC, which was its international equivalent.

Pershing's WWI Allied colleague, French Marshal Ferdinand Foch, visited America in fall 1921, and Gignilliat arranged for Culver's BHT to provide Foch's escort and for the CMA Band to march and play in his honor during his visit to Indianapolis on November 4. Bringing all 100 Troopers and the entire CMA Band, Gignilliat provided the esteemed French hero with a most dignified escort that was entirely fitting and exactly the type of courtesy Pershing wished to extend.

Gignilliat's presence and the magnificent performance of both the BHT and the CMA Band enhanced the event significantly. Foch was suitably impressed, writing to Gignilliat of how captivated he was with "the brilliant showing and bearing of the cadets of Culver Military Academy" since his visit and expressing his "heartiest felicitations" to and "highest regards" for Gignilliat, his staff, and the CMA cadets.[21] Nothing could have delighted Gignilliat or Pershing more than honoring Foch so appropriately and receiving such accolades.

Despite Foch being unable to visit Culver personally, the arrival of Foch's trusted subordinate and Gignilliat's great friend French General Payot to Culver on November 8, 1921, was another resounding success. As expected, it was characterized by Gignilliat's traditional celebratory schedule of events and the again-magnificent performance of the Culver cadets.

Given the level of importance that Pershing placed on

The BHT escorting French Marshal Foch (riding in the automobile) during his visit to Indianapolis, 4 Nov. 1921.[20]

Gignilliat with visiting French General Payot, November 8, 1921.[22]

treating Foch and his party with the highest possible level of dignity during their visit, it becomes clear that Gignilliat's actions furthered Pershing's own agenda and resulted in sustained support for Gignilliat. Within two days of Payot's visit to Culver, Gignilliat was nominated for promotion to the rank of brigadier general in the ORC on November 10.

Such a nomination could only occur with the explicit support of the Army Chief of Staff, and it is clear that Gignilliat had earned such support as a result of his performance and actions. In less than one month, Gignilliat was promoted to the rank of brigadier general in the ORC, with a retroactive date of rank of November 4, 1921. The speed of his promotion, evidenced by the exceedingly short period of time between his nomination and actual promotion, along with the decision to backdate his date of rank (which enhanced his status in terms of seniority) indicate that Gignilliat's promotion had the highest level of support.

On January 1, 1922, and befitting his new rank and status, Gignilliat assumed command of the 168th Infantry Brigade from his Culver colleague Major Harold C. Bays, which was part of the US Army's Organized Reserve tasked with providing training for officers and enlisted men in the ORC at summer Civilian Military Training Camps (CMTCs) akin to the Plattsburg camps from before the war. Intended to complement the ROTC programs as sources of reserve officers, the CMTCs allowed citizens to complete military training as either officers or enlisted during the summers in short increments along the lines Gignilliat had suggested during his 1919 testimony to the Senate Armed Services subcommittee. Given his support for the program, his experience in running similar camps at Culver, along with his own participation in one such camp at Fort Sheridan in fall 1915, Gignilliat was ideally suited for such a command.. He held this rank and served in this position until his retirement from the US Army on July 4, 1939.[23]

Gignilliat's status as a national public figure, along with the influence of *Arms and the Boy* and the performance of Culver alumni in WWI combined to further enhance Culver's already stellar national reputation as one of the nation's premier military schools. The most tangible measure of its success comes from Culver's enrollment figures during the period 1917-1920, during which it either held steady (which was a great success during the war period) or increased substantially.

Just after Gignilliat's call to active duty in May 1917, Culver's enrollment in fall 1917 was an impressive 548, which was an increase of 84 cadets from fall 1914 and about which Gignilliat had been so concerned. By the following year in the midst of America's involvement in the war, Culver's enrollment was at 596 and growing, which was quite remarkable during the war period and which was sufficient to signal the need for additional barracks. Culver constructed two additional large barracks – Argonne and Chateau Thierry – in time for use in fall 1919, which was fortunate since Culver's enrollment shot up to 728 in fall 1919 by an astonishing 22 percent, equating to an increase of 132 cadets! By fall 1920, Culver was filled to capacity even with its expanded capacity provided by the two large new barracks, welcoming 744 cadets to campus, a number which would not be surpassed until after World War II.[24]

A combination of the recognition that both Culver and Gignilliat had earned during the war period, along with a heightened sense of patriotism in some areas that helped to counter growing anti-militarist movement elsewhere, was undoubtedly responsible for much of this growth.

Gignilliat Reaches His First "Peak" of Influence as a National and Public Figure at Culver

Using his new status as a general officer and brigade commander t o Culver's advantage, Gignilliat remained quite active in promoting the value of military education and preparedness whenever and wherever the opportunity arose for him to do so. In May 1922, Gignilliat traveled to Pittsburgh, Pennsylvania to deliver a short radio address regarding the value of military training in education.[25] Gignilliat used the opportunity to reemphasize his standard themes: Its value in promoting discipline, hardiness, citizenship, and service; that it is democratic and based on merit; that it does not promote militarism; and its overall positive educational value.

Following a relaxing summer session at Culver and after beginning the winter session in fall 1922 with more than 700 cadets enrolled (706), Gignilliat was ready for (and perhaps due) an uneventful year. He learned of the death of his adopted father, Leigh Robinson, on November 4, 1922. While undoubtedly causing him some level of grief, it does not appear that he traveled to Richmond, Virginia for the funeral, indicating that the two had never truly reconciled in the years since their break while Gignilliat was attending VMI.

The Quest to Get General Pershing to Visit Culver

The personal tragedy of the passing of his adopted father notwithstanding, 1922 ended with one of the greatest personal and professional triumphs of Gignilliat's entire career: arranging for a visit to Culver by General of the Armies John J. Pershing.

Beyond his exceptional performance between mid-March and the end of June 1919 in the American sector of occupied Germany, there appear to have been at least two other reasons for Pershing's support of Gignilliat. First was the congruence between the ideas regarding the value of military training and citizenship between Pershing and Gignilliat, which included the belief by both men that military training made for better citizens and did not engender militarism.

The second had to do with the contribution that military schools made to national military preparedness, which was a topic about which both men were particularly passionate. Both men shared the belief that military officers had to lead citizen soldiers more by persuasion than coercion, and the Culver system was far ahead of schools like West Point (from which Pershing graduated in 1886 as First Captain) in creating a system to produce such leaders. It is worthwhile to examine this second reason in greater depth to gain a deeper understanding of the status of military schools in the country in the years immediately following WWI.

The process and logistics of arranging for a visit by the most famous man in America were both long and arduous, taking on the trappings of an epic quest, and the episode is worth recounting at length for what it shows about Gignilliat as a person and professional at this point in his career. As one might expect, the basis of this account of this occurrence comes not from Gignilliat himself (for he was far too modest to tell such a story about himself and his efforts) but rather from a more extroverted raconteur working at Culver at the time: Colonel Robert Rossow.

As part of a nation-wide inspection tour, General Pershing visited Chicago in 1919 just before Christmas, and Gignilliat secured from him a "tentative acceptance" of an invitation to provide the commencement address at the June 8, 1920 graduation ceremony. Gignilliat enlisted the assistance of the ever-reliable Vice President Thomas R. Marshall to act as Culver's emissary in the effort "to secure a confirmation to the tentatively accepted invitation" for General Pershing (who was the nation's most senior Army officer awaiting his appointment as the Army Chief of Staff to begin on July 1, 1921).

According to Rossow, however, sometime during "the latter part of May" 1920, a "bitterly disappointed" Gignilliat was informed by Marshall that travel delays had prevented Pershing from returning to Washington, DC in time to make the trip to Culver for what Gignilliat had designated as "Pershing Day" at the academy. Gignilliat was especially distressed by this news, as he had just received the beautifully engraved invitations he had ordered to invite people to the event, which had all been addressed and were ready to be posted.

Gignilliat remarked to Rossow, with (one hopes) some hyperbole, that this cancellation was perhaps the greatest disappointment of his entire life, and the determined Gignilliat was not going to accept the situation without doing all he could to try to rectify it. Rossow noted that this steely determination in the face of adversity was quite characteristic of Gignilliat, writing that, "When ordinary persons are ready to quit the fight, I've often found that [Gignilliat] hasn't even started to roll up his sleeves yet," and that Gignilliat's resolve in such situations was unshakable.[26]

Rossow also found that such situations brought out the very best in Gignilliat in terms of his ingenuity and ability to improvise on the spot, consider every angle and never overlook the slightest opportunities to succeed.[27] This must also have been one of the traits that impressed Pershing and made him admire Gignilliat so much.

According to Rossow's account, Gignilliat sent him on a hastily planned mission of the highest importance to Washington, DC to secure Pershing's agreement to appear as (tentatively) promised. With less than an hour to catch the express train in Plymouth, Gignilliat informed Rossow that he had already made all the travel arrangements for Rossow to make the trip and that they would be waiting for him at the ticket office in Plymouth. Authorizing Rossow to "get all the money you think you'll need at the Quartermaster's," Gignilliat instructed Rossow to rush to Washington, DC without delay and "use every influence in Washington that [he] can think of – or reach" to accomplish his mission of getting General Pershing to agree to come to Culver as planned.

Expressing his confidence in Rossow, Gignilliat closed by telling him that it was up to him to find a way to succeed, characteristically allowing him (as he did with other trusted subordinates) wide discretion in how he accomplished this critical task.[28]

The newly promoted Lieutenant Colonel Rossow was dazed by the enormity of the task he had just been assigned and sat down for a moment to process what he was being asked to do – to find a way to get General Pershing to agree to come to Culver after having already declined the opportunity to do so to the Vice President of the United States! After hurrying to Plymouth and arriving just in time to make the train, the station agent rushed out and told him that, predictably, Gignilliat wanted to talk to him on the phone with another idea. Gignilliat believed that taking a cadet with him to Washington, DC would strengthen their appeal tremendously, and Rossow agreed.

Rossow immediately identified "the finest looking boy" he could think of, Cadet Edward "Eddy" Wells, Captain of Company E, First Lieutenant of the Black Horse Troop, talented Rough Rider, athlete, and all-around exemplary cadet, as his choice for the mission. Gignilliat concurred with Rossow's choice. Wells, who possessed a tremendously likable affect and upbeat personality, turned out to be an exceptionally appropriate choice. He was also a strapping young man who, at "six feet tall, slender, and with a tapering waist that widened to perfectly stunning square shoulders," complimented by a "lean, bronzed, good-looing face" with lively gray eyes and a perpetual grin that showed his "flashing white teeth," would provide the ideal representation of a Culver cadet on this mission.[29]

It also helped that Rossow and Wells were well acquainted by virtue of Wells' involvement in the BHT, and that Wells was a "true believer" in Culver who was as fully committed to accomplishing the mission as Rossow. Rossow described him as being essential to keeping up morale as they faced a discouraging series of rejections, calling Wells both "a tonic and an inspiration" and remarking that "his never falling cheerfulness sustained me."[31] Rossow also later learned that Wells had a connection with General Pershing that would be quite fortuitous. Gignilliat used his intimate knowledge of the rail system to work out a way to have Cadet Wells meet up with Rossow in Harrisburg, Pennsylvania early the next

Cadet Edward "Eddie" Wells.[30]

morning in such a way as to cause Rossow no delay.

On the trip, Rossow determined that "the most able and determined gentlemen" of Pershing's staff needed to be the focus of his efforts, and that getting the right person to acquiesce to his request was the key to accomplishing his mission. Upon his arrival in Washington, DC, Rossow, wearing civilian clothes, began by visiting Vice President Marshall in the Senate Chamber to get a better sense of the opposition he was facing, with the "shined and shining" Cadet Eddie Wells by his side in his full-dress uniform offering "spectacularly impelling" salutes to all the officers they encountered. Having been prepared for their arrival by Gignilliat, Marshall welcomed both travelers heartily and, in keeping with his gentle personality, informed the pair that he was intimidated by military men and that "General Pershing scares me most to death." Marshall could not offer much in the way of support, but he wished Rossow luck in his endeavor.

Rossow embarked on his quest soon thereafter, calling on "every senator, every representative, every prominent Washingtonian whom I knew – or who was suggested by...Gignilliat," only to be rebuffed by each and every one with responses of "they didn't feel they could interfere in the matter" and that "they had no influence with General Pershing." He had little success at the War Department either.[32]

The following days were filled with the same kind of efforts and outcomes, going so far as going to the office of the current Army Chief of Staff, General Payton C. March, who had a son attending Culver at the time and was quite supportive of Culver, and calling on Rossow's former corps commander and division commander from the war. Having struck out in all of his efforts but knowing how determined Gignilliat was to secure General Pershing as the commencement speaker, Rossow, with a flash of inspiration worthy of Gignilliat himself, inquired if General Pershing was free on June 9, believing that Gignilliat would agree to postponing the commencement ceremony for one day in order to accommodate General Pershing's schedule.

Rossow got a message to Pershing with the amended invitation and awaited his response. While he waited, Rossow telephoned Gignilliat and told him of his efforts and situation. Gignilliat approved of his work "heartily," telling Rossow that he had come up with the same idea of postponing commencement for one day and had put the matter to the cadets for a vote. While hopeful for positive outcome, Gignilliat waited on the outcome of the vote with bated breath, fearing that the cadets might resent such an action and withhold their approval for such a drastic measure. The outcome of these two vigils was quite different: Gignilliat was gratified that the cadets were willing to postpone the commencement ceremony for one day; Rossow learned, after waiting almost an entire day, that the Pershing had declined the amended invitation for June 9th.

Massively disappointed but unwilling to admit defeat, both Rossow and Gignilliat pressed on and took unusual actions. Rossow acquired the General's unlisted home telephone number and hoped to make use of it to find a way to meet with Pershing in person on Monday morning (which happened to be Memorial Day). Meanwhile Gignilliat had arranged for Admiral Albert Ross (who happened to be in Annapolis), a well-known retired Navy officer who knew Pershing well and was running Culver's Summer Naval School at the time, to be available to help Rossow.

Agreeing reluctantly to back out of a commitment he had made to Naval Academy, Ross consented to accompany Rossow and Eddie to meet with General Pershing on Monday. Making use of Pershing' contact information, Admiral Ross' influence, and a bit of deception, Rossow was unexpectedly successful in gaining a brief audience with General Pershing at 11:00 am on Memorial Day.

All the moving pieces came together with fortuitous timing for the meeting. Delighted to see his old comrade Admiral Ross, Pershing welcomed them graciously. After pleading their case and remembering that he had met Eddie previously at a whistlestop (what are the odds of selecting perhaps the only Culver cadet to have met Pershing for this mission?), Pershing responded by telling them that while he was quite aware of Culver and its reputation, he simply could not accept their invitation to visit Culver when they were asking him to do so.

Nevertheless, Pershing was impressed by their perseverance and persistence, and wanting to take his own measure of the school about which he had heard so much, Pershing committed to doing all he could to schedule a visit to Culver, perhaps as soon as in the fall. Gignilliat seized upon this commitment and pursued it with his characteristic dogged determination. Circumstances prevented a visit in fall 1920, but Gignilliat persevered, and his persistence finally paid off.

After almost 2 ½ years of effort, the forces of the universe finally aligned to allow for Pershing to visit Culver for four hours on the morning of December 7, 1922. Having the opportunity to personally recognize the recently promoted General Gignilliat for his tremendous performance after the war in the American occupation sector in Germany and decorate Colonel Charles "Cal" Chambers with the Distinguished Service Cross (the nation's second highest award for valor) and Gignilliat with the Distinguished Service Medal provided a successful ending to this particular odyssey.

Pershing's Visit to Culver – A Personal and Professional Culmination for Gignilliat

Determined to take every advantage of the opportunity presented by his triumph, Gignilliat packed the four hours Pershing spent on campus to the hilt. After being escorted from the train station to campus by the BHT at 7:30 am, Pershing joined Gignilliat for breakfast at the Superintendent's house before receiving a 17-gun salute upon entering campus formally to meet with the cadet captains in Legion Memorial Hall and review the stirring Gold Star memorial honoring Culver men who lost their lives in WWI.

Next, Pershing greeted the Trustees, senior administrators, and the faculty and staff, along with their families, before reviewing the corps outdoors in a driving rainstorm. After a thorough inspection of the cadets in ranks, Pershing decorated Gignilliat with the Distinguished Service Medal in front of the entire community. Pershing also decorated Colonel Charles "Cal" Chambers with the Distinguished Service Cross.

The citation for Gignilliat's Distinguished Service Medal reads as follows:

General Pershing meeting with CMA Cadet Captains, December 7, 1922.[33]

"Leigh R. Gignilliat, Brigadier General, Officers' Reserve Corps, then Colonel, Infantry, United States Army. For exceptionally meritorious and distinguished service. As G-2 of the 84th Division from October 6, 1917, until November 8, 1918, and of the 37th Division from November 9, 1918, until March 15, 1919, he displayed an unusual devotion to duty and military attainments of a high order, which enabled him to place the intelligence sections of both divisions on a high place of efficiency. From March 15, 1919, to June 27, 1919, as the United States Representative on the Inter-Allied Food Commission, by rare tact, great energy and marked ability, he solved, with conspicuous success, many perplexing problems of supply in our occupied areas."

Despite the miserable conditions, the corps performed exceptionally well. As a former First Captain at West Point with an exceptionally discerning eye for military precision, Pershing found no fault with any of the passing formations and was very impressed with the cadets' discipline.

Moving indoors for much of the remainder of the visit, Pershing was treated to military displays from the infantry, artillery battery, and

General Pershing decorating General Gignilliat, December 7, 1922.[34]

the BHT in the riding hall, ROTC displays in the Recreation building, and athletic displays in the gymnasium. Pershing took time to engage kindly with a large group of children from the surrounding area that had gathered in front of the gym, addressing them briefly and even (somewhat unexpectedly) posing for photographs with them. The death of several of Pershing's own children prior to WWI had hardened him noticeably, so his willingness to engage so freely with the children indicates that he was truly at ease and enjoying his visit.

After inspecting the new Argonne barracks to see how the cadets lived, Pershing participated in a tree-planting ceremony to honor first three Culver men who gave their lives in WWI.[37]

After meeting privately with Gignilliat and the Trustees, ER Culver presented Pershing with a scroll establishing a four-year scholarship at Culver in his honor

General Pershing engaging with the children, December 7, 1922.[36]

to be awarded to the child of a WWI veteran. Pershing was escorted off campus as the band played "Over There," departing a little after 11:30 am on a train bound for Washington, DC.[39]

General Pershing inspecting the CMA Corps, December 7, 1922 (Gignilliat is at the far left).[35]

The entire visit went very well, and Pershing remarked that he would depart carrying with him "a very touching recollection" of his visit, highlighting the time he was able to spend with the cadet captains. He expressed confidence in Culver's ability to carry out the noble "ideals and purposes" of the institution as they had been demonstrated to him and thanked all for their hospitality.[40] Just before he departed campus, Pershing turned to the Superintendent and said, "General Gignilliat, I have

General Pershing planting memorial trees, December 7, 1922 [38] *(Gignilliat is just to the right of the tree being planted).*

not only been greatly impressed by what I have seen at Culver, but I have been deeply moved."[41]

Given his desires for the visit and Culver's role as a representative institution of private "essentially military" schools, Gignilliat had to be quite pleased with the visit and the powerful impression it made on Pershing. Coming near the peak of the military school movement in America and in the wake of the National Defense Acts of 1916 and 1920, it is hard to imagine an event that could bring more positive attention or be more influential on the Army Chief of Staff, who was convinced that Army officers had to be exceptionally capable instructors and leaders to be effective fighting with armies of citizen soldiers in the future.[42]

Culver Within the Context of Other Military Schools – Compared to West Point

Pershing's visit to Culver made such a positive impression on him partly because of how the Culver he experienced compared to his own alma mater at the time, when Douglas MacArthur served as Superintendent during a truncated three-year period from June 1919 to June 1922. Dashing, charismatic, and a highly decorated war hero, MacArthur was about the same age as Gignilliat, and like Gignilliat he possessed a passion for the school he led. However, and unlike Culver, West Point had become somewhat ossified for the previous half-century based upon the justification that its success in producing almost all of the generals of note on both sides of the Civil War using the time-tested system that was still in place was not only successful but, according to some, as close to perfect as possible.[43]

MacArthur, however, determined that West Point's existing system (which he had personally experienced, graduating in 1903 as First Captain, like Pershing) no longer addressed the needs of preparing officers for the demands of modern, industrialized warfare that he had just experienced. When nations had relied on relatively small professional armies consisting mostly of conscripts from the lower echelons of society who did not want to serve and had to be forced and coerced to continue doing so, officers developed rigid training methods and imposed severe discipline to maintain control over this "more or less recalcitrant" group of men in order to mold them into effective soldiers. West Point was founded in 1802 to produce just this kind of highly disciplined officer to lead these kinds of soldiers in the American army.

The methods developed, implemented, and taught at West Point may have worked well in the mid-19th century to direct armies comprised largely of reluctant soldiers from the rougher parts of society who needed rigid methods of training and discipline. Based on his WWI experience, MacArthur found it to be wholly inappropriate to lead the 20th-century citizen-soldiers who had either volunteered or been conscripted and which comprised the huge armies allowed for by the nation at arms brought about by the potent combination of the industrial revolutions and the total mobilization of a society.[44]

The main reason it was no longer appropriate was that the tone and tenor of warfare had changed since the time of the Civil War, becoming more complex and destructive. With the late-19th century rise of the "nation at arms," that combined the ability to mobilize effectively the nation's people and its total resources and the Industrial Revolution's mass-production capabilities that allowed for the provisioning of armies of unimaginable size and their rapid regeneration, the methods developed in the 19th century were no longer applicable to the large armies of citizen soldiers of the 20th century. Citizen-soldiers wanted to learn and serve, and they did not need either the rigid training methods to become effective soldiers or the severe type of discipline required to keep less-willing soldiers in line.[45]

These developments changed the requirements for effectiveness and successful leadership. Leadership still mattered, but it was no longer decisive in terms of being able to win a "decisive battle" that could settle the issue in a single afternoon enjoyed by great captains of the past like Alexander the Great and Napoleon. What many recognized as a result of their WWI experiences was that, in the age of the large citizen-solider armies, perhaps more than ever, military leadership was essential to the effective implementation of the overall strategic direction of the war that had replaced the elusive "decisive battle" as the key to winning modern industrialized wars.

Doing so with citizen-soldiers, who viewed serving in the armed forces as a privilege and responsibility of citizenship that they were only too happy to fulfill, required a style of leadership based more on persuasion and consensus than coercion and direction. As historian Stephen Ambrose put it, "now officers had to lead men who represented the sturdiest parts, not the scurviest, of society," and who required a very different style of leadership.[46] Culver's peer leadership was exactly the type needed for citizen-soldiers.

Army Chief of Staff Gen. Peyton C. March, who had hand-picked him for the assignment, charged MacArthur with the mission of reforming West Point because it was, in his professional judgment, at least "40 years behind the times." MacArthur himself often referred to the culture and institution as "the monastery on the Hudson." As a result, MacArthur arrived at West Point determined to transform the institution into one capable of producing the kind of officers needed to lead 20th century soldiers effectively and succeed on the modern industrialized battlefield.

Accordingly, MacArthur, based on his own wartime experiences, determined that the limited view of West Point's function was no longer valid or applicable.[47] Especially damaging was the unofficially sanctioned practice of hazing (which he himself had endured while a cadet at West Point), that, in MacArthur's experience and view, was antithetical to the development of the "new kind of officer" needed to lead America's citizen armies.

MacArthur, who viewed character as being just as important as intellect, wrote in his first annual report as West Point's superintendent, that the experience of WWI showed that the citizen-soldiers of America's future armies (like those he led in his beloved 42nd "Rainbow" Division in the war) possessed a greater sense of self and had to be led with dignity and respect, and that the practice of hazing was particularly detrimental in encouraging this type of leadership in cadets.[48]

Fleshing out his thoughts more completely, MacArthur argued, based on his extensive reading of military history, that WWI had demonstrated that the professional armies of the 19th century were incapable of resolving issues on the battlefield in modern industrialized warfare. Rather, wars in the 20th century were going to be titanic struggles, and the armies that modern nations fielded were not going to be composed of professional soldiers like those of the 19th century who required harsh discipline and coercion to be led effectively.

As in the war just ended, the armies of the 20th century would consist of citizen soldiers who bore little resemblance to the traditional cannon fodder of professional armies for centuries past, being instead "fresh-faced young men torn from factory and farm, classroom and office who were intelligent and quick-witted but amateurs in the art and science of warfare. The old, brutal methods of leadership would not work with them or be accepted by a modern society," and they needed to be led differently and by an entirely "new kind of officer."[49]

To summarize, MacArthur believed that the changes in warfare had created the need for "a new type of officer" who could subordinate his own needs to those of society but could also effectively lead a new type of solider – citizen-soldiers. These citizen-soldiers, as he had learned during his time with the 42nd "Rainbow" Division in WWI, "had an advanced concept of their rights and...were reluctant to accept the military ethic" unquestionably and instead needed to be "routinely and repeatedly persuaded" to do so, often as a result of an agreed-upon compromise with authorities that would have been unthinkable in the 19th century.[50]

This type of leadership required a more nuanced approach and a deft touch in such negotiations to maintain good order and discipline by achieving an appropriate balance between acceptable levels of obedience and consensus. To prepare future military officers for this type of challenge, MacArthur determined that he needed to revise and improve cadet leader and leadership training, to update and enhance the academic education provided, and to decrease the isolation and increase integration with society at West Point.

In addition, the performance of West Pointers was not as stellar in WWI as some would have liked to believe. In fact, Dr. Charles Eliot, President

Emeritus of Harvard University, offered his assessment in 1920 that "during the Great War, West Pointers were unable to adapt to new methods in the fields of supply and procurement, because of their stifling training."[51] In the conduct of modern warfare, officers have to be able to plan, organize, train, and equip their soldiers effectively to be successful, making Eliot's criticism all the more damning.

During his time as superintendent (July 1919-June 1922), MacArthur attempted to reform the West Point system to produce the leaders needed by the 20th century Army by implementing many inventive programs and approaches. What is striking is that many/most of MacArthur's desired reforms were akin to what Culver was already doing and had been implemented by Gignilliat, including Culver's peer leadership model that proved so effective in WWI.

MacArthur's most significant new programs and approaches included a formalized honor system, a comprehensive program of varsity and intramural athletics, instituting a more systemic "whole man" approach to cadet development by combining "military bearing, leadership and personality, military efficiency, athletic performance, and cadet participation" in activities, along with periodic peer assessments of their "leadership ability and other elements of military character," which, along with the assessments of their tactical officers, combined to produce their final class standings (much as Culver did).[52]

Many of MacArthur 's most significant changes also reflected practices already in place at Culver. Some of these changes included:

- Moving the tactical officers into the barracks for closer supervision over the corps

- Insisting that all treat cadets (and that cadets treat one another) with dignity and respect

- Bringing in more outside speakers to reduce the geographical isolation of West Point

- Establishing aeronautics classes for specialized training of future aviators

- Decreasing the isolation of cadets from society to do away with cadet provincialism

- Increasing West Point cadet integration with the Regular Army to connect more directly their West Point experience with what they would do as officers in the Army to bring the Academy into a newer and closer relationship with the Army at large

- Revising and improving cadet leader and leadership training by eliminating hazing and increasing cadet responsibility to produce the kind of officers needed in the future.[53]

Given that so many of these programs and approaches were already in place and thriving at Culver, it appears that the Culver military and educational system that Gignilliat helped create by the summer of 1919 indicated that Culver as an even better institution than the venerable West Point and the most innovative and effectual military school in the country.

In one particular area, MacArthur was ahead of Culver. He had his commandant develop a theory-based leadership course for which Lincoln Andrews wrote an informal text. The very enlightened premise of this course was that "commanders secured the best results by developing loyalty and intelligent initiative in their soldiers and then trusting them to execute."[54] This was likely the first theory-based collegiate leadership course of its kind in the country, and Culver did not develop something similar until Gignilliat directed his Commandant, McKinney, to develop such a course in 1938. While certainly innovative, there is little evidence that it lasted beyond the two years under Danford (1920-1922).[55]

The respectable conceptual basis of his efforts notwithstanding, MacArthur's methods of changing West Point and implementing his own ideas were somewhat disingenuous and ham-handed. Since he had not developed any level of consensus for them, they were not well-received by either West Point's powerful Academic Board or graduates like Pershing.

His decisions to relax many of the rigid regulations and practices regarding cadet conduct and behavior to encourage thoughtful engagement and meaningful development by allowing for more freedom, time away from post, and subjective discipline to develop their own sense of responsibility and accountability and enable the application of judgment and discretion (as would be needed in the Army) led to MacArthur being criticized as being "not Prussian enough" in terms of enforcing an appropriate level of discipline within the corps of cadets.[56]

In addition, the West Point community resented the changes he was making, viewing them as causing irreparable (and unpardonable) harm to the rigid 19th-century system of order that had been successful for almost 100 years and also to the existing sense of order, discipline, and community within the USMA community itself.[57] Those who opposed MacArthur's actions were not shy about voicing their objections, bringing many of their complaints to Pershing's personal attention. Criticism of MacArthur reached a crescendo and in late 1921 Pershing cut MacArthur's tenure at West Point short by a year and reassigned the troublesome superintendent at the end of the current academic year (June 1922).

It was within this context that Pershing experienced his visit to Culver and processed what he witnessed. In marked contrast to the situation at West Point, Pershing saw at Culver a mature system designed to produce the type of military leaders needed on the modern, industrialized battlefield that had been implemented successfully at an institution led by a highly capable, competent, and beloved superintendent.

The comparison could not have been more stark, and Pershing had to have recognized the difference and determined that it was Culver, and not West Point, that was the nation's premier military school. This realization had to have been sobering and helped provide justification for Pershing's decision to relieve MacArthur early as West Point's superintendent and bring in another leader who could do for USMA what Gignilliat had done at Culver. While slow to catch on, this is what occurred at West Point during the 1920s and 1930s.[58]

Reaching the Pinnacle of His Lifetime

This remarkable period of Gignilliat's life ended with the most famous man in America visiting Culver to recognize his personal accomplishments and those of his beloved institution. Gignilliat's record of individual achievements included:

- Rising from very little as an orphaned middle child of a modest family from Darien, Georgia;

- Earning a degree from a respected college;

- Creating one of the most effective military training systems in the country that elevated the school to national prominence;

- Marrying the girl of his dreams and creating the ideal family life for his children that he never experienced;

- Ascending to the top leadership position at Culver by dint of hard work and achievement;

- Serving with distinction on active duty in the Army for over two years during a war;

- Earning promotion to the rank of brigadier general in the US Army; and

- Being decorated by many nations with some of their highest military awards, earning international esteem.

In aggregate, his level of success was astonishing.

As an educator and administrator, the unique military training system he developed transformed Culver into one of the most respected institutions in the country, placing it programmatically ahead of even West Point at the time. Doing so brought renown to the institution he loved and accolades aplenty to him, including an honorary academic degree (Trinity College, 1915).

Welcoming General Pershing to campus and having the nation's attention focused on him and Culver for a brief moment was therefore an entirely suitable manner to recognize his achievements, honor his beloved institution, and bring this chapter of his life to a gratifying and most appropriate conclusion. It was perhaps the most appropriate possible method of providing such well-deserved recognition for a self-made man like Gignilliat reaching the very pinnacle of achievement in his lifetime, occurring in the presence of everyone he loved at an institution he revered and at which he was beloved, and on ground he considered to be sacred.

Part II

The Lengthening Shadow

Part II: The Lengthening Shadow

American essayist Ralph Waldo Emerson famously declared, *"Every institution is the shadow of one man."* Though this phrase may come across as being anachronistic now, it was certainly both apt and accurate for the Culver of the 1920s.

Nevertheless, and while the remaining 31 years of Gignilliat's life were impressive, they were not nearly as remarkable as the first 47 years, becoming increasingly ceremonial and based mostly on his tremendous achievements of the former period – The Lengthening Shadow.

Gignilliat's "sun," which had been waxing up to this point, was directly overhead in December 1922 during Pershing' visit to Culver – perhaps his personal apotheosis – and it began to wane thereafter, producing "a lengthening shadow" that became more pronounced for the next 20 years but also more distorted and less substantive as the years passed. However, during the period 1923-1928, Gignilliat's "shadow" was both substantial and important to Culver. While notable, his successes after 1922 were less substantial, more achievable by others, and more aesthetic than substantive in nature.

Culminating Point – A Waning and/or Loss of Initiative

- <u>Astronomically</u> - culmination occurs when a star or constellation crosses the local meridian and reaches its highest point in its orbit (apogee); the point at which a star or constellation's general appearance will be at its/their very best (and without the hindrance of the atmospheric effects, such as seeing, refraction or air mass).

- <u>Military</u> - The point at which a force no longer has the capability to continue its form of operation; for example, in the offense it is the point at which continuing the attack is no longer possible and the force must consider reverting to a defensive posture or attempting an operational pause; more generally, it is the point at which a force loses the initiative and begins having to react/respond to the situation and/or actions of its opponent(s) instead of being able to exploit a situation and/or having an opponent(s) react/respond to its actions.[1]

Process Note: Just as Gignilliat's role began to change during this period, so too does the biographer's perspective, shifting from a focus on the particular and day-to-day activities (a chronicle) to one on the more general and the larger themes that begin to emerge as the more influential aspects of the story (a narrative).

Chapter 15: Culver's Gilded Age, 1923-End of 1928

A Return to Normalcy on Campus

Gignilliat in 1923 – still virile and healthy.[2]

US presidential candidate Warren G. Harding's 1920 campaign slogan – "Return to normalcy" – captured the mood of the country quite nicely, and it also provides a very apt description of what occurred at Culver for Gignilliat in the first several years of the post-WWI period. The comforting routine returned and became commonplace, and Culver resumed its traditional rhythm of operations that it had established and adopted from the preceding decade.

During this period, there was little adjustment to the academic curriculum, and the military remained ascendent. This appeared to be a prudent approach in terms of recruitment and retention, as Culver's winter enrollment increased and averaged over 700 cadets for the entire period.

Indeed, and according to Richard Davies:

> *"Culver soon returned to its normal routine following Gignilliat's return in 1919. During the first part of the next decade, little changed at the academy in terms of its curriculum and program. Some new buildings were built and the enrollment continued to increase. By 1922, Culver had 747 cadets with a faculty and staff of eighty-three"[4]*

While perhaps accurate from the surface and regarding Culver returning to some semblance of "normal," and with respect to the areas of its academic curriculum and overall direction, Davies' observation belies some significant modifications that occurred at Culver in less visible areas as a result of its WWI experience and its increased size that impacted the institution overall and Gignilliat more specifically.

Gignilliat at Iron Gate for 1923 commencement.[3]

What became increasingly clear was that Culver had changed since before WWI. In many ways, Culver's growth should have been foreseen as the culmination of the Greater Culver Plan that realized its vision and anticipated accordingly, but the growth of both the physical plant and the corps was not supported initially with the necessary organization and administrative changes needed to oversee and manage the transformed organization.

These changes included the organizational structure of the how the school was administered, and the leadership team of Gignilliat, Glascock, and Greiner had to change with it to ensure they could continue managing the institution well and that it maintained its effective manner of operation. More specifically, Gignilliat himself had to evolve to become more of a modern executive capable of directing the larger and more complex institution that Culver had become. This required him to develop himself organizationally and administratively, which occurred with varying degrees of success during this period but always within the context of being pragmatic (i.e., finding what worked).

His personality of wanting to please others, shoulder more than his share of the load to prove his worth and validate his contributions, and avoid conflict exacerbated the challenges further, providing Gignilliat with few options to reduce his external commitments and/or redirecting his focus back on campus where it was increasingly needed. This allowed divisions to develop and fester, factions to develop and form, and set the stage for the coming period of dissention and change. However, none of that was apparent at the beginning of 1923.

As had become his practice, the demands he placed upon himself during this period, especially on behalf of FIDAC during the period 1925-1927, along with a period of debilitating illness during the first half of 1926, reduced his effectiveness fairly substantially and diverted his attention away from Culver (where it was arguably most needed during its greater period of flourishing that he had worked so hard to bring about). These conditions combined and created a crisis of sorts in terms of his own health and welfare.

In addition, Gignilliat endured a serious and extended bout of influenza beginning in January 1926 that was so incapacitating that he was able to do little else during the first six months of the year other than attend to the immediate needs at Culver. According to his own account of his health status during this period, written on February 5, 1927, he had been in "ill health" for extended periods in 1925 and 1926. Regarding the first six months of 1926, Gignilliat wrote that his condition was so severe that it required "every ounce of energy and moment of time to carry on my duties with the school," and that he was forced to delegate responsibility for all non-Culver matters to others and was unable to perform the "check ups" that he would have ordinarily made on such matters.[5] His health thus impacted his ability to function effectively at Culver, and, as will be related in the chapter addressing it, adversely on his Skyland Camps endeavor.[6]

Having witnessed the alarming decline in her husband as a result of the influenza, Minnie asserted her considerable authority in their relationship and stepped in, reducing his level of activity considerably and accompanying him on his travels to ensure he did not over-expend himself. To relive the administrative burden of remaining in contact with the myriad individuals wanting his attention and to whom he felt personally responsible to correspond (so as not to disappoint them and/ or reflect poorly on Culver), Minnie enlisted the two eldest sons (Leigh Jr. and Fred) to serve as Gignilliat's personal secretaries to take charge of the father's personal affairs.

While certainly well-intended and successful in terms of contributing to Minnie's overall efforts to allow her husband to recover his health and regain his former level of vitality, this arrangement did not turn out well overall.

Nevertheless, and having recovered his health and vitality, Gignilliat enjoyed a bit of a resurgence in 1928 that led to a second (albeit less impressive) "peak" of success in 1928.

Culver's Gilded Age – 1923-1928

Having established a sterling national reputation before the war that was burnished by the performance of its graduate s during the fighting, and perhaps especially by its remarkable superintendent, Culver settled into its post-WWI administrative rhythm, run largely by the dynamic and eminently well-paired duo of Glascock and Greiner. This arrangement worked well for both Gignilliat and Culver, as both Glascock and Greiner were primarily educators, which is what Culver needed during this period. However, this routine became increasingly inappropriate for both the new faculty at Culver and, perhaps even more importantly, for the new type of boys enrolling at Culver. Thus, the period 1923-1928 may be characterized as witnessing the apotheosis of Gignilliat the man and also the twilight of the "old" Culver during what became Culver's "Gilded Age."

After readjusting to life out of the active Army and back at Culver with his family, staff, cadets, and running the school he so dearly loved, Gignilliat became comfortable with his leadership team retaining the enhanced responsibilities they had assumed in his absence during WWI and began transitioning into a modern executive, both at Culver and in the Army as a General Officer. With things running well on campus, and after a period of respite, Gignilliat began devoting his tremendous energy to projects outside the confines of Culver, assuming more external responsibilities. While natural (and perhaps unavoidable) for him, and likely comforting to provide him with avenues to direct his inexhaustible well of energy, this process also exposed the limitations of his abilities and capabilities, bringing about a situation in which the demands placed upon him exceeded his own management and executive capacity.

The extent of his travels further exacerbated this situation, along with another round of serious illness that required him to devote all of his efforts to attending to his responsibilities at Culver. The quixotic and perplexing Skyland Camps endeavor (addressed separately) provides perhaps the best example of this development, representing a Culver-related project that he was unable to control or make successful, and which ended in failure and bringing personal harm to his own carefully maintained reputation and to the institution he so zealously guarded from defamation.

Enrollment – Highest by Far During Culver's First 50 Years

Culver's enrollment during the period 1920-1928 averaged a remarkable 726 cadets, representing the highest level of enrollments (by far) during its first 50 years. Financially, this level of enrollment generated approximately $1.3 million in tuition revenue (726 x $1,800 = $1.31 million), which was a staggering amount for a secondary school during this period. Reasons for its growth reflected the results of the "Greater Culver" strategic improvement plan for the school, along with the increased number of students attending high school. However, there was also an increased level of competition for students that was most acute in the Midwest during this same period, along with the anti-military sentiment that was manifested at this time. The ability of Culver to sustain such a remarkably high level of enrollment in such conditions must be viewed as a success and testament to both the institution's efforts to sustain its enrollment and the enduring appeal of the institution itself.

School Year	Opening Enrollment	Number of Graduates
1920 - 1921	744	124
1921 - 1922	706	147
1922 - 1923	721	156
1923 - 1924	735	162
1924 - 1925	714	147
1925 - 1926	740	162
1926 - 1927	741	151
1927 - 1928	719	146
1928 - 1929	711	142
1920 - 1929 Average	726	149

Culver Winter School Enrollment, 1920-1928.[7]

These are strong numbers for a school with a business model predicated on receiving revenue from at least 400 enrolled students (i.e., $600,000 in tuition revenue), allowing the institution to continue operating at a relative level of luxury, especially in terms of the services it provided (among the best at any school in the nation), the number of faculty and staff it employed (over 100), and of being able to do virtually all that it wanted to do without having to make the hard choices imposed by financial limitations. However, then as now, 700+ students represents a threshold that requires more sophisticated methods and a more robust administrative structure to manage, requiring Culver to make changes in both to sustain its level of performance and reputation.

This growth in enrollment also resulted in an increase in the size of the faculty and staff to over 100. The number of students and size of the faculty and staff, along with the demands of the organizational structure and the Culver system combined to transform the Culver of the 1920s into a complex institution that required a new administrative structure to sustain the Culver system for such a large number of people and manage it effectively. It was not entirely clear if the traditional Culver system could continue operating successfully under such conditions.

1922-1928: A Complex Institution Requires More Sophisticated Management -- The Making of an Executive

Organizationally, Culver's growth into a larger and more complex organization that needed a new administrative structure to manage it effectively had been recognized by Glascock and Greiner in the war years. Enrollment increased from 548 students when Gignilliat departed to 596 for the 1918-1919 winter school session (which was the largest enrollment at Culver up to that point) to a remarkable 728 by the beginning of the 1919-1920 winter school session.

Increased enrollment was generally a good thing and something that Culver desired, but it also brought with it some new challenges. The increase of almost 200 cadets required the creation of several additional 50-cadet units to maintain Culver's preferred organizational size and desired adult-to-student ratio. Doing so increased the number of cadet units and resulted in the formation of a cadet regiment at Culver comprised of two battalions shortly after WWI. Acknowledging the difficulty of sustaining Culver's distinctive approach of providing high levels of personal attention to the cadets, Glascock and Greiner created the positions of Dean of Old Cadets (Stoutenburgh) and Dean of New Cadets (Bennett) as enrollment increased and in response to this grown and expansion. Gignilliat had been part of some of these sensible organizational changes to the corps, which surely helped them to be acceptable to him philosophically as well.

Having become comfortable with his administrative team's new way of functioning, and just as they had realized that the larger number of cadets required organizational changes for the corps, Gignilliat, Glascock, and Greiner created a new administrative structure for Culver. This structure was a hybrid version of what would be known today as the dual-responsibility president-principal model of administration. This hybrid model was more accurately described as a treble-responsibility Superintendent-Headmaster-Commandant model, and it was as innovative as it was both necessary and effective.

A New Administrative Approach on Campus: Superintendent-Headmaster-Commandant Team

It is helpful to put this development in its broader context to be properly understood and appreciated. After his return, re-adjustment, and becoming comfortable with his leadership team retaining the enhanced responsibilities they had assumed in his absence during WWI, by necessity and design Gignilliat began making the transition to a modern executive, both at Culver and in the Army as a General Officer. Part of this transition was a change in focus from the tactical day-to-day operations of the school (which was his strength and preferred focus) to more strategic areas of the institution (which came less naturally to him).

Based upon the military's idea of "span of control," which seeks to limit the amount of responsibility for any one person to a manageable level, the idea was to divide the multiple administrative roles and responsibilities among the three of them to more effectively address the ever-increasing complexity of administering a large secondary school that had outgrown its existing administrative structure. The new structure was intended to provide for academic leadership and the daily operation of the school in ways that leveraged Glascock's and Greiner's long experience and educational administrative expertise, and also to allow for the school's senior leadership to be devoted to more strategic areas like management of financial resources, institutional advancement, strategic planning, fidelity to mission, and vision-building using Gignilliat's burgeoning executive abilities.

In this model, the executive functions of an institution are elegantly aligned around two distinct leadership profiles: An outward-facing institution-builder and entrepreneur (President); and an inward-facing academician championing teaching, learning, discipline, and safety (Principal). Developed 50 years later, this model was unknown to Culver leaders, but the underlying logic of its structure was readily apparent to anyone seeking to find new ways to manage a complex organization.

Culver's Superintendent-Headmaster-Commandant Managerial Model

As a result of the tremendous growth of the school (almost 200 cadets, four more units, and an increasingly complex corps organization), along with the changes to the administrative structure and the increased size of the faculty and staff (which increased to over 100 during this period), Culver's three senior administrative leaders recognized that the demands of the institution had increased such that the size that Culver became in 1920s exceeded the capability of the management structure Culver had used up to this point and the institution had outgrown the ability of any one person to exercise dominion effectively over all aspects of it. More directly, Gignilliat, Glascock, and Greiner found that an organization of 700-plus students and over 100 faculty members required a more sophisticated model of administration that was not natural for Gignilliat but which he realized was necessary.

Culver's senior leadership team was committed to adopting/creating a managerial method that was more collaborative. The organizational model needed to make the best use of the talents and personalities at Culver at the time, take advantage of the experience and abilities Glascock and Greiner had gained and honed during Gignilliat's absence during WWI, and provide ways to make use of Gignilliat's own burgeoning executive abilities.

The model they developed – the Superintendent-Headmaster-Commandant model – was similar to the innovative president-principal that would be devised by similarly motivated educational entrepreneurs a half-century later but also slightly different. Owing to its military structure, it included an additional person.

Culver's Superintendent-Headmaster-Commandant model included three individuals: an outward-facing institution-builder and entrepreneur focused on public relations, marketing, enrollment, and the long-term strategic operations (fund raising was not yet active at Culver), a Superintendent/President ; an inward-facing executive focused on academics who championed teaching and learning, a Headmaster/Principal; and an inward-facing executive focused on residential life, discipline, and safety, a Commandant). As befitted Culver, this model was as effective as it was innovative.

This approach had its roots in the challenges Glascock and Greiner had faced while running the institution together for 27 months during Gignilliat's WWI absence. Having developed effective ways to manage the school as it grew, along with establishing a smooth and effortless rapport while running Culver, Gignilliat, upon his return and once he adjusted to the new reality, supported their approach and became comfortable with this administrative arrangement. This new approach allowed Gignilliat to begin functioning as a true executive and also turn his focus outward, confident that Glascock and Greiner could handle things, would run the school as he wanted, and that the school was in good hands.

Accordingly, Gignilliat and his team began experimenting with and implementing a new model more along the lines of a modern-day president-principal model (unbeknownst to them), with Gignilliat functioning as the president and Glascock functioning as the principal. Reflecting Culver's unique needs as a military boarding school, the model developed was a hybrid and incorporated a third member, with Greiner assuming a portion of the duties normally overseen by the principle in the traditional model and thus becoming an integral member of the leadership trio.

Gignilliat as CMA's "President"

For Gignilliat, transitioning his primary role as superintendent to one of functioning more as the "president" did at other institutions was a departure from the role of Chief Operating Officer (COO) that was most comfortable for him and was instead a more completely executive role that he had to learn and develop different skills to fulfill. Fortunately, his status as a General officer in the Army required much the same of him, and the Army provided him with training and experience to help him develop into the executive he needed to be/become.

The fit for Gignilliat in this administrative structure as a functioning "president" responsible for being the institution-builder and entrepreneur with an external focus on the areas of public relations, marketing, enrollment, and the long-term strategic operations was fairly good, with most of these responsibilities being in Gignilliat's wheelhouse naturally but which he still had to learn how to do well. This was especially relevant with respect to the requirement for strategic thinking, which, unlike operations, was a skill that did not come naturally to him. When he turned his attention to the consideration of strategy, he functioned as more of a visionary/dreamer than a disciplined strategic thinker.

While traditionally associated with the president's role in this type of model, it is worth noting that there was no fund-raising being done during this period by deliberate decision, as Gignilliat (and likely ER and BB Culver) did not believe that alumni should ever be asked to contribute financially back to the school. A drawback of this approach was that it both allowed and encouraged Gignilliat to direct his attention externally, creating the potential for an institutional loss of focus (which ended up occurring as a result of the departure of Greiner and Glascock). Maintaining sufficient institutional focus by those at the very top of the organization is an essential component of success for a complex institution being administered by this type of organizational structure.

Glascock as CMA's "Principal" – A Terrific Fit

Functioning as the principal was a role that suited Glascock exceptionally well. The principal was the chief academician, champion of the institution's education function, and focused internally on the faculty, curriculum, teaching, learning, and the day-to-day running of the institution. All of these responsibilities were very much in Glascock's wheelhouse, and he was well-qualified to fulfill them. Omnipresent and affable, this role represented very little change from the role he had been fulfilling since his arrival at Culver, since partnering with Gignilliat as Superintendent, and during the years immediately preceding, during, and following WWI. In effect, Glascock became Culver's Senior COO.

What was new was the requirement for the person in this role to assume an increased level of responsibility for maintaining institutional focus. However, both by its organizational hierarchy and the personality of the leadership team, this had always been an area attended to directly, effectively, and somewhat exclusively by Gignilliat himself.

Greiner as CMA's Commandant – A Role He Grew into Exceptionally Well

Greiner's role also had to change, and due to his intimate familiarity with the demands of the Commandant's position, Gignilliat recognized this need quite intuitively. As the other member of the internally focused component of this model, Greiner, as Commandant, was responsible for focusing on the residential life, discipline, and safety functions. Given the size of the corps and that Culver was primarily a boarding school, this division of internal functions made much sense and allowed Glascock and Greiner to focus on their areas of responsibility somewhat exclusively and without becoming overwhelmed by the demands of these essential functions. While not representing a change for Culver, this allowed for a natural division of labor of the internally focused duties that suited Culver perfectly.

What did change was the managerial responsibilities of the Commandant. With the larger enrollment and more complex organization of the corps, the Commandant needed additional staff members to allow Culver to continue providing the intimate level of attention to each cadet that characterized (and perhaps accounted for) its successful approach to cadet development. It was the Commandant's responsibility to supervise and manage these additional staff members.

The expanded staff required adding another layer of management to the Commandant's organizational structure. Gignilliat was fully supportive of incorporating the changes that Glascock and Greiner had made in his absence to assist the Commandant by creating, in 1924, the positions of Dean of Cadets for winter and summer schools to help manage the larger number of students and adults to supervise them sufficiently.

This additional administrative level was essential to allow the span of control to remain manageable for the team responsible for supervising over 700 cadets in the winter school and over 1,000 cadets in the summer school. Enrollment growth at Culver overall exceeded the ability of the Commandant's office to be effective as it had been traditionally structured. Greiner became, in effect, Culver's Junior COO. Fortunately for Culver, Bert Greiner was up to the task and capable of maintaining his effectiveness while functioning in this new administrative and managerial manner.

On-campus Hierarchy

Another important aspect of this hybrid model reflected the importance of hierarchy in a military institution. When created, and owing largely to convention, personality, ability, and personal preference, the Superintendent/President was at the top, followed by the Headmaster/Principal and then the Commandant. While seemingly logical, this was different from the time of Fleet, when Gignilliat, as Commandant, was second in the institutional hierarchy, followed by Glascock as the Headmaster. Having the Headmaster functioning as the "Number 2" recognized implicitly the increasing importance of academics at the institution but become a source of tension for at least one member of the military staff as the decade progressed.

In terms of reporting structure, this model also worked quite well with the existing personalities and conventions. As an incorporated institution, the Board of Trustees bore ultimate organizational responsibility and oversaw a single employee – the Superintendent. In practice, this meant that the chair of the board – ER Culver – was responsible for overseeing Gignilliat. As a managerial approach, this worked very well for the two of them after having developed a strong, respectful, and collegial professional association, along with a warm personal relationship over the course of more than two decades and especially since ER assumed primary responsibility for overseeing the school for the Culver family in 1912 and just after Gignilliat became Superintendent in 1911.

This arrangement, based upon working with one with whom he had a close personal relationship, worked very well for Gignilliat, since this was how he preferred to and was most comfortable operating. However, as Gignilliat's role and activities included increasing levels of external focus, this method of oversight may not have been idea l in terms of directing the specific efforts of the Superintendent and/or ensuring that he provided and maintained a sufficient level of institutional focus, which are essential for a complex organization.

As one would expect in a military organization, the Headmaster and Commandant reported directly to the Superintendent, along with others having higher levels of responsibility at the school. This meant that

Gignilliat effectively supervised the entire Culver staff by directing those who reported directly to him, which is exactly as he would have wanted it but which became progressively more challenging, especially as the size of the faculty and staff exceeded 100 and the organization became increasingly complex, meaning that the number of direct-reports he supervised also increased.

Organizational Fit for the President-Principal-Commandant Administrative Structure

In the 1920s model at Culver, and even though the military program remained ascendent institutionally, the personalities involved understood the priorities, accepted the order of precedence, and made the arrangement work. As it turned out, this hierarchy was well suited for Culver in terms of structure and within the military system, and the model was well suited for Gignilliat, Glascock, and Greiner, both in terms of personalities and abilities. However, and reflecting Gignilliat's desire for harmony above all, this model may have allowed some the faculty's growing discontent during the 1920s to go unnoticed by Gignilliat, as long as Glascock was second in the hierarchy and Greiner was present to keep the military component collegial and in its proper place (according to this model and the school's educational function).

The ability of this model/approach to minimize conflict was extremely important to maintain the harmony so prized by Gignilliat, but it may not have been as effective for the school as an organization. While there were many advantages to this administrative approach and structure, it was also quite dependent upon the personalities of the key administrators to be willing and able to collaborate effectively and get along well with one another.

It is worth noting that this arrangement was not usual within the military's preference for hierarchy, with all roles subordinated to a single commander, and unity of command, with a single person in charge. Greiner (who operated at Culver more like an educator than a professional officer) functioned well within the structure, but a more traditional military officer (e.g., Rossow) might not have been so amenable to it (as we shall see). Possessing of both advantages and drawbacks, this new model nevertheless represented a significant departure from the traditional military model and how Culver had been organized and run during its first 30 years (1896-1925).

One of Glascock's greatest strengths facilitated by this hybrid model was his ability to sustain the harmony (or at least the appearance of harmony) that was so important to Gignilliat. Glascock supported Gignilliat, was content with his position and situation, and was not apt by temperament or experience to challenge Gignilliat, contributing to the pervading sense of harmony. While very affable, Glascock was also quite adept at placating the concerns of the faculty and capable of keeping other faculty members who might have challenged Gignilliat in line. It is little wonder that he was designated as a Superintendent Emeritus upon his retirement.

As Commandant, Greiner also supported Gignilliat, was content with his position and situation, and was not apt by temperament or experience to challenge Gignilliat. Trained as Commandant by Gignilliat, he was more than capable of keeping the military program running as Gignilliat wanted and as it had been under Gignilliat. Like Glascock, Greiner was also very collegial and able to get along with faculty colleagues well, who, in the egalitarian spirit of the faculty, he viewed as co-equal peers who were also a fully legitimate partners helping Culver to achieved its vision.

Also helpful was that Greiner was more of an educator than a trainer when it came to the cadets, which perhaps was not as effective in the Army but was an approach that was both well suited and quite effective at Culver. It was also precisely what the school needed from its Commandant at the time. In addition, Greiner possessed the managerial ability required of the Commandant in the new administrative model. His unexpected (and untimely) death in late-1926 would come as a shock to the institution for administrative as much as social reasons.

These changes altered the roles of the big three – Gignilliat, Glascock, and Greiner – as described above, but they were not supported by accompanying organizational change. This meant that Gignilliat was still involved intimately in the day-to-day operations by design and preference, as all the main administrators continued to report directly to him. While this may have conformed to Gignilliat's own preference, it negated many of the intended advantages of the new system and limited its effectiveness. Not until 1935 are the role changes supported by organizational changes to increase the system's effectiveness.

Gignilliat's Right-hand Man in the 1920s -- The Redoubtable Stoutenburgh

Another indicator of the need for administrative change was the increased enrollment in winter school, which became beyond the ability of the Commandant's office (as organized) to address properly. Beginning in 1924, Culver created positions of Dean of Cadets for Winter School – Major Michael V. Bennett – and Dean of Cadets for Summer School – Major Abram Sheffield Stoutenburgh. These two positions

The "Deans" M. V. Bennett (L), Dean of New Cadets & A. S. Stoutenburgh (R), Dean of Old Cadets.[8]

were also responsible for serving as Gignilliat's personal representatives for correspondence with parents and with the tactical staffs of the winter and summer schools. It is important to note that these were two vitally important aspects of Culver for Gignilliat, and he would not relinquish direct responsibility for either willingly or lightly unless and/or until he felt compelled to do so.

As mentioned above, this change was likely reflective of the increased work related to maintaining contact with such a large number of cadets, and it may have been more the idea of Glascock and Greiner, based upon their experience running Culver during WWI, since they had created similar positions had been used in winter school during the war (Dean of Old Cadets and Dean of New Cadets). This explanation makes sense, and the timing of it also lines up with the time it took for Gignilliat to become comfortable with the new arrangement and begin trusting it.

Under this arrangement, Stoutenburgh also handled the overall administration of the summer school to include the hiring of its faculty. Faculty hiring for the winter school remained an executive function of the Superintendent (Gignilliat), but he delegated much of this responsibility for summer school faculty and staff. Given the value Gignilliat placed upon employing the right people for Culver, this represented a big change and also indicated the level of trust he afforded to Stoutenburgh. While it might have been difficult for Gignilliat to accept at first, what is clear is that this managerial change took much of the administrative burden from Gignilliat, allowing him to function in more of an executive role.[9]

Another indicator of the level of trust he enjoyed was the increasing frequency with which the name "Stoutenburgh" begins to appear in Culver's published materials. It appears that Gignilliat thought enough of him to include him in his trusted inner circle during this period.

Just who was this new key assistant? Born in 1881 to an old Dutch family in New York, Stoutenburgh earned a BA from Hobart College in1905. He arrived at Culver 1908 to teach math, and by 1913, he had become Gignilliat's Summer School aide, which, given the importance placed upon the Summer School by Gignilliat, indicates the high level of trust he had in Stoutenburgh. Stoutenburgh remained on campus during WWI, serving as the Dean of Old Cadets, indicating that he had earned the trust of both Glascock and Greiner as well. He was also appointed to Culver's Publicity and Morale & Religious Activities boards during WWI, becoming further associated with areas of particular importance to Gignilliat.

By 1921, he was made Director of Summer Schools and promoted to Major. Three years later (1924), Stoutenburgh became Dean of Cadets for Summer School, followed in 1928 by his elevation to Dean of Cadets for Winter School under Rossow after Greiner died in December 1926, brought in perhaps as a leavening influence for Rossow's more "animated" personality. Stoutenburgh was thus part and illustrative of the administrative and organizational changes made at Culver during this period. It makes sense that Gignilliat would have looked to one he trusted deeply to help him administer areas that were of great importance to him but which had expanded beyond his ability to manage them without assistance.

The affable Abram Stoutenburgh, as he is most remembered.[10]

It is worth noting that when he died unexpectedly on March 11, 1935, at 54 years of age. Gignilliat wrote that Stoutenburgh was utterly devoted to work and Culver in terms of the time and effort he gave to each. Gignilliat also highlighted Stoutenburgh's attention to detail, along with his unflappable and unruffled spirit. He was, in every way possible, a true Gignilliat man and likely kindred spirit.

Becoming an Army Executive – Training and Experience as a General Officer

Having been promoted to the rank of Brigadier General in the ORC at the end of 1921, the US Army began training Gignilliat to function as the executive he was expected to be at this rank. During summer 1922 and summer 1923, after assuming command on the 168th Brigade on January 1, 1922 (from Howard C. Bays), he was introduced to the Army's new standardized approach to training as part of his command responsibilities and then brought on active duty during the period January 28 – March 18, 1924 to attend a supply course at the US Army War College in Washington, DC.[11]

At the end of that year, Gignilliat began developing his executive leadership and decision-making abilities by leading his brigade in a war game pitting his own reserve 84th Division against a rival reserve division (38th). This was the first large-scale ORC exercise, and it attracted national attention.[12] These experiences helped to develop further Gignilliat's executive abilities as a general officer, and he likely also used much of what he learned to improve Culver.

The National Defense Act of 1920

Based upon its WWI mobilization experience and a realization that the mobilization of a citizen army required a concerted effort for preparedness in times of peace, the US government determined that the National Defense Act of 1916 needed revision. Intended to "unite the Army and the people," and determined to apply the lessons of WWI to its national defense, the National Defense Act of 1920 was passed into law in June 1920, establishing the Army of the United States (AUS) comprised of three distinct components: the Regular Army; the National Guard; and the newly created Organized Reserve.

The Organized Reserve was comprised of the Officers Reserve Corp (ORC), the Enlisted Reserve Corps (ERC), and the Reserve Officers Training Corps (ROTC). However, rather than uniting the people with the Army, the act more actually united the Army with the National Guard and Organized Reserve, as almost half (49 percent) of the regular Army was involved in training non-Regular soldiers and units by 1926.[13]

A wave of pacifism began sweeping through the country almost as soon as WWI ended, fueled by the reasonable assertion that the nation had no further use for a large, standing army now that the "war to end all wars" had ended. Indeed, budget cuts, personnel reductions, and glacially slow promotions were the order of the day for much of the 1920s.

Both of these dynamics – the Army's reorganization and the influence of pacifism/anti-militarism – would have profound impacts on Gignilliat's military service in the 1920s.

Gignilliat has been part of the process of creating and implementing the National Defense Act of 1916 that had brought about fundamental changes in the Army, and the decade immediately following WWI was a time of even greater change in the nation's reserve forces. Within one year of his return, and after having been discharged from the National Army and reappointed as a Colonel of Infantry in the Officers' Reserve Corps (ORC) in December 1919, the nation adopted the National Defense

Act of 1920 in June of its namesake year. Among other things, the 1920 act created the New Citizen Army, and it established the parameters of Gignilliat's service in the army for the next 19 years until his retirement.

The Regular Army's New Mission – Creating the New Citizen Army

The National Defense Act of 1920 was all but revolutionary in that it changed the mission and character of the Regular Army. Instead of serving as the professionally trained ground force in the nation's defense structure, the military took on as its most basic mission the education and training of the civilian components of the new citizen army, making it, in Pershing's words, "a great institution of military instruction."[14] Even though Regular Army soldiers looked down on the ORC and adopted a Prussian-like attitude toward them, the Regular Army continued to regard this mission as its chief and defining responsibility during the entire interwar period, even at the expense of its own training and development.[15]

Creating this new citizen army involved three essential tasks:

- Reorganizing the Regular Army,
- Developing the citizen components, and
- Properly assembling them into the Army of the United States.[16]

It was to the second task – developing the citizen components – to which Gignilliat's efforts were directed by the Army as a general officer and commander for the remainder of his time in uniform. Given all he had done up to this point in his professional life, he was uniquely and tremendously prepared to make the same kinds of contributions in this area as he had done to the use of a military system to help educate adolescent boys. However, he began turning his attention to adult males in their 20s and 30s in this new role.

Helping Create the New Citizen Army – Gignilliat's Army Responsibilities

Within one month of his promotion to Brigadier General, Gignilliat assumed command of the newly activated US Army 168th Brigade on January 1, 1922. Intended to help address the challenges of maintaining a reliable and effective reserve force, the 168th Brigade was a reserve organization created to train and develop Reserve officers commissioned through the ROTC and CMTC programs, along with reserve NCOs, to be prepared to serve in the next large-scale conflict. As an integral component of developing its federal military reserve, this was a new endeavor for the US Army.

The function of developing officers not on active duty had been the responsibility of state militias prior to WWI, and the Army had been constantly displeased with the results. As a result of the defenses reorganization that occurred before and after WWI, the Regular Army assumed responsibility for this important task, believing it could accomplish it much better than state militias had been able to on their own. However, it was a task that would be far more challenging than perhaps anyone in the Army anticipated at the outset.

This was also substantially new for Gignilliat, who had not commanded any unit of significance in the Army. While he ostensibly "commanded" a depot responsible for training new soldiers at Camp Taylor as part of his duties as a member of the 84th Division headquarters (without formal command authority), he had no other experience serving as a commanding officer in the Army. His time at Culver as the commander of the Corps of Cadets (as Commandant) and of the school (as Superintendent) was likely the best possible preparation for this role, but assuming official command for one of the higher-level organizations in the US Army was still something that was new and unfamiliar to him, both in terms of formal preparation and experience.

The New Citizens Army – A Federally Managed Organized Reserve

The 1920 NDA established a four-part system for the New Citizen Army, which, joined with the Regular Army, formed what was called the Army of the United States (AUS). In practice, the United States Army (USA) referred specifically to only the Regular Army.

There were five components of the Army of the United States:

- *Regular army (not part of the New Citizen Army)*
- *National Guard*
- *the Officers' Reserve Corps (ORC)*
- *the Reserve Officers' Training Corps (ROTC)*
- *the Citizens' Military Training Camps (CMTC) (which had an anomalous relationship to the entire program).*

While he had served briefly with a National Guard division in WWI (the 37th Division), it is important to note that Gignilliat was quite involved with the ORC, ROTC, and CMTC components. The result was that he was also very much a part of creating America's New Citizen Army as part of the nation's first federally managed Organized Reserve.

US Army Organized Reserve

The Organized Reserve infantry divisions raised immediately after World War I continued the lineage and geographic area distribution of National Army divisions that had served in the war. They were maintained on paper with all of their officers and one-third of their enlisted men. These organizations also maintained relationships with military schools, along with civilian colleges or universities, which populated them with officers through the ROTC. In the event of war, Organized Reserve officers and enlisted men would be called to duty to form the cores of the divisions to which they were assigned and serve as the training cadre during mobilization and pre-deployment training.

Providing the training and oversight for the Organized Reserve was the responsibility of the Regular Army (both by choice and design), and the Army began creating the hierarchy of command for doing so. The effort became so large by 1926 that almost half (49 percent) of the Regular Army was involved.[17]

To establish specific jurisdictions, the country was organized into nine areas consisting of several states and called Corps Areas. Within each Corps Area, the Organized Reserves were assigned to divisions associated with each state. The Army's National Army divisions (demobilized after WWI) became the basis of the Organized Reserves as the next echelon of command. In Indiana, this was the 84th Division, in which Gignilliat has served during much of his time on active duty. The 84th Division was reconstituted as an ORC division on June 24, 1921, and activated on 6 September 1921 in Indianapolis.[18]

Organized Reserve (OR) divisions could recruit up to 100 percent of their authorized officer strength but only up to 33 percent of its authorized enlisted strength. Since there were no enlistment or pay incentives for the Enlisted Reserve Corps (ERC), few men joined. As a result, OR divisions generally had fewer than 100 enlisted men on the rolls. On the other hand, due to the many WWI-era officers and commissionees from Reserve Officers' Training Corps (ROTC) programs and Citizens Military Training Camps (CMTCs), most of these divisions were at or near full strength in officer personnel from about 1925 until 1940.[19]

In terms of timing, the organization and activation of the 84th Division occurred simultaneously with the organization and activation of similar organizations across the country. This effort was largely completed by the end of 1922. According to one historian, "Most divisional subordinate organizations achieved somewhere near full strength in authorized officers by the mid-1920s and could be considered as functional cadre units."[20]

84th "Lincoln" Division – Indiana's Organized Reserve Division

With higher-level organization complete, the Army began activating lower-level units to which it could assign members of the ORC and ERC, and into which ROTC graduates could join to satisfy their reservice requirements and continue their training. Retaining the "square" division structure used in WWI, Army divisions consisted of two Infantry Brigades, along with a Field Artillery brigade and an Engineer regiment.

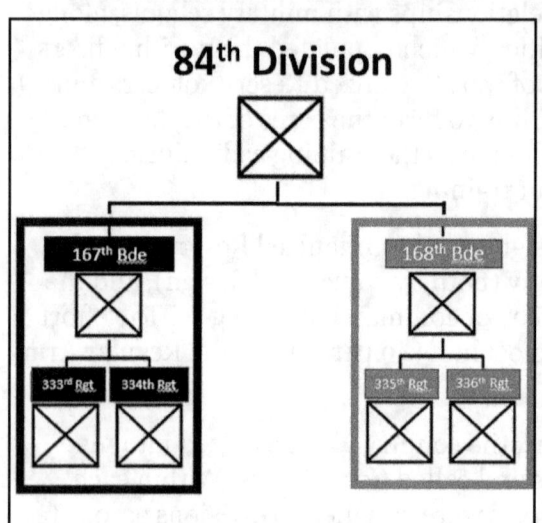

The 84th Division was reconstituted in the Organized Reserve on June 24, 1921, assigned to the Fifth Corps Area, and allotted to the state of Indiana as its home area. Headquartered in Indianapolis, Indiana, much of its training occurred within the state and also at Camp (Fort) Knox, Kentucky. The division's infantry trained at Fort Benjamin Harrison, Camp Knox, and sometimes at Fort Thomas, Kentucky.

The main two units of the 84th Division were its two largest units: the 167th and 168th infantry brigades. Both brigades had been reconstituted in the OR on 24 June 1921. The 167th Brigade was activated on 3 Nov 1921 and headquartered in Newcastle, Indiana. Intended to be commanded by a Brigadier General (one star), finding a suitable commanding officer for the unit remained a challenge, and it was commanded by a 1LT, Captain, Major, and Lieutenant Colonel during its time as an OR unit. After a brief stint being commanded by a Major (Harold C. Bays, of Culver), the division's other infantry unit – the 168th Brigade – was commanded by BG Gignilliat for almost its entire period of existence.

The 168th Brigade -- Gignilliat's Army Command

Organized to include ORC and ERC members from the northern half of Indiana, the 168th Brigade was activated on December 7, 1921. Given its regional orientation, it was headquartered at Montpelier, Indiana for the first ten years (1921-1931), moving to Culver for two years (1931-1933), and settling finally in South Bend in 1933 until activated for WWII service on 7 December 1941.

Upon its activation, the 168th Brigade was commanded by Culver's own Howard C. Bays, who was a Major in the ORC and the highest-ranking ORC officer available for assignment in the area. However, brigade-level units were intended to be commanded by Brigadier Generals. Fortunately, Gignilliat was promoted to the rank of Brigadier General in the ORC the next day on December 8, 1921 (with a date of rank of November 4, 1921,

for purposes of seniority), making him a one-star general in the OR located in north-central Indian and in need of a suitable billet. Command of the 168th Brigade, based

Officers of the 168th Brigade during its first gathering with Gignilliat as commander.[21]

in north-central Indiana, was therefore a natural assignment for him, and he assumed command of the unit on January 1, 1922.

With little precedent in terms of role and organization (much like serving as an Intelligence officer in terms of having no formal training to do so during his wartime service), Gignilliat hosted the first meeting with the leaders of his brigade on May 14-15, 1922 at Culver.

At this two-day conference, Gignilliat discussed his intention of scheduling occasional conferences throughout the year to discuss military subjects and build *esprit de corps*. The leaders agreed to commit to cooperating closely with National Guard units, to help promote efforts to increase attendance at the Citizens' Military Training Camps (CMTC) in summer 1922, and also to encourage rifle shooting in Indiana. Along with addresses from several Regular Army officers (presumably regarding the mission and role of the 168th Brigade), Gignilliat provided attendees with classroom instruction in military problems, while also allowing them to observe Culver cadets working out such problems in the field. Gignilliat established a professional and collegial environment within the unit that was both enjoyed and appreciated by its members.[22]

Using his influence and facilities, Gignilliat managed to host training for one and sometimes both of the division's infantry brigades at Culver. In addition to the unit training camps, the infantry units of the division rotated responsibility for conducting the infantry CMTC held at Fort Thomas and Camp Knox each year. Occasionally, the division participated in training with higher units, giving leaders opportunities to practice the roles they would be expected to perform in the event the division was mobilized.[23]

Training Organized Reserve Units

Having created the necessary structure, the Army developed a training plan for these new organizations. Initial training efforts occurred during the two-year period 1922-1924.

The training difficulties facing the OR divisions were substantial, due to the lack of enlisted personnel, equipment, and funding. For most years, the War Department allocated funding for about 25 percent of the OR's personnel annual training (due to shortages and based upon the notion that OR units could endure having a three-year level of training proficiency of around 75 percent, which could be increased if/when needed through mobilization). Despite sparse funding, OR units did all they could to provide adequate training for their personnel during summer training and inactive training periods (e.g., conducting map problems via mail correspondence).

At the outset of this endeavor in the early 1920s, OR divisions held division-level group camps which every person in the division, regardless of unit, attended as part of the division and not as part of any subordinate element. The training at these camps initially tended to be very general in content – e.g., close order drill, rifle marksmanship, first aid, etc., along with a few rudimentary blocks of branch-related instruction – to ensure all members possessed a common foundation of skills, knowledge, and abilities. These camps succeeded in achieving their objectives by the end of 1924.

For example, the summer (July) 1923 camp for the 84th Division divided the members into five groups, based upon their rank and specialty. More specifically, this camp provided specialized training for leaders from the Infantry, Field Artillery, and Cavalry; along with combat support elements from the engineers, military intelligence, signal corps, chemical warfare corps, and the chaplain corps; and for combat service support leaders assigned to the quartermaster, ordinance, adjutant general, sanitary, and medical corps.[24]

Each group had a number of Regular Army unit instructors who were responsible for preparing, conducting, and overseeing the training. The training took place July 12-20 in a field environment and consisted of a series of tactical walks (a tactical exercise without troops) during which participants considered notional situations and were required to propose solutions to certain aspects of the situation and make a series of decisions as it played out. Often one of the tactical walks was focused on a specific type of operation or support function—the use of the reserve or artillery support in the defense, for example.

The overall scenario for the July 1923 camp was the movement of an infantry division into the line with a follow-on attack against an enemy force. At each stage of the first seven days, various aspects of division operations were taught, explained, and/or otherwise illustrated. In some instances, a Regular Army unit would actually perform some task as a demonstration on what a given maneuver, tactic, or support function looked like. After a demonstration or class was completed, a discussion would ensue as to how each type of unit or support function fit into the overall mission or task. The final two days of the camp's training was a Command Post Exercise (CPX) designed to familiarize the officers with the functions of a command post and communications in wartime.

These types of camps lasted until 1924, after which subordinate units were developed enough that they could hold unit camps and focus on collective training at the regimental, battalion, or company level(s). After this period of mandatory division-sponsored training, individual officers were trained by serving with a Regular Army unit in garrison or with a National Guard unit during that unit's own summer training period.[25]

The primary training objective was to explore different ways to train members of the ORC and ERC so they were as prepared as possible to serve effectively with minimal training if/when mobilized in times of national emergency. Since this was a completely new endeavor for the Army, there were different ideas regarding what "prepared" meant.

The Army had experimented with methods of assessing officer candidates during its Officer Training Camps in 1917-1918, and these efforts carried over to the post-war period and provided some basis for the training efforts of OR units like the 168th Brigade. For officer candidates, the focus was to identify the most important aspects to assess during training that would be a reliable method of determining those officer candidates best suited to be commissioned and lead soldiers in battle. Having assessed its newest officers, the Army engaged in an effort to change its time-honored system of promotion based upon seniority and develop and implement a more effective and systematic way to select officers for promotion based upon achievement and merit.

The following categories were used in these efforts:

Officer Candidate		Officer	
Adaptability	10	Physical Qualities	15
Judgment	10	Intelligence	15
Habits	10	Personal Qualities	15
Leadership	10	Leadership	15
Value to the Service	10	Value to the Service	40
More general and each of equal value		More specific and of a differing value	

Comparison of Traits and Weights of Officer Candidates and Junior Officers

The Army determined that each of the five areas was of equal value for officer candidates, but that the Value to the Service area was of much greater value than each of the other four elements (but not in aggregate) for serving officers. It is also interesting to note that the Army found that defining and describing "Personal Qualities" was the most difficult, followed by describing "General Value to the Service," in terms of capturing their intended meanings from the Army's perspective. The other three headings (Physical Qualities, Intelligence, and Leadership) were considered by the Army to be more straightforward and easier to define/describe in terms of their intended meanings.[26]

Having identified the essential traits for its officers, the Army gave the units responsibility for training and developing these leaders (e.g., ROTC units, OR brigades, etc.) broad discretion for developing training programs that allowed for the assessment and enhancement of these traits. This played to Gignilliat's strengths as a trainer, both for officer candidates (as he did at Culver) and for the younger officers assigned to his OR brigade (with whom he had worked while on active duty).

The Training and Development of Gignilliat as an ORC Officer and His OR Brigade

Having to find his way in command of the organization largely on his own (since it was among the first of its kind), Gignilliat began educating himself on the Army's requirements and the needs of the members of the organization. Fortunately, the Army realized the challenges facing such units and did its best to provide them with training to help them learn their own jobs, understand the requirements and expectations of their positions, and function effectively in their new roles. In a bit of serendipity, Gignilliat's brigade was assigned administratively to his former WWI unit, the 84th Division (which had become a training division for the Organized Reserve Corps (ORC)). The 84th Division sponsored a training camp at Fort Knox, KY, for its unit leaders in summer 1923, which Gignilliat attended for two weeks from July 12-20.

The following year, Gignilliat received some intensive individual training from the Army, attending an eight-week course (January 28-March, 18, 1924) at the prestigious US Army War College in Washington, DC, related to higher-level supply issues. Just after the beginning of Culver's 1924 summer school, Gignilliat had the opportunity to apply what he had learned from the Army while hosting the 168th BDE's two-week summer training at Culver from July 7-29.

This was somewhat unusual, as most of the summer training for units like the 168th BDE occurred at Fort Knox, under the watchful eyes of members of the 84th Division's staff, but it was also eminently practical, as approximately one-third of the brigade's officers were connected with Culver. Having the training at Culver allowed Gignilliat to host his organization on his home turf, keep an eye on Summer School, and relieve a large percentage of the assigned officers from having to make the trip to far away Fort Knox and instead devote the time that would have been spent traveling to preparations and additional training.

Taking advantage of the opportunity and determined to make a good impression on both the members of his unit and his higher headquarters (who sent observers to Culver), Gignilliat applied his characteristic attention to detail and zeal to planning the event and ensured that it qualified as the highest quality of training provided to an ORC unit. The resulting training plan included lectures addressing organization and signal communications, along with more active blocks of training devoted to map problems, terrain exercises, demonstrations, drill, and sand table exercises.

Addressing the more physical aspects of soldiering, Gignilliat also made use of Culver's facilities to provide training in rifle and automatic rifle marksmanship, field training regarding the employment of machine guns and accompanying weapons, and equitation. As a common feature of the training, all members also participated in daily athletic competitions. As intended, the 168th BDE's training was quite successful, and, given how new the concept of providing planned and systemic training for Reserve officers and NCOs, it attracted great attention by the press across the country and within the War Department and CMTC leadership.[27]

In fall 1924, Gignilliat's most powerful Army patron, General of the Armies John J. Pershing, retired from active duty. While he developed a warm rapport with his VMI classmate George C. Marshall (who would become the US Army Chief of Staff on September, 1, 1939, less than two months after Gignilliat retired from the Army) during the 1920s, Gignilliat never again enjoyed the support of such a high-ranking officer. This may explain while he remained at the same rank and in the same assignment for his remaining 18 years in the Army.

Closing out the year, Gignilliat led the 168th BDE in one of the first exercises of its kind for the ORC on December 15, 1924, a wargame pitting his own 84th Division against the rival 38th Division. As the first large-scale ORC exercise of its kind, this exercise attracted national attention, and it required Gignilliat to make use of all he had learned developing and directing Culver's military training program, during his time on active duty as an intelligence officer and trainer in WWI, and from the Army as a new General Officer. His performance commanding at this level must have been sufficient, as he was retained as the commander of the unit.[28]

Gignilliat continued devoting substantial amounts of time and energy to his Army responsibilities, hosting a map exercise at Culver on February 21, 1926, and spending two weeks on active duty at Fort Benjamin Harrison (near Indianapolis) between the end of the 1925-1926 winter school session (departing soon after the June 9th commencement exercises) and the beginning of the 1926 summer session (from around June 14-28, 1926). Gignilliat again hosted the 168th BDE summer training at Culver for two weeks in July, 1927, providing training for approximately 52 officers. Gignilliat impressed his boss' boss in 1928 (the Corps Area commander, MG Dennis E. Nolan, who had created the G-2 section of the AEF and thus had much in common with Gignilliat), who designated him as the Fifth Corp s Area representee at ORC training sponsored by the Army in Washington, DC in summer 1928.

By the end of 1928, Gignilliat had settled into his role as a Brigadier General in the ORC and as the commander of the 168th BDE, and he had learned much from the Army about the executive responsibilities of serving at this level and in a command position. However, the time, effort, and energy to do so was substantial and tended to place considerable demands on him at times during which he had previously been able to relax and recharge from the demands of serving as Culver's Superintendent (which had also increased). The strain of maintaining such a pace would culminate in a collapse of his health during the first part of 1926 that would reduce his ability and effectiveness for much of that year.

Assessing the impact Gignilliat had on the development of his unit, US Army Reserve historian Dr. John "Jay" Boyd contends that Gignilliat's efforts with 168th BDE were such that "Gignilliat literally built an army for the OR."[29] While perhaps a bit overstated, Boyd's sentiment nonetheless conveys the significant impact Gignilliat, with the Culver family's support (as usual), had on bringing the 168th Brigade into being and making it as effective as possible. As during the period prior to WWI, the partnership of Gignilliat and the Culver family was yet again quite effective in contributing meaningfully to the nation's military preparedness.

Gignilliat on Leadership Development for Cadets and Junior Officers

After having become accustomed to serving as a General officer, settled into his responsibilities as a commander, and adjusted to the requirements of the Army and his role, Gignilliat was quick to recognize the similarities of his responsibilities in developing cadets while leading Culver and developing junior reserve officers in the Army. Reflecting on both, his thoughts on the type of leadership he hoped to develop and instill in both his unit and his cadets coalesced, allowing him to be better able to articulate them more comprehensibly.

The reform-minded Secretary of War Elihu Root, who started the Army on its path to modernization at the beginning of the 20th century, adopted what was a radical idea at the time: the mysterious force called leadership could be developed! In his 1899 report on the state of the Army, Root presented his vision to not only develop leadership intentionally in Army leaders (primarily officers) but to do so in a way that allowed the Army to depart from its traditional reliance on the unreliable method of developing officers with and through a "cult of personality," who may or may not be leading effectively but certainly did so memorably and with remarkable quirks.

Rather, Root wanted to implement "a systemic approach to developing what he referred to as "safe leadership," which he contrasted with the quirkiness of the existing method and meant instead a program of study that trained officers to "follow well-understood methods of staff and command" that would bring predictability to the running of units and increase the Army's overall effectiveness.[30] This vision was especially important during Root's tenure, as the Army had relatively few officers to serve as leaders. However, Root was only able to impart his vision, and it took others to develop the program, flesh it out, and implement it. The requirement to develop a large citizen army for WWI both hastened and sharpened these efforts.

During and as a result of the war, and for perhaps the first time in its history, the Army had determined that it needed its officers to be capable military managers, instructors, and leaders (called trainers, managers, and leaders by the Army), but it was still determining what it meant by each of these in the early 1920s. Even though he was a n 1886 graduate of West Point steeped in the rigid discipline practices of the 19th century Army he joined, Pershing came to a very similar conclusion, remarking in a 1923 speech to the faculty of the Army War College that "In no other Army is it so important that the officers of the permanent establishment be...prepared to serve as instructors and leaders for the citizen forces which are to fight our wars."[31] Despite the significant change in the role of officers, Pershing retained his belief in the importance of discipline, albeit in a form that differed from the more harsh version used in the frontier Army of his past.

Gignilliat lacked Pershing's experience in the Army, but he had developed his own ideas about the role of discipline during his time at Culver. Having rejected the arbitrary discipline he experienced at VMI, his time in Yellowstone and at Culver showed him the value of discipline if and when used for a purpose. Gignilliat championed the ability of discipline as an organizing function and highlighted the Prussian Baron Von Steuben's training of the Continental Army during the American Revolutionary War as an excellent example of using military discipline effectively.

Prior to WWI, Gignilliat made it clear that enhanced citizenship was one of the greatest values of military education. While maintaining his focus on citizenship, Gignilliat began to manifest an interest in leadership (which he considered to be a subset of citizenship). In fact, he developed a remarkably innovative and progressive view of the leadership required of young leaders at a time when leadership itself was just beginning to be studied systematically and better understood. This conception of leadership would be broadly applicable to the relatively inexperienced officers in the ORC who he was charged with developing in his Army role and also to the cadets he educated and trained at Culver.

Reflecting the complexity of his thinking and embracing a set of novel contradictions that allowed for far more nuance than usual, Gignilliat's view was at once cautious and empowering, realistic yet optimistic, and both skills-based and developmental, setting his views apart from most during this period. Ten years after writing *Arms and the Boy*, Gignilliat laid out his approach regarding leadership and young leader development far more explicitly and in much greater detail in a very thoughtful letter to the Superintendent of VMI, William H. Cocke, on November 5, 1927.

According to Gignilliat, "We are inclined to think of Von Steuben as a Prussian, but it would be fine if in every military school and military organization the members were required to learn by heart his instructions to the captains and lieutenants in Washington's army at Valley Forge." In line with his own beliefs, Gignilliat emphasized that Von Steuben used discipline premised on a "personal and kindly touch between officers and men" to bring "order out of chaos."

Below is an excerpt from Von Steuben's *Instructions to His Captains* that is particularly relevant to Gignilliat's point in this regard:

> *A Captain cannot be too careful of the company the State has committed to his charge. He must pay the greatest attention to the health of his men, their discipline, arms, accoutrements, ammunition, clothes and necessaries.*
>
> *His object should be, to gain the love of his men, by treating them with every possible kindness and humanity, enquiring into their complaints, and when well founded, seeing them redressed. He should know every man of his company by name and character. He should often visit those who are sick, speak tenderly to them, see that the public provision, whether of medicine or diet, is duly administered, and procure them besides such comforts and conveniences as are in his power. The attachment that arises from this kind of attention to the sick and wounded, is almost inconceivable; it will moreover be the means of preserving the lives of many valuable men....*
>
> *He must keep a strict eye over the conduct of the non-commissioned officers; oblige them to do their duty with the greatest exactness; and use every possible means to keep up a proper subordination between them and the soldiers: For which*

reason he must never rudely reprimand them in presence of the
men, but at all times treat them with proper respect.[32]

Such an approach – which is also reminiscent of Sun Tzu's leadership advice to "unite through benevolence and regulate through discipline" – was more in line with the type of citizenship Americans needed and would allow military schools to impart to cadets and ORC units to impart to junior leaders ways to "handle men" that were more effective and suitable for leading citizen soldiers.

Far from advocating softness, which he believed was too prevalent in contemporary society, Gignilliat endeavored for the Culver system he created and implemented to "develop hardihood by the good, stiff, well-ordered regime that a competent military school should carry out without instituting an un-American system of oppression under which the individual has no redress," which required, among other things, that it be properly administered. For Pershing, who was a firm believer in the value of discipline, this must have surely struck a chord, and this approach was equally applicable to Gignilliat's work with training the officers of his 168th Brigade.

Gignilliat also codified much of what he believed regarding the requirements of leaders as a result of his experience in the Army during WWI and based upon his own demeanor. Gignilliat believed that "the best type of leadership is not the bullying or bull-dozing kind," demonstrating a lack of respect for those being led, or the "swash-buckler" who was more interested in drawing attention to himself than in helping others. Rather, he determined that the most effective leader was "the quiet chap who took a real interest in his men, treated them kindly but firmly and always looked after their welfare," very much akin to the ideal leader described by Von Steuben. This was much more in line with his own approach to leadership and from what he had absorbed from Captain Bromwell at Yellowstone and other successful leaders during WWI like MG Hale (who commanded the 84th Division).

To Gignilliat, the best way to secure the voluntary obedience he sought was to provide leaders with high levels of expertise in terms of knowledge and skills so they appeared wise and had more information and a higher level of proficiency than those who they led, thereby creating a natural condition for followers to accept the leadership of those placed in charge of them based upon their higher levels of expertise and knowledge, much as someone who is ill voluntarily seeks the counsel of a doctor, as the crew of ship consents to the authority of its captain, and as a traveler willing accepts the recommendations of a knowledgeable guide.

This approach was spelled out more explicitly in some of the military leadership manuals published around the time of the US entrance into WWI (which Gignilliat may or may not have read), in guidance like the following: "To attain the confidence and respect of your men, the first requisite is *superior knowledge*. That will give you self-confidence to appear as the leader, and will justify your men in following you." The author observed that those who did not possess such "superior knowledge" were only "pretending to lead."[33]

Reflecting on what he had witnessed and learned, Gignilliat concluded that good leadership consisted of being an expert in your responsibilities, knowing your men, treating them kindly but firmly, looking after their welfare, and using persuasion instead of coercion to gain compliance. However, Gignilliat also believed that the country's military schools had failed "to instill in cadets the real spirit of leadership" based upon persuasion instead of coercion, blaming the continued practice of hazing (among other things) for giving cadets "entirely the wrong idea of handling men" effectively and respectfully.[34] He was determined that neither Culver nor the 168th Brigade would make the same mistake.

Coming to a similar conclusion, Douglas MacArthur, serving as the Superintendent at West Point, wrote:

> "*Discipline no longer required extreme methods. Men generally needed only to be told what to do, rather than to be forced by the fear of consequence of failure. The great numbers involved made it impossible to apply the old rigid methods which had been so successful when battle lines were not so extensive. The rule of this war can but apply to that of the future. Improvisation will be the watchword. Such changed conditions will require a modification in type of the officer, a type possessing all of the cardinal military virtues as of yore, but possessing an intimate understanding of the mechanics of human feelings, a comprehensive grasp of world and national affairs, and a liberalization of conception which amounts to a change in his psychology of command.*"[35]

Thus, it appears that Gignilliat's own ideas on the proper method of leadership, which he developed empirically, were shared with experienced scholars and officers in the Army and was also extent in the existing literature of the period (such as it was). Gignilliat's vision of leadership also reflects a high level of congruence and continuity among the desired attributes for officer candidates (cadets) and officers. The difference was how best to develop the desired qualities in each group. As a result of his

WWI experience and throughout the 1920s, Gignilliat found that doing so required one type of approach for cadets at a military school aged 14-19 and a slightly different approach for part-time officers aged 22-40. During the pre-WWI period at Culver he had concentrated on developing an effective way of doing so for cadets, and throughout the 1920s he focused more on figuring out how best to do so for junior Army officers.

Gignilliat's Responsibilities to FIDAC

Gignilliat remained quite involved in the activities of FIDAC during this period, functioning at its highest levels, which developed him further as an executive. He attended FIDAC meetings each year during the period 1922-1928, representing the US at high levels beginning in 1925.

In summer 1922, he attended the 1922 gathering in New Orleans, which did not require him to be away from campus for very long. The next six meetings occurred overseas, requiring Gignilliat to be away from campus from five to six weeks at a time at the end of the summer and the beginning of the winter school session. During his period, his travels took him to Brussels in August-September 1923, where he was decorated as a Commander in the Moroccan order "Nichan Ictabar" and met the Queen of Romania, and to London in 1924, where he invited FIDAC delegates to campus of the dedication ceremony of the Legion Memorial Building on November 8 of that same year.

Gignilliat and Preston Wolfe (aide) in Vienna, Austria, 1926.[36]

Gignilliat led the US FIDAC delegation as chairman to Rome in 1925, staying in Europe afterwards to meet with Foch (among other things) and then heading directly to Omaha, Nebraska upon his return for the national meeting of the American Legion. This kept him away from campus for an extended period of over seven weeks from August 19 to October 10, 1925.

The following year, as vice chairman of the American FIDAC contingent, Gignilliat attended the annual meeting in Warsaw, taking him away from campus for over six weeks (August 15 - October 2). During the 1926 trip, Gignilliat took the opportunity to travel in Europe afterwards, stopping in Paris, Switzerland, Belgium, Austria, Germany, and England. He also took a recent Culver graduate, Preston Wolfe, along as his aide.

Serving again as the vice president of the American FIDAC delegation, Gignilliat traveled to Paris for the annual FIDAC meeting. He took an extended European tour before and after the meeting, visiting Italy, Switzerland, Alsace-Lorraine, Belgium, and England. As with the previous year, he traveled directly to the annual American Legion meeting before returning to Culver, causing him to be away from campus from late August (departing on August 26) until virtually the end of October (returning on October 27), a period of almost nine weeks. He wrote an article about the 1927 adventure for the American Legion Monthly magazine that was published in March of 1928, touting the large size of FIDAC.

Gignilliat's last significant FIDAC engagement was in 1928. Serving for a final time as the vice president of the American group, he went to Bucharest, Romania and had a delightful encounter with the crown princess of Romania. Gignilliat again wrote an article about the trip for the American Legion Monthly magazine, and he also invited the princess to campus for a visit. It is noteworthy that his only publications during this period came as a result of his FIDAC trips, indicating the importance of these activities to him.

Gignilliat did not attend the 1929 FIDAC meeting, but he did attend one final FIDAC meeting in Washington, DC in 1930, bringing his involvement with FIDAC to a close. However, the 1928 trip essentially ended his decade-long involvement with FIDAC, as new members took over and a "changing of the guard" occurred," and FIDAC begins to lose its influence.

Overall, and as a result of his extended involvement with FIDAC throughout the 1920s, Gignilliat gained much executive experience in his efforts on behalf of the US and FIDAC in uniting veterans' associations established after the end of WWI in various allied countries into an international federation whose main purpose was to promote peace, continuously strengthen the brotherhood initiated on the battlefield, and provide help to the wounded, the disabled, widowers, war orphans, veterans, and also commemorate the heroes fallen in battle and the Allied war effort.

As with his Army experiences, however, this executive experience came at the cost of diverting his attention and keeping him physically away from campus for significant periods of time each year of his involvement.

Gignilliat's Responsibilities in AMCSUS

Gignilliat also gained significant executive experience while serving as an elected official in AMCSUS for three annual terms during this period. He served as the Vice President of AMCSUS for the year 1925-1926 (again) with LTC Sandy Beaver as President, helping to rebuild its enrollment and guiding the organization during the period of the anti-militarism campaign that arose in America in the mid-1920s.

Other achievements during his time as AMCSUS president included holding the annual meeting in Chicago in mid-February 1928 and away from Washington, DC for the first time. Although he personally enjoyed Washington, DC (having spent a good portion of his youth there beginning at age nine), holding the annual meeting in Chicago allowed more schools from the Midwest to attend and made the annual meeting feel more inclusive (which was a quality Gignilliat prized highly).

During the annual meetings themselves, Gignilliat focused much attention on increasing the size and effectiveness of the organization, supporting the cooperative advertising campaign by discouraging efforts by the government to publish the specific results of annual inspections and ratings and increasing membership dues. As an enhancement activity for the organization, he also brought in his long-time colleague O'Shea to discuss dangers of permissive society "over-exciting" youth and had Culver's own Colonel Hunt present on "The Stimulation of Academic Interests" (by parents, incentives, teachers, and school).

Along with the challenge of maintaining enrollment, the most significant challenge faced by AMCSUS during the second half of the 1920s came from the anti-militarism campaign. It is important to address the motives and scope of this campaign in order to understand the context and Gignilliat's role in it.

The 1920s Anti-militarism Campaign

Beginning in 1925, a group of liberal educators and pacifists formed a private Quaker organization – called initially the Committee on Military Training – based upon a common belief that military training was incompatible with the ideals of peace and international cooperation. The cause they championed blossomed into a national movement during the second half of the 1920s and continued with varying levels of intensity until the US entered WWII.

Historian James Hawkes describes the 1920s anti-militarism campaign as unfolding in three stages:

- The initial stage lasting from 1925 with the preparation and publication of the Lane pamphlet (published in 1926) to 1930 with the ruling from the US Attorney General regarding the requirements of the Morrill Act;

- The second phase lasting from 1930-1935, focused mostly on the issue of conscientious objection; and

- The final phase, lasting from 1936-1940, during which the movement became divided, lost steam, and ended.[37]

Gignilliat was involved fairly significantly in the first phase, but not as much in the second and third phases.

The initial phase began rather innocuously with the release of a small pamphlet. As a way of presenting its views (similar to Martin Luther nailing his 95 theses to the church door in Wittenberg), the committee published in 1926 a study by one if its own members, Winthrop D. Lane, contending that the War Department was covertly militarizing the youth of America through the ROTC program. The substance of their concerns rested on their questioning of the educational value of the ROTC program (which some academics shared, but for different reasons).

The Lane pamphlet (as it came to be known) argued that institutions surrendered control of part of their curriculum by sponsoring /allowing ROTC on campus. This proved to be a very appealing argument to hyper-sensitive faculty members, many of whom had been supporters of the military before the war but had since turned against the military after witnessing the catastrophic level of destruction of the Great War. Endorsed by 50 prominent citizens, including John Dewey and Jane Addams, the substance of the pamphlet resonated with many other pacifists, as well as those who wanted the US to avoid another global conflict at all costs This pamphlet was instrumental in sparking the anti-militarism debate in America that was to last until the beginning of WWII.

Soon after the release of the Lane pamphlet, the Committee on Military Training changed its name to the Committee on Militarism in Education, and it became well known for the next 15 years by its three-letter abbreviation: CME. The stated goals of the CME included the elimination of compulsory military courses in colleges and of all such instruction in high schools, along with the termination of federal funding for and War Department control of military training in educational institutions.

Each of these goals was of particular concern to Gignilliat in his various roles, but the goal of eliminating all military instruction in high schools hit especially close to home in his role as the head of the Culver Military Academy and his on-going efforts to promote military training in high schools across the nation. The CME presented a challenge that he was compelled to address, both personally and professionally.

The release of the Lane pamphlet created momentum for the CME, which it used to its advantage that same year to have bills introduced in both the House and Senate to amend the National Defense Act of 1920 to make ROTC training voluntary. This became the CME's defining issue, which it pursued doggedly until the outbreak of WWII rendered it largely moot.

The basis of the CME's opposition to military training at land-grant institutions related to the necessity for it to be mandatory, along with their interpretation of the legislation establishing it. The language in the 1862 Morrill Act was sufficiently vague to make such a question legitimate and worthy of consideration.

For those like the CME who opposed compulsory training, simply offering training as an elective choice for students to choose as they desired was sufficient, and it did not need to be mandatory. This was a strict interpretation of the letter of the act as written in 1862. However, those who were supportive of compulsory military training disagreed, arguing that no such thing as "elective" courses existed in higher education at the time of the Morrill Act (1862), meaning that the implication was that the military training offered by the institutions was mandatory for all enrolled students (as with all other courses in the curriculum at the time).

There was merit to each side of the disagreement. Both sides lined up supporters (including John Dewey and Jane Addams for the CME) and presented their arguments during congressional hearings in both the House of Representative and the Senate. According to one account, the educational organizations generally conveyed reasoned opposition to the bill, while military organizations (e.g., ROA) conveyed unreasonable opposition to the bill. Nevertheless, there was little support for the CME's argument in either chamber. As a result, neither bill made it out of committee, and the challenge they promoted was defeated rather easily.

Despite the defeat of both bills, and perhaps unwisely overstepping its area of expertise, the CME continued to push, questioning whether compulsory military training was better/more effective than relying on volunteers in terms of national defense. This was a settled question for and within the military, which believed that the effectiveness of trained reserve junior officers proved to be far superior on the battlefields of WWI when compared to the effectiveness of relatively untrained volunteer officers in previous conflicts (especially the somewhat recent Spanish-American War). If anything, the military believed that junior officers required even more training to be effective on the modern industrialized battlefield. However, the average American citizen, steeped in the mystique of the effectiveness of the Minute Man to defend America, and the false but persistent notion of Americans being natural-born fighters in need of little training to be effective, was not as certain.

For those who supported military instruction in schools, the challenge from the CME was viewed to be sufficiently threatening to warrant the formation of an organization to counter it. Ralph Mershon, a successful engineer, patriot, reserve officer, and graduate of the large and excellent ROTC program at Ohio State University, responded by forming the Citizens Military Education Fund (CMEF) in 1928.

Owing to his connections and involvement in helping create the ROTC program, writing a portion of the National Defense Act of 1916, and help in getting it passed into law, Mershon's CMEF was quite influential and had "direct connections to the War Department," serving as an unofficial lobby for the Army's position in the debate.[38] For its membership, Mershon recruited the President of AMCSUS (which happened to be Gignilliat at the time) and the leader of the Reserve Officers Association, Edward Orton, Jr. (another Ohio State colleague who was also a veteran of the 1916 NDA effort and a brigadier general in the ORC).

Mershon's action in forming the CMEF was well-timed, as the CME ramped up its anti-militarism efforts by publishing a sequel to the 1926 Lane pamphlet in 1928. By 1929, the CME was coordinating the actions of 25 national organizations opposed to required military training.[39]

Gignilliat's Role in the First Phase of the Anti-militarism Campaign, 1925-1930

Gignilliat was both opposed to the efforts of the CME and involved with efforts to counter them on many levels. As the head of one of the nation's most well-known military schools and author of the best-known book on the subject, he was adamantly opposed to the CME's efforts to eradicate military training from all high schools in America. As the elected president of AMCSUS, he represented a constituency that was decidedly in support of offering military training at both the secondary and higher education levels. As a leader in FIDAC, he was part of an international body of like-minded individuals who were convinced that military preparedness and sufficient readiness were keys to avoiding another catastrophic conflict like WWI. Finally, as a senior officer in the ORC, he was charged professionally with providing military training to individuals to ensure the country's preparedness for future crises. In every aspect of his professional life (and likely in his personal life as well), Gignilliat represented the antithesis of the CME's beliefs.

Accordingly, and given his level of national recognition, he was a natural choice to be part of the opposition to the anti-militarism campaign. He was involved in efforts to oppose it from Culver, AMCSUS, the American Legion (also representing the interests of FIDAC), and the US Army, both as the commander of an ORC unit and by virtue of his role in Mershon's CMEF. Even though he preferred collegiality and avoiding confrontation when possible, he was well-suited for this task by temperament and belief. However, the efforts to oppose the CME in which he was most involved – those lasting from 1925-1930 – were time consuming and emotionally draining, diverting his focus from Culver and sapping the energy of one who had shown himself to be, up to this point, virtually indefatigable.

During a year's respite from leadership in AMCSUS, Gignilliat chaired American Legion Committee in 1926 to address the anti-militarism campaign. His efforts focused on countering the charges levels by the CME and the Lane pamphlet in general, and helping coordinate the opposition to the 1926 bills in the House and Senate seeking to remove the requirement for military training on land-grant campuses to be mandatory.

It was as a result of his efforts on behalf of FIDAC and chairing this committee that created the opportunity for Gignilliat to be considered seriously as the National Commander of the American Legion for the 1928-1929 term (aided, no doubt, by proximity and familiarity, since both the Indiana state headquarters and the national headquarters for the American Legion were both located in Indianapolis, Indiana). This did not come to pass, but that was more due to the unchecked ambition of a single individual (Paul V. McNutt) than it was a reflection of the tremendous level of support Gignilliat enjoyed from his American Legion peers across the country (many of whom felt that Gignilliat had earned this honor and encouraged the McNutt to back down and wait his turn).

In the thick of the fight against a determined anti-militarism campaign, which had expanded to over 25 national organizations, Gignilliat was elected to two consecutive terms as AMCSUS President in 1928 and 1929. Partnering with LTC RF Farrand from St. John's Military Academy, Gignilliat directed AMCSUS efforts that carried on an advertising campaign and conducted a sustained new membership drive that succeeded in raising membership from 39 to 50 member institutions (the highest since 1923).[40] Gignilliat's membership drives made sense, given that the number of military schools was increasing significantly throughout the 1920s (reaching its peak of 280 in 1926).[41]

This was also during the period of the expansion of the initial phase of the anti-militarism campaign, shifting some of its focus to high schools. While the entire campaign was having an adverse effect on military school enrollment and creating a public relations challenge for military schools, its impact was particularly significant on high schools for which public support for military training had never been very high.[42] Gignilliat was thus drawn into the anti-militarism debate personally and significantly.

As the elected president of AMCSUS, Gignilliat felt obligated, both professionally and personally, to defend military education from the growing number of anti-military attacks occurring in the national press. One such attack appeared in a 1928 edition of *The Rotarian* during his terms as AMCUS president. Written by the pacifist Reverend Ernest Tittle (and coming on the heels of the 1926 Lane Bill debate and the release of the supplement to the Lane pamphlet), the author lamented the increase in the number of military schools in the nation in the preceding decade, rising (by his count) from 57 in 1916 to 233 in 1926 (note : the number was actually 280).[43] In terms of the number of students enrolled in some form of military training, the same period witnessed an increase from 29,976 in 1916 to 119,914 in 1926 (coinciding with the increase in high school enrollment during the High School Movement and especially during the 1920s in the Midwest).

The increase in numbers was sufficient cause for alarm on its own, but to the Reverend Tittle the implication was that a concerted effort was being made to promote an insidious and cynical interpretation of history accepting that war was inevitable, which he found to be both militaristic and unacceptably destructive to the next generation (and especially considering the devastation that had occurred to the current generation as a result of WWI). He ended by issuing a call for a nationwide protest this effort, arguing that:

> *"If the rising generation of American s should become convinced that peace is possible, there is hope for the world. But if the rising generation, even in America, becomes impregnated with the idea that war is inevitable, God help the race,"*[44]

Targeting military training high schools proved to be quite effective for the anti-militarism campaign. While college students were assumed to have at least a modicum of choice in their activities and the maturity to discern the impact of military training on them, high school students were assumed to have neither. This fueled much of the opposition to military training in high schools.

A contemporary educator, William G. Carr (Assistant Director of the Research Division of the National Endowment for the Arts) wrote in 1926:

> *"It will be observed that at no time during this period [immediately before and after WWI] has military training been popular in American high schools, Even at the peak of war excitement in 1918, not one high school in ten offered a course in military drill. In 1926 less than four per cent (sic) of high school boys received such instruction and the work was offered in less than two per cent (sic) of the high schools. There was a decided decline in interest in military drill in high schools after the close of the war."*[45]

In addition, the American public during second half of 1920s was "lukewarm about preparedness" and in some cases hostile to the military services.[46] By targeting military training in high schools, the anti-militarism campaign tapped into an area of existing popular discontent that the CME was able to both exploit and exacerbate.

Gignilliat asked his long-time colleague, Professor Michael O'Shea, for assistance in providing a suitable response. At Gignilliat's request, O'Shea prepared a report in 1928 summarizing his findings and impressions of the impact of military training on boys using input he solicited from superintendents of public instruction across the country. Acknowledging concerns that military training could feed a perceived "craving for war" that some felt existed naturally in boys, O'Shea reported that all but one of the respondents replied that military training has been a positive influence on their students, providing support for Gignilliat's main point that realistic military training, rather than some romanticized version of it, actually reduces such cravings (if they even exist) when given properly by exposing them to the true nature of military activities (and even as it contributed positively to their overall development).

O'Shea also encouraged Gignilliat to argue that military training enhances the boy's individuality and ingenuity rather than promoting an unhealthy level of conformity and crushing his initiative. This reflected another important element of Gignilliat's defense of military training.

While the issue died down somewhat in the wake of Gignilliat's response, it was far from over, emerging again the very next year with even greater force and vitriol. According to one author:

"As it turned out, the threat to compulsory ROTC diminished greatly during the middle and late 1930s. Antimilitary forces conducted no further important campaigns from 1936 to the end of World War II. Their attempts to abolish compulsion by amending the National Defense Act or by withholding federal appropriations all failed and in the 1934 case of Hamilton et al v. Regents of the University of California, the United States Supreme Court ruled against conscientious objectors to ROTC drill. [47]

The same author concluded:

Antimilitarist activities in the states were only slightly more successful. Weakened by financial problems and divided, as was the peace movement as a whole, by the issue of military resistance to fascism the Committee on Militarism in Education suspended operations in 1940. By that time, only seventeen colleges or universities and only three land grant institutions had abandoned ROTC or made in an elective subject." [48]

After the direct and very public confrontation of the 1920s, the War Department's response was to work quietly with through civilian allies and organization s (like the CMTE) and avoid attacking the anti-militarists directly.[49] By removing the "spark" of controversy, the War Department effectively extinguished the CME's "flame," and the controversy largely faded away from the public's view.

Summary of Gignilliat's Performance Opposing the Initial Phase of the Anti-militarism Campaign, 1925-1930

Gignilliat played his role well as one of the most prominent, visible, and credible AMCSUS leaders and military school proponent, and he led AMCSUS well. The anti-militarism challenge allowed him to leverage his strengths as a person, educator, and military officer, and with the retirement of his most powerful Army patron (John J. Pershing in September of 1924), this period represented his final appearance on the national stage as an Army officer of influence. However, the cost was telling to him both professionally in terms of distracting him from his usual focus on campus, and personally, resulting in a prolonged period of infirmity and sub-optimal performance.

In aggregate, Gignilliat's activities related to his US Army responsibilities, FIDAC, and AMCSUS were substantial and took much of his focus, time, energy, and effort away from Culver during the period 1922-1928. This was particularly impactful to his performance of duty as Culver's Superintendent, as CMA had become a larger and more complex organization that demanded more of him and required him to function in new roles and develop abilities that were neither inherent to nor natural for him. Lacking his steady influence and consistent attention, the simmering unrest on campus (exacerbated, in part, by his response to the anti-militarism campaign), allowed for the rise of factions and challenges to his methods that were unthinkable in the pre-WWI era.

The Cost of His Efforts

As result of his diverse and frenetic activity, Gignilliat succumbed to a debilitating bout of influenza during the epidemic of 1926 that laid him low for almost half a year. Combined with his travels on behalf of FIDAC and the Army, he ended up being ill or away from Culver for seven of the 16 months during the period August 1925 to January 1927. He contracted influenza in late January 1926. In his somewhat depleted state, he was unable to recover from the initial episode, and the lingering effects of the flu slowed him down considerably during the first half of 1926.

In fact, he did not fully recover until the following January (1927).

Coupled with FIDAC trips in 1925 to Warsaw and in 1926 to Rome (the latter of which was especially taxing on him), Gignilliat found himself overwhelmed, both mentally and physically. His condition left him so depleted that he reported having to devote "every ounce of energy and moment of time to carry on [his] duties with the school," resulting in his turning over all personal matters to a personal secretary (one or both of his sons) who he could not supervise as closely as was his usual practice and which caused problems for both Culver (allowing its insurance coverage to lapse!) and the effort to create the Skyland Camps.

Gignilliat in 1925, prior to his illness.[50]

Meanwhile, Back on Campus...

While he was absent from campus for 27 months during WWI, the situation was quite different during such a crisis, as most all tried to toe the line and not make waves during his absence. The collective effort on campus was to continue performing as they knew Gignilliat would want them to as a way of showing their support and keeping Culver operating effectively. However, during the peaceful period of the mid-1920s, with no crisis-altering behavior, Gignilliat's absence from campus, both in terms of his attention and physical presence, was felt far more keenly and with greater impact.

The simmering discontent that developed on campus during this period arose largely from the expectations of the new faculty members of a more shared sense of governance with respect to the school's operations (fanned by JS Fleet). While unusual for Culver, it was somewhat indicative of the feeling of high school faculty members across the nation at the time. There is some indication that educators began to have increased difficulty in seeing the educational value of military training even prior to WWI, and this trend only increased during the 1920s and 1930s. For example, one 1926 study by George Coe found that an overwhelming number of secondary education professors disapproved of "the wisdom of military training in high schools."[51]

On Culver's campus (and reflecting a national trend), an increasing number of educators were also having difficulty in seeing the educational value of military training, especially to the extent it existed at Culver. Having arrived after WWI and with the military system well established, they required Gignilliat's direct attention and involvement to explain the rationale for the system and address their concerns, but Gignilliat simply could not be there to provide the attention this issue deserved due to commitments to the Army, AMCSUS, and FIDAC (all of which took him and his attention away from campus) and his own precarious state of health at the time.

Instead, it was another long-time Culver institution, JS Fleet, who began to influence campus increasingly toward his own beliefs that Culver needed to be less military and more academic, and that military training needed to be reduced to make this happen. Fleet's status of being Alexander "Fred" Fleet's son, combined with his cordial nature and charismatic manner, undoubtedly appealed to the talented young faculty members hired by Culver in the 1920s. These bright young educators hired by Gignilliat himself could have and should have been influenced more positively and proactively by Gignilliat but were instead left to the tender mercies of JS Fleet. Glascock almost certainly did all he could to counter Fleet and carry Gignilliat's position, but Greiner's death and Rossow's emergence and less-than-collegial nature towards his academic colleagues likely exacerbated the situation and lent much credence to JS Fleet's criticism and arguments.

Groups need leaders, especially one as large and well-educated as the Culver faculty and staff of the 1920s, and lacking guidance from the superintendent, it was only natural for them to look elsewhere for guidance. Someone like JS Fleet was bound to emerge as an influential figure in the relative "vacuum" left by Gignilliat's absence at this critical point in Culver's development.

In fact, the effort to seek guidance was precisely the type of initiative that led to their hiring. However, the system required the steady accessibility of and to the superintendent to be effective, and that condition was lacking during the mid-1920s at Culver.

In addition, and from an organizational perspective, Culver simply grew too large for Culver family oversight in 1920s as well. As president, ER Culver should have done a better job of keeping an eye on Gignilliat and monitoring the situation on campus during this period.

Making matters much worse, just as Gignilliat was recovering from this bout of ill health, and with things on campus going along well, catastrophe struck in the form of Bert Greiner dying suddenly of a heart attack on December 1, 1926. Given just how dependent the new administrative structure was on the personalities of Gignilliat, Glascock, and Greiner to function effectively, along with the simmering discontent developing on campus and the enhanced need for the utmost collegiality from the Commandant to assuage the concerns of the newer faculty members regarding Culver's military system, Greiner's presence as a senior administrator was perhaps as critical during this period as it had been during WWI.

Greiner's loss was a devastating blow to Gignilliat, Glascock, and the entire Culver community, and it set the stage for Gignilliat to make one of his most important post-war executive decisions. Unfortunately, Gignilliat made a choice that was comfortable for him personally but ill-suited for either the situation or for Culver that would have significant consequences in the near future.

Gignilliat immediately appointed Rossow as "Acting Commandant" (as was the Culver custom), and he was the natural choice for the position from the Superintendent's point of view, as Gignilliat both liked and respected Rossow.

Within the Culver hierarchy, Glascock remained number two and the Commandant remained number three. This arrangement worked for Rossow within the existing parameters of the situation, since Glascock was far senior to him in terms of age and service to Culver. From both a military and temperament perspective, however, Rossow was less comfortable with ranking below the Headmaster, since this was not the norm in the Army (where the military commander would always be the number two). For the naturally assertive cavalryman, Rossow was most comfortable being in command or functioning as a deputy commander as the acknowledge d "Number 2."

In addition, while Greiner had been part of the process of developing the new administrative model for Culver's senior leadership, had been trained as a commandant by Gignilliat himself, and thoroughly understood his role and the part he was expected to play, Rossow had far less familiarity with such matters, and he likely viewed the situation somewhat differently than Greiner. Given how important maintaining congruence among the three senior administrators was to the effectiveness of the new system, especially lacking the corresponding organizational changes that should have accompanied its implementation, this change could upset the delicate balance maintained by the three Gs that allowed the approach to be effective. To be fair, this would have been true for any newcomer to the situation, but Rossow's aggressive personality was bound to exacerbate the situation sooner or later.

In terms of skills and abilities, Rossow was much less of an educator and more of a trainer. This worked well for him in the Army, but it was not quite in line with Culver's approach (Rossow's experience at Culver notwithstanding) and/or what Culver needed from a Commandant at this particular time. Perhaps just as importantly, Rossow, unlike Greiner, had not been trained as a Commandant by Gignilliat, so he tended to default to his own military experience, to the precedent of military hierarchy, and a cavalry officer approach, characterized as being more raucous and bold, prone more to taking action than giving a matter some thought. As a result, Rossow tended to issue directives rather than being collegial with faculty peers (who he likely viewed as subordinates whose activities were subordinate to the military in achieving the Culver vision).

This approach to the Commandant's role was very different from that of the amiable and affable Greiner, and it was likely quite unsettling to the new members of the faculty who had come to expect a more collegial relationship like that of Greiner. Rossow was thus quite capable of keeping military program running as he *thought* Gignilliat wanted and as it had been since he arrived at Culver in 1906, but he was not able to sustain the same caliber of collegiality and/or educational focus of his predecessor.

Rossow's aggressive personality and different approach that was less deferential and comfortable with the military role as being number three in the Culver hierarchy may have begun upsetting the harmony of the Glascock-Greiner era that was so highly desired and prized by Gignilliat and which worked so well for Culver. It almost certainly upset JS Fleet and his group of followers, who wanted academics to be/become paramount and believed that the military should always give way when academics needed more of the cadets' time and energy.[52]

The gifted peacekeeper Glascock was likely able to manage the simmering discontent expertly and using all of the savvy, tact, and respect he had acquired during his three decades leading Culver's academic efforts. However, and as will become evident, Glascock's retirement, and his less capable replacement, created the conditions for the process of change desired by some to become manifest on campus.

The Aviation Program and WCMA Radio Station -- Indicators of Gignilliat and Culver Reaching Culminating Points in the 1920s

Just as Gignilliat was facing the limits of his own administrative abilities, so too had he, his vision, and his success pushed Culver to come up against its own "culminating point" as an institution in terms of sustainability.

With an average enrollment of over 700 students in the winter session, Culver's net tuition revenue far exceeded its operational expenses (based upon an enrollment of at least 400 students paying full tuition). Gignilliat proposed two high-tech and high-cost programs upon his return from WWI that proved to be unsustainable during this period.

Aviation program – Began in 1920, but due to high operational costs and insurance requirements, along with the challenges of keeping the

fleet of aircraft operational, the program was discontinued in 1925 (not to be revived again until October 1971).

"Fly Ins" (planes landing on frozen Lake Maxi Maxinkuckee) remained popular at Culver, especially during the period of the aviation program.[53]

Campus radio station

Culver created a low-budget 100-watt radio station (WHBH) in early 1925 (March) that was successful and effective. Culver invested $7,000 in new equipment in 1926 (~$110,000 in contemporary dollars) to enhance it to a 500-watt station and change the designation to WCMA, which occurred and began broadcasting at the end of November 1926. However, the challenges of programing turned out to be too great to

WCMA transmission towers on the Recreation Building in the 1930s.[54]

sustain, and broadcasting was cut back to three days a week for a total of six hours by spring 1928, and to just once a month by September 1928, It was completely off air by 1930 and the equipment and call letters were sold to another entity, who kept a radio station with the call letter WCMA on air until 1934, but the station was not affiliated with Culver in any way.

The curtailment for largely financial reasons of both of these programs,

WCMA broadcast "studio" on the balcony of the Recreation Building.[55]

which were each desirable and fit within Culver's tradition of finding effective ways of incorporating cutting-edge technology into its educational approach, along with the limited financial support provided for Gignilliat's own "castle in the sky" – the Skyland Camps in Montana (discussed in its own chapter) – suggests that the1920s represented Culver's Gilded Age, characterized by recognizing that perhaps things had changed, but wanting nonetheless to keep going according to the Old Ways.

Challenging Times Financially for the Wrought Iron Range Company

It is important to understand the circumstances that produced this situation, which requires one to examine the status of the Wrought Iron Range Company in the 1920s. As the only other source of financial support for Culver Military Academy aside from its net tuition revenue, the financial status of the Wrought Iron Range Company was directly related to the ability of the Culver family's ability to provide financial resources for Culver Military Academy. Up to right before the outbreak of WWI, this had never been an issue, as the Wrought Iron Range Company had been a tremendously successful commercial enterprise. Based upon the funding model relied upon by Culver Military Academy – comprised of its net tuition revenue plus Culver family contributions – CMA's financial solvency was contingent upon the continued financial success of the Wrought Iron Range Company during the period of its governance under the Culver family's association (which began in 1902).

During WWI, BB Culver transitioned the Wrought Iron Range Company away from producing civilian products, concentrating instead on providing the military with large commercial-style ranges for mess halls, along with coffee urns and cast-iron pans, and smaller stoves for heating barracks and tents, along with a variety of other war-related equipment. With the civilian market all but discontinued, along with the need for its wagon-based sales force, the hundreds of horses and mules and the wagons they had pulled were liquidated.

The war brought an end to the Culver's slow but tried-and-true method of farm-to-farm sales operations in all but the most rural of areas, replaced afterwards by the more rapid automobiles and trucks, and large showrooms where customers could come to shop. While the Culver brothers continued to make innovations to their own products, electric and gas ranges were becoming more popular with American consumers, reducing the share of the market once dominated by the Wrought Iron Range Company.[56]

BB Culver acknowledged that the times had changed, and in mid-1925 he decided to raze the three-story factory on Washington Avenue in St. Louis that had served the company so well and replace it with a new two-story building designed as a showroom using Albert H. Knell as the architect (the same man who had designed over 20 fireproof red brick buildings on the campus of Culver Military Academy). The building, constructed using handsome but costly materials, was completed in 1926 at a cost of approximately $100,000 (approximately 1.7 million in 2024 dollars). BB

New Wrought Iron Range Company showroom building, 1926.

intended to rent out excess space to other tenants as a way of helping to alleviate the cost of the structure.

However, while attractive, eye-catching, and popular in residential dwellings at the time, its nine peaked gables arranged in three sections separated by two faux-chimney piers was, according to one author, a "bold, almost alien, choice" for a building design in downtown St. Louis.

As a result, the structure was somewhat out of place in the neighborhood in which it was constructed, and it had difficulty attracting and retaining reliable tenants. Occupancy began dwindling almost immediately, and by 1929, BB had to make the difficult but necessary decision to move the Wrought Iron Range Company showroom out of the building, presumably relocating it to the company's factory location elsewhere in St. Louis.[57]

Along with declining revenue for the company and the expense of the new building, BB and ER completed the drawn-out and convoluted buy-out of their siblings in 1928 (begun as early as 1902) at the astronomical cost of $2 million (which equates to over $35 million in 2023 dollars).

The infighting between and among the surviving siblings had been sustained but fairly civil during much of this period, and it centered largely on disagreement with ER and BB's consistent determination to direct much (if not all) of the company's stock dividends back to support Culver Military Academy, which they believed honored their deceased father's wishes. The passing of the family matriarch Emily Jane in 1923, however, gave license to some of the children to discard any pretext of civility they may have retained up to that point in their dealings with ER and BB regarding their share of the inheritance.

While worth the cost to the Culver brothers in terms of ending the sibling conflicts and securing their father's legacy, the combined impact of the declining revenue and considerable expense of the new building and the sibling buy-out produced significant financial challenges for the company. As a result, the Culver family could provide sufficient but no

Payson Map depiction of the Culver campus in 1927 (used by permission of Colonel Payson's living descendants).

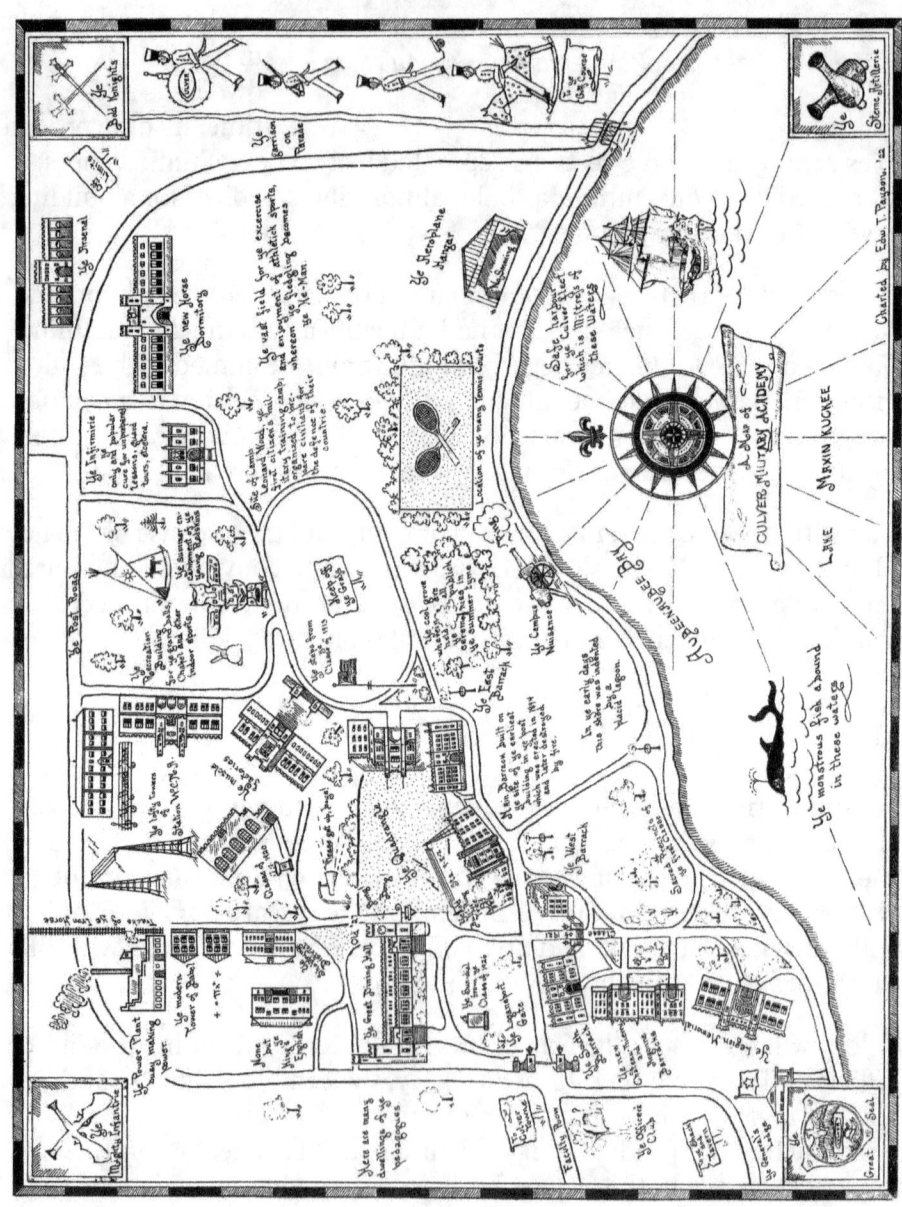

longer virtually unlimited funding for Culver Military Academy. ER and BB concluded that they needed to create a non-profit foundation and transfer ownership of Culver Military Academy to it to ensure that the school their father had established could remain viable and in existence in the future.

Culver' Physical Plant at the Height of Gignilliat's Influence

The well-known "Payson map" does an excellent job of portraying Culver at the height of Gignilliat's influence. Long-time Culver band director Colonel Edward T. Payson (CMA 1922) drew the map in 1927, and it shows the breadth of campus that Gignilliat had helped develop by then, from the Superintendent's quarters in the southwest to Arsenal building in the northeast.

Impacts on CMA and Gignilliat

As an institution, Culver appears to have reached its financial "culminating point" during the 1920s, with an average enrollment of over 700 students in the winter session and a faculty of over 100. This created a situation in which it was in a solid financial position that allowed it to do some but not all of what it wanted to do (in terms of financing) based upon its available financial resources.

Even though enrollment was quite high, there were financial challenges to keep Culver operating while relying primarily on net tuition revenue and the Culver family's preferred level of financial support, and without support from fundraising and/or the safety net of an endowment.

The Culver system developed during its first three decades was heavily dependent upon sustaining a large number of faculty and staff to provide the cadets with the level of sufficient and individualized attention that had come to characterize and distinguish the Culver approach. This method proved to be increasingly costly to sustain, especially and becoming increasingly apparent when the institution began enrolling an average of over 700 cadets during the winter session (which has served as an empirical threshold, then as now, for differentiating meaningfully between the size and complexity of a secondary educational institution).

Administratively, Gignilliat's approach and skills were better suited to a smaller (i.e., under 700 students) and less complex organization (i.e., the "old" Culver) that could be administered using his preferred method –

Organizational Leadership – which focuses more on the operational and day-to-day concerns of the institution. The same appears to hold true for Culver's oversight model of governance and financial model as a family-own association, which did not have much of a strategic component at this point.

While Gignilliat (and, presumably, ER and BB Culver) remained enthralled with new technology and determined to keep Culver on the cutting edge in terms of providing the very latest innovations, Culver faced very real (albeit self-imposed) limitations to its ability to do so during the 1920s, despite its relatively strong financial situation.

This began a new era for Culver of having to make choices among various desires based upon financial means available, for which Culver had not developed a process and that Gignilliat may not have been particularly well suited to superintend. His desire for harmony was placed at odds with the requirement to make hard choices that inevitably disappointed some. In addition, he was not sufficiently present during this period to guide the process and selections (as he had been in the past, and which he should have been and needed to be during this period).

Given his financial savvy and acumen, BB Culver surely recognized this situation for what it was. These contributing factors, along with Emily Jane's death on June 23, 1922, provided the impetus for the decision by ER and BB Culver towards the end of the 1920s (beginning in 1928) to start buying up all the remaining shares for other family members to transform Culver from a family-owned association into an educational foundation in 1930 (delayed by ER Culver's untimely death until June 1932 and not completed until June 1933).[58] This development would bring about a change in the governance of the institution that was necessary but which introduced an approach that was less comfortable for Gignilliat and/or suited to his abilities.

A Similar Crossroads in His Military Career – Gignilliat's Challenging Involvement with The Reserve Officers Association

As with so many of his other activities during this period, Gignilliat became involved with the national organization established for the ORC, the Reserve Officers Association (ROA). Gignilliat was present at the ROA's creation in Washington, DC in October 1922, making him a founding member of it.[59] He remained involved with the ROA for the next several years, and he was called to Washington, DC in February 1924 to support ROA Congressional testimony.[60] While he did not speak, the request for his presence indicates his level of influence in the organization.

By 1926, he was no longer officially associated with the ROA, likely due to his competing demands from his numerous other activities (especially FIDAC and AMCSUS).

Gignilliat re-engaged with the ROA in 1928 when he was appointed as the V Corps Area representative by the Corps Commander, MG Dennis Nolan, who he had impressed by his work with the 168th Brigade. Gignilliat continued to serve as the V Corps Area ROA representative for several more years, but his most meaningful engagement in this capacity occurred during his first year in 1928.

On May 14, 1928, Assistant Secretary of War Robbins appointed a committee of Reservists to consider Reserve policy. Known as the "July Advisory Committee," it was comprised of one Reserve officer, named by the Corps commander, from each of the country's nine Corps Areas. Gignilliat was the V Corps representative, and likely due to seniority was named chairman of the committee.

This appointment was so important that it caused Gignilliat to miss the 168TH Brigade's summer drill, hosted at Culver during the final two weeks of July 1928 and involving 56 officers.[61] Accompanied by Minnie and her mother, Gignilliat departed Culver in early July, 1928, and traveled by car to Virginia, where he dropped off his wife and mother-in-law at the Fleet family home and then continued on to Washington, DC.[62] His assignment kept him away from campus for an entire month, and he returned on August 9, 1928, in time to participate in Culver's first celebration of Founders Day (on the anniversary of HH Culver's birthday).

Once in Washington, DC, the July Advisory Committee met for three days (July 9-12, 1928). Several members (including Gignilliat) continued working in Washington, DC for another week, wrapping up the effort by around July 19, 1928.

The main task of the committee was to provide input to the office of the Secretary of War regarding the proper method of providing official oversight for the newly created federal reserve forces. Most in the Regular Army believed that the Army's existing structure was sufficient to provide the necessary oversight, while the ROA believed that the Secretary of War should create a separate bureau – referred to as a "Reserve Division" – to provide oversight for the Army's reserve forces, as had been done for the National Guard.

The committee requested to hear from the Secretary of War and the Army Chief of Staff on the matter, but neither was available to meet with the committee during the three days of its deliberation. The committee did its best to obtain the information it hoped to get from the War Department's leadership by alternate means, but a disagreement arose among the members of the committee regarding the sufficiency of its efforts in this regard.

The majority (six out of nine, including Gignilliat), believed that its efforts had provided it with sufficient information upon which to base its decision and elected to complete its task and issue a recommendation at the conclusion of its three-day period of deliberation on the issue. The minority (three out of nine) dissented based upon their belief that a separate agency within the War Department was needed to coordinate the activities of the newly created Federal Reserve (comprised of the Officers' Reserve Corps (ORC) and the Enlisted Reserve Corps (ERC)).

The crux of their dissent related to their belief that the majority opinion failed to consider all of the relevant information, which they believed could only be obtained from the Secretary of War and Army Chief of Staff, and that it did not represent the wishes of the majority of the members of the ROA. They accused the majority of coming to a hasty and ill-informed decision and of having refused to confer with the Secretary of War and the Army Chief of Staff on the matter.

Gignilliat worked as the chairman with both sides to try to resolve the dispute and gain the consensus that he and the War Department leadership desired. However, he was not successful, and he dutifully forwarded the majority recommendation and minority dissent to the War Department on July 19, 1928.

The War Department leadership was dissatisfied with the committee's work, wanting a more clear consensus from the ROA on the matter. Accordingly, the Secretary of War referred the matter to the ROA's top leadership on August 29, 1928, requesting a more definitive expression of the ROA's position on the matter and that they advise him of it accordingly.

The ROA responded by assembling its National Council in Chicago on September 18, 1928. Dissented from and essentially discrediting the July Advisory Committee's majority report that Gignilliat had supported and signed, the ROA National Council instead expressed its unanimous support from the ROA for the creation of a Reserve Bureau in the War Department. Going a step further, the ROA's National Council communicated to its own membership that it did not believe that the July

Advisory Committee's majority opinion supported the building up of the ROA and was actually working at cross purposes for doing so, and that its supporters were being misled a select few with nefarious intentions.[63]

While it is likely that Gignilliat was invited to the meeting, he was in Bucharest for the FIDAC meeting and not available to attend. His absence from the ROA National Council meeting was unfortunate, as he was unable to support the majority position and/or provide the rationale for his own position on the issue, but also likely largely irrelevant (since the ROA did not agree with the July Committee's recommendation supported by Gignilliat).

Overall, Gignilliat's position was not in support of the ROA, but it was very much in line with US Army's position (as reflected in the fact that it did not create a Reserve Division within the War Department prior to WWII). Nevertheless, his position on this issue ended up impacting him negatively as a Reserve officer, as he was virtually excommunicated from the ROA and was never allowed to have any meaningful association with it again (despite being a founding member of it).

This episode and its outcome illustrate the strength of Gignilliat's convictions, as even when his desire for consensus and harmony came into conflict with his principles, he acted (as he always had) in accordance with his own convictions and supported his principles. It also reflected how he understood the role of a commander as having an essentially "free hand" in most aspects, and how he operated at Culver up to this point, collegial but without any evidence of a "shared governance" approach. Gignilliat's inherent trust and support in authority made the position he took understandable, but the coming Age of the Consultants (1929-1934) at Culver would put him in a very different position and expose him to something like the minority approach in this episode.

Losing the support of the ROA and largely being excluded from it (except if/when acting in an official capacity when appointed as V Corps representative by MG Nolan) was both unfortunate and unfair, as Gignilliat was very much in support of the ORC and Reserve forces. He showed this time and again through his actions in AMCSUS and the American Legion, his command of the 168th Brigade, his support for ROTC and CMTC, and his advocacy for the ROA resulted in Indiana consistently having the second highest level of ROA members in the country.[64]

Gignilliat as an "Institution Man"

This outcome sheds light on another aspect of Gignilliat: That of being a certain kind of an "Organization Man.," more accurately identified as an "Institutional Man." William H. Whyte, Jr. published his seminal work, *The Organization Man*, in 1956, in which he introduced the notion of the "organization man" into the American lexicon. Described as a new breed of worker who not only worked for an organization but also "belonged" to it physically, mentally, emotionally, and spiritually, the organization man takes the view of the organization as his own and views life through the prism of the organization for which he works. According to Whyte, organization men are "the mind and soul of our great self-perpetuating" organizations."[65]

Since the publication of *The Organization Man*, a new idea has emerged, that of the "institution." This concept was identified by Tom Peters and Robert Waterman and introduced in their own seminal work, *In Search of Excellence*, as being an organization with values.[66]

Typically ahead of his time while also hearkening back to simpler times, Gignilliat was an "organization man" attached to institutions, making him an "institution man." He identified with and belonged physically, emotionally, and spiritually to the institutions of Culver and the ORC, having taken on their views as his own and becoming the mind and soul for them. This is clearly the case for Culver, and it also appears to apply to him as a Reserve officer.

The impact of his complete devotion to institutions had a profound impact on Gignilliat, shaping him as much as he shaped the institutions to which he was devoted. These powerful institutions to which he attached himself – Culver and the ORC – became part of his identity and allowed him to experience the sense of belonging to something larger than himself that he craved throughout his entire life (perhaps to make up for the lack of connection he felt to his own family growing up).

It was thus tremendously jarring for him to be essentially rejected by the ROA, which as an arm of the ORC institution to which he had been attached to since its founding. While he found ways to remain connected to and part of the ORC until his retirement from the Army in 1939 and even afterwards, this rejection hurt him deeply and substantively. Only his perceived rejection by Culver in early 1942 would eclipse the hurt he felt from this episode.

Gignilliat's Second "Peak"

Despite some setbacks, Gignilliat experienced a second "peak in the late 1920s. The post-WWI period began with Gignilliat in command of a powerful majority on campus who supported (if not entirely shared) his views and approach. However, as the decade progressed and his attention was directed elsewhere, his campus majority began to dwindle. While his personal influence remained strong, his absences from campus allowed for the influence of others – most of whom were not entirely in support of all of Gignilliat's views and support – to increase and become more pronounced.

As an individual, Gignilliat enjoyed what may be characterized as his second (and final) "peak" in 1928 – as a culmination of his own personal influence. This height of influence spans the four-year period lasting from 1927-1930. Highlights of this second pinnacle include:

- o FIDAC American representative – 1928

- o Elected AMCSUS President in 1927 and 1928 and serving two consecutive terms– 1928-1929 (in the midst of the first phase of the anti-militarism campaign)

- o Serious consideration to become the American Legion National Commander 1928-1929

- o ROA July Advisory Committee Chairman.

Gignilliat reached another zenith during this period; he had an effective administrative organization and team that was ideally suited to assist him in continuing to guide Culver in directions and ways that he saw fit. However, his willingness to take on more projects than was reasonable also brought him face-to-face with his limits as an administrator and his physical limits, as he experienced setbacks in both areas and saw his shadow of influence over the institution begin to lengthen.

While he maintained his ability to achieve remarkable outcomes when provided with the right circumstances and the opportunity to perform, this second "peak" was not quite at the level of his previous "peak" in 1921-1922, as the circumstances were not as ideal and there was not the same level of opportunity for him. His overall level of ability remained high, but it was also just beginning to show signs of decline (perhaps related to illness and/or age). Along with his level of preparation (when he had time for it), Gignilliat's overall level of performance remained impressive, since many of the challenges he faced were still largely within his areas of expertise and training.

However, as evidenced by the anti-militarism campaign and the Skyland Camps adventure (more about that in another chapter), Gignilliat was also beginning to face challenges that moved beyond his areas of expertise and natural abilities. As a result, the outcomes he achieved during this period were good, but most were not beyond what could be reasonably expected, and his direct influence on them were not as discernible and/or substantial (meaning that perhaps someone else could have achieved similar outcomes during this period). Gignilliat's character remained consistently sterling throughout all of the trials and tribulations of this period. This was one of the reasons that accusations of malfeasance and misdeeds related to the Skyland Camps endeavor upset him so greatly (as addressed in the chapter addressing this episode in greater depth). Having his loyalty questioned by the ROA was similarly disconcerting to him.

Chapter 16 – The Quixotic and Perplexing Skyland Camps Endeavor: An Unnecessary Distraction and Preventable Failure

Of the many ventures undertaken by Gignilliat throughout his life, the quixotic and perplexing Skyland Camps endeavor is perhaps the most unusual and disappointing. The idea was to establish a location for a somewhat informal summer camp for boys deep in the wilderness as a place to go for an adventure while also learning valuable Culver lessons.

The theory for this undertaking may have been sound, but the execution of the idea in a remote and inaccessible location over 1,600 miles way from Culver was anything but sensible, and it became what appears to have been an inexplicable failure at first glance. However, upon further consideration and analysis, the endeavor was founded on an unstable premise that was exacerbated by poor decision-making and circumstances that make the lack of success more comprehensible (if not palatable).

According to the National Parks Service (NSP) description of it,

> *"One of the unusual camps to operate within the park was the Skyland Camp, with headquarters on Bowman Lake. It opened for business in 1922, serving mainly as a boys' camp from July 2 to August 27 and as a tourist camp for the remainder of the time between June 15 and snowfall. The camp was operated by the Culver Military Academy of Culver, Indiana, and catered to teenage boys who could take care of themselves in the woods with the proper leadership and guidance... This camp operated for several years, but finally closed down because of lack of business."*[1]

Data from Glacier National Park (GNP) shows that the failure of the Skyland Camps venture was not due to low visitation at GNP, which increased steadily and substantially during the period of its operation.[2] In the absence of such an explanation to explain the venture's unsuccessful outcome, one must look instead to Gignilliat for reasons why it failed.

There appear to have been three main reasons why this endeavor failed:

- Gignilliat made a poor initial decision locating the camps;

- He put his trust in people in whom he had confidence (two sons), but who lacked the experience to succeed in such a situation; and

- He did not have the time to provide proper supervision of their efforts to guide them and help them succeed.

In the only scholarly treatment of it, the author characterized the Skyland Camps venture as being ill-advised, ill-fated, and as Gignilliat's "enthusiastic [but] shattered dream."[3] While a more accurate description might be one referring to it as a quixotic and perplexing endeavor that was as grand and ambitious as it was puzzling and ill-conceived, it nevertheless represents the least successful endeavor undertaken by Gignilliat in the 1920s, and perhaps of his entire professional career.

It is certainly hard to argue with Gignilliat's methods and level of success pre-WWI, but his record of achievement beginning in the post-WWI was simply not as impressive. The unexpectedly disappointing outcome of the Skyland Camps episode – which appeared to have been tailor-made to Gignilliat's exceptional abilities to create a compelling vision, generate national interest, and market an idea exceedingly well – along with the financial challenges being faced by the Culver family and the unrest being fomented on campus by JS Fleet related to his (perhaps unfounded) concerns about performance of Culver graduates in college, along with other organizational and institutional concerns beginning to percolate on campus among rising stars like Gregory, Chambers, and others, began to expose Gignilliat's limitations as an administrator and made him vulnerable to challenges to his authority.

Making a poor initial decision regarding the location of the camps, along with taking on far too many responsibilities to be able to manage effectively during the period, and exacerbated by his inability to provide his usual level of oversight and supervision, long absences from campus to attend to external duties, and the breakdown of his health, all contributed to an outcome that was as unexpectedly disappointing for Culver as it was uncharacteristic of the efforts of its renowned Superintendent.

Within the context of this biography, this episode portrays Gignilliat's performance as a burgeoning executive, highlights some of his limitations, illustrates the impact of his overcommitment during this period, and serves as a harbinger of things to come.

Skyland – From Rejuvenating Respite to Visionary Quest

At the end of the 1921 summer school session, Gignilliat found himself feeling somewhat "below par physically" and decided to accompany Colonel Rossow on what had become an annual horseback trip away from campus for his first real vacation since returning from WWI. The purpose of these trips was to provide an optional opportunity for cadets to visit unpopulated areas on horseback, camping in the woods and enjoying a respite from the demands of their lives prior to the beginning of the winter school session. Since Minnie, Leigh Jr., and Hank were touring

Virginia, Gignilliat took his middle son Fred with him on the trip. Fred's Culver classmate, A. H. "Frank" Denton '18, accompanied them as well, having gained access by signing up for Colonel Rossow's trip.

Rossow's destination in 1921 was the distant and isolated Glacier National Park. Established in 1910 and consisting of over 1,500 square miles of territory, Glacier National Park was located in northern Montana, abutting the Canadian border, at an elevation of approximately 4,000 feet. Rossow made the transportation and logistical arrangements, which included securing the use of a suitable number of horses for the group. Being approximately 1,600 miles from Culver, it was a destination that was as ambitious as it was remote.

After completing Rossow's portion of the trip, Gignilliat decided to remain in the wilderness extracting "all the ozone available" and away from campus until his "strength and vigor [were] fully restored." Fred and Frank Denton remained with him while Rossow and the remainder of the group returned to Culver to begin the 1921-1922 winter school session.[4] At this point, what began initially as a way to recover his health on one of Rossow's summer horseback trips transformed into something far more consequential.

The Creation of the Skyland Camps Idea – Fall 1921

The trip had an invigorating effect on both Gignilliat and Fred. As a result, "Fred conceived the idea of a unique boys camp conducted along informal lines which would admit the taking in of parents who did not object to roughing it."[5] Enamored with the notion of creating his own "castle" in the farthest northwester portion of the country (much as HH Culver had done at Culver), Gignilliat immediately expressed his support for his son's suggestion. This transformed the excursion from a leisurely tour into an expedition with a purpose of identifying the best possible location for such a camp.

Led by GNP guide Jack Monroe, the group began exploring GNP for possible camp sites.

Gignilliat (R), guide Jack Monroe, and Fred Gignilliat (L) scouting for a camp site.[6]

Glacier National Park, with North Forks and Two Medicine areas highlighted.

Monroe guided them to explore two regions of the park as possible locations for the camp: the more accessible Two Medicine Lake area in the southeast portion of the park; and the more remote and less-accessible Bowman Lake area in the extreme northwest portion of the park.

Gignilliat was quite impressed with the Two Medicine Lake area, and he initially selected the very accessible locale as site for a camp for approximately 50 boys. Always thinking bigger, Gignilliat envisioned growing the camp to be able to accommodate as many as one thousand boys (or more) rather quickly.

However, after the tourist season closed in mid-September 1921, Monroe led the trio into the northwestern portion of the park to the North Forks Area that was not yet open to regular tourist traffic. Here they found a group of the most beautiful lakes in the world, anchored by the primeval Bowman Lake that was "chock full of gamey trout just aching for an opportunity to snap at a fly." During their visit to this area, Fred tells of pulling 15–20-pound fish out of the lakes, and he described the clean, sweet smell of the forest as transforming the air into "an invigorating tonic."[7] The pristine beauty they encountered was magnificent and unlike anything they had encountered previously on the trip, and it impacted the three of them deeply.

The picture shows the spectacular vista that captivated Gignilliat and moved him and the others so deeply. While its beauty is undeniably breathtaking, it was also remarkably inaccessible. GNP was straightforward in telling Gignilliat that it had no plans to improve the roads leading to this area of the park.

Bowman Lake and Rainbow Peak on the right (9,895 ft) looking north from the location of Skyland Camps.[8]

Nevertheless, the majesty and setting of Bowman Lake enthralled the group and took hold of their imaginations as no other location had.

As a rugged outdoorsman, Monroe was likely partial to the pristine splendor of the North Forks area, which, despite its inaccessibility by wheeled vehicles, was quite accessible on horseback (which was Monroe's preferred mode of travel in the park). Inspired by Gignilliat's notion of finding a location for the camp that would support the experience of having an adventure in the wilderness, the remote and unspoiled North Forks area had a tremendous appeal to it. It is likely that the environment and experience of reconnoitering the area from horseback exerted a powerful influence over Gignilliat, Fred, and Frank that may have subconsciously skewed their thinking (as it has for countless others exposed to such primordial magnificence).

By end of the visit, which had by now stretched into October 1921, Gignilliat determined that the more accessible Two Medicine Lake location was "too tame" for his proposes. This may have come from either the influence of Monroe and/or the experience itself.

Instead, he selected instead the less accessible, more remote, and more pristine and breathtakingly beautiful Bowman Lake location as the base of operations for his own "castle in the sky" that he dubbed "Skyland Camp." Here he believed that he would be able to create the idyllic wilderness retreat conceived of by Fred and which he was determined to make manifest.

In addition to being captivated by its undeniable beauty, and despite the inaccessibility of the location, Gignilliat was perhaps inspired to select the Bowman Lake location based upon a belief that it would be more suitable to accommodate the growth he envisioned for the venture (from 50 to 1,000 or more in a few years). Given its location in the park, this surely appealed to him as well.

Upon their return to Culver, the idea gained momentum, and plans were developed throughout fall 1921. In true Gignilliat fashion, he had successfully marketed the idea, gaining the interest of "a notable list of advisors" that was a virtual "who's who" of important outdoor enthusiasts, including former President and noted outdoorsman Theodore Roosevelt, the commissioner of Major League Baseball Judge Kenesaw Mountain Landis, famous football coach and "Father of American football" Walter Camp, founder of the Woodcraft Scouts and leading figure in the Boy Scouts of American Ernest Thompson-Seton, along with several famous writers. By the end of the year, Gignilliat has secured the support of ER Culver for the project, along with a concession from the US Parks

Department (which is how the government granted permission to private entities) to formally establish Skyland Camps in GNP and construct several cabins on the shore of Bowman Lake.[9]

Clearly captivated by the idea, Gignilliat devoted considerable time and effort to the Skyland Camp venture in 1921-1922. The record of his correspondence indicates a lively exchange of letters with administrators at both GNP and at the National Park Service through the end of 1922, when the record stops and does not become active again until mid-1926 (by which time things at the camps and with the leaders at GNP had deteriorated badly and virtually beyond repair). This period coincides with the beginning of Gignilliat's command of the 168th Brigade and of his extensive FIDAC involvement, perhaps accounting for his inattention.

Buoyed by his father's interest in and support for his idea, Gignilliat's middle son had found a purpose, and threw himself into the endeavor with all the zeal one would expect from his energetic father. Consumed by the effort, Fred was quite busy working to bring his vision to reality in a manner he had seen his father do many times before. Using what he learned at Culver, he and Frank collaborated to draft a master plan for the site and develop myriad other ideas for the camp. The sketch below provides some insight into the Skyland Camp idea as it first developed in Fred's mind.

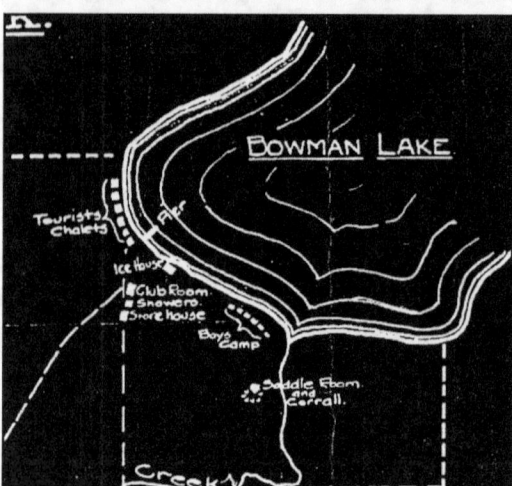

Sketch plan by Fred Gignilliat and Frank Denton for Skyland Camp at Bowman Lake.[10]

With Fred's plan in hand by December, Gignilliat himself sprang into action to begin realizing the Skyland Camp vision. He began by hiring the man who held the Park's boat concession on several lakes (including Two Medicine Lake), known as "Captain" Billy Swanson, to build the durable log structure at the Bowman Lake site Gignilliat had designed himself. Gignilliat directed Swanson to construct a central log chalet to be used as the camp's dining hall and recreation building, which could be used as a storage facility in the off season. Swanson used "massive" tamarack logs and native stone to build the structure. Swanson also constructed some simple wooden bases over which 16-foot pyramidal tents were erected to serve as sleeping quarters for the campers. He completed these efforts in August 1922.

Skyland Camp Begins Operations in Summer 1922

1922 Skyland Camp Rainbow Lodge.[11]

Since the facilities were not completed by the time the first camp began in July 1922, Gignilliat established a rustic temporary tent site at the Two Medicine Lake location he had first identified for the camp in July 1922 before moving to the Bowman Lake site in August when Swanson had completed his construction efforts.

Under the stewardship of CMA graduates Fred Gignilliat '19 and Frank Denton '18 (a University of Kansas graduate as well), Skyland Camp began operations in summer 1922 as a remote location for summer adventures for boys desiring an escape from the dull, sedate, and predictable attractions of civilization.

A bit about Fred: born Frederick Fleet Gignilliat at Culver on March 4, 1901, he was an outstanding athlete and an exceptional tennis player, capturing the singles championship at Culver in 1916 and 1917, along with the double's championship in 1917. After his third year, Fred departed Culver to serve his country in WWI. After serving 6 months as a 2nd Lieutenant in the infantry, he returned to finish his Culver education, graduating with the class of 1919. He was, by all accounts, an excellent cadet at Culver. The year after he graduated, Fred accompanied his father on the trip to the 1920 BSA Jamboree in London, serving as one of the group leaders for the trip. By 1923, having completed three years of college (one at Massachusetts Institute of Technology and two at Princeton University) but uninterested in continuing or completing his undergraduate studies, he appeared ready for his first adult position of responsibility.

Fred Gignilliat, Skyland Camp Director, at Bowman Lake.[12]

Fred Gignilliat (left) and Frank Denton at Skyland Camps, circa 1922.[13]

The 1922 boys' camp ran from July 2 to August 27, and a tourist camp running simultaneously for the remainder of the time between June 15 and the first snowfall (which could come as early as mid-September). The first group of boys was small. The boys found the 16-ft pyramidal canvas tents with floors (used at Culver's own summer camp) and the log dining hall (once completed) to be satisfactory for their purposes. The camp also hosted some tourists during its first summer of operation. Despite appealing to the more adventurous boys, the facilities proved to be a bit too primitive for tourists. Overall, it was a modest initial effort, and there were approximately 20 or so people at Skyland Camp (including staff) at any one time during that first summer of operation.

While not quite the triumph he had initially envisioned, Skyland Camp was nevertheless up and running. Gignilliat was both thrilled with its establishment and, applying what he had learned at Culver throughout his experience with the "Greater Culver" building program on campus, determined to make improvements to the facilities so that the camp would be even more successful in future summers.

Making Improvements during the 1922-1923 Off Season

During 1922-1923 off season, Gignilliat had Swanson enhance the facilities in response to the desires expressed by the tourists. By the beginning of the 1923 season, Swanson had added six small cabins of one to five rooms (designed by Fred), an office building, a store, an icehouse, shower facilities, a vegetable garden, and a flotilla of "sturdy wooden row boats." He also made arrangements to have the camp staffed from the beginning of June to mid-October each year. The venture began taking on an appearance of permanence, despite Gignilliat's initial plan for the camp to remain small "for a number of years" "until a first-class road was built from Belton to Bowman Lake."[14]

Thinking long-term, and hoping to create sufficient room for the realization of his vision for up to 1,000 visitors to make use of the camp, Gignilliat also had Swanson establish two branch camps at the nearby Lower Kintla Lake and Upper Kintla Lake (12 miles north of Bowman

Lake and three miles apart from one another). Campers lived in canvas tents at both locations, and Gignilliat had Swanson build a small log cabin as a dining location at the Lower Kintla Lake site.

These improvements transformed the Skyland Camps (now referred to in the plural, as there were actually three camp sites), creating the opportunity for the Bowman Lake site to serve as a base

Cabins at Bowman Lake.[15]

camp on its own and also to support excursions to the Lower and Upper Kintla Lakes locations for hiking, fishing, and/or on horseback using animals and equipment available at Bowman Lake. These developments were right in line with Gignilliat's vision for this endeavor.

Tents at one of the Skyland Camps branch camps.[16]

During the offseason, Gignilliat also promoted and marketed the Skyland Camps, sharing brochures with travel agencies in the east and soliciting groups of campers (at discounted rates) from various schools and organizations with which he engaged. As was his practice, and adding to his marketing efforts, Gignilliat also lined up a group of notable figures to provide testimonial support for the camp he was creating, including Theodore Roosevelt, writer Mary Roberts Rinehart (known as America's Agatha Christie), and railroad executive Louis Hill, along with scouting's Ernest Thompson Seton and his own PMS&T and fellow VMI alum, Colonel Fitzhugh Lee.

The 1923 Skyland Camps Operations

As an extension of the Culver program, Gignilliat had Fred bring the Culver methodology and awards program to the 1923 camp (in the spirit of the TUXIS method). Each boy was assigned responsibility for caring for his own horse, and Gignilliat created a system of camp insignia that

Culver cadets "throwing the diamond hitch" while packing a horse.[17]

could be earned by demonstrating proficiency in tasks such as packing a horse properly, tying a diamond hitch correctly, clod-shoeing their horse, navigating using the Park map, and identifying the prominent geological formations and types of vegetation around the camp, much like the practices at Culver's own summer camps and schools.

Since the Culver system was based upon competition, campers also competed with one another for the coved top award by proving that they were the "best all-around camper and horseman" who also "exemplified the spirit of comradeship and helpfulness," with a handsome saddle awarded to the best overall camper.

Along with the Skyland camps, the Glacier Park Transport Company tried to establish a transport service to the Bowman Like site in June 1923. However, they found that the final six miles of the existing road to be too difficult to traverse without causing significant (and costly) damage to their existing fleet of vehicles, and the company suspended the service that same month. Reflecting what would remain one his enduring concerns, Gignilliat had written to the GNP park superintendent earlier that year requesting some park maintenance on the road to make it more trafficable, "so that the average car can get into Bowman Lake without getting stuck." While desirable from Gignilliat's point of view, GNP had little interest in enhancing the accessibility of this remote part of the park and even fewer funds to do so.

Raising the flag at Bowman Lake camp.[18]

Things Begin to Unravel at Skyland Camps, 1924-1925

After two fairly successful iterations, both Gignilliat and the GNP administrators were ready to move from the annual permit to a more lasting agreement. On January 1, 1924, Gignilliat and the Park Service signed a five-year operating contract. While receiving little apparent consideration from Gignilliat at the time, the contract stipulated that all "buildings,

Cadets and their horses at Skyland Camps.[19]

Boys swimming at Bowman Lake.[20]

equipment, and fixtures" at the camp would become the property of the US Government in the event that the agreement was canceled and/or terminated. This was standard practice for government contracts, which also exempted the US Government from any claim that might be brought against in as related to the agreement.

Thrilled to have secured a long-term agreement for the venture, and reflecting his natural enthusiasm and confidence in his own abilities, Gignilliat gave little thought to such provisions, certain that his creation would grow to "a thousand or more [boys] in a few short years."

Boys using row boats on Bowman Lake.[21]

Fred Gignilliat (L) and Frank Denton.[22]

Fred accompanied Gignilliat to sign the contract, and Gignilliat left Fred, along with Frank Denton, in charge of the endeavor. Being given such responsibility and out from under the watchful eye of his father must have been exhilarating for Fred. However, and as many just starting out on their own in such circumstances find, the allure of making less-than-desirable choices when able to do so -- referred to as having "agency" -- can be as powerful as the responsibility of being in charge.

Unfortunately for both him and his father, Fred's level of maturity did not match up to the level of responsibility to which he had been entrusted. Operating largely on his own in the remote wilderness of Montana, he quickly lost his way and succumbed to his baser instincts. Active by nature, having ridden horses from an early age at Culver, and bored by the mundane responsibilities of administering the sparsely attended Skyland Camps, Fred signed on as a mounted guide for the Glacier Park Saddle Horse Company and neglected his administrative duties related to Skyland Camps. It appears that Denton did not serve as either a steadying influence or as a reliable partner to help direct Fred's attention back where it belonged.

With an appreciation for discipline more along the lines of Gignilliat himself and concerned about an apparent lack of commitment to the Skyland Camps, the new Glacier Superintendent, Charles J. Kraebel (who, in 1924, had replaced J. Ross Eakin, with whom Gignilliat had established a warm personal relationship) felt compelled to reprimand Fred twice during the 1923-1924 period for actions involving excessive drinking and associated inappropriate behavior (and in which Denton appears to have been complicit as well).

Having no prior relationship and assessing his performance on its own and according to what he expected from other professionals of the period, Kraebel advised that the young man needed to "steady down and demonstrate an earnest effort to improve his service" if he was to succeed in his current role. Such a remonstration would have surely chagrined Fred's father, but it appears that the elder Gignilliat was never made aware of his son's lapses in professionalism at the Skyland Camps.

Failing to heed Kraebel's counsel, Fred's neglect began having an adverse impact on the condition of the facilities at Bowman Lake and the two branch camps, but there is little evidence that he made any effort to address the situation. Rather, Fred's behavior worsened. He was cited for being "drunk and disorderly" in mid-August 1925, leading him to be expelled from Glacier National Park in mid-September 1925 by Kraebel for repeated incidents of inappropriate conduct and inattention to his duties. This incident occurred at precisely the time that Gignilliat's attention was divided and directed elsewhere, preventing him from intervening on his son's behalf and/or becoming involved to rectify the situation and restore good order and discipline to the undertaking (as he surely would have done had he been informed of the situation).

However, another elder Gignilliat was available to address the situation. In an apparent turn of good fortune, Fred's older brother, Leigh Jr. was at the Skyland Camps at the time with a friend and Culver classmate, Richard H. Nesbit. With Fred's departure, Leigh Jr. and Nesbit remained at Bowman Lake and took over responsibility for administering the Skyland Camps for the remainder of the 1925 season.

It is unclear what happened next with Fred and the extent to which Gignilliat himself was made aware of what had occurred, but the outcome was that Leigh Jr. took over responsibility for managing the Skyland Camps at that point. Gignilliat later reported that he had no knowledge of the situation occurring at Skyland Camps during this period.

Here is where it is plausible to question Gignilliat's denial of knowledge of Fred's behavior, as it is difficult to believe that all this occurred without his knowledge and/or consent. However, he had other concerns during that period that took him out of the country for an extended period of time, since he was engaged that summer as the chairman of the American delegation at the FIDAC meeting in Rome, and then he proceeded directly to the national meeting of the American Legion (in which he was also quite involved) in Omaha, Nebraska and was therefore away from Culver for almost two months (16 August – 10 October 1925), which coincided with the events related to Fred's disciplinary episode that led to his expulsion from Glacier National Park. The travel associated with these events required him to spend much of it out of routine communication on board ships and in Europe, making it is quite conceivable that he was as ignorant of the events as he claimed to be later.

Leigh Jr. Steps in to Run Skyland Camps – 1925

Further exacerbating the situation was the disreputable behavior of Leigh Jr. and Nesbitt during the 1925-1926 offseason. According to reports he had received from the GNP staff, Kraebel was made aware of frequent trips made by Leigh Jr. and Nesbitt at high speed along the treacherous road from Bowman Lake to the entrance at Belton (and elsewhere) in a "high powered Packard Roadster" to attend "wild parties in places where they would be in no danger of breaking Park regulations" and being subject to the same fate as Fred. In addition, both Leigh Jr. and Nesbitt had also passed numerous "worthless checks bearing their signatures" in the area that summer. Having never met the elder Gignilliat, Kraebel's opinion of the Gignilliat family was therefore based upon the tremendously irresponsible behavior of Fred and Leigh Jr., and he was both disappointed in and fed up with them and the entire Gignilliat family by the end of the 1925 season.

An Unfortunate Reckoning in 1926

While these events may have escaped Gignilliat's notice, they served to solidify Kraebel's negative opinion of the entire Skyland Camps venture. Writing to his boss in January 1926, Kraebel, who shared Gignilliat's own affinity for efficiency and proper conduct, observed that the Skyland Camps operations had been unsatisfactory for the preceding two seasons (1924 and 1925). Kraebel also noted that Culver had not paid the 1925 $1,000 concessions bond, required from all park utility operations to retain their status and access to the park, and that Skyland Camps had outstanding debts for its $10 yearly licensing fees for the preceding three years (1923, 1924, and 1925). Nor had Skyland Camps ever submitted the required reports disclosing its financial status and the status of its facilities.

Concluding that the experiment of the Skyland Camps, which he acknowledged had begun so auspiciously, had failed to live up to expectations and had become instead "a convenient summer camp for the Gignilliat family and their friends," and based upon the disappointing and unprofessional behavior of Fred and Leigh Jr., Kraebel recommended terminating the contract for the Skyland Camps and association with the Gignilliat family immediately.

Agreeing with the compelling case presented by Kraebel that the entire situation had become "exceedingly unsatisfactory," the Director of National Parks (Stephen Mather) wrote to Gignilliat in February 1926 expressing his disappointment and informing him that he had 60 days to correct the deficiencies identified by Kraebel or the Park Service would terminate the Skyland Camps' concession contract. Receiving no response within 90 days, the Park Service sent Gignilliat a final notice by registered mail in May 1926, which also failed to elicit a response.

According to a well-researched study of this episode by historian Michael J. Ober, "Just as Superintendent Kraebel was about to being proceedings to close the camp," a telegram arrived from General Gignilliat on the evening of June 14, 1926 in which he explained that "through a curious combination of an incapacitating illness and a secretary who purportedly had neglected to deliver any correspondence relative to the camp," he was completely unaware of the seriousness of the situation.

In the absence of any contradictory information, Gignilliat had believed that all was well at Glacier, and he shared that he was "astonished" when he had been informed of the unfortunate status of the Skyland Camps and mortified regarding the regrettable behavior of his two sons. Knowing his sensitivity to bringing any slights to the reputation of Culver or those associated with it (including himself; recall the 1913 Presidential Inaugural incident involving Vice President-elect Marshall), there could be little news that would cause him greater dismay, especially from the actions of trusted members of his own family.

It is important to know that this part of the episode occurred just as Gignilliat was recovering from the bout of influenza he had contract ed in late-January 1926. This was when Minnie stepped in and placed one or both of the older Gignilliat sons – Leigh Jr, and/or Fred – in charge of attending to their father's personal correspondence (which included activities associated with Skyland Camps). While it is difficult to know for certain without more definitive evidence, it appears as though Gignilliat's sons were the secretaries who had "neglected to deliver any correspondence relative to the camp" to him. This explanation is all the more plausible, given that they were primarily responsible for the causes of the Park's displeasure as well as the subjects of to complaints related to Skyland Camps.

Wishing to take all measures necessary to rectify the situation immediately, Gignilliat informed Kraebel that he was sending the very capable and trusted Captain M. W. Armstrong (a retired US Army First Sergeant who had been a beloved cavalry instructor at Culver for several years beginning in 1917) to Glacier immediately to assume responsibility for running the Skyland Camps, and he quickly paid the outstanding licensing fees related to the Skyland Camps. He also provided his personal assurance that Glacier would receive payment for the outstanding $1,000 concession fee very soon. He hoped that all these measures would salvage the situation and put the endeavor back on the solid foundation upon which he had believed it to rest prior to learning of these unfortunate events.

While these actions were laudable, Kraebel remained steadfast in his recommendation to terminate the concessions contract for the Skyland Camps. Kraebel had clearly had enough from Culver and wanted no more to do with it or the Skyland Camps endeavor. However, upon direction from Mather, Kraebel relented and agreed reluctantly to allow Captain Armstrong to open the Skyland Camps for the 1926 season.

Due to lack of promotion and preparation by the Gignilliat boys, there was no boys camp that summer. After spending $4,000 dollars to rehabilitate the facilities that had been neglected by Fred and Leigh Jr., the cursed luck of the Skyland Camps appeared again in the form of widespread forest fires in the area that drove away all tourists, forcing Armstrong to close the camps after being open for a mere three weeks. A proud professional used to succeeding in difficult circumstances and with high expectations for himself and for Culver graduates (especially the sons of the Superintendent), Armstrong made his way back to Culver discouraged, somewhat embittered, and determined to find out how the affairs at the camp "had been so badly misrepresented to him when he was asked to take charge" of the operation earlier that year.

In responding, Gignilliat discovered that things at the Skyland Camps were far worse than he could have imagined. He had not been provided with accurate information regarding the status of the facilities when he sent Captain Armstrong to assume responsibility for the venture. For one who placed the highest value in trust and honest collaboration (especially from his own sons), this discovery must have come as a devastating blow to him, both personally and professionally.

From a strategic perspective, the smart play at this point was to cut his losses and close the camp for good. However, his resolution and sense of duty took control, and he resolved to make the Skyland Camps a success.

After talking with Armstrong upon his return, gathering all possible information, and likely discussing the situation with ER Culver, Gignilliat decided to ask for another chance to salvage the situation. He wrote to the Acting Director of the Park Service, Arno B. Cammerer, on February 5, 1927, insisting that he was "unaware of the disreputable condition of the camp" and requesting the opportunity to run the camp for one more season in 1927 and give a true accounting of Culver's effectiveness in such endeavors (based upon its 25 years of running successful summer camps on its own grounds). Impressed by Gignilliat's sincerity and renewed vitality, Cammerer decided that Gignilliat deserved one more season to make good on his promises and demonstrate the ability to run a proper camp at Glacier.

A Final Try at Salvaging the Skyland Camps Endeavor – 1927

Reinvigorated with such support, Gignilliat sent Armstrong back with renewed hopes for success in the summer of 1927. However, after receiving Cammerer's approval on February 9, 1927, there was little time to promote the boys' camp, and for the second summer in a row the Skyland Camps failed to sponsor what Gignilliat believed and hoped would be the centerpiece of the effort.

While an exceptionally accomplished horsemanship instructor and able administrator, Armstrong's overly regimented approach (as a retired US Army First Sergeant of 30 years) was ill-suited for tourists and made him a disappointing camp manager. The 1927 season saw very few visitors to the Skyland Camps – with none at all visiting either of the branch camps – and the season ended with little to show for Armstrong's efforts and even less financial profit. This outcome was all the more disappointing, coming as it did with all of Gignilliat's promises of renewed vitality and as a result of Cammerer's leap of faith.

This outcome was all the more disappointing, as the Culver family was becoming increasingly less able to provide financial support for the endeavor. Facing reduced revenue from the Wrought Iron Range Company, along with mounting expenses related to building the new Wrought Iron Range Company building and showroom and buying up the remaining company shares from their siblings, brothers ER and BB had little funding available to support Gignilliat's efforts at the Skyland Camps during this period. It appears that Gignilliat was forced to fund the efforts in 1926 and 1927 on his own.

A New Master Concessions Plan for GNP in Late-1927 Makes Skyland Camps Untenable

At the conclusion of the 1927 season, Glacier produced a new master plan that clarified its concession policy that it had been developing for the previous decade as being focused on supporting the efforts of a few organizations dedicated to providing multiple concessions in the park instead of partnering with larger numbers of organizations providing single concessions (which had been its practice in the past). This decision made sense for the park in terms of efficiency, but it made Culver's precarious situation with respect to the Skyland Camps almost untenable in terms of policy, as Culver was struggling to provide meaningful contributions at Bowman Lake, let alone at the branch camps it sponsored.

The folks at Glacier concurred with this assessment, concluding that the Skyland Camps experiment had been "premature" and showed "very little prospect of becoming a paying proposition" for the park. The events of the previous three seasons had caused the Glacier leadership to become "unfavorably disposed" to the Skyland Camps venture, and they revoked recognition for the branch camps at Lower and Upper Kintla Lakes (based on a lack of use) and determined that they would no longer provide support for the Skyland Camps venture, including (and perhaps most importantly) related to making any improvements to the access road to Bowman Lake.

In effect, Glacier had deemed the Skyland Camps experiment a failure and hoped that Gignilliat would recognize their November 1927 decisions for what they were: a vote of "no confidence" in him and the once-promising public-private Skyland Parks venture.

Gignilliat's Response – Predictable Dogged Determination but with Little Success

Having two more years remaining on the five-year contract, Gignilliat chose to ignore the message and tried his best to make a go of it at the Skyland Camps during the 1928 and 1929 seasons with very little success. Operating again without a boys' camp (as it had been doing since 1926), the paltry number of tourists who visited were not sufficient even to cover the camp's meager operating costs, and the venture lost at least $1,000 each season (likely incurred by Gignilliat himself). Gignilliat was perhaps the final remaining believer in the venture, which ended in debt and closed with a whimper at the end of the 1929 season.

Skyland Camps Goes on Hiatus Beginning in 1930 and Ends Officially in 1939

There was little hope that GNP would renew the five-year contract. Recognizing the reality of the situation, Gignilliat requested instead an annual "special use permit" that allowed him to retain control of the facilities and equipment at the Skyland Camps. Without a concessions contract, Gignilliat was forced to sell the horses and much of the equipment to the Saddle Horse Company in 1930. In the wake of the death of ER Culver in 1930, the beginning of the Great Depression that reduced enrollments in both the winter and summer schools, and the enacting of the Culver Covenant in 1932, the CEF Board, under the direction of the very fiscally minded BB Culver (who was far less indulgent of Gignilliat's schemes and dreams), refused to provide any further funding to the Skyland Camps, ending its official support for the project.

To remain active or even viable, Gignilliat would have to fund the venture on his own. It appears that he sunk as much as $20,000 of his own money to keep it afloat (which equates to ~ $330,000 in 2023 dollars).

In the wake of these developments, the camps remained dormant throughout the 1930s and fell into disrepair, unsellable and becoming an increasing financial burden to Culver and fire hazard to GNP. According to assessments by GNP, the facilities had fallen into such a state of disrepair after years of neglect that they were unusable and so unsightly that they "would scarcely warrant the cost of demolition." Gignilliat finally acknowledged reality and declined to apply for an annual special use permit in 1939, selling off what equipment remained.

Relieved that Gignilliat had finally relented, the Park Service notified Gignilliat in 1940 that it would begin dismantling the facilities at the Skyland Camps. Gignilliat protested (with some validity) and requested partial reimbursement from the government based upon what he believed to be a shared responsibility for the endeavor's failure. Despite Gignilliat raising some valid objections, the Park Service refused his request and began dismantling all of the structures except the Rainbow Lodge in spring 1940, working through the summer to return the area to its original state.

Thus ended the unfortunate Skyland Camps experiment and the opportunity for Gignilliat to create his own "castle in the sky."

One Scholar's Assessment – The Failure of an Over-ambitious Military Man

Ober cites the following reasons for the failure of the Skyland Camps venture:

- GNP's concession policy that veered away from single private contracts
- The inaccessibility to Bowman Lake area
- Management and supervisory difficulties
- Lack of patronage (both from boys and tourists)
- "[A] kaleidoscope of other obstacles."[23]

Ober's perspective is from the National Parks' perspective, and it is based completely upon sources related to and available from the National Parks archives. While technically accurate, this account fails to consider the character and personality of Gignilliat, and Ober concludes in places, and based upon the evidence available to him, that Gignilliat was "an aging zealot" who was deceitful and both duplicitous and disingenuous in much of his dealings with GNP and the National Park Service.

This author finds little evidence to support this negative assessment of Gignilliat himself, as he was almost never either "duplicitous" or "disingenuous" in his dealings with anyone. In fact, the idea of being deceitful in any way was anathema to him. Explaining Ober's determination, for which he provides no justification, requires one to engage in speculation, but it may simply be a result of him having a negative opinion of humans overall, believing the worst about them in the absences of countervailing evidence.

However, and when considering additional material, and the person and situation more broadly, it become evident that beginning in 1923 (when things begin to go badly and with Fred in charge), Gignilliat no longer had time in the summers to devote to the Skyland Camps venture, based upon his military training requirements as the commander of the 168th Brigade and also on his lengthy trips to FIDAC meetings (all of which are in Europe 1923-1929). Being constantly distracted, away from campus, and/or engaged with other important activities, it was simply not possible for him to devote his customary time and/or attention to the Skyland Camps endeavor (as he almost certainly desired to do).

More specifically, Gignilliat's summer responsibilities during this period prevented him from taking the extended periods off as he had done pre-WWI and which allowed him to regain his health. His new and enhanced post-WWI responsibilities kept him going at a terrific pace year-round, which ground him down and made him less effective overall and susceptible to illness (as shown in 1925-1926). It is also important to note that Skyland Camps operated in July-August, just when he was required to be either focused on Culver's own summer camps and/or away from campus most summers attending to other matters (and sometimes both).

The challenges of making the Skyland Camps venture successful were exacerbated further by the location being over 1,600 miles away from Culver in a largely inaccessible location, the personal secretary actions that kept Skyland Camps-related correspondence from him, and the requirements of the public-private partnership nature of his vision for Skyland Camps. Regarding the final issue, it would have been far easier and cheaper to be able to focus solely on boys and Culver's needs instead of trying to make the camps accessible to the general public as well, but that was simply not possible given the arrangements Gignilliat agreed to with GNP and the National Parks Service.

Ober adds that the Skyland Camps idea was both out of its time (i.e., too soon) and out of place for Culver (i.e., too far away from campus to be managed effectively). These two aspects are important and were exacerbated by the poor initial decision to locate the camps around the highly inaccessible Bowman Lake area, which was terrible and doomed the venture to failure.[24]

When considered holistically, the reasons for failure become more evident. The National Parks Service administrators should have never agreed to Culver using the inaccessible North Forks area for its concession (knowing that roads would not be built to service it); the GNP leaders should have insisted on a more responsive method of executive oversight from Culver; Gignilliat should have resisted the appeal of the North Forks area and established the camps around Two Medicine Lake; and ER Culver should have been more proactive in his supervision of Gignilliat and discerning in his decision to support the endeavor.

A Cautionary Tale – The Impact of Distraction, Lack of Oversight, and Misplaced Trust

While innovative and demonstrating that he still "had it" in 1921, this episode represents one of the very few missteps for Gignilliat, and it tells us much about him during this period.

To begin with, the proximate cause of many of the problems related to the unsuccessful venture stem from two actions directly related to Gignilliat:

- The decision to locate the Skyland Camps in the remote and largely inaccessible North Forks area around Bowman Lake; and

- Placing the entire venture under the control of his inexperienced sons and not providing them with his characteristic level of oversight.

The first decision resulted from him thinking more with his heart – attracted more by the allure of the location than the practicality of it, and perhaps also a desire to support and please his middle son Fred – than with his head. This is not the first time Gignilliat engaged in this type of decision-making, having done so when making the critical decisions in the 1900 "Big Fire" and 1913 "Logansport Flood" episodes addressed previously. While it is unrealistic to expect executives to get every major decision right, it is nonetheless enlightening that Gignilliat tends to make relatively poor strategic decisions – those involving how to make the best use of available means in ways to achieve desired ends while accounting for risk (both operational, in terms of safety, and strategic, arising from a mismatch of means and ends) – as compared to the more operational decisions he made (which tended to turn out much better).

It is also clear in hindsight that Gignilliat's Skyland Camps idea was never a particularly good fit for Glacier National Park, especially after the change in policy regarding park concessions that occurred at the end of 1925. Gignilliat's idea was perhaps too grand for GNP, and while he had never gotten in trouble for thinking too big at Culver, this approach was not right for dealing with GNP, especially with Kraebel. This was especially true when relying on his sons to run the camp's operations. While he had ample reason to trust them, they had not yet accumulated the life experience to warrant such discretion as they were given. Placing such a high level of trust and responsibility on them without an appropriate level of supervision turned out to be a mistake that contributed directly to the endeavor's failure, both administratively and financially.

The lack of supervision provided to his sons also highlights Gignilliat's uncharacteristic lack of attention to the venture, and it is more indicative of his level of distraction arising from his tendency to over-commit himself by never saying "no" to those who ask him for assistance. This is a laudable characteristic in many respects, and it is the basis for some of the success Gignilliat achieved, both personally and for Culver (he was one of the hardest working administrators at Culver and in AMCSUS); however, it is an approach with limitations that is not appropriate for all roles and/ or situations and which must be controlled (as we have seen).

In the case of Culver, this approach would only work if the necessary organizational changes in responsibility were made to accompany it so that the person functioning in the "principal" role was empowered to make most/all of the necessary day-to-day operational decisions. Owing to Gignilliat's personal preference and being adopted informally, this change did not occur at Culver during the 1920s (it would not occur until mandated by the CEF Board in 1935). The result was that Gignilliat's approach of being intimately involved in every routine decision at Culver continued even though it was no longer practical for the "president" in the new administrative model Culver adopted in the 1920s as a result of its growth and expansion.

More directly, Gignilliat was too busy to be as involved in the day-to-day functioning of Culver as he had been previously (which he acknowledges directly in his letter to the National Parks Superintendent when he became aware of the true state of affairs at Skyland Camps in summer 1926), and the result of him trying unsuccessfully to do so meant that no one was making such decisions. One has to imagine that Glascock did so in an ad hoc manner and likely in a reactionary mode, removing opportunities to make better decisions and allowing the institution to operate sub-optimally (which was not desirable for anyone and/or the institution). However, and perhaps more practically, Gignilliat simply did not have the time or energy to focus on persuading GNP to build the access road needed by the Skyland Camps to improve its accessibility, and he did not delegate responsibility for this task to anyone else, meaning that it (like an increasing number of other things under his responsibility during this period) simply did not get accomplished.

This led to the next aspect revealed by the Skyland Camps episode: the Culver family governance method was no longer effective for overseeing the post-WWI Culver. Many of Gignilliat's decisions, and much of the resulting turmoil caused by them and his inattention, could have and should have been foreseen, addressed, and averted by an effective method of governance and oversight, but this was not the case for Culver in the 1920s. Based upon their intimate personal relationship, ER Culver and Gignilliat continued to operate during the post-WWI period largely as they had during the pre-WWI era, which was likely both comfortable and their preferred approach to managing the institution but which became evident that it was no longer a suitable approach for doing so.

ER Culver needed to do a better job of overseeing Gignilliat to ensure that he focused on the most important aspects of his role as "president" of CMA, even while attending to the external duties this new role entailed and encouraged. Similarly, ER Culver should have insisted that Gignilliat relinquish his operational decision-making responsibilities in the new administrative model to Glascock, with whom ER had worked in a similar manner during Gignilliat's absence in WWI. Doing so would have curtailed many of the issues that arose on campus at the end of the 1920s and into the 1930s (after his death).

This situation was exacerbated by the Culver family' increasing inability to support the Skyland Camps endeavor financially beginning in the mid-1920s. Perhaps its inability to provide the project with sufficient fiscal resources should have served as a sign that it was an idea that was no longer feasible (as with the efforts at Culver related to its radio station and the school's aviation program), especially after 1925 when it was clearly not succeeding. However, and as noted previously, Culver had no administrative method for making such choices during the 1920s, and Gignilliat himself was ill-suited for such a task.

It is noteworthy that BB Culver made quite different financial decisions regarding Skyland Camps when he resumed his role as the chief overseer of CMA. BB cut the financial support for it rather abruptly (and likely to Gignilliat's chagrin), in the face of institutional challenges Culver faced as a result of the Great Depression, along with the dormant nature of Skyland Camps (no longer operating and under a "special use permit"), the enacting of Culver Covenant, and BB's more financially focus ed priorities. These conditions combined to convince the newly created CEF Board to dissociate itself with Skyland Camps venture.

Finally, this episode also highlights the role of Minnie in Gignilliat's life. Her decision to step in and assert herself during Gignilliat's period of infirmity during the first half of 1926 was not unusual, as she had often insisted that he take a break and relax when he had worked himself to a frazzle in times past (in fact, this may have been one of the ways she contributed most directly to her husband's success throughout their marriage).

However, her decision to put one or both of her elder sons in charge of his/their father's personal correspondence (including all related to the Skyland Camps venture) was quite unusual and represented the most intrusive step she had yet taken (eclipsed only by her insistence that her husband remain away from campus for over four months during the period November 1933-March 1934 in the next decade). While well-meaning and correct in terms of taking care of her overwhelmed husband, the selection of her sons proved to be disastrous for the Skyland Camps endeavor, resulting in Gignilliat suffering a substantial blemish on his otherwise sterling reputation.

Thus, in each of these areas – strategic decision-making, ambitious idea that was a poor fit strategically, lack of supervision, incorrect board oversight, and unwise personnel decisions – the Skyland Camps venture is an important episode to consider in order to gain a more complete understanding of Gignilliat as a strategic leader and administrator in the 1920s. While remarkably talented and decisive operationally, and unquestionably committed and devoted to Culver's success, he was perhaps no longer the best choice to superintend his beloved institution in the enhanced form it assumed in the post-WWI decade. This became increasingly evident to others associated with Culver as well, and the period 1929-1934 would make it even more obvious and result in significant changes at Culver as a result.

Chapter 17 – The Age of the Consultants and Challenges to Gignilliat's Reign, 1929-1934

Despite still looking youthful and vibrant (at least from the perspective of the artist of his portrait for the 1929 *Roll Call*), the five-year period 1929-1934 would become one of the most challenging of Gignilliat's life, both personally and professionally. In some respects, this period has a Shakespearian aura to it.

In Shakespeare's play, *King Henry IV*, a beleaguered and anxious leader speaks these lines:

Likeness of Gignilliat circa 1929, by unknown artist.[1]

"And in the visitation of the winds,
Who take the ruffian billows by the top,
Curling their monstrous heads and hanging them
With deafening clamour in the slippery clouds,
That, with the hurly, death itself awakes?
"Canst thou, O partial sleep, give thy repose
To the wet sea-boy in an hour so rude,
And in the calmest and most stillest night,
With all appliances and means to boot,
Deny it to a king? Then happy low, lie down!
Uneasy lies the head that wears a crown."

Henry IV, Part 2 (emphasis added)

Taking Shakespeare's observation regarding a particular situation – a character's insomnia – and elevating it to a more general statement about the burden of responsibility, the final line is often now phrased now as, *"heavy is the head that wears the crown."* It has become an English idiom meaning that those charged with major responsibility carry a heavy burden that makes it difficult for them to relax. This means that a person with great power must take responsibility for what happens, which exposes one to criticism and judgment by others. Whereas empathy is expected from a leader, it is seldom given to one, which prevents a leader from finding peace and enjoying any sort of repose. The demands are unrelenting.

Being a leader is challenging, and Gignilliat faced many hardships during the period 1929-1934 that drove this point home for him and established the context for the breakdown of his health as a result of the unrelenting pressure and his gradual phasing out as a meaningful figure in terms of providing substantive guidance and making meaningful decisions, leading ultimately to his departure from Culver.

The challenges he faced came primarily from four areas: administrative; organizational; professionally at both Culver and in the Army; and personally, in terms of his health. This chapter uses these challenges as the framework to examine the period 1929-1934.

Administrative Challenges –
The 1929 Culver Self-Study and Harvard Study

Just as Gignilliat and Culver were preparing to resume the 1929 winter school session after the holidays, an influenza epidemic swept across the country in late December 1928. Wanting to avoid the challenges involved in managing the spread of a contagious condition on campus, Gignilliat made the decision to delay the resumption of the academic session by ten days, meaning that the cadets' return would be postponed. However, most of the faculty and staff had already returned by the time the decision was made, presenting a challenge but also providing for a unique opportunity.

JS Fleet had been urging such an undertaking for several years, but it was Gignilliat's trusted Executive Officer, Cal Chambers, who had laid the groundwork for the ensuing self-study. Seeking assistance to address Culver's existing tutorial program, and its highly unpopular punitive study hall, he had written to the American Council on Education asking for advice in early December 1928. The response he received suggested conducting an internal self-study as a first step prior to bringing an outside agency to campus to provide further assistance.

The notion to begin by collaborating among themselves made sense, and Chambers took this recommendation to Gignilliat. The delayed resumption of the winter school session provided the faculty with the unusual opportunity to devote attention to conducting a self-study without any other distractions.

Culver's first-ever self-study occurred during the second week of January 1929, with the intention of conducting "a thorough discussion and study of the whole educational machinery" of Culver.[2] The study used a framework of inquiry developed by Fleet, Gregory, Chambers, and others to examine the effectiveness of Culver's existing practices and programs.

The scope of the self-study was quite extensive, touching on virtually every aspect of the Culver system as it existed at the time. Specific topics included:

- The possible re-adjustment of the daily schedule to eliminate the long period between breakfast and lunch ;
- Preparation of an agenda for the coming self-study on "Academic Policies and Methods";
- Discussion of the study hall, directed study, and the tutorial programs;
- Consideration of possible structural changes in the headmaster's office;
- The possibility of new academic classrooms and facilities;
- Consideration of a variety of topics ranging from the length of the academic year and the grading system to whether academic instructors should be allowed to wear civilian clothes instead of uniforms ;
- Whether Culver should continue offering both a college prep and commercial curriculum.[3]

Department heads broke into subcommittees to consider each topic more thoroughly.

To make it even more comprehensive, the self-study also included interviews conducted by selected instructors with boys having academic difficulties and parents of incoming boys. Sent out during the same week as the subcommittee meeting occurred, the purpose of these interviews was to solicit their input from the cadets, prospective cadets, and parents pertaining to the issues being considered by the subcommittees on campus.

Validating Fleet's suspicions and Chambers' efforts, the results acknowledged that Culver had done much to reduce obstacles to education associated with military schools but also revealed much discontent with Culver's existing system and approaches suspected by some at Culver but wholly unanticipated by Gignilliat. Based upon the attacks on military education that had been occurring during the period 1925-1930 and the results of self-study indicting significant faculty concern regarding the adequacy of Culver's educational approach and programs, the outcome made clear, according to Davies, that "Gignilliat's ideals of military education were no longer self-evident," that "the halcyon days of military schooling had passed – both in the nation and at Culver," and that the time for significant changes at Culver had come for many.[4]

Much of this information came as a shock to Gignilliat, but if he had been paying closer attention to the trends in secondary education in the 1920s, he would have been less surprised. Two trends had emerged that provided the context for the self-study results: shared governance and the High School Movement.

Shared Governance

On college campuses and in some of the more prestigious prep schools during the 1920s, the notion of a single, all-powerful head of school was giving way to the notion of "shared governance." Under this concept, the faculty were given access to administrative aspects of the institution, based upon the understanding that they knew what was occurring in the classrooms and with the students better than anyone and that the group doing the most important work of a school – teaching the students – deserved a say in how it was run.

This notion appealed to JS Fleet intrinsically, and it was also a notion brought to campus by many of the high-quality faculty members hired in the 1920s. Many were disappointed with the governance situation they encountered when they arrived on campus, perhaps confirming some of their suspicious and/or worst fears about a military high school. Finding a kindred spirit and a sympathetic colleague in JS Fleet, many of the new faculty members were drawn to him, and Fleet made use of his position as chairman of the Committee for Academic Improvement (formed in 1927) to begin making strides towards a greater level of shared governance for Culver.

The American High School Movement

The other contributing factor was what became known as the "High School Movement" that occurred in America during the 1920s. During this movement, secondary schools spread across the country and became an established part of the American educational landscape.

Established in the early 1880s, the American public high school was an innovative and unique institution. Taking root after a generation in existence, the rise of the public high school during the period from 1910 to 1940 had a dramatic impact on education in the country and brought about the second great transformation of American schooling. America had experienced its first great transformation in the mid-nineteenth century with the spread of the common school (grades 1-8), and the third would come in the post-WWII period with the rise of college education. However, in terms of the impact on American society regarding increased access to meaningful learning, the rise of the public high school was the most spectacular by far.

During this early part of the 20th century, a significantly increased number of American youth attended high schools. According to the closest study of this issue, only 18 percent of children aged 14 to 17 years old were enrolled in high school, and only nine percent graduated. By 1940, 73 percent of American youths were enrolled in high school and more than half (51 percent) had earned a high school diploma.[5] The same study determined that both attendance rates at and graduate rates from secondary schools "increased spectacularly in much of the United States from 1910 to 1940," and that these increases were particularly high "in the non-southern states," meaning that Culver was impacted by them.[6]

As the early leaders of Culver found, pre-college education in the United States was and remains a very local affair, the purview of municipal government and local school boards. During the early decades of the 20th century, neither federal legislation nor state funding had any appreciable impact on the substance or numbers of secondary education institutions. In fact, there was not even a standard format established and prescribed for America's high schools with respect to graduation requirements until 1902. This meant that high schools differed greatly from one another, preventing any sort of "standard high school experience" from emerging.

During the period of the High School Movement, the American high school "assumed its familiar shape and characteristics" such that by 1920, the four-year high school for grades 9-12 had become the norm.[7] However, the 40-year period of its development (spanning the period 1880-1920) was anything but smooth and experienced substantial changes before it assumed the form we recognize today.

What remained constant through the period was the belief that the primary aim of high schools was to develop the intellect and character of students, based upon the belief that education was the best way of producing better citizens for the nation (which remained the guiding purpose of public education in the country). Since many were no longer working side-by-side with their parents as America became more industrialized, the ability for teens to be placed in situations in which they would be under constant adult supervision during their period of what came to be known as *"strum und drang"* ("storm and stress") and mold their intellects and character helped to give high schools more appeal and greater support from parents.[8]

What remained in dispute was the main overall purpose of a high school education: to prepare the student for college or for the workforce. At the beginning of the high school movement, this was viewed in largely Manichean "either/or" terms. However, as ideas about the institution itself developed, and based upon the opportunities presented by society and the desires of the increased number of students, this perennial issue acquired additional nuance as both educators and the market made their desires more apparent.

Culver's governing association functioned in the role of both the municipal government and the local school board, allowing educators like Alexander Fleet and Hugh Glascock tremendous leeway in determining the substance and requirements of Culver's curriculum. As a private school, Culver had the luxury of witnessing the developmental trends as they appeared and choosing which to embrace, ignore, and/or alter as it saw fit, as the dominant personalities desired, and based upon its understanding of its own mission. Nevertheless, Culver could not avoid facing the issue of college prep vs. vocational training as an education institution.

In the first decade of the 20th century, a primary reason to attend high school was to gain entrance to college, and most high schools offered the classical (or Latin/Scientific) curriculum required by many colleges to prepare students for admission and success in higher education. While attractive to those bound for college, it nevertheless limited the overall appeal of a high school education for most. Indeed, and according to Goldin's research, the number of public high school graduates intending to further their own education beyond high school actually declined during much of the period of the high school movement, beginning at a of high of around 50 percent in the 1910s, dropping to 44 percent by 1923 and to 25 percent by 1933 before rebounding slightly to 29 percent by 1937. During the same period, the proportion of all American youths entering college had expanded, meaning that fewer of the new entrants treated high school as a prelude to college and confirming the unusual trend of decreased numbers of high school graduates pursuing higher education (a trend which did not see a reverse until the 1970s).[9]

Building and staffing public high schools in the early part of the 20th century were largely grass-roots efforts reacting to (and in some cases, anticipating) the increased numbers of teens no longer employed in manufacturing jobs. While the federal government certainly encouraged such efforts, these local initiatives were intended to engage children meaningfully in their teens, prepare them for the demands of modern life and citizenship in the 20th century, and both improve and increase economic opportunities for graduates.

Accordingly, many of the students attending high school during the 1910-1940 period sought an education that would prepare them for employment, not college. Not only had the demand for juvenile manufacturing workers declined substantially, but the new American economy created the need for large numbers of workers with more formal education to develop the enhanced cognitive skills (e.g., the ability to read manuals, interpret blueprints, use complex formulas, etc.) required of the workplace and that were not provided by the common school (grades 1-8) but which also did not require a college degree. A shared desire coalesced among students, educators, and employers for a curriculum that was more vocational in nature and which prepared students for the workforce by training them not in the liberal arts but instead in the practical arts required for these new positions.[10]

In the view of many (especially at the municipal levels and on local school boards), public high schools were ideally suited to supply this demand, and as a result, one of the most significant impacts of the high school movement was therefore to transform secondary schools from being institutions primarily focused on providing college preparation into schools that prepared students for the responsibilities of modern life and citizenship. The resulting high school curriculum became more skill-based, intended to provide graduates with academic preparation sufficient to meet the responsibilities required of the 20th century workplace and function as informed and active citizens of the nation.

A decrease in transportation costs, combined with the reduced demand for juvenile manufacturing workers and the resulting increase in high school enrollments that necessitated the building of more public high schools, along with a change to a more vocational curriculum, further spurred the High School Movement. The changes to secondary schooling in America during this period were "quantitatively...significant" in terms of their effectiveness in preparing students for the demands of modern life and citizenship in the 20th century, along with improving and increasing economic opportunities for graduates.[11]

The growth of U.S. secondary schooling varied across the country during the 1910-1940 period. As compared to other regions of the country, the Midwest experienced its greatest increase in high school enrollment during the 1920s, in the decade immediately preceding the Great Depression. The greatest rates of increase occurred in areas involved in farming, ranching, and/or mining, which were relatively homogeneous in terms of income and wealth, and where residents enjoyed a relatively good standard of living.

These conditions existed in the Midwestern states of Indiana, Iowa, Kansas, Nebraska, all of which had relatively high levels of wealth per capita, homogeneous levels of income and wealth, and widely dispersed populations that required local high schools, as the vast distances between population centers precluded more centralized schools.[12] They were particularly prevalent in the Midwest and in the areas from which Culver drew a majority of its students during this period.

Impact of the High School Movement on Culver

Even though it enjoyed a national reputation by this time, enrollment still came predominantly from the Midwest, meaning that Culver was located in an area which experienced the greatest relative increase in competition for high school students in the country during the 1920s. This helps explain Culver's robust but relatively flat enrollment numbers for the period, and it actually suggests that Culver was quite successful in sustaining its enrollment during a period of significantly increased competition for students from institutions that did not charge tuition.

Nevertheless, during the period of the High School Movement, and along with becoming more numerous and witnessing increased enrollment and graduate rates, there remained a demand for secondary institutions focused on providing students with "college preparation," whether preparing graduates to succeed on college entrance exams (required by many institutions) and/or providing them with a legitimate and respected academic credential that could grant them access to higher education. This created a niche for private high schools, many of which were only too happy to embrace what they perceived to be a more educationally noble mission that they had fulfilled traditionally.

Such institutions intentionally eschewed the "vocational" nature of providing preparation for the responsibilities of life and citizenship using a more skills-based curriculum and approach, which American public high schools were more than capable of providing.

The decentralized nature of US education policy and decision-making systems further increased the competition, especially when combined with school-building initiatives. Being free and generally accessible, the new high schools posed a distinct potential threat to Culver, unless Culver could offer something different and appealing that would be viewed by parents as being of value and worth the tuition they paid at Culver (~ $1,000, or ~ $17,000 in contemporary dollars) instead of enrolling their sons in the free high schools in their local areas.

Since time of Alexander Fleet, Culver had provided its students with choice from curricula focused on classical and scientific (for college preparation), and a vocationally focused business curriculum more oriented on preparation for the responsibilities of life and citizenship. However, the faculty hiring that occurring in the 1920s was more oriented to educators able to provide the more academically demanding classical and scientific, slanting Culver's faculty more towards college preparation.

It is interesting to note that during the period of Gignilliat's tenure as Culver's head, the overwhelming majority of adults had just over 8 years of formal education.[13] For many parents with such a limited education, the most valuable gift they could provide their sons was the very best secondary education available to increase their economic opportunities and prepare them for broadest spectrum of opportunities (e.g., either business and/or college). For such parents, the cost of a private secondary education was a price they were willing to pay to help their offspring improve their lot, making it more than worth the return on the investment they could expect for their sons.

Challenges in Enrollment – A First for Culver

Coinciding with the Great Depression in America, this period also saw Culver's first decline in its winter school enrollment in 30 years. Winter school enrollment at Culver did not begin declining significantly until 1931, becoming quite pronounced by 1933, when total enrollment dropped to about half of what it had been before the crash (1929 – 695; 1933 – 355). In response, the CEF Board lowered the tuition from $1,500 to $1,100 in 1935, resulting in an increase in enrollment to 443 for the next school year.

While the tuition reduction resulted in a decrease of around $45,000 in annual net tuition revenue, the accompanying increase in enrollment was nevertheless critical, as Culver's business model was predicated on receiving revenue from at least 400 enrolled students (i.e., $600,000 in revenue). To offset the loss in net tuition revenue, Culver reduced its number of faculty from 113 to 73 (addressed later), resulting in significant savings in terms of operating costs that allowed the school to sustain operations at the reduced tuition rate.[15]

Years	Winter School Enrollment	Tuition	Faculty/Staff
1929-30	695	$1,500	105
1930-31	646	$1,500	107
1931-32	551	$1,500	113
1932-33	402	$1,500	103
1933-34	335	$1,500	93
1934-35	335	$1,500	73
1935-36	443	$1,100	73
1936-37	551	$1,100	82
1937-38	581	$1,100	78
1938-39	605	$1,100	84
1939-40	606	$1,100	91

Winter School Enrollment, Tuition, & Faculty/Staff Numbers, 1929-39.[14]

Research indicates that a similar trend occurred in summer school during the early 1930s.

As with winter school, it is logical to assume that Culver reduced tuition for Summer Schools/Camps sometime after summer 1932, when

Summer Year	Enrollment
1929	1017
1930	878
1931	641
1932	437
1933	471
1934	512
1935	584
1936	681
1937	786
1938	743
1939	743
1940	768

Summer Schools and Camps Enrollment, 1929-40.[16]

enrollment bottomed out at 437. If this occurred, it appears to have helped enrollment to begin increasing in summer 1933. One also suspects that there was a corresponding reduction in the number of faculty and staff members in the summer schools and camps during this period as well (as had occurred in the winter school).

The combined loss of revenue from the winter and summer schools, coupled with the tremendous reduction in the number of faculty and staff in winter school (and which likely in the summer schools and camps faculty and staff as well) indicates that the mid-1930s were very difficult for Culver.

According to Richard Davies, Gignilliat decided deliberately to be away from campus during the period 1933-1935 for a number reasons (many of which related to the changes occurring on campus during the Age of Consultants that will be addressed below, but also due to his health changes at the end of 1933 spring 1934), but one of the most important reasons for his absences were to reassure the alumni that the core of the Culver system remained intact and to encourage them to act as ambassadors for the school and recruit promising candidates.

As the charts above show, enrollment in Culver's winter and summer schools did not rebound until 1935.While Gignilliat's trips certainly had some effect (and not to shortchange his efforts), it was more likely due, then as now, to the determined efforts of the talented Director of Admission s, John Henderson, along with a host of other unnamed individuals who did the hard work required for recruiting success.

Challenges in Affording Faculty – Another First for Culver

As a result of the reductions in cadet enrollment and the concomitant impact on the school's net tuition revenue, CMA had to make reductions in its faculty as well for the first time in its history and during one of the most challenging economic times imaginable. As mentioned previously, between end of 1931-1932 winter school session and end of 1934-1935 winter school session, Culver was forced to reduce its overall faculty and staff by over one-third (35.4 percent, which equated to the loss of 40 members of its faculty and staff (40/113)).[17]

The 1933-1934 and 1934-1935 sessions must have therefor e been very difficult for faculty/staff and cadets. Prizing harmony and consensus above all, these sessions must have also been excruciatingly difficult for Gignilliat, having to let go many valued colleagues with whom he had worked for many years. In addition, the affable Hunt was likely not good at making such cuts, and with Gignilliat away from campus for much of this period, one suspects that the duty of informing the individuals who were separated from the institution may have fallen to the unfortunate Post Adjutant, Allen Elliot.

It is also significant to note that Gregory was away from campus 1934-1935 school year, missing most of the biggest personnel cuts, and returned to a depleted (and likely dispirited) faculty and staff. While he was not on campus during this period his habit of remaining in close contact with a group of influential members of the faculty and staff ensured that he heard all about the cuts and was well apprised of the terrible impact they must have been having on the Culver community.

While none of this may have been Gignilliat's fault, it is the tradition in the military to hold a commander responsible for everything his/her units does or fails to do (as alluded to by the Shakespeare quotation at the beginning of this chapter). Enrollment and faculty retention are two of the most important indicators of success in education, and some may have ascribed blame for Culver's challenges in each of these essential areas to its leader, bringing into question his ability to continue leading the school effectively.

Given his tendency to internalize and take personal responsibility for all areas under his supervision, it is likely that Gignilliat was experiencing some similar doubts about his own abilities. This was also the first crisis Culver faced without ER Culver's calming presence, and while it is not known how BB Culver responded personally, it was almost certainly different from how ER Culver had responded previously. It was the confluence and combination of all of these circumstances during a concentrated period of time and challenge unprecedented for the institution that contributed to the rise of the Age of Consultants at Culver.

Inaugurating the Five-Year "Age of the Consultants," 1929-1934

As far back as 1910, and regularly since, Gignilliat solicited impact from outside experts, like Michael O'Shea from Wisconsin, to obtain support for his style of military education. Faced with the most substantial challenge he had yet encountered, he responded in much the same manner. Between 1929 and 1934, Gignilliat invited experts from respected colleges of education (including Harvard, Michigan, and Wisconsin) to study the Culver program, subjecting the curriculum to intense reviews. The consultants provided recommendations addressing the school's administrative structure, curriculum, and counseling program. Gignilliat intended for them to support his methods and approach, as they had in the past, but others like JS Fleet and Gregory used the recommendations as the basis for implementing changes that they and others wanted to make at Culver.

As was his custom, Gignilliat responded by looking to outside experts to address the issues raised by the self-study. The use of the external experts initiated a five-year period of intense outside scrutiny of virtually every aspect of Culver's educational approach, programs, and practices, referred to by this author as The Age of the Consultants. This period would have substantial and lasting impacts on both Gignilliat and Culver. Gignilliat began by contacting Mather Abbott, the head of the Lawrenceville School (a renowned East coast boarding school), who recommended bringing in outside experts from the Harvard Graduate school of Education (which had recently done a study of Lawrenceville that Abbott found helpful). Gignilliat was delighted that the head of the Harvard Graduate School of Education and a leading progressive educator in the country, Dean Henry W. Homes, agreed to lead the study team, comprised of three additional members of the Harvard Graduate School of Education:. The four-person team he formed was comprised of the following individuals: Professor Bancroft Beatley; Professor F. G. Nichols; and Professor L. L. Dudley.[18]

In relatively short order, the team formed and conducted its first visit to Culver during the period April 8-12, 1929, a short three months after the initial self-study. Upon their arrival, the members of the Harvard team met with faculty, administrators, and department heads; conducted classroom visits; and examined the school's structure and curriculum in detail, along with its significant co- and extra-curricular programs. After gathering as much information as possible in person, the team returned to Harvard and began analyzing the data. Over the course of the next ten months, the members of the team kept up a steady stream of correspondence with academic and administrative leaders at Culver to clarify information they had gathered, request additional data, and refine the focus of their final report. The engagement between the Harvard team and Culver leaders was dynamic, collaborative, and collegial. Although they presented their final 217-page report to Culver in April 1930 (one year after their initial visit), they provided Culver with the substance of their recommendations in early December 1929 to enable the Culver leadership to consider over the holidays and prior to the resumption of the winter school session in January 1931. Their feedback was divided into two sections: the first provided their assessment of Culver's education offerings as they existed; and the second presented the group's recommendations for changes to the school's academic programs and structure.

The Harvard group's overall assessment was as follows:

> *[The program] included a curriculum preparatory for immediate entrance into business and opportunities for well-rounded general education with continuous and integrated study in any one of several fields, such as English, science, fine arts, music, and military science. The Academy can serve best by setting up its own aim in substantive terms."*

Based upon their assessment, Culver would be better served by educating "a body of young men of high ideals, good habits, active interests, and well-informed minds – an aim implied in the whole tradition and leadership of the school."[19]

In effect, the Harvard group believed that a high school diploma should be a terminal degree for Culver graduates, and that Culver should endeavor to ensure that its approach "finished the job" of educating them at the Academy.

The overall theme of the report encouraged Culver to "take a stand against limiting its work to the preparing of candidates for entrance to college" and to instead:

> *"Assign to college preparation less importance than it now has ... [and] ...accept as a general principle the idea that the program of instruction is to fit the needs and aptitudes of individual cadets and the instruction adapted to their differing powers, so that every cadet who graduates has actually achieved an educational goal within his own competence, even if he is not prepared for a particular college."*

Overall, the Harvard group's recommendations come across as being paternalistic and patronizing when read today, reflecting an East-coast bias and a belief that Midwestern students were not capable of completing the work necessary to prepare them for admission to and success at the nation's best colleges and universities.

The college-level faculty Culver had assembled in the 1920s was likely offended by the tone (if not the substance) of the report, knowing not only what their students would be expected to do in college but also what they were capable of doing in high school. Indeed, the group's assessment of Culver's faculty reflected the same paternalistic and patronizing bias, observing that the Academy had "a few outstanding teachers and many others who under proper supervision could develop a much higher degree of competence," but that much of the teaching they observed was "on the whole uninspired," with many instructors failing "to exhibit a proper understanding of their functions as teachers." One wonders how the recently departed headmaster, Hugh Glascock, reacted to this assessment. Curiously and also somewhat disingenuously, the authors concluded this section by commending the efforts of Culver administrators "to secure and retrain only superior teachers."

Harvard Report's Assessment of Gignilliat as School Head

Perpetuating the patronizing and paternalistic tone, the authors of the Harvard report commended Gignilliat "as an educator" while simultaneously damning him with faint praise. Observing that he was neither schooled in "the technical aspect of education" nor did he "possess those points of view, appreciation of value, and skills that a leader would possess whose approach to his position is educational rather than military," the authors nevertheless felt that a military man had an advantage when leading a military school, since "they did not believe that the superintendent of the academy need have an educational, rather than a military, background."[20]

While this assessment was quite complimentary, it did not even persuade its subject. Gignilliat himself recognized and acknowledged that he was a relative amateur, writing later that he never considered himself to be an "educator"; rather, he viewed himself as more of an administrator who was fortunate to work with talented educators (who did the real work of Culver).[21]

This self-assessment is a quite telling, perhaps helping to explain Gignilliat's initial acceptance of the Harvard group's recommendation for Culver to eschew the college prep aspect of its curriculum and adopt a more general preparation approach to its education program. For one who did not consider himself to be a full-fledged educator, the Harvard group's assessment makes some sense, indicating that institutions devoted to something other than college preparation could be well-led by a head administrator lacking an educational background and unschooled in "the technical aspect of education" and/or the capabilities of a legitimate educator, especially one leading a military school.

From a somewhat different vantage point, both in terms of time and perspective, Culver historian Richard Davies makes the rather surprising case that, Gignilliat, as head of a large Midwestern military school with a predominantly upper-class clientele (at this point it its history), embraced some (but not all) aspects of the period's "progressive education" trends.[22] According to Davies, Gignilliat did so out of both a sense of pragmatism and also as a way of showing that Culver was adaptive and on the cutting edge of educational practices of the time. As he had done with the "Greater Culver" plan, Gignilliat co-opted the progressive ideology as a way of supporting the way in which he had made Culver's military system central to the school's educational approach.[23]

Harvard Report's Seven Main Recommendations for Culver

The Harvard group made seven main recommendations for Culver:

1. That Culver should not make college preparation its primary purpose.
2. That changes in the curriculum and in the teaching techniques should be made in terms of this main proposition.
3. That the military character of the school should continue to be maintained.
4. That academic officers should not wear uniforms.
5. That the department of guidance should be set up.
6. That a department of measurement and appraisal should be developed.
7. That to aid in making the necessary changes involved in the above recommendations, the Academy should retain the services of professional consultants.

The Harvard report was quite significant in terms of its impact, but not in the way intended by the authors of it. The recommendations were received with various levels of acceptance, with some being adopted verbatim (such as the recommendations to form an education foundation to govern the school and to revise the school's counseling program), others modified, and others discarded altogether. Overall, the substance of the Harvard report initiated a five-year period of change within Culver's curriculum, administrative structure, faculty management, and counseling program, which, in aggregate, impacted the very structure of Culver itself.

It is useful to examine Gignilliat's own position on these recommendations, which was fairly clear, before considering how Culver as an institution responded to them.

1. That Culver should not make college preparation its primary purpose – *Gignilliat supported it, since it fit within his own ideas about the purpose of secondary education and allowed him to validate much of the system he had developed and implemented at Culver.*

2. That changes in the curriculum and in the teaching techniques should be made in terms of this main proposition. – *Gignilliat supported making alteration curriculum to more general and vocational preparation, but, as he had done with Glascock, he left these matters up to the Headmaster/Dean of the Faculty.*

3. That the military character of the school should continue to be maintained. – *Gignilliat strongly supported (and may have influenced this recommendation).*

4. That academic officers should not wear uniforms. – *Gignilliat did not support but acquiesced, with the caveat that they would still be referred to by their military ranks and that cadets would salute them.*

5. That department of guidance should be set up – **This recommendation repudiated his own longstanding belief that an effective counselor was a good "man who likes boys," suggesting that counselors needed to be professionalized and** *be/become an expert in counseling/guidance (more along Gregory's idea), Gignilliat went along with the majority view and authorized the establishment of this office in 1930 under L. R. Kellam. Gignilliat watched it very closely and became delighted with this endeavor when Kellam created in 1933 what became the famous "Culver Guidance Chart," consolidating a tremendous amount of information about each boy on a single chart and allowing for a far more systematic (Gignilliat would have used the word "scientific") method of developing each boy individually.*

6. That a department of measurement and appraisal should be developed. – *Gignilliat enthusiastically supported (based upon his penchant for trying to quantify all things and his support for embracing "scientific" approaches to as many parts of Culver as possible). With Gignilliat's support, this department was established in 1933 under Gregory as the Department of Supervision and Research (Gregory was also very involved in the Guidance Department).*

7. That to aid in making the necessary changes involved in the above recommendations, the Academy should retain the services of professional consultants. – *supports strongly, since it fit precisely within his preferred method of bringing in outside experts to help Culver remain on the cutting edge of education that he had been using since at least 1910 (and even earlier for the military program)*

Overall, Gignilliat initially supported five of the seven recommendations – numbers 1, 2, 3, 6, and 7, and he came around to supporting number 5. He never really got on board personally with number 4 – faculty members not wearing military uniforms – at what he always considered to be an "essentially military school," but he accepted it grudgingly and with the caveat noted above.

For Culver's first 30 years of existence, Gignilliat's approach reflected the desires of many/most parents, who were willing to pay for a Culver education as an investment in their son's overall development and wellbeing. However, his personal opinions on the recommendations were not necessarily in line with how many of the other members of the faculty and staff felt at the time. Nor were they in line with the times. As the 1920s drew to a close, and especially as a result of the Great Depression, parents wanted a more tangible return on their investments, meaning that they desired and expected the education they funded for their sons to prepare them to be admitted to the universities of their choosing and to succeed in college.

Institutional Responses to the Harvard Group's Seven Recommendations

As a way of highlighting the differences of how the recommendations of the Harvard report were received on campus, the list below reflects that overall feeling of the Culver faculty and staff to the Harvard group's seven main recommendations:

1. That Culver should not make college preparation its primary purpose – *Divided opinion (some supported, but most opposed).*

2. That changes in the curriculum and in the teaching techniques should be made in terms of this main proposition – *The crux was a recommendation to alter curriculum to more general and vocational preparation; divided opinion (some supported, but most opposed).*

3. That the military character of the school should continue to be maintained – *Most supported, but some small minority wanted Culver to discard its military system and adopt an approach similar to the east coast prep schools.*

4. That academic officers should not wear uniforms – *Most all faculty supported, and most military opposed, exposing a clear divide; accommodation for doing so was that faculty members would be required to continue using military titles and to be saluted by cadets.*

5. That department of guidance should be set up – *Most supported, but more out of their displeasure with the somewhat superior attitude of the Tactical Officers. The hope was that professionalizing them would make them more collegial and reduce the existing divide between the members of the military and academic staffs.*

6. That a department of measurement and appraisal should be developed – *Most supported, as it appears to be a tailor-made position for Gregory (who also enjoyed great support among the faculty and staff). With Gignilliat's support this department was established in 1933 under Gregory as the Department of Supervision and Research (Gregory was also very involved in the Guidance Department).*

7. That to aid in making the necessary changes involved in the above recommendations,
   the Academy should retain the services of professional consultants – *Most supported, believing (contrary to Gignilliat) that outside consultants would agree with them and help them change the Culver system for the better.*

As becomes apparent, the Harvard report's recommendations brought to light the differences in educational philosophy between Gignilliat and many others that had arisen at Culver during the 1920s. It catalyzed and crystallized a triumvirate of opposition to Gignilliat – comprised of JS Fleet, William E. Gregory, and Cal Chambers – that was to have momentous impact for the remainder of the decade and beyond. While Fleet's opposition had been quite apparent since the mid-1920s and especially through his leadership of the Committee for Academic Improvement beginning in 1927, the lack of support from Gregory (who he had hired, respected, mentored, and promoted swiftly) and Chambers (who had served as his Executive Officer for nine years and with whom he had a very close personal relationship) must have been quite surprising.

As the differing opinions became manifest, it became apparent that Gignilliat favored an approach that prepared students broadly for the outside world, whether attending college or going directly into the work force, while Fleet, Gregory, and Chambers were more in support of a college preparation approach in which the military system played an important but less prominent role. More specifically, Gregory was strongly committed to the military system but felt that it needed some significant revisions, whereas Fleet had been clamoring for changes to the military program through the 1920s to de-emphasize it in favor of placing more emphasis on academics.

As a more recent Culver graduate than Fleet, Chambers developed the most nuanced position of all, siding with Gregory in terms of the military system needing significant revisions and also with Fleet in terms of enhancing the focus on academics at the expense of the military system. All three agreed that Culver's military system was very effective in developing a sense of civic responsibility in cadets that was sorely needed in America at the time.

Gignilliat's involvement in Culver's consideration of the Harvard Report

In what had become a fairly predictable response to both the situation and to the seventh recommendation from the Harvard study, Gignilliat brought in a group of experts to help address the issues, including:

- B. Moehlman – University of Michigan (Professor of Administration and Supervision); recognized expert on school management (author of six books on education science); visiting consultant to address administrative issues and academic facilities[24]

- S. A Courtis – University of Michigan (Professor of Education since 1924); recognized expert on effective educational practices (author of two books on education science); focused on addressing individualized teaching at Culver[25]
- H. Edgerton – University of Wisconsin; technical advisor to the faculty committee on counseling, guidance, measurement, and appraisal.[26]

It is important to note that the process was not something that was being "done to Culver" and which took on a life of its own; rather, it was one in which Gignilliat himself was quite involved, considering all aspects of Harvard Report and chairing meetings to discuss them in which he both allowed and encouraged free and open discussion of the issues. However, from reading the minutes that were recorded of the discussions, it is clear that Gignilliat's involvement was more as that of an administrator and not as a faculty member and/or educator. His comments during the sessions indicate that he was genuinely interested in considering all of the Harvard group's recommendations and that he truly encouraged a frank and open dialogue about them, both in sessions with the department heads and in sessions with the members of the faculty.[27]

Below is a summary of the actions Culver took in response to the seven main recommendations of the Harvard group:

Outcomes and Deliberations

Regarding the Harvard group's seven main recommendations:

1. That Culver should not make college preparation its primary purpose – ***Rejected.***
2. That changes in the curriculum and in the teaching techniques should be made in terms of this main proposition – ***Tried and modified.***
3. That the military character of the school should continue to be maintained – ***Adopted.***
4. That academic officers should not wear uniforms – ***Adopted (with caveats).***
5. That department of guidance should be set up – ***Adopted, and established in 1930 under L R Kellam.***
6. That a department of measurement and appraisal should be developed – ***Adopted and established in 1933 under Gregory as the Department of Supervision and Research.***

7. That to aid in making the necessary changes involved in the above recommendations, the Academy should retain the services of professional consultants – ***Adopted and continued through the end of 1934.***

In summary, four of the seven recommendations were adopted and implemented, one was adopted with caveats, one was tried and modified, and one was rejected. This outcome indicates that the recommendations of the Harvard group were consequential and had a substantial impact on Culver. However, the most significant outcome of the Harvard report and the five years of intense internal scrutiny that occurred was that by 1934, CMA determined that it would be a college preparatory school operating within a military framework. This vision – quite different from Gignilliat's own idea – guided the development of Culver for the next 20 years (at least). This outcome is especially significant and worth exploring in greater detail.

Whereas Gignilliat conceived of CMA as an "essentially military school" with excellent academics suitable for providing general preparation for all, along with the training to allow graduates to enter into the work force immediately and/or gain acceptance and find success at the best colleges and universities in the country, his focus was always principally on the formation of character by (primarily) the military system, but also through academics and athletics. This vision, reflecting the pre-High School Movement "general preparation" (whether for work or college) way of thinking within secondary education, held sway up to WWI and proved its worth in the Great War. However, the changes in society, the faculty, and in boys in the decade following WWI made such an approach increasingly anachronistic and out of step with the times.

Rumblings of discontent with Gignilliat's system began on campus in the mid-1920s, when Gignilliat was away from campus for extended periods of time (and perhaps longer than he should have been), gaining purchase with the 1927 formation of the Committee for Academic Improvement, chaired by JS Fleet. Fueled by his support and exacerbated by the departure of many of Culver's "old guard," the discontent grew, finding voice in the opportunity presented by the propitious January 1929 self-study. This activity was the catalyst for generating the momentum that resulted in the Harvard group's study of 1929-1930 and the involvement of several external consultants during the period 1930-1934, culminating with Moehlman's final report in November 1934.

It is noteworthy that this process may have been even more open and candid had it occurred a decade earlier, prior to Gignilliat's apotheosis on campus. Many of the newer faculty members, while quite capable, had not had the opportunity to get to know Gignilliat well and develop a personal relationship with him. For many of the newer members of the faculty, he was simply "the General" who had helped build the school from its beginning, served as its most prominent and successful exemplar in peace and war, and was the guardian of the existing Culver way.

Gignilliat's Changing Views on Education during this Period – The Evidence

Gignilliat was nothing if not pragmatic, and he was almost certainly able to take in all of this information and input, and realize that his current educational thinking was perhaps somewhat dated, out of step with both the times and with Culver, and needed to change. He had demonstrated such abilities as a trainer on numerous occasions previously, and it stands to reason that he remained capable of doing so as an educator at this point in his career.

We see his views on Culver's education system evolve, reflected in a new outlet he began using to connect with the Corps in 1930 – the *Roll Call* (CMA's yearbook). Coincidently (or perhaps intentionally), this practice began immediately after his youngest son – Hank – graduated from CMA in 1929, severing the intimate connection he had with the Corps in that regard since Leigh Jr. became a cadet in 1912, just after Gignilliat become Superintendent.

More evolutionary than revolutionary, the changes in Gignilliat's thinking regarding education reflected more of a change in degree than in kind, never fully embracing or opposing either pole – general preparation or college preparation – and instead drifting from one to another mostly out of pragmatism rather than philosophical conviction. Writings of his that appeared in the *Roll Call* bear out his changes of opinion. He observed in the 1930 *Roll Call*, tellingly, that "*Culver is quite grown up, like a young man in his thirties,*" with the vision and drive of youth but a new purpose.

He goes on to write that, "The old machinery [will soon be] entirely overhauled, the obsolete courageously scrapped, the new assemblage functioning for a new decade to meet the needs of a new concept of secondary education," suggesting the beginnings of the new Culver. This was also the first year that Culver instructors did not wear uniforms (although they did retain military rank and were required to be saluted by cadets), which came as a direct result of the Harvard group's recommendations. Given the timing, it was almost certainly a reflection of the results of the self-study and the work of the Harvard group.

In 1931, Gignilliat suggests in his *Roll Call* article that Culver's previous education program was less than ideal, and conveys that Culver was working to develop "... an ideal [educational] program that will achieve as far as possible the summum bonum in mental, physical, social and emotional accomplishment. It readily offers a hand in solving some of the difficult problems that education means in the best sense of the word."

Expounding on this theme, Gignilliat wrote that, "The new philosophy of trying to adapt education to a natural process of growth, to the end that the individual may become a properly rounded person within the outer bounds of his own limits," echoing the language of the Harvard report, while also "adhering to the laws of psychological growth about which we are becoming increasingly well informed" and better able to implement "is...a powerful challenge," and "we will not be satisfied...until we educate a youth far better fitted than at present to attain 'the durable satisfactions of life,' which certainly includes keeping in step with the times."

This is a very powerful statement regarding the changes occurring, which were a blend of old and new and intended to improve graduates' preparation for life and also keep "*in step with the times,*" suggesting that Culver had been out of step with the times and not preparing its grads for the world as well as it could and should have been doing and was adopting a new philosophy to allow it to do so better. Coming as it does after the final Harvard group's report, it is highly likely that these comments reflect the efforts related to the external consultants as well.

A study of Culver's marketing material reveals that around 1932, the standard messages of Gignilliat regarding the school's military system (training must be made real and given properly...) began to change, deviating from the main points he had been emphasizing since they coalesced in his own mind in the five years prior to American's entry into WWI, and began instead to reflect a bit more ambiguity and flexibility. This provided additional evidence regarding two things: the changes occurring in Gignilliat's thinking regarding education, and that he was inexorably ceding leadership in the design of Culver's overall program.

Organizational Challenges – The 1932 Culver Covenant

As the final act of the 1911 "Greater Culver" plan, the Culver Covenant represented a culmination in that it demonstrated the Culver family's confidence in the ability of the institution to endure as a suitable memorial to their father and mother. The family had always wanted to use the school as a way to memorialize their father, but with matriarch Emily Jane's death in June 1922 they realized that CMA could perpetuate the memories of both and that only a non-profit foundation could do so.

The family, led by brothers ER and BB, became determined to "divest the Academy of all personal ownership, realizing that the dispersion of private stock ownership by inheritance or otherwise might create situations inimical to the welfare of the institution."[28] This was the animating spirit behind what became the largest single philanthropic gift in American secondary education history at the time.

Culver's history regarding the Culver Covenant is quite well known. What is perhaps less well known is the level of Gignilliat's involvement in developing the CEF and Culver Covenant. Richard Davies crafted the most thorough description of Gignilliat's role in Culver's transition of governance that culminated with the publishing of the Culver Covenant on June 7, 1932, which tells a story of far greater involvement by Gignilliat than has been previously acknowledged.[29]

It was one of the consultants that Gignilliat engaged as result of the Harvard study, Arthur B. Moehlman, who was the true driving force behind this endeavor, but Gignilliat's role and contributions to it were also significant. Moehlman had been involved in a previous land dispute among some members of the Culver family, and the acrimony he witnessed during their engagements with one another (perhaps exacerbated by the financial challenges being faced by the Wrought Iron Range Company at the same time) created concern in his mind regarding the viability of the family's continued and future governance of the institution.

Moehlman visited with Gignilliat in January 1930 to discuss his role with respect to addressing the Harvard group's recommendations, raising concerns about the viability of Culver remaining a family-run enterprise through stock ownership. Moehlman recommended to Gignilliat that Culver consider adopting the best practice of governance at the time, which involved establishing a non -profit educational foundation to replace the stock-owning corporation as the school's highest level of governance. The head of the Harvard group – Dean Homes – made a similar suggestion to Gignilliat separately.

Based upon his own observations and experience, Gignilliat agreed with this assessment, telling Moehlman that at least two members of the Culver family – ER and BB – shared this desire. In fact, ER and BB had been actively pursuing such an option by purchasing the stock options from other Culver family members since the time of Emily Jane's death in 1922, and they had completed the process of doing so by the beginning of 1930. Controlling all of the stock options related to CMA allowed ER and BB to put the plan into effect. While waiting for the opportune moment to present this aspect of the Harvard group's recommendation to the Culver family, Gignilliat instructed Moehlman to draft up plans for transferring CMA from private family ownership to a more appropriate type of non-stock and non-profit educational foundation, and to act as a consultant for the process of doing so.

By some accounts, the Culver brothers were ready to execute the transfer in 1930. However, ER Culver's untimely death on October 3, 1930, both slowed down and accelerated the process. It slowed it down because ER controlled much of the CMA stock, and his assets had to go through the process of probate. There may have also been the issue of a potential inheritance tax that had to be addressed for such a considerable bequest (Davies concluded that there is scant evidence to assess the validity of this claim). As it turned out, the stock went to his widow, who supported the idea of transferring ownership from the family and donating the assets to an educational foundation, thereby negating any issue of inheritance tax.

The process was accelerated by creating an even greater sense of urgency, since only BB was left to carry out the plan. It may also have been hurried along by concerns related to the potential of having to remit a considerable inheritance tax on ER's estate (if this was even an issue).

Moehlman worked quickly, presenting Gignilliat with a draft plan in November 1930, but neither BB nor ER's eldest surviving son, ER Jr., were ready at that point to implement the plan. In January 1931, Moehlman discussed his plans with the Culver Board of Trustees, reviewing the issue more deeply with BB in a private session. Armed with BB's perspective, Moehlman re-worked his initial draft and presented a revised version of it to Gignilliat in September 1931.

BB happened to be visiting Culver at the time, informed Moehlman that he was ready to carry out the idea, and took a copy of Moehlman's revised plan to consider. After making additional revisions to the plan based upon input from Gignilliat and BB, Moehlman, Chambers, and BB met with a Judge Sprague in February 1932 to begin the formal process of transferring control of CMA from the Culver family to a non-stock and non-profit education foundation.

Favorably impressed by the concept and meticulous nature of Moehlman's work, the Culver family agreed to execute the transfer of ownership at the end of the 1931-1932 winter school session. On June 7, 1932, during commencement activities, the Culver family formally transferred their holdings related to Culver Military Academy – valued at approximately $6,000,000 (equating to ~ $122 million in 2023 dollars), to the Culver Education Foundation. As with all such ceremonies, Gignilliat staged this momentous occasion in his usual flamboyant manner at a lakeside ceremony near Founder's Rock, where Culver lore has it that H. H. Culver first dreamed of founding the academy.

According to a newspaper article regarding the event, brief addresses were given by Dr. Robert M. Hutchins, president of the University of Chicago; Dr. George Van Santvoord, headmaster of the Hutchins school; Major General, H. A. Drum; Admiral Hugh Rodman; Albert R. Erskine, president of the Studebaker Corporation; William A. Brooks, president of the Culver Legion; and Gignilliat, as the CMA Superintendent. [30] However, the majority of the speeches came from five members of the Culver family, culminating with the unveiling of a plaque on Founder's Rock which read:

> *Here in 1894, with his boulder as his work bench and nature's own out-of-doors for his shop, Henry Harrison Culver fashioned out of the mists of his boyhood dreams the framework of a school – a school where the youth of coming years should be forged into men for the citizenship of the morrow.*

The new arrangement – referred to as the Culver Covenant – created a ten-member Board of Directors to control the newly created non-stock and non-profit Culver Education Foundation, responsible for overseeing Culver Military Academy and the Culver Summer Schools (Naval, Cavalry, and Woodcraft). While the Culver family remained a strong presence on the board it did not hold a majority, allowing others like Gignilliat, Chambers, and four alumni to have direct involvement into the formal governance of CMA.

The Culver Covenant legal transfer took effect on March 9, 1933. The process of transferring control from the Culver family was completed on June 1, 1933, with the formal dissolution of the "Culver Military Academy" corporation and the activation of the Culver Education Foundation to assume control of CMA and the Culver summer program.[31]

The Culver Covenant Brings Organizational Modernization

The implementation of the Culver Covenant was indicative of the Progressive Era process of organizational modernization impacting Culver. The dawn of the twentieth century saw the convergence of industrialization, urbanization, and rapid immigration, producing a period characterized more by change related to modernization than by continuity with the past. This environment energized many in American society even as it unsettled those more comfortable with sustaining time-tested practices from previous eras that had been successful.

Pre-modernization organizations rooted in 19th century practices were informal and decentralized organic partnerships organized horizontally that functioned through individual consultation between/among self-taught non-professionals with fairly loose areas of responsibility and lines of authority, aimed at achieving harmony and cooperation. These organizations relied on familial connections, engaged in informal deliberations, and used largely unstructured decision-making processes to arrive at their determinations, which were based as much on emotion and personal preference as on logic and rationality.

Personality played a large and important role in the functioning of such organizations and how decisions were made.[32] The organizational dynamic was one of getting along, working together, and contributing where you could in ways that were personal and unique. This caused the organization to change in unexpected ways as the people changed.

The characteristics of the pre-modernization organization reflect the way that Gignilliat and ER Culver functioned. Gignilliat was comfortable and effective functioning in such an environment -- he thrived in it.

By contrast, 20th-century modernized organizations were more formal and centralized managerial corporations organized vertically that had clear areas of responsibility and unambiguous allocations of authority, stressing rationality, efficiency, and predictability. They engaged in formal deliberations and adopted rational planning and structured decision-making processes directed at clearly definable and predictable outcomes to arrive at their logical and rational determinations. Process – not personality – was the driving force in the functioning of such organizations and how decisions were made.[33]

Overall, the organizational dynamic was one of ensuring that all made their defined and specific contributions as important "cogs" in machine that were somewhat impersonal and interchangeable, resulting in an organization that remained the same in spite of people changing.

The characteristics of the modernization organizations reflect much of the way that Culver functioned beginning with the establishment of the Culver Covenant.

Gignilliat's practical executive development by Alexander Fleet and ER Culver had not prepared him to function in this manner. As became more apparent in the coming years, the somewhat less personal nature of governance via the CEF Board turned out to be less conducive to Gignilliat's style and preferred method of interaction, and he began to lose his effectiveness as the school's chief executive officer in such an environment, never floundering but becoming reactive instead of proactive for the first time in his professional life at Culver.

The organizational change was also difficult for others to accept. As mentioned previously, Gignilliat decided to be away from campus for extended periods of time to meet with alumni, explain the new arrangement, assure them that Culver was still in good hands and would continue doing the important things they valued, and encourage them to recruit for Culver.[34]

This decision highlights the conundrum he faced: although he knew that there was growing unrest on campus needing his presence and attention to address, he also felt a responsibility to support the CEF Board, demonstrate his ability to function effectively under the new organizational arrangement, and cater to his alumni constituency. There was no perfect solution to this dilemma, and Gignilliat acted as he saw best.

His decision to absent himself from campus during this critical period created the opportunity for increased influence from others not within his own trusted circle of supporters and/or ideas that differed from his own and better able to function well in the modernized organizational structure inaugurated by the Culver Covenant, setting himself up for the decreased level of influence on campus and role he played during his final decade at Culver.

Personal Challenge 1: JS Fleet as Gignilliat's Nemesis?

There is some evidence to suggest that an adversarial relationship developed beginning in the mid-1920s between two of the most cordial and polite people at Culver: Gignilliat and John Seddon (JS) Fleet. According to Culver historian Bob Hartman, JS Fleet was noted for his "gentle and humble nature," but this should not be misread as and/or confused with a lack of strength arising from his passion for Culver and devotion to the intellectual development of the cadets. In fact, one may surmise that JS Fleet became Gignilliat's institutional nemesis during the decade spanning 1924-1934. The word "nemesis" is used to convey professional conflict between two individuals over the proper direction of the institution and is not intended to suggest personal animosity between the two.

JS Fleet was a CMA graduate from the class of 1898. His father, Alexander "Fred" Fleet, was a highly educated and respected scholar who is recognized as one of Culver's "giants." The intellectual genes ran in the family: JS Fleet's younger brother, William A. "Billy" Fleet (CMA '00), was one of America's first Rhodes Scholars. JS Fleet was himself quite bright, graduating from his father's alma mater, the University of Virginia, in 1902. Upon graduation, JS Fleet taught foreign language at Culver until 1908, when he left and became head of several small schools in the South. He also became a highly respected Latin instructor in his own right, serving as a long-time reader for the College Board.

JS Fleet returned to Culver 1918 as a highly respected professional educator and took over the Latin department as its head/chair. He became Acting Superintendent in April 1942, when Gregory was called to active duty in the Army. Reaching the mandatory retirement age at Culver of 65, he retired in September 1943 (replaced by Allen Elliot for the remainder of WWII until Gregory's return). Throughout his career, JS Fleet met and mixed with many high-level academics at both secondary and higher education levels, He was as accomplished an educator as it was possible to be in his time.

As the eldest son of Alexander Fleet, JS Fleet likely saw himself as the keeper of the Fleet vision at Culver, especially the academic component to which his own father had devoted so much of his attention and effort to creating. Beginning in the mid-1920s, it became apparent that JS Fleet represented the academic pole of the Culver debate, while Rossow as Commandant represented the military pole. Their fundamental disagreement regarding the proper role of the military at Culver created tension between the two, and also made Gignilliat uncomfortable (he valued harmony and disliked confrontations) if/when he had to choose between the two. Gignilliat's own discomfort likely exacerbated this tension further.

As one example of his academic focus, JS Fleet was the driving force behind Culver getting a *Cum Laude* chapter to help put Culver on the level of the best East-coast schools. Founded in 1906, the Cum Laude Society was and remains dedicated to honoring scholastic achievement in secondary school s. Modeled intentionally on Phi Beta Kappa in higher education, including its distinctive "key," it is the most prestigious

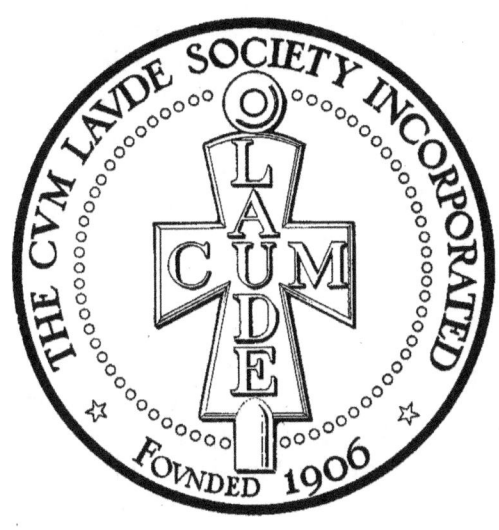

Distinctive Cum Laude key and seal.

academic society for secondary schools.

Fleet's initial effort in 1924 was not successful, as *Cum Laude* administrators were "suspicious" of Culver's commitment, ability, and "sincerity" to do quality "college-preparatory work." One suspects that much of this hesitancy came from Culver being a military school, as there were few high-performing schools of this type operating in the country at the time, and also a Midwestern institution, as the nations' best college prep schools were almost all located on the East coast.

Fleet responded to this initial rebuff by highlighting Culver's rigorous curriculum and the impressive credentials of its faculty members (including his own), reasoning that these were two strengths of the school that he could promote and which would have purchase with *Cum Laude* administrators. In doing so, the conflicts between the academic and military programs must have become even more starkly apparent to him, and this realization may well have been the basis for the somewhat adversarial professional relation that developed between Fleet and Gignilliat over the course of the ensuing decade. This work may also have been the basis for his dissatisfaction with the performance of Culver graduates in college (despite AMCSUS statistics to the contrary).

The success of his efforts to get a *Cum Laude* chapter at Culver in 1925 was the academic equivalent of Gignilliat's efforts to gain recognition for Culver as a "distinguished military institution" two decades earlier, and it represented one of the great triumphs for Culver in the 1920s. JS Fleet was justifiably proud of this achievement, and the prestige he acquired as a result was almost certainly the basis of creating the Committee for Academic Improvement and naming him its chair in 1927. Indeed, one has a hard time identifying a more qualified and suitable candidate to lead this committee, and his appointment was almost certainly supported by Gregory and many of the other newer and highly qualified academic members of the faculty.

Along with being an excellent use of his talents, this appointment also likely made JS Fleet the champion of the newer faculty and unofficial leader of it. It was only natural for Fleet to feel a special kinship with highly qualified faculty that came to Culver in 1920s, much as Gignilliat did with the members of the military staff. This was probably most important for its impact on the relationship between Fleet and Gregory, who arrived in 1924 and shared a nuanced educational vision embracing both the academic and military poles but which was more in line overall with that of Fleet.

As the relationship developed between Fleet and Gignilliat, and based on what he had experienced at and learned from other institutions and professional educators, Fleet, like his professional colleagues on the Harvard group, likely viewed Gignilliat as the educational "amateur" that he was and did not agree with the prominence given to the military at, in his view, the expense of academics. Fleet and Gregory likely shared many similar views and bonded in the late 1920s and 1930s over efforts to make changes at Culver that enhanced its academic program. The master peacemaker Glascock was able to placate Fleet and keep him in check, but Hunt was not able to so as effectively, which, along with the circumstances that arose in the late 1920s, helps explain why the professional disagreement between Fleet and Gignilliat became adversarial by the end of the 1920s.

The forum for these disputes became the Committee for Academic Improvement, formed in early 1927. Toward the end of Glascock's tenure, it is possible that Gignilliat viewed JS Fleet as a likely and highly qualified successor to Glascock as Headmaster. However, it appears that Fleet viewed the situation somewhat differently. For example, it was in this committee that faculty rumblings about dissatisfaction with how Gignilliat was running Culver began with respect to one particular issue: the performance of Culver graduates in college.

Data collected by AMCSUS member institutions throughout the 1920s indicated that not only were Culver graduates among the highest performing military school graduates in colleges and universities, their performance compared favorably with graduates from well-known East coast prep schools. However, during this same period, JS Fleet became convinced that Culver graduates were underperforming in higher education, which he increasingly attributed to what he believed to be Culver's misguided overemphasis on its military program that was coming increasingly at the expense of the cadets' academic educations.

It is unclear why the AMCUS data failed to impress JS Fleet, but what is clear is that Fleet got it into his mind that this was a serious issue that needed to be addressed and he began recruiting others to support his position. Perhaps this reflects a desire of Fleet's on some level to make his own substantial mark on what he considered to be his father's institution. Since Fleet considered himself an educator (and Gignilliat, according to his own admission did not consider himself to be an educator), perhaps their conflict represented a true difference of philosophy – preparation (Gignilliat) vs. education (JS Fleet). It might also reflect the influence of the High School Movement on Fleet (which largely bypassed Gignilliat's notice). Nevertheless, and despite there being scant evidence of Culver graduates not doing well at college, Fleet used the committee to make his point and gain supporters.

Regardless of the origins and parameters of their professional disagreement, it is important to note that JS Fleet and Gignilliat remained cordial toward one another, and that Fleet's influence on campus with both the faculty and the students continued to grow. It culminated in an informal way in 1936, with the *Roll Call* being dedicated to JS Fleet and identified by the cadets as being a scholar, gentleman, and a friend. Nevertheless, the impact of this division was that Culver's faculty and staff became divided over a substantive issue for perhaps the first time and at the very time when they needed to be even more unified to face the coming challenges. For one who valued harmony above all, it was also quite disconcerting for Gignilliat personally as well as professionally.

Professional Challenges – Gignilliat's Engagement with the 168th Brigade and the Army's CMTC Program, 1929-1934

Gignilliat also faced the challenges of balancing his Army duties as a General officer and brigade commander with his responsibilities as Culver's superintendent, along with his other activities regarding war-veteran societies (e.g., FIDAC and the American Legion), post-WWI military preparedness, and countering the anti-militarism campaign that appeared in the 1920s.

Besides being demanding, Gignilliat's role in helping create America's New Citizen Army during this period was both substantial and time-consuming. Much of his work in these areas drew him away from campus, both physically and mentally, diverting his attention from Culver during a period in which it was perhaps most sorely needed. This period taxed his energies and abilities as no other had, bringing him to a physical breaking point that required Minnie's firm intervention to rectify.

Gignilliat's professional military responsibilities during this period related to his duties leading the 168th Brigade of the New Citizens Army. Created by the National Defense Act of 1920, the New Citizens Army was comprised of an organized reserve of trained citizen-soldiers who, along with the National Guard and units like the one commanded by Gignilliat, could be mobilized rapidly in times of crisis to augment the smaller Regular Army.

The officers for these units came from two main sources: the Reserve Officers Training Corps (ROTC) and the Citizens Military Training Camps (CMTC). Gignilliat had been involved with ROTC since its beginning, helping to draft the legislation that brought it into being in 1916 and hosting one of the very first ROTC units at Culver. Beginning in the late 1920s, he became involved with the CMTC as a way of providing training opportunities for the members of his 168th Brigade and of contributing meaningfully to the national defense.

The program for the Citizens' Military Training Camps drew its lineage and inspiration from the pre-WWI Plattsburgh Camps. Intended to provide training that was more thorough and systematic, the purpose of the Citizens' Military Training Camps was "to bring together men of all types, both native and foreign born; to develop closer national and social unity, to teach the privileges, duties, and responsibilities of American citizenship."

In addition, the CMTC program was intended "to show the public by actual example that camp instruction of the kind contemplated will be to the liking of their sons" by developing them "physically, mentally, and morally" to "teach Americanism in its true sense." By "Americanism," the CMTC program a form of citizenship meant to instill a sense of patriotism "and all that makes for clean, healthy, vigorous American manhood" in its participants.[35] The parallels with Culver's approach to development are remarkable, making the appeal to Gignilliat quite understandable.

Within the national defense establishment, the CMTC provided a way for young men of at least 16 years of age (17 beginning in 1923) and "of good character, intelligence and physical condition" not enrolled in college with the opportunity to "increase his worth to the nation" as a citizen while also obtaining "priceless value to himself and to the community in which he lives." This training was provided at no cost to the participants.[36] No service obligation was associated with the program, except with the final course, but the expectation was that those who participated would be inclined to enlist and/or serve in their country's Organized Reserves or the National Guard.

The CMTC program began as a three-summer course of instruction consisting of one-month camps, with each year designated by a different color: red for the first year; white for the second year; and blue for the third year. The Army added a fourth year of training to the CMTC program, resulting in a program comprised of the Basic Course, followed by the Red, White, and Blue courses.[37]

The initial course was intended for beginners with no previous military experience. The second course continued the training of the initial course by providing opportunities to apply basic military concepts in rudimentary field. Completion of the first two courses (Basic and Red) equated essentially to completing the Army's basic training and qualified a participant to enlist in the Organized Reserves with the rank of private and also to progress to the next course.

The third course (White) provided advanced military training that prepared participants to become non-commissioned officers in the Officers Reserve. Successful completion of the third course would qualify the CMTC cadet for appointment as a non-commissioned officer in the Organized Reserves and eligibility for the final course. As the culminating event, the final course (Blue) enhanced the training provided in the first three courses to qualify graduates for appointments as junior officers (i.e., second lieutenants) in the Organized Reserve Corps (ORC).[38]

The training emphasized physical health and development, with elementary infantry drill activities in the morning and more specialized training in the evenings, delivered mostly via lectures. This left much of the day open for a variety of athletic sports intended to improve the cadets' physical health, enhance their physical development, and encourage a commitment to a lifetime of habits promoting physical health and vigor.

The Army decided in 1928 to assign Organized Reserve units – like Gignilliat's 168th Brigade – to assist with CMTC training. This decision was quite pragmatic, allowing for Reserve Officers to provide a sizable and relatively effective cadre for the program. It also provided excellent leadership training opportunities and experience for ORC officers (like Gignilliat), which was perhaps the greatest contribution of the CMTC to national defense and Army military preparedness.[39]

Gignilliat took full advantage of this opportunity to provide the best and most abundant training opportunities for the officers of his 168th Brigade. He also used his abilities as a trainer and familiarity with the training requirements and abilities as a trainer, both of which were quite substantial, to improve the CMTC training provided by his officers. In addition to making his own officers into more capable trainers, this also helped improve the CMTC training overall.

Personal Challenge 2 – The Departure of the "Old Breed" and "Gignilliat Men," Change, Facing His Own Limitations

In many ways, 1929 was the final year of the "old" Culver. The Culver family owned the school, and ER Culver providing oversight of it as he has since 1912. Glascock was still the steadfast and reliable headmaster, the faculty still wore uniforms, and Chambers continued serving as Gignilliat's Executive Officer. His son Hank was in his final year at Culver, providing Gignilliat with instant access to the happenings and mindset of the corps. This was perhaps the last comfortable year for Gignilliat, as changes began occurring rapidly beginning with commencement in June 1929.

One momentous change occurred with Glascock's retirement in 1929. Although he had been grooming Hunt to take over for years, Glascock was an extraordinarily capable administrator who had the respect of the entire Culver community – including the Culver family, faculty, staff, and cadets – and was able to sustain the harmonious environment on campus so prized by Gignilliat. Hunt was quite capable in terms of his knowledge of education, but he was also quite conflict-adverse, preferring to "go along and get along" with his colleagues. This was comfortable for him and made for an outwardly collegial appearance, but the forces and personalities present on campus conspired to exploit this affable approach, leading to disruption and unrest.

In particular, JS Fleet and Rossow were able to take advantage of Hunt's desire for friendly relations among all to begin advancing their own agendas and increasing their own levels of influence. This dynamic developed such that it resulted, perhaps inevitably, in pitting the cordial JS Fleet against the more aggressive Rossow as the battle for dominance at Culver between academics and the military came to a head in the coming years.

Just as the most visible impact of the Harvard study's recommendation – the faculty no longer wearing military uniforms (but still referred to by their military ranks and saluted by cadets) – took effect beginning with the 1929-1930 winter school session, Rossow began challenging the authority of Hunt. Rossow believed, as a military school, that Culver should reflect a more traditional military hierarchy in which the commandant was the second-in-command.

Perhaps he believed that he would have Gignilliat's support for this arrangement, since it reflected the hierarchy that existed on campus when Gignilliat was commandant. However, the situation had changed significantly in the ensuring years, and Gignilliat's tenure as superintendent had established for almost two decades that the headmaster was the rightful and legitimate second-in-command, manifest most notably when Glascock served at acting superintendent during Gignilliat's 27-month absence for WWI.

Rossow's personality, however, was far more forceful and aggressive, and he found it fairly easy to prevail over the more meek and affable Hunt. It became Rossow's custom to "run over" Hunt if and when he disagreed with him and/or wanted a different outcome. Wanting to have the best person in charge in his absence and somewhat oblivious to the inequitable power dynamic between Rossow and Hunt, Gignilliat began to rely more and more on Rossow to be in charge in his absence. Fairly well behaved in Gignilliat's presence, Rossow became quite directive and forceful with his colleagues in Gignilliat's absence and when placed in charge. This was a shocking and disturbing development for many of the faculty members hired during the 1920s who were used to having the calm and collegial Glascock in charge during the General's frequent absences.

The disharmony among his senior staff was occurring at the same time as the unrest within the organization began on campus. This unrest was manifested by the surprisingly negative results of the January 1929 self-study, the first visit by the Harvard group in April 1929, and the final disappointing session at Skyland Camps and decision to essentially discontinue the endeavor.

The death of ER Culver in October 1930 was perhaps the greatest shock for Gignilliat, as the two had worked very closely since 1912 and developed an intimate relationship. An excerpt from the 1931 *Roll Call* does well in conveying the impact of ER's death.

> *Mr. Culver for many years has given his every energy to bringing the highest state of perfection to the school he loved so dearly. His gentleness, his unselfishness, his utter devotion to work for others have won for him love and admiration that is given to few men to attain.*

> *All who have worked with him in the cause of building this great school have some to look to him for inspiration and courage, and have learned to love him as a rare and tired friend. To them and the entire school his going is a stunning blow and a source of infinite grief.*

> *No tribute of written or spoken words could compare with the*
> *unspoken tribute in the hearts of those who knew him, nor to the*
> *testimonial to his labors that will live in the school to which he*
> *gave so richly from his creative and vigorous mind and from his*
> *loyal and kindly heart.*[40]

Indeed, this tribute could have just as easily been applied to Gignilliat and reflects much of what was written about him upon his passing in 1952.

This loss, unexpected as it was and hitting so close to home, must have been a tremendously difficult blow for Gignilliat to endure. Gignilliat enjoyed a good relationship with BB Culver, but the younger Culver brother's focus was much more business-oriented than the more creative approach embraced by ER.

Soon thereafter, Gignilliat also lost his own "right-hand man," Cal Chambers, as his Executive Officer and close confidant. Chambers accepted a position as the Secretary for the CEF Board in December 1930, which took effect in June 1931. Chambers was replaced with Allen Elliot, who was a very cable CMA graduate with long service at Culver (he would become acting superintendent from 1943 -1946). Nevertheless, Gignilliat never developed the warm and intimate relationship with Elliot that he enjoyed with Chambers.

The Departure of the "Old Breed" and the "Gignilliat Men"

In retrospect, these transitions were perhaps more significant in aggregate than they appeared individually. By the end of 1929, Gignilliat had lost five of his 11 direct reports. Greiner's death in December 1926 was still likely keenly felt, and the long-serving (25 years) Morale Officer, Howard Frank (H.F.) Noble, resigned in 1927.

The year 1928 brought the departures of former Dean of Cadets M. V. Bennett and Dr. P. J. Trentzsch, whom Gignilliat had employed as his Consultant in Mental Hygiene, along with the death of the long-serving Post Surgeon C. E. Reed on December 21, 1928. Combined with the retirement of Glascock as Headmaster in 1929, the death of ER Culver in October 1930, and the departure of Chambers in June 1931, it is fair to conclude that the members of "old Guard" upon whom Gignilliat had come to rely to run Culver with, for, and in his absence, were no longer present on campus by the early 1930s.[41]

The 1932 departure of Quartermaster W. M. Hand and the death of Harold C. Bays contributed further to the loss of Gignilliat's "old guard." Indeed, the departure of Hunt as Headmaster and the death of Stoutenburgh as his aide in 1935 completed the process of changeover for

Seven of the 1920s "Old Breed" of "Gignilliat Men." [42]

Gignilliat's "old guard" by the mid-1930s.

The loss of Chambers in 1931 pushed the level of change over the halfway point. A 1908 CMA graduate, Chambers came to Culver in 1922 as a liaison officer and quickly became Gignilliat's Executive Officer by the end of that year and by the time of Pershing's visit in late December 1922. Gignilliat's span of control involved 11 individuals, which was likely too large for him to manage on his own, and he relied upon the talents of the highly organized Chambers to manage them effectively.

Chambers' departure in 1931 was likely difficult for Gignilliat, as it upended the smooth-running operation he had created upon his return from WWI and upon which he had come to rely. It was also significant because it meant that Gignilliat was no longer heading his own ideal team to lead Culver, tipping the scales to the influence of the "new breed" of administrators and educators guiding CMA.

Given the scope and impact of the changes occurring during the period 1929-1932, it is perhaps no wonder that Gignilliat became run-down and fell ill again. One suspects that the insightful Minnie dreaded the impact this would have on her husband and perhaps even saw it coming.

Losing His Grip on Culver Marketing Efforts – Indicator of Waning Influence

With his genius for marketing, one of the places that Gignilliat's influence was present most consistently was in Culver's marketing material, especially since 1911 when he became superintendent. Since that time, Culver's marketing materials had reliably conveyed Gignilliat's core messages regarding the purpose and benefits of its unique military program that he was most responsible for developing and implementing. These messages included providing necessary structure, guidance, and purpose that was beneficial for boys; developing initiative; needing to be given properly and constructively; and that military training does not either dampen a boy's ingenuity or produce militaristic tendencies in them. The consistency of this messaging was as remarkable as it was unchanging for twenty years (1912-1932).

A study of Culver's marketing material reveals that around 1932, the standard messages of Gignilliat regarding the school's military system (training must be made real and given properly…) began to change, deviating from the main points he had been emphasizing since they coalesced in his own mind in the five years prior to American's entry into WWI and began instead to reflect a bit more ambiguity and flexibility.

According to the 1933 catalog, while *"Mr. Culver was not a military man…He saw in military training some of the moral equivalents of his own early battle with life. He sensed their need for the privileged boy, who, because of lack of necessity ordinarily had no such opportunity for the development of his sinews. For that reason he made the school military, and in that spirit the military training at Culver has been carried forward and adapted to educational needs."*[43]

Gignilliat's ideas for how Culver's military training should be *"carried forward and adapted to educational needs"* held sway during Culver's first three decades of existence (the period 1897-1927); however, as it entered its fourth decade in the mid-1930s, there began to be questions as to whether Gignilliat's methods remained the best way for Culver to do so. Indeed, many of the very educators brought to the school by Gignilliat to keep in the Avant Garde (e.g., Gregory supported by JS Fleet from the old guard, and, increasingly, Cal Chambers) were most responsible for fostering this reexamination. Their own ideas were validated and confirmed by many external experts and consultants brought to Culver during this period by Gignilliat, who believed and hoped that they would substantiate his own ideas and approach.

It is important to note that this development coincided with the beginning of decline in enrollment at Culver, starting in 1931 and becoming quite pronounced by 1933, when total enrollment dropped to about half of what it had been before the stock market crash of 1929. This decline in enrollment resulted in a substantial tuition reduction from $1,500 to $1,100 in 1935.

While there is not sufficient evidence to establish a legitimate cause-and-effect relationship, it appears that Culver's "tried and true" methods that had worked for three decades were losing their effectiveness and needed to change with the times and be adapted to the needs of a new generation of boys. The 1935 *CMA Catalog* reflects this trend in the following statement:

> *"The training that was effective with the boy of a generation or so ago, for whom riding a bicycle was the zenith of action, cannot hold the interest of the boy today, who drives an automobile and longs for an airplane."*[44]

Looking to the future, the catalog stated that Culver:

> *"..offers to boys of today the best of the old in tradition and seasoned experience coupled with the thoroughly tested new in procedures, developed from modern research in educational methods."*[45]

These statements suggest that a changing of the guard was occurring at Culver as much in its approach and system as in its educators and administrator.

Making Movies at Culver

Despite the school's literature looking forward, the most visible media efforts related much more to Culver's past. There were three motion pictures made about Culver during the period 1927-1939, two of which were filmed on campus.

Prep and Pep – A 1928 Silent Movie

The movie, *Prep and Pep*, was a silent picture filmed at Culver during the final two weeks of the 1927 -1928 winter school session and, according to Gignilliat, became known to the cadets as "The Battle Creek Serial."[46] The plot of the movie involved a bashful, timid 17-year-old boy coming to his father's *alma mater* and struggling to live up to his father's reputation. The boy's father was considered to be the school's finest athlete, but the son discovers that he possessed other gifts. After failing on the athletic field, the boy finds success with horses and earns his way into the school's prestigious cavalry, thus establishing his own identity and reputation.

While Culver is not referred to directly the film is dedicated to Culver Military Academy, and a contemporary review referred to the picture as being a "thrilling story" of the "famous Culver Military School." Released on November 18, 1928, both the filming and the premier were exciting events, but the movie had little impact on Culver. Reaction to the film on campus was decidedly negative especially among the cadets, who felt that it portrayed CMA as being too "soft" and referred to it derisively as "The Battle Creek Serial."[47]

PREP AND PEP

FOX MOVIETONE FULL-LENGTH FEATURE
with

DAVID ROLLINS *and* NANCY DREXEL
Young Love and High Jinks at Prep School

THE PERFECT FEATURE FOR THE HOLIDAYS

Produced by DAVID BUTLER
the man who made
THE HIGH SCHOOL HERO

Prep and Pep *movie poster.*[48]

Tom Brown of Culver – A Triumph

While the first movie had little impact on Culver, the same cannot be said for the next movie, *Tom Brown of Culver*. The filming of this picture was much more of a significant event at Culver, and the resulting movie had a far larger impact on the school. Involving virtually the entire Culver community, the 10-day filming schedule in May 1932 (with the crew residing on campus in the open-air barrack) was as disruptive as it was exhausting.

Determined to get each aspect of the CMA experience as close to right as possible, the leadership threw themselves into every aspect of the production. So much extra footage was shot that Gignilliat later remarked that 300,000 feet of film was shot but only 7,000 feet of it was used in the final cut of the picture.

Gignilliat contributed to the stirring finale, filmed at the Soldiers and Sailors Monument in Indianapolis, by arranging for a number of American Legion posts to provide their color guards and drum and bugle units to participate in the scene and add to the background of it. Gignilliat entertained the cast in their quarters, and Minnie became particularly impressed with one of the unknown young actors named Tyrone Power.[49]

To ensure the project's fidelity, Culver retained final script approval. In addition, Gignilliat sent Rossow to Hollywood for several weeks to supervise the off-campus filming. Reflecting Gignilliat's own attention to detail, Rossow brought uniforms made at Culver and two cadet wardrobes with him to ensure the authenticity of the cadet rooms for the picture. He also drilled

Colonel Rossow (left) in Hollywood on the set of Tom Brown of Culver.[50]

Tom Brown of Culver *movie poster.*[53]

the high school ROTC cadets being used as extras to ensure they represented the high standard of Culver as nearly as possible. It becomes easy to see why Gignilliat had such confidence in Rossow during this period.

The resulting picture was a triumph for both Culver and for the film itself, which was released on July 1, 1932, to excellent reviews.[51] The story was so well done that the final movie about Culver, *The Spirit of Culver*, released in 1939, was essentially a remake of the 1932 picture.

Premiered at Culver on July 15, 1932, the picture was "enthusiastically received by the capacity crowd." According to a review appearing in the *Culver Citizen*, "the film not only gave excellent views of the academy and ably depicted the molding of a boy's life, but the acting was of the highest type," "the directing of the picture was unusually good," and "the theme kept the interest of the audience at a high point throughout."[52]

Coming just as enrollment was beginning to decline at Culver, it also provided some welcome publicity, useful for increasing awareness of the school across the country and to a new generation of boys.

Physical Challenges: Illness, November 1933 – April 1934

Gignilliat's health was beginning to fail in late 1933. He developed a sinus infection in late November 1933 that settled into a deep chest cold that he could not shake. After suffering for two weeks, he determined that his illness was so severe that he had to reschedule a ceremony by the Italian government to knight him at Culver for his work with FIDAC. Determined to recover,

Gignilliat being knighted at Culver in May 1934.[54]

he departed during the first week of December 1933 for Tucson, Arizona to recuperate in the warmer and drier climate of the southwest. Viewing this as his first vacation in two years, Gignilliat intended to return shortly after Christmas. However, his recovery did not occur as rapidly as he had hoped. Concerned for her husband, and perhaps fearing a reoccurrence of his illness in the mid-1920s, Minnie joined him two weeks later.

The couple took up residence in a small, rustic cottage just outside of Phoenix, Arizona, where they remained until mid-April 1934. However, during this period, Gignilliat was not entirely incapacitated. He traveled from Arizona to Chicago in mid-January 1934 for a CMEF meeting and remained in fairly constant contact with George C. Marshall regarding their work with the CMEF, including exploring the possibility of creating a lobbying organization for the CMTC program in the wake of the War Department's 1933 funding cut to it.

Gignilliat also remained in contact with Pershing during this period, suggesting that he may have been quite ill but not completely incapacitated, and that his absence from Culver during this period may have been a repeat of Minnie's influence during his previous period of illness in the mid-1920s when she essentially took over the direction of his daily activities and became his personal "chief of staff," especially after he tried to return to duty at Culver in early 1935 and was told to return to Arizona for four to six weeks to recover fully.

By the time he returned to Culver in mid-April, he was able to resume his normal duties. However, he returned to campus looking ghastly, old, fragile, and even more gaunt than usual.

Despite his diminished appearance, the knighting ceremony was something special. The ceremony took place at Culver on Sunday, May 13, 1934, at which Gignilliat was actually "knighted" by the Italian consul for Indianapolis, Dr. Vincent Lapenta, on behalf of the King of Italy (Victor Emmanuel III and not Mussolini).[55] This represented his public installation into an Italian honor organization of those who made significant contributions to the benefit of humanity known as the "Crown of Italy" in the rank of "Knight Commander" for his "outstanding work as a solider and an educator" on behalf of FIDAC (which Italy supported).

Gignilliat was allowed to accept the honorary title (which was quite common after WWI) although he was not referred to as "Sir" Gignilliat (in keeping with the custom associated with being allowed to accept foreign honorary titles). It is hard to imagine anything that could have captured the imagination of boys more completely than this ceremony, and being led by a general who had actually been knighted became and remained a great source of pride for cadets and the entire Culver community.

Looking at him in the photo (and in the video of the ceremony that also exists[56]), Gignilliat appears drawn, pale, and old, showing clearly that the illness had taken quite a toll of him physically. According to Marshall, who had seen him in both January and May of 1934, Gignilliat looked much better by then, although he still needed to regain some weight. Despite his recovery, this episode must have surely concerned both the Culver family and the members of the CEF Board. Seeing how gaunt he had become and how much the illness had aged him at the knighting ceremony, the CEF Board took up the issue of succession in earnest and began efforts to identify a suitable successor for Gignilliat and get him in place as soon as possible.

Never one to remain idle for long, the indefatigable Gignilliat was able to squeeze in time for a visit to Purdue in May 1934 and felt well enough to discuss holding an ROTC gathering at Culver the following month.

Coming to a Head –
The Impact of the Organizational Unrest on Campus in 1934

During his prolonged absence from campus in late 1933 and early 1934, Gignilliat placed Rossow in charge (as mentioned previously). This decision had a disastrous impact on campus, exacerbating the struggle for control and influence on campus. According to Davies, Rossow mishandled many aspects of administration when placed in charge. As an example, and most egregiously, Rossow reinstituted "the Bull Ring" as standard punishment for cadets sometime in early 1934. Requiring cadets to march for specific periods of time carrying all of their field equipment and rifles during their rare free time, his decision was so upsetting because Gignilliat had ended this practice in the early 1920s at the behest of the faculty. While the faculty and most of the staff had been delighted by the curtailing of this disciplinary method, most of the military staff still supported the practice and likely lobbied Rossow for its return in Gignilliat's absence.

In fact, Rossow had not informed Gignilliat that he had done so, despite remaining in contact with Gignilliat during his absence. Gignilliat also remained in close correspondence with the consultant Moehlman during this period, who informed Gignilliat of the situation in a letter dated February 8, 1934 (while Gignilliat was still recovering in Arizona).

Moehlman was appalled by Rossow's actions for several reasons, including that it was a violation of Rossow's authority when acting in

Gignilliat's stead. When functioning in an "acting" capacity, one was expected to make the decisions Gignilliat would have made and not his own (since he was not in command). Rossow's decision was also quite detrimental to the learning process at Culver. This method was understandably (and perhaps rightly) detested by cadets, and Moehlman reported hearing "vulgar and profane" comments under their breaths when he walked close enough to the cadets in the Bull Ring.

Moehlman determined (as have many other educators since) that "the boys were not being disciplined in any effective sense of the word by this practice and were instead gaining a 'thorough distaste for military life'" that was antithetical to both Culver's educational approach and military system and an anathema to Gignilliat and his intent for Culver's military system. He concluded that Rossow's action was "thoroughly out of step with recent tendencies and institutional changes at Culver," and he pleaded with Gignilliat to address the situation immediately.

Gignilliat was distressed by this news (perhaps hearkening back to being excluded from the information regarding Skyland Camps), and he contacted his Executive Officer, Colonel Elliot (now functioning as the Post Adjutant in yet another organizational change) via letter on February 12, 1934. Gignilliat directed Elliot to "take the matter up in a tactful manner with Rossow" as soon as practicable, informing Rossow that Gignilliat did not support this decision and wanted it to cease immediately.[57] Rossow's ascendance had been based on Gignilliat's respect and admiration for him as a solider, but both must have been damaged seriously by this episode. It also likely exacerbated Gignilliat's own feeling of having been out of touch with what was occurring on campus during his absence.

This situation represented a regression back to the old way of doing things at Culver that many considered to be no longer acceptable, and it brought up the greatest fears of many on campus determined to transform Culver along the lines of the recommendations of the consultants. It also highlighted the need for clearer guidance for the formal hierarchy on campus and the succession of command in the absence of the superintendent. While this was a matter that had been left to the superintendent's discretion during the time of the Culver family's ownership and direct oversight of the school, the new governance model of the CEF Board no longer supported such practices, which needed to be considered, formalized, and written into policy by the CEF Board.

Prelude to Gignilliat's Dénouement

The Age of the Consultants, during the period 1929-1934, saw the end of the "old" Culver and beginning of period of significant change for the school. While impacting many aspects of the institution, this period had specific and explicit impacts on Gignilliat, both personally and professionally.

Moehlman's final report in November 1934 was the culmination of the Age of the Consultants. With the submission of Moehlman's final report in November 1934, the Age of the Consultants came to an end at Culver. Gignilliat's hold on the institution had been weakened as a result, but there was no thought of replacing him. Rather, the concern about developing a succession plan for him became paramount. Culver was also preparing to launch it junior college.

This period also brought the twenty-year "Greater Culver" plan, and its accompanying efforts, to a close, and it ushered in the new "Culver Plan" to be implemented by Gignilliat's successor. The next chapter will address the process of identifying and installing a suitable successor, and the inevitable "changing of the guard" resulting from and accompanying this process.

Guest Poem as a Fitting Denouement for Gignilliat

Written by renowned poet Edgar Guest in 1930 just after Gignilliat had reached his second "peak" and at the very beginning of the Age of the Consultants, the poem captures the reverence and esteem Gignilliat had earned from the community since his arrival on campus in 1897. Guest's work was tremendously popular in the 1930s, and he was renowned at the time as being the "People's Poet" for his uncanny ability to convey the wonder of everyday life. It is noteworthy that he was sufficiently inspired by the remarkable impression Gignilliat made on him during a brief visit to campus. The work's three stanzas capture the "splendid truth" of Gignilliat's actions and example as only poetry can. It also has the feel of a valedictory that presaged a wonderful and natural exit for Gignilliat.

General L. R. Gignilliat
By Edgar A. Guest

NEVER MIND THAT NAME OF HIS,
    PRONOUNCE IT HOW YOU WILL.
THOUGH YOU WRITE HIM FORTY LETTERS
    YOU MAY SPELL IT WRONGLY STILL.
HE HAS SEEN THE SMOKE OF BATTLE,
    HE HAS SEEN BRAVE SOLDIERS DIE
AND THERE'S MANY A TIME THEY'VE CAUGHT
    HIM WITH A TEAR–DROP IN HIS EYE.
FOR THAT HEART OF HIS IS TENDER,
    AND THAT DREAM OF HIS IS FINE
AND YOU'LL FIND HIS FAME AT CULVER,
    NOT ALONG THE BATTLE LINE.

OH, HIS LIFE IS WRAPPED IN BOYHOOD,
    IN THEIR MISCHIEF IN THEIR PLAY;
HE WELCOMES THEM AS YOUNGSTERS
    AND AS MEN SENDS THEM AWAY.
ON HIS SLEEVES ARE STRIPES OF SERVICE,
    THERE ARE RIBBONS ON HIS BREAST,
BUT THE GLORY OF HIS RECORD CANNOT
    EASILY BE GUESSED,
FOR HIS INFLUENCE IS MARCHING
    IN AN ENDLESS LINE OF YOUTH
AND HIS VICTORIES ARE MANY
    ON THE BATTLEFIELD OF TRUTH.

OH, I STOOD WITH HIM AT CULVER,
    AND THE MIST WAS IN HIS EYE
AS THOSE MANLY YOUNGSTERS PASSED HIM
    AND HE BADE THEM ALL GOOD–BYE.
AND I THOUGHT SOME LIVE IN BUILDINGS
    WHICH THEIR SKILL AND WEALTH HAVE
    REARED,
AND SOME PUT WORDS ON PAPER,
    AND THEIR MEMORIES ARE REVERED,
SOME FIND IN WEALTH BRIEF SPLENDOR,
    BUT A MATCHLESS FAME HAS HE
WHO GIVES HIS LIFE TO BOYHOOD AND THE
    MEN THOSE BOYS WILL BE.

Chapter 18 – The Denouement: Gignilliat's Final Years at Culver, 1935-1942.

The tremendous energy released by the self-study and the Harvard report during the first half of the 1930s upset the façade of serenity on campus and began a period of significant change for Gignilliat. Combined with the challenges of the Great Depression, this period might be described as one in which Gignilliat was in the unusual position of reacting more to changes at Culver than initiating and/or precipitating them.

In addition, Gignilliat's physical appearance after his illness and upon his return after his extended absence from campus during the period December 1933 -- April 1934 shocked the other members of the CEF Board, causing them to think seriously for the first time of a Culver without Gignilliat as its head. In response, and as one of its more important early actions, the CEF Board began developing a succession plan for CMA's superintendent.

Gignilliat with his beloved dog Mussolini (Moussi) in his beloved garden at the beloved Superintendent's Quarters at his beloved Culver.[1]

A "Changing of the Guard" Begins at Culver -- Rossow and Hunt Relieved

While motivated by the circumstances mentioned above, attending to the matter of Gignilliat's succession at Culver was also a prudent measure for the CEF Board to consider. This issue was addressed by the external consultants examining Culver during the Age of the Consultants, bringing even more attention to it. Taking action on this issue would be consistent with the advice offered by the consultants to begin replacing the older heads with younger men who were more steeped in practices of "modern" education and possessing of the energy required to keep pace with adolescent boys and the increasingly challenging demands of secondary education.

The process of replacing older department heads began rather abruptly, with doing so for Culver's two main departments – the academic and military departments – in June 1935. The *beau ideal* but controversial military man Rossow was replaced as Commandant of Cadets by the more bookish-looking and relatively sedate Charles F. McKinney. Three months later, at the beginning of the 1935-1936 winter school session, the venerable but somewhat ineffective Hunt was replaced as Dean of the Faculty by the energetic and well-credentialed William E. Gregory.

Ostensibly, Rossow was rotated out to head the summer Woodcraft Camp, and Hunt was replaced to allow him to focus his efforts on developing Culver's nascent (and short-lived) junior college. However, it was quite clear that there was more to it than the justification let on, and it represented the beginning of what became a wholesale "changing of the guard." The perceptive (and quite disappointed) Rossow corroborated this aspect in his memoirs, writing that his transition was a deliberate decision related to succession to bring in new blood as the heads of the academic and military departments while Gignilliat was still around.[2]

This particular change was also significant because it was not initiated by Gignilliat, as had been the practice at Culver since HH Culver made the decision to replace the Superintendent / Commandant in fall 1896. As the most significant personnel changes in over two decades since then, it was notable that they were not directed by Gignilliat himself but instead by the CEF Board. Rossow provides corroborating evidence that Gignilliat was directed to make these changes when relating how Gignilliat broke the news to him that he was being replaced as Commandant. It is worth quoting Rossow directly to convey the gravity and nuance of this episode.

Several days after receiving a very official-looking document from the Superintendent's office informing him that he was to be relieved as Culver's Commandant of Cadets (the same documents Hunt received informing him that he was to be replaced as the Dean of Faculty), a stunned and bewildered Rossow was called to Gignilliat's office for a face-to-face discussion about the situation. It turned out that Rossow's wife, Ethel, unable to bear her husband's suffering any longer, informed Gignilliat about how much this decision had hurt the proud but privately vulnerable Rossow (who would never think to question the decision of his highly respected superior on his own).

When he arrived, Rossow was surprised by the "grief-stricken look" in Gignilliat's "kindly eyes."

According to Rossow, the meeting proceeded as follows :

> "'Bobby,' he said, with harrowed feeling showing in every line
> in his thin, aesthetic face, 'this had been the hardest job that has
> ever confronted me. It is my fault that you were notified of this
> by letter. The board of directors – Mr.[B.B.] Culver especially
> – wanted to send for you and tell you about this necessary act,
> face to face,' he paused, then and smiled gently, 'knowing your
> violent temper, as I think I have every reason to know, I warned
> them against telling you of this face to face. I was afraid that
> you'd blow up – that you'd say things that couldn't be recalled –
> and that; then, ever thing (sic) would be over."[3]

The manner in which Gignilliat informed Rossow of his relief was
compassionate, and it also helped Rossow understand the organizational
rationale for the action. While this was a convenient explanation that
partially accounted for it, it is also highly likely that Rossow's own
behavior as Commandant (mentioned previously) had contributed to this
outcome as well.

A "Changing of the Guard" -- Gregory Replacing Gignilliat

As momentous as these changes were, the most significant result was
the decision to identify and prepare a replacement for Gignilliat himself.
While there were several well-qualified individuals to consider (e.g., J. S.
Fleet, Allen Elliott, etc.), Gregory was the clear and consensus choice by
all involved in this decision.

The plan developed by the CEF Board was both effective and efficient. It
involved installing Gregory as Culver's chief academic officer in fall 1935
and allowing him to serve in this capacity for five years, during which he
could be apprenticed, developed, and prepared to replace Gignilliat in
July 1940, when Gignilliat turned 65 years of age and was no longer able
to continue serving on the CMA staff (according to Culver's own policies).

This approach also had the added benefit of allowing Gregory to begin
taking on some of Gignilliat's tasks, reducing Gignilliat's work load to
make it more manageable and allowing him to focus on the things he did
particularly well – alumni relations, marketing, and public relations. This
aspect of the plan was all the more attractive to the members of the CEF
Board after being shocked by how much the illness has aged the General
and diminished his storied capacity for hard work (some of which may
have been the result of Minnie's influence).

In Gignilliat's mind, this transition would be gradual and involve the type of close mentoring he had used with Greiner when preparing him to become the new Commandant of Cadets back in 1911-1912. Believing that the Culver system he had developed and implemented was largely effective and required only minor adjustments, Gignilliat's idea for the transition period was that it would be smooth and comprised of measured and incremental changes thoroughly considered and discussed by the two men before being implemented that would do little to upset the equilibrium and harmony on campus he treasured so greatly.

However, the more ambitious, headstrong, and somewhat impatient Gregory had other ideas. As he had shown by his leadership during the Age of Consultants and in helping Culver develop and implement its response to the Harvard group's recommendations, he was lacking in neither ideas nor the willingness to take action. He also felt exceptionally and especially prepared to function in his new role, having just completed a year of study at Harvard's prestigious Graduate School of Education. In addition, he believed that the time for making more substantial changes at Culver was overdue, and he was anxious to begin implementing the ideas and policies he had been developing on his own and discussing with others for nearly a decade. It was a fortuitous convergence of opportunity and ability for both the individual and the institution, and Gregory was determined to act decisively to take advantage of it.

Acting under the CEF Board's specific directive to reduce Gignilliat's workload by assuming responsibility for the routine and day-to-day operations of CMA, and according to his own desire to take advantage of his new role to bring about necessary changes to the institution quickly, Gregory proceeded decisively in his new role and in the same manner that Gignilliat had done when he became superintendent. Gregory's approach was quite different from what Gignilliat had envisioned, and Gignilliat had never had a subordinate at Culver who challenged him in this manner. Gignilliat's desire to avoid confrontation and maintain harmony among his senior staff, along with his inexperience in dealing with such an aggressive subordinate, resulted in him responding by doing little else but providing support and going along with Gregory.

Gregory's approach was likely best for Culver, but the result, intended or otherwise, was that Gignilliat was not afforded the gradual and collegial transition period he envisioned. Rather, Gignilliat was respectfully but decidedly pushed aside, as the new breed took over and assumed responsibility for directing Culver almost immediately upon Gregory's elevation to the position of Dean of the Faculty in September 1935. While he retained the decision-making authority appropriate for the Superintendent, this organizational change institutionalized the Superintendent-Headmaster-Commandant approach in that it essentially (and rightfully, from the CEF Board's perspective) removed the Superintendent (as the chief executive officer) from direct involvement in the routine decisions of the Headmaster/Dean of the Faculty and Commandant of Cadets (who functioned collectively as the chief operating officers).

Shortly, and in accordance with the CEF Board's desires, Gregory was identified as the Dean of the Academy, and he became Culver's Chief Operating Officer with authority to direct the actions of all others except the Superintendent. This placed the Commandant in an officially subordinate role, which would not have worked with Rossow as Commandant. However, this new arrangement worked quite well for the more amenable McKinney as Commandant (suggesting another motive for Rossow's somewhat sudden relief as Commandant).

A Changed Role as Superintendent

Under this new organizational arrangement, Gignilliat had more time to focus on the things he did particularly well -- alumni relations, marketing, and public relations – just as the CEF Board intended. However, this was a somewhat strange situation for him, as he had never functioned as the head of the institution with such responsibilities while being largely divorced from the day-to-day operations of the school. His strength had always been as an operational leader who focused on the routine operations of Culver. In addition, the level of autonomy afforded to Gregory was also quite different from how his previous subordinates had operated, and he had become accustomed to being both consulted on and

deferred to with respect to important decisions regarding Culver. As a result, this new role was quite a change that required some significant adjustments for him.

The role was new for Gregory as well. Relying on his training as a military officer, Gregory's approach was to treat Gignilliat as the executive leader and

With Minnie having a portrait painted on campus.

general officer he was. This meant presenting Gignilliat with decisions to endorse rather than issues to discuss and ponder. While this approach was very much in line with Gregory's training as an Army officer with respect to interacting effectively with general officers and reflective of existing business practices regarding dealing effectively with executives, it was also a very good way to reduce Gignilliat's workload and allow him to focus his energy and efforts on the most important aspects of the institution.

Nevertheless, Gregory's approach ran counter to how Gignilliat had become accustomed to operating for almost four decades at Culver, and it had the effect of leaving Gignilliat feeling disconnected, left out, and marginalized. While this was likely not the intent of Gregory and others, who were more focused on doing their best to help Culver navigate through the challenges of the Great Depression and implement the changes coming from the Age of the Consultants, it couldn't have been easy for Gignilliat to accept and remain effective.

As one indicator of his marginalization, Gignilliat was away from campus for over seven weeks at the end of December 1936 to early February 1937. Traveling widely in the Southeast with Minnie during the period December 18, 1936, to February 5, 1937, Gignilliat made stops in Washington, DC, Georgia, South Carolina, and Florida. While he was routinely away from campus for up to six weeks when traveling internationally on behalf of FIDAC, the previous leadership team at Culver understood that he wanted to remain involved in the decision-making process regarding routine matters at Culver and facilitated this approach.

Gregory and the new leadership team had no such understanding and were not interested in sustaining such an approach. In the view of Gregory, functioning officially as the Acting Superintendent in Gignilliat's absence, he had the responsibility and authority for making the decisions that were within his purview and did so. While there is no indication that Gregory ever acted counter to what he knew to be Gignilliat's wishes (as Rossow had done when re-instituting the "Bull Ring" as punishment for cadets in Gignilliat's absence), it was also the case that many decisions were made on campus about which he was largely unaware. This situation added to and exacerbated Gignilliat's feelings of being increasingly sidelined.

It is also somewhat remarkable to note that this absence from campus for such an extended period of time was essentially a personal vacation that was unprecedented. One suspects that this was largely the result of

Minnie's influence, but this absence may have also been indicative of his need to remove himself from the situation in the face of his mounting feelings of marginalization. Going out on the road enabled him to engage in alumni relations and public relations efforts, allowing him to feel useful and make contributions he felt were both of value and within his new scope of responsibilities.

Changes Bring About an Alumni Crisis of Confidence

It became clear almost immediately that Gregory's changes began addressing the balance between academics and the military, as he intended. Gregory supported Culver's military program completely, but he had become convinced that the military program retained a level of influence it no longer warranted or was necessary to sustain its status as a distinguished military school. The overemphasis on the military – in the assessment of Gregory and others – was also no longer desirable in terms of achieving the institution's overall goals. Accordingly, and with his authority as the fully empowered deputy on campus superior to all others (including the Commandant), Gregory's first acts involved adjusting the existing balance between the military and academics.

While Gignilliat had needed to marshal the efforts of the entire school to achieve the coveted "distinguished military school" designation at the beginning of the 20th century, changes to the US military program since then, and especially since the end of WWI, meant that this level of effort was no longer necessary to retain this designation. Prior to WWI, the Army had imposed strict limits restricting this designation to the top ten percent of all schools with Army officers assigned to them to conduct military training. The number of such institutions was small – around 120 – which meant that the number of schools that could achieve such a designation was quite small – around a dozen or fewer institutions. However, in the aftermath of the National Defense Act of 1916 (establishing ROTC), the end of the WWI, and the National Defense Act of 1920 (expanding the ROTC program), the number of ROTC programs grew exponentially. This meant that Culver had a relatively easier time sustaining its status as one of the nation's distinguished military schools, since the number of designations increased by a factor of two or three in the post-WWI period.

Gignilliat believed that sustaining Culver's focus on its unique military program was desirable as an end unto itself, even if it was no longer necessary to sustain its distinguished military school designation. It was his nature to design systems to achieve what he wanted, which often involved significant changes and innovation, but then to sustain the systems and resist efforts to change them unless and/or until he was convinced of the rationale to do so. This represented an intriguing combination of progressive and conservative tendencies that both contributed to his success and also frustrated others at Culver.

In the assessment of Gregory and others (especially JS Fleet), however, the changed situation referred to above meant that Culver did not have to devote such an enormous effort to retaining its status as a distinguished military school and could do so with relatively less effort while also sustaining its status as one of the nation's premier military schools. The reduced effort required in the military area thus freed up time to devote to academics, which had become increasingly important during the Depression and desired by parents as a return on their investment from Culver. Fully empowered to proceed as he saw fit, Gregory began making such changes at Culver and implementing them during his first two years as Dean during the 1935-1936 and 1936-1937 winter school sessions.

Gregory's Changes Elicit Alumni Concerns – A First for Culver

While fully warranted in Gregory's own mind and in those of his supporters, and justified on the grounds of doing what was required to keep Culver on the forefront of adolescent education in the country, these changes had a very different impact on other constituencies, especially the alumni. The substance and impact of them caused some alumni to become concerned about the well-being of Culver's military program, which, during their time as cadets, was of paramount concern on campus. Gignilliat (who perhaps privately shared some of their concerns) likely began hearing about alumni concerns during his travels in late-1936 and early 1937, and word of the alumni concerns likely continued to filter into his office upon his return to campus and throughout the remainder of the spring 1937 winter school session.

One dynamic that arises within high-performing organizations is a certain level of pride in the difficulty of becoming and remaining a member of it, even when some of the difficulty may not be entirely necessary to the process. Such a feeling tends to become more pronounced the longer one is away from the institution and heightened when the sanctity of the process comes under scrutiny, is questioned by outsiders, or appears to be threatened by changes to it.

Culver certainly qualifies as high-performing organization, making it reasonable to assume that such a dynamic applied to its alumni at this time. The tremendous level of changes in personnel and polices in the mid-1930s appear to have triggered this dynamic among its alumni, creating a crisis of confidence among the alumni and which required Gignilliat's direct and personal involvement to resolve.

Reviewing the relevant literature of this period, the following concerns about Culver become apparent:

- Gignilliat being marginalized

- Gregory's changes

- McKinney's kinder and gentler approach

- Overall impact on Culver's military system.

Some of this came from the noticeably reduced number of references and attention to Gignilliat and his actions in contemporary Culver publications during the 1920s (which were substantially less than during the pre-WWI period), suggesting, and perhaps even conveying, that Gignilliat was functioning in a more ceremonial role at this point in his career. The revered "old man" made appearances at important occurrences and for alumni events, but his influence in and on the substantive aspects of running CMA was no longer nearly as evident as it had been in the pre-WWI era.

However, during his travels and upon his return to campus in early 1937, he must have become aware that there was concern arising among the alumni that his diminished role in the school's daily operations, combined with the changes being implemented by Gregory, might have been (or perhaps was actually) having an adverse impact on the system he had spent his life developing and that was so ingrained in the institution and cherished by graduates.

Gignilliat decided to respond by addressing their concerns directly. He wrote a remarkable article for the *Culver Alumnus*, titled "Books and Bugles," that appeared as the lead article in the June 1937 edition. The main purpose of the article appears to have been to assuage fears that CMA's military program was being diminished in favor of academics. Gignilliat asserted that Culver was capable of being both an outstanding military school and a superb academic institution, and he reiterated that "the Culver Board of Directors believes emphatically in the benefits of military training for boys of preparatory school age," validating Culver's continued commitment to providing the very best military training for high school boys in the country.

Coming directly from the person responsible for creating the Culver military system and using brilliant rhetoric to make his case, most alumni were inclined to accept the judgment of the person at Culver they most respected. The article was a masterpiece in terms of achieving its intended purpose, and it showed how adept he had become at writing and how polished and effective his prose had become.

One wonders just how upset the alumni had become over the changes implemented during the year-and-a-half of Gregory's tenure as Dean of the Faculty, but the directness and tone of "Books and Bugles," along with its placement as the lead and feature article in the June 1937 edition of the *Culver Alumnus* magazine, suggests that alumni discontent had certainly become worrisome to some at Culver. The outcome also indicates that while Gregory may have better at navigating the new CEF Board governance system, he had not yet gained the trust of the alumni to the level achieved by Gignilliat, making the latter far more effective in alumni relations.

While Gignilliat largely diffused the alumni concerns with his timely article assuring them that the Culver system was still intact and effective, it is worth noting that this is perhaps the first time in Culver's history that its alumni had expressed such concerns. This makes this episode important on its own and worth exploring in greater depth.

The Revised Military Program

In "Books and Bugles," Gignilliat assured the alumni that there was no cause for concern that Culver was losing it military edge. He wrote that while the methods may be changing, the outcomes remained the same.

Gignilliat addressed the concerns of the alumni even more directly, reminding them that it was equally important to the CEF Board that Culver "maintain a place second to none in preparing boys for college and in excellence of scholarship," conveying the outcome of the institution's vision for its future as a result of the reflection and assessments of the Age of the Consultants. Being even more explicit, Gignilliat assured the alumni that the newly implemented six-day academic schedule still allowed for Saturday morning B.I. and Sunday morning

Gignilliat in his field uniform with Admiral Rodman – still influential.

G.I., occurring on alternating weeks, and that the standards for these inspections remained as high as ever, with rooms, rifles, and appearance achieving the established Culver standards despite having half as many inspections. In fact, the current corps of cadets was, if anything, more efficient and effective in attending to its military duties.

He defended the incorporation of academic requirements for cadet officers to hold and retain rank in the corps. Gignilliat also expressed his support for the discontinuance of "borrowing" time from academic hours for additional military preparations for big events and/or important ceremonies, assuring this constituency that the "leadership and soldierly bearing" of the cadet officers and the "snap and dash" of cadet drill had not diminished and remained reflective of Culver's high standards in these important areas of its military system.

In fact, Gignilliat informed the graduates that both the integration and balance between the military and academic programs were better than ever, emphasizing that "the military has lost nothing in esprit or performance" and had actually increased in terms of its educational effectiveness, allowing for the academic program to reach a standard "where it has nothing to apologize for in comparison with the top preparatory schools of the country." He cited the input he received from alumni returning to campus for visits as evidence to support his claims. Few, if any, alumni would doubt Gignilliat's word in such matters (which all knew were of utmost importance to him), and none were prepared to dispute his claims.

Somewhat tellingly, Gignilliat acknowledged that his practice of using time earmarked for academics to improve military performance for certain events was no longer going to be allowed, had been perhaps somewhat ill-advised previously, and that Culver's academic program had not been at the level of its military program and needed improvement to achieve parity. As a professional educator who was also a committed solider, Gregory was ideally suited to lead these efforts, and the alumni could be assured that Gregory would ensure that the distinctive Culver military system remained intact and would continue to produce the results to which the alumni had become accustomed in terms of performance and outcomes.

More specifically, Gignilliat wrote that, "cadet officers have learned that laxity in the performance of academic duties is just as much neglect of duty as laxity of military nature," and that "the rank and file (sic) respect academic standards that apply equally to captain and plebe." The latter point spoke directly to one of Gignilliat's most oft-cited benefits of using a military system within an educational institution: the "meritocracy" value of holding all to the same standards, regardless of their social station.

Addressing perhaps the alumni's greatest concern directly, Gignilliat wrote that, "In attaining these ends that there have been no sudden or violent changes of policy inaugurated by some administrative officer" (almost surely an oblique reference to Gregory), taking responsibility by assuring all concerned that the changes occurring on campus had originated with his own recommendation to the Board that Culver conduct a comprehensive survey of its entire educational program and that the deliberation and decisions that came as a result during the five-year period that followed (referred to here as the Age of the Consultants).

The resulting program and strategic plan – the Culver Plan – had been very effective at improving the school, allowing it to be even more selective in its admissions and retention decisions, and ensuring that it remained among the very best college preparatory schools in the nation. Speaking directly to alumni concerns as parents, Gignilliat assured them that their sons enrolling at Culver would continue to get the "stiffening of fibre (sic), the poise, and self-confidence" by and from its military system while also being well prepared to succeed in college within an environment of "discipline and hardihood so essential in this complex world" and valued by Culver grads.

Gignilliat also pointed out that Culver had made the deliberate decision to forgo possible revenue by limiting its enrollment to ensure that its resources and means were sufficient to maintain the standards for its enrolled cadets. This may have been more indicative of the tremendous reduction in faculty (- 40) that had occurred over the most recent years, almost certainly resulting in the departure of instructors who were familiar if not also beloved by the cadets.

He closed by citing from a letter he received from a pacifist mother who had been quite skeptical of the Culver approach but who, upon witnessing its impact on her own son, became the staunchest supporter of it. It is worth noting that the rise of pacifism/anti-militarism in the 1920s had been viewed as one of the most worrisome threats to Culver specifically and American military schools more generally. Gignilliat had spent much time and effort in the 1920s countering their concerns on behalf of both Culver and AMCUS, so this aspect was of particular relevance to him.

Gignilliat's conclusion is worth presenting in its entirety, and it does well identifying the most important issues he addressed and concerns he hoped to allay.

"In conclusion may I say to the many thousands of alumni whose interest in Culver continues so gratifyingly unabated, that I have never felt happier over the Culver outlook, never more confident of Culver's ultimate destiny, never more confident that to achieve that destiny the maintenance of the distinctive excellence of Culver's military training is as essential as its constant striving for the top place in scholarship among the preparatory schools of the country. Let no Alumnus feel anxiety lest the bugle call of the military tradition of snap, precision, duty, discipline will disappear or sound less clearly on the Culver campus of the tomorrows."

The final sentence is as masterful as it is elegant in speaking to the basest concerns of alumni with respect to changes being implemented allowing academics to supersede Culver's military system

This was, in its entirety, a full-throated statement of support for the changes occurring at Culver and the new program that was emerging as a result that established a new level of integration and balance between the military and academic programs that was every bit as effective as the previous program had been in terms of the military and even more so in terms of academics. It was quite magnanimous of Gignilliat to take responsibility for the changes occurring at Culver by saying that the y originated with decision he made as far back as 1929, and it was also an unalloyed show of support for Gregory and his efforts, despite the fact that many/much of them occurred without much opportunity from Gignilliat to comment on them or have the opportunity to dissent (as they were presented largely as *faits accompli* to him).

Concerns about McKinney and His Approach as the New Commandant

Alumni concerns were not solely focused on changes being made by Gregory. Another source of concern appears to have stemmed from what appeared to some as a more gentle approach to discipline adopted by Rossow's successor, Charles F. McKinney. The Culver Legion Board of Visitors, which had been directed the previous year to make several visits to observe the activities of the school during its normal schedule of academic, military, and athletic activities (instead of during special periods, e.g., Thanksgiving, Easter, etc.) to get a better idea how it operates routinely, admitted as much in its report, which also appeared in the June 1937 Culver Alumnus magazine.

The report has this to say regarding the current status of the military program and discipline within the corps of cadets:

> *"An excellent standard is being maintained in the Military Department and we wish to commend Colonel McKinney and his wholesome attitude in enforcing rigid discipline and at the same time commanding the respect of the entire corps. The discipline is obviously of a more understanding nature than in the past. While life has been made a little more pleasant for cadets, they appear to be none the less manly because of this. They are receiving the same benefits at Culver as they ever have in the past plus a better cultural background, and far better academic training."[4]*

The phrases *"wholesome attitude," "obviously of a more understanding nature," "made life a little more pleasant," "appear to be none the less manly,"* and *"are receiving the same benefits at Culver as they ever have in the past"* are quite telling and indicate that they referred to the some of the most significant concerns of the alumni.

In its own 1937 assessment of the state of the corps of cadets, the Culver Legion Board of Visitors reported that:

> *"We think the spirit and appearance of the Corps are excellent, the best that they have been for many years. The boys are happy and enthusiastic and working remarkably well as a unit. This year's Corps of Cadets has an exceptionally high morale, is snappy in military appearance, and apparently as proficient in the military work as ever in the past. They appear happy yet serious-minded about the job at hand, are polite, and seemingly thoroughly full of the Culver Spirit."[5]*

It is significant that the report addressed the appearance and moral e of the cadets so directly and explicitly. The tone of this portion of the report suggests that it was in response to specific concerns expressed in these areas by alumni.

To provide some context, enrollment at Culver had reduced substantially beginning in 1929 when Rossow began asserting himself more forcefully on campus. Enrollment reached its nadir for the period at the beginning of the 1933-1934 winter school session and remained at this level for the 1934-1935 winter school session.

While much of this had to be attributed to the onset of the Great Depression, it was also almost certainly due to reduced levels of retention among the cadets. It is significant to note that enrollment increased substantially for the 1935-1936 winter school session, when tuition was reduced from $1,500 to $1,100. This tuition reduction also coincided with

Years	Total Boarding Students	Tuition	Faculty
1929–30	695	$1500	105
1930–31	646	$1500	107
1931–32	551	$1500	113
1932–33	402	$1500	103
1933–34	335	$1500	93
1934–35	335	$1500	73
1935–36	443	$1100	73
1936–37	551	$1100	82
1937–38	581	$1100	78
1938–39	605	$1100	84
1939–40	606	$1100	91

CMA enrollment and tuition figures, 1929-1940.[6]

the relief of Rossow as Commandant of Cadets and the appointment of McKinney as his replacement, who, Gignilliat acknowledge d, ushered in a "more understanding" type of discipline that made the lives of cadets "a little more pleasant" but remained nonetheless "manly."

Taken together, the evidence appears to suggest that Rossow's approach was not good for cadet morale and that cadets were not happy with his approach, despite his own high level of personal charisma. The reduced level of retention may have also been a proximate cause of the CEF Board's decision to reduce tuition for the 1935-1936 winter school session by $400 dollars (from $1,500 to $1,100), exacerbating its financial situation. If Rossow's approach did have an adverse impact on cadet retention (and perhaps enrollment), it would provide even more compelling rationale for his relief as Commandant of Cadets in summer 1935.

The direct and explicit nature of the Culver Legion Board of Visitors' comments indicate that it was responding to specific concerns of its constituency. While perhaps not as outwardly harsh, it also appears that McKinney's somewhat "kinder and gentler" approach to cadet discipline and performance was achieving the desired results (despite the initial skepticism of its ability to do so by some). As with Gignilliat's "Books and Bugles" article, this determination provided further support for Culver's new direction under Gregory's leadership.

Providing further validation, the results of the 1937 Arm annual inspection in mid-May (May 17-18) were excellent, resulting in Culver retaining its coveted designation as an "honor military school" for 1937 and thus appearing to corroborate the assessments that the changes were not having an adverse impact on its military program and/or performance. The CEF Board noted that the current cadets were *"apparently as proficient in their military work as ever in the past"* (emphasis added). That may have been the case, but it could also have been a reflection of less rigorous inspection standards that focused instead more on achieving satisfactory performance (as opposed to exemplary) and/or a reduction in the value of being designated as an "honor military school," as there was no longer a limitation placed upon the number of schools allowed to earn this distinction.

As mentioned previously, the designation as a distinguished military school was no longer as difficult to achieve as it had once been in terms of relative numbers, but it still represented the top ten percent of all ROTC programs in the country, which is impressive even if it was not quite at the level of the previous distinction. Growth during the interwar period required the Army to allocate more resources to ROTC than it desired (along with having to create JRTOC programs and also run the Civilian Conversation Corps (CCC)). In addition, the anti-militarism campaign brought unwanted attention.

By the mid-1930s, the Land-Grant Association (which had partnered with the Army during the pre-WWI period to help create the ROTC program) determined that the Army had become largely "indifferent" to the ROTC program.[7] Nevertheless, while educator and cadet support for the program as an elective course of study was down from its peak in the early 1920s and no longer supported compulsory military training as a graduate requirement, one historian concluded that by the mid-1930s "the universities supported ROTC much more intensely than the Army did."[8] The same could be said for Culver during this period.

The Revised Academic Program

Changes in the classroom may have also elicited concerns from alumni, as the faculty no longer wore uniforms, which would be difficult for alumni to accept and might have led them to conclude that the school had "gone soft" and was losing its military character and edge.

Turning its attention to academics, the Culver Legion Board of Visitors report lauded both the new faculty members and academic program in terms of how cadets were being instructed.

In particular, the report noted that the barriers between instructors and cadets that had existed previously had been removed (perhaps as a result of the faculty no longer being in uniform) and that cadets were now being taught to think instead of simply memorizing information. This assessment suggests that taking the faculty out of uniform and promoting more engaging forms of instruction (two reforms championed by Gregory) were having the desired effects of creating better and more meaningful relationships between instructors and cadets.

The Overall Impact of "Books and Bugles"

What becomes clear is that the alumni expressed a crisis of confidence in the new approach and mobilized their resources to convey its concerns to the administration and to conduct its own inspections to see for itself and make its own determination. Culver responded by employing its "big gun" in Gignilliat to respond to its concerns. While his assessment was largely unimpeachable, the corroborating evidence offered by the Culver Legion Board of Visitors further reinforced the General's assessment, likely helping to ameliorate much of the anxiety expressed by the alumni.

Preparing to Retire

As Gignilliat became increasingly sidelined by Gregory regarding the Academy's day-to-day operations, the Culver family became increasingly worried about the succession of the leadership of the CEF Board in the latter third of the 1930s. While he retained the respect of the members of the CEF Board, Gignilliat's "Books and Bugles" article may well have been the catalyst for them to begin thinking of Gignilliat as a possible successor to BB Culver as the CEF Board president.

In the wake of the 1937 crisis of confidence he (very presidentially) helped to alleviate, Gignilliat took time to visit his failed Skyland Camps location with Minnie one final time in September 1938. It was perhaps a fitting venture, as Gignilliat's actions during this period indicate that he was preparing to retire in 1940 as planned. Nevertheless, he retained considerable influence in some areas.

One example of how he exerted his considerable influence occurred at the very end of his time as superintendent and in an area in which he excelled: marketing. Hollywood decided that it was time to remake *Tom Brown of Culver*, and Gignilliat assigned himself the role played by Rossow during the production of the previous film, spending several weeks away from campus in Hollywood during 1939 as the new movie's on-set technical advisor (along with a recent CMA graduate who

Gignilliat and Minnie in campus garden.[9]

functioned as the drill master for the extras). However, the cast never quite attained the level of discipline or proficiency that Gignilliat would have liked (perhaps not surprisingly!).

Much like Gignilliat's time at Culver during this period (1935-1942), there was little new in the *Spirit of Culver*, and it essentially rehashed *Tom Brown of Culver* with a new cast and a bit more flash, hearkening back to Culver's "glory days" of the 1920s. Starring newcomers Freddie Bartholomew, Andy Devine, and Jackie Cooper, the 1939 remake may have been a bit more polished but many at Culver felt that it lacked the charm of the 1932 original film.

Whereas Gignilliat had always been willing to prioritize military ceremonies over academics, it is indicative of the changes that had occurred on campus in that the decision was made to film the remake on a reconstructed set in Hollywood to avoid disrupting the operation of the school. While this decision accomplished its objective and the production values may have been a bit improved by it, *The Spirit of Culver* was nowhere nearly as impactful for Culver as the 1932 original film version had been, suggesting in yet another way that the Gignilliat era at Culver was coming to a graceful, if inevitable, close.

The Spirit of Culver poster.[10]

Culver's New Power Trio -- Gregory, Elliott, and McKinney

The elevation of Gregory to Dean of the Faculty/Academy and McKinney's promotion to Commandant of Cadets, both occurring in 1935, constituted two-thirds of the transfer of power from the Old Guard to the New Breed of Gregory, McKinney, and Elliott. The final member of the new trio – Allen Elliott, required two promotions to complete the process.

Allen R. Elliott was a 1904 Culver graduate who had been with the school professionally since 1910 and was likely hired by Gignilliat in his role as Acting Superintendent. Gignilliat had confidence in him, naming him as Post Adjutant in 1931 and also as the chair of the Department of Health and Athletics, which were two areas in which Gignilliat retained significant interest. Becoming the Executive Officer of the Academy in 1938, Elliott reported directly to Gignilliat and was responsible for running the support operations of the Academy, supervising all non-instructional activities, and also remaining the chair of the Department of Health and Athletics.

While Gregory may have been groomed explicitly to succeed Gignilliat, the level of responsibly given to Elliott was also excellent preparation for him as a potential successor. Gignilliat, however, likely viewed Elliott as a capable "number two" but not of the caliber of himself and perhaps not even capable of serving well as a "number one." In addition, the dour, stern, visually formidable (if not severe), and physically intimidating Elliott was Gignilliat's polar opposite, and the two had an uneasy relationship far different from Gignilliat's close and intimate associations with the affable Cal Chambers and Abram Stoutenburgh.

As chair of the Department of Health and Athletics, Elliott removed the Director of Athletics responsibility that had been part of the Commandant's duties from McKinney, and he provided direct oversight of cadet physical training and athletics.

It is possible that this change came as a result of the untimely death in 1935 of Stoutenburgh's (who kept a close eye on these areas for Gignilliat) and/or in response to McKinney's assessment that this was too much for the Commandant to oversee. Regarding the latter, it is important to know that Elliott, although a few years older, had been a cadet at Culver at the same time as McKinney, and the two were close and lifelong friends. Regardless of the impetus for this action, it was yet another organizational change that brought to an end to one of the final vestiges of the "old Culver" way.

Elliott was appointed Executive Officer in 1938, serving directly under Gignilliat and responsible for "all non-instructional activities including the operations of finance, service of supplies and equipment, operations and upkeep of the physical plant and grounds, and operations of the mess, uniform department, Academy store, and canteen, placing him essentially in charge of all CEF property and equipment. Elliott also functioned as the Director of Alumni activities.

The assumption of these duties by Elliott was the final step in removing Gignilliat from having direct responsibility over any of Culver's routine activities. It also completed the process of transforming the Superintendent's position into a true executive role (which was good for Culver but which did not work best for Gignilliat and/or to his own strengths).

Elliott worked closely with Gignilliat, but the two had a somewhat volatile relationship. Blunt almost to the point of rudeness, Elliott told Gignilliat the truth (as he saw it), which Gignilliat appreciated, but he was far less cordial and deferential than Chambers had been, eliciting volatile responses from Gignilliat at times.

In a tribute written after his death, Elliott recalled that he had been called into Gignilliat's office on many occasions to provide the General with his reaction to something he had written or some plan he had devised. When providing any sort of disagreement, Elliott reported that Gignilliat's *"reactions on such occasions bordered on the violent. He would tell me that I didn't ever approve of, or agree with, anything, or words to that effect; and I, having expressed myself, would withdraw to the other side of the door – to my office."* More characteristic of Gignilliat, Elliott wrote that the General would invariably open Elliot's door within minutes to apologize.[11]

Gignilliat (looking decidedly older and somewhat uncomfortable) with Culver's new leaders: Gregory (L), McKinney (standing), and Elliot (r).[12]

Culver historian Richard Davies related another story about a disagreement Gignilliat had with Elliott regarding the premier of the 1939 movie *The Spirit of Culver* that illustrates the volatility of their relationship. According to Davies, Gignilliat learned in the winter of 1939 while still in Hollywood that Elliott had declined to premier the film on campus, prompting, in Davies' words, *"an irate and spirited letter to Elliott voicing his displeasure at the decision."* Since it is so out of character for the normally reserved, cordial, and polite Gignilliat, it is worth quoting portions of the letter at length.

On February 19, 1939, Gignilliat wrote:

> *"For God's sake, Allen! Have I gone haywire or Hollywood or is Culver going the 'holier than thou,' unimaginative, dry rot route, to win approval from such as never made Culver though they made the West, made history, though they may not have made a university club, or made their sons bond salesmen.*
>
> *I am truly worried about something more than a picture and its premier. I am concerned about the 'Spirit of Culver.'*
>
> *Perhaps I am out of step, and the time has come for me, not for a premier, but a final bow, yet until I make it, I shall strive to keep Culver non complaisant (sic), conscious of the great medium of expression of our times, the movies, the radio, included, even though they seem academically undignified, for the moment... Perhaps because I have tried to put so much of that sort of thing into this picture; the spirit of all you people I have worked with, all the boys of Culver, the ones upstairs, their pictures, over and past the saluted gold stars, in a room just to the left of the Allied flags; perhaps because of all that I have thought that Culver should launch into this picture, that so nicely depicts fine young American boyhood, and Culver's product, not, surely not, with Hollywood ballyhoo but with a Culver benediction..."*[13]

This episode is indicative of how Gignilliat was less consulted than informed of decisions and provided the opportunity to assent only to what had already been decided by others. Gignilliat accepted the situation in most instances, confident that those charged with the responsibility of leading Culver would do so with its best interests in mind. However, in this case, he did not see evidence of such and could not reconcile the decision to decline to premier the movie on campus with Culver's best interests, and he fired off an uncharacteristically fiery letter in response. The "Old Man" still had some fire in him.

Elliott responded a month later on March 19, 1939, admitting he had made an error in judgment and that the film presented Culver in a dignified manner that was in keeping with the *Spirit of Culver* and could not do the school any harm. In fact, Elliot observed that it might actually do Culver some good in terms of increased enrollment over the next five to ten years.[14]

It appears that the New Breed did not share Gignilliat's zeal for using the media – especially movies and the radio – to promote Culver widely, viewing such efforts as being "academically undignified." It is likely that their view permeated campus in Gignilliat's absence, perhaps contributing to the rather tepid reception of the film once it was shown on campus and the review of it appearing in *The Vedette*. Elliot assured Gignilliat that *"the reaction of faculty and cadets was much more positive at the second showing of the film."*[15]

As with Rossow's decision to reinstitute the Bull Ring in Gignilliat's absence in early 1934, the New Breed appear to have not supported Gignilliat in his marketing efforts (which were ostensibly what he was supposed to be focusing on as Superintendent) and instead worked actively against them in his absence. Just as Rossow's decision effectively ended his period of being one of Gignilliat's closest and most trusted advisors, the tone of his letter to Elliott suggests that Elliott and the others involved in the initial decision to not premier *The Spirit of Culver* on campus broke faith with the General and lost his trust.

This was the situation in spring 1939 when the CEF Board began considering a suitable replacement for BB Culver as its president.

The Gignilliats serenaded on campus around the holidays.[16]

A Second Succession Decision – President of the CEF Board

By spring 1939, BB Culver (who was the same age as Gignilliat, having been born on June 14, 1875, was becoming exhausted by the efforts required of leading both the Wrought Iron Range Company and the CEF Board. This is understandable, as he had assumed responsibility for overseeing CMA since ER's unexpected death on October 3, 1930.

In addition, he was perhaps becoming overwhelmed by his duties after serving as President of the Wrought Iron Range Company since the unexpected death of his older brother, HH Culver Jr, on January 22, 1912, starting a new business enterprise – Texas Foundries – in 1938, and also serving as the director of the First National Bank of St. Louis as well as the St. Louis Union Trust Company. This was a level of responsibility that would have overwhelmed even the heartiest individual, and BB was in his mid-60s by this time of his life.

Up to this point, there does not yet appear to have been any suggestion that Gignilliat may have been poised to become the CEF president. This development appears to have come as quite a surprise to both Gignilliat and likely to the new ruling triumvirate of Gregory, McKinney, and Elliott as well, and it is worth exploring in greater detail based upon what can be discerned from the existing sources.

As Gignilliat became increasingly sidelined regarding the Academy's day-to-day operations by Gregory, the Culver family became increasingly worried about the succession of the leadership of the CEF Board in the latter third of the 1930s. Gignilliat's actions indicate that he was preparing to retire in 1940 as planned, suggesting that becoming the CEF President had not occurred to him or anyone else much prior to the decision.

Looking to the Culver family, the 43-year-old ER Jr may have been judged to be not quite ready to take on the level of responsibility associated with overseeing CMA. It could also have been the case that it was just a better idea to have Gignilliat serve as CEF President so he could remain at Culver after reaching mandatory retirement age. Regardless of the rationale, it became apparent that Gregory was fully prepared to become Culver's Superintendent, that the time for elevating Gregory was fast approaching, and that waiting until summer 1940 to do so was no longer the best plan.

It also may have been that there were no suitable candidates within the Culver family to succeed BB Culver, and since Gignilliat has worked so closely with both ER Culver and BB Culver for the four decades since the death of HH Culver, it was natural for the Culver family to look to the aging superintendent to replace BB Culver, who had likely intended to step down as president earlier and was himself becoming somewhat aged. Gignilliat's role in helping to quell alumni unrest in 1937 may have provided the impetus for some to begin considering Gignilliat as a possible successor to BB Culver as the CEF board president.

Upon surveying the possibilities, it is almost certain that the Culver family determined fairly quickly that Gignilliat was the only possible candidate in whom they would have enough trust to replace BB and shepherd the institution they all loved so dearly and viewed as a living monument to HH and Emily Jane Culver.

It could also have been the case that making Gignilliat CEF board president was more of a way to keep him involved with the school after he rejected the board's offer to exempt him from the mandatory retirement requirement (according to Gignilliat's own telling). Making Gignilliat the CEF president may have been more of an expedient to keep him at Culver, and the creation of the chairman position for BB Culver was a necessity (even if it wasn't desired). It could also have been a way to allow BB Culver to give up the CEF president role, elevating him to a higher and largely ceremonial role in the governance structure. Regardless, this somewhat unusual and certainly unexpected arrangement was initiated and desired by others on behalf of Gignilliat.

A New Strategic Direction – The Culver Plan

It was also becoming more clear that it was time for a new superintendent to lead Culver and implement its new strategic plan. Since becoming Dean of the Faculty/Academy, Gregory had been working closely with the CEF Board to develop a replacement for the "Greater Culver" strategic plan that had guided Gignilliat and the institution for the twenty-year period from 1910-1930. Developed by the Culver family, the Greater Culver plan had been mostly about building better facilities, but Gignilliat co-opted it to encompass the entire Culver system, which set the stage and propelled Culver's success and growth before and after WWI.

Using the Greater Culver plan as a guide, the CEF Board and Gregory developed its successor – the Culver Plan – during and shortly after the Age of the Consultants.

The new strategic plan addressed the following areas:

- o Type of school
- o Course of study
- o Balance – military training must remain real, purposeful, and of high quality
- o Diagnosis and guidance
- o Quality of staff.

By 1935, it was time to begin implementing the new Culver strategic plan, and it became Gregory's guide (much as the Greater Culver plan had been Gignilliat's guide).[17]

Unlike its predecessor, the new strategic plan needed a much more academically focused and professional academician to implement it effectively, and Gregory was perfectly suited to begin doing so in 1935 as Dean of the Faculty/Academy. Blending what had worked at Culver in the past with the latest trends, Gregory's task was to guide Culver to become the type of school it was determined to become as a result of the Age of the Consultants – a college preparatory school – with appropriate courses of study and a modified balance with the military program that allowed it to become more academically focused, driven by diagnosis, data, and guidance efforts, and staffed with the highest quality faculty possible (which required a certain level of reduction in the school's military program). These change were also necessary to respond to the demands of the faculty, the changes in society, the expectations of parents that their sons would be as well prepared for college as they were in terms of citizenship, and the changes of the new generation of boys.

It is important to note that all involved in making these changes – especially Gregory – were committed to maintaining Culver as a preeminent military school. However, the way to do so while responding to the myriad competing demands outlined above was a matter of interpretation, and what became clear was that Gregory and the New Breed of educators at Culver had very different ideas from Gignilliat and Culver's Old Guard about the best way of doing so.

However, by 1939, Gregory had accomplished all he could as Dean of the Academy and needed to become Superintendent in order to complete the work of fully implementing the Culver Plan. It was these circumstances that converged to create the conditions for Gignilliat's final role and period at Culver.

Bringing His Army Career to a Close

Gignilliat was also close to completing his own military career during this period. For his active duty in summer 1937, Gignilliat reported to Camp Knox with Minnie (still keeping a watchful eye on her husband) to serve as the acting commander of the 84th Division (normally a two-star Major General) for a Command Post Exercise. Having served as a brigade commander for 15 years, the opportunity he was provided to command at the highest level of the ORC was a culmination for him from a military perspective. Accounts of his performance in this role indicated that he acquitted himself quite well in the exercise, and this event was his final significant act as a serving military officer prior to the completion of his military career.

Upon reaching the mandatory retirement age of 64, Gignilliat retired from the US Army Reserve with the rank of Brigadier General. Culver honored him with a special parade on his 64th birthday on July 4, 1939, and many of his officers from the 168th Brigade, which he had commanded since 1921, were in attendance.

The Army did not assign a permanent commander of the 168th Brigade to replace Gignilliat. Given the situation in the country and the pre-war planning, preparations, and training that was occurring, it is almost certain that the two regiments of the 168th Brigade continued to conduct training for their members and also provide training for others, even in the absence of an assigned brigade commander. The CMTC program remained quite popular throughout the second half of the 1930s, so there were likely ample opportunities for the 168th Brigade in terms of continuing to provide training in the summers. However, there is little record of such training opportunities or where they may have taken place.

Based upon his seniority, it is likely that Allen Elliott (commander of the 168th Brigade's 336th Regiment and Gignilliat's long-time colleague at Culver) functioned as the acting commander, representing yet another aspect of transition Gignilliat was experiencing on campus at Culver. The 168th Brigade did not continue as an ORC for much longer, and its activation the day after the attack on Pearl Harbor brought the Army's experiment with such ORC units to a close.

Gignilliat in his Army uniform for one of the final times.[18]

Promotion to CEF President and Service in The Role, June 1939-April 1942

As a result of the complex confluence of events and considerations, the CEF board appointed Gignilliat as its president in June 1939. It is likely that a combination of BB Culver's desire to relinquish his responsibilities as the CEF board president as soon as possible, Gregory's increasing involvement in the Academy's daily operations, Gignilliat's age and impending mandatory requirement date, and Gignilliat's own desire to focus on areas more appropriate for a board president are the main influences that brought about his change in status in summer 1939. This was the first time someone served in this position who was not a member of the Culver family, so it stands to reason that it was a decision that was as considered as it was deliberate.

The announcement was made in early June 1939 while Gignilliat was traveling in San Francisco for a previously scheduled alumni event, catching many by surprise. Gignilliat, however, reported that he was fully aware and supportive of the changes in both his own status and that of Gregory, who was named Acting Superintendent (as was Culver's custom) as his successor.

BB Culver was elevated to the newly created and somewhat lofty position of Chairman of the CEF Board. These changes completed the transition of leadership at CMA that began in the summer of 1935 with the appointment of McKinney as Commandant, followed by Gregory's appointment as Dean of the Faculty/Academy, and Elliott's elevation to the institution's top tier of leadership. Gregory was confirmed as Culver next superintendent in 1940, removing the "acting" from his title.

Examining the Change in His Role

Gignilliat wrote to his former VMI roommate and current Superintendent of VMI on June 23, 1939, that:

> *"Since I last wrote you my status with the institution has undergone a change. I have been promoted to the job of President of the Board of Directors of The Culver Educational Foundation. This does two things: It relieves me of the burden of the detailed internal administration and, confidentially, it obviates my retirement from the Culver scene, which is mandatory for members of the Culver faculty upon reaching the age of sixty-five. My sixty-fifth birthday occurs a year from this July 4th."* [19]

Gignilliat was undoubtedly aware of the mandatory retirement requirement, as he likely implemented it as superintendent.

Gignilliat characterized this development quite positively when writing to his close personal friend. If he was upset with the change in any way, Gignilliat would have almost certainly shared such feelings in a confidential letter to such an intimate friend, but he does not.

Several very interesting themes become apparent from the text of this letter:

- Gignilliat shared that his status had "*undergone a change*" since last wrote to Kilbourne, indicating that this change was somewhat unexpected (assuming that the two remained in relatively frequent contact, as it appears they did);

- Gignilliat characterized the move as a "*promotion*," indicating that he welcomed the change and viewed it positively;

- Gignilliat wrote that the change "*relieves me of the burden of the detailed internal administration*," indicating that he welcomed being relived of such responsibilities and that he viewed this as a positive outcome of his promotion;

- Gignilliat shared with Kilbourne that this promotion also "*obviated my retirement from the Culver scene*," indicating that he wanted to remain at Culver and that he would have had to retire by July of the following year if he remained as the superintendent.

Despite it being somewhat unexpected, Gignilliat characterized the move in three different ways as being positive, indicating that he supported it, welcomed it, and was happy with it.

Gignilliat addressed the situation directly in a letter to his sister Helen. Very soon after the change was announced and in response to Hellen's concerns, Gignilliat wrote:

> *Dear Sister,*
>
> *I am glad that the special edition of the Culver Alumnus answered for you so many questions that you had in mind. I know how you feel about not wanting to think of anyone else Superintendent at Culver. Of course emotionally I share that feeling and the giving up of the intimate internal direction of the Institution is tough after so many years at the helm. Yet there must be such things as age limitations <u>and</u> the distress of reaching them.*

In the Army and Navy, retirement is mandatory at 64. I am more fortunate than the Army and Navy officers in a way, since for the present at least instead of flat retirement I draw a new job, which while it does not give me the close contact and administrative duties I have so much enjoyed, yet retains for me a post of distinction and a hand in shaping the broader policies of the school. Nor does it for the present at least seriously affect my income.

We have an annuity and retirement plan at Culver under which actual members of the school staff must retire at 65. While the Board spoke of not applying the rule to me, it would have been a mistake to have made an exception in any case and I so expressed myself to the Board. They thereupon devised a plan under which I would pass from the Academy staff to the Board where I would not be subject to the mandatory retirement clause.

Of course how long I remain in my present status depends on my health, usefulness, the pleasure of the Board and my own wisdom. My present job still involves a good deal of work and thought and the time may come when I shall voluntarily wish to take things in more leisurely fashion.

If the Board had waited until next year to take the action they have taken, it would have looked more like just a subterfuge to keep from retiring me and the effect on other members of the staff long in the employ of the school might not have been so good. I really feel that the Board gave the matter a great deal of thought and consideration and that their action is a real expression of appreciation of the services I have rendered Culver and is also an expression of their belief that I can still render them service of value. Even though I retired outright my annuity would be such as to enable me to live comfortably although on a much more modest scale than in the past.

Now as to your inquiry about Col. Gregory. He is a highly trained, capable young educator. I say "young," he is several years older than I was when I became Superintendent. As Dean of the Academy he has been second in command to myself for several years and has done an outstanding piece of work in bringing the academic phases of the school to the very top in the whole country. He is the very modern type of educator, very businesslike and efficient and highly trained professionally. He is much more thoroughly academic in outlook than I am, whether he sees as well or better than I have done the complete picture and the broader concept of the school's function in training the whole boy remains to be seen. He may or may not possess those indefinable nuances of personality and imagination that are necessary to build up and maintain a great school. I do feel, however, that he has a lot on the ball and I concurred in the recommendation of the Board that he should be made acting Superintendent to succeed me.

It would only be human of me to have baser moments when I hope they are going to have a hard time filling my place, but I try to put them promptly out of mind. My main concern is that the school to which I have given, and Myn has given, so many years of our lives, shall continue to grow in usefulness and fame and I shall do everything to that end.

Now Sis, that is the lowdown, written at considerable length because I am deeply appreciative of your love and interest. Thank you for sending me Beth's very sweet letter, I shall write to her at once.

I am so sorry that you have been feeling a bit under the weather. I know your trip to Birmingham from Kentucky will do you a lot of good. I hope to be back about the middle of August so let me know when you get to Murray. It is not such a terribly long drive from here and we would love to come down and bring you to Culver.

Lots of love from Myn and me to you and yours,

Affectionately,

Leigh.[20]

This undated letter to his sister Helen was almost certainly written in summer 1939 just after the announcement. In the letter, Gignilliat expresses that he felt as though the CEF board was quite thoughtful and found a way for him to continue serving Culver. It also emphasizes the money aspect several times, indicating that while not paramount, money was still an important concern for him. The substance of the letter further indicates that Myn was in it with him completely and that they were a team.

Regarding Gregory being named as his replacement, Gignilliat conveyed that he believed that Gregory was a *"highly trained,"* *"capable,"* and *"young"* individual who had done quite well with academics, was *"very modern," "very businesslike and efficient,"* had a *"more thoroughly academic outlook"* and had *"a lot on the ball."* These comments present a very positive assessment and the outward appearance of support. While admitting that he supported the board's decision for Gregory to be his replacement, Gignilliat did not conclude with a ringing endorsement of Gregory, indicating that he was still somewhat unsure if Gregory had what it took to be a successful superintendent for Culver (despite having hired him and worked with him for 16 years).

Gignilliat also acknowledged to his sister that part of him wanted it to be hard for Culver to replace him. His admission of wanting his transition as superintendent to be felt was eminently human and may be another indicator of his introvert's aversion to conflict.

Even though he may not have wanted to give up the superintendent's position (for which he was born to serve), he was more willing to agree to give it up and accept the offer of becoming the CEF president from the board than to resist and try to remain as the superintendent for the one final year he had left (or perhaps more if the board suspended the 65 cutoff for him), which may have led to some level and/or type of conflict. He was also clearly still very committed to serving Culver in whatever role he could to continue to help the school thrive, even if that role could no longer be as its superintendent.

A New Role – President of the CEF Board

As President, Gignilliat relinquished all pretense of any responsibility for the school's routine operations, allowing him to focus on ensuring the school remained financially solvent and viable in at least three areas of great strength for him: alumni relations, recruitment, and public relations.[21] There truly was no better spokesman for the institution, and allowing Gignilliat to prioritize and focus his efforts in these three essential areas was not only the best use of his tremendous talents in his mid-60s but also the very best way to set Culver up for success in the coming years.

Having also completed his own military service, mid-1939 was thus a tremendous transition for Gignilliat, bringing to an end both his superintendency of Culver and his long service in the Army Reserve. What the future would hold for him was anyone's guess, but the prospect of embarking a new adventure as the President of the CEF was likely exciting and invigorating as he looked back on the highlights of a wonderfully successful career serving both Culver and Army.

The change to serving as president at Culver required some adjustment for Gignilliat. He addressed his new role at the school during the Summer 1939 board meeting, observing that his perspective was much changed and that it allowed him to look at the school anew and with the benefit of having time for reflection that did not exist when burdened with the daily responsibilities of being the superintendent. Believing that it was good for the school to have a member of the board present on campus on a full-time basis, Gignilliat planned to meet informally with members of the faculty and staff periodically to keep in touch with the pulse of the institution while also allowing them to share their thoughts directly with a board member.

This conception of his new role appears to have been sufficient to satisfy him for the first six months, if for no other reasons that its novelty and potential. However, and once the novelty wore off and his actual situation became unavoidably clear, it quickly became apparent to him than the reality of the situation was not anywhere close to what he had imagined or wanted it to be.

When the drums of war began sounding louder on the eve of WWII, the institution took on new energy. Gregory was called to active duty in March or April 1942 with a report date of May 1, 1942, and Colonel John S. Fleet, Gignilliat's brother-in-law and son of Colonel Alexander Fleet, was named Acting Superintendent in his absence. While this must have been disappointing to Gignilliat, he likely realized that not only was Fleet quite capable of guiding the institution well – Gignilliat had hired him and had worked with him for many years, and Flee t was serving as the Chairman of the Faculty – but that his own role as President might become even more essential and that he could be serve the institution in that role.

However, it must have been quite a blow to Gignilliat to learn that he was not the first choice to serve in Gregory's stead and also tremendously disappointing for the institution to not look to him to serve again as superintendent as a wonderfully suitable expedient during the school's wartime exigency. It had to have also been and all the more galling for him to have to be part of the process of authorizing someone who was not a military man to serve as acting superintendent.

For a man who had dedicated his entire life to serving an institution that was clearly in need of a steady hand to guide it through the tumultuous war years ahead, such a development likely brought all of his frustration and disappointment to a head. Given Gignilliat's exasperation in his largely inactive role as president of the Culver Educational Foundation, it appears to have been the final straw convincing him Culver no longer seemed to want or need his service. Conversely, it was probably quite a relief to Minnie that her aged husband had not been called to serve in such a capacity.

Gignilliat had been the one called to active duty during WWI, and he left the Academy in the hands of Hugh Glascock, who, while serving as Culver's headmaster, was a staunch advocate of the military system. Signifying that the transformation was complete, during WWII the school was to be guided by an academic rather than a military man in the absence of its superintendent.

His hopes for his role as CEF president to become more significant failed to materialize. Just prior to Fleet being named as Gregory's replacement, Gignilliat wrote the following to his close friend Charles Kilbourne, who was still serving as the superintendent of VMI, on February 23, 1942:

> "As you know, I have been in a more or less inactive capacity
> for the last two years as President of the Board of Directors,
> and am thinking very seriously now of living away from
> Culver. It is very difficult to be sitting on top of a place where
> one has been active most of his life and not have a finger in the
> pie, which of course I could not do without making it difficult for
> my successor. Therefore, my wife and I have about concluded to
> move away from Culver." [22]

Gignilliat characterized his previous two years as president as one of his being "in a more or less inactive capacity," indicating that his vision for his role as president, which was still a fairly new position that had as yet little organizational purchase or import at Culver, had not panned out as he had hoped. His frustration at "sitting on top of a place where one has been active most of his life and not have a finger in the pie" indicates that he not involved or asked to be involved in the operations of the school and that the roles he had envisioned for himself in terms of engaging in alumni relations, recruitment, and public relations were not as fulfilling as he had hoped.

It is doubtful whether his plan to meet informally with members of the faculty and staff periodically to remain connected to the school panned out either, leaving Gignilliat isolated and alone in his large office on the second floor of the Legion Memorial building and largely disconnected from the school he loved so dearly (despite still being on campus).

It also shows how much of a gentleman Gignilliat was, choosing to be miserably uninvolved rather than surrendering to temptation and involving himself, which would have made things quite difficult for

Gregory (as Gignilliat points out). Richard Davies surmised that the relationship between Gignilliat and Gregory had become cool after Gregory became superintendent, bringing to an end the "warm and friendly correspondence" between the two and replacing it with exchanges that were *"formal but not friendly."*[23]

Given the insight in the letter cited above, however, it appears more likely that Gignilliat was, in keeping with the best military traditions, intentionally keeping his distance and allowing his successor all possible room and latitude to succeed without interference from his predecessor. Gignilliat was still living in the superintendent's quarters and was almost certainly aware of his status on campus and of the necessity for him to be both mindful of his presence and also to limit himself to impacting only those areas suitable for involvement by the president of the board. Perhaps this would have been more difficult for him to do with Fleet serving as Acting Superintendent, prompting Gignilliat to make the decision to retire as President of the CEF Board very soon after learning of Fleet's appointment.

The Decision to Retire and Depart Culver

Rather than continue on in such a state, Gignilliat and Minnie, who were entering their fifth decade in residence at Culver, made the unexpected decision to "move away from Culver" to either Lexington, Virginia and close to VMI and the Fleet homestead or to Fort Worth, Texas, to be close to their son Fred. This rather sudden decision is perhaps the clearest indicator of the level of frustration Gignilliat was experiencing at being left out of any substantive role at Culver. That Minnie supported the decision to leave provides further evidence that the situation for Gignilliat at Culver was difficult and no longer tenable.

Gignilliat in front of the Superintendent's quarters.[24]

Gignilliat arranged to travel to Lexington and contacted a realtor to look at some properties in the area in March 1942. For whatever reason, the move to Lexington did not happen, despite Minnie's strong desire to return to what she considered to be her native state (in terms

The Gignilliat family gathering at the superintendents' quarters during happier times. [25]

of family heritage, despite being born in Missouri).

In the wake of Gregory being called to active duty and the board's decision to appoint JS Fleet as Acting Superintendent early April 1942, Gignilliat resigned as president on April 25, 1942. He and Minnie moved over 1,000 miles away to Fort Worth, Texas, where they took up residence in a small but comfortable apartment in the Blackburn Hotel. Being in Fort Worth allowed the couple to be close to their son Fred, who worked at Consolidated Aircraft Corporation, and to Fred's family. Despite having to depart the superintendent's quarters that served as their own homestead, the move allowed the elder Gignilliats to be doting grandparents to Fred's children.

Designated immediately as President Emeritus, Gignilliat was granted a generous annuity of $10,000 for the first two years of his retirement (a little over $170,000 in contemporary dollars) and then $7,500 for the remainder of his life (which is almost $125,000 in contemporary dollars). This amount allowed him to live comfortably without having to work if he so chose.

Gignilliat continued to serve as a member of the CEF Board, returning dutifully to Culver for meetings, but his presence was almost non-existent as he receded into the background. Sometime during this period, Gignilliat sought permission to return to Culver and use the Superintendent's quarters to have a family reunion, since this was the home in which he had lived for over 20 years. However, Culver denied the old man permission, adding insult to injury.

The completed Gignilliat couple portrait, showing them in all their glory and highlighting three things of greatest importance to him: Minnie, cadets, and Culver.

ER Culver, Jr. '15 replaced Gignilliat as the president of the CEF board, benefiting perhaps from the three years Gignilliat served in this position and ready to assume the responsibilities in a way that he was not perhaps ready to do in 1939. JS Fleet served as Acting Superintendent for just over one year until he reached the mandatory retirement age of 65, retiring on September 1, 1943. Allen Elliott was appointed to replace Fleet, and Elliott served ably as Acting Superintendent until Gregory's return on July 13, 1945, committed to continuing the work begun by Gregory, McKinney, Fleet, and himself, serving in Gregory's stead and not as the superintendent in his own right.

While Gregory may have been groomed explicitly to succeed Gignilliat, the level of responsibly given to Elliott proved to be excellent preparation for him as a potential successor as well. True to his nature, Gignilliat likely supported this change, but it was likely made more palatable by his being over 1,000 miles away from campus when it occurred.

The Gignilliat Era at Culver Concludes

Thus concluded the Gignilliat era at Culver. It had begun on a snowy night in January 1897 and ended on a spring day in April 1942, in a manner that Gignilliat neither preferred nor could have possibly anticipated. The finality and impact had yet to sink in for either Gignilliat or Culver.

Chapter 19 – Gignilliat's Life After Culver and Final Decade, 1942-1952.

Gignilliat relaxed, circa 1940.[1]

Upon resigning as the CEF President, Gignilliat moved, along with Minnie, to Fort Worth, Texas, where they took up residence in a small but comfortable apartment in the Blackburn Hotel. Beginning this new chapter of their life in Fort Worth allowed the Gignilliats to be close to Fred, who worked at Consolidated Aircraft Corporation, and to Fred's family. Despite having to depart the community in which they had lived since 1897 and the superintendent quarters that served as their homestead since 1919, the move was a positive event, allowing the elder Gignilliats to be doting grandparents to Fred's children as they considered their futures.

The Engineering, Science, and Management War Training Program

After an unsuccessful bid to secure a recall to active military service, in good health and not yet ready for full retirement or being one to rest on his own laurels, the restless Gignilliat soon found another impactful way to the war effort. With the US entering WWII in early December 1941, the nation's mobilization for war began in earnest in 1942.[2] The accompanying industrialization produced a demand for skilled workers, providing an opportunity for Gignilliat to use his experience as an educator to continue serving the nation in this time of peril.

Germany's ability to defeat multiple Allied nations in the early years of the war was due in part to the success of its modernization and mobilization programs. This also made it clear that the war would not be short. Victory would require America to harness all of its tremendous intellectual, industrial, and technological power.

During the process of mobilizing for WWII, the military identified the need for a program capable of providing specialized training via short, intensive college-level courses designed to prepare individuals for technical and scientific work in war industries. Recognized as being essential to the coming war effort, the Engineering, Science, and Management Defense Training (ESMDT) program was established under the sponsorship of the U. S. Office of Education at the beginning of October 1940. Expanded in July 1941, it was renamed the Engineering, Science, and Management War Training (ESMWT) program.[3]

The Blackstone Hotel, Fort Worth, Texas. The design is somewhat castle-like, perhaps providing comfort to Gignilliat.

As part of the country's total mobilization effort, the United States substantially expanded its industrial capacity, requiring many more workers with specialized training. The ESMWT program was one way of supporting this aspect of wartime mobilization. Modern industrialized total warfare relies every bit as much on a nation's scientific and engineering capacities, and technical manufacturing skills, as it does on the actual fighting.[4]

One of the most pressing needs that became immediately apparent was for trained engineers and skilled technicians. Accordingly, the program was designed to produce scientific and technical specialists for crucial defense industries as rapidly as possible. The program offered courses in Engineering (75%), production supervision (21%), Physics and Chemistry (both around 2%), along with Business, Radio Science, Personnel Management, Accounting, Office Management (among others). As part of their autonomy, the classes offered were different at each institution, determined by each school based upon their capabilities and the needs of the region in which they existed.

Courses offered practical training for specific tasks and were intended to "give specific, intensive training to meet specific and definitely determined needs of defense and war industries," so students did not receive college credit for them.[5] They were offered mostly at night (to accommodate the work schedules of the enrolled students) and taught by faculty members from participating higher education institutions (along with some special teachers).

The program was free and open to all who qualified. With many male students leaving school to serve in the military, this program provided an avenue of advancement previously unavailable to many groups. According to one author, a distinct attribute of the program was the diversity of its participants due to the prohibition of discrimination on the basis of race, sex, or age, which allowed for groups that has been traditionally excluded, such as women and people of color, to participate in industries and educational fields in which they were historically not prevalent. It also allowed them to join and make meaningful contributions to the war effort.

This aspect of the program provided an opening for the aged but still very capable former Superintendent and President of the Board of Culver Military Academy. Having reached the mandatory age of retirement and retired from the Army in July 1939, Gignilliat had been appointed as an advisor to Secretary of War Henry L. Stimson on July 31, 1941. This appointment likely gave him some added visibility within the War Department, and with his extensive experience with education, he was an ideal candidate to help the military get the newly designated ESMWT program into high gear.

In order to run the program on a nationwide level the country was divided into 22 regional areas, with each region having an appointed advisor. This advisor was then responsible for forming a regional committee made up of representatives for the institutions in his or her area which would coordinate the program's training.[6] The first regional advisors "were recognized leaders in engineering education" who worked for no compensation and were mostly left to their own devices.[7] Each region was responsible for contacting the industries in their area and determining the respective training needs, but in order for the class to be approved and funding allocated it was required for them to contact the federal staff through the regional committee.

According to the ESMWT program final report, the individuals selected as regional advisors "had the confidence and respect of their colleagues in the program," and they were, ideally, "intimately acquainted with each of the institutions in their respective areas."[8] This was not the case with Gignilliat, but he served as a local coordinator for the highly respected Dean of the University of Texas Engineering school. Still, it suggests that the confidence and respect he enjoyed that led to his being appointed to this position made up for his relative lack of association with any of the member organizations for which he was responsible for coordinating.

Acting as friends and colleagues, rather than supervisors, directors, or administrative officials, administrators like Gignilliat "rendered service of inestimable value throughout the program" and were "a source of inspiration and help" to their member institutions. Significant responsibilities included planning and conducting meetings among member institutions, discerning the local institutions' ability to provide for the regional needs for training, suggesting ways in which participating institutions could be helpful in meeting those needs, promoting institutional cooperation, and enhancing effectiveness. Engaged advisors like Gignilliat contributed further by maintaining an active interest in the work of each participating institution and by "counseling on problems," all of which did much to raise the general morale of the participating institutions.[9]

Regional advisors met with the national director in Washington, DC quarterly, helping to form policies, design and clarify procedures, and enhancing collaboration between the individual colleges and the Office of Education. Operating in this capacity, regional advisors "greatly facilitated a two-way exchange of information which resulted in a clear conception of the program as an integrated nation -wide cooperative enterprise of the colleges in aid of the war effort, and brought to the Washington staff important current information on local problems in the several parts of the country, and a continuous appraisal of the general effectiveness of the program in expediting defense and war production."[10] In essence, they helped the colleges feel connected to the larger effort, and they helped ensure that the federal oversight was well and accurately informed about the activities of the participating institutions and regional efforts.

Working with one of the 22 regional advisors, Dr. W. R. Woolrich, who was the Dean of Engineering at the University of Texas Austin, enrollment peaked just about the time that Gignilliat became involved in the program (i.e., between 1942-1943), when the number of trainees was around 600,000 taking almost 13,000 classes offered at 214 institutions across the United States.[11]

Serving the Nation in WWII – Fort Worth Local ESMWT Program Coordinator

Since it was considered to be a highly industrialized metropolitan area served by several different institutions, the Texas region determined that it made sense to have a local coordinator in the Dallas-Fort Worth area "to effect a closer degree of coordination of the program than was feasible through the usual regional committee."[12]

Shortly after his move to Forth Worth in spring 1942, Gignilliat was appointed as the Local Coordinator for the Fort Worth, Texas area of the Texas Regional ESMWT program. He was responsible for coordinating the actions of the following four institutional campus ins the Dallas-Fort Worth area: the University of Texas, Texas A & M, Southern Methodist University, and Texas Tech University. There may have been at least two other institutions participating in some capacity (e.g., providing faculty and/or classroom space). The Dean of the University of Texas Engineering school served as the Regional Coordinator for the Texas ESMWT regional program, and a board was formed using professors from each participating institution.

Gignilliat's specific role was "to handle such matters as promotion and publicity," which was a great strength of his, along with "joint registration of trainees, designation of the institution to conduct a particular course, and the general coordination of all ESMWT training in the area." He was further charged with the responsibility of "preventing overlapping of activities by neighboring institutions and in promoting the over-all efficiency of the program in the area served by the coordinator."[13] The requirements of the position appeared to be ideally suited for Gignilliat's skill set, and he engaged in his responsibilities with his typical zeal and high level of energy.

Unlike in WWI, when the military arrived and virtually took over college campuses as part of the wartime efforts associated with ROTC and especially, the Student's Army Training Corps (SATC) program (and about which many college officials remained bitter), a guiding principle of the ESMWT program was that it would be a program of the institutions assisted by the Office of Education, not a program of the Office of Education assisted by the institutions. Thus, each program retained a high level of autonomy, and the influence of the officials from the participating institutions was particularly acute.[14] As such, the person in the role in which Gignilliat served had to have tremendous interpersonal skills to be able to work with educators from across the entire spectrum of beliefs and abilities, and do in ways that were as collegial as they were effective. This was yet another aspect of this role for which Gignilliat was particularly well suited and at which he excelled.

Having participated in and benefited from the rapid training programs implemented by the US military during WWI, Gignilliat was now on the other end of the effort, helping to provide rapid and effective academic training to support the industrial efforts of WWII. Part of his responsibilities included discerning the training needs of the local industries, many of which were devoted to aircraft manufacturing, and helping the Fort Worth ESMWT program design and offer courses able to produce individuals trained for such duties. Efficiency was also important to ensure that there was no overlap or duplication of efforts in the vocational and shop training offered by area high schools to make the best use of the available resources for the program. Given that it took the US almost two years to reach full industrialization, this aspect of his role was especially important. With his eye for detail and penchant for organizational leadership, it was also a role for which he was particularly well suited.

Reuben Fleet – An Especially Beneficial Culver Connection During This Period

Gignilliat's Culver connections were also quite beneficial in his new role. One of the more important companies in the area was Ruben Fleet's Consolidated Aircraft Corporation, which designed and built the B-24 Liberator for the US military. Gignilliat was well-acquainted with Fleet, who was the nephew of Colonel Alexander "Fred" Fleet, the Culver superintendent who hired Gignilliat as commandant in 1897, whose daughter he married and who he replaced as Superintendent. Ruben Fleet was a Culver cadet during the time Gignilliat served as Commandant, amassing an outstanding record during his four years on campus as a superb athlete, editor-in-chief of *The Vedette*, and military leader, commanding one of the infantry companies and graduating as a cadet captain.

During World War I and afterwards, Fleet gained substantial renown as an aviator. He served as a Major in the US Army Air Service from 1917-22, commanding 34 flying fields as executive officer for flight training in the United States. He earned the distinction of being named "Air Mail Pilot Number One" when he was appointed officer in charge of the first air mail flights between New York, Philadelphia, and Washington, D.C. This distinction was given at a special inauguration on May 15, 1918, with President Woodrow Wilson in attendance.

After his military service concluded, Fleet founded Consolidated Aircraft Corporation in 1923 and served as its president. His company was quite successful, later becoming the Convair Division of General Dynamics Corporation.

Fleet remained connected to Culver throughout his entire life. After graduating from Culver, he served two terms as president of the Culver Legion and was a lifetime member. Two of his sons and two of his grandsons were Culver graduates (David Girton Fleet, CMA '29, Preston Mitchell Fleet, CMA '52, David Fulton Fleet, CMA '54, and Allen Mitchell Fleet, CMA '74). Fleet's eldest son David graduated Culver with Gignilliat's youngest son, Henry "Hank" Gignilliat, in 1929. Later, he became a member of the Board of Directors of the Culver Educational Foundation from 1948 until his retirement in 1966. In fact,

Culver's airfield -- Fleet Field -- was named in honor of the Fleet family. In recognition of his numerous contributions to Culver, Reuben was presented Culver's Distinguished Service Award Sabre in October 1974.[15]

Contributions to the War Effort as an ESMWT Local Coordinator

The Culver connection brought Gignilliat and Fleet together again in Fort Worth during WWII. Having such a close relationship with someone as important in the aircraft industry as Ruben Fleet, especially in the Fort Worth area, provided Gignilliat with an exceptional advantage in terms of function as an effective ESMWT Local Coordinator.

In a letter written in summer 1942, Gignilliat described the work as being "altogether absorbing and stimulating," which must have been a welcome relief from the relatively unchallenging duties of serving as the CEF Board President for the preceding 18 months. Although it is unknown how long Gignilliat was involved with this endeavor, given his strong duty ethic, and lacking any evidence to the contrary, it is likely that he served until its conclusion at the end of June 1945, when there was no longer a need for the regional advisors.

By the time it ceased operations, 227 different institutions officially offered classes as part of the program, training 1,795,716 students.[16] The actual number of institutions was likely much higher as many institutions often subcontracted with other non-participating schools for additional faculty and classroom space.

The intense and rapid modernization of the United States Armed Forces could not have been accomplished at the pace and scale they were if not for the ESMWT program and other defense training programs. Reports from the period make this fact abundantly clear, including numerous quotes from industrial executives about the benefits their plants and industries gained through ESMWT training of personnel. A quantitative report from 1944 found a correlation that was "positive and large enough to be regarded as significant."[17] The contributions of the EMSWT program provided both tangible benefits to the war effort and also allowed for countless individuals to make their own intangible contributions to it. It also increased efficiency indirectly through the increased efficiency of other employees thanks to their presence and training.

The ESMWT program was a three-part relationship between higher education, the federal government, and industry, each of which benefited from it. Unlike WWI efforts, the ESMWT program was conducted with far better cooperation and collegiality, fostering a close and positive relationship between the higher education institutions and the government. This opened up many post-war education opportunities, including the GI Bill and the expansion of ROTC programs. Countering its traditional apprentice and vocational approaches, industry learned that colleges were capable of providing the kind of courses it needed more effectively than it could do on its own, and higher education institutions were able to do with less interference with production.

As impactful as it was on industry and the war efforts in the short term, the greatest impact of the ESMWT program was more long term and on the people. Over 1.5 million men and women were given the chance to obtain and/or further their educations, in some cases for the first time since elementary school! They were able to acquire the training and skills necessary to work in vital industries, while also making their own significant contributions to the war effort.[18]

Many were pleasantly surprised at how well they were able to succeed in such roles, boosting both their self-esteem and confidence in their own abilities. For many, there was no going back to their pre-war selves, and the ESMWT experience both motivated and encouraged them to seek a better life for themselves and their families, contributing to the general sense of improvement and positive momentum that developed in America during the ensuring post-war era.

For Gignilliat, who retained his preference for a more generalized approach to education (as opposed to the more specialized approach to college preparation adopted by Culver in the mid-1930s), the confluence of people, industry, and higher education that occurred in the ESMWT program provided an ideal venue for him to be able to again answer the nation's call for mobilization and continue serving during the Second World War. It allowed him to place his tremendous interpersonal and organizational talents in service to the country during a time of war in a manner that appropriate for him after having devoted over 40 years of his life to Culver. It must also have been quite refreshing for him to part of a larger efforts working toward a common purpose in a role in which he was valued and making a meaningful contribution.

After having relied on the military system as the foundation of his program at Culver, it was an intriguing opportunity for him to help develop individuals to benefit through the knowledge gained by schooling that gave them the capability and purpose to assist their nation in war without wielding a weapon of any kind.

Culver Ambassadors in Texas – Minnie Continues to Serve as the "Mother to the Corps"

As a couple, Gignilliat and his wife were equally wedded to the Academy's growth and success, and almost all Culver men considered the General and Mrs. Gignilliat as an inseparable pair and as being the very essence of Culver Military Academy. Minnie's role as Culver's "social arbiter" for the Corps, along with her uncompromising requirement that all young men demonstrate the highest qualities of gentlemanly behavior, enshrined her indelibly in the hearts of thousands of Culver men.

According to Hank Gignilliat, even when she was no longer on campus, Minnie continued functioning, as she had been at Culver, as "a mother figure" to Culver men who came to visit the Gignilliats in Fort Worth. With her phenomenal memory, it took little more than a specific turn of a phrase in conversation or a glance from her to recognize a distinctive gesture of a person she had known years before as an awkward boy or developing young man. Instantly, she was able to recall details of the man's time at Culver long forgotten by almost everyone else (including, perhaps the visitor himself!). The mutual delight in their small reunions at the Blackstone apartment home of the Gignilliats were occasions of great joy and shared reminiscences.[19]

The Gignilliats continued to serve Culver as welcoming ambassadors in Texas. According to an October 1944 double-column article in the *Fort Worth Press*, the General and Minnie were "constantly entertaining service men in their suite at the Blackstone Hotel," undoubtedly comprised of many Culver-affiliated young men. Remaining the incomparable hostess, the article reported that one guest commented that Minnie ran "the best USO in the USA." Not even the press of wartime duties could dampen Minnie's indomitable spirit to continue serving as the "Mother to the Culver Corps of Cadets," and Gignilliat himself continued to demonstrate his sincere commitment to his boys, despite no longer being an official part of Culver and residing far away from campus.

The General and Minnie in retirement and as likely encountered in Fort Worth (notice the cigarette Minnie is holding/hiding behind her back!).[20]

This photograph is labelled "The Author and His Son [Hank], in the Earlier Days of Their Collaboration" in Gignilliat's memoirs. It was likely from one of the scrapbooks Gignilliat created during this period. The photo behind the two men is of a young Fred Fleet Gignilliat.[23]

Gignilliat's duties as the Local ESMWT Coordinator for the Dallas-Fort Worth area were meaningful but not nearly as taxing as the job of Culver's Superintendent. With more time on his hands away from Culver, Gignilliat became somewhat reflective and decided to take the opportunity to record his memories of his life, both in writing and in scrapbooks with pictures.

According to his son, Hank, Gignilliat wrote his memoirs a chapter at a time during his time in Fort Worth, sending them to Hank to be edited.[21] He wrote seventeen chapters, and he added short post-scripts to the final version of the manuscript. From a close personal inspection by this author, all of the draft chapters of what became *Unfurling the Colors* appear to have been reviewed by Hank and edited (at least with changes and corrections penciled in on chapter drafts), but the final product was not published during Gignilliat's lifetime.[22] Hank selected the chapters for inclusion, and he also worked with his father (and later, Culver Historian Robert B. D. "Bob" Hartman) to determine their order in the published version.

Hank chose not to include seven chapters into the final version, most of which related to events from his father's life that were not connected to Culver, but he did incorporate relevant material from three of these chapters into other chapters to flesh out certain aspects of Gignilliat's memoirs that had not been addressed elsewhere. While understandable in terms of keeping the focus on Culver, Hank's selections were intriguing, as he left out several interesting chapters, one of which dealt with a fascinating episode from his childhood about which we know little ("The Boston Stereopticon Company," addressed previously in the chapter regarding Gignilliat's youth), and the other providing a summary of his life and achievements ("The Summing Up," addressed in the final chapter of this biography).

These chapters have been reviewed by only a few close family members since they were written, and it was important to include the substance of them throughout this biography, since they provide rare glimpses into little-known and/or previously unknown episodes in Gignilliat's life in his own words.

The focus of much of his memoirs, understandably, was on his role, activities, and achievements at Culver. As a reverie, the substance and overall theme of his memoirs reinforces the central nature that Culver played in his life. They also show him to be a witty storyteller and deft writer, providing evidence of growth in both of these areas from his beginnings as a shy lad and man who had little confidence in his ability to craft respectable prose.

1944 –1947 – Settling in at Fort Worth and To His Post-Culver Routine

According to Culver historian Bob Hartman, even though he was "a thousand miles from Culver, Gignilliat's concern for the Academy and its alumni remained strong." For example,

> *"When support among alumni and friends of the Academy for a Memorial Chapel began to develop in 1944, he became a leader in the campaign to raise the necessary funds. His constituency net swept across the nation and his contacts were important in garnering financial support for the project. One of his close contacts in Fort Worth was Amon Carter, his former cadet aide and a member of the Class of 1938. When pledges were being made for two of the chapel's most important gifts, the carillon and the organ, Carter pledged the magnificent 51-bell carillon. Alumnus Reuben H. Fleet '06 gave the latter."*[24]

While physically away from campus, Gignilliat was never apart from the school in spirit.

1944 – Minnie Diagnosed with Breast Cancer

While residing in Fort Worth, Minnie's health became a concern. A check-up revealed that she had sarcoma of the breast, a rare form of breast cancer. Added to her chronic arterial sclerosis (i.e., hardening of the arteries; diagnosed around 1937), this equated to the couple having to begin paying attention to her health as well as his.

According to information from Johns Hopkins Medical Center (which specializes in the treatment of cancer), breast sarcomas are a very rare form of breast cancer because the location of the affected cells in the connective tissue causes it to act differently than more common kinds of breast cancer. It can also be quite aggressive. Breast sarcomas manifest as tumors, and treatment can include radiation therapy and/or chemotherapy.[25]

During the initial two years, Minnie likely underwent some initial treatment while in Fort Worth, which prevented her from engaging with others and required an excuse of an unnamed "illness" to explain (which would have been all that polite society of the period allowed or required). It is likely that her "illness" of which others became aware around 1946 was related to this condition.

1946 – Another Manuscript for Bobbs-Merrill – *A School and a Family*

In addition to writing his memoirs, Gignilliat also wrote another manuscript during this period. He had maintained sporadic contact with Bobbs-Merrill after his return from World War I regarding *Arms and the Boy*, mostly involving other books published by Bobbs-Merrill related in some way to Culver. Perhaps spurred by the memories stirred up while writing his memoirs, Gignilliat drafted his second book-length manuscript for Bobbs-Merrill. Titled, *A School and a Family,* this work was intended to highlight the impact of the Culver family on the institution, along with providing a tangible artifact of his lifelong love for and of Culver.

With more time on his hands during the second half of 1945, after the ESMWT ended in June, Gignilliat worked on and completed the manuscript for Bobbs-Merrill, submitting it in 1946 for consideration. The review of it indicated that it was mostly a discursive collection of stories that would need substantial editing to be publishable. However, the reviewer believed that the manuscript did show promise for publication if Gignilliat was willing to make the necessary revisions.[26] Unfortunately for posterity, Gignilliat was unable to follow through (likely due to health reasons), the revisions were never made, and the manuscript is lost to history.[27]

1946 – Culver's Loss of Senior ROTC Status

In what had to be a blow to Gignilliat, Culver lost its authorization to host "Senior" ROTC programs that qualified its graduates to become commissioned military officers. However, the reasons for this decision had little, if anything, to do with Culver itself, and it is worth exploring these reasons further.

Unlike prior to WWI, the senior ROTC programs were now well established. They had developed (and even flourished) on college campuses across the nation, providing the military with a predictable and reliable source of reserve officers in time of war.

The experience of WWII had also shown that officers needed to be older than the typical high school graduate for both cognitive and practical reasons. It is worth noting that affording the opportunity for recent high school graduates had been a source of concern for the military since before WWI, but the demands for large numbers of reserve officers for the war and during the ensuing decade (i.e., the 1920s) meant that restricting reliable sources of reserve officers was simply a luxury the military could not afford during that period.

In addition, the US military was in the midst of its most massive reduction-in-force in its history. At the time of the decision, the US did not envision needing to maintain a large peacetime military. Taken together, these considerations meant that the military could afford to be far more selective in terms of the sources for its reserve officers it decided to retain.

Accordingly, in November 1946, the US Army reclassified all military preparatory schools, including Culver, as "Junior" ROTC programs and denied them the privilege of awarding commissions. Despite having nothing to do with the value of the military training provided at Culver and/or the performance of its graduates in WWII, this decision had a significant impact on Culver, which had been awarding direct commissions to its qualified graduates for 30 years since first authorized to do so in November 1916, and it was likely viewed by many at Culver as an unnecessary and indefensible reduction in status.[28]

1946 – Minnie Receives Treatment for Breast Cancer

Accounts of the period refer to an unnamed "illness" that Minnie suffered in 1946. It stands to reason that this "illness" was referring to cancerous sarcoma of the breast condition that had been diagnosed in 1944 that had almost certainly not been acknowledged publicly and for which she had been receiving treatment. This condition and the treatment for it prevented Minnie from engaging in her usual duties of hosting and socializing that she so enjoyed and for which she was renowned.

According to information from Johns Hopkins Medical Center, both the staging and treatment of breast sarcomas differ from other types of breast cancer. Breast sarcomas do not typically spread through the lymphatic system, meaning that removal of the underarm lymph nodes is usually not required (as it is for other types of breast cancer). This means that much of the initial treatment is non-surgical and can be performed on an outpatient basis.

Treatment aimed at preventing the spread of the cancer elsewhere could be provided via radiation therapy, which did not require hospitalization. However, if/when the sarcoma became too large to treat in this manner and/or metastasizes, treatment progressed to include surgery to remove the tumor and any affected tissue, or a mastectomy, which removed the entire breast.

1947 – A Year of Decision and the Beginning of the End

A Final Appearance on Behalf of Culver

With the war over, his duties as the Dallas-Fort Worth area Local ESMWT Coordinator concluded, and both his memoirs and the initial draft of his second Culver-related manuscript completed, Gignilliat had more time to travel on behalf of Culver. The "Old Man" remained in high demand for alumni events, and he traveled to Detroit to speak at a Culver alumni event on March 28, 1947.

Gignilliat made this trip on his own, as Minnie had taken a bad fall in their apartment earlier in the month, resulting a broken pelvis which largely incapacitated her while it healed. Recovery must have been long for the aged dame, and it likely made it more difficult for her to take care of her ailing husband. It is likely that traveling on his own made what may have been ignored up to this point quite evident: Gignilliat's physical condition was deteriorating and needed treatment.

Parkinson's Diagnosis

A subsequent visit to the doctor confirmed what he and Minnie had perhaps suspected: Gignilliat was suffering from the effects of Parkinson's Disease. Manifestations include the characteristic palsy, or tremors, associated with this condition, along with a significant reduction in mobility. Many suffering from Parkinson's Disease find that their gait is reduced to a shuffle, making it increasingly difficult for them to remain ambulatory. This would make it quite challenging to remain living in a high-rise apartment building like the Blackstone Hotel in Fort Worth. These aspects of his condition likely became increasingly pronounced throughout the remainder of 1947 and into 1948, forcing the couple to consider alternative living arrangements.

Furthermore, and as his own condition worsened, Minnie's breast cancer reduced her ability to provide her husband the care he needed, including helping him in the bathroom, bathing, and even eating. While able to provide him the assistance he needed as his Parkinson's Disease symptoms began manifesting themselves, her ability to continue doing so became progressively reduced as his needs increased and her own condition continued to worsen.

The deterioration of motor functions associated with Parkinson's Disease begins well prior to the physical manifestation of its symptoms, so it makes sense that the Culver event in Detroit at the end of March 1947 would be Gignilliat's final official appearance on behalf of Culver, as his symptoms likely began manifesting around this period. For the appearance-conscious Gignilliat, this diagnosis, coupled with the reduced mobility and uncontrollable tremors that are characteristic of the condition, likely resulted in him determining that he no longer felt comfortable representing Culver in public.

The Decision to Move to Chicago

With Minnie receiving treatment for her breast cancer and the broken pelvis she suffered in 1947, along with Gignilliat's own worsening physical status and diagnosis with a progressively degenerative condition, it was time for the couple to reassess their living situation. It also became apparent that apartment living was no longer feasible for either of them, given their mobility challenges. Accordingly, they had to make a move to a place where his ability to receive the medical care he needed was co-located with her ability to live comfortably.

The effects of Parkinson's Disease are both chronic, meaning they persist, progressive, and degenerative, meaning the symptoms grow worse over time. In many cases, by the time a diagnosis is made, the effects may have already progressed to a point where people are beginning to experience difficulty controlling the movement of their bodies due to the involuntary shaking brought about by the tremors, the diminishing of reflexes that is another impact of the condition, and a progressive stiffening of the limbs and/or the trunk of the body, all of which contributes to an overall slowness of movement, impaired balance, and reduced mobility. As these symptoms progress, walking, talking, swallowing, and completing other simple tasks can become challenging.

The Parkinson's diagnosis made the couple acutely aware that Gignilliat would be invalided at some point, and that Minnie would need some place to live. Discussions with family members almost certainly resulted in offers of lodging and assistance from the three children: Leigh Jr. living in Chicago; Fred living in Fort Worth; and Hank living in Delafield, Wisconsin. The older Gignilliats were fully aware of what living with Fred in the Fort Worth Area offered, and they likely considered living with Hank in Delafield to be a bit too remote (even though it was close to Milwaukee).

However, the prospect of living with Leigh Jr. in Chicago presented real advantages, as the Hines Medical Center was renowned for its treatment of veterans, and Leigh Jr. had just moved to with in 15 miles of the facility. Needing to be near both excellent medical care, since Minnie could no longer provide him the care he needed, and also family (for a place to live), Chicago, which satisfied both, became the obvious choice for relocation.

The type of care he would require was likely more along the lines of palliative care (which is quite common for Parkinson's Disease patients). Intended to improve quality of life by helping with symptoms, enhancing current care, and focusing on quality of life for them and their family, palliative care can be helpful at any stage of illness but is best provided soon after a person is diagnosed.

With the capacity to care for over 3,000 patients by the time of Gignilliat's arrival, Hines also had a medical research division and partnered with five medical schools to become a training center, along with the capability to manufacture some of its own medical equipment. It was also a state-of-the-art facility that offered unparalleled care and treatment for those who had served the nation.

Becoming a veteran's hospital almost immediately upon opening, the hospital at Hines specialized in providing just such care, allowing Gignilliat to receive assistance using the bathroom, bathing, and helping him eat (which was always a concern for the ever-gaunt man). Designed so that every room could have sunlight, and along with a magnificent Doughboy Fountain honoring World War I veterans like Gignilliat, and extensive landscaping that appealed to the gardener in him, Hines hospital was a perfect fit for Gignilliat to be infirmed. Such a facility satisfied Minnie's requirement that he receive the best possible care and be comfortable.

Leigh Jr. had just moved from New Trier into an apartment in the Near Northside neighborhood of downtown Chicago (12 East Scott Street) that was located near the Hines medical facility (within 15 miles). Along with providing an excellent government hospital in Hines, and the ability to live with Leigh Jr. and his family, Chicago also allowed Minnie to continue receiving the treatment she needed. Accordingly, and once Minnie was able to travel, the Gignilliats departed Fort Worth for Chicago in 1948.

A New Reality – The Challenges of Living with Parkinson's Disease in a Hospital

The move to Chicago in 1948 allowed for the couple to live with Leigh Jr, and for Gignilliat to receive excellent care at the renowned Hines veteran medical center. After getting settled in the area, and probably as expected, Gignilliat's condition had deteriorated to the point that he was admitted to Hines on April 20, 1949, where he resided for the remainder of his life (departing for short periods in 1950, 1951, and 1952), while Minnie continued to live with Leigh Jr. and his family and received outpatient treatment for her cancer.

It is important to note that, while many people with Parkinson's Disease eventually develop dementia, which is also a leading reason for Parkinson's patients to transition from independent living at home to long-term care facilities, Gignilliat appears to have retained his mental faculties to the end (based upon the credible assessments of people able to observe him in action, like Allen Elliott).

Culver Provided Two Compelling Events for Gignilliat to Be Away from the Hospital

Once admitted, Gignilliat was largely invalided and lived most of his days in Hines in relative comfort. He did leave for special occasions, both related to the construction of a new building on Culver's campus: Memorial Chapel.

The construction effort for Memorial Chapel was part of the new strategic plan – the Culver Plan – developed and implemented by Gregory, and the building represented the first major addition on Culver's campus with which Gignilliat had not been directly involved since the rebuilding of Main Barrack in 1895. He had been involved in the fundraising efforts for the building, but this was clearly an effort associated with and guided by Gregory. As such, it was an unusual situation for Gignilliat to return to campus for the laying of a cornerstone of a building that had not been one of his own initiatives. Gignilliat made two visits to Culver related to this structure:

- October 22, 1950, for the laying of the cornerstone for Memorial Chapel.

- October 22, 1951, for the dedication of Memorial Chapel and a brief inspection.

He was not a speaker at either event, and his presence was barely mentioned in contemporary accounts, indicating both that he was likely quite incapacitated and that his presence was largely ceremonial. Nevertheless, he appears differently at each, and it is worth exploring these episodes more closely, since they represent his final public appearances at Culver.

October 22, 1950 – Laying of the Cornerstone for Memorial Chapel – Looking His Age

Gignilliat's presence on campus for the event on October 22, 1950, reflected his overall marginalization with respect to Culver and to this particular project. He was not part of the official stage party for the event. Shunted instead off to the side in civilian clothes and a wheelchair, Gignilliat was as unremarkable as possible. Nor was his presence mentioned in the school's coverage of the event, and he was

Laying of the cornerstone, October 22, 1950.[29]

Gignilliat to the side of the official party at the cornerstone laying, October 22, 1950.³⁰

Gignilliat looking old, frail, and somewhat isolated at the cornerstone laying, October 22, 1950.³¹

not visible in any of the published photographs of the event. The only way one would know that he was present was if one had attended the ceremony in person and/or had access to uncropped photographs of the events, like the one below.

Perhaps, based on his own health, his diminished role was as he wanted it to be. He looks particularly frail, and his countenance lacks its usual vitality, suggesting that he may have been struggling in terms of his health. Nor does it appear that Minnie was with him, suggesting that her health was not sufficient to allow her to accompany her husband (as she almost always had). If this was the case, it helps to further explain Gignilliat's marginalization and non-vital presence at such an important Culver event.

What is certain is that the ceremony itself followed the framework he had implemented and perfected at Culver, ensuring that the event was treated with an appropriate level of dignity and that the entire Culver community was involved in its conduct and celebration. While his physical presence may have been diminished, his spiritual presence was as strong as ever at the event in this regard.

October 22, 1951—The Dedication of Memorial Chapel – The Old Man Rallies!

One year later, however, for the official dedication of the Memorial Chapel, was a very different story. Even though Minnie was too ill to accompany him, but perhaps sensing that this might be his "final curtain call" on the Culver stage, the old man rallied for the dedication of Memorial Chapel on October 22, 1951, having sufficient energy to conduct of a brief inspection of it.

Gone were the civilian clothes and the wheelchair. In their place,

A gaunt but mobile Gignilliat at the Memorial Chapel dedication ceremony, October 22, 1951.[32]

Gignilliat arrived resplendent in his military uniform, standing ramrod straight and striding purposefully around campus..

Gignilliat looks thin (more thin than usual) but better in the 1951 photo, compared to the 1950 photos of him in a wheelchair.

As one can tell from the photograph below, his presence appears to overshadow even that of Gregory, who was most responsible for bringing the idea of a memorial chapel into reality.

Looking much hardier, Gignilliat appears to be more comfortable and at ease among the notable dignitaries gathered on the reviewing line than does Gregory (at his left), feeling perhaps back in his element and among his colleagues and friends in the place he most loved. Indeed, the photograph above suggests that Gignilliat is the true "man of honor" at the ceremony.

A more robust and mobile Gignilliat at the Memorial Chapel dedication ceremony, October 22, 1951.[33]

A direct comparison of his appearance is illustrative. The contrast between his condition on the same date exactly one year apart is as striking as it is counterintuitive, as one would expect his condition to have been better in 1950 and worse in 1951. Gignilliat's health appears to be nearing its nadir in 1950 and more akin to how most remembered him in 1951. He conducted a brief inspection after the 1951 dedication ceremony, indicating that he was in better health.

October 22, 1950   *October 22, 1951*

Perhaps Gignilliat had an inkling that this would be his final public appearance at Culver and in uniform and rose to the occasion once more. Thus ended his 55-year tenure at Culver that began on a snowy evening on January 13, 1897, and ended on a crisp fall afternoon on October 22, 1951.

A Final Anniversary Celebration with Minnie

The *Culver Citizen* reported that the Gignilliats celebrated their 53rd wedding anniversary on August 2, 1951, together in Leigh Jr's apartment in Chicago. This occasion was especially significant because Gignilliat was brought from the hospital (where he lived) to join Minnie in their son's apartment. This was a very pleasant surprise for Minnie, who was beginning to be more impacted by her cancer at the time. As it turned out, it was fortuitous that they found a way to celebrate what would be their final wedding anniversary together.

Minnie's health continued to decline, and she died on March 20, 1952, bringing to an end a remarkable love story and relationship of over 50 years. Gignilliat left the hospital to attend Minnie's funeral service and internment at Culver on May 20, 1952. This was likely his final visit outside the hospital.

Thus it was that only the two great loves of his life – Culver and Minnie – could coax him out of the hospital during his final years.

Minnie's Death

Despite Gignilliat being the one confined to the hospital, it was the slightly older Minnie (born January 27, 1873) who passed away first. Her health appears to have taken a substantial turn for the worse in late 1951 or at the beginning of 1952, likely involving the tumor(s) in her breast(s) having grown too large to treat effectively and/or having metastasized and requiring surgical excision. Her condition required a greater level of care than Leigh Jr. and his family could provide, so Minnie took up residence at Maple Wood Rest Home near Wheaton, Illinois, in January 1952.

The trauma of the procedure must have been significant, as she remained anemic and was never able to return to Leigh Jr.'s house. Succumbing to her eight-year battle with cancer, she died at 7:30 pm on March 20, 1952, at Maple Wood Rest Home. She was 77 years old.

Culver men around the world felt a pang of loss at her passing that brought a flood of memories of the gracious First Lady of Culver and Mother to the Corps whose queenly spirit, infectious goodness, gladsome heart, and tireless energy ensured that she would remain "forever alive in their minds" that were "made better by her presence" in influence.[34]

According to one of the many tributes written on her behalf, for many young men who, during their first weeks at Culver became homesick plebes who felt the world had deserted them, it was from Mrs. Gignilliat that they received their first morale boost at her plebe parties. According to the stirring tribute written by Frederick Hunt, "With unerring tact, with ready wit and keenest skill, she flitted among her charges, somehow managed to talk with each one, to unearth some common tie with his home town, and to brace him up with her cheering words."[36]

Mrs. Gignilliat – "First Lady of Culver and Mother to the Corps" – looking marvelous.[35]

Her impact was not limited to first-year cadets, persisting among the "Old Men" as recipients of her hospitality, talking with her of their homes, hopes, and dreams. Hunt observed that, "It was a genuine interest in people, and above all, in these cadets that passed through Culver year after year that brought this intimate relationship with 'her boys.'" Minnie was a source of comfort to anxious Culver parents as well, being welcomed by her into the extended Culver "family" while their sons were on campus and long afterwards in life-long friendships.

According to another tribute to her from the period, "As the daughter of one superintendent of Culver Military Academy and as the wife of another superintendent her life spanned two periods in its development; the early beginning and later the development and

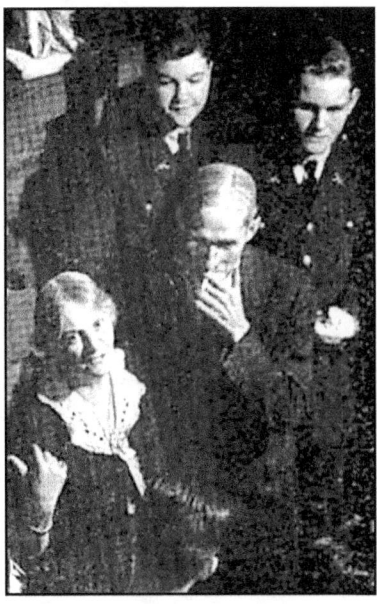

Mrs. Gignilliat, hosting cadets at the Superintendent's quarters, as countless Culver cadets encountered her and remembered her fondly.[37]

expansion of a great educational institution." She was, as much as her renowned husband, an "Institutional Woman."

Her many roles as Culver's First Lady and Mother to the Corps included:

- Welcoming guests in her own home;
- Receiving at the Academy balls;
- Supporting the teams as keenly as the boys;
- Decorating the Gold Star flag on Memorial Day;
- Greeting generals, foreign and domestic;
- Doing the honors for distinguished visitors that came and went.

Hunt wrote, "She did it all with a vivacity of spirit that never flagged," reflecting, in her own way, the indefatigable energy of her husband.[38]

Hunt's tribute makes reference to a particular trait of Mrs. Gignilliat that impressed many and made her an invaluable partner for her husband: her remarkable memory. According to Hunt:

> *"Not least of Mrs. Gignilliat's qualities was an almost uncanny memory that sometimes startled and always amazed. Long years after they had passed from Culver she would encounter old boys whose rotund shape and receding brows bore little resemblance to the striplings she had known. But only a moment was needed for her agile mind to leap the years; reminded by some glint of the eye, a familiar smile, or a characteristic gesture – presto! She would call their names and amaze them with some lively recollection of their cadet days."*[39]

The cadets' affection and admiration for her is conveyed touchingly in the special honor they bestowed upon her by dedicating the 1916 *Roll Call* to her:

> *"To the lady of the open door and the outstretched hand; mother of us all at Culver; whether Plebes or Old Men, privates, non-comms or commissioned officers; friend to us when in trouble and fount of hope to those of us who were faint of heart; a guide to many along life's highway; genial hostess, wise counselor and kind friend; the Class of Nineteen Sixteen affectionately dedicates this Roll Call to you, Mrs. Gignilliat."*[40]

This sentiment for her was shared by scores of associates and friends.

According to Hartman,

"For 54 years she had been an integral part of her husband's endeavors and was, in her own way, as influential as her husband in establishing traditions at the Academy. The gala cotillions which became part of the spirit of Culver were largely her creation, and her place as the arbiter of social graces and the expectation of gentlemanly behavior for all cadets at the Academy was unquestioned. She was the perfect wife for the head of the school and her loss was keenly felt by hundreds of winter and summer students.[41]

According to a journalist from Texas, Minnie "lived well " and had "the gift of bringing home to her family wherever she happens to be. Boys from all over the world seem to find their way to this lovely couple; Chinese, British, and American men, who have seen service all over the world." Minnie "always seems to have a helpful word for all of them." According to one account, if/when she encountered a boy who appeared to be bored, she would remark with her characteristic energy and positivity:

For heaven's sake don't ever let this become a habit. There are too many beautiful things in the world to see, too many interesting people to meet and too many necessary things to be done.

She was, for more than fifty years, Gignilliat's spouse, confidante, and devoted partner who enjoyed with her husband what one referred to as *"a beautiful companionship."* Their pairing was such that he had to have felt her passing viscerally, becoming somewhat lost without her steadying presence and ability to instantly commiserate with him, sharing both his sorrows and joys as only a partner of such long standing could do.

Honoring Culver's First Lady – A State Funeral on Campus

Minnie was given the equivalent of a state funeral at Culver, with the service occurring in the newly dedicated Memorial Chapel and the interment occurring at the local Masonic cemetery in Culver. Minnie's funeral service was conducted in the Memorial Chapel by the Academy Chaplain, Dr. Hardigg Sexton.

The honor of helping to lay her to rest fell to many longtime friends of the Gignilliat family, but there were too many vying for the privilege. To accommodate as many as possible, the family agreed to designate two types of pallbearers: Active and Honorary. Active pallbearers included

Minnie's headstone at the Culver cemetery.[42]

Edwin R. Culver III, B. L. Curry, Richard Gimbel, Patrick H. Hodgkin, John Mars, and Russel Oliver. Honorary pallbearers included ER Culver Jr, William E, Gregory, Robert Rossow, J. W. Henderson, C. A. Whitney, Frank Brooke, W. G. Johnston, L. R. Kellam, C. C. Mather, George L. Miller, W. O. Osborn, and L. J. Stone. In aggregate, they represented the most impressive gathering of Culver's most distinguished individuals assembled on campus in recent memory.

The End for Gignilliat

Gignilliat's own health continued to decline, perhaps exacerbated by the loss of his beloved Minnie. He had been living in the hospital for three and one-half years. He suffered a heart attack on October 28, 1952. Lingering for two days, he died of natural causes at 6:58 am on October 30, 1952, at Hines hospital at the age of 77. The cause of death was listed as "cardiac failure" brought on by arteriosclerotic heart disease, likely exacerbated by his smoking and/or high cholesterol. In addition, he had Parkinson's Disease for at least five years (and perhaps longer), which may have contributed to his death but was not related to the disease or condition causing his death.

His passing marked the end of one of Culver's most remarkable influencers. It also brought to a close a six-decade era, stretching back to Culver's founding, that had defined the school and would continue to influence it for the next six decades and beyond. Scarcely anyone associated with Culver during the period 1894-1952 could conceive of the school without Gignilliat, or Gignilliat apart from Culver. Such was his impact, influence, and legacy.

The Passing of a Culver Giant – Gignilliat's Campus Funeral

As he would have done for anyone of similar stature at Culver, Gignilliat was given the equivalent of a state funeral at Culver, and it was attended by many luminaries who came to pay tribute to one of the century's great secondary educators.

As reported by Hartman:

> *His funeral service was conducted in the Memorial Chapel.*
> *Following the sermon, cadet pallbearers carried the coffin to the*
> *chapel plaza where the band played ruffles and flourishes and*
> *"The General's March." The funeral cortege then moved across*
> *the campus to Logansport Gate, led by the Infantry Honor*
> *Guard and Band as an 11-gun salute was fired in his honor. This*
> *Culver giant among giants was laid to rest at the local Masonic*
> *Cemetery beside his beloved Mamie.*[43]

Gignilliat's casket inside Memorial Chapel.[44]

Culver pulled out all the stops for this occasion. As it had been for Minnie seven months prior, the funeral service was conducted by the Academy Chaplain, Dr. Hardigg Sexton. Inside Memorial Chapel, the cadet choir sang the Bach hymn "Come, Sweet Death," and Sexton reminded the cadets that they were the beneficiaries of the efforts of the man being honored and laid to his final rest.

Upon completion of the service inside the chapel, the service moved outside to the terrace in front of the chapel, with the Color Guard on the west side and the Band on the east side. Flanked by six cadet captains as pallbearers, the Color Guard came to "present arms" while the Band played ruffles and flourishes and the "General's March."

Moving down the west walk toward the Recreation Building between two lines of the Honor Guard, the casket was placed in the funeral car. The remainder of the corps lined the route from the chapel through Sally Port to Logansport Gate and the funeral procession moved between them as the great Bourdon bell of the carillon tolled slowly and an eleven-gun salute was fired by the battery in his honor. Departing campus through Logansport Gate, the funeral procession made its way to the Masonic cemetery and the remainder of the corps was dismissed.

At the cemetery, the funeral part was joined by members of Gignilliat's family and the Culver faculty. The General was laid to rest by the cadet pallbearers, and an eight-cadet firing detail fired a final salute. His final response was in a family plot next to the woman he loved, near the school and lake he treasured, and in the community that he had made his home for almost 50 years.[47]

Gignilliat's casket outside Memorial Chapel during his funeral service, Nov 2, 1952.[45]

A military perfectionist and gifted showman, he would have appreciated the pomp and precision of the ceremony that was entirely appropriate for the occasion and which provided a most fitting send-off for him.

Alumni and students visit his grave site occasionally. A recent tradition has been for the Black Horse Troop to mark his passing with a ride and brief ceremony at his graveside on the Sunday closest to the anniversary of his death, surely warming the heart and soul of this "giant" of Culver.

Gignilliat's funeral procession on campus.[46]

Gignilliat family plot marker for both Gignilliat and Minnie, Culver Masonic Cemetery.[48]

Headstone for Gignilliat's grave, Culver Masonic Cemetery.[49]

While the school bears the Culver name, it was the spirit of Gignilliat that animated it for most of its existence until his death. No single individual has had comparable impact on the school, either in terms of significance or duration. Indeed, the *Spirit of Culver* became synonymous with the Spirit of Gignilliat on campus and for a half-century of Culver men. Culver historian Bob Hartman was perhaps most successful in capturing the essence of Gignilliat's influence and impact on Culver, dubbing him Culver's "giant of giants."

Epilogue

How to capture the essence of a man who was as thin as a sapling but as sturdy as an oak? Perhaps the best way of doing so is to consider his own assessment of his worth, identify the crux of his achievements, and then position his accomplishments within a broader context of the times and milieu in which they occurred to weigh their lasting impact.

Gignilliat's Own Assessment

Gignilliat titled the unpublished final chapter of his memoirs, "The Summing Up," which contains the only known record of his own assessment of his accomplishments and impact. Ascribing minimal weight to his personal efforts regarding Culver's achievements as an educational institution, Gignilliat took little credit for its success.

He believed that the honors bestowed upon him were "unreal," mostly unwarranted, and far more than he deserved. According to his assessment, he was simply *"a school man who succeeded because he had a good many breaks."* In true Gignilliat fashion, he shifted the attention away from himself, offering that *"the real credit goes to the many unsung teachers of the Academy...who have worked in such close personal contact with the boys"* and who had *"dedicated their lives to the education of our youth."*[1]

Through his rhetoric and emphasis, Gignilliat concluded his memoirs in the same manner in which he served Culver: Minimalizing attention on him and championing the efforts of those who had the most impact on the cadets and, by extension, on the school itself.

Positioning His Accomplishments Within a Broader Context

As portrayed in this biography and the historical record upon which it is based, the picture of him that emerges is far more acclamatory. Gignilliat comes across as being an honest man and indefatigable worker able to elicit trust, confidence, and respect from others, and a gifted organizational leader with an instinctive understanding of what appealed to boys and young soldiers and a genius for marketing. Neither a natural intellect, strategic thinker, nor a visionary in the traditional sense, he was a talented individual who succeeded by dint of hard work, perseverance, determination, persistence, common sense, and genuine care for others, all in the pursuit of the common and/or greater good.

Overall, Gignilliat is perhaps best characterized as being a morally righteous "strategic opportunist" who was particularly well suited to function in many of the positions he held. The innovation and growth that arose from this noble strategic opportunism fostered a corresponding culture on campus among the faculty and staff that was as generative and it was synergistic, driving Culver to ever-greater levels of performance and achievement, and furthering Culver's competitive advantage. This culture brought with it flexibility and adaptability, making Culver an exceptionally nimble institution able to change quickly, encouraging continuous growth and innovations that allowed it to continue to thrive in dynamic and uncertain times both prior to WWI and for the ensuing decades afterwards.

What remained constant was the core of who Gignilliat was: An honorable gentleman devoted to the success of those institutions with which he was associated. While his legendary level of energy may have flagged on occasion, and his level of influence decreased steadily throughout the 1930s internally and externally, his character, integrity, zeal, selflessness, and devotion to Minnie and family remained constant and consistent.

The Crux of Gignilliat's Achievements – The Culver System + Personal Example

The system Gignilliat developed at Culver and his personal example as an exemplar of that system were most responsible for his tremendous impact and account for his enduring legacy.

Based upon a collective ethos while also allowing for a certain amount of individualism essential to adolescent boys and fostering creativity, the system he developed was as innovative as it was ingenious. Gignilliat cleverly melded the Protestant social ethic of "rugged individualism" with a belief that the proper role for the individual was to be subsumed within the institution and a community ethos that stressed cooperation and high-mindedness. There was also some of Adam Smith's emphasis on the value of individual excellence incorporated into the method. Cadets excelled based upon their own merit and performance, and not at the expense of others, within the context of promoting and perpetuating the success of a larger institution for a greater good, championing a sustained collectivist culture and character.

Competition was an intrinsic part of this approach. Unlike most other military schools, it was competition that was measured against defined standards of excellence for individual honors instead of against one another. At Culver, as with Gignilliat, all were "self-made men" based upon their talents, abilities, and efforts.

Wearing a common uniform while also being able to express their individualism meaningfully in the rank and awards they earned for themselves as a result of their individual efforts in the military, academic, athletic, and extracurricular programs enabled them to develop their own identities even as they remained bound together communally. This somewhat insulated community was oriented on the Culture of Character, providing a righteous scaffolding within which they could exist and progress as their unique personalities emerged.

His approach also allowed for wholesome contests among the various groups to which cadets belonged, centered around their home units. These aspects allowed boys to pursue individual goals to establish their own identities while also providing them with a collective purpose, enhancing their sense of belonging to something larger than themselves and the value of both earning and retaining acceptance. Appealing to the primordial needs of boys, these features made Gignilliat's system constructive and ennobling.

Operating the system without the developmentally destructive adversarial component and adopting a more constructive approach that encouraged care and respect within a challenging and safe environment was yet another distinctive feature of Gignilliat's system that contributed mightily to its effectiveness and distinctiveness. This tempered the damaging aspects of adolescent male competition and served to bring out the very best in boys.

Within such a system, the impetus for the individual was to be/become the best version of the "institutional" person idealized within the culture. This ingenious system allowed the boy to make his greatest contribution to the community through self-improvement efforts. Stated a bit differently, individual excellence in the areas that mattered to such a society were intrinsic goods, and striving for them became as much an individual goal as it was a collective effort.

This rigorous and respectful scheme was quite attractive to many parents of the period. Mothers and fathers believed that the ever-trustworthy Gignilliat would use his tough but fair system to help transform their sons into the honorable and capable young men they were destined to be.

It was, in many ways, as ideal of a utopia as was possible to conceive for adolescent lads at the time. Boys thrived in such a system, became the best versions of themselves, and derived immense satisfaction from their efforts and status as accepted members of a community that they valued and which had tangible benefits for them. It was Gignilliat's masterpiece.

Subjecting himself to this system and becoming its exemplar was a complementary masterstroke. Besides enabling Gignilliat to accomplish things and achieve a level of success far beyond anything that either anyone could have predicted for him, doing so allowed him and his success to exemplify the power of the Culver system he designed and implemented to do the same for boys who embraced it. One had to look no further than Gignilliat himself to get an idea of the possibilities and potential of embracing the "Culver Way" of Gignilliat's system.

Considering Gignilliat's Lasting Impact

The story of Leigh Robinson Gignilliat is one of symbiosis between a leader and institution, of each making the other better and helping one another to realize their full potential. This process relied upon character, integrity, selflessness, and duty, none of which ever go out of style. Gignilliat was a truly remarkable person, and his example and achievements serve as enduring beacons of light and hope for all to emulate.

His true genius was his sincere ability to use his intellect, intuition, energy, and experience to lead young men through persuasion to want to accept an arduous program that improved them individually and which allowed them to make meaningful contributions to the greater good. Using the institution of CMA, the organization of the corps of cadets, and the community of Culver as models and examples, he tried to do extend his influence with the US Army brigade he commanded for almost 20 years.

Throughout his life, he personified the *Spirit of Culver*, demonstrating an indefatigable *hope to win* and *zeal to dare*, along with *contempt for what is base and mean, pride in achievement that is fair, and high regard for what is clean.* Promoting and perpetuating *the strength that is in brotherhood* across many organizations, he showed time and again that he *possessed the courage that proclaims success* in almost every endeavor. At his core resided *the will to strive for what is good,* and his slender figure epitomized embodied for many in the Culver community what they considered to be *first and always, manliness.* Indeed, Samuel Ellsworth "S. E." Kiser could scarcely have imagined a more fitting exemplar for his stirring 1912 couplet verse.

In terms of social impact, Gignilliat was able to navigate the challenges of the anti-militarists successfully by countering efforts to characterize Culver as being overtly and/or overly "militaristic," focusing instead on the constructive and ennobling educational value of the military model. He did so, not by engaging in the fear-mongering rhetoric of the perils of being unprepared, but rather, by focusing on the positives of using a military system to improve young men and prepare them deliberately and intentionally to be a well-educated and capable citizens willing and able to make meaningful contributions to society.

As part of this effort, he was able to co-opt the emerging understanding of adolescence and concerns about industrialized American society making its young men too "soft" into a justification for using a challenging military approach to mold young men of value by imparting desirable character, values, citizenship, and leadership abilities.

An Exceptional Institution Requires an Exceptional Leader

An exceptional institution needs an exceptional leader, and Gignilliat was more than able to satisfy that requirement. His personal performance and success helped to establish and sustain Culver's reputation for excellence, providing manifestations of it in numerous ways. Belief in the effectiveness of Gignilliat's system transformed into a form of exceptionalism at Culver, and Gignilliat's achievements demonstrated, illustrated, reinforced, and perpetuated it.

The essence of the Culver system he developed has remained largely unchanged, and given the essentially immutable nature of boyhood and adolescence, it has retained its fundamental value up to the present day. There is a certain amount of comfort in that continuity. In addition, its historical and continued impact on Culver is perhaps the main reason we should perpetuate the memory of him.

Do Times Make the Man or Does the Man Make the Time?

A perennial issue in the scholarship regarding "great men" addresses the issue of whether it is the times that make the man or if it is the man that makes the times. For Gignilliat, it began as the former and evolved into the latter. He worked tirelessly on behalf of Culver and the Army for his entire life. In the end, Gignilliat was a man perfectly suited for the times, both at Culver and in the Army, and he in turn helped to make the times what they became for both.

Endnotes

Introduction

1. Charles Mather, *History of Culver Military Academy, 1894.1956*, unpublished manuscript, Culver Archives, 1959. Richard Gwyn Davies, *Of Arms and the Boy: A History of Culver Military Academy, 1894-1945*, unpublished PhD dissertation, Indiana University, 1984.

2. Robert B. D. "Bob" Hartman was the Official Culver Historian, and he wrote (at least) 46 different works regarding Culver and its history, addressing myriad topics. I have made use of many of these works in this biography and provide specific references for them throughout the work.

Ch. 1 – Leigh R. Gignilliat Family Background and Early Life

1. Image posted by Davis E. McCollum to *Find a Grave* website on July 29. 2021.

2. Much of this information came from three sources: William Harden, *History of Savannah and South Georgia*, (The Lewis Publishing Company, 1913), pp. 1016-1022; Robert Gignilliat Kenan, *History of the Gignilliat Family of Switzerland and South Carolina*, (Southern Historical Press, 1977), *passim*; and information provided to the author by the Georgia Historical Society, "Gignilliat Family Papers," (MS2077), Series 1, 2, 3, 5, Boxes 1, 2, 11

3. Courtesy of Google Images (in the public domain).

4. Joy Fisher, "Gignilliat, William Robert, 1839-1995," McIntosh-Chatham-Baldwin County, Georgia Archives Biographies, pp. 1016-1022, 31 October, 2004.

5. Most of this information was combined by the author from three sources: William Harden, *History of Savannah and South Georgia*, (The Lewis Publishing Company, 1913), pp. 1016-1022; Robert Gignilliat Kenan, *History of the Gignilliat Family of Switzerland and South Carolina*, (Southern Historical Press, 1977), *passim*; and information provided to the author by the Georgia Historical Society, "Gignilliat Family Papers," (MS2077), Series 1, 2, 3, 5, Boxes 1, 2, 11.

6. According to a contemporary appearing in the *Savannah Moring News*, the gunshot wound came a result of a heated quarrel occurring at Stokes Bluff, South Carolina (on the border between Georgian and South Carolia) between Gignilliat and an African American named Elmund Stevenson, Jr. over the status of a business arrangement to transport a horse owned by Gignilliat. After returning the next morning to attempt to resolve the issue, Gignilliat became quite angry and struck Stevenson with a switch or stick, and Stevenson responded by reaching for his shot gun. Gignilliat drew his pistol and fired, striking Stevenson in the groin and severing a vein. Before dying, Stevenson returned fire and shot Gignilliat in the face with a full load of Number 4 buckshot. About 40 pieces of shot struck Gignilliat in the head and face, tearing his left eye completely out of his head and rendering him unconscious. Mortally wounded, the doctor could do nothing for Gignilliat, who was transported to the boarding house in which he was residing in Brighton, Georgia, and made as comfortable as possible. Gignilliat survived for about 12 hours after the shooting before dying from the wound around midnight on December 11, 1890. "Stokes Bluff Tragedy," *Savannah Morning News*, December 13, 1890, p. 8.

7. Leigh R. Gignilliat , unpublished chapter from manuscript, *Unfurling the Colors: Reminiscences of a Culver Superintendent*, circa 1947, copy provided to author by Mary Margret Gignilliat.

8. Gignilliat , unpublished chapter from manuscript, *Unfurling the Colors: Reminiscences of a Culver Superintendent*, circa 1947, copy provided to author by

736

Mary Margret Gignilliat. Winning a silver medal for declaiming from "Emerson Institute" article in *The Evening Star: Washington, DC*, June 17, 1891, p. 7.

9. Image courtesy of Find a Grave (in the public domain).

10. Gignilliat, *Unfurling the Colors: Reminiscences of a Culver Superintendent*, p. 44.

11. Gignilliat, *Unfurling the Colors: Reminiscences of a Culver Superintendent*, p. 44.

12. *Report of the Commissioner of Education for the Year 1898-99*, vol. 2, Washington, DC: Government Printing Office, 1900), pp. 2064-2065.

13. "The Emerson Institute" article in *The Evening Star: Washington, DC*, June 19, 1889, p. 8; "Emerson Institute" article in *The Evening Star: Washington, DC*, June 17, 1891, p. 7.

14. Gignilliat, *Unfurling the Colors: Reminiscences of a Culver Superintendent*, p. 75.

15. "Emerson Institute" article in *The Evening Star: Washington, DC*, June 17, 1891, p. 7.

16. Image courtesy of VMI Archives.

17. William C. Davis, *The Battle of New Market*, (Louisianna State University Press,1975), pp. 52-53.

18. Shipp had also (briefly) served as President of Virgina A&M (now Virgina Tech) in August 1880. William Couper, *One Hundred Years at VMI*, Vol. 4, (Garrett and Massie, Inc, 1939), p. 105.

19. Couper, *One Hundred Years at VMI*, Vol. 4, p. 105; Wise, *Drawing Out the Man*, pp. 71-76.

20. VMI historian Henry Wise provides corroboration for Shipp's prioritization of discipline. Henry A. Wise, *Drawing Out the Man: The VMI Story*, (University Press of Virginia, 1978), p. 77. Historian Ed Cray provides further support for Shipp's focus on discipline within his uncharacteristically harsh assessment of VMI during this period in his otherwise remarkably objective biography of George C. Marshall, likely stemming from Marshall's own experience while attending VMI and self-identified preference for the "military aspects of life at VMI" at the time. Ed Cray, *General of the Army: George C. Marshall, Solider and Statesman*, (W. W. Norton & Company, 1990), pp. 24-25, 27.

21. Letter from Robinson to Shipp, June 5, 1891, VMI Archives.

22. Couper, *One Hundred Years at VMI*, Vol. 4, p. 48.

23. *Educational Attainment and Achievement Chartbook*, Russell Sage Foundation, 2010, p. 2, accessed on August 16, 2017; see also Theodore Caplow, Louis Hicks, and Ben J. Wattenberg, *The First Measured Century: An Illustrated Guide to Trends in America, 1900-2000* (Washington, DC: AEI Press, 2000), p. 52.

24. Image courtesy of the VMI Archives.

25. Description and explanation of the VMI method of calculating the General Order of Merit (GOM) provided by Colonel Diane B. Jacob, head of archives and records management at the Virginia Military Institute's Preston Library, August 16, 2017.

26. Cadet Record of Leigh R. Gignilliat, provided to author by the VMI Archives.

27. Letter from Leigh Robinson to General Scott Shipp, January 8, 1892, VMI Archives.

28. Cadet Record of Leigh R. Gignilliat, provided to author by the VMI Archives.

29. W. J. Rorabaugh, *The Alcoholic Republic: An American Tradition* (NY: OUP, 1979), pp. 187, 191-218; James L. Morrison, *The Best School in the World: West Point, the Pre-Civil War Years, 1833-1866* (Kent, OH: Kent State University Press, 1986), p. 79; (both quoted from *Custer's Trials* (p. 36 electronic)); Wise, *Drawing Out the*

Man, pp. 233. 296-297.

30. Special Orders, VMI, February 29, 1892, VMI archives.

31. Letter from Leigh Robinson to General Scott Shipp, March 7, 1892, VMI Archives.

32. Gignilliat , unpublished chapter from manuscript, *Unfurling the Colors: Reminiscences of a Culver Superintendent*, circa 1947, copy provided to author by Mary Margret Gignilliat.

33. Gignilliat , "The Old Rat," unpublished chapter from manuscript, *Unfurling the Colors: Reminiscences of a Culver Superintendent*, circa 1947, copy provided to author by Mary Margret Gignilliat.

34. "Fourth Class cadets, 1891-1892," Publications Collection, *Catalogs*, Virginia Military Institute archives, Lexington, Virginia.

35. Image from Robert Gignilliat Kenan, *History of the Gignilliat Family of Switzerland and South Carolina*, (Southern Historical Press, 1977).

36. Gignilliat , "The Boston Stereopticon Company," unpublished chapter from manuscript, *Unfurling the Colors: Reminiscences of a Culver Superintendent*, circa 1947, copy provided to author by Mary Margret Gignilliat.

37. *Register of Former Cadets of VMI*, 1989, p. 112.

38. Gignilliat was the lowest academically ranked cadet in his class to receive that designation in his class that year. "Third Class cadets, 1891-1892," Publications Collection, *Catalogs*, Virginia Military Institute archives, Lexington, Virginia.

39. Cadet Record of Leigh R. Gignilliat, provided to author by the VMI Archives.

40. Image courtesy of the VMI Archives.

41. "Third Class cadets, 1891-1892," Publications Collection, *Catalogs*, Virginia Military Institute archives, Lexington, Virginia.

42. *VMI Bomb* (which is the VMI yearbook), 1895.

43. Wise, *Drawing out the Man*, p. 57.

44. Letter from Leigh Robinson to General Scott Shipp, December 20, 1892, VMI Archives.

45. Image courtesy of the VMI Archives.

46. Gignilliat, *Unfurling the Colors: Reminiscences of a Culver Superintendent*, p. 42.

47. Letter from Leigh Robinson to General Scott Shipp, July 1, 1893, VMI Archives.

48. Gignilliat Letter to Robert A. Marr, August 11, 1893, VMI Archives.

49. *Register of Former Cadets of VMI*, 1989, p. 114.

50. *VMI Bomb*, 1895.

51. "Second Class cadets, 1891-1892," Publications Collection, *Catalogs*, Virginia Military Institute archives, Lexington, Virginia.

52. Letter from Leigh Robinson to General Scott Shipp, January 17, 1894, VMI Archives.

53. Image courtesy of VMI Archives.

54. Letter from Leigh Robinson to General Scott Shipp, January 17, 1894, VMI Archives.

55. Image courtesy of VMI Archives.

56. *VMI Bomb*, 1895.

57. Timothy J. Williams, *Intellectual Manhood: University, Self, and Society in the Antebellum South* (Chapel Hill, ND: The University of North Carolina Press, 2015), p. 87.

58. Leigh Robinson Gignilliat, editor, *The Bomb* (VMI yearbook), (Philadelphia, PA: Huston, Ashmead, Wilson Co. Ltd., 1895), pp. 123-124.

59. Timothy J. Williams, *Intellectual Manhood: University, Self, and Society in the Antebellum South* (Chapel Hill, ND: The University of North Carolina Press, 2015), p. 88.

60. Letter from General Scott Shipp to William S. Gignilliat (brother), October 16, 1894, VMI Archives.

61. Telegram from Leigh Robinson to General Scott Shipp, May 26, 1894, VMI archives.

62. Letter from Gignilliat to General Scott Shipp, July 2, 1894, VMI archives.

63. Letter from Gignilliat to VMI, July 6, 1894, VMI archives.

64. Letter from Thomas H. Gignilliat (brother) to General Scott Shipp, September 25, 1894, VMI archives.

65. Letter from William S. Gignilliat (brother) to General Scott Shipp, October 12, 1894; Letter from Leigh Robinson to General Scott Shipp, October 15, 1894, VMI archives.

66. Letter from General Scott Shipp to William S. Gignilliat (brother), October 16, 1894, VMI Archives.

67. Letter from William S. Gignilliat (brother) to General Scott Shipp, January 11, 1895, VMI archives.

68. *Register of Former Cadets of VMI*, 1989, p. 113.

69. "First Class Graduates, 1895," Publications Collection, *Catalogs*, Virginia Military Institute archives, Lexington, Virginia.

70. Image courtesy of the VMI Archives.

71. Leigh Robinson Gignilliat, editor, *The Bomb* (VMI yearbook), (Philadelphia, PA: Huston, Ashmead, Wilson Co. Ltd., 1895), pp. 59, 61, 123-124, 134, 137, 140.

72. "Special Order No. 3," Headquarters, Virginia Military Institute, January 8, 1895, pp. 10-13, Virginia Military Institute archives, Lexington, Virginia.

73. Special Order, VMI, January 16, 1895, VMI Archives.

74. William S Gignilliat (brother) letter to General Scott Shipp, January 11 1895, VMI archives.

75. Special Order, VMI, January 16, 1895, VMI Archives.

76. Letter from General Scott Shipp to William S. Gignilliat (brother), February 1, 1895, VMI Archives.

77. Letter from Gignilliat to VMI Board of Visitors, February 6, 1895, VMI Archives.

78. *VMI Bomb*, 1895.

79. "First Class Graduates, 1895," Publications Collection, *Catalogs*, Virginia Military Institute archives, Lexington, Virginia.

80. *VMI Bomb*, 1895, preface.

81. Charles Mather, *History of Culver Military Academy, 1894.1956*, unpublished manuscript, Culver Archives, 1959, p. 81. Mather notes that he acquired this information directly from a letter from Gignilliat, dated August 7, 1947.

82. Ari Hoogenboom, "The Pendleton Act and the Civil Service," *The American Historical Review*, 64: 2, Jan 1959), pp. 301-318; p. 313.

83. "Married at Pineora: Mr. Robert D. Gignilliat Weds Miss Lila C. Seabrook," *Savannah Morning News*, April 24, 1896, p. 8.

84. Image is from the color-applied lantern slide of "What a National Park will bring -- A bear dinner," courtesy of Wikipedia, Yellowstone National Park in the public domain.

85. The image is of Horace M. Albright in Yellowstone National Park in 1922 from the National Park Service historic photograph collection.

86. Henry Wellge (1850-1917) - David Rumsey Map Collection (in the public domain).

87. *Fourteenth Report of the United States Civil Service Commission, July 1, 1896 to June 30, 1897* (Washington, DC: Government Printing Office, 1898), p. 73.

88. Ibid., p. 74.

89. According to the records, only 29,474 of the 50,571 applicants passed the exam, equating to a pass rate of 58.3 percent. *Fourteenth Report of the United States Civil Service Commission, July 1, 1896 to June 30, 1897* (Washington, DC: Government Printing Office, 1898), p. 15.

90. *Fourteenth Report of the United States Civil Service Commission, July 1, 1896 to June 30, 1897* (Washington, DC: Government Printing Office, 1898), p. 74.

91. Gignilliat Letter to General Scott Shipp, August 22, 1896, VMI archives.

92. Robert B. D. Hartman, "Gignilliat...As in Giant," Culver Education Foundation, n.d.

93. Charles C. Mather, *History of Culver Military Academy, 1894-1956*, (Culver Education Foundation, 1959), p. 80.

94. Hartman, "Gignilliat...As in Giant."

95. Mather, *History of Culver Military Academy, 1894-1956*, pp. 80-81.

96. Hartman, "Gignilliat...As in Giant."

97. Hartman, "Gignilliat...As in Giant."

98. Hartman, "Gignilliat...As in Giant."

99. Mather, *History of Culver Military Academy, 1894-1956*, p. 81; Mather attributes this information to a letter from he received from Gignilliat on August 7, 1947.

100. Image courtesy of Culver Archives.

101. IIartman, "Gignilliat...As in Giant."

102. Hartman, "Gignilliat...As in Giant."

103. Mather, *History of Culver Military Academy, 1894-1956*, p. 81.

104. Hartman, "Gignilliat...As in Giant.

105. Image from Google Images (in the public domain).

Ch. 2 – The Situation at Culver at the Time of Gignilliat's Arrival

1. "The Life of H. H. Culver," an anonymous document discovered by the author in the Culver Archives that appears to have been written circa 1907 to commemorate the ten-year anniversary of HH Culver's passing, p. 4.

2. Image courtesy of the Culver Archives.

3. *1922-1923 CMA Catalog*, "The Founder," p. 24.

4. Image courtesy of the Culver Archives.

5. Image courtesy of the Culver Archives.

6. This author's sense is that the true reason for HH adopting a military system is unknowable.

7. Image from Robert R.D. Hartman, "To be or Not to be: J. H. McKenzie and C. H. Tebbetts," (Culver Education Foundation, n.d.), p. 1.

8. Image courtesy of the Culver Archives.

9. Bertram B. "BB" Culver Jr., *Those Towers Lofty: A Narrative History of the Culver Campus*, (Culver Education Foundation, 1992), p. 5.

10. BB Culver, *Those Lofty Towers*, p. 5.

11. Robert B. D. Hartman, "Brick, Stone, Steel, Iron...and Lots of Vision," (Culver Education Foundation, n.d.), p. ; *Plymouth Tribune*, 14 June 1906, p. 1.

12. CMA Catalog, 1922-1923, "The Buildings – Fireproof Construction," p. 27.

13. *Plymouth Tribune*, 14 June 1906, p. 1.

14. Robert B. D. Hartman, *Footfalls Through the Century*, Culver Education Foundation,

1994, p. 5.

15. Image from *Culver Alumnus*, "When Culver Was Very Young, Oct 1930, p. 47.

16. Image from *Culver Alumnus*, "The Lengthening Shadow," Jan 1937, p. 2.

17. Letter from FT Neal (Culver Business manager) to HH Culver reporting that Tebbetts had been let go (28 Sept, 1896; #241, CMA Official Correspondence, 1896-1898, Culver Archives). This is the first definitive version of this story based upon credible archival sources ever presented. The author was able to piece it together through a painstaking review of over 500 messages from the period contained in the Culver Archives.

18. Letter from FT Neal (Culver Business manager) to HH Culver reporting that Tebbetts had been let go (28 Sept, 1896; #241, CMA Official Correspondence, 1896-1898, Culver Archives).

19. Image courtesy of the Culver Archives.

20. Image from *The Sigma Chi Quarterly*, Volume 14, 1894-1895 (Chicago, IL, 1895), p. 306.

21. Alexander F. Fleet Letter to General Scott Shipp at VMI, March 18, 1897, (VMI Archives).

22. George W. Cullum's *Register of Officers and Graduates of the United States Military Academy*; Cullum Record; Vol. IV, p336 [Supplement, Vol. IV: 1890 1900]). Goode was a highly experienced cavalryman who had served extensively on the frontier (~ 15 years) prior to coming to MMA, and his service appeared to have prepared him well for an assignment as a PMS&T.

23. *The Culver City Herald*, 23 October 1896, p. 1; based on account from the *St. Louis Post-Dispatch*.

24. *The Culver Vedette*, November 1896, p. 5.

25. Image courtesy of the Society of the Military Horse (in the public domain).

26. *Army and Navy Journal*, Vol 34, October 17, 1896, p. 108.

27. *The Culver Vedette*, November 1896, pp. 10-11; *Army and Navy Journal*, Vol 34, November 21, 1896, p. 197.

28. *The Culver Vedette*, November 1896, p. 11.

29. *The Culver City Herald*, 23 October 1896, p. 1; based on account from the *St. Louis Post-Dispatch*.

30. Image courtesy of the Culver Archives (modified by author).

31. *Congressional Record*, 56th Congress, March 17, 1900, p. 3010.

32. Image from 1909 CMA *Roll Call*, p. 6.

33. *1897 CMA Catalog*, p. 20.

34. *1897 CMA Catalog*, pp. 22-23. (According to the Bureau of Labor Statistics consumer price index, prices in 2023 are 3,571.11% higher than prices in 1897. The dollar experienced an average inflation rate of 2.90% per year during this period, making $2,000,000 in 1897 equivalent to $73,422,208.84 in 2023. The period covered is significant, as it curiously does not include the fire at Culver in February 1895 but does include the fire that destroyed MMA in September 1896. Ending on April 22, 1897, instead of either finishing out the school year or accounting for an entire year up to August 24, 1897, also indicates that the statistics were collected with an eye on getting the catalog printed and published by summer 1897, which coincided very closely with Fleet's time at the school (and also Cook's arrival).

35. *1897 CMA Catalog*, p. 39.

36. *1897 CMA Catalog*, pp. 28-29; G. Stanley Hall, *Adolescence*, Vol. 1, 1904, p. xiii.

37. *1897 CMA Catalog*, p. 30.
38. Ibid.
39. *1897 CMA Catalog*, pp. 30-31.
40. *1897 CMA Catalog*, p. 31.
41. *1897 CMA Catalog*, p. 32.
42. *1897 CMA Catalog*, p. 33.
43. *1897 CMA Catalog*, p. 44.
44. *1897 CMA Catalog*, p. 34.
45. *1897 CMA Catalog*, pp. 34-35, 38, 39.
46. *1897 CMA Catalog*, p. 32.
47. *1897 CMA Catalog*, p. 34.
48. *1897 CMA Catalog*, p. 44.
49. *1897 CMA Catalog*, p. 51.
50. Image from *1907 CMA Catalog*, p. 9.
51. *1897 CMA Catalog*, pp. 52-54.
52. *1897 CMA Catalog*, p. 55.
53. *1897 CMA Catalog*, p. 52.
54. Rex Bowman and Carlos Santos, *Rot, Riot, and Rebellion: Mr. Jefferson's Struggle to Save the University That Changed America,* (Charlottesville, VA: University of Virginia Press, 2013), p. 5.
55. Bowman, *Rot, Riot, and Rebellion*, pp. 133-134.
56. Bowman, *Rot, Riot, and Rebellion*, p. 157.
57. Bowman, *Rot, Riot, and Rebellion*, pp. 4, 135. The University of Virginia did this with undergraduates beginning ~1840s; Culver does it with prep school boys 60 years later beginning in 1897.
58. Major E. B. Garey, *The R.O.T.C. Manual: Freshman Course (1ˢᵗ Year Basic) – A Text Book for the Reserve Officers Training Corps* (Baltimore, MD: Lord Baltimore Press, 1921), p. 3.

Ch. 3 – Gignilliat Takes Charge as Commandant, 1897-1900

1. Robert B. D. Hartman, "Leigh Robinson Gignilliat," unpublished biography of Gignilliat, p. 3, courtesy of the Culver Archives.
2. Hartman, unpublished Gignilliat biography, pp. 3-4.
3. Image from *1897 CMA Catalog*, p. 42.
4. Image from the collection of Mary Margaret Gignilliat, used with permission.
5. Hartman, unpublished Gignilliat biography, p. 4.
6. Image from 1908 *Roll Call.*
7. Hartman, unpublished Gignilliat biography, p. 4.
8. Image courtesy of the Culver Archives.
9. Image from the collection of Mary Margaret Gignilliat, used with permission.
10. Gignilliat, *Unfurling the Colors*, p. 2.
11. Ibid.
12. Hartman, unpublished Gignilliat biography, p. 5.
13. Gignilliat, *Unfurling the Colors*, p. 2.
14. *The Culver Vedette*, 1:3, January 1897, p. 62.
15. Image from *1896 CMA Catalog*, p. 17.
16. Gignilliat, *Unfurling the Colors*, p. 73.
17. Photo from collection of Mary Margret Gignilliat, used with permission.
18. Gignilliat, *Unfurling the Colors*, p. 73.

19. Image from *Culver Alumnus*, "The Lengthening Shadow," Jan 1937, p 5.
20. Image from *1896 CMA Catalog*, p. 12.
21. Hartman, unpublished Gignilliat biography, pp. 7-8.
22. Hartman, unpublished Gignilliat biography, pp. 9-10; Gignilliat, *Unfurling the Colors*, pp. 2-3.
23. Ibid.
24. Hartman, unpublished Gignilliat biography, p. 10.
25. Gignilliat, *Unfurling the Colors*, p. 4.
26. *The Culver Vedette*, 1:3, January 1897, p. 56.
27. Gignilliat, *Unfurling the Colors*, p. 14.
28. Ibid.
29. Photo in the public domain from *Find a Grave* website; information comes from links from *Find A Grave* entry and also from *WikiTree* sources.
30. I found no specific references to Powell anywhere in the Culver Digital Vault, beyond the listing of his name in the CMA catalog from 1902.
31. Powell's name does not appear as Culver's PMS&T in the 1903-1904 CMA Catalog (the entry for that position is blank). Information regarding his death from obituary in *The New York Times*, May 12, 1905.
32. Gignilliat contributed an extensive report of the Culver military system and activities associated with it, providing the best overview of it as it existed during his first year at Culver, along with his initial ideas for how he intended to develop it further. Gignilliat, "Report of the Commandant, 1898 *CMA Catalog*, pp. 53-74.
33. Keith R. Widder, *Reveille Till Taps: Solider Life at Fort Mackinac, 1780-1895*, (Mackinac Island, MI: Mackinac State Historic Parks, 1972), p. 13.
34. *1898 CMA Catalog*, p. 78.
35. Gignilliat, *Unfurling the Colors*, p. 13.
36. *1899 CMA Catalog*, p. 91.
37. *1899 CMA Catalog*, p. 92.
38. Gignilliat, *Unfurling the Colors*, p. 14; Robert B. D. Hartman, "When the Rails Hummed, Part 1," (Culver Education Foundation, n.d.), p. 4.
39. Gignilliat, *Unfurling the Colors*, p. 13.
40. Gignilliat, *Unfurling the Colors*, p. 14.
41. Ibid.
42. Ibid.
43. Ibid.
44. Ibid.
45. Ibid.
46. Image from *1900 CMA Catalog*, p. 68.
47. Gignilliat, *Unfurling the Colors*, p. 15.
48. Photo courtesy of the Culver Archives.
49. 1898 CMA Catalog, p. 81.
50. 1898 CMA Catalog, pp. 81-82.
51. 1902 CMA Catalog, p. 42.
52. Gignilliat Letter to General Scott Shipp, December 2, 1902, VMI Archives.
53. Gignilliat, *Unfurling the Colors*, p. 73.
54. Ibid.
55. Ibid.
56. Ibid.

57. Leigh Robinson Letter to General Scott Shipp, April 20, 1897, VMI Archives; Gignilliat, *Unfurling the Colors*, p. 73.
58. Gignilliat Letter to General Scott Shipp, February 16, 1898, VMI Archives.
59. Colonel Alexander Fleet Letter to General Scott Shipp, March 18, 1897, VMI Archives.
60. Leigh Robinson Letter to General Scott Shipp, April 20, 1897, VMI Archives.
61. Gignilliat, *Unfurling the Colors*, p. 73.
62. Photo from the collection of Mary Margaret Gignilliat; used with permission.
63. Gignilliat, *Unfurling the Colors*, p. 74.
64. Gignilliat Letter to General Scott Shipp, February 16, 1898, VMI Archives.
65. "Wedding at the Academy: Miss Fleet Becomes the Wife of Major L. R. Gignilliat," *The Culver Herald*, August 5, 1898, p. 1.
66. Gignilliat, *Unfurling the Colors*, p. 74.
67. Photo from the collection of Mary Margaret Gignilliat; used with permission.
68. Gignilliat, *Unfurling the Colors*, p. 74.
69. Gignilliat, *Unfurling the Colors*, p. 75.
70. Ibid.
71. Hartman, "When the Rails Hummed, Pt 1," p. 4; 1900 CMA Catalog, p. 49.
72. 1900 CMA Catalog, pp. 49-50.
73. Image from *1900 CMA Catalog*, p. 50-1.
74. As reported in the *Culver Citizen*.
75. Image from *1900 CMA Catalog*, p. 46-1.
76. Image from *1900 CMA Catalog*, p. 46-1.
77. Image from *1900 CMA Catalog*, p. 48-1.
78. *1900 CMA Catalog*, p. 46.
79. *1900 CMA Catalog*, p. 47.
80. *1900 CMA Catalog*, p. 48.
81. *1909 CMA Catalog*, p. 16.
82. Gignilliat, *Unfurling the Colors*, p. 17.
83. Rex Bowman and Carlos Santos, *Rot, Riot, and Rebellion: Mr. Jefferson's Struggle to Save the University That Changed America,* (Charlottesville, VA: University of Virginia Press, 2013.
84. Henry A. Wise, *Drawing Out the Man: The VMI Story*, (University Pres of Virginia, 1978), pp. 58, 77.
85. Gignilliat, *Unfurling the Colors*, p. 18.
86. Mather, "The History of Culver Military Academy, 1894-1956," p. 94.
87. Gignilliat's recollections of the actual number of cadets varies a bit. In the text of a speech he gave in November 1915, Gignilliat related that 105/201 cadets were dismissed as a result of the incident LRG, Nov 1915 Wisconsin Teachers' Association Speech). In his memoirs, Gignilliat recalled that 102/205 cadets were dismissed (UFTC, pp. 15 & 20). The November 1900 edition of The Vedette places the number of cadets who departed campus at 105 (p. 27). The Culver Citizen reports that Culver's enrollment at the time of the Big Fire was 235. (Culver Citizen reports 235 in Dec 1900) Culver's own published enrollment statistics report a total enrollment of 260 cadets for the 1900-1901 school year (1909 CMA Catalog, p. 16). Given corroboration from *The Vedette* and the proximity in time to the actual event of each figure, I used the numbers Gignilliat included in his 1915 speech (105/210), believing them to be more reliable. Regardless, the important point is that Culver dismissed one-half of its enrolled students as a result of the episode.

88. Gignilliat, *Unfurling the Colors*, pp. 18-19.

89. Hartman, "When the Rails Hummed, Part I, p. 5.

90. Image from Hartman, "When the Rails Hummed, Part I, p. 5.

91. Cadet Scrapbook, Culver Archives.

92. *The Vedette*, November 1900, p. 28.

93. Ibid; Gignilliat, *Unfurling the Colors*, p. 20.

94. *The Vedette*, November 1900, pp. 27-28.

95. *The Vedette*, November 1900, pp. 30-31.

96. Gignilliat, *Unfurling the Colors*, p. 18.

97. Wise, *Drawing Out the Man*, p. 57.

98. Wise, *Drawing Out the Man*, p. 58.

99. Wise, *Drawing Out the Man*, p. 77.

100. Ibid.

101. *The Vedette*, January 1901, pp. 67-68.

102. Gignilliat, *Unfurling the Colors*, pp. 20-21.

103. *The Vedette*, January 1901, p. 67.

104. 1902 CMA Catalog, p. 42.

105. Image from *1899 CMA Catalog*, p. 66.

106. *The Vedette*, December 1900, p. 48.

Ch. 4 — Creating Culver's Unique Military System, 1900-1906

1. *1900 CMA Catalog*, p. 51.

2. *1909 CMA Catalog*, p. 16.

3. Photo from *1907 CMA Catalog*, p. 9.

4. *1902 CMA Catalog*, p. 42.

5. *1903 CMA Catalog*, p. 46.

6. *1902 CMA Catalog*, p. 44.

7. *1902 CMA Catalog*, pp. 45, 48, 49-53.

8. *1902 CMA Catalog*, p. 47.

9. Gignilliat, *Unfurling the Colors*, p. 15.

10. Gignilliat, *Unfurling the Colors*, pp. 22-23.

11. Gignilliat, *Unfurling the Colors*, p. 22.

12. Hartman, *Unfurling the Colors*, p. i.

13. Image from *1905 Culver Summer Naval School (SNS) Catalog*, p. 26.

14. *1904 SNS Catalog*, p. 4.

15. Ibid.

16. Photo from *1906 SNS Catalog*, p. 5.

17. *1906 SNS Catalog*, p. 5.

18. Photo from *1906 SNS Catalog*, p. 14.

19. Photo from *1906 SNS Catalog*, p. 10.

20. Photo from *1907 SNS Catalog*, p. 6.

21. *1910 SNS Catalog*, p. 3.

22. Photo from 1910 SNS Catalog, p. 3.

23. According to Culver Archivist Jeff Kenney, there were articles regarding Culver's Summer naval program in three different Logansport papers in the summer of 1902. Two of the articles (appearing in the *Pharos* and the *Logansport Reporter*) were positive or neutral about it, but the article appearing in the *Logansport Chronicle* was scathing, calling Thomas Gignilliat a fake naval officer and claiming that the US Navy provided Culver with the cutters as a favor to Senator Charles W. Fairbanks (who

went on to serve as the Vice President of the United States). I am indebted to Jeff Kenney for this research and information.

24. *1903 CMA Catalog*, pp. 42, 44.
25. *1903 CMA Catalog*, p. 44.
26. Ibid.
27. *1903 CMA Catalog*, p. 43.
28. *1903 CMA Catalog*, p. 44.
29. It was the convention at Culver to use first and middle initials when providing names in official publications. The author has made every effort to determine the correct first name for individuals, and used the first and middle initials provided in official publications in cases where the correct first name could not be determined.
30. Photo from 1903 *Roll Call*.
31. Image from Hartman, "When the Rails Hummed, Part 1," p. 6.
32. *1907 Summer Cavalry School (SCS) Catalog*, p. 16.
33. *1906 CMA Catalog*, pp. 58-60; "Cadets Celebrate Culver Day at Fair," *St. Louis Republic*, June 3, 1904, appearing in the *1906 CMA Catalog*, p. 62.
34. "Military Ball Ends Culver Day," *St. Louis Globe-Democrat*, June 3, 1904, appearing in the *1906 CMA Catalog*, pp. 62-63.
35. "Cadets Celebrate Culver Day at Fair," *St. Louis Republic*, June 3, 1904, appearing in the *1906 CMA Catalog*, p. 62.
36. *1906 CMA Catalog*, p. 60.
37. "Gov. Durbin Returns from St. Louis – Proud of Culver Cadets," *Indianapolis Journal*, June 6, 1904, appearing in the *1906 CMA Catalog*, p. 61.
38. 1906 CMA Catalog, p. 58.
39. Hartman, "When the Rails Hummed, Part 1," p. 6.
40. Image from Hartman, "When the Rails Hummed, Part 1," p. 6.
41. Photo from 1906 *Roll Call*.
42. *The Vedette*, January 1906, p. 83.
43. Image from *1907 CMA Catalog*, p. 56.
44. Gignilliat made mention of this often, for example in his 1914 remarks during the Logansport Gate dedication in 1914, and in his 1915 speech to the Wisconsin Teachers' Association speech; Logansport.
45. *1907 CMA Catalog*, p. 48.
46. Photo from *1907 CMA Catalog*, p. 48.
47. Photo from *1908 CMA Catalog*, p. 66.
48. Images from *1907 CMA Catalog*, p. 48.
49. Photos from *1907 CMA Catalog*, p. 52.
50. Photo from *1907 CMA Catalog*, p. 46.
51. Photo from *1907 CMA Catalog*, p. 44.
52. *1907 CMA Catalog*, p. 49.
53. Gignilliat, *Arms and the Boy*, (Bobbs-Merrill, 1916), pp. 16-17.
54. Image from *1907 CMA Catalog*, p. 50.

Ch. 5 – Institutionalizing Success and Serving as Acting Superintendent, 1907-1910

1. *1907 CMA Catalog*, p. 50.
2. Photo from *1907 CMA Catalog*, p. 50.
3. Photo from *1907 CMA Catalog*, p. 52.
4. "Culver Again in the Big Six," *The CMA Vedette*, October, 1907, Vol. XII, No. 1, p. 8.

5. Along with VMI, Norwich University, Pennsylvania Military College, St. John's School (Manlius), and Shattuck School. "Culver Again in the Big Six," *The CMA Vedette*, October, 1907, Vol. XII, No. 1, p. 8.

6. Photo from *1910 CMA Catalog*, p. 46-2.

7. "Again in the Big Six: Culver Military Academy Retains Position With the Leading Institutions in the Country," *The Culver Citizen*, August 8, 1907, p. 4.

8. Gignilliat, *Unfurling the Colors*, p. 30.

9. *1907 SCS Catalog*, p. 5; Gignilliat, *Unfurling the Colors*, p. 30

10. *1907 SCS Catalog*, p. 5.

11. *1909 CMA Catalog*, p. 16.

12. "Cadets at Richmond," from the *Richmond-Times Dispatch*, appearing in *The Culver Citizen*, August 29, 1907, p. 5; and Hartman, "When the Rails Hummed, Part 1," p. 7.

13. Hartman, "When the Rails Hummed, Part 1," p. 7. The specific train information comes from "Off for Jamestown, *The Culver Citizen*, August 22, 1907, p. 1.

14. "Cadets at Richmond," from the *Richmond-Times Dispatch*, appearing in *The Culver Citizen*, August 29, 1907, p. 5.

15. Hartman, "When the Rails Hummed, Part 1," p. 8.

16. Photo from *1907 SCS Catalog*, p. 12.

17. Images from *1908 SNS Catalog*, p. 14.

18. Photo from *1908 SNS Catalog*, p. 29.

19. *1908 SNS Catalog*, p. 29.

20. Image from *1908 SNS Catalog*, p. 4.

21. Gignilliat, *Unfurling the Colors*, p. 31.

22. Photo from *1908 SCS Catalog*, p. 3.

23. *The Culver Citizen*, September 5, 1907, p. 5.

24. Gignilliat, *Unfurling the Colors*, p. 31.

25. Photo from *1908 SCS Catalog*, p. 17.

26. Gignilliat, *Unfurling the Colors*, p. 31.

27. Image from *1908 SCS Catalog*, p. 18.

28. Comments from an article appearing in the *Annapolis Capital; 1908 SCS Catalog*.

29. Hartman, "When the Rails Hummed, p. 9; "The Jamestown Trip: Summer Schools Leave Next Monday on Their Ten Day (sic) Tour of Eastern Points of interest," *The Culver Citizen*, August 15, 1907, p. 1.

30. *The Culver Citizen*, September 5, 1907, p. 1.

31. Photo from *1910 CMA Catalog*, p. 48-4.

32. Photo from *1909 CMA Catalog*, p. 48-3.

33. Photo from *1910 CMA Catalog*.

34. "Dismissal for Culver Hazers: Thirteen Cadets Found Guilty and Expelled from Military Academy," *The Culver Citizen*, May 10, 1906, p. 3.

35. *1907 CMA Catalog*, "Report of the Commandant," p. 52.

36. Photo from *1908 SCS Catalog*, p. 17.

37. Photo from *1909 SNS Catalog*, p. 11.

38. Ibid.

39. "Cruise of Summer School on Continual Ovation," *The Culver Citizen*, Sept 10, 1908, p. 4.

40. Ibid.

41. Photo from 1910 *Roll Call*.

42. *The Vedette*, June 1909, pp. 238-239.

43. Image from *1910 CMA Catalog*, p. 18.

Ch. 6 – Assuming the Mantle of Leadership, September 1910 – December 1912

1. 1900 US Census data, obtained with the assistance of Don W. Jones.
2. Ibid.
3. His first publications addressed and explained the Culver system he was developing and implementing.
4. L. R. Gignilliat, "What We Leave Behind," *The Vedette*, Vol 7, No. 4, January 1903, p. 80.
5. L. Robinson Gignilliat, "An Inland Naval School," *Munsey's Magazine*, June 1903, pp. 420-423.
6. See Major R. L. Gignilliat, "Education of Boys by the Military Method," *Scientific American*, 92:9, March 4, 1905, pp. 184-185, (Notice the incorrect identification of Gignilliat's initials in the first article that was corrected for the second article.) and Major L. R. Gignilliat, "Manning Oars and Halyards as a Summer Outing," *Scientific American*, 92:18, May 6, 1905, pp. 360-361. Two photographs of Culver Summer Naval School cadets appeared on the cover of the May 6, 1905 Scientific American, no doubt to the great delight of Gignilliat and the Culver family.
7. Major L. R. Gignilliat, "Military Schools in America," *The Times Magazine*, February 1907, 1:3, (NY: Times Magazine Company), pp. 287-294.
8. *A Handbook of Schools*, (Garden City, NY: Doubleday, Page, & Co., 1911), pp. 16-21.
9. Robert B. D. Hartman, "To Your Good Health, Sirs, Part I," p. 5.
10. Photo courtesy of the Culver Archives.
11. Photo courtesy of the Culver Archives.
12. BB Culver Jr., *Those Towers Lofty: A Narrative History of the Culver Campus*, (Culver Education Foundation, 1992), p. 9.
13. Photo courtesy of the Culver Archives.
14. Photo courtesy of the Culver Archives.
15. Photo courtesy of the Culver Archives.
16. Hartman, "To Your Good Health, Sirs, Part I," p. 5.
17. Content deleted.
18. Photo courtesy of the Culver Archives.
19. Hartman, "To Your Good Health, Sirs," Part I, pg. 6.
20. *1907 CMA catalog*, p. 19.
21. Hartman, "To Your Good Health, Sirs," Part I, pp. 4-5.
22. Image from *1907 CMA Catalog*, pg. 56-3.
23. Hartman, "To Your Good Health, Sirs," Part I, p. 2.
24. Hartman, "To Your Good Health, Sirs," Part I, pp. 1-2.
25. BB Culver, Jr., *Those Lofty Towers*, p. 9.
26. Photo courtesy of Georgia Historical Society (used with permission).
27. From the description of Thomas Heyward Gignilliat and Thomas Heyward Gignilliat, Jr. papers, 1890-1956. (Georgia Historical Society).
28. Gignilliat, *Unfurling the Colors*, p. 23.
29. Photo from *1909 SNS catalog*, p. 25.
30. Hugh Glascock, "Colonel Fleet: A Sketch," 1907 *Roll Call*, pp. 26-27.
31. "In Memorium: Colonel Alexander Frederick Fleet," *The Vedette*, XVI:1, September 1911, p. 1.
32. CMA Special Order, Sept 27, 1911, Culver Archives.
33. Photo courtesy of the Culver Archives.

34. Photo courtesy of the Culver Archives.

35. Photo courtesy of the Culver Archives.

36. Hartman, *Footfalls Through the Century: A Visual Salute to the Culver Campus*, p. 7.

37. Photo courtesy of the Culver Archives.

38. Hartman, *Pass in Review: Culver*, p. 88.

39. Photo from *Culver Alumnus*, "16 Years Ago in Washington," p. 8.

40. *Culver Alumnus*, "16 Years Ago in Washington," pp. 8-9.

41. Photo courtesy of the Culver Archives.

42. 1911 CMA catalog, p. 41.

43. Hartman, "The Iron Gate and the Graduation Arch," pp. 1-2.

44. Hartman, "The Iron Gate and the Graduation Arch," p. 1.

45. Photo from Hartman, "The Iron Gate and the Graduation Arch," p. 3.

46. Hartman, "The Iron Gate & the Graduation Arch," p. 1.

47. Photo courtesy of the Culver Archives.

48. "Interesting Bits of News about the Faculty, Past, Present, and Future," *Culver Alumnus*, November 1950, p. 17.

49. "Who Was the First to Crash 'the Old Iron Gate?", *Culver Alumnus*, January 1928, p. 20.

50. Hartman, "The Iron Gate and the Graduation Arch," p. 2.

51. Photo courtesy of the Culver Archives.

52. Mather, *History of Culver Military Academy*, p. 96.

53. Mather, *History of Culver Military Academy*, p. 96; "Who Was the First to Crash 'the Old Iron Gate?", *Culver Alumnus*, January 1928, p. 20; and Hartman, "Gignilliat...as in Giant," p. 4.

54. Mather, *History of Culver Military Academy*, p. 96.

55. Photo from the collection of Mary Margret Gignilliat (used with permission).

56. Photo from Find a Grave (in the public domain).

57. Mather, *History of Culver Military Academy*, p. 101.

58. Ibid.

59. Photo from Find a Grave (in the public domain).

60. Gignilliat, *Unfurling the Colors*, p. 31.

61. 1912 Woodcraft catalog, p. 4.

62. Gignilliat, *Unfurling the Colors*, p. 32.

63. Ibid.

64. Gignilliat, *Unfurling the Colors*, p. 33.

65. Ibid.

66. Photo from cover of Beard's book (in public domain).

67. 1912 Woodcraft catalog, p. 4.

68. Image courtesy of the Culver Archives.

69. 1912 Woodcraft catalog.

70. Hartman, "The Founding of Culver's Woodcraft School," *Culver Citizen*, July 10, 2008, p. 7.

71. Gignilliat, *Unfurling the Colors*, p. 33.

72. Photo from an article about Seton (in the public domain).

73. *1912 Woodcraft catalog*, p. 5.

74. Image from *1912 Woodcraft catalog*, p. 4.

75. Photo courtesy of the Culver Archives.

76. Robert B.D. Hartman, "A Salute to the Woodcraft Camps," p. 3.

77. Gignilliat, *Unfurling the Colors*, p. 33.

78. 1911 BSA Handbook, p. 3.

79. 1911 BSA Handbook, pp. 4, 7.

80. 1911 BSA Handbook, p. 9.

81. 1911 BSA Handbook, p. 10.

82. Ibid.

83. 1911 BSA Handbook, p. 12.

84. 1911 BSA Handbook, p. 8.

85. 1911 BSA Handbook, p. 4.

86. Photo from the public domain.

87. Image courtesy of the Culver Archives.

88. *The Vedette*, February 1912, p. 135. Additional information about this event came from Posted on the La Salle Council Boy Scouts of American, Aug 1, 2019, reposted on Culver Academies History Blog, Aug 3, 2019.

89. *The Vedette*, February 1912, p. 135.

90. *The Vedette*, October 5, 1912, p. 2; October 12, p. 3.

91. *The Vedette*, October 12, 1912, p. 1.

92. *The Vedette*, November 23, 1912, p. 1.

93. *The Vedette*, November 23, 1912, pp. 1-2.

94. Image from *The Vedette*, November 23, 1912, p. 2.

95. *The Vedette*, November 23, 1912, p. 3.

Ch. 7 – 1913 – The Year of Destiny

1. *Culver Alumnus*, "16 Years Ago in Washington," pp. 8-9.

2. Gignilliat, *Unfurling the Colors*, "Inaugural Escort," p. 1, unpublished portion, draft provided to author by Mary Margret Gignilliat.

3. Robert B. D. Hartman, "Nine Decades Ago...The Troop Goes to Washington," p. 3.

4. Photo from US Department of Defense, in public domain.

5. Gignilliat, *Unfurling the Colors*, "Inaugural Escort," unpublished portion, p. 2.

6. Image courtesy of Culver Archives.

7. Image courtesy of Princeton University Archives.

8. "16 Years Ago in Washington," *Culver Alumnus*, April 1929, p. 10.

9. Gignilliat, *Unfurling the Colors*, "Inaugural Escort," unpublished portion, p. 3.

10. Ibid.

11. Gignilliat, *Unfurling the Colors*, "Inaugural Escort," unpublished portion, p. 4.

12. Ibid.

13. Gignilliat, *Unfurling the Colors*, from an unpublished portion, pp. 160-161.

14. Gignilliat, *Unfurling the Colors*, "Inaugural Escort," unpublished portion, p. 160.

15. Photo from *1913 Inaugural Scrapbook*, produced by Culver Military Academy, courtesy of the Culver Archives. Gignilliat ensured that each cadet who participated in the 1913 Presidential Inaugural received a copy of a scrapbook loaded with pictures to ensure they had a suitable keepsake to remember this momentous occasion.

16. Photo from *Pittsburg Chronicle Telegraph*, March 1, 1913, p. 1.

17. Photo from *1913 Inaugural Scrapbook*, produced by Culver Military Academy, courtesy of the Culver Archives.

18. Photo from *1913 Inaugural Scrapbook*, courtesy of the Culver Archives.

19. Photo from Wikipedia (in the public domain).

20. Photo from *1913 Inaugural Scrapbook*, courtesy of the Culver Archives.

21. Ibid.

22. Ibid. This photo also appeared in an article about the 1913 Presidential Inaugural in the *Culver Alumnus*.

23. Ibid.

24. Ibid.

25. Ibid.

26. Ibid.

27. Gignilliat, *Unfurling the Colors*, "Inaugural Escort," unpublished portion, p. 161.

28. Photo from *1913 Inaugural Scrapbook*, courtesy of the Culver Archives.

29. Photo from *New York Tribune*, March 5, 1913, p. 1.

30. Photo from *1913 Inaugural Scrapbook*, courtesy of the Culver Archives.

31. *The Vedette*, 15 March, 1913, p. 3.

32. *The Vedette*, 3 May, 1913, p. 2.

33. *The Vedette*, 3 May 1913, p. 1.

34. Ibid.

35. Photo courtesy of the Culver Archives.

36. *The Vedette*, 17 May 1913, p. 1.

37. Photo courtesy of the Culver Archives.

38. Photo courtesy of the Culver Archives.

39. Photo courtesy of the Culver Archives.

40. *The Vedette*, 10 May 1913, p. 1.

41. Hazel Felleman, ed., *The Best Loved Poems of the American People*, (NY: Doubleday, 1936, p. 132.

42. *Culver Alumnus*, January 1929, p. 7.

43. *The Vedette*, 26 October 1912, p. 2.

44. *The Vedette*, 9 November 1912, p. 2; 23 November, p. 4.

45. *The Vedette*, 31 May, 1913, p. 2.

46. Image from *1914 SNS catalog*, p. 3.

47. *The Vedette*, 31 May 1913, p. 2.

48. "Enrollment Statistics, 1911-12 – 1931-32, Central Files, Culver Academies.

49. Letter from Michael V, O'Shea to Gignilliat, October 14, 1913, WHS 3:4.

50. *The Vedette*, October 4, 1913, p. 3.

51. Ibid.

52. John Gary Clifford, *The Citizen Soldiers: The Plattsburg Training Camp Movement, 1913-1920*, (University Press of Kentucky, 2015), p. 2.

53. Clifford, *The Citizen Soldiers*, pp. 6-8.

54. Clifford, *The Citizen Soldiers*, pp. 22-23.

55. *The Vedette*, 8 November 1913, p. 1; Van Horn info p. 4.

56. *The Vedette*, 15 November 1913, p. 1.

57. The Michigan Army National Guard had conducted its annual training encampments at Ludington's Lincoln fields between 1904 and 1912, demonstrating that the site was quite suitable for such an event. When the Michigan Army National Guard moved their training to a more northern site in 1913, Lincoln Fields became available to host the Army student military training camp in the Midwest. "Inspect Camp Site," *The Ludington Chronicle*, Vol 13, No. 34, March 4, 1914, p. 1.; James L. Cabot, *Ludington: 1830-1930*, Images of America Series (Charleston, SC: Arcadia Publishing, 2005), p. 90.

58. *Vedette* 25 Oct 1913; corroborated in letter from MVO to LRG, 13 Jan 1914, WHS 4:1.

59. USS Arkansas (Battleship # 33) Photo Album: "Our European Cruise. October 25th, to December 15th, 1913, S-582 USS Arkansas (BB-33) Collection, Naval History and Heritage Command.

60. *Army-Navy Journal*, September 6, 1913, p. 289.

61. Image from USS Arkansas Photo Album, p. 1.

62. Image from USS Arkansas Photo Album, p. 15.

63. *The Vedette* 18 July & 22 August 1914.

64. Image from *The Vedette*, Dec 6, 1913, p. 1.

65. Image from USS Arkansas Photo Album, p. 83.

66. Image from USS Arkansas Photo Album, p. 30.

67. Image from USS Arkansas Photo Album, p. 31.

68. Image from Wikipedia (in the public domain).

69. Image from USS Arkansas Photo Album, p. 40.

70. Gignilliat, *Unfurling the Colors*, p. 49.

71. *The Vedette*, 17 Jan 1914, pp. 2-3, p. 2.

72. *The Vedette*, 23 May, 1914, p. 1.

73. Gignilliat, *Arms and the Boy*, p. 125.

74. Image from USS Arkansas Photo Album, p. 86.

75. *The Vedette*, 17 Jan 1914, p. 1.

Ch. 8 – The "Schoolboy Epic Supreme" of the 1913 Logansport Flood Rescue Adventure

1. Trudy E. Bell, *The Great Dayton Flood of 1913*, (Arcadia Publishing, 2008), p. 8. Bell's account is of the same flood that impacted Logansport, Indiana in 1913, but from the perspective of its impact on Dayton, Ohio. Thus, much of the information pertains to the Logansport flood as well.

2. Bell, *The Great Dayton Flood of 1913*, p. 8.

3. Ibid.

4. Geoff Williams, *Washed Away: How the Great Flood of 1913, America's Most Widespread Disaster, Terrorized a Nation and Changed It Forever*, (Pegasus Books, 2013), pp. 204-205).

5. Bell, *The Great Dayton Flood of 1913*, p. 8.

6. Williams, *Washed Away*, pp. 204-205.

7. Bell, *The Great Dayton Flood of 1913*, p. 9.

8. Williams, *Washed Away*, p. 205.

9. Gignilliat, "Schoolboy Epic Supreme," *Unfurling the Colors*, pp. 35-40.

10. Gignilliat, "Schoolboy Epic Supreme," *Unfurling the Colors*, p. 35.

11. Photo courtesy of the Culver Archives.

12. Gignilliat, "Schoolboy Epic Supreme," *Unfurling the Colors*, p. 35.

13. Photo courtesy of the Culver Archives.

14. Gignilliat, "Schoolboy Epic Supreme," *Unfurling the Colors*, p. 35.

15. The *Vedette*, April 12, 1913, pp. 2, 4.

16. According to an article about the 1913 flood appearing in *Logansport Press*, June 4, 1956.

17. According to an article appearing around the one-year anniversary of the 1913 Logansport flood in the *Logansport Journal-Tribune*, May 21, 1914, p. 1.

18. Gignilliat, "Schoolboy Epic Supreme," *Unfurling the Colors*, pp. 35-36.

19. According to an article about the 1913 Logansport flood on the Maxinkuckee History Past Tracker.

20. *Logansport Journal-Tribune*, May 21, 1914, p. 1.

21. Williams, *Washed Away*, p. 58.

22. Williams, *Washed Away*, p. 47.

23. Ibid.

24. Image courtesy of the Cass County Historical Society, modified by the author.

25. Gignilliat, "Schoolboy Epic Supreme," *Unfurling the Colors*, p. 36.

26. Williams, *Washed Away*, p. 204.

27. Gignilliat, "Schoolboy Epic Supreme," *Unfurling the Colors*, p. 36.

28. Image from the 1913 *Roll Call*, front piece.

29. Gignilliat, *Arms and the Boy*, 1916, p. 4.

30. Photo from Hartman, "When the Rails Hummed," Part 1, p. 11.

31. Gignilliat, "Schoolboy Epic Supreme," *Unfurling the Colors*, p. 36.

32. Hartman, *Logansport – The Flood*, (Culver Education Foundation, 1994), p. 22.

33. Photo of Glascock from the 1913 *Roll Call*, p. 13; photo of Greiner from the 1913 *Roll Call*, p. 92.

34. Williams, *Washed Away*, p. 30.

35. Gignilliat, "Schoolboy Epic Supreme," *Unfurling the Colors*, p. 37.

36. Hartman, *Logansport – The Flood*, p. 25.

37. This information is corroborated by Williams in *Washed Away*, p. 203.

38. Gignilliat, "Schoolboy Epic Supreme," *Unfurling the Colors*, p. 37.

39. Hartman, *Logansport – The Flood*, p. 24.

40. Williams, *Washed Away*, pp. 55, 56.

41. Williams, *Washed Away*, p. 58.

42. Photo from 1911 *Roll Call*, p. 10.

43. Gignilliat, "Schoolboy Epic Supreme," *Unfurling the Colors*, p. 37. The terrific pull of the current in the flooded streets is corroborated in Peru in Williams, *Washed Away*, p. 238.

44. Photo courtesy of the Culver Archives.

45. Gignilliat, "Schoolboy Epic Supreme," *Unfurling the Colors*, p. 37.

46. Gignilliat, "Schoolboy Epic Supreme," *Unfurling the Colors*, pp. 37-38.

47. Gignilliat, "Schoolboy Epic Supreme," *Unfurling the Colors*, p. 38.

48. Ibid.

49. Photo courtesy of the Cass County Historical Society (used with permission).

50. Gignilliat, "Schoolboy Epic Supreme," *Unfurling the Colors*, p. 38.

51. According to Rossow, the cutter he was commanding became caught in a current and came very close to capsizing. Only the quick thinking of Rossow and the determined efforts from the cadets, along with some external assistance from some locals on the scene, prevented the episode from ending in catastrophe. Hartman, Logansport – The Flood, pp. 27-29; Rossow, unpublished memoirs , pp. 130-134.

52. Photo courtesy of the Cass County Historical Society (used with permission).

53. Gignilliat, "Schoolboy Epic Supreme," *Unfurling the Colors*, p. 39.

54. Ibid.

55. Ibid.

56. Gignilliat, "Schoolboy Epic Supreme," *Unfurling the Colors*, p. 38.

57. Photo courtesy of the Cass County Historical Society (used with permission).

58. Photo from 1912 *Roll Call*, p. 3.

59. 1914 *Roll Call*, p. 17.
60. Williams, *Washed Away*, p. 123.
61. Gignilliat, *Arms and the Boy*, p. 5.
62. Photo courtesy of the Cass County Historical Society (used with permission).
63. 1913 *Roll Call*, p. 134.
64. Hartman, *Logansport – The Flood*, p. 43.
65. Williams, *Washed Away*, p. 204.
66. *The Vedette*, April 5, 1913, p. 1.
67. Gignilliat, "Schoolboy Epic Supreme," *Unfurling the Colors*, p. 40.
68. Photo courtesy of the Culver Archives.
69. *The Vedette* printed a copy of Gignilliat's remarks at the ceremony. *The Vedette*, May 23, 1914, p. 1.
70. *The Vedette*, 23 May, 1914, p. 1.
71. Ibid.
72. Ibid.
73. *The Vedette* printed a copy of Jenkins' remarks at the ceremony. *The Vedette*, May 23, 1914, p. 1.
74. Photo courtesy of the Culver Archives.
75. Photo courtesy of the Culver Archives.
76. Gignilliat, *Arms and the Boy*, p. 6.
77. *Logansport Journal-Tribune*, May 21, 1914, p. 1.
78. Gignilliat, "Schoolboy Epic Supreme," *Unfurling the Colors*, p. 39.
79. Gignilliat, "Building Character through Military Training", p. 12.
80. Williams, *Washed Away*, p. 254.
81. Williams, *Washed Away*, p. 341.
82. Gignilliat, "Schoolboy Epic Supreme," *Unfurling the Colors*, p. 36.
83. Gignilliat, *Unfurling the Colors*, pp. 18-19.
84. Gignilliat, "Schoolboy Epic Supreme," *Unfurling the Colors*, p. 36.
85. Gignilliat, *Unfurling the Colors*, pp. 18, 36.
86. Gignilliat, "Schoolboy Epic Supreme," *Unfurling the Colors*, p. 36.

Ch. 9 – Finding His Voice: Becoming an Evangelist of Military Preparedness, 1914 - 1915

1. Alan M. Bunner," Chapter 2: The Culver Honor Code," text for instructing new cadets and students at Culver, p. 18, n.d.; Bunner was a long-time math teacher at Culver (began in January 1957) who also served as an advisor to the Cadet Honor Council for many years; the Bunner text is still used for this purpose on campus.
2. "Cadet Council Assuming Form," *The Vedette*, March 7, 1914, p. 1.
3. "Articles of Organization for Cadet Council," 1914 *Roll Call*, p. 153.
4. *The Culver Citizen*, March 5, 1914, p. 1.
5. "Articles of Organization for Cadet Council," 1914 *Roll Call*, p. 154.
6. "Council Taking Final Form," *The Vedette*, March 28, 1914, p. 1.
7. "Council Has Been Chosen," *The Vedette*, April 18, 1914, p. 1.
8. 1914 *Roll Call*, p. 152.
9. "Council Has Been Chosen," *The Vedette*, April 18, 1914, p. 1.
10. "Articles of Organization for Cadet Council," 1914 *Roll Call*, p. 153.
11. 1914 *Roll Call*, pp. 17, 152-154.
12. 1914 *CMA Catalog*, p. 16.
13. John A. Coulter, *Cadets on Campus: History of Military Schools of the United*

States, (College Station, TX: Texas A&M University Press, 2017, pp. 3, 17).

14. LRG Ltr to MVO, 30 Mar 1914 (WHS 4:3) and 8 Apr 1914 (WHS 4:4).

15. RS to MOV, 9 Apr 1914 (WHS 4:4).

16. RS to MVO, 13 Apr 1914 (WHS 4:4).

17. O'Shea was an ardent supporter of other authors, especially inexperienced ones, helping many to develop the writing skills necessary to present their own work in ways that were professional and effective. Gignilliat was one of several scores of young authors with whom O'Shea worked and upon whom he had a tremendously positive impact.

18. Michael V. O'Shea, Letter to Gignilliat, April 16, 1914 (WHS 4:4).

19. LRG to MVO 18 Apr 1914 (WHS 4:4).

20. MVO to LRG 29 Apr 1914 (WHS 4:4).

21. *The Log*, 11 July 1914, p. 1.

22. *The Vedette*, Oct 10, 1914, p. 1.

23. Richard Davies, *Arms and the Man*, unpublished Ph.D. dissertation, 1984, p. 79.

24. Letter, LRG to ERC, January 6, 1915, Culver Archives.

25. The AMCSUS annual meeting Washington, DC, during the periods January 19-21, 1915. This was the second meeting of AMCSUS, and Gignilliat would remain involved in the organization throughout most of his time at Culver, serving as President and Vice President of the organization twice in the 1920s.

26. Letter LRG to MVO, January 16, 1915, WHS 6:2.

27. Photo from 1910 *Roll Call*.

28. AMCSUS had formed and held its first meeting in December 1913, but Gignilliat was unable to attend because he was still on the Mediterranean. Cruise. Minutes from a later AMCSUS meeting identify a "Jim Lass" as being Culver's representative at the meeting, but the author has been unable to corroborate this claim or discover any information about anyone with this name associated with Culver.

29. All quotations and much of this information comes from Alvan Cordell Hadley, Jr., "Military Schools: The Association of Military Colleges and Schools of the United States (AMCSUS) and the Historical Struggle for the Survival of Military Preparatory Schools in America," unpublished Ph.D. dissertation, University of Kentucky, 1999, pp. 25-26.

30. Hadley, "Military Schools," pp. 214.

31. It is unclear if AMCSUS members met in 1914.

32. Letter, LRG to ER Culver, January 11, 1915, Culver Archives.

33. Gene M. Lyons and John W. Masland, *Education and Military Leadership: A Study of the ROTC*, reprint of the edition published by Princeton University Press, Princeton, NJ, 1959, (Westport, CT: Greenwood Press, Publishers, 1975), p. 38.

34. Photo of Garrison from public domain.

35. United States Bureau of Education, *Federal Laws, Regulations, and Rulings Affecting the Land-grant Colleges of Agriculture and Mechanic Arts* (Washington, DC: US Government Printing Office, 1911), pp. 3-5.

36. Arthur F. McClure, James R. Crisman, and Perry Mock, *Education for Work: The Historical Evolution of Vocational and Distributive Education in America* (Cranbury, NJ: Associated University Presses, Inc., 1985), pp. 42-43.

37. Lyons and Masland, *Education and Military Leadership*, pp. 36-39.

38. Staff study of the War College Division of the US Army General Staff Corps prepared as a supplement to *The Statement of a Proper Military Policy for the United States*,

"Study on Educational Institutions Giving Military Training as a Source of Supply of Officers for a National Army," WCD 9053-121, Document No. 510 (Washington, DC: War Department, Office of the Chief of Staff), pp. 8-9.

39. Lyons and Masland, *Education and Military Leadership*, p. 39. War College, "Study on Educational Institutions Giving Military Training as a Source of Supply of Officers for a National Army," p. 9.

40. War College, "Study on Educational Institutions Giving Military Training as a Source of Supply of Officers for a National Army," p. 9.

41. Letter LRG to MVO, June 4, 1915, WHS 7:2.

42. Wilfred B. Shaw, ed., *The University of Michigan, an Encyclopedic Survey: Part I – History and Administration, The University in War Service*, (Ann Arbor, MI, University of Michigan, Digital Library Production Service, 2000), p. 198.

43. Letter MVO to LRG, March 15, 1915, WHS 6:4.

44. Letter MVO to LRG, May 10, 1915, WHS 7:1.

45. Letter LRG to MVO, May 18, 1915, WHS 7:1.

46. Letter LRG to MVO, March 17, 1915, WHS 6:4.

47. Ibid.

48. Ibid.

49. Ibid.

50. The Michigan Army National Guard had conducted its annual training encampments at Ludington's Lincoln fields between 1904 and 1912, demonstrating that the site was quite suitable for such an event. When the Michigan Army National Guard moved their training to a more northern site in 1913, Lincoln Fields became available to host the Army student military training camp in the Midwest. "Inspect Camp Site," *The Ludington Chronicle*, Vol 13, No. 34, March 4, 1914, p. 1.; James L. Cabot, *Ludington: 1830-1930*, Images of America Series (Charleston, SC: Arcadia Publishing, 2005), p. 90.

51. Letter LRG to MVO, March 17, 1915, WHS 6:4.

52. Ibid.

53. Ibid.

54. Letter LRG to MVO, March 24, 1915, WHS 6:4.

55. *The Log*, August 26, 1915, p. 1.

56. *Ibid.*

57. *The Vedette*, March 6, 1915, p. 1.

58. Gignilliat, *Arms and the Boy*, p. 61.

59. Photo courtesy of the Culver Archives.

60. Photo courtesy of the Culver Archives.

61. *The Vedette*, May 29, 1915, p. 1.

62. "Military Academy Chief's Experiment a Surprise to Gen. Wood," *Salina Daily Union*, May 25, 1915, p. 3.

63. Photo courtesy of the Culver Archives.

64. Robert B. D. Hartman Gignilliat Sets the Stage: Culver's Schoolboy Training Program, 1915-1917," CEF, n. d.; *Culver in the World War* p. 17.

65. William Mather Lewis, "One Way to Prepare," *Seven Seas*, September 1915, Vol I, No. 4 (New York: Seven Seas Co. Inc., 1915), p. 33.

66. Lewis, "One Way to Prepare," p. 33.

67. Lewis, "One Way to Prepare," p. 34.

68. Ibid.

69. Ibid.

70. Ibid.

71. Ibid.

72. Ibid.

73. "Lincoln Fields Transformed Again Into a Tent City," *The Ludington Chronicle*, Vol. 15, No. 2, July 22, 1915, p. 6.

74. *The Ludington, Chronicle*, March 4, 1914, p. 1.

75. "Lincoln Fields Transformed Again Into a Tent City," p. 6.

76. James L. Cabot, *Ludington: 1830-1930*, (Charleston, SC: Arcadia Publishing, 2005), p. 90.

77. *Culver Citizen*, June 17, 1915, p. 1.

78. Ibid.

79. Gignilliat, *Unfurling the Colors*, p. 49.

80. Photo courtesy of the Culver Archives.

81. Gignilliat, *Unfurling the Colors*, p. 49.

82. Ibid.

83. K. G. Karsten, "The Collegiate Anti-Militarism League," *The Cosmopolitan Student*, Vol 5, No. 11, June 1915, pp. 351, 365.

84. Karsten, "The Collegiate Anti-Militarism League," pp. 348-350.

85. Military Training Camps Association of the United States, *Roster of Attendants at Federal Military Training Camps 1913-1916* (NY: Anderson & Ruwe, Inc., December 1916), pp. 134, 406, 407.

86. Col. L. R. Gignilliat, "Military Training for the Boy," *Chicago Daily Journal*, Wednesday, October 6, 1915.

87. Ibid.

88. John G. Clifford, *The Citizen Soldiers: The Plattsburg Training Camp Movement, 1913-1920*, (Lexington, KY: University Press of Kentucky, 2015), p. 96.

89. Letter, Gignilliat to Howland, November 24, 1915, p. 2, file 1, Bobbs-Merrill archival material, Lilly Library, University of Indiana.

90. Gignilliat, "Military Training for the Boy."

91. Letter, Gignilliat to Howland, November 24, 1915, file 1, Bobbs-Merrill archival material, Lilly Library, University of Indiana.

92. "Two Parables at Sheridan," *The Chicago Evening Post*, October 19, 1915.

93. *The Vedette*, October 30, 1915, p. 1.

94. Ibid.

95. Ibid.

96. Ibid. I am grateful to Culver Archivist Jeff Kenney for helping make the connection with Jensen's concurrent landscaping work on campus.

97. *The Vedette*, December 4, 1915, p. 5.

98. Hartman, "Boots-Saddles - and the Giants Who Made the Culver Summer Cavalry School a Legend," p. 8.

99. *The Vedette*, October 30, 1915, p. 1.

100. Hartman, "Boots-Saddles," pp. 8-9.

101. *The Vedette*, October 30, 1915, p. 1.

102. Colonel L. R. Gignilliat, "Building Character through Military Training," appearing as, "Utilizing the Military System for Moral Development" (a title likely created by an editor) in *Proceedings of the Sixty-third Annual Session of the Wisconsin Teachers' Association*, (Madison, WI: Cantwell Printing Company, State Printer, 1916), pp. 73-

81.

103. Richard Davies, *Arms and the Man*, unpublished Ph.D. dissertation, 1984, pp. 55-56.

104. Gignilliat, "Building Character through Military Training," pp. 74-75.

105. George C. Herring, "James Hay and the Preparedness Controversy, 1915-1916," *Journal of Southern History*, Vol. 30, No. 4, Nov 1964, p. 390.

106. Herring, "James Hay and the Preparedness Controversy, 1915-1916," pp. 390-391.

107. War Department Document No. 510, "Study on Educational Institutions Giving Military Training as a Source for a Supply of Officers for a National Army," Washington, DC: Army War College, November 1915, p. 9.

108. War Department, "Study on Educational Institutions," p. 5.

109. Ibid.

110. Ibid.

111. Alfred E. Stearns, L. R. Gignilliat, Milo H. Stuart, Eric Parsons, and J. J. Findlay, *Types of Schools for Boys*, a volume in the *Childhood and Youth Series* edited by M. V. O'Shea (Indianapolis: The Bobbs-Merrill Company, 1917), p, 60.

112. These "many and varied" successes of 1915 included the following: Using the Culver military system to train 200 schoolboys so well and in less than half the time allocated for the Lincoln Fields camp in Ludington, Michigan; his recent experience at the Fort Sheridan camp 20 September – 17 October 1915; and the synthesis of his thinking that occurred as a result of his address to the Wisconsin Teachers' Association on November 5, 1915 (which likely also served as a culmination of all of his other Preparedness Movement activities).

113. Letter Gignilliat to Howland, November 19, 1915, WHS 8:2.

114. Ibid, emphasis added.

115. While the author was unable to find this particular letter, it is quite clear from Howland's subsequent letter to Gignilliat that this was his suggestion. Cf to Howland letter to O'Shea, December 1, 1915, Bobbs-Merrill archival material, Lilly Library, University of Indiana.

116. Hand-written note from William Conrad Bobbs, President of Bobbs-Merrill, November 27, 1915, Bobbs-Merrill archival material, Lilly Library, University of Indiana.

117. Letter, US Army Chief of Staff to New Orleans Superintendent of Schools, subject, "Military Training in High Schools," Feb 8, 1915, cited in Marvin A. Kreidberg and Merton G. Henry, *History of Military Mobilization in the United States Army, 1775-1945*, (Washington, DC: Department of the Army, November 1955), p. 211.

118. Letter Gignilliat to Howland, November 24, 1915, Bobbs-Merrill archival material, Lilly Library, University of Indiana.

119. Ibid.

120. John G. Clifford, *The Citizen Soldiers: The Plattsburg Training Camp Movement, 1913-1920*, (Lexington, KY: University Press of Kentucky, 2015), p. 105.

121. Letter Gignilliat to Howland, November 24, 1915, Bobbs-Merrill archival material, Lilly Library, University of Indiana.

122. Letter Gignilliat to O'Shea, November 24, 1915, WHS 8:2.

123. Letter, O'Shea to Gignilliat, November 29, 1915, WHS 8:2.

124. Letter, O'Shea to Howland, November 29, 1915, Bobbs-Merrill archival material, Lilly Library, University of Indiana.

125. According to Alvin C. Hadley, Jr., who has done the most extensive work on the history of AMCSUS, he was unable to locate the minutes from the "first nine Annual

meetings from 1914 through 1922," and they have not been located since he searched for them. However, Gignilliat confirms that these two events occurred in a letter to Howland in December 1915. Hadley, "Military Schools," pp. 26-27. Letter, Gignilliat to Howland, December 13, 1915, Bobbs-Merrill archival material, Lilly Library, University of Indiana.

126. Letter, Howland to Gignilliat, December 10, 1915, Bobbs-Merrill archival material, Lilly Library, University of Indiana.

127. Letter, Gignilliat to Howland, December 13, 1915, Bobbs-Merrill archival material, Lilly Library, University of Indiana.

128. Ibid.

129. Letter from Howland to Gignilliat, December 15, 1915, Bobbs-Merrill archival material, Lilly Library, University of Indiana.

Ch. 10 – Using His Voice: Publishing *Arms and the Boy* and Military Preparedness in 1916

1. According to John B. Coulter, who has done the most extensive work on this topic, this was the period during which the number of military schools peaked in America. Coulter writes, "Between 1903 and 1926, no fewer than 278 to 280 military schools operated in the United States. This was the peak for the number of military schools in the United States." According to Coulter's information, the number of military schools in American in 1915 was around 170. John B. Coulter, "History of Military Schools of the United States: Origin, Rise, decline, Resurgence, and Potential in Future Public Secondary Education," unpublished Ph.D. dissertation, the University of the Incarnate Word, May 2013, pp. 184, 290. This number was further refined to 173 in Congressional testimony offered in January 1916. "To Increase the Efficiency of the Military Establishment of the United States," *Hearing Before the Committee on Military Affairs, House of Representatives*, Sixty –fourth Congress, first session, (Washington, DC: Government Printing Office, 1916), vol. 1, p. 218.

2. Letter, Gignilliat to Howland, January 15, 1916, Bobbs-Merrill archival material, Lilly Library, University of Indiana.

3. Ibid.

4. Ibid.

5. *The Vedette*, Jan 15, 1916, p. 1.

6. Letter, Gignilliat to Howland, January 15, 1916, Bobbs-Merrill archival material, Lilly Library, University of Indiana.

7. Letter, Howland to Gignilliat, January 19, 1916, Bobbs-Merrill archival material, Lilly Library, University of Indiana.

8. Having served in this role since the earliest Colonial times, one can understand their opposition.

9. George C. Herring, "James Hay and the Preparedness Controversy, 1915-1916," *Journal of Southern History*, Vol. 30, No. 4, Nov 1964, p. 394.

10. Garrison testimony on January 6, 1916. "To Increase the Efficiency of the Military Establishment of the United States," *Hearing Before the Committee on Military Affairs, House of Representatives*, Sixty –fourth Congress, first session, (Washington, DC: Government Printing Office, 1916), vol. 1, pp. 10, 11, 64.

11. "To Increase the Efficiency of the Military Establishment of the United States," *Hearing Before the Committee on Military Affairs, House of Representatives*, Sixty –fourth Congress, first session, (Washington, DC: Government Printing Office, 1916), vol. 1, pp 20-22.

12. "To Increase the Efficiency of the Military Establishment of the United States," p. 218.
13. "To Increase the Efficiency of the Military Establishment of the United States," p. 445.
14. "To Increase the Efficiency of the Military Establishment of the United States," pp. 45-446.
15. "To Increase the Efficiency of the Military Establishment of the United States," p. 447.
16. "To Increase the Efficiency of the Military Establishment of the United States," pp. 449-450.
17. "To Increase the Efficiency of the Military Establishment of the United States," pp. 462-472, 473-474.
18. "To Increase the Efficiency of the Military Establishment of the United States," pp. 472-473.
19. Edwin L. Kennedy, Jr., "Mass-Producing Leaders: WWI Army Needed a Lot of Officer – Quickly (*ARMY*, July 2017), pp. 47-48.
20. Gignilliat testified before the committee on January 21, 1916. "To Increase the Efficiency of the Military Establishment of the United States," pp. 472-473.
21. Letter, Gignilliat to E.R. Culver, January 23, 1916, Culver archives.
22. Ibid.
23. Gignilliat, *Army and the Boy*, pp. 226-227.
24. Major General Leonard Wood (USA), "Preparedness," appearing in *National Service Library, Vol. 1, Universal Military Training*, Major Charles E. Kilbourne, ed., (P. F. Collier & Son, 1917), p. 21; Gignilliat, *Arms and the Boy*, pp. 224-228.
25. George Creel, "Wyoming's Answer: Five Years of Training Schoolboys," *Everybody's Magazine*, Vol. 34, No. 2, February 1916, p. 154.
26. Ibid.
27. Creel, "Wyoming's Answer," pp. 152-53.
28. Creel, "Wyoming's Answer," p. 156.
29. *Everybody's Magazine*, April 1919, Vol. 40, No. 4, p. 86. The "unity of racial sympathies" phrase comes from George Creel, the editor of *Everybody's Magazine* who was expressed decidedly populist views and rhetoric.
30. Ibid.
31. Ibid.
32. Ibid.
33. "HSVUS," *Everybody's Magazine*, June 1917, p. 720.
34. Ibid.
35. Edgar Z. Steever and James L. Frink, Introduction, *The Cadet Manual: Official Handbook for High School Volunteers of the United States*, ((Philadelphia, PA: J. P. Lippincott Company, 1918), p. xx.
36. *Everybody's Magazine*, July 1917, 142-43.
37. *Everybody's Magazine*, January 1917, Vol 36, No. 1, p. 113.
38. Letter, Gignilliat to Howland, February 16, 1916, Bobbs-Merrill archival material, Lilly Library, University of Indiana.
39. Letter, Gignilliat to Howland, February 16, 1916, meet with the Chicago School Board regarding military training the following day (6 Mar 1916). Gignilliat traveled to Bloomington, Indiana by invitation to speak about military training in schools at Indiana University on February 23, 1916.

40. *Fort Wayne Daily News*, March 10 and March 11, 1916.

41. *The Vedette*, 19:18, 11 Mar 1916, p. 1.

42. *The Vedette*, 19:12, 19 Feb 1916, p. 1.

43. "The Battle Cry of Peace," *American Film Institute Catalog of Feature Films: The First Hundred Years, 1893 to 1993.*

44. Letter, Gignilliat to E. R. Culver, March 4, 1916, Culver archives.

45. Ibid.

46. Letter, Gignilliat to Howland, March 5, 1916; , Bobbs-Merrill archival material, Lilly Library, University of Indiana.

47. Letter, Howland to Gignilliat, March 7, 1916, Bobbs-Merrill archival material, Lilly Library, University of Indiana.

48. Max Boot, *The Savage Wars of Peace: Small Wars and the Rise of American Power*, (NY: Basic Books, 2002), p. 183; *The Vedette*, 19:18, 11 Mar 1916, p. 1.

49. Boot, *The Savage Wars of* Peace, p. 183.

50. Boot, *The Savage Wars of Peace*, p. 185.

51. Boot, *The Savage Wars of Peace*, p. 189.

52. LRG Ltr to ex-member of the BHT, March 16, 1916, Culver archives.

53. The substance reported related to this episode comes from a letter that Gignilliat sent to BHT alumni on March 16, 1916, Culver Archives.

54. Photo courtesy of the Culver Archives.

55. Clifford, *The Citizen Soldiers*, pp. 134-35.

56. *The Vedette*, 28 Apr 1916, p. 1

57. *Culver Citizen*, August 24, 1916, p. 2. For some reason, Noble is not listed as the author in *Arms and the Boy*.

58. *Illustrated Catalog of the Culver Military Academy*, (Culver, IN: Culver Military Academy, 1916), p. 7.

59. *Illustrated Catalog of the Culver Military Academy*, (Culver, IN: Culver Military Academy, 1916), p. 8.

60. *Culver Citizen*, August 24, 1916, p. 2.

61. *The Vedette*, 18:24, 1 May, 1915, p. 1.

62. Photo from 1905 *Roll Call*, p. 6.

63. Content deleted.

64. Gignilliat, *Arms and the Boy*, p. 226.

65. Letter, Gignilliat to Howland, March 23, 1916, Bobbs-Merrill archival material, Lilly Library, University of Indiana.

66. The weekly magazine, *Arms and the Man*, provided readers with articles regarding the military and shooting, reporting the results of shooting matches as well, during this period. Beginning in late December 1915, *Arms and the Man* began providing excellent articles regarding preparedness that undoubtedly appealed to Gignilliat. See, for example, National Rifle Association of America, *Arms and the Man*, Vol. 59, No. 24, March 9, 1916, which provided an excellent summary of the status of the Hay and Chamberlain bills in Congress on pages 467 & 470, and which Gignilliat almost certainly read with great interest. These articles began appearing in *Arms and the Man* at the same time that Gignilliat was revising his manuscript, adding plausibility to the notion that this publication provided him with the contemporary inspiration for his suggested title for his book of *Arms and the Boy*.

67. Letter, Gignilliat to Howland, March 23, 1916, Bobbs-Merrill archival material, Lilly Library, University of Indiana.

68. Letter, Howland to Gignilliat, March 25, 1916, Bobbs-Merrill archival material, Lilly Library, University of Indiana.

69. Letter, Gignilliat to Howland, March 23, 1916, Bobbs-Merrill archival material, Lilly Library, University of Indiana.

70. Ibid.

71. Ibid.

72. L. R. Gignilliat, "Culver's Contribution to National Defense," *Culver in the World War*, The Culver Legion, (South Bend, IN: Peerless Press, 1930), p. 27.

73. Ibid.

74. The author was skeptical of this information until he located it in the *Congressional Record*, and it provides yet another example of the remarkable influence of Gignilliat and Culver during this period.

75. Photo from Wikipedia, in the public domain.

76. Smoot's testimony on behalf of Culver is recorded in from the *Congressional Record*, "First Session of the Sixty-fifth Congress of the United States of America," vol. LIII, part 6, (Washington, DC: GPO, 1916), p. 5629. The specific impact on Culver comes from L. R. Gignilliat, "Culver's Contribution to National Defense," *Culver in the World War*, The Culver Legion, (South Bend, IN: Peerless Press, 1930), pp. 27-28.

77. *Congressional Record*, "First Session of the Sixty-fifth Congress, p. 5629.

78. Ibid.

79. Ibid.

80. Gignilliat, "Culver's Contribution to National Defense," p. 28.

81. Wilfred B. Shaw, ed., *The University of Michigan, an Encyclopedic Survey: Part I – History and Administration, The University in War Service*, (Ann Arbor, MI, University of Michigan, Digital Library Production Service, 2000), p. 198.

82. While seemingly trivial, the Senate's concern regarding nitrate plants was legitimate, based upon fears that "the United States might be cut off from its Chilean source in time of war." Herring, "James Hay and the Preparedness Controversy, 1915-1916, p. 402.

83. Herring, "James Hay and the Preparedness Controversy, 1915-1916, pp. 401-402.

84. Letter, Steever to Gignilliat, April 3, 1916, , Bobbs-Merrill archival material, Lilly Library, University of Indiana; Letter, Gignilliat to Howland, April 4, 1916, , Bobbs-Merrill archival material, Lilly Library, University of Indiana.

85. Letter, Gignilliat to Bobbs-Merrill, April 7, 1916, Bobbs-Merrill archival material, Lilly Library, University of Indiana.

86. Letter, Gignilliat to Howland, April 6, 1916, Bobbs-Merrill archival material, Lilly Library, University of Indiana.

87. Letter, Gignilliat to Bobbs-Merrill, April 7, 1916, Bobbs-Merrill archival material, Lilly Library, University of Indiana.

88. Letter, Bobbs-Merrill to Gignilliat, April 10, 1916, Bobbs-Merrill archival material, Lilly Library, University of Indiana.

89. Letter, Gignilliat to Bobbs-Merrill, April 12, 1916, Bobbs-Merrill archival material, Lilly Library, University of Indiana.

90. Ibid.

91. Letter, Howland to Gignilliat, April 15, 1916, Bobbs-Merrill archival material, Lilly Library, University of Indiana.

92. Letter, Gignilliat to Howland, April 17, 1916, Bobbs-Merrill archival material, Lilly Library, University of Indiana.

93. There were at least ten letters exchanged between Gignilliat and Bobbs-Merrill regarding corrections, revisions, photographs, and suggestions for revisions during the period April 17-28, 1916. On one particular day, April 20, 1916, Gignilliat send four letters to the editors at Bobbs-Merrill. Letters, Gignilliat to and from Bobbs-Merrill, April 17-28, 1916, Bobbs-Merrill archival material, Lilly Library, University of Indiana.

94. Letter, Gignilliat to Howland and to Bobbs-Merrill, May 5, 1916, Bobbs-Merrill archival material, Lilly Library, University of Indiana.

95. Letter, Gignilliat to Howland, May 11, 1916, Bobbs-Merrill archival material, Lilly Library, University of Indiana.

96. Letter, Fleet to Gignilliat, May 10, 1916, Bobbs-Merrill archival material, Lilly Library, University of Indiana.

97. Ibid.

98. Photo from NARA public domain archive.

99. "Lincoln Fields Transformed Again into a Tent City," *The Ludington Chronicle*, Vol. 15, No. 2, July 22, 1915, p. 6.

100. Herring, "James Hay and the Preparedness Controversy, 1915-1916," p. 402.

101. Herring, "James Hay and the Preparedness Controversy, 1915-1916," pp. 402-403.

102. Culver Alumni Bulletin, 1916, p. 7.

103. Ibid.

104. Ibid.

105. One of the participants was awarded the Distinguished Service Cross, the nation's second-highest award for heroism in ground combat, and one was awarded the Silver Star, the nation's third highest award for heroism in ground combat. Robert, B. D. Hartman," Gignilliat Sets the Stage: Culver's Schoolboy Training Program, 1915-17" (Culver, IN: Culver Academies, June 24, 2008), p. 6. See also Gignilliat, "Culver's Contribution to National Defense," pp. 28-31.

106. Content deleted.

107. Letters, Howland to Gignilliat, May 23, 1916, and May 24, 1916, Bobbs-Merrill archival material, Lilly Library, University of Indiana.

108. Letter, Gignilliat to Howland, May 25, 1916, Bobbs-Merrill archival material, Lilly Library, University of Indiana.

109. Letter, Howland to Gignilliat May 29, 1916, Bobbs-Merrill archival material, Lilly Library, University of Indiana.

110. Letter, Gignilliat to Howland, May 30, 1916, Bobbs-Merrill archival material, Lilly Library, University of Indiana.

111. Letter, Gignilliat to Howland, May 31, 1916, Bobbs-Merrill archival material, Lilly Library, University of Indiana.

112. Letter, Howland to Gignilliat, June 2, 1916, Bobbs-Merrill archival material, Lilly Library, University of Indiana.

113. Letter, Bobbs-Merrill to Gignilliat, June 3, 1916, Bobbs-Merrill archival material, Lilly Library, University of Indiana.

114. Letter, Gignilliat to Bobbs-Merrill to, June 5, 1916, Bobbs-Merrill archival material, Lilly Library, University of Indiana.

115. Culver Alumni Bulletin, 1916, p. 3.

116. 1917 *Roll Call*, p. 80,

117. 1919 *Roll Call*, p. 67.

118. *Culver Alumni Bulletin* 1916, pp. 1, 8.

119. Photo courtesy of Mary Margaret Gignilliat.

120. Regarding the advance sheets, letter, Gignilliat to Howland, July 20, 1916, Bobbs-Merrill archival material, Lilly Library, University of Indiana; regarding the special leather-bound editions, letter, Gignilliat to Howland, July 21, 1916, Bobbs-Merrill archival material, Lilly Library, University of Indiana.

121. Letter, Gignilliat to Chambers, July 20, 1916, Bobbs-Merrill archival material, Lilly Library, University of Indiana; letter, Chambers to Gignilliat, July 21, 1916, Bobbs-Merrill archival material, Lilly Library, University of Indiana.

122. Letter, Howland to Gignilliat, July 22, 1916, Bobbs-Merrill archival material, Lilly Library, University of Indiana.

123. Letter, Chambers to Gignilliat, August 7, 1916, Bobbs-Merrill archival material, Lilly Library, University of Indiana.

124. Letter, Gignilliat to Chambers, August 8, 1916, Bobbs-Merrill archival material, Lilly Library, University of Indiana.

125. Letter, Chambers to Gignilliat, August 1, 1916, Bobbs-Merrill archival material, Lilly Library, University of Indiana.

126. Letter, Gignilliat to Chambers, August 4, 1916, Bobbs-Merrill archival material, Lilly Library, University of Indiana.

127. Invoice, Bobbs-Merrill, August 11, 1916, Bobbs-Merrill archival material, Lilly Library, University of Indiana.

128. Letter, Chambers to Gignilliat, August 14, 1916, Bobbs-Merrill archival material, Lilly Library, University of Indiana.

129. Content relocated.

130. Content relocated.

131. Letter, Gignilliat to Chambers, August 18, 1916, Bobbs-Merrill archival material, Lilly Library, University of Indiana.

132. Letter, Gignilliat to Chambers, August 12, 1916, Bobbs-Merrill archival material, Lilly Library, University of Indiana.

133. Letter, Gignilliat to Chambers, August 18, 1916, Bobbs-Merrill archival material, Lilly Library, University of Indiana.

134. Ibid.

135. Letter, Gignilliat to Howland, August 22, 1916, Bobbs-Merrill archival material, Lilly Library, University of Indiana.

136. Gignilliat's first correction related to "an erroring the classification of military schools" that he discovered on page 14. His second correction involved inserting the word "military" in the cation under the Picture of Norwich facing page 13 so that it identified Norwich correctly as the "first private military school in America." Letter, Gignilliat to Howland, August 26, 1916, Bobbs-Merrill archival material, Lilly Library, University of Indiana.

137. Letter, Howland to Gignilliat, August 28, 1916, Bobbs-Merrill archival material, Lilly Library, University of Indiana.

138. Letter, Gignilliat to Howland, August 26, 1916, Bobbs-Merrill archival material, Lilly Library, University of Indiana.

139. Letter, Gignilliat to Chambers, October 5, 1916, Bobbs-Merrill archival material, Lilly Library, University of Indiana.

140. I used the most comprehensive bibliography from the period available to corroborate Gignilliat's claim regarding the uniqueness of *Arms and the Boy* at the time. See W. R. Burgess, H. B. Cummings, & W. P. Tomlinson, "Military Training in the Public

School: An Annotated Bibliography, *Teachers College Record*, vol. XVII, James E, Russell, ed., (NY: Teachers College, Columbia University, 1917), pp. 141-157.

141. Letter, Gignilliat to Chambers, October 17, 1916, Bobbs-Merrill archival material, Lilly Library, University of Indiana.

142. Letter, Chambers to Gignilliat, October 19, 1916, Bobbs-Merrill archival material, Lilly Library, University of Indiana.

143. Letter, Gignilliat to Chambers, October 28, 1916, Bobbs-Merrill archival material, Lilly Library, University of Indiana.

144. "Colonel Gignilliat Discusses the Value of Military Training in Schools and Colleges," *New York Times*, October 8, 1916.

145. Noor Qasim, "The Evolution of the Book Review," *New York Times*, April 4, 2021, p. 2.

146. Letter, Gignilliat to Howland, November 18, 1916, file 4, Bobbs-Merrill archival material, Lilly Library, University of Indiana.

147. Letter, Gignilliat to Chambers, October 28, 1916, Bobbs-Merrill archival material, Lilly Library, University of Indiana.

148. Letter, Chambers to Gignilliat, November 9, 1916, file 4, Bobbs-Merrill archival material, Lilly Library, University of Indiana.

149. Handwritten memo from JRC (?) to Chambers, October 31, 1916, file 4, Bobbs-Merrill archival material, Lilly Library, University of Indiana.

150. Letter, Chambers to Gignilliat, November 9, 1916, file 4, Bobbs-Merrill archival material, Lilly Library, University of Indiana, emphasis added.

151. I have transcribed Gignilliat's hand-written note as well as I could, and I have presented it as closely to how it appears in the letter as possible. Letter, Gignilliat to Chambers, November 10, 1916, file 4, Bobbs-Merrill archival material, Lilly Library, University of Indiana.

152. Letter, Gignilliat to Chambers, November 10, 1916, file 4, Bobbs-Merrill archival material, Lilly Library, University of Indiana.

153. Ibid.

154. *The Culver Citizen*, November, 1916, p. 1.

155. Letter, The Hollenbeck Press, Indianapolis, IN, to Bobbs-Merrill, November 14, 1916, file 4, Bobbs-Merrill archival material, Lilly Library, University of Indiana.

156. Hand-written memorandum, Chambers to Howland, November 14, 1916, file 4, Bobbs-Merrill archival material, Lilly Library, University of Indiana.

157. Letter, Chambers to Gignilliat, November 17, 1916, file 4, Bobbs-Merrill archival material, Lilly Library, University of Indiana, emphasis added.

158. Letter, Gignilliat to Chambers, November 18, 1916, file 4, Bobbs-Merrill archival material, Lilly Library, University of Indiana.

159. Letter, Chambers to Gignilliat, November 20, 1916, file 4, Bobbs-Merrill archival material, Lilly Library, University of Indiana.

Ch. 11 – Gignilliat's Aeneid: The Content and Argument of *Arms and the Boy*

1. Gignilliat, *Arms and the Boy*, preface.

2. Ibid.

3. Ibid.

4. Gignilliat, *Arms and the Boy*, pp. 2-3.

5. Benjamin Rene Jordan, *Modern Manhood and the Boy Scouts of America: Citizenship, Race, and the Environment, 1910-1930* (Chapel Hill, NC: The University of North Carolina Press, 2016), pp. 4-10; see also Gignilliat, *Arms and the Boy*, pp.

18-19, 43.

6. Gignilliat, *Arms and the Boy*, p. 3.

7. Gignilliat, *Arms and the Boy*, pp. 196-205, 307-312.

8. Gignilliat, *Arms and the Boy*, p. 8.

9. Gignilliat, *Arms and the Boy*, p. 19.

10. Gignilliat, *Arms and the Boy*, pp. 19, 59-60.

11. Gignilliat, *Arms and the Boy*, pp. 19, 25.

12. Gignilliat, *Arms and the Boy*, p. 29.

13. Gignilliat, *Arms and the Boy*, p. 31.

14. Ibid.

15. Gignilliat, *Arms and the Boy*, p. 35.

16. Gignilliat, *Arms and the Boy*, p. 32.

17. Gignilliat, *Arms and the Boy*, p. 43.

18. Gignilliat, *Arms and the Boy*, p. 45.

19. Gignilliat, *Arms and the Boy*, pp. 44-45.

20. Gignilliat, *Arms and the Boy*, p. 46.

21. Gignilliat, *Arms and the Boy*, p. 61.

22. Gignilliat, *Arms and the Boy*, pp. 46-47.

23. Gignilliat, *Arms and the Boy*, p. 50.

24. Gignilliat, *Arms and the Boy*, p. 48.

25. Ibid.

26. Gignilliat, *Arms and the Boy*, p. 53.

27. Gignilliat, *Arms and the Boy*, pp. 55-57.

28. Gignilliat, *Arms and the Boy*, p. 56.

29. Gignilliat, *Arms and the Boy*, p. 58.

30. Gignilliat, *Arms and the Boy*, p. 55.

31. Gignilliat, *Arms and the Boy*, p. 60.

32. Gignilliat, *Arms and the Boy*, p. 61.

33. Ibid.

34. Gignilliat, *Arms and the Boy*, p. 63.

35. Gignilliat, *Arms and the Boy*, pp. 70-71.

36. Gignilliat, *Arms and the Boy*, pp. 72-80.

37. Gignilliat, *Arms and the Boy*, pp. 66-67.

38. Gignilliat, *Arms and the Boy*, p. 81.

39. Gignilliat, *Arms and the Boy*, p. 82.

40. Gignilliat, *Arms and the Boy*, pp. 83-85.

41. Gignilliat, *Arms and the Boy*, p. 81.

42. While not reflected in the Congressional record, Jones' comment likely elicited at least one guffaw from those in attendance. Sebastian C. Jones, Superintendent of New York Military Academy and President of AMCSUS testimony on January 21, 1916. "To Increase the Efficiency of the Military Establishment of the United States," *Hearing Before the Committee on Military Affairs, House of Representatives*, Sixty–fourth Congress, first session, (Washington, DC: Government Printing Office, 1916), vol. 1, pp. 460.

43. Gignilliat, *Arms and the Boy*, p. 86.

44. Gignilliat, *Arms and the Boy*, pp. 91-93.

45. Gignilliat, *Arms and the Boy*, p. 90.

46. Gignilliat, *Arms and the Boy*, p. 91.

47. Gignilliat, *Arms and the Boy*, p. 98.
48. Gignilliat, *Arms and the Boy*, pp. 97.
49. Gignilliat, *Arms and the Boy*, p. 95.
50. Letter, Howland to Gignilliat, December 10, 1915, Bobbs-Merrill archival material, Lilly Library, University of Indiana.
51. Gignilliat, *Arms and the Boy*, p. 101.
52. Gignilliat, *Arms and the Boy*, pp. 108-111.
53. Gignilliat, *Arms and the Boy*, p. 122.
54. Gignilliat, *Arms and the Boy*, p. 122-123.
55. Gignilliat, *Arms and the Boy*, pp. 112-119.
56. Gignilliat, *Arms and the Boy*, p. 53.
57. Gignilliat, *Arms and the Boy*, pp. 131-134.
58. Gignilliat, *Arms and the Boy*, pp. 135-138.
59. Gignilliat, *Arms and the Boy*, p. 142.
60. Gignilliat, *Arms and the Boy*, pp. 170-173, 184-186.
61. Gignilliat, *Arms and the Boy*, pp. 176-184.
62. Letter, Howland to Gignilliat, December 10, 1915, Bobbs-Merrill archival material, Lilly Library, University of Indiana.
63. Gignilliat, *Arms and the Boy*, p. 209.
64. Gignilliat, *Arms and the Boy*, p. 226.
65. Gignilliat, *Arms and the Boy*, p. 237.
66. Gignilliat, *Arms and the Boy*, p. 243.
67. Gignilliat, *Arms and the Boy*, p. 246.
68. Gignilliat, *Arms and the Boy*, pp. 252-253.
69. Gignilliat, *Arms and the Boy*, p. 270.
70. Gignilliat, *Arms and the Boy*, p. 273.
71. Gignilliat, *Arms and the Boy*, p. 281.
72. Gignilliat, *Arms and the Boy*, p. 288.
73. Gignilliat, *Arms and the Boy*, p. 295.
74. Gignilliat, *Arms and the Boy*, p. 297.
75. Gignilliat, *Arms and the Boy*, p. 305.
76. Gignilliat, *Arms and the Boy*, p. 307.
77. Gignilliat, *Arms and the Boy*, p. 313.
78. Gignilliat, *Arms and the Boy*, p. 320.
79. Gignilliat, *Arms and the Boy*, p. 324.
80. Gignilliat, *Arms and the Boy*, p. 326.
81. Gignilliat, *Arms and the Boy*, p. 332.
82. Gignilliat, *Arms and the Boy*, p. 336.
83. Constructivism is the view that students are actively involved in constructing the worlds of meaning they inhabit.
84. Lance Betros, *Carved from Granite: West Point Since 1902*, (Texas A&M, 2012), p. 240.
85. Michael Neiberg, *Making Citizen Soldiers: ROTC and the Ideology of American Military Service*, (Harvard University Press, 2000), p. 180.
86. Robert Kegan, *In over Our Heads: The Mental Demands of Modern Life*, (Harvard University Press, 2994), pp. 37-43.
87. There was an article published in 1955 identifying military schools explicitly as "assimilating institutions." See Sanford M. Dornbusch, "The Military Academy as an

Assimilating Institution," *Social Forces*, (published by Oxford University Press) Vol. 33, No. 4, May, 1955, pp. 316-321.

88. Much of the substance regarding formation and assimilation comes from the author's own work, "The Modern American Military Education Model: A New Approach for a New Century," Ch. 6 in Mark Patrick Ryan and Timothy L. Weekes, eds., *Handbook of Research on Character and Leadership Development in Military Schools*, (IGI Global, 2021), pp. 116-145.

Ch. 12 – Preparing Culver and Himself to Answer the Nation's Call to Arms in 1916 and 1917

1. *Culver Alumni Bulletin*, 1916, p. 4.
2. "Name Five Schools for Army Training," *Chicago Daily News*, November 15, 1916, p. 1. According to Gignilliat, the orders establishing the senior units for the infantry, cavalry, and field artillery at Culver were issued by the War Department on November 18, 1916. Gignilliat, *Culver in the World War*, p. 28.
3. St. Thomas College educated both high school and college-aged students at the time. Beginning in 1903, military training became mandatory for all students, and the War Department designed it a "military school" in 1906. The school was quite good in terms of its military performance, earning recognition from the War Department as a "Distinguished Institution" three times in the years 1908, 1909, and 1915. The high school program became its own entity as St. Thomas Military Academy in 1922. When it moved to its own campus in 1965, it separated from the University of St. Thomas. It remains in existence today in Mendota Heights, MN (a suburb of St. Paul) as St. Thomas Academy, an outstanding all-male, Roman Catholic, college preparatory, military high school, educating middle school boys in a non-military program and high school boys school in its own independent military program.
4. Image for the US National Archives in the public domain.
5. Image for the US National Archives in the public domain.
6. Letter, Gignilliat to E. R. Culver, November 16, 1916, Culver archives, 1916 general correspondence file.
7. Ibid.
8. Gignilliat, *Culver in the World War*, p. 24.
9. *Everybody's Magazine*, April 1919, p. 86.
10. *The Vedette*, XX: 12 27 Jan 1917, p. 1.
11. Ibid.
12. *Everybody's Magazine*, July 1917, 143-144.
13. J. M. H. Frederick, "Superintendent of Schools Annual Report for the 1916-17 School Year," Cleveland, OH, January 7, 1918, pp. 71-75.
14. Steever had established programs in the following states: CO, DC, FL, GA, IA, ID, IL, KY, MI, MO, NC, NJ, OH, OR, PA, TX, WI, WY. Note that he had not yet established a program in Indiana. Steever, "Quarterly Report to President HSVUS," June 1917, appearing in *Everybody's Magazine*, Vol. 36. No. 6, June 1917, pp. 719-720.
15. *The Vedette*, XX; 13, 3 Feb 1917, p. 1.
16. H. L. Durborow, "Preparing While We Wait," *The School Review*, Vol. 25, No. 3, March 1917, pp. 151-156.
17. *The Vedette*, March 17, 1917, p. 1.
18. Ibid.
19. Ibid.
20. Ibid.

21. Ibid.

22. Ibid.

23. *The Vedette*, March 17, 1917, p. 2.

24. Image from *The Vedette*, March 17, 1917, p. 1.

25. *The Vedette*, March 17, 1917, p. 3.

26. *The Vedette*, March 17, 1917, p. 2.

27. *The Vedette*, March 17, 1917, p. 3.

28. 1917 *Roll Call*, p. 149.

29. Rodney Carlisle, "The Attacks on U. S. Shipping that Precipitated American Entry into World War I," *The Northern Mariner/Le marin du nord*, XVII No. 3 (July 2007), p. 41.

30. Letter, Gignilliat to Bobbs-Merrill, March 23, 1917, file 4, Bobbs-Merrill archival material, Lilly Library, University of Indiana.

31. "Arms and the Boy," Roster, dated initially October 12, 1916 and amended to July 2, 1919, "Arms and the Boy" file, Culver archives, Culver Academies, Culver, IN.

32. "Memorandum of Agreement" regarding the production and sale of Arms and the Boy between L. R. Gignilliat and the Bobbs-Merrill Company, undated copy signed by Gignilliat and Howland (on behalf of the Bobbs-Merrill Company), "Arms and the Boy" file, Culver archives, Culver Academies, Culver, IN.

33. Statement, Bobbs-Merrill to Gignilliat, March 30, 1917, file 4, Bobbs-Merrill archival material, Lilly Library, University of Indiana.

34. Gignilliat, *Culver in the World War*, p. 36.

35. Gignilliat, *Culver in the World War*, p. 36.

36. Ibid.

37. Gignilliat, *Culver in the World War*, pp. 36-37.

38. Gignilliat, *Culver in the World War*, p. 36.

39. David Kennedy, *Over Here: The First World War and American Society*, (NY: Oxford University Press, 1980), pp. 148-49.

40. Gignilliat, *Culver in the World War*, p. 35.

41. Gignilliat, *Culver in the World War*, p. 36.

42. Gignilliat, *Culver in the World War*, p. 37.

43. Gignilliat, *Culver in the World War*, p. 25.

44. Articles attesting to Denny's work appeared in the Wabash College student newspaper, *The Bachelor*, several times during April and May, 1917, when he was present on campus and working with cadets. The following editions of *The Bachelor* for specific references to Denny's work: "Drill Progresses Under CAPT Denney," April 21, 1917, p. 1; "Guard Instruction Set for Friday Postpones," April 25, 1917, p. 1; "Weather Interferes with Drill During Past Week," April 28, 1917, p. 4; "Wabash Battalion Can Not Train in Manual of Arms," May 2, 1917, p. 4; "Wabash Battalion Plays Important Role in Parade," May 5, 1917, pp. 1, 3; "Wabash Plays Large Part in Lafayette Celebration," May 9, 1917, p. 4.

45. Photo from 1917 *Roll Call*.

46. Gignilliat, *Culver in the World War*, p. 25.

47. Photo from Culver Archives.

48. Gignilliat, *Culver in the World War* p. 25; see also *The Vedette*, May 1917.

49. Ibid.

50. The information was provided by Vera J. Snook, Librarian at the Reddick Library in Ottawa, IL. "These Books Are Barred in Germany," *Ottawa Free Trader-Journal*,

April 21, 1917, p. 2.

51. George Creel, "Preface (written in January 1918)," *The Cadet Manual: Official Handbook for High School Volunteers of the United States*, (Philadelphia, PA: J. B. Lippincott Company, 1918), pp. vii-viii.

52. Howard Wheeler, "Foreword," *The Cadet Manual: Official Handbook for High School Volunteers of the United States*, (Philadelphia, PA: J. B. Lippincott Company, 1918), pp. ix-x.

53. Edgar Z. Steever, *The Cadet Manual: Official Handbook for High School Volunteers of the United States*, (Philadelphia, PA: J. B. Lippincott Company, 1918), p. xvii.

54. Steever, *HSVUS Cadet Manual*, p. 47.

55. Photo from *1918 CMA Catalog Supplement*, p. 3.

56. Official War Department Report of 1917 CMA Annual Inspection, *1918 CMA Catalog Supplement*, p. 3.

57. *The Vedette*, May 12, 1917, p. 1.

58. Photo from 1917 *Roll Call* Entry, p. 80.

59. Ibid.

60. Image from 1917 *Roll Call* Entry, p. 80.

61. Photo from 1917 *Roll Call* Entry, p. 80.

62. 1919 *Roll Call*, p. 67.

Ch. 13 – Combining Voice and Action, May 1917-July 1919

1. Photo from Culver Archives.

2. *Culver in the World War*, p. 1026.

3. Dr. John "Jay." Boyd. (2015). "The Great War of 1932: Making the Organized Reserve a "Going Concern." Office of Army Reserve History, p. 11.

4. Boyd, p. 13.

5. Jennifer Keene's *Doughboys, the Great War, and the Remaking of America*, pp. 68-81.

6. Keene, p. 76.

7. Keene p. 81.

8. Keene, pp. 68-69.

9. Keene, p. 75.

10. Keene, p. 79; Boyd, p. 13.

11. Edward M. Coffman, *The War to End All Wars: The American Military Experience in World War I* (Madison, WI: The University of Wisconsin Press, 1986), p. 55.

12. Captain X (Edward L Fox). (1918). *Our First Half Million: The Story of Our National Army*. (The H. K. Fly Company), p. 188.

13. *US Army Special Regulations No. 49*, "Training Camps for Reserve Officers and Candidates for Appointment as Such, May 15 – August 11, 1917," (Washington, DC: US Government Printing Office, 1917), p. 12.

14. *US Army Special Regulations No. 49*, p. 15.

15. John A. Almstrom, "Learning to Live: Tactical Training for the AEF, 1917-1918," (unpublished MA thesis, Rice University, 1972), pp. 35, 37.

16. *US Army Special Regulations No. 49*, p. 12.

17. Ibid.

18. *US Army Special Regulations No. 49*, p. 15.

19. *US Army Special Regulations No. 49*, p. 32.

20. *US Army Special Regulations No. 49*, pp. 11, 12, 14.

21. *The Culver Citizen*, May 23, 1917, p. 1.

22. Robert Rossow, *Rossow's Reminiscences*, unpublished manuscript, n.d., pp. 171-172.

23. These included the following Culver personnel: Harold C. Bays, Bennett, Elliot, Gignilliat, Hackler, Harris, Johnston, Kennedy, Kutchinski, Charles F. McKinney, Miller, Howard F. Noble, Ramsey, Reitz, Charles Ainsworth Rockwood, Robert Rossow, Ralph G. Sickles, Starbuck, Sutherlin, Thomas. 1918 *Roll Call*, p. 31.

24. Almstrom, "Learning to Live: Tactical Training for the AEF, 1917-1918," p. 37.

25. Photo from US National Archives in the public domain.

26. *US Army Special Regulations No. 49*, pp. 33-35.

27. *US Army Special Regulations No. 49*, pp. 36-40.

28. *US Army Special Regulations No. 49*, pp. 40-56.

29. Richard S. Faulkner, *Pershing's Crusaders: The American Soldier in World War I* (Lawrence, KS: University Press of Kansas, 2017), p. 263.

30. Gignilliat, *Arms and the Boy*, p. 106.

31. Bryon Farwell, *Over There: The United States in The Great War, 1917-1918* (NY: WW Norton, 1999), pp. 67-68.

32. "Lieut.-Col. Gignilliat Relieved of His Post," *Indianapolis News*, October 2, 1917, p. 3.

33. *Culver in the World War*, pp. 112, 1026.

34. "Military Record of General L. R. Gignilliat," Gignilliat files, Culver archives, Culver Academies, Culver, IN.

35. Major J. A. Hillman, "The Building Up of the American Army," *Culver in the World War* (South Bend, IN: Peerless Press, 1930), p. 68.

36. Hillman, "The Building Up of the American Army," p. 70.

37. Hillman, "The Building Up of the American Army," p. 69.

38. Ibid.

39. "Bids his Boys Godspeed," *Indianapolis News*, 15 August 1917, p. 11.

40. Hillman, "The Building Up of the American Army," p. 69.

41. "Bids his Boys Godspeed," *Indianapolis News*, August 15, 1917, p. 11.

42. Colonel C. C. Chambers, "Introduction," *Culver in the World War* (South Bend, IN: Peerless Press, 1930), p. xi.

43. Hillman, "The Building Up of the American Army," p. 70.

44. First OTC Company Training Roster, 5th Company, 9th Provisional Training Regiment, Aug 1, 1917, Box 2, Fort Benjamin Harrison, Misc, First OTC, 8th and 9th PTR, National Archives, St. Louis, MO.

45. *US Army Special Regulations No. 49*, p. 10.

46. *US Army Special Regulations No. 49*, p. 7.

47. Almstrom, "Learning to Live: Tactical Training for the AEF, 1917-1918," pp. 36-37.

48. "Lieut.-Col. Gignilliat Relieved of His Post," *Indianapolis News*, October 2, 1917, p. 3.

49. Ibid.

50. Hillman, "The Building Up of the American Army," p. 67.

51. Colonel August C. Nissen was a USMA 1895 graduate who served as a Regular cavalry officer before being commissioned as an infantry officer in the National Army on August 5, 1917. Nissen served as the commander of the 333rd Infantry Regiment, assigned to the 84th Division's 167th Infantry Brigade, from August 29, 1917 to June 6, 1918. Colonel Fredrik L. Knudsen was also a long-serving senior officer who also served in the 167th Infantry Brigade. It is likely that both Nissen and Knudsen were impressed with Gignilliat while observing him as instructors at the First Series OTC

at Fort Harrison and recommended that the 84th Division request that Gignilliat join their division. Information on Nissen comes from the *USMA Register of Graduates*.

52. *Full Text Citations for Award of the Army Distinguished Service Medal, U.S. Army for World War I*, "Gignilliat, Leigh R.," War Department, General Orders No. 43 (1922); "National Army" referred to units formed during the war. These divisions were numbered 76-91, and all of the National Army divisions formed during the war went overseas. Richard A. Rinaldi, *The US Army in World War I: Orders Of Battle – Ground Units 1917-1919* (Takoma Park, MD: General Data LLC, 2004), p. 6.

53. Michael E. Bigelow, *A Short History of Army Intelligence* (U.S. Army Intelligence and Security Command, 2012), p. 17; James L. Gilbert, *World War I and the Origins of U.S. Military Intelligence* (Lanham, MD: Scarecrow Press, 2012), pp. 125-126.

54. *Infantry Training*, US War Department (Washington, DC: US Government Printing Office, 1917), p. 5.

55. *Infantry Training*, pp. 5-7.

56. *Infantry Training*, pp. 8-9.

57. *Infantry Training*, p. 12.

58. *Infantry Training*, p. 8.

59. *Infantry Training*, p. 5.

60. *Infantry Training*, pp. 5, 18-24.

61. Faulkner, *Pershing's Crusaders*, pp. 83-84.

62. *Infantry Training*, pp. 18-24.

63. *Infantry Training*, pp. 18-29.

64. Faulkner, *Pershing's Crusaders*, p. 83.

65. Photo from US National Archives in the public domain.

66. Faulkner, *Pershing's Crusaders*, p. 95.

67. Ibid.

68. LRG Ltr to ER Culver, 19 Oct 1917, Culver Archives.

69. LRG Ltr to ER Culver, 9 Oct 1917, Culver Archives.

70. LRG Ltr to ER Culver, 20 Jan 1918, Culver Archives.

71. Ibid.

72. LRG Ltr to ER Culver, 9 October 1917, Culver Archives.

73. LRG Ltr to ER Culver, 19 Oct 1917, Culver Archives.

74. *Indianapolis News*, March 16, 1918, p. 13.

75. Gignilliat, *Arms and the Boy*, *passim*, especially pp. 90, 148.

76. "What Men Take: Overseas List Issued to Soldiers at Camp Sherman," *Indianapolis News*, August 8, 1918, p. 8.

77. Photo from US National Archives in the public domain.

78. "What Men Take: Overseas List Issued to Soldiers at Camp Sherman," p. 8.

79. Photo from US National Archives in the public domain.

80. LRG Ltr to ER Culver, January 20, 1918, Culver Archives.

81. Ibid.

82. Letter, Howland to Gignilliat, November 26, 1917, file 4, Bobbs-Merrill archival material, Lilly Library, University of Indiana.

83. Letter (handwritten), Gignilliat to Howland, November 27, 1917, file 4, Bobbs-Merrill archival material, Lilly Library, University of Indiana.

84. "What Happens to the Drafted Man at Camp Zachary Taylor," *South Bend News-Times*, April 19, 1918, p. 17.

85. Ibid.

86. Ibid.

87. Ibid.

88. Ibid.

89. *The Vedette*, XXI: 26, April 27, 1918, pp. 1-2.

90. US Army Center of Military History, *American Expeditionary Forces: Divisions Volume 2*, in the *Order of Battle of the United States Land Forces in the World War* series, reprint; first printed in 1931 as CMH Pub 23-2, (Washington, DC: US Army Center of Military History, 1988), p. 368.

91. *The Vedette*, XXI:38, August 17, 1918. p. 1.

92. Benjamin F. Shearer, "An Experiment in Military and Civilian Education: The Students' Army Training Corps at the University of Illinois," *Journal of Illinois State Historical Society*, Vol. 72, No. 3, August 1979, pp. 213-224; citation comes from p. 213.

93. United States War Department, "Special Regulations No. 103," *Students' Army Training Corps Regulations*, (Washington, DC: Government Printing Office, 1918), pp. 5-9; United States War Department, *The Students Army Training Corps Descriptive Circular*, second edition, (Washington, DC: Government Printing Office, corrected to October 14, 1918), pp. 10-32.

94. United States War Department, *The Students Army Training Corps Descriptive Circular*, see especially pp. 12-13 & 30 for information pertaining to the state of Indiana.

95. LRG Ltr to ER Culver, 29 June 1918, Culver Archives.

96. LRG Ltr to ER Culver, 2 Sept 1918; LRG Ltr to Glascock, 2 Sept 1918, Culver Archives.

97. LRG Ltr to Glascock, 2 Sept 1918, Culver Archives.

98. Photo from US National Archives in the public domain.

99. Cover letter and manifest of *SS Melita*, Headquarters Port of Embarkation, Hoboken, NJ, US Army Adjutant General's Office, released 4 October 1918, provided by Don W. Jones via research on Ancestry.com, 23 Jan 2019.

100. Photo from US National Archives in the public domain.

101. Photo from US National Archives in the public domain.

102. Passenger List of SS Antrim, provided by Don W. Jones via research on Ancestory.com, 23 Jan 2019.

103. CMH, *American Expeditionary Forces: Divisions Volume 2*, pp. 368-371.

104. CMH, *American Expeditionary Forces: Divisions Volume 2*, p. 371.

105. Ibid.

106. *Full Text Citations for Award of the Army Distinguished Service Medal, U.S. Army for World War I*, "Gignilliat, Leigh R.," War Department, General Orders No. 43 (1922); *Culver in the World War*, p. 1026; "National Guard" referred to state militia units that existed prior to the war. These divisions were numbered 26-42, and all of the National Guard divisions called to active duty during the war went overseas. Richard A. Rinaldi, *The US Army in World War I: Orders Of Battle – Ground Units 1917-1919* (Takoma Park, MD: General Data LLC, 2004), p. 6.

107. French Marshal Ferdinand Foch was appointed Supreme Allied Commander on April 3, 1918. This appointment allowed him to issue operational orders to all of the forces of the Allied and Associated powers.

108. *Culver in the World War*, p. 1026.

109. American Battle Monuments Commission, *37ᵗʰ Division Summary of Operations*

in the World War (Washington, DC: US Government Printing Office, 1944), pp. 20-21, 27-31; US Army Center of Military History, *American Expeditionary Forces: Divisions Volume 2*, p. 237.

110. American Battle Monuments Commission, *37th Division Summary of Operations in the World War,* pp. 27-31; see also map of Ypres-Lys Operation, Lieut. Col. Frank W. Weed, M. C., ed., *Field Operations, Volume VIII*, in the series *The Medical Department of the United States Army in the World War*, (Washington, DC: US Government Printing Office, 1925), Ch. 36, Plate LII, appearing between p. 870 and p. 871.

111. CMH, *American Expeditionary Forces: Divisions Volume 2*, p. 239.

112. LRG Ltr to ER Culver, 12 March, 1919, Culver archives.

113. *Culver in the World War*, p. 1026.

114. Hillman, "The Building Up of the American Army," p. 112.

115. *Culver in the World War*, pp. 112, 1026.

116. *United States Army in the World War 1917-1919*, Vol. 10, Part 2, p. 1201.

117. *United States Army in the World War, 1917-1919, Vol. 11, American Occupation of Germany,* (Washington, DC, US Army Center of Military History, 199), p. 3. Zone identifications added by author.

118. F. L. Carsten, F.L. (1944). "The British Summary Court at Wiesbaden, 1926-1929," *Modern Law Review*, (Oxford: Blackwell Publishing, 1944), p. 215.

119. *United States Army in the World War 1917-1919*, Vol. 10, Part 2, pp. 1201-1202.

120. Charles G. Dawes, *A Journal of the Great War*, Vol. 1 (NY: Houghton Mifflin, 1921), pp. 333-335.

121. Image of French General Charles Jean Marie Payot, in the public domain.

122. Dawes, *A Journal of the Great War*, Vol. 1, p. 333.

123. *United States Army in the World War 1917-1919*, Vol. 10, Part 2, pp. 1201-1202.

124. *United States Army in the World War 1917-1919*, Vol. 10, Part 2, p. 1205; Nick Lloyd, The Western Front: A History of the Great War, 1914-1918, (Liveright Publishing, 2021), p. 496.

125. *United States Army in the World War 1917-1919*, Vol. 10, Part 2, pp. 1205-1206.

126. *The United States Army in the World War, 1917-1919: Vol. 11*, p. 167.

127. Passenger List of Organization, USS Von Steuben, Headquarters Port of Embarkation, Brest, France, Major P. H. Charlton, US Army 37th Division Personnel Adjutant, Adjutant General's Office, provided by Don W. Jones via research on Ancestory.com, 23 Jan 2019; LRG Ltr to ER Culver, 12 March, 1919, Culver archives.

128. Ibid.

129. Ibid.

130. Ibid.

131. Ibid.

132. LRG Ltr to ER Culver, undated continuation of Ltr begun on 12 March, 1919, Culver archives; *Full Text Citations for Award of the Army Distinguished Service Medal, U.S. Army for World War I*, "Gignilliat, Leigh R.," War Dept, General Orders No. 43 (1922).

133. LRG Ltr to ER Culver, 12 Mar 1919, Culver archives.

134. Joachim Schröder and Alexander Watson, "Occupation during and after the War (Germany)," *International Encyclopedia of the First World War*, as of 23 June 2016.

135. Brian F. Neumann, and Shane D. Makowicki, *Occupation and Demobilization, 1918-1923*, The US Army Campaigns of World War I Commemorative Series, (US Army

Center of Military History, 2019), p. 11.

136. The population of the American occupation zone was reported to be 893,000 in 1919. Neumann, and Makowicki, *Occupation and Demobilization, 1918-1923*, p. 11.

137. The population of Coblenz was reported to be 65,434 in 1919. Neumann and Makowicki, *Occupation and Demobilization, 1918-1923*, pp. 11. 19.

138. The population of Trier was reported to be 53,248 in 1919. Neumann, and Makowicki, *Occupation and Demobilization, 1918-1923*, p. 11.

139. *Culver in the World War*, p. 1026.

140. *The United States Army in the World War, 1917-1919: Vol.*, p. 167.

141. Neumann, and Makowicki, *Occupation and Demobilization, 1918-1923*, p. 21.

142. LRG Ltr to ER Culver, 15 April 1919, Culver archives.

143. LRG Ltr to ER Culver, 12 Mar 1919; LRG Ltr to ER Culver, 15 April 1919, Culver archives.

144. LRG Ltr to ER Culver, 12 Mar 1919, Culver archives.

145. *Full Text Citations for Award of the Army Distinguished Service Medal, U.S. Army for World War I*, "Gignilliat, Leigh R.," War Dept, General Orders No. 43 (1922).

146. LRG Ltr to ER Culver, 15 April 1919, Culver archives.

147. Ibid.

148. *The Vedette*, November 5, 1921, p. 1.

149. LRG Ltr to ER Culver, 15 April 1919, Culver archives.

150. *The United States Army in the World War, 1917-1919: Vol. 11*, pp. 191-192.

151. *The United States Army in the World War, 1917-1919: Vol. 11*, p. 193.

152. Ibid.

153. *The United States Army in the World War, 1917-1919: Vol. 11*, p. 191.

154. *The United States Army in the World War, 1917-1919: Vol. 11*, pp. 191-192.

155. *The United States Army in the World War, 1917-1919: Vol. 11*, p. 191.

156. *The United States Army in the World War, 1917-1919: Vol. 11*, pp. 190-191.

157. *The United States Army in the World War, 1917-1919: Vol. 11*, p. 192.

158. Ibid.

159. *Full Text Citations for Award of the Army Distinguished Service Medal, U.S. Army for World War I*, "Gignilliat, Leigh R.," War Dept, General Orders No. 43 (1922).

160. *The United States Army in the World War, 1917-1919: Vol. 11*, pp. 191-193.

161. Photo modified by author slightly for clarity. Used courtesy of Culver Academies archives.

162. *Full Text Citations for Award of the Army Distinguished Service Medal, U.S. Army for World War I*, "Gignilliat, Leigh R.," War Dept, General Orders No. 43 (1922).

163. *Culver in the World War*, p. 1026; Passenger List of SS Imperator, provided by Don W. Jones via research on Ancestory.com, 23 Jan 2019.

164. *The Vedette*, XXIII:35, July 19, 1919, p. 1.

165. Brigadier General L. R. Gignilliat, "Culver's Contribution to National Defense," *Culver in the World War* (South Bend, IN: Peerless Press, 1930), p. 12.

166. *The Vedette*, XXIII:35; July 19, 1919, p. 1.

167. *The Vedette*, XXIII:36, July 26, 1919, pp. 1-2.

168. *Culver in the World War*, p. 1026; *The Vedette*, August 23, 1919, p. 2.

169. Photo courtesy of Culver Archives.

170. *US Army Special Regulations No. 49*, p. 10.

171. Colonel C. C. Chambers, "Introduction," *Culver in the World War* (South Bend, IN: Peerless Press, 1930), p. i.

172. 52 Culver men served in two or more services, causing the number of Culver men to appear to be 3,552. Chambers, "Introduction," *Culver in the World War*, p. xi.

173. Ibid.

174. Ibid.

175. Robert B. D. Hartman, *Lest We Forget: Culver – Two Great Wars and the Years Between* (Culver, IN: Culver Education Foundation, 2007), pp. 22-23.

176. *Culver in the World War*, front plates. Of the 85 total Gold Star men, 56 were from CMA Winter School, and 29 were from Culver Summer School. All numbers corroborated in 2018 by Gary Christlieb, Senior Humanities Instructor, Culver Academies (email from Gary Christlieb, to author, January 21, 2019).

177. Chambers, *Culver in the World War*, p. xi.

178. Chambers, *Culver in the World War*, pp. vii, xi, 128.

179. Photo used courtesy of Culver Academies archives.

180. Hartman, *Lest We Forget*, pp. 22-23; corroborated in *Culver in the World War*, pp. 114-117.

Ch. 14 – Resting His Voice, August 1919 – December 1922

1. *The Vedette*, 5 October 1918, p.1, and 9 August 1919, p. 1.

2. *The Vedette*, 7 June 1919, p. 1

3. Forrest C. Pogue, *George C. Marshall: Education of a General*, (Penguin Books, 1963), p. 205-06.

4. *Hearings Before the Subcommittee of the Committee on Military Affairs, United States Senate, Sixty-Sixth Congress, First Session, Part 8*, testimony recorded from session on August 28, 1919 (Washington, DC: US Government Printing Office, 1919), pp. 461-462.

5. *Hearings Before the Subcommittee of the Committee on Military Affairs*, p. 460; "The History of Officer Candidates School," (n.d.), p. 1.

6. *Hearings Before the Subcommittee of the Committee on Military Affairs*, p. 466.

7. Photo courtesy of Mary Margaret Gignilliat

8. Content deleted.

9. A. B. Smith, "Helping the Colonel Lead the Boy Scouts," *The Vedette*, 2 Oct 1920, pp. 1, 3.

10. Donald F. Duncan, CMA 1905-1907 (Cadet Captain of Company C), Captain, USMC, KIA Chateau Thierry 6 June 1918, DSC and Navy Cross (*Culver in the World War* 1930, p. 961); Charles H. "Willie" Ulmer, CMA 1913-1916 (Cadet Captain of Company F), SNS 1910-1911, SCS 1912, 2LT, USMC, WIA near Chateau de l'Orange 8 June 1918, and died of wounds same day, SS and French Croix de Guerre (*Culver in the World War* 1930, p. 974); Note that Duncan and Ulmer were in the same USMA regiment (6th) and dies within two days of each other; John G. "Jack" Schneider, CMA 1915-1917 (Cadet Captain and Battalion Adjutant), SNS 1916, 1LT, USMC, WIA near Vierzy 19 July 1918, WIA in Argonne forest 1 November 1918, died of wounds 3 November 19198, DSC, Navy Cross, SS, and French Croix de Guerre (*Culver in the World War* 1930, p. 971).

11. Photo from *The Vedette*, 16 Oct 1920, p. 2.

12. Photo courtesy Mary Margaret Gignilliat.

13. Image from Wikipedia in the public domain.

14. Photo courtesy of Mary Margaret Gignilliat.

15. D. H. Rathbun, "Through France and Belgium with Colonel and the Scouts," *The Vedette*, 9 Oct 1920, pp. 1, 3; D. H. Rathbun, "Colonel Gignilliat in Legion of Honor,"

The Vedette, 16 Oct 1920, pp. 1, 2.

16. Photo courtesy of Mary Margaret Gignilliat.

17. Rathbun, "Colonel Gignilliat in Legion of Honor," *The Vedette*, 16 Oct 1920, pp. 1-2.

18. James M. Sellers, Jr., "A Brief History of The Association of Military Colleges and Schools of the United States," unpublished, compiled at Wentworth Military Academy, Lexington, Missouri, March 12, 1990, p, 4; Alvan C. Hadley, "Military Schools: The Association of Military Colleges and Schools of the United States (AMCSUS) and the Historical Struggle for the Survival of Military Preparatory Schools in America," unpublished EdD dissertation, University of Kentucky, Lexington, KY, 1999, pp. 36-38.

19. "Pershing Visits Culver," *The Culver Builder*, Vol 3, No. 1, 22 Dec 1922, p. 5.

20. Photo from *The Vedette*, Pictorial Supplement, 26 Nov, 1921.

21. Ltr from Marshall Foch to Gignilliat, 15 Nov 1921, *The Vedette*, Pictorial Supplement, 26 Nov, 1921.

22. Photo from *The Vedette*, Pictorial Supplement, 26 Nov, 1921.

23. "Military Record of General L. R. Gignilliat," Gignilliat files, Culver archives.

24. "Enrollment Statistics, 1911-12 – 1931-32, Central Files, Culver Archives.

25. Brig. Gen. L. R. Gignilliat, "The Value of Military Training in Education," An address broadcasted from station KDKA Westinghouse studio, Pittsburgh, PA, May 20, 1922.

26. Robert Rossow, "Chapter XIII – A Message to Garcia," "Rossow Reports," unpublished manuscript, circa 1939, p. 248. This manuscript was later edited and published by Robert B. D. Hartman as the book, *Rossow Reports: Colonel Robert Rossow, Cavalryman and Raconteur, His Stories*, Culver Education Foundation, 2007.

27. *Rossow Reports*, p. 250.

28. *Rossow Reports*, pp. 248-49.

29. *Rossow Reports*, p. 250.

30. Photo from 1920 *Roll Call*, p. 153.

31. *Rossow Reports*, p. 250.

32. *Rossow Reports*, p. 253.

33. Photo from *The Vedette*, Pictorial Supplement, 20 Jan 1923.

34. Ibid.

35. Ibid.

36. Ibid.

37. The three individuals memorialized were Arthur B. McCormick '15 (Canadian Army), William A. Fleet '00 (British Army), and Donald F. Duncan '07 (USMC).

38. Photo from *The Vedette*, Pictorial Supplement, 20 Jan 1923.

39. "Pershing Visits Culver," *The Culver Builder*, Vol 3, No. 1, 22 Dec 1922, pp. 1, 5, 6.

40. "Pershing Speaks to Cadet Captains in Memorial Hall," *The Vedette*, Dec 9, 1921, p. 3.

41. "Pershing Visits Culver," p. 1.

42. Pogue, *George C. Marshall: Education of a General*, 1963, p. 220.

43. Lance Betros, *Carved from Granite: West Point Since 1902*. Texas A&M University Press, 2012, p. 220; Geoffrey Perret, *Old Soldiers Never Die: The Life of Douglas MacArthur*, (Random House, 1996), p. 117.

44. Douglas MacArthur, quoted in USMA *Annual Report of the Superintendent*, 1920, 3; Betros, 244.

45. Stephen E. Ambrose, *Duty, Honor, Country: A History of West Point*, (The Johns

Hopkins University Press, 1966), pp. 264-65.

46. Ambrose 1966, 264.

47. Geoffrey Perret, *Old Soldiers Never Die: The Life of Douglas MacArthur*, (Random House, 1996), p. 116.

48. Perret 1996, 117; based on MacArthur quotation from 1920 Superintendent's Report, 4-5; Ambrose 1966, p. 276, 280.

49. Perret 1996, pp. 116-117; emphasis added.

50. Ambrose 1966, p. 273; emphasis added.

51. Ambrose 1966, p. 263.

52. Ambrose 1966, pp. 280-81.

53. Ambrose 1966, p. 281.

54. Betros 2012, p. 246.

55. Betros 2012, fn 27, p. 409.

56. Ambrose 1966, pp. 272-73, 282.

57. Ambrose 1966, pp. 272-73.

58. Ambrose 1966, p. 284.

Ch. 15 – Culver's Gilded Age, 1923 to the End of 1928

1. This military definition comes from current (2024) US military doctrine.

2. Photo from *The Vedette*, pictorial section, 31 March 1923.

3. *The Vedette*, 26 May 1923, pictorial supplement

4. Davies unpublished PhD dissertation, p. 79.

5. Letter from Gignilliat to Arno B. Cammerer, Assistant Director, National Parks, United States Department of Interior, dated February 5, 1927. Document provided to the author from archivist Jean Tabbert at the Glacier National Part archives, July 25, 2020.

6. Correspondence between Gignilliat and Charles J. Kraebel, Superintendent of Glacier National Park, corroborate the duration and seriousness of Gignilliat's illness during the first half of 1926. This correspondence began with a telegram from Gignilliat on June 14, 1926 and continued with several more letters over the course of the next six months, culminating with a letter from Kraebel to Gignilliat on January, 28, 1927. Documents provided to the author from archivist Jean Tabbert at the Glacier National Park archives, July 25, 2020.

7. Enrollment Figures Source: "Enrollment Statistics, 1911-12 – 1931-32," Central Files, Culver Archives. I have used these figures through this work for the sake of consistency, since enrollment figures reported elsewhere (e.g., *The Vedette*; Culver alumni magazines; *The Message Center*; etc.) vary widely and the sources of them are not apparent and/or verifiable, whereas the consistency of using figures from a single document provide a more reliable source that are also verifiable as being recognized as "official" figures by Culver.

8. Photo from 1918 *Roll Call*, p. 30.

9. *The Vedette*, 12 January 1924, p. 1.

10. Photo from Culver Archives.

11. *The Vedette*, 19 Jan 1924, p. 1; account of his time at the US Army War College in *Vedette*, 29 March, 1924, pp. 1-2.

12. *The Vedette*, 13 Dec 1924, p. 1.

13. Edward M. Coffman, *The Regulars: The American Army, 1898-1941*, (Belknap Press, 2004), p. 235.

14. William J. Woolley, *Creating the Modern Army: Citizen Soldiers and the American*

Way of War, 1919-1939 (University Press of Kansas, 2022), p. 43.

15. Woolley, *Creating the Modern Army*, p. 43; Faulkner, *School of Hard Knocks*, p. 221.

16. Woolley, *Creating the Modern Army*, p. 43.

17. Coffman, *The Regulars*, 2004, 235.

18. Steve E. Clay, *U.S. Army Order of Battle 1919-1941. Volume 1: The Arms: Major Command and Infantry Organizations* (Fort Leavenworth, KS: Combat Studies Institute Press, 2010), p. 203.

19. Clay, *U.S. Army Order of Battle 1919-1941. Volume 1*, p. 203.

20. Clay, *U.S. Army Order of Battle 1919-1941. Volume 1*, p. 204._

21. Photo from *The Vedette*, Pictural Supplement, 10 June 1922.

22. Report of 168th BDE's first organizational meeting at Culver, *The Vedette*, 20 May 1922, p. 1.

23. Clay, *U.S. Army Order of Battle 1919-1941. Volume 1*, pp. 225-226.

24. Clay, *U.S. Army Order of Battle 1919-1941. Volume 1*, pp. 204-205.

25. Ibid.

26. *The Personnel System of the United States Army, Vol. I: History of the Personnel System*, Washington, DC, 1919, pp. 543-580. The post-WWI information comes from material developed by influential early sociologist Walter D. Scott, who pioneered this work for the US Army during and after WWI, gathered by the author at the Scott archives at Northwestern University.

27. *The Vedette*, 12 July 1924, pp. 1, 3; further account in Vedette, 19 July 1924.

28. *The Vedette*, 13 December 1924, p. 1.

29. Dr. John "Jay" Boyd, The Great War of 1932: Making the Organized Reserve a "going concern," Office of Army Reserve History, 2015, p. 12.

30. Coffman, *The Regulars*, 2004, 191.

31. Stephen E. Ambrose, *Duty, Honor, Country: A History of West Point*, (Johns Hopkins University Press,1966), p. 286.

32. Frederick William Augustus, Baron von Steuben, *Regulations for the Order and Discipline of the Troops of the United States*, "Part I: Instructions for Captains (partial)," February 1778.

33. Lincoln C. Andrews, *Leadership and Military Training*, (Philadelphia, PA, 1918, pp. 26. 51). Andrews was a professor at West Point, and MacArthur turned to him to write the first leadership textbook used for teaching leadership to cadets at USMA during 1922 and 1923. According to military historian Richard S. Faulkner (who has written extensively on the Army's training of its officers during this period), the best examples of such books include Andrews', along with James A. Moss, *Manual of Military Training* (Menasha, WI: George Banta Publishing, 1914), both of which were quite popular during this period. Richard S. Faulkner, "What Price Glory, Captain Flagg?' Leader Competence in the American Expeditionary Forces," (unpublished MA thesis, Fort Leavenworth, KS, 2000), pp. 10, 103.

34. LRG Ltr to General William H. Cocke, Superintendent VMI, 5 Nov 1927, pp. 1-3, VMI Archives.

35. Douglas MacArthur, quoted in [USMA] "Annul Report of the Superintendent," 1920, 4; cited in Lance Betros, *Carved from Granite: West Point Since 1902*, (Texas A&M University Press, 2012), p, 244.

36. Photo from *The Vedette*, 2 October 1926, p. 1.

37. James H. Hawkes, "Antimilitarism at State Universities: The Campaign Against

Compulsory R.O.T.C., 1920-1940," *Wisconsin Magazine of History*, Autumn 1965 (49:1), pp. 41-54.

38. Ronald Schaffer, "War Dept's Defense of ROTC 1920-1940," *Wisconsin Magazine of History*, Winter 1969-1970 (53:2), pp. 108-120; pp. 112-113.

39. Hawkes, p. 45.

40. James M. Sellers, Jr., "A Brief History of The Association of Military Colleges and Schools of the United States," unpublished, complied at Wentworth Military Academy, Lexington, Missouri, March 12, 1990, p, 4; Alvan C. Hadley, "Military Schools: The Association of Military Colleges and Schools of the United States (AMCSUS) and the Historical Struggle for the Survival of Military Preparatory Schools in America," unpublished EdD dissertation, University of Kentucky, Lexington, KY, 1999, pp. 36-38.

41. John B. Coulter, Cadets on Campus: History of Military Schools of the United States, (Texas A&M University Press, 2017), p. 254.

42. William G. Carr, *Education for World Citizenship. Stanford University*, 1925, cited in Louis H. Chaney, "Military Training in the Secondary Schools," unpublished MA thesis, Butler University, 1940, p. 20.

43. Coulter, *Cadets on Campus*, 2017, 254.

44. Reverend Ernest Tittle, "Military Training in Civil Schools," *New York Christian Advocate* 103 (November 8, 1928), 1363-1364; cited in Davies 1982, 90-91.

45. Carr, *Education for World Citizenship*, p. 20.

46. Schaffer, "War Dept's Defense of ROTC 1920-1940," p. 120.

47. Schaffer, "The War Department's Defense of ROTC, 1920-1940," pp. 108-120, p. 119 (citing Hawkes, "Antimilitarism").

48. Ibid

49. Schaffer, "The War Department's Defense of ROTC, 1920-1940," pp. 108-120, pp. 119-120.

50. Photo from *The Vedette*, 17 Oct 1925, p. 1.

51. N=47; 33/47 "Definite disapproval" 70.2%. Louis H. Chaney, "Military Training in the Secondary Schools," unpublished MA thesis, Butler University, 1940, p. 28.

52. Robert B.D. Hartman, "The Grand Parade: Volume 1," (CEF, 1994) p. 49.

53. Photo from the Culver Archives.

54. Photo from the Culver Archives.

55. Photo from the Culver Archives.

56. Robert B.D. Hartman, "Home on the Wrought Iron Range, Part II: Cookbooks, Clocks, and the End of an Era," (Culver Education Foundation, 1994), pp. 4-8.

57. "Wrought Iron Range Company," Lake Maxinkuckee Its Intrigue History & Genealogy Culver, Marshall, Indiana.

58. Mather, *History of Culver Military Academy*, 1894-1956, p. 101.

59. John T. Carlton and John F. Slinkman, *The ROA Story: A History of the Reserve Officers Association of the United States*, (Reserve Officers Association of the United States, 1982), p. 33.

60. Carlton & Slinkman 1982, p. 37.

61. *The Vedette*, 14 July 1928, p. 1.

62. *The Vedette*, 21 July 1928, p. 2.

63. Carlton & Slinkman 1982, pp. 86-92.

64. Wisconsin – 44%; Indiana – 42 %; Carlton & Slinkman 1982, p. 98.

65. William H. Whyte, Jr., *The Organization Man*, (Simon and Schuster, 1956), p. 3.

66. Thomas J. Peters and Robert H. Waterman, Jr., *In Search of Excellence: Lessons from America's Best-Run Companies*, (Warner Books, 1982), pp. 98-99.

Ch. 16 – The Quixotic and Perplexing Skyland Camps Endeavor, 1921-1939

1.   *National Park Services Description of Parks*, 1942, 108-109.
2.   Glacier National Park attendance figures: 1920 – 22,449; 1930 – 73,776; 1940 – 177,307; GNP Official Fact Sheet.
3.   Michael J. Ober, "Glacier's Skyland Camps: The Enthusiastic, Shattered Dream of a Culver Colonel," *Montana The Magazine of Western History*, Summer 1973, pp. 30-39.
4.   *The Culver Builder*, September 1921, p. 2.
5.   "Fred Gignilliat to Invade the Montana Rockies," *The Culver Builder*, May-June 1922, p. 6.
6.   Photo from *The Culver Builder*, May-June 1922, p. 6.
7.   *The Culver Builder*, May-June 1922, p. 6.
8.   Photo from Wikipedia, in the public domain.
9.   *The Culver Builder*, May-June 1922, p. 6.
10. Image from Glacier National Park Archive; used with permission.
11. Image from Glacier National Park Archive; used with permission.
12. Photo from *The Culver Builder*, May-June 1922, p. 6.
13. Photo courtesy of Mary Margaret Gignilliat.
14. Recorded in a letter from Eakin to Cammerer, 13 Dec 1922, GNP archives.
15. Image from Glacier National Park Archive; used with permission.
16. Image from Glacier National Park Archive; used with permission.
17. Ober 1973, p. 35.
18. Image from Glacier National Park Archive; used with permission.
19. Ober 1973, p. 33.
20. Image from Glacier National Park Archive; used with permission.
21. Image from Ober 1973, p. 33.
22. Ober 1973, p. 35.
23. Ober 1973, p. 39.
24. Ibid.

Ch. 17 – The Age of the Consultants and Challenges to Gignilliat's Reign, 1929-1934

1.   Image from 1929 *Roll Call*, p. 14.
2.   Davies 1984, 109.
3.   Davies 1984, 110.
4.   Davies 1984, 111.
5.   Claudia Goldin, "America's Graduation from High School: The Evolution and Spread of Secondary Schooling in the Twentieth Century," *Journal of Economic History*, 58(2), 1998, pp. 345-374, p. 347; citations from abstract.
6.   Goldin 1998, 347.
7.   Edward A. Krug, *The Shaping of the American High School, 1880-1920*, (The University of Wisconsin Press, 1969), xi.
8.   Krug 1969, 10.
9.   Goldin 1998, 350-51.
10. Goldin 1998, 352, 372.
11. Goldin 1998, 347.
12. Goldin 1998, 358-360, 363-64, 368.

13. Theodore Caplow, Louis Hicks, and Ben J. Wattenberg, *The First Measured Century: An Illustrated Guide to Trends in America, 1900-2000*, (The AEI Press, 2001), pp. 52-53.
14. Davies 1984, 154; extrapolated by Richard Davies from CMA catalogs.
15. Davies 1984, 154, 155.
16. Figures collated from information in the Culver Archives by Carolyn Saft of the Culver Academies Museum, September 13, 2023.
17. Davies 1984, 154; extrapolated from CMA catalogs.
18. "Academic Progress: Modernizing the curriculum for Culver Cadets," *Culver Alumnus*, Oct 1930, p. 22.
19. Davies 1984, 116-117.
20. Davies 1984, 120.
21. Gignilliat, "The Summing Up," unpublished chapter in *Unfurling the Colors*, n.d., manuscript provided to author by Mary Margret Gignilliat.
22. Davies 1984, 114-116.
23. Davies 1984, 116.
24. "Academic Progress: Modernizing the Curriculum for Culver Cadets," p. 22.
25. Ibid.
26. "The Academic Growth of Culver," *Culver Alumnus*, April 1937, pp. 1-3; p. 2.
27. Transcription of Meeting Notes on Faculty Discussions of the Harvard Report Recommendations, 1930-1931, Culver archives.
28. Mather, *History of Culver Military Academy, 1894-1956*, p. 103.
29. Davies 1984, pp. 136-140.
30. *The News-Sentinel*, (Fort Wayne, IN), Tuesday, May 24, 1932.
31. Mather 1959, pp. 94, 104.
32. Daniel R. Beaver, *Modernizing the American War Department: Change and Continuity in a Turbulent Era, 1885-1920*, (The Kent State University Press, 2006), pp. ix-xii.
33. Ibid.
34. Davies 1984, 156.
35. P. S. Bond. O. O. Ellis, E. B. Garey, and T. L. McMurray, *The Red, White, and Blue Manual: Volume One – Red Course*, (Johns Hopkins Press, 1921), authors preface and p. 1.
36. *Red Course Manual*, 1921, p. 1.
37. Donald M. Kington, *Forgotten Summers: The Story of the Citizens' Military Training Camps, 1921-1940*, (Two Decades Publishing, 1995), p. 66.
38. *Red Course Manual*, 1921, p. 1.
39. Neiberg 2000, pp. 42-43.
40. 1931 *Roll Call*, p. 5.
41. The 1932 departure of Quartermaster W. M. Hand and the death of Harold C. Bays contributed further to the loss of Gignilliat's "old guard."
42. Image from 1926 *Roll Call*.
43. 1933 CMA Catalog, p. 12.
44. 1935 CMA Catalog, p. 9.
45. 1935 CMA Catalog, p. 9.
46. Gignilliat, *Unfurling the Colors*, p. 65.
47. Information regarding the negative reaction to the film on campus courtesy of Jeff Kenney, Culver archivist. Kenney also notes that this is a "lost" movie, meaning that

no known copies exist. Cadet derisive name for the film from Gignilliat, *Unfurling the Colors*, p. 65.

48. Image from image from the Internet Movie Database (IMDB).
49. Gignilliat, *Unfurling the Colors*, p. 66.
50. Photo courtesy of Paul Gignilliat.
51. The film was also an early directorial effort for Williiam Wyler, who went on to direct the award-winning film, "Ben Hur" (written by native Hoosier Lew Wallace).
52. "Film about CMA Premiers at CMA," *The Culver Citizen*, July 20, 1932, p. 1.
53. Image from the Internet Movie Database (IMDB).
54. Image from *Culver Alumnus*, November 1952, p. 15.
55. Dr. Vincent A. Lapenta was also a knighted member of the same Italian order, the "Crown of Italy." "Raised to Knighthood," *Indianapolis Star*, April 23, 1924, p. 10.
56. A brief video clip of Gignilliat being knighted in May 1934 exists in the Culver archives.
57. Davies 1984, 146-147.

Ch. 18 – The Denouement: Gignilliat's Final Years at Culver, 1935-1942

1. Photo from front cover of *Culver Alumnus*, November 1952.
2. Robert Rossow, untiled memories of his life and experiences at Culver, unpublished manuscript, not dated, provided to author by Paul Gignilliat, p 342.
3. Rossow, pp. 340-342.
4. *Culver Alumnus*, June 1937, p. 12.
5. Ibid.
6. Davies, "Arms and the Man," 1984, p. 154.
7. Neiberg, *Making Citizen-Soldiers*, 2000, p. 31.
8. Ibid.
9. Photo courtesy of Mary Margret Gignilliat.
10. Image from the Internet Movie Database (IMDB).
11. Allen R. Elliott, "In Tribute to 'The General,'" *Culver Alumnus*, November 1952, front piece.
12. Photo from Culver Archives.
13. Richard Davies, "Portrait of a Culver Man, *Culver* Magazine, Spring/Summer 2009, pp. 22-23.
14. Davies, "Portrait of a Culver Man," p. 23.
15. Ibid.
16. Postcard from Culver Archives.
17. Davies 184; *Culver Alumnus*, April 1937.
18. Photo courtesy of Mary Margret Gignilliat.
19. Gignilliat letter to Charles Kilbourne, June 23, 1939, VMI archives.
20. Robert Gignilliat Kenan, *History of the Gignilliat Family of Switzerland and South Carolina*, (Easley, SC: Southern Historical Press, 1977), pp. 54-55.
21. Note: Fundraising is usually included in such duties, but Culver had not yet begun soliciting alumni for financial contributions, mostly due to Gignilliat's own opposition to doing so. Culver would not begin soliciting alumni donations for another 20 years.
22. Gignilliat letter to Charles Kilbourne, February 23, 1942, VMI Archives.
23. Davies, "Arms and the Man," 1984, p. 196.
24. Photo from Culver Archives.
25. Photo courtesy of Mary Margret Gignilliat.

Ch. 19 – Gignilliat's Life After Culver and Final Decade, 1942-1952

1.   Photo from *Culver Alumnus*, November 1952, p. 14.
2.   There is evidence that Gignilliat tried to return to active duty in the Army after being retired for several years, but he was well past the mandatory retirement age in 1942 for this to be a possibility (even though he was close friends with the US Army Chief of Staff, George C. Marshall). Ltr from Gignilliat to E. C. Wirtz, February 5, 1942, Culver Archives. Having no success in this endeavor, Gignilliat turned his attention to finding a way to serve the war effort as a "coordinator for defense training in Fort Worth, Texas. Ltr from Gignilliat to E. C. Wirtz, June 2, 1942, Culver Archives.
3.   Henry H. Armsby, "Engineering, Science, and Management War Training Program Final Report, Bulletin 1946, No. 9, (US Office of Education, 1946), pp. VIII, XI.
4.   Armsby 1946, p. 8.
5.   Armsby 1946, p. 3.
6.   Armsby 1946, pp. 12-14.
7.   Armsby 1946, p. 16.
8.   Armsby 1946, p. 96.
9.   Ibid.
10.   Ibid.
11.   Armsby 1946, pp. 47-51.
12.   Armsby 1946, p. 98.
13.   Ibid.
14.   Armsby 1946, pp. 4-5. Much of the information regarding the ESMWT program was corroborated by as second source: Dieter Ostermann, "The Engineering, Science, and Management War Training Program: Higher Education and the Second World War," Honors Thesis in History, University of Iowa, Fall 2020.
15.   Much of this information comes from William Wagner, *Reuben Fleet and the Story of Consolidated Aircraft*, (Aero Publishers, 1976), *passim*.
16.   Armsby 1946, p. 36.
17.   Armsby 1946, p. 133.
18.   Armsby 1946, pp. VIII-X.
19.   Henry C. Gignilliat, "Introduction," Leigh R. Gignilliat, *Unfurling the Colors: Reminiscences of a Culver Superintendent*, (Culver Education Foundation, 1993), pp. iii-iv.
20.   Photo courtesy of Mary Margret Gignilliat.
21.   Henry Gignilliat, "Introduction," *Unfurling the Colors*, p. iii.
22.   Draft chapters provided to the author courtesy of Mary Margret Gignilliat.
23.   Photo courtesy Mary Margret Gignilliat.
24.   Robert B. D. Hartman, "Gignilliat...As in Giant!," (CEF Education Foundation, n.d.), p. 6.
25.   Information regarding breast sarcomas obtained from Johns Hopkins Medical Center.
26.   Review notes on Gignilliat's manuscript, *A School and a Family*, March 19, 1946, file 5, Bobbs-Merrill archival material, Lilly Library, University of Indiana.
27.   I have searched for it among his descendants without success.
28.   Robert B.D. Hartman, *(J)ROTC – Its Place in the Military History of the Culver Military Academy*, Part II, (CEF Education Foundation, n.d.), p. 2.
29.   Photo courtesy of the Culver Archives.
30.   Photo courtesy of the Culver Archives.

31. Photo courtesy of the Culver Archives.

32. Photo courtesy of the Culver Archives.

33. Photo courtesy of the Culver Archives.

34. Frederick L. Hunt, "Mrs. Gignilliat: As One Remembers," *Culver Alumnus*, May 1952, front piece.

35. Photo provided courtesy of Mary Margret Gignilliat.

36. Hunt 1952, front piece.

37. Photo from Hunt 1952, front piece.

38. Ibid.

39. Ibid.

40. 1916 *Roll Call*, p. 7.

41. Hartman, "Gignilliat...As in Giant!", p. 6.

42. Photo of headstone from "Find a Grave," modified to improve clarity.

43. Hartman, "Gignilliat...As in Giant!", p. 6.

44. *Culver Alumnus*, November 1952, p. 2.

45. Ibid.

46. *Culver Alumnus*, November 1952, p. 3.

47. *Culver Alumnus*, November 1952, p. 1.

48. Photo of Gignilliat family plot marker from "Find a Grave."

49. Photo of headstone from "Find a Grave."

Epilogue

1. Gignilliat, "Summing Up," p. 6; emphasis added.

Works Cited

Primary Sources

Cass County Historical Society (Indiana)
1913 Logansport Flood material – accounts and photos

Culver Archives
1913 Inaugural Scrapbook, produced by Culver Military Academy, courtesy of the Culver Archives
"Enrollment Statistics, 1911-12 – 1931-32, Central Files, Culver Academies.
"Military Record of General L. R. Gignilliat," Gignilliat files, Culver archives, Culver Academies, Culver, IN
Transcription of Meeting Notes on Faculty Discussions of the Harvard Report Recommendations, 1930-1931, Culver archives.

Georgia Historical Society
Georgia Historical Society, "Gignilliat Family Papers," (MS2077), Series 1, 2, 3, 5, Boxes 1, 2, 11.
Thomas Heyward Gignilliat and Thomas Heyward Gignilliat, Jr. papers, 1890-1956. (Georgia Historical Society); https://www.findagrave.com/memorial/102000321/thomas-heyward-gignilliat

Gignilliat Family
Gignilliat, Leigh R. Unpublished chapters from manuscript, *Unfurling the Colors: Reminiscences of a Culver Superintendent*, circa 1947, including
- "The Boston Stereopticon Company"
- "Old Rat"
- "Inaugural Escort"
- "The Summing Up"
Family photos

Glacier National Park Archives
Skyland Camps, 1921-1940
Letter from Gignilliat to Arno B. Cammerer, Assistant Director, National Parks, United States Department of Interior, dated February 5, 1927. Document provided to the author from archivist Jean Tabbert at the Glacier National Part archives, July 25, 2020.
Correspondence between Gignilliat and Charles J. Kraebel, Superintendent of Glacier National Park, corroborate the duration and seriousness of Gignilliat's illness during the first half of 1926.

> This correspondence began with a telegram from Gignilliat on June 14, 1926 and continued with several more letters over the course of the next six months, culminating with a letter from Kraebel to Gignilliat on January, 28, 1927.

Documents provided to the author from archivist Jean Tabbert at the Glacier National Part archives, July 25, 2020.

Correspondence during the period 1921-1940 between/among National Park invidiucals and also with Gignilliat

Research material cited by Michael J. Ober for his 1976 article regarding Gignilliat and the Skyland Camps, "Glacier's Skyland Camps: The Enthusiastic, Shattered Dream of a Culver Colonel," *Montana The Magazine of Western History*, Summer 1973, pp. 30-39.

IU Lilly Library (Indian University) -- IU Lily Library Archives

Gignilliat correspondence with Bobbs-Merril, 1913-1938, Bobbs-Merrill mss., Lilly Library, Indiana University, Bloomington, Indiana.

NARA St. Louis, MO – Text Gignilliat service in First Officer Training Camp, 1917

First OTC Company Training Roster, 5th Company, 9th Provisional Training Regiment, Aug 1, 1917, Box 2, Fort Benjamin Harrison, Misc, First OTC, 8th and 9th PTR, National Archives, St. Louis, MO.

VMI Archives

Jacob, Colonel Diane B. Description and explanation of the VMI method of calculating the General Order of Merit (GOM) provided. Head of archives and records management at the Virginia Military Institute's Preston Library, August 16, 2017.

Cadet Record of Leigh R. Gignilliat, Virginia Military Institute archives.

"Fourth Class cadets, 1891-1892," Publications Collection, *Catalogs*, Virginia Military Institute archives, Lexington, Virginia.

"Third Class cadets, 1891-1892," Publications Collection, *Catalogs*, Virginia Military Institute archives, Lexington, Virginia.

"Second Class cadets, 1891-1892," Publications Collection, *Catalogs*, Virginia Military Institute archives, Lexington, Virginia.

"First Class Graduates, 1895," Publications Collection, *Catalogs*, Virginia Military Institute archives, Lexington, Virginia.

"Special Order No. 3," Headquarters, Virginia Military Institute, January 8, 1895, pp. 10-13, Virginia Military Institute archives, Lexington, Virginia.

Special Order, VMI, January 16, 1895, VMI Archives.

Wisconsin Historical Society

Michael V. O'Shea papers

Yellowstone National Park Archives

Memoirs

Gignilliat, L. R. (written circa 1947/published 1993). *Unfurling the Colors: Reminiscences of a Culver Superintendent*. Culver Education Foundation.

Rossow, Robert, *Rossow's Reminiscences*, unpublished manuscript, n.d.

Unpublished Manuscripts

Almstrom, John A., "Learning to Live: Tactical Training for the AEF, 1917-1918 (unpublished MA thesis, Rice University, 1972).

Bunner, Alan M., " Chapter 2: The Culver Honor Code," n.d.

Chaney, Louis H. (1940). "Military Training in the Secondary Schools," unpublished MA thesis, Butler University, https://digitalcommons.butler.edu/cgi/viewcontent.cgi?article=1084&context=grtheses

Christlieb, Gary, Senior Humanities Instructor, Culver Academies, verification of numbers of Culver's Gold Star men in 2018, email from, to author, January 21, 2019.

Davies, Richard Gwyn. *Of Arms and the Boy: A History of Culver Military Academy, 1894-1945*, unpublished PhD dissertation, Indiana University, 1984.

Faulkner, Richard S., "What Price Glory, Captain Flagg?' Leader Competence in the American Expeditionary Forces," (unpublished MA thesis, Fort Leavenworth, KS, 2000.

Fisher, Joy, "Gignilliat, William Robert, 1839-1995," McIntosh-Chatham-Baldwin County, Georgia Archives Biographies, pp. 1016-1022, 31 October, 2004, http://www.genrecords.net/email registry/vols/00001.html#0000031

Gignilliat, Leigh R. Unpublished chapters from manuscript, *Unfurling the Colors: Reminiscences of a Culver Superintendent*, circa 1947, including
- "The Boston Stereopticon Company"
- "Old Rat"
- "Inaugural Escort"
- "The Summing Up"

Hadley, Alvan Cordell Jr., "Military Schools: The Association of Military Colleges and Schools of the United States (AMCSUS) and the Historical Struggle for the Survival of Military Preparatory Schools in America," unpublished Ph.D. dissertation, University of Kentucky, 1999

Hartman, Robert B. D. H., "Leigh Robinson Gignilliat," unpublished biography of Gignilliat, p. 3, courtesy of the Culver Archives.

"The Life of H. H. Culver," an anonymous document discovered by the author in the Culver Archives that appears to have been written circa 1907 to commemorate the ten-year anniversary of HH Culver's passing

Mather, Charles C. (1959). *History of Culver Military Academy, 1894.1956*, unpublished manuscript, Culver Archives.

Ostermann, Dieter, "The Engineering, Science, and Management War Training Program: Higher Education and the Second World War," Honors Thesis in History, University of Iowa, Fall 2020, file:///C:/Users/kelly/Downloads/The%20Engineering%20Science%20and%20Management%20War%20Training%20Program_%20Hi.pdf

Sellers, James M. Jr., "A Brief History of The Association of Military Colleges and Schools of the United States," unpublished, complied at Wentworth Military Academy, Lexington, Missouri, March 12, 1990.

Transcription of Meeting Notes on Faculty Discussions of the Harvard Report Recommendations, 1930-1931, Culver archives.

Secondary Sources

Books

A Handbook of Schools. (1911). Doubleday, Page, & Co.

Ambrose, S. E. (1966). *Duty, Honor, Country: A History of West Point*. The Johns Hopkins University Press.

American Battle Monuments Commission. (1944). *37ᵗʰ Division Summary of Operations in the World War*. US Government Printing Office.

Andrews, Lincoln C., Brig Gen, US Army. (1918). *Leadership and Military Training*. J. B. Lippincott Company.

Barnes, A. (2011). *In a Strange Land: The American Occupation of Germany, 1918-1923*. Schiffer Military History.

Beard, Dan. (n.d.). *The Books of/Daniel Beard*. Pamphlet in public domain, https://www.historyforsale.com/daniel-c-beard-pamphlet-signed/dc176074

Beaver, Daniel R.. (2006). *Modernizing the American War Department: Change and Continuity in a Turbulent Era, 1885-1920*. The Kent State University Press.

Bell, Trudy E. (2008). *The Great Dayton Flood of 1913*, (Arcadia Publishing).

Betros, Lance. (2012). *Carved from Granite: West Point Since 1902*. Texas A&M University Press.

Bigelow, Michael E. (2012). *A Short History of Army Intelligence*. U.S. Army Intelligence and Security Command

Bond, P. S., O. O. Ellis, E. B. Garey, and T. L. McMurray. (1921). *The Red, White, and Blue Manual: Volume One – Red Course*. Johns Hopkins Press.

Boot, Max. (2002). *The Savage Wars of Peace: Small Wars and the Rise of American Power*. Basic Books.

Bowman, Rex and Carlos Santos, *Rot, Riot, and Rebellion: Mr. Jefferson's Struggle to Save the University That Changed America,* (Charlottesville, VA: University of Virginia Press, 2013).

Boy Scouts of America. (1911). *The Official Handbook for Boys*. Nash Publishing.

Cabot, James L. (2005). *Ludington: 1830-1930*, Images of America Series. Arcadia Publishing.

Caplow, T., Hicks, L., and Wattenberg, B. J. (2000). *The First Measured Century: An Illustrated Guide to Trends in America, 1900-2000*. AEI Press, 2000.

Carr, William G. (1928). *Education for World Citizenship*. Stanford H. Press.

Carlton, John T. and John F. Slinkman. (1982). *The ROA Story: A History of the Reserve Officers Association of the United States*. Reserve Officers Association of the United States.

Child, Paul W., ed. (1987). *Register of Graduates and Firmer Cadets*. Association of Graduates USMA.

Clay, Steve E. (2010). *U.S. Army Order of Battle 1919-1941. Volume 1: The Arms: Major Command and Infantry Organizations*. US Army Combat Studies Institute Press. https://www.armyupress.army.mil/Portals/7/combat-studies-institute/csi-books/OrderofBattle1.pdf

Clifford, John Gary. (2015). *The Citizen Soldiers: The Plattsburg Training Camp Movement, 1913-1920*. University Press of Kentucky.

Coffman, Edward M. (2004). *The Regulars: The American Army, 1898-1941*. Belknap Press.

----- (1986). *The War to End All Wars: The American Military Experience in World War I*. The University of Wisconsin Press.

Coulter, John A. (2017). *Cadets on Campus: History of Military Schools of the United States*. Texas A&M University Press.

Couper, William. (1939). *One Hundred Years at VMI*, Vols. 1-4. Garrett and Massie, Inc.

Cray, E. (1990). *General of the Army: George C. Marshall, Solider and Statesman*. W. W. Norton & Company.

Cullum, George W. (1901). *Biographical Register of the Officers and Graduates of the U.S. Military Academy at West Point, N.Y., from its Establishment, in 1802; Vol. IV: 1890 1900, Supplement*. Edited by Edward S. Holden. The Riverside Press. https://usma.primo. exlibrisgroup.com/view/delivery/01USMA_INST/12178578040005711

Culver, Bertram B. Jr. (1992). *Those Towers Lofty: A Narrative History of the Culver Campus*. Culver Education Foundation.

Culver in the World War. (1930). Peerless Press.

Davis, William C. (1975). *The Battle of New Market*. Louisianna State University Press.

Dawes, Charles G. (1921). *A Journal of the Great War*, Vol. 1. Houghton Mifflin.

Educational Attainment and Achievement Chartbook (2010). Russell Sage Foundation.

Farwell, B. (1999). *Over There: The United Sates in The Great War, 1917-1918*. WW Norton.

Faulkner, R. S. (2017). *Pershing's Crusaders: The American Soldier in World War I*. University Press of Kansas.

----- (2012). *The School of Hard Knocks: Combat Leadership in the American Expeditionary Forces*. Texas A&M University.

Felleman, Hazel, ed. (1936). *The Best Loved Poems of the American People*. Doubleday.

Garey, Major E. B. (1921). *The R.O.T.C. Manual: Freshman Course (1st Year Basic) – A Text Book for the Reserve Officers Training Corps*. Lord Baltimore Press.

Gignilliat, L. R., editor. (1895). *The Bomb* (VMI yearbook). Huston, Ashmead, Wilson Co. Ltd.

----- (1916). *Arms and the Boy*. Bobbs-Merrill.

Gilbert, James L. (2012). *World War I and the Origins of U.S. Military Intelligence*. Scarecrow Press.

Harden, W. (1913). *History of Savannah and South Georgia*. The Lewis Publishing Company.

Hartman, Robert B. D. (2007). *Lest We Forget: Culver – Two Great Wars and the Years Between*. Culver Education Foundation.

----- (1994). *Footfalls Through the Century: A Visual Salute to the Culver Campus*. Culver Education Foundation.

----- (1993). *Pass in Review: Culver, a Century in the Making*. Culver Education Foundation.

Hartman, Robert B. D., ed. (1994). *Logansport – The Flood, March 1913*. Culver Education Foundation.

Jordan, Benjamin Rene. (2016). *Modern Manhood and the Boy Scouts of America:*

Citizenship, Race, and the Environment, 1910-1930. The University of North Carolina Press.

Keene, J. D. (2001). *Doughboys, the Great War, and the Remaking of America*. The Johns Hopkins University Press.

Kegan, Robert. (1994). *In over Our Heads: The Mental Demands of Modern Life*. Harvard University Press.

Kenan, R. G. (1977), *History of the Gignilliat Family of Switzerland and South Carolina*. Southern Historical Press.

Kendall, P. M. (1967). *The Art of Biography*. Norton.

Kennedy, David. (1980). *Over Here: The First World War and American Society*. Oxford University Press.

King, Spencer B. (1981). *Darien:The Death and Rebirth of a Southern Town*. Mercer University Press.

Kington, Donald M. (1995). *Forgotten Summers: The Story of the Citizens' Military Training Camps, 1921-1940*. Two Decades Publishing.

Kreidberg, Marvin A. and Merton G. Henry. (1955), *History of Military Mobilization in the United States Army, 1775-1945*. Department of the Army.

Krug, Edward A. (1969). *The Shaping of the American High School, 1880-1920*. The University of Wisconsin Press.

Lloyd, Nick. (2021). *The Western Front: A History of the Great War, 1914-1918*. Liveright Publishing.

Lyons, Gene M. and John W. Masland. (1959/1975). *Education and Military Leadership: A Study of the ROTC*. Reprint of the 1959 edition published by Princeton University Press, published in 1975 by Greenwood Press.

McClure, Arthur F., James R. Crisman, and Perry Mock. (1985). *Education for Work: The Historical Evolution of Vocational and Distributive Education in America*. Associated University Presses.

Military Training Camps Association of the United States. (1916). *Roster of Attendants at Federal Military Training Camps 1913-1916*. Anderson & Ruwe.

Morrison, J. L. (1986). *The Best School in the World: West Point, the Pre-Civil War Years, 1833-1866*. Kent State University Press.

Moss, James A. (1914). *Manual of Military Training*. George Banta Publishing.

Neiberg, Michael. (2000). *Making Citizen Soldiers: ROTC and the Ideology of American Military Service*. Harvard University Press.

Neumann, Brian F. and Shane D. Makowicki. (2019). *Occupation and Demobilization, 1918-1923*, The US Army Campaigns of World War I Commemorative Series. US Army Center of Military History.

Perret, G. (1996). *Old Soldiers Never Die: The Life of Douglas MacArthur*. Random House.

Peters, Thomas J. and Robert H. Waterman, Jr. (1982). *In Search of Excellence: Lessons from America's Best-Run Companies*. Warner Books.

Pogue, F. C. (1963). *George C. Marshall: Education of a General*. Penguin Books.

Rinaldi, Richard A. (2004). *The US Army in World War I: Orders Of Battle – Ground Units 1917-1919*.General Data.

Rorabaugh, W. J. (1979). *The Alcoholic Republic: An American Tradition.* Oxford University Press.

Rossow, Robert. (2007). *Rossow Reports: Colonel Robert Rossow, Cavalryman and Raconteur, His Stories.* Robert B. D. Hartman, ed., Culver Education Foundation.

Shaw, Wilfred B., ed. (2000). *The University of Michigan, an Encyclopedic Survey: Part I – History and Administration, The University in War Service.* University of Michigan, Digital Library Production Service.

Stearns, Alfred E., L. R. Gignilliat, Milo H. Stuart, Eric Parsons, and J. J. Findlay. (1917). *Types of Schools for Boys,* M. V. O'Shea, ed. The Bobbs-Merrill Company.

Steever, Edgar Z., and James L. Frink. (1918). *The Cadet Manual: Official Handbook for High School Volunteers of the United States.* J. P. Lippincott.

Steuben, Frederick William Augustus, Baron von. (1778). *Regulations for the Order and Discipline of the Troops of the United States,* "Part I: Instructions for Captains. Discover Lewis & Clark. https://lewis-clark.org/a-military-corps/army-regulations/von-steubens-regulations/

US Army Center of Military History. (1991). *United States Army in the World War 1917-1919,* Vol. 10, Part 2, *The Armistice Agreement and Related Documents,* CMH Pub 23-16. US Army Center of Military History).

US Army Center of Military History. (1991). *United States Army in the World War, 1917-1919, Vol. 11, American Occupation of Germany.* US Army Center of Military History.

US Army Center of Military History. (1988). *American Expeditionary Forces: Divisions, Volume 2,* in the *Order of Battle of the United States Land Forces in the World War* series, reprint; first printed in 1931 as CMH Pub 23-2. US Army Center of Military History.

USS Arkansas (Battleship #33) Photo Album: "Our European Cruise. October 25th, to December 15th, 1913, S-582 USS Arkansas (BB-33) Collection, Naval History and Heritage Command, https://www.history.navy.mil/our-collections/photography/alphabetical---donationso/a/s-582-uss-arkansas--bb-33--collection.html

Wagner, William. (1976). *Reuben Fleet and the Story of Consolidated Aircraft.* Aero Publishers.

Weed, Frank W., Lieut. Col., M. C., ed. **(1925).** *Field Operations, Volume VIII,* in the series *The Medical Department of the United States Army in the World War.* US Government Printing Office; accessed at http://history.amedd.army.mil/booksdocs/wwi/fieldoperations/chapter36.html.

Wentz, Robert W., Kathryn A. Wise, and Shiela R. Turregano, eds. (1989). *Register of Former Cadets of the Virginia Military Institute, Sesquicentennial Edition. VMI.* The VMI Alumni Association.

Whyte, William H. Jr. (1956). *The Organization Man.* Simon and Schuster.

Widder, Keith R. (1972). *Reveille Till Taps: Solider Life at Fort Mackinac, 1780-1895.* Mackinac State Historic Parks.

Williams, Geoff. (2013). *Washed Away: How the Great Flood of 1913, America's Most Widespread Disaster, Terrorized a Nation and Changed It Forever,.* Pegasus Books.

Williams, T. J. (2015). *Intellectual Manhood: University, Self, and Society in the Antebellum South.* The University of North Carolina Press.

Wise, H. A. (1978). *Drawing Out the Man: The VMI Story.* University Press of Virginia.

Woolley, William J. (2022). *Creating the Modern Army: Citizen Soldiers and the American Way of War, 1919-1939*. University Press of Kansas.

Captain X (Edward L Fox). (1918). *Our First Half Million: The Story of Our National Army*. The H. K. Fly Company.

Journals and Periodicals

Arms and the Man: The National Military and Shooting Weekly, National Rifle Association of America Journal.

Army and Navy Journal, Vol 34, October 17, 1896, November 21, 1896, September 6, 1913

The Sigma Chi Quarterly, Volume 14, 1894-1895 (Chicago, IL, 1895),

Journal and Periodical Articles

"Academic Progress: Modernizing the curriculum for Culver Cadets, *Culver Alumnus*, October 1930, p. 22.

"The Academic Growth of Culver," *Culver Alumnus*, April 1937, pp. 1-3.

"Articles of Organization for Cadet Council," 1914 *Roll Call*, p. 153.

"The Battle Cry of Peace," *American Film Institute Catalog of Feature Films: The First Hundred Years, 1893 to 1993*, https://catalog.afi.com/Catalog/moviedetails/17305.

Boyd, Dr. John "Jay." (2015). "The Great War of 1932: Making the Organized Reserve a "Going Concern." Office of Army Reserve History, https://history.army.mil/events/ahts2015/presentations/seminar5/sem5_DrJayBoyd_text_GreatWarOf1932.pdf

Breast sarcomas information, https://www.hopkinsmedicine.org/kimmel_cancer_center/cancers_we_treat/breast_cancer_program/treatment_and_services/rare_breast_tumors/breast_sarcomas.html

Burgess, W. R., H. B. Cummings, & W. P. Tomlinson, "Military Training in the Public School: An Annotated Bibliography, *Teachers College Record*, vol. XVII, James E, Russell, ed., (NY: Teachers College, Columbia University, 1917), pp. 141-157.

Carlisle, Rodney, "The Attacks on U. S. Shipping that Precipitated American Entry into World War I," *The Northern Mariner/Le marin du nord*, XVII No. 3 (July 2007), 41-66.

Carsten, F.L. (1944). "The British Summary Court at Wiesbaden, 1926-1929," *Modern Law Review*, (Oxford: Blackwell Publishing, 1944), p. 215.

Chambers, Colonel C. C., "Introduction," *Culver in the World War* (South Bend, IN: Peerless Press, 1930), pp. I-XII.

Creel, George, "Wyoming's Answer: Five Years of Training Schoolboys," *Everybody's Magazine*, Vol. 34, No. 2, February 1916, p. 154.

Creel, George, "Preface (written in January 1918)," *The Cadet Manual: Official Handbook for High School Volunteers of the United States*, (Philadelphia, PA: J. B. Lippincott Company, 1918), pp. vii-viii.

Davies, Richard, "Portrait of a Culver Man, *Culver* Magazine, Spring/Summer 2009, pp. 21-25.

Dornbusch, Sanford M., "The Military Academy as an Assimilating Institution," *Social Forces*, (published by Oxford University Press) Vol. 33, No. 4, May, 1955, pp. 316-321. Stable URL: http://www.jstor.org/stable/2573000

Durborow, H. L., "Preparing While We Wait," *The School Review*, Vol. 25, No. 3, March

1917, pp. 151-156.

Elliott, Allen R., "In Tribute to 'The General,'" *Culver Alumnus*, November 1952, front piece.

"Fred Gignilliat to Invade the Montana Rockies," *The Culver Builder*, May-June 1922, p. 6.

Frederick, J. M. H., "Superintendent of Schools Annual Report for the 1916-17 School Year," Cleveland, OH, January 7, 1918, pp. 71-75.

Gignilliat, Henry C., "Introduction," Leigh R. Gignilliat, *Unfurling the Colors: Reminiscences of a Culver Superintendent*, (Culver Education Foundation, 1993), pp. iii-iv.

Gignilliat, L. Robinson, "An Inland Naval School," *Munsey's Magazine*, June 1903, pp. 420-423.

Gignilliat, Major L. R. "Education of Boys by the Military Method," *Scientific American*, 92:9, March 4, 1905, pp. 184-185.

Gignilliat, Major L. R. "Manning Oars and Halyards as a Summer Outing," *Scientific American*, 92:18, May 6, 1905, pp. 360-361.

Gignilliat, Major L. R. "Military Schools in America," *The Times Magazine*, February 1907, 1:3, (Times Magazine Company), pp. 287-294.

Gignilliat, Colonel L. R. "Building Character through Military Training," appearing as, "Utilizing the Military System for Moral Development" (a title likely created by an editor) in *Proceedings of the Sixty-third Annual Session of the Wisconsin Teachers' Association*, (Madison, WI: Cantwell Printing Company, State Printer, 1916), pp. 73-81.

Gignilliat, L. R. "Military Schools in America," eight chapters appearing in Michael V. O'Shea, ed., *Types of Schools*, (Bobbs-Merrill, 1917), pp. 53-125.

Gignilliat, L. R., "Culver's Contribution to National Defense," *Culver in the World War*, The Culver Legion, (South Bend, IN: Peerless Press, 1930), pp. 11-39.

Gignilliat, Brig. Gen. L. R. "The Value of Military Training in Education," An address broadcasted from station KDKA Westinghouse studio, Pittsburgh, PA, May 20, 1922.

Goldin, Claudia, "America's Graduation from High School: The Evolution and Spread of Secondary Schooling in the Twentieth Century," *Journal of Economic History*, 58(2), 1998, pp. 345-374.

Hawkes, James H. "Antimilitarism at State Universities: The Campaign Against Compulsory R.O.T.C., 1920-1940," *Wisconsin Magazine of History*, Autumn 1965 (49:1), pp. 41-54.

"The History of Officer Candidates School," (n.d.), https://www.quantico.marines.mil/portals/147/Docs/History_of_OCS.pdf

Hoogenboom, Ari "The Pendleton Act and the Civil Service," *The American Historical Review*, 64: 2, Jan 1959), pp. 301-318; p. 313.

Hugh Glascock, "Colonel Fleet: A Sketch," 1907 *Roll Call*, pp. 26-27.

Herring, "George C. "James Hay and the Preparedness Controversy, 1915-1916," *Journal of Southern History*, Vol. 30, No. 4, Nov 1964, p. 390

Hillman, Major J. A., "The Building Up of the American Army," chapter in *Culver in the World War* (South Bend, IN: Peerless Press, 1930), pp. 39-128.

"In Memorium: Colonel Alexander Frederick Fleet," *The Vedette*, XVI:1, , p. 1.

Interesting Bits of News about the Faculty, Past, Present, and Future," *Culver Alumnus*,

November 1950, p. 17.

"Who Was the First to Crash 'the Old Iron Gate?", *Culver Alumnus*, January 1928, p. 20.

Hartman, "The Founding of Culver's Woodcraft School," *Culver Citizen*, July 10, 2008, p. 7.

"HSVUS," *Everybody's Magazine*, June 1917, p. 720.

Jordan, Kelly C., "The Modern American Military Education Model: A New Approach for a New Century," Ch. 6 in Mark Patrick Ryan and Timothy L. Weekes, eds., *Handbook of Research on Character and Leadership Development in Military Schools*, (IGI Global, 2021), pp. 116-145.

"The Lengthening Shadow," *Culver Alumnus*, Jan 1937, p. 2.

"Military Training in Public Schools," in *Issues of the Day; Being a Text-Book on the Political Situation, Past and Present* (Chicago, 1903), p. 432.

Karsten, K. G. "The Collegiate Anti-Militarism League," *The Cosmopolitan Student*, Vol 5, No. 11, June 1915, pp. 348-350.

Kennedy, Edwin L. Jr., "Mass-Producing Leaders: WWI Army Needed a Lot of Officer – Quickly (*ARMY*, July 2017), pp. 47-48.

La Salle Council Boy Scouts of American, Aug 1, 2019, reposted on Culver Academies History Blog, Aug 3, 2019 https://www.facebook.com/pg/culverhistory/posts/

Lewis, William Mather "One Way to Prepare," *Seven Seas*, September 1915, Vol I, No. 4 (New York: Seven Seas Co. Inc., 1915).

Letter, US Army Chief of Staff to New Orleans Superintendent of Schools, subject, "Military Training in High Schools," Feb 8, 1915, cited in Marvin A. Kreidberg and Merton G. Henry, *History of Military Mobilization in the United States Army, 1775-1945*, (Washington, DC: Department of the Army, November 1955), p. 211.

The 1913 Logansport flood, Maxinkuckee History Past Tracker, http://www.maxinkuckee.history.pasttracker.com/lots_barnes/barnes_family.htm

Ober, Michael J., "Glacier's Skyland Camps: The Enthusiastic, Shattered Dream of a Culver Colonel," *Montana The Magazine of Western History*, Summer 1973, pp. 30-39.

Orton, Edward Jr., "The Status of the Military Department in the Land-Grant Colleges," appearing in *The Proceedings of Twenty-Seventh Annual Convention of the Association of American Agricultural College and Experiment Stations*, (Montpelier, VT: The Capital City Press, 1914), p. 181.

"Pershing Speaks to Cadet Captains in Memorial Hall," *The Vedette*, December 9, 1921, p. 3.

"Pershing Visits Culver," *The Culver Builder*, Vol 3, No. 1, December 22, 1922, p. 5.

Qasim, Noor, "The Evolution of the Book Review," *New York Times*, April 4, 2021, p. 2.

Rathbun, D. H., "Through France and Belgium with Colonel and the Scouts," *The Vedette*, 9 Oct 1920, pp. 1, 3.

Rathbun, D. H., "Colonel Gignilliat in Legion of Honor," The Vedette, 16 Oct 1920, pp. 1, 2.

Schaffer, Ronald, "War Dept's Defense of ROTC 1920-1940," *Wisconsin Magazine of History*, Winter 1969-1970 (53:2), pp. 108-120.

Schindel, S. J. Bayard, "Address of Captain S. J. Bayard Schindel, War College Division General Staff, United States Army," delivered on November 13, 1913 and appearing in J.

L. Hills, ed., *Proceedings of the Twenty-Seventh Annual Convention of the Association of American Agricultural Colleges and Experiment Stations* (Montpelier, VT: The Capital City Press, 1914), p. 186.

Schröder, Joachim and Alexander Watson, "Occupation during and after the War (Germany)," *International Encyclopedia of the First World War*. Accessed at https://encyclopedia.1914-1918-online.net/article/occupation_during_and_after_the_war_germany]

Shearer, "Benjamin F. An Experiment in Military and Civilian Education: The Students' Army Training Corps at the University of Illinois," *Journal of Illinois State Historical Society*, Vol. 72, No. 3, August 1979, pp. 213-224.

"16 Years Ago in Washington," *Culver Alumnus,* April 1929

Smith, A. B., "Helping the Colonel Lead the Boy Scouts," *The Vedette*, 2 October 1920, pp. 1, 3.

Steever, Edgar Z., "Quarterly Report to President HSVUS," June 1917, appearing in *Everybody's Magazine*, Vol. 36. No. 6, June 1917, pp. 719-720.

Tittle, Reverend Ernest, "Military Training in Civil Schools," *New York Christian Advocate* 103 (November 8, 1928), 1363-1364.

Wheeler, Howard, "Foreword," *The Cadet Manual: Official Handbook for High School Volunteers of the United States*, (Philadelphia, PA: J. B. Lippincott Company, 1918), pp. ix-x.

"When Culver Was Very Young, *Culver Alumnus,* Oct 1930, p. 47.

Wood, Leonard, Major General (USA), "Preparedness," appearing in *National Service Library, Vol. 1, Universal Military Training*, Major Charles E. Kilbourne, ed., (P. F. Collier & Son, 1917), p. 21.

"Wrought Iron Range Company," Lake Maxinkuckee Its Intrigue History & Genealogy Culver, Marshall, Indiana, http://www.maxinkuckee.history.pasttracker.com/culver_family/wrought_iron_range.htm)

Monographs

Hartman, R. B. D., published by the Culver Education Foundation
    "Gignilliat...As in Giant!"
    "To be or Not to be: J. H. McKenzie and C. H. Tebbetts"
    "Brick, Stone, Steel, Iron...and Lots of Vision"
    Footfalls Through the Century
    "When the Rails Hummed, Part 1"
    "To Your Good Health, Sirs, Part I"
    "The Iron Gate and the Graduation Arch"
    "A Salute to the Woodcraft Camps"
    "Nine Decades Ago...The Troop Goes to Washington"
    "Boots-Saddles - and the Giants Who Made the Culver Summer Cavalry School a Legend"
    "Gignilliat Sets the Stage: Culver's Schoolboy Training Program, 1915-17"
    "The Grand Parade: Volume 1"

"Home on the Wrought Iron Range, Part II: Cookbooks, Clocks, and the End of an Era"

(J)ROTC – Its Place in the Military History of the Culver Military Academy, Part II

Newspapers
Georgia
Savannah Morning News (GA)
Illinois
Chicago Daily Journal (IL)
Chicago Daily News (IL)
Ottawa Free Trader-Journal (IL)
Indiana
The Bachelor, Wabash College student newspaper
The Culver Citizen
The Culver Herald
Fort Wayne Daily News (IN)
Indianapolis Journal (IN)
Indianapolis News (IN)
Indianapolis Star (IN)
Logansport Journal-Tribune (IN)
Logansport Press (IN)
The News-Sentinel (Fort Wayne)
Plymouth Tribune (IN)
South Bend News-Times (IN)
Kansas
Salina Daily Union (KS)
Michigan
The Ludington Chronicle (MI)
Missouri
St. Louis Globe-Democrat (MO)
St. Louis Republic (MO)
New York
The New York Times (NY)
New York Tribune (NY)
Pennsylvania
Pittsburg Chronicle Telegraph (PA)
Washington, DC
The Evening Star (Washington, DC)

Newspaper Articles
"Again in the Big Six: Culver Military Academy Retains Position With the Leading Institutions in the Country," *The Culver Citizen,* 8 Aug 1907, p. 4.
"Bids his Boys Godspeed," *Indianapolis News,* 15 August 1917, p. 11.

"Cadets at Richmond," from the *Richmond-Times Dispatch*, appearing in *The Culver Citizen*, August 29, 1907, p. 5

"Cadets Celebrate Culver Day at Fair," *St. Louis Republic*, June 3, 1904.

"Colonel Gignilliat Discusses the Value of Military Training in Schools and Colleges," *New York Times*, October 8, 1916.

"Cruise of Summer School on Continual Ovation," *The Culver Citizen*, Sept 10, 1908, p. 4.

"Drill Progresses Under CAPT Denney," *The Bachelor*, Wabash College student newspaper, April 21, 1917, p. 1.

"Dismissal for Culver Hazers: Thirteen Cadets Found Guilty and Expelled from Military Academy," *The Culver Citizen*, May 10, 1906, p. 3.

"The Emerson Institute" article in *The Evening Star: Washington, DC*, June 19, 1889, p. 8; "Emerson Institute" article in *The Evening Star: Washington, DC*, June 17, 1891, p. 7.

"Film about CMA Premiers at CMA," *The Culver Citizen*, July 20, 1932.

"Gov. Durbin Returns from St. Louis – Proud of Culver Cadets," *Indianapolis Journal*, June 6, 1904.

"Guard Instruction Set for Friday Postpones," *The Bachelor*, Wabash College student newspaper, April 25, 1917, p. 1.

"Inspect Camp Site," *The Ludington Chronicle*, Vol 13, No. 34, March 4, 1914.

"The Jamestown Trip: Summer Schools Leave Next Monday on Their Ten Day (sic) Tour of Eastern Points of interest," *The Culver Citizen*, August 15, 1907, p. 1.

"Lieut.-Col. Gignilliat Relieved of His Post," *Indianapolis News*, Oct 2, 1917, p. 3.

"Lincoln Fields Transformed Again Into a Tent City," *The Ludington Chronicle*, Vol. 15, No. 2, July 22, 1915, p. 6.

"Married at Pineora: Mr. Robert D. Gignilliat Weds Miss Lila C. Seabrook," *Savannah Morning News*, April 24, 1896, p. 8.

"Military Academy Chief's Experiment a Surprise to Gen. Wood," *Salina Daily Union*, May 25, 1915, p. 3.

"Military Ball Ends Culver Day," *St. Louis Globe-Democrat*, June 3, 1904.

"Military Training for the Boy," Col. L. R. Gignilliat, *Chicago Daily Journal*, Wednesday, October 6, 1915.

"Name Five Schools for Army Training," *Chicago Daily News*, November 15, 1916, p. 1.

"Off for Jamestown, *The Culver Citizen*, August 22, 1907, p. 1.

"Raised to Knighthood," *Indianapolis Star*, April 23, 1924, p. 10.

"Stokes Bluff Tragedy," *Savannah Morning News*, December 13, 1890, p. 8.

"These Books Are Barred in Germany," Vera J. Snook. *Ottawa Free Trader-Journal*, April 21, 1917, p. 2.

"Two Parables at Sheridan," *The Chicago Evening Post*, October 19, 1915.

"Wedding at the Academy: Miss Fleet Becomes the Wife of Major L. R. Gignilliat," *The Culver Herald*, August 5, 1898, p. 1.

"Wabash Battalion Can Not Train in Manual of Arms," *The Bachelor*, Wabash College student newspaper, May 2, 1917, p. 4.

"Wabash Battalion Plays Important Role in Parade," *The Bachelor*, Wabash College student newspaper, May 5, 1917, pp. 1, 3.

"Wabash Plays Large Part in Lafayette Celebration," *The Bachelor*, Wabash College student newspaper, May 9, 1917, p. 4.

"Weather Interferes with Drill During Past Week," *The Bachelor*, Wabash College student newspaper, April 28, 1917, p. 4.

"What Happens to the Drafted Man at Camp Zachary Taylor," *South Bend News-Times*, April 19, 1918, p. 17.

"What Men Take: Overseas List Issued to Soldiers at Camp Sherman," *Indianapolis News*, August 8, 1918, p. 8.

"What We Leave Behind," L. R. Gignilliat. *The Vedette*, Vol 7, No. 4, January 1903, p. 80.

Unpublished Manuscripts

Almstrom, John A., "Learning to Live: Tactical Training for the AEF, 1917-1918," unpublished MA thesis, Rice University, 1972.

Chaney, Louis H. (1940). "Military Training in the Secondary Schools," unpublished MA thesis, Butler University, https://digitalcommons.butler.edu/cgi/viewcontent.cgi?article=1084&context=grtheses

Christlieb, Gary, Senior Humanities Instructor, Culver Academies, verification of numbers of Culver's Gold Star men in 2018, email from, to author, January 21, 2019.

Davies, Richard Gwyn. *Of Arms and the Boy: A History of Culver Military Academy, 1894-1945*, unpublished PhD dissertation, Indiana University, 1984.

Faulkner, Richard S., "What Price Glory, Captain Flagg?' Leader Competence in the American Expeditionary Forces," unpublished MA thesis, Fort Leavenworth, KS, 2000.

Hadley, Alvan Cordell Jr., "Military Schools: The Association of Military Colleges and Schools of the United States (AMCSUS) and the Historical Struggle for the Survival of Military Preparatory Schools in America," unpublished Ph.D. dissertation, University of Kentucky, 1999

Mather, Charles C. (1959). *History of Culver Military Academy, 1894.1956*, unpublished manuscript, Culver Archives.

Ostermann, Dieter, "The Engineering, Science, and Management War Training Program: Higher Education and the Second World War," unpublished honors thesis in history, University of Iowa, Fall 2020.

Sellers, James M. Jr., "A Brief History of The Association of Military Colleges and Schools of the United States," unpublished, complied at Wentworth Military Academy, Lexington, Missouri, March 12, 1990.

Government Documents

Armsby, Henry H. "Engineering, Science, and Management War Training Program Final Report," Bulletin 1946, No. 9, (US Office of Education, 1946), pp. VIII, XI. https://files.eric.ed.gov/fulltext/ED543335.pdf

Congressional Record, 56th Congress, March 17, 1900, p. 3010.

Congressional Record, "First Session of the Sixty-fifth Congress of the United States of America," vol. LIII, part 6, (Washington, DC: GPO, 1916), p. 5629.

Official War Department Report of 1917 CMA Annual Inspection, 1918 CMA Catalog Supplement, p. 3

Cover letter and manifest of *SS Melita*, Headquarters Port of Embarkation, Hoboken, NJ, US Army Adjutant General's Office, released 4 October 1918, provided by Don W. Jones via research on Ancestory.com, 23 Jan 2019.

Fourteenth Report of the United States Civil Service Commission, July 1, 1896 to June 30, 1897 (Washington, DC: Government Printing Office, 1898) https://babel.hathitrust.org/cgi/pt?id=nnc1.cu09006931;view=1up;seq=5

Full Text Citations for Award of the Army Distinguished Service Medal, U.S. Army for World War I, "Gignilliat, Leigh R.," War Department, General Orders No. 43 (1922) http://www.homeofheroes.com/members/03_DSM/army/citations/04_WWI-armyAd.html

Glacier National Park Official Fact Sheet https://www.nps.gov/glac/learn/news/fact-sheet.htm)

Hearings Before the Subcommittee of the Committee on Military Affairs, United States Senate, Sixty-Sixth Congress, First Session, Part 8, testimony recorded from session on August 28, 1919 (Washington, DC: US Government Printing Office, 1919), pp. 461-462.

Infantry Training, US War Department (Washington, DC: US Government Printing Office, 1917).

National Park Services Description of Parks, 1942.

1900 US Census data, 1910 US Census data obtained with the assistance of Don W. Jones

Passenger List of SS Antrim, provided by Don W. Jones via research on Ancestory.com, 23 Jan 2019.

Passenger List of Organization, USS Von Steuben, Headquarters Port of Embarkation, Brest, France, Major P. H. Charlton, US Army 37th Division Personnel Adjutant, Adjutant General's Office, provided by Don W. Jones via research on Ancestory.com, 23 Jan 2019.

Passenger List of SS Imperator, provided by Don W. Jones via research on Ancestory.com, 23 Jan 2019.

Report of the Commissioner of Education for the Year 1898-99, vol. 2, Washington, DC: Government Printing Office, 1900), pp. 2064-2065.

Staff study of the War College Division of the US Army General Staff Corps prepared as a supplement to *The Statement of a Proper Military Policy for the United States*, "Study on Educational Institutions Giving Military Training as a Source of Supply of Officers for a National Army," WCD 9053-121, Document No. 510 (Washington, DC: War Department, Office of the Chief of Staff), pp. 8-9.

The Personnel System of the United States Army, Vol. I: History of the Personnel System, Washington, DC, 1919

"To Increase the Efficiency of the Military Establishment of the United States," *Hearing Before the Committee on Military Affairs, House of Representatives*, Sixty –fourth Congress, first session, (Washington, DC: Government Printing Office, 1916), vol. 2, p. 844.

US Army Special Regulations No. 49, "Training Camps for Reserve Officers and Candidates for Appointment as Such, May 15 – August 11, 1917," (Washington, DC: US Government Printing Office, 1917).

United States Bureau of Education, *Federal Laws, Regulations, and Rulings Affecting the Land-grant Colleges of Agriculture and Mechanic Arts* (Washington, DC: US Government

Printing Office, 1911), pp. 3-5.

United States Military Academy *Annual Report of the Superintendent*, 1920.

United States War Department Document No. 510, "Study on Educational Institutions Giving Military Training as a Source for a Supply of Officers for a National Army," Washington, DC: Army War College, November 1915.

United States War Department, "Special Regulations No. 103," *Students' Army Training Corps Regulations*, (Washington, DC: Government Printing Office, 1918).

United States War Department, *The Students Army Training Corps Descriptive Circular*, second edition, (Washington, DC: Government Printing Office, corrected to October 14, 1918).

Culver Publications

Culver Alumni Bulletin, 1916.

Culver Alumnus, January 1929, April 1937, June 1937, November 1952.

The Culver Builder, September 1921, May-June 1922.

Culver Military Academy Catalogs: 1895, 1896, 1897; 1898, 1899, 1900, 1902, 1903, 1906, 1907, 1908, 1909, 1910, 1911, 1914, 1918 (Supplement), 1922, 1933, 1935.

Culver Military Academy *Roll Call*, 1903, 1905, 1906, 1907, 1908, 1909, 1910, 1911, 1912, 1913, 1914, 1916, 1917, 1918, 1919, 1929, 1931.

Culver Summer Cavalry School (SCS) Catalog, 1907.

Culver Summer Naval School (SNS) Catalog, 1904, 1905,1906, 1907, 1908, 1909, 1910, 1914, *Illustrated Catalog of the Culver Military Academy*, 1916).

The Culver Vedette, November 1896, January 1897, November 1900, December 1900, January 1901, January 1906, October, 1907, June 1909, September 1911, February 1912, October 5, 1912; October 12, October 26, 1912, November 9, 1912, November 23, 1912, 15 March, 1913, April 5, 1913, April 12, 1913, May 3, 1913, 10 May 1913, May 17, 1913, May 23, 1914, May 31, 1913, October 4, 1913, October 25, 1913, November 8, 1913, November 15, 1913, December 6, 1913, January 17, 1914, March 5, 1914, March 7, 1914, March 28, 1914, April 18, 1914, May 23, 1914, 18 July 18, 1914, August 22, 1914, October 10, 1914, May 1, 1915, May 29, 1915, October 30, 1915, December 4. 1915, January 15, 1916, February 19, 1916, March 11, 1916, April 28, 1916, January 27, 1917, February 3, 1917, March 17, 1917, May 12, 1917, April 27, 1918, October 5, 1918, June 7, 1919, July 19, 1919, July 26, 1919, August 9, 1919, August 23, 1919, October 2, 1920, October 9, 1920, 16 Oct 1920, October 16, 1920, November 5, 1921, November 26, 1921 (, Pictorial Supplement), May 20, 1922, June 10, 1922 (Pictural Supplement), January 20, 1923 (Pictorial Supplement), March 31, 1923, May 26, 1923 (pictorial supplement), January 12, 1924,January 19, 1924, March 29, 1924, July 12, 1924, July 19, 1924, December 13, 1924, October 17, 1925, October 2, 1926, July 14, 1928, July 21, 1928.

Culver Woodcraft Catalog, 1912.

Images

Cass County Historical Society (Indiana)
Culver Archives
Find a Grave

Image posted by Davis E. McCollum to *Find a Grave* website on July 29. 2021, https://www.findagrave.com/memorial/17747114/william-robert-gignilliat/photo

Image courtesy of Find a Grave (in the public domain), https://www.findagrave.com/memorial/21112318/leigh-robinson

Photo in the public domain from *Find a Grave* website, https://www.findagrave.com/memorial/49300613/philip-pendleton-powell; information comes from links from *Find A Grave* entry and also from *WikiTree* sources, https://www.wikitree.com/wiki/Powell-16810.

https://www.findagrave.com/memorial/38423173/mary-seddon-gignilliat

https://www.findagrave.com/memorial/38423228/leigh-robinson-gignilliat/photo

https://www.findagrave.com/memorial/38423228/leigh-robinson-gignilliat/photo

Georgia Historical Society

Gignilliat family

Paul Gignilliat collection

Mary Margaret Gignilliat collection

Glacier National Park

Skyland Camps images

Google – In the Public Domain

Civil War artillery battery, courtesy of Google Images (in the public domain), https://www.google.com/search?q=confederate+civil+war+artillery+battery&rlz=1C1CHBF_

About the Author

Dr. Kelly C. Jordan is a retired U.S. Army Lieutenant Colonel, Professor of Military and National Security Studies at American Military University, and former Commandant of Cadets at Culver Military Academy, 2008-2013. Dr. Jordan received his B.A. from the Virginia Military Institute, graduating with academic distinction and as a Distinguished Military Graduate. He holds a M.A. and a Ph.D. in military history from The Ohio State University and is also a graduate of the U.S. Army Command and General Staff College. As an academic, Dr. Jordan is an award-winning professor who has served on the faculties of the United States Military Academy at West Point, the United States Army Command and General Staff College, the United States Naval War College, and the University of Notre Dame. As a scholar, he is the author of numerous military history and leadership studies publications.

www.ingramcontent.com/pod-product-compliance
Lightning Source LLC
Chambersburg PA
CBHW071656120626
46550CB00001B/2